Game Time

ALSO BY ROGER ANGELL

The Summer Game

Five Seasons

Late Innings

Season Ticket

Once More Around the Park

A Pitcher's Story:
Innings with David Cone

The Stone Arbor

A Day in the Life of Roger Angell

ROGER ANGELL

GAME TIME

A Baseball Companion

Edited by
Steve Kettmann

Harcourt, Inc.
Orlando   Austin   New York   San Diego   Toronto   London

www.HarcourtBooks.com

Library of Congress Cataloging-in-Publication Data
Angell, Roger.
Game time: a baseball companion/Roger Angell;
edited by Steve Kettmann.—1st ed.
p.   cm.
"A Harvest original."
ISBN 0-15-100824-8
1. Baseball—United States. 2. Baseball—United States—History.
I. Kettmann, Steve.   II. Title.
GV863.A1 A533 2003
796.357—dc21   2002152611

Text set in Stempel Garamond
Designed by Scott Piehl

Printed in the United States of America

First edition
K J I H G F E D C B A

Contents

Introduction

Richard Ford

Loving baseball is (or once was) easy. The game offers regular-sized humans performing oversized, occasionally glorious feats with grace and precision, all of it viewable in normally nice weather, pretty surroundings, and in real time. Nobody monotonously beats everybody (bad teams regularly win); competition is heated but rarely hostile. Mostly people don't get hurt, and performing excellently means you do something notable every third try. Meanwhile, the game's nature doesn't change much over a lifetime but maintains its casual, elemental sturdiness reminiscent of pastoral, patriotic origins. Repetition becomes consoling. Older players play and are venerated. Eccentricity is allowed. Uniforms are colorful. No one plays to a tie. And when a game's over you can, if you choose, happily forget all about it without paying it an insult. It's why they call it a pastime.

On the other hand, writing about baseball, at least in ways that enhance the actual experience of the game (as though you are watching it from some good seat, and also playing it) while providing a reading experience interesting enough to make a stranger put aside something more important, say Middlemarch, for the hope of finding comparable pleasure and refreshed awareness—well, that's challenging.

Baseball, of course, invites writing to its door by providing plenty of "openings" through which writing can enter, then create and satisfy a reader's need. Baseball is usually a slow and sometimes tedious game that can profit from shrewd, inventive commentary attesting to how it's also a good and occasionally beautiful game. At the same time, many baseball events happen fast and rely on subtly nuanced strategies and interreliances that can always stand to be illuminated. The game also embraces an almost limitless artichoke of layered rituals and protocols (many obscure even to the most practiced watchers), and the revelation of these can add to whatever else we may know of the game—thereby helping to create baseball's pleasurable *density*—an ingredient to making it lovable. Plus, baseball seems easy to play but isn't; its history is always problematically impinging on its present; many people take it too seriously and need to be told to lighten up. And finally it's often just good to be able to relive games we might already have seen or heard. Writing's good for all of these. And when writing *itself* is good—accurate, words chosen well, when it's thorough, proportioned, good-spirited—then the game is returned to us better than first we knew it, making us ready and eager to watch or even play it again.

Roger Angell has been writing about baseball for more than forty years—mostly for *The New Yorker* magazine—and for my money he's the best there is at it. There's no writer I know whose writing on sport, and particularly baseball, is as anticipated, as often reread and passed from hand to hand by knowledgeable baseball enthusiasts as Angell's is, or whose work is more routinely and delightedly read by those who really aren't enthusiasts. Among the thirty selections in this volume are several individual essays and profiles (the Bob Gibson profile, "Distance," for instance) which can be counted in that extremely small group of sports articles that people talk over and quote for decades, and which have managed to make a lasting contribution to the larger body of American writing.

Writing for *The New Yorker* has, of course, afforded Angell leniencies unavailable to his colleagues on the *Daily Planet*. He's had the luxury (and the talent) to write what he likes without hurrying, and to reconsider his words in relative peace—the gratitude good writing deserves. When William Shawn gave Angell his first *New Yorker* sports assignment in 1960, the editor expressed—perhaps in a memo—his view that sports shouldn't be written about either cynically or romantically (as though these two were essentially different). And Angell has gone along through the years to interpret Shawn's charge the way a gifted short-story writer might put his personal stamp upon an elder practitioner's words of moral guidance: say, to "forge in the smithy of my soul the uncreated consciousness of my race." In Angell's case, of course, the race in question has mostly been a pennant race.

Angell has written felicitously (always), and he has written acutely (always). He hasn't always written short, but he's written with a sense of providing a reader what the reader will need properly to appreciate the game. To read Roger Angell is never to feel condescended or shown off to, or to feel that reading is a privileged overhearing of some superior sports savant. One never senses that Angell imagines himself essential to the game, but rather the opposite—that his is "amateur expertise," an "insatiable vicariousness," and that baseball (uncynically) is good enough to be interested in.

Angell's words seem to come and be chosen for their places one at a time, not like bricks to a bricklayer or diamonds to a jeweler but like words to a writer who's found a means and subject to engage his full freedom and best self—what every writer longs for—and that allow him to write about sports from within a groove where he's limber, graceful, witty, intelligent, restrained, smoothly allusive, proportionate, and thoroughly satisfied to be doing just this work. Here is Angell on the subject of Fenway Park, from the year 2001:

"Writers waiting to gain postgame admission to the Red Sox manager's office at Fenway Park line up outside the clubhouse, separated by a metal rail from the jammed-together, slowly departing right-field-side patrons, who are headed home in the opposite direction. If the Sox have won, the crowd is noisy and uninteresting, but when they have lost again, as they do by habit in late summer, this year and every year, the tableau becomes weighty and shadowed, with more irony and history and atmosphere to take in than any mere game can account for. It's dark down here under the stands, for one thing, and the shuffling, oppressed humanity, the dingy lighting, the food smells, the bunched strands of wires and cables running haphazard overhead, and the damp, oddly tilting stone floor cast a spell of F Deck aboard the Titanic." Anyone, it should be said, who can make *me* feel a frisson when reading about the loss-obsessed Red Sox and their goofy (Oh, I'm sorry…their lovable, interestingly eccentric, history-ennobled) little urban ball yard has done a good trick indeed.

But, aside from his affinities for fine, evocative writing, and a long career at a fancy magazine, it is by getting those previously enumerated baseball essentials (strategies, nuances, protocols) down onto the page, and cementing the hard foundation without which sportswriting can't earn your time away from the game itself, that Angell has made his bones. Roger Angell's most rightful writerly seat is in the press box and the clubhouse and behind the batting cage with his friends, the shirtsleeve beat writers and the twice-a-week pundits who carry us fans the long way around from pitchers-and-catchers, till the day after the fat lady sings in the fall. "I could listen to this stuff all day," Angell has said, about the story-swapping and tall-taling that accompany the sportswriter's life—so much of which is spent simply waiting, but which (if you're good at your job) is never time wasted. Owner of a sports memory reaching back to Ott and Ruth, confident minder of the game's boundaryless stats, possessor of grave insights into the game's fluid mechanics, master of the wry trope, the *mot juste,* the running story, and confident practitioner of baseball's *poetics,* whereby managers stand at the *helm* of teams, winning streaks come in *skeins,* home runs are *launched,* wins *garnered,* Angell first and always gives good baseball to the boys in the cheap seats. And he does the hard slog: he gets bulldogs (like Pete Rose) to say interesting things, saving them thereby from being just bulldogs. And he gets good guys like David Cone to now and then sound like philosophers. "Cone's first start after Tampa…," Angell wrote in his chronicle of the slightly bemused Yankee hurler coming to the end of his time in the bigs, "came in two parts. Working with a pared-down, tauter motion, he threw early strikes to the tough Seattle batters but kept running up his pitch counts thereafter, straining for the K. At one stretch he went to the full count against eight straight batters. Much was at stake, and there was something like a groan or a sigh in the press rows when Alex Rodriguez pounced on a fastball that had drifted over the plate and drove it into the right-field stands for the second and third runs of the inning. Down by 3–2, Cone now persevered, perhaps recalling the look on Joe Torre's face when he'd taken him up the tunnel between innings for a talk about body language. But Torre kept him in the game for a full six— no more runs, six strikeouts, and a startling hundred and thirty-seven pitches. When Cone fanned Mike Cameron in the fifth, the announcement came that it had been his twenty-five-hundredth career strikeout—a level he shared only with Clemens and Randy Johnson, among all active pitchers—and the fans delivered a sustained full minute of applause: an ovation of all things. They'd been waiting weeks for the chance. The Yanks lost the game in the end, going down in the ninth, 6–5...." A few lines later Angell observes that Cone "didn't believe that illusions about his strikeouts or sliders would haunt him, once he decided to retire. It was the other way around. 'I've always been a super-realist,' he said. 'I go over things in my mind—I can't let them alone. It's how bad I've been that gets me. I could use a little fantasy right now. Guys who can kid themselves are much better off.'"

Back in the late sixties, a teacher of mine—now a famous novelist—used to say that baseball was just a stylized enactment of the basic Freudian paradigm: the catcher was the mother, the pitcher the father, the batter the hapless son, seeking with his waggling appendage to intercept the father's pitch and give it a pasting before the ball got in between the catcher's legs, after which... well, after which I seem to remember the formulation kind of broke down and everyone lost interest.

But ever since then, I've stayed watchful of the deft balance sportswriting must achieve between its preoccupation with "the game" and the game's context, the outside world, where moms and dads and sons really do struggle, and where things matter a lot and are rarely soluble, and where baseball—its rules, history, conduct—isn't a very useful microcosm, and life's lessons can't be taught very well by overpaid twenty-two-year-old phenoms. Sport may occasionally be a little like life and occur within it. But it's a game. That's its fun part, its privileged irrelevancy and occasionally its beauty.

Roger Angell, entirely consonant with his affection for the game, writes about baseball from a viewing stand that's conspicuously *in* life and society, and he understands, as the few great sportwriters do, that to achieve his craft's highest expression, a writer must bring along his loftiest values, moral and lexical, yet somehow do it without tying his slender subject to weights and galactic significances it can't persuasively bear. To make sport be more than itself threatens to make it boring, and almost always turns the writing absurd and bad. "Baseball memories are seductive," Angell has written, "tempting us always toward sweetness and undercomplexity." And he might as well have said it about baseball itself with regard to its relevance to life at large. And so, when Angell's gaze travels outside the lines, it is not to make the smaller realm instruct the wider one, or mirror it, but rather from within baseball's interior to credit life, for which the game stands not as allegory but as a pretty reprieve. That's the game's bargain with us, its proffer and appeal. And we trust Roger Angell because he knows that, and because he sees what we see.

"I went back to Shea the day after the eleven-inning loss to the Expos," he wrote last year, "but this time sat jam-packed in the stands in short left, where patches of pale sunshine and mild booing (while Mets starter Steve Trachsel gave back an early 3–1 lead) and the shrilling of kiddie fans kept us cheerful. Fans in every style and vintage of Mets gear paraded up and down the aisles, and returning, view-blocking food-bearers, in ancient ritual, paused to ogle the field in response to the smallest hint of action. A busy dad in front of me missed Alomar's first-inning homer while on forage, and then blew Robbie's next dinger, in the third, when he'd gone down again for ice cream. Some mini-minors near me had to stand on their seats, teetering and peering—and sometimes grabbing my shirt or ear to keep balance—to catch fractional glimpses of the batter, way off to our right. Now and then one of the standees would step on the wrong part of his seat and disappear from view, like a wader taken down by a shark, but then resurface smiling, with peanut dust and bits of popcorn in his hair. The noise was amazing, and not much like the apprehensive or vengeful sounds of Yankee Stadium, where every game must be won."

Of course, when it does actually mimic life, as almost all institutions now and then will (think stock market, think government), then baseball suddenly doesn't seem as seductive or as sweet. And Angell is typically ready, if not very eager, to look beyond the web of baseball, see over the fence, and tell us what's there—since what's there inevitably affects the game.

"Sports were different in my youth," he wrote in 1992. "A series of events to look forward to and then to turn over in memory, rather than a huge, omnipresent industry with its own economics and politics and crushing public relations" [again, think stock market, think government]. Now, though, he goes on, "we are wary of sentiment and obsessively knowing, and we feel obliged to put a spin of psychology or economic determinism or bored contempt on all clear-color memories [and] it is because most of American life, including baseball, no longer feels feasible."

This is surely enough to say, though perhaps there's a better note to end on.

Sometime along in the middle of October, 1981—a dreary season for me in almost all respects—my wife was sitting in our house in Princeton, staring moodily out the living-room window at the maple's seeming to change leaf by leaf, and with it the year, its dour end game begun. The Series had just finished. The Dodgers had defeated the Yankees in six games. No one's back was any longer against the wall. The fat lady'd sung. There *was* a tomorrow, and this was it. No one who fancies baseball ever feels very good about things on this day, no matter who's become champ.

"Ho-hum," my wife said, resigned, her nose to the cool glass, her eyes gray and unblinking.

"Right. Ho-hum," I said, offering her some company.

"Well," she said. "That's all over now." She nodded. But suddenly her face brightened. "In a week, though, we'll have Roger Angell to read, and I'll probably feel better again. It's the only good thing about the end of the season—Roger Angell comes along and makes it go alive again. I wish it could be today."

"Me, too," I said.

And baseball, by these simple acts, was tucked away for another quilted winter, to be attended to properly, lovingly in the interval. So that come March we'd all find it again, renewed and much as it was—the way we like it.

My wife smiled at me, happy for this prospect. Together we commenced our wait.

Richard Ford
2002

Preface

One morning in the mid-nineteen-eighties I was sitting with manager Sparky Anderson in his office at Marchant Stadium, the Tigers' spring-training park, in Lakeland, Florida. We were alone except for a life-size photograph of Ty Cobb sullenly staring from one wall. The Georgia Peach was wearing a thick cardigan sweater, with that imposing Gothic "D" over the heart, and I may have lowered my voice when I nodded toward the old Tiger, still the holder of the highest lifetime batting average in the books, and said, "What about this guy, Sparky? Where would he fit into your plans if he could be back here right now?" Anderson took his pipe out of his mouth and leaned forward from his chair. "I know he's not starting for me," he whispered. "I just hope he makes the Opening Day roster."

Baseball, despite our wishes, changes all the time, and this collection, which encompasses more than forty years of reporting on the game, may suggest some reasons for its shifting place in our estimation. Maybe not. While I was covering this long run of memorable or trifling moments and innings, it never occurred to me that I was putting down history or looking for something to say about the American psyche. It was only about the games and the players, and how I felt, watching. This book is a personal selection from almost a million words about baseball, and, taken as a sampler, may only illustrate one writer's progress from young fan (youngish: I was forty-one when I went down to St. Petersburg in March, 1962, for *The New Yorker* and nervously tied on my first credential) to decidedly senior reporter. Some of these chapters have appeared in previous collections, but a larger share of the contents has not been seen in book form. The shorter "Takes" sections carry an old pressbox tag, from the days when beat writers banged out their game stories on portable typewriters and handed their running copy, page by page, to Western Union messengers, who relayed it to desk and rewrite men at their home papers. Clif Keane, a fixture with the Boston *Globe,* used to watch me filling up a notebook with pages of stuff that might later be turned into a line or two in a piece weeks or months away, and would rag me for my pains. "How many takes tonight, Rahj?" he would call over cheerfully. "Ten? Twenty?"

Baseball pressboxes are quieter now, thanks to laptops, but much more crowded. Each writer follows the action below and then checks it out in replay on one of the television monitors, where the game story is going out to America without any effort from him. Perpetually scooped, he has become a skilled feature writer or celebrity critic, and part of the entertainment media blitz. Because of television's technical wizardry and its range of commentators, most of whom are former big-league players, we fans have become more expert about how the game is played, and more argumentative as we sense ourselves slipping into an electronic tavern, open at all hours, where every sport is equal and every athlete the subject of a ceaseless and irritable attention. Major-league ballgames are played to a rock-concert blast of sound and light; statistics hover near each pitch and at-bat and play, prepared to certify another first-ever, to feed our appetite for greatness. ESPN keeps us up to the moment, even as the rarity of the moment slips away, and instant replay supplants memory. When I asked Carlton Fisk once whether he still had any private recollection of his celebrated twelfth-inning home run off the foul pole at Fenway Park in Game Six of the 1975 World Series, and his frantically gesturing dance up the first-base line as he waved the ball fair, he said, "It's very interesting you asked that, because, you know, I've only seen that shot four or five times in my life. Every time it comes on my television set, I turn it off or leave the room, because I'm trying to keep a crystal memory of what that was like."

We've all made these adjustments—we have no other choice—and we labor each day to recognize a few names in the lineups of thirty teams, where once there were sixteen, and not to care too much that these enormous players are making more money in a season or a month or an at-bat than we will in our entire working lives. I don't think we're much surprised when Ty Cobb slips out of the all-time batting order, or the day arrives when we must weigh Randy Johnson and Barry Bonds and Alex Rodriguez against the best two or three who ever played their positions. It's thrilling, in fact. What we ask in return, though—we almost insist on it—is that the stars be good guys, too. In an ironic, fractious age, we crave a less distracted view of baseball, and cling to the notion that the game can still be as sweet as we imagined it when we were kids, and the players still country lads or gallant Gehrigs or jovially naughty, like the Babe. Major League Baseball holds out this hope in its misty P.R. on the pastime, and last fall kept screening that excerpt from "Field of Dreams" in which James Earl Jones says, "This field, this game, reminds us of all that once was good and that could be again." Get a grip.

Some fans are inconsolable about this imagined loss. Last summer they were so distressed to find baseball once again in the middle of a labor standoff and incipient strike that they threatened—here and there in noisy numbers—a lifetime boycott of the sport. They'd gone bonkers. A year or so after the previous strike, which wiped out the latter part of the 1994 season and the World Series, I was a participant in an onstage baseball reading and discussion in San Francisco. When we were done, a man in the audience put his hand up during the Q. and A. and said he'd had it with baseball forever. The owners were pigheaded and self-destructive and the players all spoiled, overpaid babies. He'd never go back again.

For once, the right answer came to me—there on the spot, instead of later. I said I'd heard that the San Francisco Symphony was also out on strike just then. How was that going?

"Yes, they are," he responded. "It doesn't look good. They've been out for a couple of months now."

"And you?" I said. "You've given up on Mozart and Chopin and Schubert forever?"

My wiseguy answer drew a mixed response—there were some laughs and a few boos, and then applause—but suddenly I felt great about baseball again and terrifically lucky to be a part of it. For me, the music was still playing.

I am grateful to my friend and fellow baseball correspondent Steve Kettmann, who first conceived the plan for this collection, and proved an enthusiastic and imaginative collaborator in its preparation. My thanks go as well to four successive editors of *The New Yorker*, who extended encouraging and almost limitless grants of space and time: William Shawn, Robert Gottlieb, Tina Brown, and David Remnick.

—R.A.
December, 2002

SPRING

The Old Folks Behind Home

1962

This winter, a local mortician named Willie Robarts sent Sarasota residents and visitors a mailing of cards printed with his name
and with the schedule of baseball games to be played here by the
Chicago White Sox, who conduct their spring training in Payne
Park, right in the middle of town. This must be interpreted as a
pure public service, rather than as an attempt to accelerate business
by the exposure of senior citizens (or "senior Americans," as they
are sometimes called here) to unbearable excitement; only last
night I was informed that a Sarasota heart specialist has ordered
one of his patients to attend every Sox game as a therapeutic measure. Big-league ball on the west coast of Florida is a spring sport
played by the young for the divertissement of the elderly—a sun-
warmed, sleepy exhibition celebrating the juvenescence of the year
and the senescence of the fans. Although Florida newspapers print
the standings of the clubs in the Grapefruit League every day, none
of the teams tries especially hard to win; managers are looking
hopefully at their rookies and anxiously at their veteran stars, and
by the seventh or eighth inning, no matter what the score, most of
the regulars are back in the hotel or driving out to join their families on the beach, their places taken by youngsters up from the minors. The spectators accept this without complaint. Their loyalty to
the home club is gentle and unquestioning, and their afternoon
pleasure appears scarcely affected by victory or defeat. If this attachment were deeper or more emotional, there would have been

widespread distress here three years ago when the Boston Red Sox, who had trained in Sarasota for many years, transferred their spring camp to Scottsdale, Arizona, and the White Sox moved down from Tampa, but the adjustment to the new stocking color, by all accounts, was without trauma. The Beach Club Bar, out on Siesta Key, still displays photographs of Bobby Doerr and Dom DiMaggio and other members of the fine Red Sox teams of the forties, and at the ballpark I spotted a boy of ten or twelve wearing a faded junior-size Red Sox uniform (almost surely a hand-me-down from an older brother), but these are the only evidences of disaffection and memory, and the old gentlemen filing into the park before the game now wear baseball caps with the White Sox insigne above the bill.

Caps are the preferred millinery for both male and female fans in Payne Park—baseball caps, long-billed fishing caps, perforated summer-weights, yachting caps with crossed anchors, old-fashioned John D. Rockefeller linen jobs. Beneath them are country faces— of retired farmers and small-town storekeepers, perhaps, and dignified ladies now doing their cooking in trailers—wearing rimless spectacles and snap-on dark glasses. This afternoon, Payne Park's sixteen-row grandstand behind home plate had filled up well before game time (the Dodgers, always a good draw, were here today), and fans on their way in paused to visit with those already in their seats. The ushers greeted the regulars by name, and I saw one of them offering his arm to a very old lady in a blue hairnet and chatting with her as he escorted her slowly to her seat. Just after the national anthem, the loudspeaker announced that a lost wallet had been turned in, and invited the owner to come and claim it—an announcement that I very much doubt has ever been heard in a big-city ballpark.

There were elders on the field, too. Early Wynn, who has spent half of his forty-two years in the major leagues and has won two hundred and ninety-two games, started for the Sox. He pitched carefully, slowly wheeling his heavy body on the windup and glowering down on the batters between pitches, his big Indian-like face almost hidden under his cap. He has a successful construction business in Venice, Florida, south of here, but he wants that three-hundredth game this year; as for the Sox, if they are to be contenders they must have ten or fifteen wins from him. Duke Snider led off the Dodger second. He is as handsome and cheerful-looking as ever—he has the classic ballplayer's face—but he is a bit portly now, and beneath his helmet the sideburns were white. As he stepped up, a man some-where behind me shouted, "C'mon, Duke! C'mon, Grandpa—belt one!" and a lady just in front of me murmured to her companion, "Now, really, I think that's *very* offensive." (Clapping and small, en-couraging cries are heard in Florida parks, but boos and personal ep-ithets are bad form.) Duke's feelings didn't seem hurt; he swung viciously and grounded out to second, running it out fast all the way.

Wynn pitched three innings, shutting out the Dodgers and giv-ing up only two hits, and was succeeded by Herb Score. The crowd was pulling for Score with every pitch; they knew his story, which is the saddest in modern baseball. Although he has entirely recov-ered from the terrible injury he suffered when he was struck in the face by a line drive hit by Gil MacDougald in 1957, Score's confi-dence, his control, and, finally, his form have vanished, and he has never again approached the brilliance of 1956, when he won twenty games for the Indians, struck out two hundred and sixty-three bat-ters, and finished with an earned-run average of 2.53. Now he is up from the minor leagues, battling for a job. Today, at least, he was getting batters out, but watching him work was a nervous, un-happy business. Most of his pitches were high, and it was difficult to see why the Dodgers weren't hitting him harder. He kept run-ning into bouts of wildness, and his delivery was a painful parody of what it used to be, for his arm would come to a full, hitching halt at the end of his windup, and he appeared to be pushing the ball. He escaped his four innings with only a lone, unearned run scored against him. Meantime, the White Sox were bleeding for runs, too, as they will be all season. They have traded away their power, Mi-noso and Sievers, for pitching and defense, hoping for a repetition of their 1959 surprise, and the run they scored in the seventh came

on two singles and a stolen base—the kind of rally their supporters will have to expect this year.

The tension of a tied, low-scoring game appeared to distract
rather than engross the crowd. The sun slid behind the grandstand
roof, and there was a great stirring and rustling around me as
sweaters were produced and windbreakers zipped up; seats began
to be vacated by deserters, and the fans in the upper rows, who had
been in the shade all afternoon, came down looking for a warmer
perch. Brief bursts of clapping died away, and the only sound was
the shrill two-note whistle of infielders encouraging their pitcher.
The old people all around me hunched forward, their necks bent,
peering out at the field from under their cap bills, and I had the curious impression that I was in a giant aviary. Out in right-field foul
ground, members of the Sox' big pitching squad began wind sprints.
They stood together in clusters, their uniforms a vivid white in the
blaze of late sun, and four or five at a time would break away from
the group and make a sudden sandpiper dash along the foot of the
distant sea-green wall, all the way into deep center field, where they
stopped just as quickly and stood and stared at the game. At last, in
the bottom of the twelfth, the White Sox loaded the bases on some
sloppy Dodger fielding, and Nellie Fox, his wad of tobacco bulging,
delivered the single that broke the bird spell and sent everyone
home to supper. "*There,* now," said the woman in front of me,
standing up and brushing her skirt. "Wasn't that nice?"

Sarasota, March 21

Watching the White Sox work out this morning at Payne Park
reassured me that baseball is, after all, still a young man's sport and
a cheerful one. Coach Don Gutteridge broke up the early pepper
games with a cry of "Ever'body 'round!" and after the squad had
circled the field once, the ritual—the same one that is practiced on
every high-school, college, and professional ballfield in the country—began. Batters in the cage bunted one, hit five or six, and

made room for the next man. Pitchers hit fungoes to the outfielders, coaches on the first and third baselines knocked out grounders to the infield, pepper games went on behind the cage, and the bright air was full of baseballs, shouts, whistles, and easy laughter. There was a raucous hoot from the players around second when a grounder hopped over Esposito's glove and hit him in the belly. Two young boys with fielders' gloves had joined the squad in the outfield, and I saw Floyd Robinson gravely shake hands with them both. Anyone can come to watch practice here, and fans from nearby hotels and cottages wandered in after their breakfasts, in twos and threes, and slowly clambered up into the empty bleachers, where they assumed the easy, ceremonial attitude—feet up on the row in front, elbows on knees, chin in hands. There were perhaps two dozen of us in the stands, and what kept us there, what nailed us to our seats for a sweet, boring hour or more, was not just the *whop!* of bats, the climbing white arcs of outfield flies, and the swift flight of the ball whipped around the infield, but something more painful and just as obvious—the knowledge that we had never made it. We would never know the rich joke that doubled over three young pitchers in front of the dugout; we would never be part of that golden company on the field, which each of us, certainly for one moment of his life, had wanted more than anything else in the world to join.

The Cardinals, who have been having a fine spring, were the visitors this afternoon, and their high spirits infected everyone. Minnie Minoso, grinning extravagantly, exchanged insults with his former White Sox teammates, and Larry Jackson, the big Cardinal right-hander, laughed out loud on the mound when he got Joe Cunningham, who was *his* teammate last year, to miss badly on a big curve in the first inning. Stan Musial had the day off, and Al Lopez, the Sox' manager, had filled his lineup with rookies. My eye was caught by the Chicago shortstop, a kid named Al Weis, who is not on the team's regular roster but who was having a nifty day in the field. He started double plays in the first and second innings, and in the third he made a good throw from deep short to get

Jackson, and then robbed Gotay with a diving spear of a low liner. At the plate, though, he was nervous and uncertain, anxious to succeed in this one short—and, to him, terribly important—afternoon. He struck out in the first inning and again in the second, stranding two base-runners.

At about this time, I began to pick up a dialogue from the seats directly behind me—a flat, murmurous, continuous exchange in Middle Western accents between two elderly men.

"Look at the skin on my hands, how dry it is," said one.

"You do anything for it?" asked the other.

"Yes, I got some stuff the doctor gave me—just a little tube of something. It don't help much."

I stole a look at them. They were both in their seventies, at least. Both were sitting back comfortably, their arms folded across their stomachs.

"Watch that ball," said the first. "Is that fair?"

"No, it's foul. You know, I haven't seen a homer this year."

"Me neither."

"Maybe Musial will hit one here tomorrow."

The White Sox, down one run after the first inning, could do nothing with Jackson. Weis struck out again in the fifth, made a wild throw to first in the sixth, and then immediately redeemed himself with another fast double play. The voices went on.

"This wind melts your ice cream fast, don't it?"

"Yes, it does. It feels nice, though. Warm wind."

In the top of the eighth, with the bases loaded, Weis grabbed another line drive and doubled up the runner at second base. There were chirps from the stands.

"It don't seem any time at all since spring training last year."

"That's because we're older now. You take my grandson, he's always looking forward to something. Christmas and his birthday and things like that. That makes the time go slow for him. You and me, we just watch each day by itself."

"Yes. You know, I didn't hardly think about life at all until I was sixty-five or seventy."

"I know."

Weis led off the bottom of the eighth, and popped up to left. He started still another double play in the ninth, but his afternoon was ruined. The Cardinals won the game, 2–0.

That evening, I looked up Al Weis's record. He is twenty-two years old and was an All-Scholastic player at Farmingdale High, on Long Island. In his three years in organized baseball, he has played with Holdrege, in the Nebraska State League; with Lincoln, in the Three-I League; and with Charleston, in the Sally League. His batting averages in those years—.275, .231, .261—tell the story: good field, no hit. Time has run out for him this spring, and it must seem to him that it went too quickly. Next week, he will report to the White Sox farm camp in Hollywood, Florida, for another year in the minors.

St. Petersburg, March 22

This is Gerontium, the elders' capital—city of shuffleboard courts, city of sidewalk benches, city of curious signs reading "Youtharama," "Smorgarama," and "Biblegraph." Today it was also the baseball capital of the world, for the game at Al Lang Field was the first encounter between the Yankees and the New York Mets, the new National League team that sprang—not simply full-grown but middle-aged—out of the forehead of George Weiss last winter. Some of the spectators' curiosity and expectancy about this game resembled the unbecoming relish with which party guests watch a newly divorced couple encountering each other in public for the first time, for they could watch General Manager Weiss, in his box behind the home dugout, and Casey Stengel, in the dugout, staring over at the team that had evicted them so scandalously two years ago. But there was another, more valid tension to be tasted; one sensed that this game was a crisis for the Mets—their first chance to discover, against the all-conquerors, whether they were truly a ball team. A rout, a laugher, a comedy of ineptitude might destroy them before the season ever began.

St. Petersburg fans are elderly, all right, but they are noisier, keener, and more appreciative than their counterparts to the south. For one thing, they know more baseball. Al Lang Field has for years been the late-winter home of two good teams, the Yankees and Cardinals; when the Yankees moved to new quarters at Fort Lauderdale this year, the Mets moved in to take their place. I had guessed that this switch of home teams might cause some confusion of loyalties, but I was wrong. There was a respectable burst of applause when Mickey Mantle stepped up to the plate in the second inning, but this was almost immediately smothered by a full roar of pleasure when Charlie Neal collared Mantle's streaking grounder in short right and threw him out. Groans and headshakings followed when the Yanks collected three singles and a run off Roger Craig's pitching, but the Mets failed to collapse. Frank Thomas hit a double in the Mets' half of the inning—the first hit given up by Bill Stafford, the Yankees' starting pitcher, all spring—and there was another startled shout a few minutes later when Hodges and Chacon pulled off a 3-6-3 double play on Maris's bouncer. The Mets not only belonged, they were winning converts every minute.

The Mets are an attractive team, full of echoes and overtones, and one must believe that George Weiss has designed their clean, honest, but considerably frayed appearance with great care. Gus Bell, Frank Thomas, Eddie Bouchee, and Richie Ashburn are former headliners whose mistakes will be forgiven and whose accomplishments will win sentimental affection. Coach Cookie Lavagetto and pitchers Roger Craig and Clem Labine will bring the older Dodger fans up to the Polo Grounds this summer. Neal and Don Zimmer looked unchanged—Neal intense, withdrawn, talented, too tightly wound for an ideal infielder, and Zimmer eager and competitive, angrily trying to make pugnacity compensate for what he lacks in size, skill, and luck. Gil Hodges still cannot hit pitches over the outside corners, but his stance and his mannerisms at the plate are a cup of limeflower tea to those with memories: the bat is held in the left hand while he fiddles with his eyelashes with his right hand, then settles his helmet, then tucks up his right pants leg, then sweeps the hand the full length of the bat, like a duelist wiping blood off a sword, and then at last he faces the pitcher. Finally, there is Casey himself, a walking pantheon of evocations. His pinstripes are light blue now, and so is the turtleneck sweatshirt protruding above his shirt, but the short pants, the hobble, the muttering lips, and the comic, jerky gestures are unaltered, and today he proved himself still capable of the winning move.

The Mets went ahead, 3–2, in the sixth inning, on two Yankee errors, two walks, and Zimmer's single. After that, the St. Petersburg fans began a nervous, fingers-crossed cry of "Keep it up, Mets!" and welcomed each put-out with shouts of incredulity and relief. In the ninth, though, the Mets' second pitcher, a thin young left-hander named Al Jackson, up this year from Columbus, gave up four singles and the tying run after Neal messed up a double play. With the winning runs on base, Stengel showed how much he wanted this game for his team, for he came out to the mound and relieved Jackson. (Pitchers are almost never yanked in mid-inning in spring training.) The relief man, Howie Nunn, retired Blanchard on a pop behind second for the last out. More wonders followed. Joe Christopher, another unknown, led off the Mets' ninth with a triple, and after Zimmer had fouled out, Stengel looked into his closet of spare parts, which is far less well stocked than his old Yankee cornucopia, and found Ashburn there. Richie hit the first pitch into right field for the ball game, and George Weiss nodded his head, stood up in his box, and smiled for the first time today.

I doubt whether any of the happy six thousand-odd filing out of Al Lang Field after the game were deluding themselves with dreams of a first-division finish for the Mets this year. The team is both too old and too young for sensible hopes. Its pitchers will absorb some fearful punishment this summer, and Elio Chacon and Neal have yet to prove that they can manage the double play with any consistency. Still, the Mets will be playing in the same league with the Houston Colt .45s, another newborn team of castoffs, and with the Phillies, who managed to finish forty-six games out of first place last year and will have eight more games this year in which to disimprove that record. The fight for the National League cellar this summer may be as lively as the fight for the pennant. What cheered *me* as I tramped through the peanut shells and discarded programs and out into the hot late sunlight was not just the score and not just Casey's triumph but a freshly renewed appreciation of the complexity and balance of baseball. Offhand, I can think of no other sport in which the world's champions, one of the great teams of its era, would not instantly demolish inferior opposition and reduce a game such as the one we had just seen to cruel ludicrousness. Baseball is harder than that; it requires a full season, hundreds and hundreds of separate games, before quality can emerge, and in that summer span every home-town fan, every doomed admirer of underdogs, will have his afternoons of revenge and joy.

Tampa, March 24th

The population of Tampa is two hundred and seventy-five thousand. I looked it up this morning, but I could have saved myself the trouble. Anyone attending a game in the big, modern reinforced-concrete-shell grandstand of Al Lopez Field (named for the White Sox manager, who is a Tampa native) could figure out that this is the big town in these parts; he could tell it, by the sound of the crowd alone—a steady, complex, cosmopolitan clamor made up of exhortation, laughter, outright booing, the cries of vendors, and the hum of garrulous city talkers. Today the old people in the stands were outnumbered. There were young women in low-cut sundresses, children of all ages (two boys near me were wearing Little League uniforms with "Western Fertilizer" emblazoned on the back), and blacks and Cubans in the grandstand. The sun was hot and summery, and I felt at home: this was July in Yankee Stadium. Nevertheless, I had trouble concentrating on the first few innings of the game, which was between the Cincinnati Reds, who train here, and the visiting Dodgers. My mind kept returning to an incident—a sudden visual snapshot of a scene—in the game I saw yesterday in Bradenton, where Milwaukee had beaten the Yankees.

Bradenton yesterday was nothing like Tampa today. The weather was cold early spring, with low clouds and a nipping wind blowing in from left field. The stadium might have been a country fairgrounds, and the elders who had come early and filled up the park to see the mighty Yankees had the gravity, the shy politeness, and the silence of a rural crowd at a tent show. A rain the night before had turned the infield into a mudpie, and while we waited patiently for it to dry, three bearded men wearing plumed Spanish helmets, silvery chest plates, short striped pants, and high boots trooped out in front of the dugout, carrying swords, to have their picture taken with Mickey Mantle. They were local citizens participating in Bradenton's annual de Soto celebration. Mickey grinned and brandished one of the swords for the photographer, and the conquistadors looked awed. At last, the game began, in tomblike silence. No one complained when Mantle, Howard, Boyer, and Berra failed to appear in the opening lineup. Hardly anyone cheered when the Braves got to Jim Coates for a run in the third. A man standing in front of the scoreboard in deep center field hung up a numbered placard for each ball, strike, and out. When the sun began to break through, another employee came out of the Braves' clubhouse beside left field and hung a dozen sweatshirts—white, with black sleeves—out to dry on a clothesline strung between two palm trees. The game turned out to be a good one; there was some small shouting when the Braves came from behind to tie the score in the bottom of the ninth on a home run by Tommie Aaron, Hank Aaron's kid brother, and some guffaws when the Yanks lost it on an error in the tenth. In spite of the score, and perhaps only because of the peacefulness and stolidity of the fans, I came away with the impression that the Braves have become a middle-aged team, now somehow past the point of eagerness and energy that has made them champions or fearsome contenders for the last nine years.

The incident that startled me at Bradenton was one of those juxtapositions that are possible only in spring training. In the seventh inning, with the sun now fully out and the grass turning soft and emerald as it dried, Whitey Ford came in to pitch for the Yankees. At the same moment, in the Braves' bullpen in deep left field,

Warren Spahn began throwing—not warming up but simply loosening his arm. Suddenly I saw that from my seat behind first base the two pitchers—the two best left-handers in baseball, the two best left- *or* right-handers in baseball—were in a direct line with each other, Ford exactly superimposed on Spahn. It was a trick photograph, a *trompe-l'oeil:* a hundred-and-fifty-eight-game winner and a three-hundred-and-nine-game winner throwing baseballs in the same fragment of space. Ford, with his short, businesslike windup, was all shoulders and quickness, while, behind him, Spahn would slowly kick his right leg up high and to the left, peering over his shoulder as he leaned back, and then deliver the ball with an easy, explosive sweep. It excited me to a ridiculous extent. I couldn't get over it. I looked about me for someone to point it out to, but I couldn't find a recognizable fan-face near me.

The Tampa crowd this afternoon would have spotted it. They knew their baseball, and they were tough and hard to please. Joey Jay, the Reds' top starter, was having all kinds of trouble on the mound. His control was off, he had to throw too many pitches, and he kept shaking his head disgustedly. After the first two innings, the Dodgers were waiting for him to get behind and come in with a fat pitch. They batted around against him in the third inning, scoring five runs; two of them came on a home run by Daryl Spencer, and then in the fifth Spencer knocked another pitch over the fence. Manager Hutchinson left Jay in, letting him take his punishment while he got the work he needed. The fans, though the Reds are their team, seemed to enjoy it all. They booed Jay lightly; they didn't mind seeing him suffer a little—not with that $27,500 salary he won after a holdout this spring. They applauded Koufax, the Dodger pitcher, who was working easily and impressively, mixing fast balls and curves and an occasional changeup, pitching in and out to the batters, and hitting the corners. Koufax looked almost ready for Opening Day.

There were fewer rookies and scrubs in the lineups today; the season begins in just over two weeks. These two teams will almost certainly fight it out with the Giants for the pennant, and I was tempted to make comparisons and private predictions. But then I reminded myself that baseball would be competitive and overserious soon enough. The city crowd around me here, the big park, and the approaching time for headlines, standings, and partisanship have almost made me knowing and Northern again. Already I had begun to forget the flavor of Florida baseball—the older, easier pleasures of baseball in the spring in the country.

Sunny Side of the Street

1975

It was raining in New York—a miserable afternoon in mid-March. Perfect. Grabbed my coat and got my hat, left my worries on the doorstep. Flew to Miami, drove to Fort Lauderdale, saw the banks of lights gleaming in the gloaming, found the ballpark, parked, climbed to the press box, said hello, picked up stats and a scorecard, took the last empty seat, filled out my card (Mets vs. Yankees), rose for the anthem, regarded the emerald field below (the spotless base paths, the encircling palms, the waiting multi-tudes, the heroes capless and at attention), and took a peek at my watch: four hours and forty minutes to springtime, door to door.

The journey and the arrival and then a few innings of mild, meaningless baseball would have been more than enough for my first day of spring training, but this particular evening promised a treat. It was the middle meeting of a three-game set between the Yankees and the visiting Mets, and the starting pitchers were Cat-fish Hunter and Tom Seaver. The ballpark was sold out, and there were rows of standees three or four deep along the fences in left and right field. Yankee manager Bill Virdon and Met manager Yogi Berra contributed to this sudden party by starting their first-stringers—two lineups that looked to be very close to the teams that would take the field four weeks later, on Opening Day. Both New York front offices had been avid participants in an off-season of exceptionally complex trading activity, and as I studied the old names and the new names I had written on my scorecard, I sensed

myself already awash in the kind of deep-water baseball speculation that usually becomes possible only in August or September.
Among the new Mets were Del Unser (a useful if unbrilliant center
fielder who had come over from the Phillies as part of a trade that
had taken away Tug McGraw) and Joe Torre, who was with the
Cardinals last year—a lifetime .300 hitter and a former Most Valuable Player, now thirty-four years old and well past his peak but
perhaps still better than any previous Met third baseman. Starting
in left field was Dave Kingman, a tall free-swinger and erstwhile
(very recently erstwhile) Giant, who had just been picked up for
$125,000 in a straight cash deal. Last of all, most of all, there was
Tom Seaver, the Mets' champion, who would be trying out the sci-
atic hip that afflicted him all last summer—a disability now tentatively but anxiously regarded as cured by rest and osteopathy.

The Yankee alterations were even more noticeable. Gone was
the familiar and overburdened Bobby Murcer, who had been dealt
to the Giants for another outfielder—another *kind* of outfielder—
Bobby Bonds, a swift, powerful, mercurial, and not altogether reliable courser, who had never quite attained the superstar status expected of him. Thurman Munson, the Yankee catcher, would be
making his first appearance of the year and would be testing the
damaged forearm that limited his effectiveness last year. And, best
of all, there was Catfish Hunter, the ex-Oakland ace, a twenty-
game winner over four consecutive seasons, last year's American
League Cy Young Award winner (he was 25-12, with an earned-
run average of 2.49), undefeated in seven World Series games, et
cetera, et cetera, who was cut free from the A's last December by an
arbitrator's decision, as a result of Oakland owner Charles O. Finley's failure to make payments on a deferred portion of his salary.
Thus suddenly empowered to sell his fealty and right arm to the
highest or most attractive bidder, Hunter settled upon the Yankees,
after receiving unimaginable cajoleries ("You want Helen of Troy,
Cat? Listen, we'll fix Helen up with a beautiful annuity and throw
in a li'l old Dodge Charger for her, and...") from almost every
other club, for a sum in the neighborhood of three and a half million

dollars in salaries and deferrals and shelters and other considerations, to be paid over the next five years, and more. Inevitably, some sportswriters have begun to refer to him as Goldfish Hunter.

Beyond these individual athletic and fiscal histories was the interesting business of the two clubs themselves and their impending summer-long fight for the affections of the same enormous and demanding baseball audience—the battle of Shea Stadium, the war for New York. There has been nothing quite like this since the departure of the Giants and the Dodgers, for the swift decline of the once mighty Yankees in the past decade and the even more precipitous ascent of the darling Mets had seemed utterly independent of each other. Now a big-city baseball reversal may be in progress, with the young and star-enriched Yankees, who were a close second in their division last year, apparently the possessors of the best pitching and the best outfield in their half-league, on the rise; and with the aging Mets, pennant winners in 1973 but a fifth-place club last year, apparently in pitching difficulties and thus possibly in very bad trouble indeed. This spring meeting was part of a good subway summer to come.

The game began, and baseball replaced speculation. Hunter in pinstripes was about the same as Hunter in green and gold—the flowing hair, the flowing motion, the big, oversized cap resettled between each pitch. Seaver, too, restored memory—the cold, intelligent gaze; the unwasteful windup; the sudden forward, down-dropping stride off the rubber. He struck out two of the first three Yankee batters, without really trying his fastball. Now, with one out in the top of the second, Dave Kingman stood in for the Mets, occasioning a small hum of interest because of his height, which is six feet six inches, and his batting style, which is right-handed, tilted, and uppercutting. The hum was replaced by an explosion of sustained shouting as Kingman came around on a high Hunter change-up, caught all of the ball—every inch and ounce of it— with his bat, and drove it out of the park and out of the lights in a gigantic parabola, whose second, descendant half was not yet perceptible when the ball flew into the darkness, departing the premises about five feet inside the left-field foul line and about three palm trees high. I have never seen a longer home run anywhere.

There were further entertainments and events—two hits by Munson; the Mets winning the game, 3–0, on sterling shutout pitching by Seaver and his young successors, Craig Swan and Rick Baldwin; and *another* homer by Kingman, also off Hunter—this one a high, windblown fly just over the fence, giving him a total of four round-trippers in his first five games as a Met. He also fanned weakly on his last two times up. In the fourth inning, Joe Torre took a backward step near third base as Bobby Bonds came down the base path from second (there was no play on him), and somehow severely sprained his right ankle. It was an inexplicable, almost invisible little accident that nonetheless ruined Torre's spring, and the kind of pure bad luck that can sometimes darken a club's entire season.

Nothing, however, could touch or diminish Kingman's first shot. Catfish Hunter, after his stint, sat in the training room with his shoulder encased in an ice bag and his elbow in a bucket of ice water, and reminisced cheerfully about other epochal downtowners he had given up. There had been a preseason one by Willie McCovey and perhaps, years ago, a Mickey Mantle five-hundred-footer. Mantle, now a Yankee springtime coach, could not remember it. "I know I never saw one longer than this," he said. Bill Virdon guessed that the ball had flown an additional two hundred and fifty feet beyond the fence, into an adjacent diamond, which might qualify it as a simultaneous homer and double: a six-base blow. The Yankees were still talking about the home run the next day, when Hunter told Ron Blomberg he hoped he hadn't hurt his neck out there in left field watching the ball depart. Others took it up, rookies and writers and regulars, redescribing and amplifying it, already making it a legend, and it occurred to me that the real effect of the blast, except for the memory and joy of it, might be to speed Catfish Hunter's acceptance by his new teammates. There is nothing like a little public humiliation to make a three-and-a-half-million-dollar executive lovable.

That night, the press clustered thickly around Kingman in the visiting clubhouse. He is a shy, complicated young man, twenty-six years old, and he seemed embarrassed by his feat, although he was noted for similar early-season tape-measure blows while with the Giants, as well as for his strikeouts. "I'm just trying to win a job here," he said. "I'm putting home runs and strikeouts out of my mind. They're not in my vocabulary." Well, yes. Every spring is a new beginning, especially for a ballplayer with a new team, but in his three and a half major-league seasons to date, Dave Kingman has hit seventy-seven home runs while striking out four hundred and twenty-two times—once for every three trips to the plate— and his batting average is .224.

Rusty Staub, dressing in front of his locker, looked over at the tall newcomer and the eight or ten writers around him, and laughed. "The trouble with you, Dave," he called over, "is you're just having a slow start. You'll get going once the season rolls along."

Postcards

Saw Eddie Kranepool hit three singles today, against the Yanks. Eddie Kranepool always hits. Last year, he hit an even .300. Eddie will always be a Met. Mrs. Payson loves him, and, besides, why would you ever get rid of him? Eddie has it made. He has twelve years in as a major leaguer, twelve years on the pension. Eddie Kranepool is thirty years old. Good old Eddie.

Ron Blomberg came up the steps from the clubhouse and into the dugout, and saw a *Times* reporter reading the Mets' press pamphlet. "Hey," he said, "can I see that for a minute?" "Sure," the writer said, tossing it to him. "Don't drop it." Blomberg nearly did drop it. "Jesus!" he muttered. Terrible hands. Bill Virdon said, "You got him thinking." Everyone nearly died laughing. . . . Maybe you had to *be* there.

———

Watched Los Angeles taking batting practice before the next game at Fort Lauderdale. A young Dodger was looking at three girls sunning themselves behind home. Coach Monty Basgall said, "Get out of the stands; you're married now."

The ballplayer said something short.

"You still married?" Basgall asked.

"I think so. Why?"

"I don't know," Basgall said. "I figure you for the kind's going to get married three, four times."

Bobby Bonds, sitting on a trunk in the clubhouse before the Dodger game, talking about his old Giant teammate Dave Kingman: "If you see him hit two singles, it's amazing. If he's making contact, the ball's going to go. You know he's a great bunter? People don't know everything about him... I'm the d.h. today. Never did *that* before. What does the d.h. do when he isn't up swinging?... It's funny—I looked over at the Dodgers there today and I didn't get that old feeling. We used to be so up for those games. They really counted."

Straight Arrows

A slim, tan, dark-eyed young man with a very thin mustache turned up in the Yankee clubhouse. He was not in uniform, but most of the Yankee regulars came over to shake his hand. "Hey," they said. "Way to go. I just heard. Go get 'em there, now." He was Ray Negron, a nineteen-year-old Queens resident, who was a Yankee batboy last year. This winter, he was taken on by the Pirates in the second round of the free-agent draft, and now he was on his way to report to Pirate City, in Bradenton, for the opening day of minor-league training camp. He hopes to play second base with the Pirates' Class A club, in Charleston, South Carolina.

"Leaving home yesterday was the hardest thing I ever did in my life," he said. "Everybody came to the airport to see me off. My father, my mother, my two sisters, my grandfather, my girlfriend, and me—everybody was there, everybody was crying. I'm not afraid of what will happen. I know I can pick it in the infield, so the only question is whether I can hit the pitching. I'm very thrilled. This is what I've wanted all my life. Being around the big leaguers last year on the Yankees got my attitude together. Watching guys like Alex Johnson and Lou Piniella made me learn to be positive. Before last year, I was a sure out. Couldn't hit, couldn't win. Since then, I've hit over .500 in every league I've been in. I know how hard a major leaguer has to work, so I'm ready. I told my girl Barbara I wouldn't see her until September, no matter what happens. I said, 'You go out, have a good time. You're free. But if you want to wait, I'll be waiting, too. I'll wait for you in September.' " He looked down at the floor, suddenly shy.

Steve Garvey, the young Dodger first baseman, shook hands with two New York writers near the batting cage. Last year, he batted .312, hit twenty-one homers, and knocked in a hundred and eleven runs, and was voted Most Valuable Player in the National League. Garvey's hair is short and neat, and he is always clean-shaven. He is friendly and extremely polite. "It was a busy winter for me," he said. "I spoke at thirty-five or forty lunches and dinners, and made sixty or seventy appearances in all. I also did P.R. work for Pepsi-Cola. I missed being with my family, but on the whole it was a very satisfying experience. It was a real opportunity for me to be a good-will ambassador for baseball and for the club. There were a lot of father-and-son dinners and Y.M.C.A. affairs, so there was the opportunity to influence young people, to show them there are people in the world they can look up to and pattern their lives after. The kids do listen to you—I was amazed. I think they're ready to get away from the antiheroes of the nineteen-sixties and move on to the heroes of the seventies. Anyway, I don't care if they listen or not, because I believe this and I practice it in my life. Excuse me for a second, please. It's my turn to bat."

He stepped into the cage. The writers watched him in absolute silence.

———

Randy Tate, a tall young right-handed pitcher, was throwing hard on the mound at Huggins-Stengel Field, the Mets' training headquarters in St. Petersburg. He was being watched by Rube Walker, the Mets' pitching coach, and by a videotape camera. There was a long orange-colored electric cord snaking across the field from the sidelines to the machine, which bore the name Video Logic. It was a cool, bright morning, and the grass was still dark with dew and early shadow. Rube Walker shook his head and called Tate in from the mound. His place was taken by Jon Matlack. "Seven minutes, Jon babe," Walker said.

Tate pulled on a silky blue warm-up jacket and joined Rube Walker beside the machine. The camera operator began the playback, and we all watched Tate pitching in slow motion on the little screen. "You still think you're pushin' off the rubber?" Rube said. "You call that pushin' off? Look at that. This machine does the trick, Randy. I could talk to you about it all day, but this damned machine don't lie. Run it back again."

Huggins-Stengel is a modest double diamond in the middle of one of the St. Petersburg public parks. The field is surrounded by trees. There is a lake out beyond right field, and a tiny strip of bleacher seats next to the low clubhouse building. An old-fashioned water tower behind home plate. On this morning, there were about thirty spectators sitting in the stands; some of them were watching the infield workout, and some were reading newspapers. There were six or eight schoolboy ballplayers there, wearing sneakers and pale-blue pin-striped uniforms with "Cardinals" across the shirtfronts in blue script. Birds were twittering. It was so quiet that when one of the coaches tapped a grounder out to a shortstop you could hear the sound the ball made as it hit the infield grass.

Del Unser was inside the batting nets, out in left-field foul territory. He stood about ten feet in front of the plate, making things harder for himself, and swung left-handed against the characterless offerings of the pitching machine. Phil Cavarretta, the Mets' batting coach, stood behind him, with his arms folded. Cavarretta has a deeply tanned face and white hair. The machine stopped, and

Unser and Cavarretta began collecting the dozens of balls scattered about the rope enclosure; they looked like park attendants picking up after a holiday. They reloaded the machine and then dusted it with a rosin bag. "I turned this wrist just a little and opened up on it," Unser said, picking up his bat again. Cavarretta nodded. "If I keep my hands back, I can bail on a pitch and still hit the ball," Unser said.

"You're damn right you can," Cavarretta said.

Randy Tate began throwing again, and I walked back and stood beside Rube Walker, behind the backstop. Rube watched a few more pitches. "He ain't doin' a damn thing different," he murmured to himself. "How am I going to get *through* to him?"

In time, batting practice began, with coach Joe Pignatano throwing from behind a low screen on the mound. Jay Kleven, a young nonroster catcher, hit two pop flies to center, and coach Eddie Yost said, "Try to loosen up that top hand, Jay. Just throw the bat at the ball."

Kleven hit a liner over second base.

"That's it," Yost said. "Good!"

The next pitch broke down sharply over the plate, and everyone cried, "Spitter! Hey, a spitter!"

"Aw, it just got a little wet on the grass," Piggy said, laughing.

I drove downtown to Al Lang Field, the ancient, iron-beamed park where the Mets and the St. Louis Cardinals play their home games in the spring. The White Sox, who had come up from Sarasota to play the Mets that day, were taking batting practice, observed from behind the batting cage by their manager, Chuck Tanner, and by Harry Walker, a special-assignment scout for the Cardinals. The Cards were off in Lakeland for a game against the Tigers, but Walker was here. He was wearing a faded Cardinal road uniform, and he was talking earnestly to Tanner. From time to time, he pointed to a batter in the cage and then touched Tanner's arm or pointed to his knees. He held up an imaginary bat and cocked his hands and hips and swung the bat forward in different planes, talking all the while. Tanner watched his batters, but he nodded as Walker went on talking. A number of players and writers looked at this tableau in delight.

Harry Walker is a tall, deep-bellied man who has at various times managed the Cardinals, the Pirates, and, most recently, the Houston Astros. As a player, three decades ago, he was known as Harry the Hat; he won the National League batting title in 1947, with an average of .363. He is Dixie Walker's brother. Harry Walker is reputed to be one of the finest theoreticians of hitting in baseball, and several players who have come under his tutelage have given him credit for an increase of twenty or thirty points in their batting averages—astounding figures, for batting is considered the most difficult of all athletic techniques to learn or to teach. Some other players, however, have admitted that they found it impossible to take advantage of Walker's wisdom, simply because they could not force themselves to stay within earshot of him—to go on listening to the hundreds of thousands of words that pour from Harry Walker every day. Harry Walker talks like a river. He is easily capable of as many words per hour as Hubert Humphrey or Buckminster Fuller—which is to say that he is in the Talkers' Hall of Fame. A few summers back, one of the Houston infielders is reported to have said to a teammate, "I'm worried about Harry. He's a natural .400 talker, and these last few days he ain't talked more than about .280."

Three years ago, before an Astros-Dodgers game in Los Angeles, I casually asked Harry Walker why his young pitchers and catchers seemed to be giving up so many stolen bases to enemy runners. Harry Walker has no casual answers, and his reply, which took the better part of twenty minutes, encompassed the American public-school system, permissiveness in the American home, Dr. Spock, our policies in Vietnam, great pick-off deliveries of various right-thinking pitchers of the past, the high rate of divorce in America, umpiring then and now, the inflated American economy, the exorbitant current bonuses paid to young baseball prospects, taxation, growing up in the Great Depression, how to protect home plate with your bat during the run-and-hit, and various other topics. At one point I recall his crying, "Whah, hell-fahr, when Ah was goin' after mah battin' title in '47 and Ah got the sign to lay down the bunt 'cause we was down a run late in the game and needed to move that runner up, Ah didn't come stormin' and hollerin' back to the dugout to tell the old man how much Ah wanted mah at-bats in order to qualify for that title and whah Ah'd ruther have hit away, and Ah didn't slam mah battin' helmet down on the ground like those kids do here today. No, sir! Whah, God damn it, we din' even *have* any battin' helmets back then!"

Here, in time, the Mets and the umpires and the fans appeared, and the batting cage and Harry Walker were taken off the field, and the game began, and the visitors demolished the Mets, in a somnolent, sun-filled time-killer, by 4–1. Jerry Koosman pitched three good innings, and Randy Tate pitched, too, and gave up five runs and six hits; I am not a camera, but it seemed to me that Tate was still not driving off the rubber. Between these two hurlers, there was an appearance by a good-looking Mets sprout named Jeff Grose, who is only two years out of high school. Grose, a southpaw, showed us a live fastball and a smooth, high-kicking motion, and he hid the ball behind his hip while on the mound, like Sandy Koufax. He seemed poised, but he was working a little too quickly, and he gave up three hits and a run in his first inning of work. In the next inning, his fastball began missing the corners. He kept falling behind the hitters, and then forcing things and overthrowing to make up for it. He gave it a battle, though. With two out and a run in, he went to three and two, saw the next pitch barely tipped foul, then threw the fourth ball way inside, to load the bases, then swiftly walked in another run and gave up a single, and was lucky when Rusty Staub threw out a base runner at the plate. It was painful to add up his totals: four runs, six hits, and four walks in two innings. Spring training is good young pitchers falling behind on the count and then disappearing until next year.

Postcards

Saw the Phillies beat the Cards at Al Lang Field by 1–0, in a game illuminated by wind, sun, and young baseball stars. The newcomers include twenty-three-year-old Alan Bannister, a swift Phillie outfielder, and twenty-one-year-old Keith Hernandez, the new Cardinal first baseman, who batted .351 last year in the American Association. Before the game, I saw the Cards' Reggie Smith and the Phillies' Dave Cash in earnest conversation near the batting cage. As I walked by, Reggie was saying, "And the rest I got in tax-exempts."

Al Lang Field is to be demolished next fall, and a more modern ballpark will be built on the same site. It seems a pity, since the stands, which look like a leftover segment of Ebbets Field, perfectly match the style and antiquity of the fans. And what will happen to the ushers? When an Al Lang usher escorts an elderly female fan to her seat, it is impossible to tell who is holding up whom.

"Pick it" is this year's "in" baseball phrase. It means playing the infield well. Ken Reitz, the Cardinal third baseman, can really pick it.

Veteran

The speaker is Ray Sadecki, thirty-four, who is beginning his fifteenth year as a major-league pitcher. His lifetime totals are a hundred and twenty-nine victories and a hundred and twenty-seven losses, and an earned-run average of 3.77. His best year was 1964, when he won twenty games for the Cardinals and also won a World Series start. The next year, he slipped to six and fifteen. He has also pitched for the Giants and, in the last five years, for the Mets. He was sent back to the Cards last winter, as part of the Joe Torre trade. He sat in the dugout at Al Lang Field one afternoon, wearing a bright-red warm-up jacket, and talked about baseball. He has a quizzical, amused expression and an easy manner. He is left-handed.

"It seems to take me every single day of the spring season to get ready now," he said. "I make all the same moves, but I come up a little short. Then, of course, when the season starts a man like me who isn't a front-line pitcher anymore has to do all his training all over again, throwing on the sidelines. You get caught in those rain-outs and before you know it you've only pitched two or three innings in three weeks. The most starts I had with the Mets was twenty, and the least was two. You get to know all the conditions, all the possibilities. You know about that year when I lost fifteen games, right after my best year? Well, a man has to be pitching pretty well to get the *chance* to lose fifteen.

"Every time I'm traded, I figure the other club wants me. I went once for a pretty fair player named Orlando Cepeda. This trade from the Mets—you know they had to make it. Getting a chance at Torre doesn't mean they dumped me. The thing about trades is it's an opportunity for most players. An awful lot of trades end up helping the people involved. Look at Nolan Ryan. Look at Dave Cash. Torre came over to this club from Atlanta and won an M.V.P. Too many people get it wrong and think, Boy, what a rotten thing to do. Fans don't understand trades.

"The only tough part about being traded—the worst part—is when it happens during the season. Seventy-two hours to report. Your family is all upset, your wife has to do all the moving. You walk into your new dugout and they're playing the anthem. Hell, when I went over to the Giants I walked out onto the mound, and Tom Haller and I had to get together on our *signs*. A pitcher and a catcher need a lot of time to get used to each other.

"I'm a completely different kind of pitcher than I was when I was with this club the last time. But I don't figure I'm down here to let them see what I can do. They're looking at the young pitchers. I got together with Red [Schoendienst, the Cardinal manager] and Barney [Schultz, the pitching coach], and said I'll get ready in my own time. I pitched two and two-thirds yesterday. They weren't the best ever, but they were just right for me. I'm just where I want to be. That's what spring training is for. Anyway, we all know about a pitcher who gets hammered all spring and then walks out there on Opening Day and nobody can touch him. Another one has it the other way around—once the bell rings, he can't get any-body out. It's awful hard to make a decision about people in the spring. I've been out there at times in March and couldn't do *any-thing*. I embarrassed myself. But you can't start throwing harder and mess yourself up. That's what a kid will do.

"It's the young players I'm sorry for. It's awful hard for a rookie to make a ball club in the spring. If you're a pitcher, you've pretty well got to throw all scoreless innings. If you're a batter, you've got to hit about .400. Even so, they'll all say, 'Hell, it's only spring training.' Spring is hard on people."

The Cactus League consists of four small ballparks attached to a ribbon of motels, moccasin shops, trailer sales lots, and Big-Boy burger stands in and around Phoenix, Arizona—plus outlying baseball stockades in Tucson, Yuma, and Palm Springs, California. (The air service to Palm Springs, where the Angels train, is sketchy, and when one of the Phoenix-area clubs—the Cubs, say—plays there, the visitors can count on a good twelve hours, round-trip, in which to study the desert from the windows of their bus.) The mo-tels are functional to the spring baseball scene. Generally, they fea-ture an enclosed central swimming pool and lawn and patio, plus restaurant and bar and dance floor and shuffle courts and lobby and coin-operated electronic Ping-Pong games, all of them variously patronized by players, managers, league executives, front-office people, writers, scouts, and fans, and attendant wives, children, ba-bies, parents, in-laws, girlfriends, hookers, and Baseball Annies. (Lounging at poolside one morning, I noticed a nearby gathering of cheerfully forward, heavily tanned ladies, of indeterminate age and affiliation. I asked a fellow-writer about them. "Groupies," he said. "They've been coming here for years and years. They used to hang out with the players, then with the coaches. Now I think they're umpire groupies.")

The Giants' park, Phoenix Municipal Stadium, is an agreeable, half-sunken field, with a concrete grandstand offering a prospect of distant mountains, a nearby highway, and, in between, several weirdly twisted, buttelike rock formations suggesting dinosaurs or

Boschian damned souls or Horace Stoneham's baseball hopes. The Giants, by general consensus, in recent years have led their league in finding and developing the greatest talent and then employing it to the smallest possible ends. This year, they have come up with another one of their nearly irresistible Spring Specials—a new (almost) manager, a lineup stripped of last year's disappointing stars, and a stimulating catalogue of young arms and great wheels. Gone is the charming, moody skipper, Charlie Fox, who plainly lost control of things last summer and was replaced in mid-campaign by the calm and approachable Wes Westrum. Gone are the high-strung, well-paid Bobby Bonds and Dave Kingman. A veteran hot-dog second baseman, Tito Fuentes, was sent to the Padres in return for a new hot dog, Derrel Thomas. The pitching staff is young and strong but without a true stopper—with the possible exception of a second-year fireballer named John D'Acquisto. The holdover regulars afield, including Chris Speier and Garry Maddox and Gary Matthews, have dash but not much power, and there is a terrific catching prospect named Marc Hill.

I watched this bright-eyed entering class in action against the World Champion A's, whom they defeated by 7–2, thus pleasing an underflow crowd of 2,802 and persuading me that another summer of high, dashed hopes was in the making at Candlestick Park. Steve Ontiveros, a former outfielder, does not exactly pick it at third base for the Giants; in the fourth inning, he played a one-hopper by Joe Rudi off his shoulder, and he later threw the ball away while attempting an easy double play. (The Giants have had forty-six third basemen since they came to the Coast, in 1958.) The A's, for their part, seemed to be suffering from similar tinkering. Joe Rudi, the best defensive left fielder in the American League, has been moved to first base in order to make room for Claudell Washington, who is a good hitter but cannot field much. He played a fly ball by Matthews into a double and later threw behind a runner. The best poke of the day was a triple in the fifth by Bobby Murcer—a Murcer Special into the deepest right-field corner. A week or two earlier, Bobby had delivered himself of a bad-tempered public blast against the Yankees for shipping him off to San Francisco in the Bonds trade, but now, after the game, he appeared to be in splendid humor, as befits a man currently batting .500. I asked him if the trade might not in fact be one of those that ended up helping both principals. "Don't know," he said. "Ask me in September."

The most heavily reported news at the Indians' camp in Tucson this spring was fundamentally unreportable—the fact that Frank Robinson, the new Cleveland manager, is black. Like several dozen visiting scribes before me this year, I sought him out in his office at Hi Corbett Field (where he was lunching on two Cokes and some saltines crumbled into a cup of soup), shook hands, asked him some questions, and concluded that he was going about his duties in a responsible if inescapably predictable fashion. He admitted to some innovations—no team curfew, the appointment of two team captains (one white, one black; or, rather, as Robinson put it, one an outfielder and one an infielder)—and said he had turned over a great deal of detail work to his coaches, so that he might have more time to watch and get to know his players. "I want things done right," he said. "That is, I want them done my way."

He hadn't had time to do much batting himself, and thus prepare himself for his additional duties as a designated hitter. Robinson spoke with alternate gravity and humor, exuding the same sense of weight and presence I have always observed in him. We chatted a little, and then I said goodbye and wished him luck, and made room for three more out-of-town reporters, who had come for the same unspoken and unspeakable purpose: How does a black manager manage? What is black managing? How does it, uh, *feel* to be the first black manager?

It was nice and hot in Tucson, and I sat in the stands that afternoon and caught some rays. There was a grove of trees out beyond center field, and the distant outfield fences were covered with old-style billboards—Jim Click Ford, Coors Beer, Ralph Hays Roofing, Patio Pools. (Arizona outfields are spacious, to make room for the great distances that fly balls carry through the dry desert air; a few years ago, in Mesa, Curt Blefary ducked away from an inside pitch, and the ball struck his bat and flew over the right-field fence for a homer.) Two veteran flingers, the Indians' Fritz Peterson and the Angels' Chuck Dobson, had at each other, with the visitors enjoying all the best of things. The Angels have only speed and pitching, and their left fielder, Mickey Rivers, a skinny blur on the base paths, stretched two routine singles into doubles. In the California fourth, Cleveland center fielder George Hendrick fielded a single and threw the ball over the cutoff man's head. The Indians, who have insufficient pitching, may have a long summer of it.

There was a good mix taking the sun in the stands that day: high-school girls with long, clean hair; a lot of young men—probably students at the University of Arizona—with beards and tanned bare chests and cutoff jeans and silver bracelets; and, of course, old folks. At one point, somebody behind me said, "I understand they gave Homer a pacemaker, but it was sort of out of pace with his heart." A pause, and then "Oh, well, Homer has more money than Carter has little pills."

Just before I left, in the seventh, I recorded a personal baseball first: Most Fans Seen Wheeling a Bicycle Up Aisle of Grandstand—1.

Postcards

Spotted Alvin Dark's car parked outside Rendezvous Park, in Mesa—a big, mocha-colored Imperial LeBaron, with Florida plates and two rear bumper stickers. "A's World Champions" was on the left side and "Jesus Is Coming Soon! Every Knee Shall Bow" on the right. Dark, the Oakland manager, is a direct man. Last winter, he mailed several revivalist tracts to Ron Bergman, who covers the team for the Oakland *Tribune*. Bergman is Jewish.

Rollie Fingers, watching the Padres take infield practice: "There's that Hernandez, at short. I'll never forget that year he had five hundred and something at-bats and drove in twelve runs."

Ray Fosse: "*What?* That's impossible."

Fingers: "Look it up."

I looked it up. The year was 1971. Enzo Hernandez drove in twelve runs in five hundred and forty-nine trips to the plate.

Before an Indians-Brewers game at Sun City, Gaylord Perry, the Cleveland pitcher who is starting his fourteenth year in the majors, spotted Del Crandall, who put in sixteen years as a player and is starting his fourth year as the Brewers' manager.

"Hey there, Big Del," Perry said. "I see we made it to another year."

"Yeah," Crandall said. "Let's hope it don't run out on us."

Easy Lessons

1984

There's nothing like an all-expenses-paid late-winter vacation under the palms and within sight and sound of batted baseballs to give a sensitive man a deeper appreciation of the nature of guilt. Each year in March, I journey to Arizona and then to Florida, or vice versa, to watch a sampling of the current and future major-league ballplayers do their morning stretching exercises on dew-dappled outfield lawns (lately these workouts are being done to bouncy aerobic-rock sounds and are led by a young woman in shorts and leg-warmers who is clearly in better shape than anyone else on the field) and then test and disport themselves in batting cages and on practice mounds—engaging in B.P. and Infield and Shagging and Flip—and eventually play a few innings of morning B-Squad ball or an afternoon exhibition game, and each year this excursion brings me such freshets of pleasure that I must find new excuses within myself to justify the dulcet bystanding. Duty, for instance. I am there at the camps as a reporter, to be sure, having been dispatched sunward to search out the news and the special sense of the coming season, and there is no sterner or more assid-uous newshawk to be found on the demanding Scottsdale-to-Sarasota beat than yours truly. Even the most casual morning invitation to take a dip in my motel pool or to make a fourth at middle-aged doubles finds me puritanically glum. "Not a chance!" I cry. "I'm *working* today." And work I do, carefully noting in my notebook the uniform number and the unremarkable batting mannerisms of some hulking young stranger now taking his hacks in the cage, and checking his thin line of stats (.266 and eight home runs in Danville in 1981) in my team press guide, and then eliciting clubhouse quotes from a grizzled bullpen millionaire about the current state of his damaged wing ("Hurts like a bastard..."), and, later in the day, raising my mid-game gaze from the diamond to observe the gauzy look of departing rain clouds lifting from the jagged rim of some distant desert peak, and then entering *that* in my notebook (with the pen slipping a little in my fingers, because of the dab of Sea & Ski I have just rubbed on my nose, now that the sun is out again and cooking us gently in the steep little grandstand behind third base). I watch and listen and write, filling up almost as much space in my copybooks as I do in October at the World Series, and entering on my scorecard the names of third-string non-roster substitutes who filter into the game so late in the day that even the geezer fans and their geezerettes have begun to gather up their backrests and seat cushions and head off home for beer and naps. Guilt, as I have said, is the spur, for it is my secret Calvinist fear that baseball will run dry on me some day and I will find nothing fresh at the morning camps, despite my notes and numberings, or go newsless on some sun-filled afternoon, and so at last lose this sweet franchise. Baseball saves me every time—not the news of it, perhaps, so much as its elegant and arduous complexity, its layered substrata of nuance and lesson and accumulated experience, which are the true substance of these sleepy, overfamiliar practice rituals, and which, if we know how and where to look for them, can later be seen to tip the scales of the closest, most wanted games of the summer. Almost everything in baseball looks easy and evident, but really learning the game, it turns out, can take a lifetime, even if you keep notes.

Let's face it: spring training is a misnomer. Thanks to aerobics, racquetball, high-tech physical-fitness centers, California-chic wives, and a sensible wish to extend their very high salaries through as many years as possible, most major-league ballplayers stay in terrific shape all year round now. Back in the straw-suitcase days, it took a month to six weeks to work off winter beer bellies and firm up poolroom-pale bodies, but contemporary players have told me that a single week of batting practice and rundown drills would make them absolutely ready for Opening Day. What with performance records, autumn visits to the Instructional Leagues, and almost daily reports from the winter-ball leagues in Latin America, most managers have a pretty good notion of the capabilities of the rising minor leaguers in their organizations, and are not likely to be badly startled (or much convinced) by a .485 spring average put together by some anonymous rookie outfielder during the exhibitions. The pitchers, to be sure, do require all of March and a little bit more in order to get their arms in shape, and the process—early stretching and tossing, the first three-inning stints, then harder stuff and longer outings—cannot be hurried or shortened, since there must be days of recuperation after each game or batting-practice workout. Spring training is really for the pitchers, then—and for the writers, who need this slow, sleepy time in which to sweeten their characters and enlarge their perceptions of what truly matters in our old game. I offer as example an apothegm uttered by a friend from the *Chronicle.* It was in a week of dazzling weather in Arizona, and we were sitting side by side in the narrow pressbox of Scottsdale Stadium, watching the Giants vs. (I think) the Brewers. Late in the sixth inning, he looked irritably at his watch and said, "Damn. Yesterday's game was already over by this time."

"Right," said I, arising and gathering up my notebook, media guides, pencils, and scorecard. (My deadline was weeks away.) "And thanks, Dave. See you at the pool."

In Winter Haven, on the very first day of this spring jaunt, I found Ted Williams out in right-field foul ground teaching batting to Von Hayes—a curious business, since the Splendid Splinter, of course, is a spring batting instructor for the Red Sox, and Hayes is the incumbent center fielder of the Phillies. Hayes was accompanied by Deron Johnson, the Philadelphia batting coach, and the visit, I decided, was in the nature of medical referral—a courtesy second opinion extended by a great specialist to a colleague from a different hospital (or league). Von Hayes is a stringbean—six feet five, with elongated arms and legs—and his work at the plate this year will be the focus of anxious attention from the defending National League Champion Phillies, who are in the process of turning themselves from an old club into a young one in the shortest possible time. Since last fall, they have parted with (among others) Pete Rose, Joe Morgan, Tony Perez, and veteran reliever Ron Reed, and later this spring they traded away Gary Matthews, their established left fielder (Matthews, in fact, was intently listening in on Ted Williams' talk to his teammate Hayes), to the Cubs. Two years ago, in his first full year in the majors, Von Hayes hit fourteen homers and batted in eighty-two runs for the Cleveland Indians—sufficient promise to encourage the Phillies to give up five of their own players (including the wonderful old Manny Trillo and the wonderful young Julio Franco) for him. Last year, Hayes, troubled with injuries (and perhaps unsettled by the nickname Five-for-One, bestowed on him by Pete Rose), batted a middling-poor .265, with six homers—reason enough for a call to Dr. Ted.

"Lemme see that," Ted Williams was saying, and he took Hayes' bat and then hefted it lightly, like a man testing a new tennis racquet. "Well, all right, if you're really strong enough," he said, giving it back. "But you don't need a great big bat, you know. Stan Musial always used a little bitty drugstore model. So what *do* you want? You know what Rogers Hornsby told me forty-five years ago? It was the best batting advice I ever got. *'Get a good ball to hit!'* What does that mean? It means a ball that does not fool you, a ball that is not in a tough spot for you. So then when you are in a tough spot, concede a little to that pitcher when he's got two strikes on you. Think of trying to hit it back up the middle. Try not to pull it every time. Harry Heilmann told me that he never became a great hitter until he learned to hit inside out. I used to have a lot of trouble in here"—he showed us an awkward inside dip at the ball with his own bat—"until I moved back in the box and got a little more time for myself. Try to get the bat reasonably inside as you swing, because it's a hell of a lot harder to go from the outside in than it is to go the other way around."

Hayes, who looked pale with concentration, essayed a couple of left-handed swings, and Williams said, "Keep a little movement going. Keep your ass loose. Try to keep in a quick position to swing. When your hands get out like that, you're just making a bigger arc."

Hayes swung again—harder this time—and Williams said, "That looks down to me. You're swingin' down on the ball."

Hayes looked startled. "I thought it was straight up," he said. He swung again, and then again.

"Well, it's still down," Ted said quietly. "And see where you're looking when you swing. You're looking at the ground about out here." He touched the turf off to Hayes' left with the tip of his bat. "Look out at that pitcher—don't take your eyes off him. That and—" Williams cocked his hips and his right knee and swung at a couple of imaginary pitches, with his long, heavy body uncocking suddenly and thrillingly and then rotating with the smooth release of his hips. His hands, I saw now, were inside, close to his body, while Hayes' hands had started much higher and could not come back for a low inside pitch with anything like Ted's ease and elegance. Nothing to it. Hayes, who has a long face, looked sepulchral now, and no wonder, for no major leaguer wants to retinker his swing—not in the springtime, not ever—and Williams, sensing something, changed his tone. "Just keep going," he said gently to the young man. "Everybody gets better if they keep at it."

Hayes kept at it, standing in and looking out at an imaginary pitcher, and then cocking and striding, while Williams stood and watched with Deron Johnson, now and then murmuring something to the other coach and touching his own hip or lifting his chin or cocking his fists by way of illustration—a sixty-five-year-old encyclopedia of hitting, in mint condition: the book.

When I left, he was deep in converse with Gary Matthews, who had asked about the best response to a pitcher's backup slider after two fastballs up and in. "Why, *take* that pitch, then!" Ted cried. "Just let it go by. Don't be so critical of yourself. Don't try to be a .600 hitter all the time. Don't you know how hard this all is?"

I accompanied the Red Sox down to Sarasota to watch Tom Seaver work against them the following afternoon—his first American League innings ever. Seaver, as most of the Northern Hemisphere must know by now, was snatched away from the Mets over the winter when that club carelessly failed to place him on its protected twenty-six-man roster prior to a "compensation draft"— a process that permits a team (in this case, the White Sox) that has lost a so-called Type A player to free agency to select as recompense a player from a pool of players with other teams that have signed up for the plan. This misshapen schema is a monster child spawned by the owners as part of the settlement of the player strike of 1981, and there is considerable evidence that its headstrong fathers may now wish to disinherit it. Shortly after the Mets' humiliation, the Yankees experienced a similar shock (the circumstances were a little different) when they lost a freshly signed top pitching prospect, Tim Belcher, to the Oakland A's in another compensation kidnapping. The Mets, in any case, suffered a horrendous double embarrassment: first, for the forfeit of their old hero figure—an Odin brought back to the fold last year, amid many trumpetings, to finish his days in Shea-Valhalla as the steadfast elder leader of a corps of shining young Baldurflingers—and, second, for the clear evidence that it somehow did not occur to them that the pennant-hungry and publicity-hungry White Sox might find some use for a highly motivated and splendidly conditioned veteran star pitcher (Seaver is thirty-nine) with a lifetime earned-run average of 2.73. The Mets people, to their credit, have rent asunder their blazers and strewn dust upon their razor-cut pates in public penance for their gaffe, and no further criticism of them will be put forward here.

The first glimpse of Tom in Chisox motley—neon pants-stripes, the famous No. 41 adorning his left groin—was a shock,

though, and so was the sight of him in pre-game conversation with
his new batterymate, Carlton Fisk. I took a mental snapshot of the
two famous Handsome Harrys and affixed to it the caption "Q:
What's wrong with this picture?" (A: Both men are out of uniform.) Then the game started, and Seaver's pitching put an end to
all such distractions. It was a prime early-spring outing—three
swift, harm-free innings that included a couple of bases on balls
and four strikeouts. There was a good pop to his fastballs, and he
wheeled in some thoughtfully located sliders and curveballs as
well, and once it was clear that he was going to be all right out there
I sat back and took pleasure in all the old looks and ways of him—
the thick, strong legs and droopy shoulders, the grave gaze catcher-
ward for the sign, the audible "*Hunh!*" that sometimes accompanied the in-driving thrust of his big body in mid-delivery (Ted
Williams had said that he doesn't hear enough grunts from the
mound nowadays), and then the mitt flipped up vertically to take
the catcher's return peg.

In the clubhouse after his stint, Seaver declared himself satisfied
with his work—perhaps more than satisfied. There had been some
small technical problems—his release point was a little flat at
times—but that wasn't surprising, because he'd been nervous about
this outing. "I wanted to prove to the guys that I can help this ball
club," he said. "They don't care who you are. They want to know if
you can still pitch—especially at the age of thirty-nine. This is a team
that wants to win. They've had a taste of it, and they want more.
What our game is all about is proving things to your own team."

He went over the three innings almost pitch by pitch, making
sure that the writers had their stories, and they thanked him and
went off. A couple of us stayed on while Tom unwrapped the big
icepack from his shoulder and started to take off his uniform. I
think we wanted reminiscence or philosophy from him now—
something about motivation or the shocks of unexpected trades or
the wearing down of an athlete's will with the years—but what we
got was much better: mechanics. He talked about tempos of early
throwing in the first few days of spring—a murmured "*one, two,*

three-four…one, two, three-four" beat with the windup as his body relearned rhythm and timing. He went on to the proper breaking point of the hands—where the pitching hand comes out of the glove—which for him is just above and opposite his face. Half undressed, he was on his feet again and pitching for us in slow motion, in front of his locker.

"What you don't want is a lateral movement that will bring your elbow down and make your arm drop out, because what happens then is that your hand either goes underneath the ball or out to the side of the ball," he said. "To throw an effective pitch of any kind, your fingers have to stay on top of the ball. So you go back and make sure that this stays closed and *this* stays closed"—he touched his left shoulder and his left hip—"and this hand comes up *here.*" The pitching hand was back and above his head. "It's so easy to get to here, in the middle of the windup, and then slide off horizontally with your left side. What you're trying to do instead— what's right—is to drive this lead shoulder down during the delivery of the ball. That way, the pitching shoulder comes up—it *has* to go up. You've increased the arc, and your fingers are on top of the ball, where they belong."

I said I'd heard pitching coaches urging their pupils to drive the lead shoulder toward the catcher during the delivery.

"Sure, but that's earlier," Tom said. He was all concentration, caught up in his craft. "That's staying closed on your forward motion, before you drive down. No—with almost every pitcher, the fundamentals are the same. Look at Steve Carlton, look at Nolan Ryan, look at me, and you'll see this closed, this closed, *this* closed. You'll see this shoulder drive down and this one come up, and you'll see the hand on top of the ball. You'll see some flexibility in the landing leg. There are some individual variables, but almost every pitcher with any longevity has all that—and we're talking now about pitchers with more than four thousand innings behind them and with virtually no arm troubles along the way."

Someone mentioned Jerry Koosman, who had gone along from the White Sox to the Phillies over the winter, and Seaver reminded us that he and Koosman and Tug McGraw and Nolan Ryan had been together on the 1969 World Champion Mets and that they were all still pitching in the majors, fifteen years later. "Nolan Ryan's still pitching *and then some,*" he said. "We all had good fundamentals, and our pitching coach, Rube Walker, stressed the right things—don't overthrow, stretch out your work with a five-day rotation, and keep those sound mechanics."

There are other ways to pitch and pitch well, to be sure, Seaver said, and he mentioned Don Sutton as an example. "Sutton's exceptionally stiff-legged," he said, "but he compensates because he follows through. He doesn't do this." He snapped his right arm upward in a whiplike motion after releasing an imaginary ball. "The danger with a stiff front leg is recoiling."

He picked up the remaining pieces of his discarded uniform and underwear and tossed them into a canvas hamper. "What is the theory of pitching?" he went on. He sounded like a young college history lecturer reaching his peroration. "All you're doing is trying to throw a ball from here to here." He pointed off toward some plate behind us. "There's no energy in the ball. It's inert, and you're supplying every ounce of energy you can to it. But the energy can't all go there. You can't do that—that's physics. Where does the rest of it go? *It has to be absorbed back into your body.* So you have to decide if you want it absorbed back into the smaller muscles of the arm or into the bigger muscles of the lower half of your body. The answer is simple. With a stiff front leg, everything comes back in *this* way, back up into the arm, unless you follow through and let that hand go on down after the pitch."

"But isn't that leg kick—" I began.

"The great misnomer in pitching is the 'leg kick,'" he interrupted. "That's totally wrong. Any real leg kick is incorrect. Anytime you kick out your leg you're throwing your shoulders back, and then you're way behind with everything. You've got to stay up on top of this left leg, with your weight right over it. So what is it, really? It isn't a leg kick, it's a *knee lift!* Sure, you should bend your back when you're going forward, but—" He stopped and half-shrugged, suddenly smiling at himself for so much intensity. "I give up," he said. "It's too much for any man to do. It's too much even to remember." He laughed—his famous giggle—and went off for his shower.

I got lucky in Arizona three days later, because here was Don Sutton working five sharp innings for the Brewers against the Giants in Scottsdale, and I could think about mechanics some more. Sutton gave up two singles and a solo home run (to Jeffrey Leonard), and got a passel of ground-ball outs with his down-breaking curve, which he throws, oddly, with his forefinger crooked up on the ball and the fingernail cutting into a seam. For a while there, I thought he *was* snapping his arm on the recoil—he comes straight over the top, right-handed, bobbing over the front leg and finishing with so little twist or drop to his body that it almost appears to be attached to a vertical wire somewhere—but when I concentrated I thought I could see his pitching arm moving so fast after the release that his hand, a blur, actually did come down past his left knee before it slowed, stopped, and rose again. I wasn't sure, though, and I checked this with him when we met in the dingy wooden visiting-team clubhouse after his outfield sprints. Sutton has fashionably cut gray curly hair and a lean, humorous face; he looks and sounds like his pitching style—slick, spare, smart. Within a couple of weeks, he would turn forty and begin his nineteenth season as a big-league starter.

"Yes, my arm comes way down," he said at once. "I transform the strain. My mechanics are fundamentally sound, because I do what comes naturally to me. We're all unique. To take a guy like me and turn him into a drop-and-drive pitcher like Tom Seaver would have made for about a one-year career, and to make Tom into an over-the-top curveball pitcher would have done the same to him. Seaver has powerful legs and butt muscles and a strong upper body. All my effort in pitching comes from my upper legs and lower back, and I've worked over the years to keep them strong."

Sutton's shirt was off by now, and I could see the lean, tightly drawn shoulder muscles moving beneath his skin. His body looked tailored. He told me that Red Adams, his pitching coach with the Dodgers years ago, had worked with him to establish and refine his pitching form—"He found my slot" was the way he put it—and had given him four checkpoints to watch for during his delivery. Raising his arms, he faced me and went through a slow-motion delivery. "One: Start square," he said. "Two: Quarter-turn. Three: Pause at the top and tap. Four: Go on through and *don't stop.*" He did it all again, even slower this time. "Starting square, looking directly at the plate, and making no more than a quarter turn is important, because if I do this"—he bent his body a little farther away from me on the pivot, going from nine o'clock to about ten-thirty—"if I get that far, I can't make up for all that body action by the time I turn the ball loose. The quarter turn keeps me together. The tap at the top"—he wiggled the toes of his right foot, the mound foot, while his hands were still together above his head— "allows the upper part of my body to catch up with the bottom half and then throw and follow through. It's a one-beat pause. If I *don't* tap, then I'll just rush ahead, so I'm twisted way over here, while my arm is still behind. When I do tap, it's—" And he finished his motion beautifully, with the arm going down and through and then rising again. He had looked almost nothing like Seaver during all this—he was more of a machine, less menacing—but then, near the end of it, I saw the lead shoulder drive down and the back shoulder fly up, bringing the pitching arm up high and through, exactly like Seaver's. They were the same, after all.

That was enough mechanics for the moment, and I asked Sutton how he felt about baseball now, in this last, or latter, part of his career.

"I don't care any more or any less about the game than when I started," he said. "I still think it's a fabulous profession to be in. Sometimes we get a little unrealistic about the role we play in things. Being a professional athlete doesn't solve world hunger or stop crime. It's not going to cure cancer or build houses for people. It's not as important as we think it is. What I do for a living isn't that big a deal to me, then, but the fact that I can do it is a real big deal, because it was the goal I set for myself. I love the competition. It's as simple as that."

I found Reggie Jackson playing in a B-game between the Angels and the A's the next morning. He'd been waiting out a pulled leg muscle, and these were his first at-bats of the spring. He rapped a little single to right, struck out, and stroked a double against Ray Burris, which the center fielder, out by the 410-foot mark on the wall, gloved but could not hold: a real Reggieblow. He was d.h.-ing for the Angels—it's his regular position now—and between his turns on deck and at bat he came out and stood in the sun with some of the writers along the low right-field fence and took care of the day's ink. Reggie loves to talk—we all love what we're good at—but now, for the first time, he was talking about the end of his playing days, or the chance of that. He had an abysmal season in 1983—a .194 average, with fourteen home runs, the last of which came in July. In the campaign just previous, he had tied for the league lead with thirty-nine downtowners. He has four hundred and seventy-eight lifetime home runs, and Angel-watchers last summer had the impression that he was so eager to reach the five-hundred plateau (he would be the thirteenth player there, ever) that his big stroke came apart under the strain. He will be thirty-eight later this spring, and there can't be many seasons ahead. He looked the same as ever—large and friendly and anxious to please, and in great shape—and it was hard to ask him how he felt about closing down his career.

"I often think about coming to the end," he said. "It's fairly real—it's a possibility—and I can't say it doesn't bother me. It isn't a big event or anything, but what I'd like now is to leave on my terms. If I had another year like last year—and that wasn't a bad year, it was *horrible*—then I'd have to go. I'd feel defeated. It isn't just slowing down, not being able to do what you've done— that's understood and accepted. You can deal with that. But we're talking about maybe not being able to play baseball at all—the end. In some ways, I won't mind. The position I've been in is that of an offensive leader who is counted on to produce. If I play in a hundred and fifty games, I'm expected to put a number on the board in a hundred of those games. That's the kind of pressure you don't mind doing without, especially if you've accomplished some goals along the way. So if I can do what I think I can do this year—hit maybe twenty-five home runs and eighty-five R.B.I.s, just get back in Reggie's groove—then I don't think I'd miss the game after that. But if I didn't—if I was asked to leave—it would be a whole lot different. I'd miss baseball if it came to that. It's *how* you go."

I asked if he felt that people expected him to fail now, where once they had expected him to succeed.

"I'm always under pressure," he said. "I always feel that. Even in this game—a little B-game. I got that base hit and everybody reacted to that. I could feel it. Then I struck out—it was the first changeup I'd seen all year—and I could feel the pressure of *Uh-oh, you didn't succeed. What are people thinking?* The pressure goes on and off for me now even from one at-bat to the next."

Someone asked if most older players didn't have to bear this sort of burden, and Reggie agreed.

"If you're over thirty-five and you've done some things in this game, you develop—if I'm using the word right—you develop a certain braggadocio, a bravado about yourself, but you know you're being watched in a special way, because this is a young man's game. If you do have some bad games, people notice it and write about it and talk about it, and you begin to think, Hey, why are you knocking me now? Even when I'd had a good season, like two years ago, I'd be asked how I measured it, how I felt about it, and that brought defensive responses. You can understand that. So listen. If I get one more good year, give me a pat on the back. Give me a feather and I'll wear it in my cap."

One of the umpires in that morning game was Pam Postema—a quick, slim, cheerful arbiter from the Pacific Coast League, who is the only woman ump in the business. I'd seen her work some games last year. The word on her is that she is an outstanding ball-and-strike ump and that she doesn't take any guff out there. At one point in the spring, there was a rhubarb on the field, and coach Herm Starrette, of the Giants, told her to go back to her needle and thread, and she threw him out of the game. Here in Phoenix, she was talking to some friends after the game—she said she'd been hit on the toe with a foul the day before and was dying to get off her feet—when a fan leaned out of the stands and handed her a ball to sign. "Just give me your autograph, will ya, honey?" the man said.

Postema took the ball and the pen and said, "You want me to sign it 'Honey' or do you want my name?"

Lucky kids get to be batboys in the spring games—mostly the sons of coaches or club executives or older players, who come and visit their fathers during the spring break at school. For a while in March, the Oakland batpersons were Kacey and Carey Schueler, the daughters of Ron Schueler, who is the pitching coach for the A's. Another A's sprout on hand was Jim Essian III, the son of the veteran backup catcher, who was the smallest batboy on view anywhere. He is four years old, and he wore a green sunsuit on the job, with manager Steve Boros' No. 14 inked on it, fore and aft. He had all the moves out there. Dave Kingman, who has caught on with the club as a designated hitter this year, bombed a moon shot up onto the left-field embankment against the Cubs' Scott Sanderson, and when Kong came around third James III was waiting about ten feet up the line from home, with Kingman's bat under his arm, and he gave him a high five—high for him, low for Dave—as he came by.

As it turned out, I did have a scheme of study this spring, and that was to listen to older ballplayers talk about their trade. I didn't plan it that way, but once it began to happen I was ready to go back for more. Rookie fireball flingers and unknown nineteen-year-old sluggers who can hit the ball five hundred feet into the mangrove swamp are the prime drawing cards of spring baseball— the equivalent of royal palms to Florida or giant cactus to Arizona—but over the years I have discovered that while it is exciting to watch the kids and think about their futures, it does not nearly match the pleasure of listening to the older players tell you what they have learned over many thousands of major-league innings. Tom Seaver, Don Sutton, and Reggie Jackson don't have much in common at first glance except their age and their long success, but what I picked up from them all was an absorbed pride in work that accompanies, and sometimes even exceeds, the self-pride and love of challenge that lie somewhere near the center of every professional athlete. We envy and admire ballplayers because they get to do brilliant things under contrived but excruciatingly difficult circumstances; if they like themselves in the end, we can forgive them, I think, for it is much clearer to them than to anyone else how truly hard it was, every day, to play this game well, or at all.

Rusty Staub, the old man of the young Mets, had an amazing season in 1983. Employed almost exclusively as a pinch-hitter, he batted .296 over a hundred and four games, and rapped twenty-four pinch hits—one short of the all-time record. His eight consecutive pinch hits, in June, tied another record, and so did his twenty-five pinch runs-batted-in for the season. All this came to pass in his twenty-first season; he started as an outfielder with Houston in 1963, when he played a full season, with more than five hundred at-bats, at the age of nineteen. Along the way, he became the first people's favorite—*le Grand Orange*—with the newborn Montreal Expos; then held down right field for the Mets in the early seventies (I can still see him catching a drive by the Reds' Dan Driessen and crashing heavily into the wall out there—and holding the ball), batting .423 in their second World Series, in 1973; then played for the Tigers, the Expos again, and the Rangers; and came back to the Mets in 1981. (Staub has put on a few pounds over the years, which isn't surprising since he is a restaurateur and a renowned chef on the side; during his second stint with the Expos, some of the writers began calling him Julia Child—though never, I think, to his face.) I talked with Staub one bright, breezy morning while we sat on a little green bench outside the clubhouse at Huggins-Stengel Field, where the Mets train. He is a large, thickly built man, with pink eyelashes and oddly pale skin and a self-contained, polite way of speaking. He was a few days short of his fortieth birthday.

"Most of the men who have played into their forties have been pitchers," he said. "The players who have made it that long are a group that's had talent and a tremendous dedication to staying in shape. People like Yastrzemski, Pete Rose, Joe Morgan, and myself took pride in how they played every day. They didn't give in. They never said the hell with today, we'll get 'em tomorrow. Every game mattered. As my career went along, I saw a lot of players with great ability who didn't stay in the game as long as they could have, because they seemed to lose their desire. Even way back when I was with Houston, people were saying I only had a couple of years left, but I knew better. I'm pleased and proud I've been able to stay in this game and still play with the young guys."

Staub said that he had found it much easier to accept his role as a pinch-hitter once Keith Hernandez came over to the Mets from the Cardinals last June. Before that, Dave Kingman had been playing first, although Staub was convinced that he himself could have helped the club more at that position. Hernandez deserved the job, in Staub's estimation, and that made a difference in his own mental adjustment to his limited duties. "You've really got to have a positive attitude about yourself to be a pinch-hitter," he said. "As frustrating as hitting is, there's just no comparison between it and pinch-hitting. You're going to come up to bat in a great many situations where the game is on the line, and no matter what sort of streak you're on you're going to make some outs, and they'll be outs that hurt. You're going to let down your teammates. It's wonderful when you do get up there and put your team back in the game, or get the hit that ties it up, or the hit that wins it, but when you make the out, that's *tough*. You have to be mentally strong about it, because you can't redeem yourself until the next opportunity, and that may not be until a week from now. You have to have a great belief in your own abilities and worth to go through that and not get down."

He talked a little about the more technical side of the work— staying loose in the clubhouse during the game with exercises and a skip-rope, so as to be in gear when called upon, and keeping his short stroke (a thing of beauty; how well I can see it!) at the plate. "If there's anything I've worked at, it's to be intelligent about the pitchers," he said. "I try to give the outstanding pitchers full credit and not do too much with the ball. Take what's there. If there's a really good left-hander with a breaking ball"—Staub is a left-handed batter—"you can't be up there wheeling for the fences. Most of the time when I'm up, I'm only after a base hit. Going after an extra-base hit is a little different, and sometimes you can have that in mind and succeed. Not a *lot*, though." He shook his head.

"I don't get to play in the field much now," he went on, "but I used to work on that part of the game as much as I did on my hitting. It's strange, but quite a few people who are known as hitters do the same thing. That's why I spent so many hours thinking about the other aspects of the game. One of the greatest compliments I ever got was when Ron LeFlore called me one of his top ten base stealers in the game, not because of my record"—Staub has forty-seven lifetime stolen bases—"but because I'd studied it so much. I knew the pitchers and their moves, and I think I was able to help him become such an outstanding man on the base paths."

I told Rusty that I'd always had the impression, watching him, that no part of the game had come naturally to him. Every aspect of it—running, hitting, picking up the ball and throwing it—looked to me as if it had been studied and practiced endlessly and somehow mastered.

"What you saw is right," he said. "I discovered at a very early age that nothing was going to come easy for me, that I'd have to work to have any success. I compliment my dad and my mom and my kid coaches and high-school coaches, who all made me want to do things the right way—and to know myself. *That's* the biggest challenge for any player: to know in what situation you might have a tendency to back off a little and not do very well—from an injury, say, or for any reason—and then to learn to overcome that. Learning to face the people you have to face and how to do things then. It's—well, I don't think I want to get into that. It's rough."

What he did want to get into, it turned out, was the part of the game from which he is now exiled—playing outfield, that is. "I probably got as much pleasure from playing defense as anyone who ever played this game," he said. He was smiling a little now. "I took great pride in being able to throw the ball hard and with real accuracy. For ten or twelve years there, I probably threw the ball from the outfield as well as anybody in my league, and I definitely threw as accurately as anyone. I know I made myself into an outstanding outfielder, and when I slowed down a little I found that I loved playing first base well. When I made an outstanding defensive play, that was as good as a base hit any day. As good or better."

Afterword: Rusty retired after the 1985 season and so missed out on the Mets' glorious pennant season and World Championship the following year; he has joined the Mets' broadcasting crew. He rapped out nineteen more pinch hits over his last two seasons—each under extreme duress, for the Mets had risen into serious contention in their division by then. To me, his finest moments came in late September of 1984. I was at Shea Stadium when he smote an eighth-inning two-run pinch-hit single that beat the Phillies and clinched second place for the Mets. He came out of the dugout for a standing O (a practice he deplores), waved his cap, and disappeared—done for the year, I assumed. *Almost* done. The next night (I was away, worse luck), with the Mets again in the soup, manager Davey Johnson again rang for the specialist, and Staub whacked a game-winning two-run homer in the bottom of the ninth. It was Rusty's only home run of the year (and his two-hundred-and-ninety-first lifetime), and the first for him since he turned forty, back in April. He struck his very first home run back on June 3, 1963—Don Drysdale was pitching—when he was a nineteen-year-old first baseman with the Houston Colt .45s. Rusty Staub thus qualifies as the second player ever to hit major-league homers as a teen-ager and in his forties; his companion in this feat is Ty Cobb. Stat of the year.

Takes: Waltz of the Geezers

1990

It's funny about spring training: everyone looks forward to it, but before it ends, everyone is dying to have it over with and get on to the regular games and the real action. Then you look back at the spring and remember how special it was. There must be more to it than sunshine and a sense of fresh beginnings. Spring training is also baseball's social season—the only extended stretch of the year when old-timers in the game can meet old friends and have a drink, have a meal, play a round of golf: catch up. Old baseball guys are sociable in the same way that actors are, and perhaps career military types as well; like them, they have come to know large numbers of fellow-professionals under vivid and demanding conditions, which are almost always followed by long stretches of separation or exile. All their lives, ballplayers keep running into old friends or old enemies; they hug and bury paws and emit low, growly noises. They are forever reuning.

No one has more friends than my friend Bill Rigney, a former manager and onetime Giants infielder, who is now senior adviser to the Oakland high command. He and I go back about ten years, I think, which still makes me a rookie friend. I told Rig once that I could remember how he'd looked playing infield for the Giants at the Polo Grounds—skinny and quick and strong, with glasses, and an eager little lean out there. But I couldn't quite recall how he'd looked up at bat. I said that wasn't in my mind's eye but I was trying to bring it back, and he said, "Don't try too hard." Rigney is quotable long and quotable short, and as a writer I appreciate this.

Rig was talking one night about a time back in the nineteen-sixties when he was managing the California Angels and had to depend on some pitchers perhaps past their prime. "I had Jack Sanford, the old Giants right-hander," he said, "and then, along about 1967, I got Lew Burdette, who'd been so great for the Braves all those years. Everybody said Lew used to throw a spitter, and they were right. He'd load up by putting his hand up to his mouth on the mound, which was legal and O.K. in those days, so long as you then went to the rosin bag. Lew would wet up just the bottom of his front two fingers—'It only takes a bitty dab, Skipper,' he'd say—and then he'd pick up the bag with the tips of his fingers and never touch the wet part at all. Just rub the ball up and it was ready to fly.

"When I got Burdette, he was just about at the end of the line. He and Sanford were roommates, and there was a day when Lew was pitching for us against the Twins out in the old Metropolitan Stadium, in Bloomington. He threw Killebrew a fastball and Harmon hit it up into the back of the upper deck—you remember those open stands out there. The ball hit a seat in just about the last row, *way* up. No one in local history had ever hit one that far. I didn't even look up when it was hit—you could tell by the sound. It was such a big home run that when we came back the next day they'd already painted that seat gold, to commemorate the spot. Well, you can imagine that Jack Sanford had had a few things to say to his friend about the home run that night—'Roomie, you must have some stuff to get a ball to go *that* far.' And the rest of it. The next day, Jack was pitching, and I'll be a son of a gun if he didn't throw one that Harmon hit just as far and just as deep. The ball hit the *adjoining seat* to the one they'd painted, so now they had to go out and paint that one, too. They probably used the same can of paint."

Rigney said that Burdette came to the end of the line later that summer, and it fell to him to break the bad news. "I told him I was sorry, but this happened to us all, sooner or later, and we were letting him go. I said I hoped he'd land with some other club and prove what a dummy I was. I felt bad about it, I don't mind telling you. Well, Lew didn't say a word. Just looked at me and shook his head and got up and walked out of my office. I was surprised, because we'd been sort of close. When we signed him, he'd even pasted a photograph of me inside the door of his locker, which was something I'd never seen before. After he left, I hung around a few minutes and then I walked out into the clubhouse, but the boy said Lew had packed up and gone—just walked off without saying a word to anybody. I went over and took a look in his locker, and that was when I saw he'd driven this big nail through the picture of me. Right through the heart. He just didn't want it to happen— didn't want to say goodbye. I ran into him somewhere a few months later, and I asked where he'd ever found a hammer to drive that spike in my heart. He said, 'Skip, I used a bat.' "

If you and Rigney are leaving a spring-training restaurant together, you might as well go on ahead and get the car out of the lot, because he will have been stopped at three or four or five tables on his way out. Same thing at the ballpark. Sitting with Rig at a morning B-game, say, you know you'll soon be introduced to some ballplayer you haven't thought about for thirty years: George Zuverink, Mickey McDermott, Walker Cooper. This spring, it came to me that these were rarely the *same* old guys; the supply seemed bottomless, and so did Rig's pleasure over each meeting.

"George Zuverink?" he said when I asked. "Well, George pitched against me a lot, but always in spring training, because he was over in the other league, with the Indians. I don't think I ever got a hit against him—that's what *he* says, anyway. No wonder I'm his friend!" (Zuverink, it should be added, is the very last name in the Baseball Encyclopedia—the other bookend to Hank Aaron.) Mickey McDermott, by contrast, was a batting-practice coach for Rigney when he was managing the Angels. "A super guy," Rigney said. "He's had some problems over the years, but everything's O.K. for him now, I imagine. His wife won five million dollars in the state lottery here last month."

I asked about his closest baseball friends, and Rigney said that most of his intimates seemed farther away these days. "They're scattered all over," he said. "I still see a fellow who played for the Giants a little ahead of me—Johnny Vergez. He lives up in Oroville, California, and he and I go fishing every year. He was the manager of the Oakland club when I came up in the Coast League. I played for him a couple of years. I have friends I played *against,* too, like Bucky Walters. You remember, he was with that good Cincinnati club, with Ernie Lombardi and the rest. Somebody reminded me the other day that in 1939 Bucky and Paul Derringer pitched fifty-nine complete games between them. Can you imagine that!"

I can listen to stuff like this all day, but when there was a pause (there are a million pauses at spring games) I asked Rigney if he thought that contemporary players had the same sort of friendships today, and if they would remember their own playing days with the clarity and pleasure that he did.

"I've wondered about that myself," he said. "Everything is different for them, in a way, with all this money, and you can't help wondering if it means as much to them. Maybe it does. I think baseball friendships were close in my time because you started with the knowledge that you'd all made it in the game—you'd done something you'd dreamed about when you were a kid. Is that the same now?"

Before long, he was talking about the spring of 1951, when the Giants and the Yankees exchanged spring-training sites, and he and some teammates found tiny cottages to rent on Lido Beach, in St. Petersburg. "Forty-three bucks a week, right on the beach," he said. "Soon there was a whole bunch of us: Herman Franks, Chub Feeney—he was our young G.M.—and Ernie Harwell and his wife. Paula [Rigney] was there, with our three kids, and Chub and Margaret Ann had two or three little ones along. Lefty Gomez and June were there—he was finished with the Yankees by then, and was working for the Wilson sporting-goods company. Alvin Dark was new to our team, but after a while he heard about us and *he* moved in. It was funny about the Yankees' being away and us Giants' being there, because that fall we played each other in the World Series. Oh, we were so young that spring! Maybe that's why you remember. I'll tell you one thing about those cottages: If you went to call on somebody, you had to bring two things. A glass and a chair."

He didn't quite want to leave the subject, and a few moments later he said, "Sometimes I see somebody I haven't laid eyes on in years, and it just gets me. I can see the way they looked on the field or up at the plate, I mean. Bert Blyleven—I watch him pitch and I can still see the way he looked when he was in his rookie year and did so well for me on the Twins. He had that great breaking stuff even then. He still calls me 'Mr. Rigney.' Orlando Cepeda—I saw *him* just the other day in Scottsdale, and it..." He seized himself around the throat. "It's the same with guys like Enos Slaughter or Andy Seminick—I remember them because I had such big fights with them, some real rhubarbs. Seminick slid into me that once, and his spikes caught part of my jersey and tore it in half—took the uniform right off me." He considered recounting this epic battle scene once again but then thought better of it. "I guess we remember because those things felt important to us," he went on. "Like the time I was in an argument with some umpire when I was managing. I was out there yelling and jumping up and down and waving my arms, and he said, 'Hey—take it easy. It's only a game, you know.' And I said, 'Only a *game*? It's my life!'"

Put Me In, Coach

1993

Big-league baseball, to hear Merv Rettenmund talk, used to be
a lot less interesting. "I broke in with the old Orioles at the end of
the sixties," he said one morning in Arizona. "And by the time I'd
made it up to that level I'd been in the Baltimore system for four
years, and I really knew the game. We were a boring club to watch,
because on the routine plays—the cutoffs, the relays, the rundowns—everyone did it right. No exceptions. Nowadays, the routine infield pop-up is no longer routine on some occasions—it's an
adventure. With free agency and with players moving around so
much now, you have two or three regulars on your club each year
who are new faces, and you have to start again from scratch. In
some places, the only way management can keep costs down is to
bring up kids, and sometimes you do that too fast. You work on
fundamentals every day in the spring, even at this level, because the
big leagues have become a developmental league. The old days are
gone. On that Baltimore organization, there might be one roster
change each season. The club was winning a hundred games, year
after year, and spring training was more a question of going out
there and getting prepared for the World Series."

Rettenmund will turn fifty this year, but he doesn't look all
that different from our first impressions of him when he arrived in
the American League, in 1968, as a midsized, thick-bodied outfielder and deadly line-drive hitter with Earl Weaver's Orioles;
we'd been hearing scary reports about him for years, it seemed,

from the Orioles' Triple-A Rochester Red Wings. He played thirteen years in the majors, with six Championship Series and four
World Series along the way. He is still in uniform, as hitting coach
with the San Diego Padres, and the change in him you notice most
might be the high-style sunglasses he wears now. He has been
teaching hitting almost as long as he practiced it—with the Angels,
the Rangers, and the Athletics, before moving over to the Padres
three years ago. Listening to him in Arizona this spring and last, I
had the notion that he remembered the old days in baseball but
without longing. His conversation switched from then to now and
back again, and he was at pains that I would not leap to any easy
conclusions along the way. "Today's established players work
much harder than guys did in the old days, and they listen more,"
he said at one point. "Work habits are wonderful now. You can't
find a guy who works harder than a Tony Gwynn, a Rickey Henderson. Players like Fred McGriff, Jose Canseco, Paul Molitor—
they're never not working, they stay later than anybody. There's a
big misconception about this, I think."

But when our conversation got around to lesser players—say,
batters who were expected to have mastered specific skills in order
to make up for less evident talent—Rettenmund admitted that
there were some contemporary deficiencies. "Down in the bottom
of the order, the job description is handling the bat," he said. "And
once again there are some jobs that are going to be lost in the major
leagues because there'll be some guy who can hit but he can't play
the game."

Baserunning has declined as well, he thought, in spite of the
quickness of modern players and the vastly increased number of
bases stolen. "Earl Weaver was a hard man, and he always let you
know how he wanted things done," he went on. "He said to do the
job right or he'd get somebody else—and you could *do* that in
those days. One of the things he insisted on was that you not get
doubled off base on a caught line drive. That's a tough situation,
but Earl would simply not accept excuses. Every time you got on
first base with one out or no outs, you had that in mind and

thought about it. It was even harder on our fast guys, like Al Bumbry and Paul Blair—real aggressive base runners—but they knew what to do. If you watch baseball today, you'll see base runners get doubled off first over and over again. It's like they think nothing can be done about it." He paused for a moment—a good coach always waits to see if a prospect knows a little something—and when I shook my head he explained. "You have to read it off the bat. You watch the pitch. If it's going to be high in the strike zone, you're in business—when that ball comes off the bat six to eight feet high, you can be running. If there's a low pitch, down in the strike zone, more than likely it's going to be a low line drive or a ground ball, so you know to hold on, ease up to protect yourself. If you're concentrating on that strike zone, you can usually read it right. But it takes years and years to learn that skill, and it still isn't easy. We coaches can talk about it and talk about it, but some players will never know what they're doing when they get on base."

Another major-league season, fresh text to the old book that Rettenmund was talking, is here, already fulfilling its traditional functions as a season harbinger and as promise that the endless winter-sport schedules will come to a close someday—well, some *month*—soon. Once again, baseball instantly showed us its appetite for surprise, when the Indians' slugger Carlos Baerga, in a game against the Yankees, knocked two home runs in the same inning from opposite sides of the plate; no one in the majors had ever done *that* before. But the fresh season has been most welcome of all as a perfect and ironic distraction from the gnarled difficulties and accumulating doubts afflicting baseball itself. Some of the sport's intractable problems have hung around for so long that their history and esoteric workings are now as familiar to us fans as the principles of the hit-and-run play, albeit without the fun. A spring checklist of baseball's chronic or worsening ailments would find the same old management-labor pangs, the revenue-sharing blockage, the television-money collywobbles, the free-agent and salary-escalation syndrome, the ever-rising salary-arbitration readings, the low-grade discriminatory-hiring infections (with the ugly flareup of the Marge Schott affair), and so forth. None of these need be further addressed now, but the bad news does not stop there. A serious decline in fan interest, particularly among the younger sectors of the audience, is at last being openly discussed, along with baseball's shortage of star performers at the topmost, Nike-commercial levels of the sport and the equally distressing diminishment of talent at the rookie stage. In addition, we have lately been seeing what one might call the Balkanization of baseball, as evidenced by the arrival of the expansion-team Florida Marlins and Colorado Rockies in the National League this year; the midwinter scramblings and finaglings over the removal and last-minute restoration of the ancient Giants franchise, from San Francisco to St. Petersburg and back again; and the recently announced and apparently unalterable plan to reconfigure the leagues into three divisions instead of two, with an accompanying new, third tier of post-season championship games which will require the admission of an inferior, "wild card" fourth team to each playoff. Lastly, but not separately from any of the above, one must note the unspoken refusal of the owners to select a new commissioner to succeed the departed Fay Vincent, whom they fired eight months ago, for more or less the same reasons that now keep them from replacing him: because they wish to remain distant from the media and the fans, accountable to no one but themselves.

With or without a commissioner, these deadweight issues and slipshod resolutions feel far removed from the game itself, which is where we fans might better direct our gaze, if we don't want to find ourselves simply giving up on baseball. With this in mind, I decided last year and this to sign myself up for some remedial baseball coaching and listening. I was impelled in this direction by a feeling that had been growing on me over the past several summers that there were plenty of other things amiss in baseball—things I could see plainly, out there on the field. The game was changing in small ways, and mostly for the worse. It wasn't the tactics or the hitting or the pitching—not in particular, I mean. I couldn't quite prove it with statistics, or necessarily find it in a single game, or two or three games, but it was clear to me that major-league baseball was no longer being played at its old rigorous and imperial best— at a level that seemed to eliminate carelessness and faulty execution and faulty thinking. It was losing the everyday dramatic tautness that had once prevailed: the expectation that almost perfect baseball would be played, inning after inning, and that winning a game would therefore require something exceptional to happen out there—a succession of stifling infield plays; a huge strikeout or an induced pop-up in the right place; a throw to an unexpected base which allowed a run to score but assassinated a big inning; a stroked single to the opposite field, off a tough pitch from a tough, knowing hurler. These were the moments you could look back on later that evening, or the next day, thinking, *That was the ballgame.* Everyday good baseball was important because the central emotion of the game was satisfaction. The thrills would come along in due course, almost on their own; what mattered was playing the game right—playing the way Merv Rettenmund talked about.

Too often now, the games I go to are not played well. I am not alone in this feeling, of course: among my friends and fellow-fans, griping about slovenly or mindless big-league ball has grown to such insistent levels in recent years that it's like a locust chorus in full summer, which one notices only when it stops. What we have seen much of is a lead-off man who doesn't want to win a base on balls; a batter in the three or four slot who is too impatient to try to work the count his way, and a fifth or sixth man in the order who will strike out, looking, twice in succession on exactly the same three-and-two slider, thrown by the same pitcher to the same corner of the plate, and will then walk back to the dugout without the smallest visible sign of concern. I am tired of seeing a well-paid six-year man once again swing from his heels (the one I have in mind bats right-handed), with a teammate on second late in a tied game, and hit a fly ball to left field instead of to right, with zero ensuing effect on the game. I'm almost startled when I notice a batter who can actually foul off a pitch that is too much for him—foul it off on purpose, I mean. I am weary of the extempore bunt attempt that means nothing, and simply passes the burden of the inning to the next man coming up to bat; and I'm even more burned up about the talented batter (this one—hint, hint—switches, and recently changed teams for the third time in three years) twice butchering an essential bunt during an at-bat and then cheering up, almost grinning, because now he is free to swing away, as was not needed.

Many fans I hear from blame these shortcomings on the inflated player salaries (the average major-league stipend is a million one hundred thousand dollars these days) and on an arbitration system that can double a player's salary after a glaringly mediocre season. They don't have to play well anymore, the complaint goes, and so they don't even try. I understand these feelings, because I have shared them at times, but I'm far from certain that money has a great deal to do with most of what goes on out on the field. And if fans are aware of a decline in skills and desire in today's game, then the clubs themselves, one must conclude, know it much better and must worry about it ceaselessly, because the financial stakes for them are so high. For evidence of this, one need go no farther than the increased attention given to coaching in the modern game. Coaches are better paid than they were even five years ago, with some of them at the major-league level now pulling down six-figure salaries. A couple of managers, Tom Lasorda and Tony La Russa, have reached the million-dollar range. Old-time coaches had the job stability and distinguished anonymity of tenured faculty members; Frankie Crosetti spent twenty-two years in the third-base box for the Yankees, patting pin-striped rumps as they rounded his corner after another Bronxian thunderclap. Modern-day coaches become celebrated and sought-after when their team has had some success; four coaches or mentor-players who served on La Russa's Oakland staff—Jim Lefebvre, Rene Lachemann, Don Baylor, and Dusty Baker—are current managers, and another coach, Ron Schueler, is in charge of major-league operations for the White Sox.

There are more coaches than there used to be, at every level of the game, and they are younger and more articulate than their predecessors; some of them have graduate degrees, and many more have had motivational training. Without exception, they regard the work as a profession, rather than simply a means of hanging on in baseball, as was once the case. Friendship still comes into play when a manager selects his coaching staff—skipper-loyalty is a prime consideration, everyone agrees—but capability outweighs palship. The deep-chested local monuments who stood at the corners of the diamond year after year (and sat beside the manager in the hotel bar every night) have gone the way of the straw suitcase.

Contemporary coaches use contemporary tools—for instance, video libraries of every at-bat by every player on the team, cross-referenced by pitcher and situation. Rene Lachemann, who is managing the newborn Florida Marlins, compiled a celebrated personal Smithsonian of tapes as a coach with the Athletics and the Red Sox over the past decade and while managing the Brewers and the Mariners before that. Larry Hisle, the batting coach for the World Champion Toronto Blue Jays, is a computer hacker who can present each batter in his lineup with a pre-game printout showing his prior tendencies and situation performances against today's starting sinker-slider right-hander with the visiting team.

Stats and tactics are always alluring, but knowing what coaches are trying to teach these days may be a more useful way of keeping up with what's going on. With that in mind, I made an effort last year not to be wholly distracted by the standings and the daily rush of game news, by super-statistics and celebrity performers; instead, I hung around coaches and managers (who are head coaches, after all) and some older active players—a couple of dozen of them, in the end—most of last spring and this spring, and in parts of last season as well, asking questions and trying to find out what *they* thought of the state of the game. All of them, of course, had been young players once themselves, and their concerns about the high level and perhaps the ultimate survival of high-quality baseball, I kept finding, ran as deep as my own. Deeper.

"In the old days, managers never got to the park early," Johnny Pesky said. "You had a pitching coach and a batting coach in the minors, and that was it. They were more workers than teachers. They put you out there and left you alone. We had those leagues to work in—the D-leagues, the Cs, the Bs, the As, the double As, and the triple As—and you went one league at a time."

Pesky, I should add, is more totem than coach these days: he is seventy-three, with a lifework tan, a needle nose, and gleaming, pinpoint eyes, but, trim in his snowy Red Sox uniform, he still looks ready to play. He is at the Sox camp in Florida every day in the spring, and although there is always a bat in his hands, you sense that he is there as exemplar—a shiny vintage-car exhibit to give the rookies and the regulars a look at baseball history, since it is a subject about which many of them appear wholly ignorant.

"In those days, you always looked for other players to model yourself after," Pesky said one morning. "Johnny Frederick—he's the one who hit six pinch-hit home runs one year—came out of the majors and back to the Pacific Coast League and was a great hitter there. I saw him when I was a kid, and tried to change myself to be a little like him. Later on, when I'd begun to play, Heinie Manush, the Hall of Famer, spotted me in a pepper game one day and called me over. He told me I was just a little guy, so I'd have to stand up a bit closer in the box and choke up a little more. He said, 'Look, those guys are going to knock the bat out of your hands, so let's just give this a try.' He convinced me, and I had a great year. Rocky Mount, North Carolina, in the old Piedmont League—it must have been 1940."

Pesky didn't make it to Fenway Park until his eighth year in organized ball, but it could be argued that he was ready. His rookie-year two hundred and five hits led the American League in 1942, but he always discounts the feat by pointing out that he was hitting just ahead of Ted Williams in the Red Sox lineup. "We had advantages then," he said to me. "Now we have all this coaching instead, and it's needed, because these kids come up so fast—a year, two years in the system, for some of them—that they haven't had the experience. Me, I'd still like to see an infielder or an outfielder play about three hundred games and *then* maybe take a step up."

John Wathan is thirty years younger than Pesky but came along in baseball in almost exactly the same manner, putting in six years in the minors (San Jose, Waterloo, Omaha, Jacksonville) before he matriculated, in 1976, as a catcher and sometime first baseman with the Royals; he played ten years in Kansas City, melding almost imperceptibly into a coach at the end, as smart catchers often seem to do, and then managed the club for five years. He is bench coach with the Angels now, after filling in as skipper again last year, when their manager, Buck Rodgers, was severely injured in a team bus crash.

"You have no idea how much instruction goes on at the major-league level now," Wathan told me in Tempe this year. "Kids are short on bunting, on hitting the cutoff man, reading a pitcher's moves when they're on base, moving a guy from second to third with no outs, when to hit away, when not to hit away—all that stuff."

Wathan said that when he made it onto the Royals' roster it was before the era of team motivational meetings. "Now all of us are working on kids' heads as well as their mechanics. You need to keep them positive all the time—I'm a firm believer in that. Players used to be self-motivated, but now— You'd almost believe it would be the other way around, but I've heard players who are making millions complain that they're not appreciated."

He recalled that managers had more authority in the old days. "Everyone knew that if you screwed up, or didn't play hard when they put you out there, you'd be back on the bench or out of there," he said. "He had that hammer."

Roger Craig is back on his horse ranch in Southern California these days, having stepped down as the Giants manager when the club was sold this winter. Last spring, in his dugout in Scottsdale, he told me that when he pitched in the Dodger system as a young man he'd had some managers who never spoke a word to him from the first day of the season to the last. Not a word of conversation, that is. "What they did was chew your ass all the time," he said. "You do that now, and the player will call his agent. It just makes everything worse. Now you've got to talk to all your players every single day. They've got to be stroked more. Maybe they're less mature, but mostly they're just different."

Craig, like Johnny Pesky, came up in the game during baseball's peak years—there were fifty-nine minor leagues in the late nineteen-forties, and perhaps ten thousand professional players in all—but I couldn't pick up any sounds of resentment or resignation when he talked about the new order of things in the clubhouse. "Players used to get paid for what they did. Now they get paid by a system," he said. "They may have that multiyear contract. They may be younger, and some of them may have less talent, but you still have to try to reach them. It's a real challenge to do that every day. Some of them may have stayed up late with a baby, or something, and then they feel, Why should I play today? I'm tired, and, besides, I'm getting paid anyway. If I see a coach who can get inside that young man's head for a hundred and sixty-two games and find a way to let him use his ability, then that's the coach I want. That's what coaches are for."

Bob Brenly, a carryover coach with the Giants this year under their new manager, Dusty Baker, was a Giants catcher for the better part of a decade—a hardworking pro and a terrific favorite with San Francisco fans and San Francisco pitchers. He is seamed and strong-looking, with a dark mustache and a cheerful manner. "When I came into baseball, things were done sort of on gut instinct," he said when we sat down together. "Coaches said, 'This is the way we've always done it,' and you were supposed to learn from that. I remember Hank Sauer, who would always yell 'Can you hit, kid?' and you had to answer 'You bet your ass!' He insisted on it."

Brenly said he thought that younger coaches, the ones most recently off the field, might be the best communicators with today's young players. Players like him, I suggested, and he said, "It was probably true back then, too, only no one tried it. We have more problems now, because the players get up here and they seem unwilling to change. They don't want to bat some other way, or try anything different on the field. They feel, This is what got me here, so why should I try anything different?"

The best help for this, in Brenly's mind, is to urge the newcomers to watch older players on the club who are working on *their* games. Will Clark, for instance. A year ago in Scottsdale, Clark (if the Dalai Lama is reading this, Will Clark is the Giants' All-Star first baseman and nonpareil left-handed swinger) had been lining a lot of pitches foul into right field, and late one afternoon Brenly and I, from behind the batting cage, watched him repeatedly hitting outside pitches toward left field and then a bit toward center: working his way back around, in the parlance. This year, standing behind the same cage one morning, I noticed that Clark was doing exactly the opposite. The B.P. pitcher was throwing inside, on Will's instruction, and he was doggedly trying to inside-out the ball: keep his bat level and hit the pitch off his fists into left field. He kept talking to himself and gesturing to the pitcher to keep the ball in tight. He wasn't doing well at first, and finally he lost patience. "*Don't* come off the ball like that, Will Nuschler Clark!" he growled, stepping back. "*Stay* in there!" He made some rumbling noises and set his jaw—his mouth looks like an upside-down jack-o'-lantern's when he's up at bat—and yelled to the pitcher, "I'm going to inside you if it takes all fucking *day!*" The next pitch was on his hands again, but he inside-outed it like a mirror-image Roberto Clemente, and the ball flew hard down the left-field line and bounced on the white foul line. Clark said, "There. *Whatcha* think now?" He was staring at me but clearly still talking to Will Nuschler Clark. I looked around to see if anyone else had seen all this, perhaps even some young Giants, but no one seemed to be paying attention.

Bunting is a whole lot easier than inside-outing the ball, but several coaches told me that contemporary players don't seem to have much interest in the art. Some of them blamed the aluminum bat—now universally employed in college ball—because the ball pings off its surface too quickly to make for a readily controlled bunt. Others mentioned artificial turf, which is likewise unconducive to the maneuver. Rod Carew, however, discards such excuses. "They're just plain not interested," he told me. "I look at these players who can run, and they never work on the bunt. I see kids with speed who are hitting about .220, and I tell them that they could be hitting .280 if they'd just add that bunt. They don't want to discipline themselves and stay with something. It's discouraging."

Carew, the stick-thin long-term batting coach with the Angels, has style: dark curly locks and seemingly permanently affixed shades, which he wears low on his nose, like a character actor. No one could ever do so many stylish things with a bat (one of his old managers, Bill Rigney, remembers a year when Carew had twenty bunt base hits over the season), and I said that it amazed me that young players didn't sense that there was something convincing about what he was telling them.

"I think they're not all that sure of themselves," Carew said quietly. "You try to throw out suggestions, but... In the end, you have to find out what a player has and work with *that.*"

Ten days later, on a rainy morning at the Mets' camp, in Port St. Lucie, Florida, I watched another lanky grand master working on bunts inside one of the batting cages. It was the new Mets shortstop, Tony Fernandez—a ten-year veteran who came over from the Padres in a winter trade to serve as a fresh sill for the team's crumbly left side. Fernandez is a switch-hitter, but after he gathered up the loose balls in the cage and reloaded the machine I noticed that he was staying lefty, batting from one side only, and still squaring around and tapping the ball again and again, laying each bunt down like a necktie on a bed. Then I remembered that Fernandez's usual stroke from that side of the plate loops the ball toward left field—a pretty thing to see but not much use whenever there might be a Mets base runner on first base whom he wanted to move along in a close game. The bunt, of course, would do just that—*will* do it, this year. Once again, though, there didn't seem to be any young players around taking in the lesson.

Gloomy thoughts about the next generation have always been endemic in baseball, as elsewhere, and it should be pointed out that a freshet of exciting, talented, hardworking, and presumably attentive young ballplayers has come into the majors in the past three or four years and is already making a considerable mark. Mike Mussina, Steve Avery, Travis Fryman, Carlos Baerga, Gary Sheffield, Chuck Knoblauch, Ken Griffey, Jr., John Olerud, Delino DeShields, and the current American League home-run champion, Juan Gonzalez, are all twenty-four years old or under, and have brilliant careers in full momentum. Several almost guaranteed future stars (the Braves' Javy Lopez and Chipper Jones come to mind) are just down the road, and clubs like the Indians and this year's Angels have put their fortunes in the hands of some very young major leaguers, in part as a maneuver against the huge costs of veterans' salaries. But my spring tours convinced me that a visible broad fault line, dividing one generation of ballplayers from the next, has fallen across clubhouses within the past decade.

Dave Righetti, the spirited southpaw battler, is still only thirty-four years old (he is hanging on in the Giants' bullpen, after a 1992 season that cost him his job as the left-handed stopper for that club), but when he talks about his 1981 Rookie of the Year season, with the Yankees, it sounds like another baseball era altogether. "We had Lou Piniella and Bobby Murcer with the team then," he said. "Those guys couldn't run anymore, but they saw to it that guys played their positions properly. They knew when to sneak up on the infield. They always hit the cutoff man, because they knew they couldn't get the ball to the plate by themselves. Up at bat, they moved people over. Most of all, they made contact. Outside of Reggie, we never had a big swinger in the order, and we all hated strikeouts in the middle of an inning—that killed rallies."

Rags said he was amazed at the number of mistakes that were made on big-league teams nowadays, especially since every event on the field was so closely watched today, thanks to television. (In the old days, he almost whispered, if mistakes were made you never heard about it the next day.) He said he was impressed with the quality of coaching at the major-league level now, but believes that most of those coaches should be sent down to the A-level minors, where they are most needed. And he thinks that large signing bonuses for young prospects are a particular hazard. "The pressure to win is everywhere now, and it affects everyone, from the manager on down, but it's worst on the kids," he said. "You see guys come out of college ball now with a big name and maybe a lot of money—I mean, a lot—and there's this sense that they want to make it pay off for the club right away. I see them out there every day in the spring, trying to do too much. Sometimes I try to tell them, 'Hey, don't do *that!*' But they never listen—I'm just a pitcher."

Another old young pitcher in Arizona this spring was Ron Darling. Suddenly, he is thirty-two, and a ten-year man. He won fifteen games for the Athletics last year, with three two-hit shutouts along the way. He told me that on the first day of early spring training this year—pitchers and catchers only—he and Bob Welch, Dennis Eckersley, and Rick Honeycutt were in the locker room together after practice ended, and they noticed that all the younger players had dressed and departed. "It's half an hour after the workout, and we're alone," he said. "We were wondering where they'd all gone—I mean, you can only go to the mall so many times. That's a big difference, you know. Young players don't hang around and talk baseball anymore, and they don't hang around to listen. It used to be—and I'm not all *that* old—it used to be that you'd sit there for an hour and hope that maybe Tom Seaver would say hi, and maybe you could get him to talk about pitching. Or you'd be in the training room and somebody like Keith Hernandez was getting iced, and you'd hear some baseball. I used to think that if I waited around for an hour and a half and picked up one new thing I was way ahead."

I asked him what he thought had happened—I had first seen him pitch when he was in college, and now he felt like an envoy between my own baseball generation and the newest one—and he shrugged and said this was the way life went now, for the young. "Everything is visual," he said. "Everything is this minute, and the kids can't wait. They say, 'Tell me five things I need to know and tell them to me *now.*' You've got a hundred and fifty channels, and it's snap-snap, click-click. It's MTV, and they can't slow down."

I said this sounded all wrong for anyone trying to learn baseball.

"That's the thing of it," he said. "You know, you have to watch a whole ballgame to appreciate it—you can't go switching to another one if a pitcher happens to be going good and there's not much action out there. That's when you could be learning. A lot of players can't be appreciated right away, either. You take a Jose, a Rickey, and you see right away what they can do. But a Carney Lansford—you can watch him play over a whole season and keep picking up little things every day about how to win a ballgame. The other morning, I was telling some of our young players here how I used to wait all week for Saturday when I was a kid, to watch the old 'Game of the Week' on television. They couldn't get over that: 'One game—get out of here!' They couldn't believe it."

Bill Rigney, unmistakable under his straw planter's hat, is to be found every March afternoon in the first or second row behind home plate at an Athletics game (he is a senior adviser with the club). Between pitches, he talks baseball, with gestures. I sometimes think I have heard every one of his baseball stories, but then he surprises me; besides, he is constantly adding fresh material, here at the front end, so I happily expect never to catch up. (I have noticed, by the way, that he shares Merv Rettenmund's favorable opinion of Rickey Henderson's and Jose Canseco's work habits, if not their maturity; back before Canseco was traded away last summer, Rigney sometimes referred to the two as Frick and Frack, after a pair of comedy skaters with the old Ice Follies.)

When Rigney came up in the game, in the late thirties and early forties, on his way to the New York Giants (and then along to an extensive managerial career), the word was that a veteran player would never help a rookie, for fear the kid would grab his job. He didn't find it that way, though. On the contrary, he kept running into old-timers—Dick Bartell, Charlie Gehringer (a teammate on a Navy service team in wartime), Ernie Lombardi—who seemed to go out of their way to pass along a little hint about grabbing off ground balls, quickening the double-play flip to second, or dealing with Ewell Blackwell's crossfire fastball up at the plate. Nowadays, Rigney believes, you almost never see an older player take a kid aside and offer a tip. "We have all those coaches to do that now," he said. "The feeling isn't the same."

Almost the biggest change, in Rigney's view, has been the loss of baseball talk. "During the great '51 Giants season, we'd be on the road, all that time on trains and in hotels, and there'd be six or seven players—Stanky, Dark, Maglie, Westrum, Thomson, Whitey Lockman, me—in somebody's room, having a beer and a sandwich and talking about the next day's game. We were looking for that little edge—something about the other team's pitcher, or about some batter, that might give us that little edge. Now it's done differently. When our coaches and the manager finish each day, they're watching games on TV, watching those tapes, to see what the opposition is doing. We never had *that* advantage."

Rigney believes that kids who have grown up watching baseball on television acquire knowledge of the game but not experience. "Getting here happens so quickly for them, you forget how few games they have under their belt," he said. "A player arrives in a year and a half sometimes, and you can see he's got a lot of ability but he's still lost in the game. You can't help noticing how different it is with some of the Latin-American kids, because they've grown up playing ball when they were young, the way we all used to. They know why the game is played right to left, from first base to third, instead of the other way around, and some of our young players still don't."

I brought up the geographical phenomenon of the dozen-odd wonderfully accomplished infielders from the Dominican Republic who have come into the majors in the past decade or so, and Rig said, "Yes, all those quick guys from—what's that place? San Pedro de Macoris. That one city. Well, it isn't the drinking water down there that's turning out shortstops—it's sandlot ball fields. No tennis courts, no swimming pools, no weight rooms, no Little League. They're playing ball all day and all night. They're ready when they get up to the big leagues, because they've all had the little problems along the way and learned what you do to get around them, how to adjust. When you have that happen after you get up here, it can be tough on a young player, believe me."

Money seldom came into these conversations and speculations, I noticed, and when it did it presented itself as another sort of pressure or a complicating obstacle to change. Established veteran players have to deal with slumps and off years, of course, which can be as painful and baffling as anything that a rookie runs into, and a two- or three-million-dollar salary under those circumstances adds a stifling, onerous factor to the puzzle. Coaches want to help, but they hesitate to speak to a veteran without invitation.

Mark McGwire, the massive Athletics basher, went through the 1991 season hopelessly locked into a batting stance that appeared to give him very little chance against breaking pitches on the far side of the plate, and finished at .201, with a bare twenty-two home runs: his worst season in the majors. The A's staff circled the problem warily, concerned but unable to break the spell; radical alterations to a famous mechanism can be fatal. Rene Lachemann, for one, believes that many big-league hitters do far too much tinkering with their swing once things begin to go wrong. Last spring, a new Oakland batting coach, Doug Rader, held extended private conversations with McGwire that resulted in a stance an inch or two closer to home plate, a more closed-up front shoulder, an infinitesimal toeing-in of his front foot, and further minute ingredients that neither man would divulge—armed with which Big Mac batted .268 over the ensuing 1992 season, with forty-two home runs and a hundred and four runs batted in: nothing to it. When I asked Rader why it had taken so long for McGwire to change, he said, "Maybe it depends on who a player is listening to. If you have something to say that's worthwhile, he'll listen. If you're a nincompoop, he *shouldn't* listen. The key is to be qualified."

Fear of change and fear of failure are commonplace in any profession, one may suppose, but sports punish failure so swiftly and with such grisly results that the spectre of debacle attends every game, waiting ghoulishly to climb up on this or that player's back and hitch a ride. Long-term players, however brilliant, are never surprised by that clammy hand on their necks, but it's far worse when you're young. Duffy Dyer, the old, square-jawed Mets backstop, coaches third base for the Brewers these days, and in Chandler one morning he remarked that the best of the young players rise so rapidly in today's narrow tier of minor leagues that they sometimes arrive in the majors entirely untouched by doubt. "Then something might go wrong for them all at once," he said. "Maybe there are hitters who can handle one of their best pitches at this level, or, if they're hitters, there's a kind of pitching they've never seen before. They're in trouble, but they don't want to change, because they've never *had* to change. For some of them, this is the first failure they've ever experienced in their lives. Then you notice less talented players who have struggled or failed at the minor-league level and had to learn to make changes, so when they get up here they're more flexible. They're better off than the kid who's been a star all along and can't understand it when he runs into trouble."

Wherever I went these mornings in Arizona and Florida, I gravitated toward coaches and watched them going about their homely tasks: throwing batting practice or knocking out ground balls to the infielders, or running one of the endless early-spring drills—pickoffs, rundowns, pitchers covering first base; cutoff plays with a runner on second, cutoff plays with runners at first and third, cutoff plays with the ball hit to right field, to center field, to left field, and to deep foul ground, right and left (and all with the assembled, standing-around older players groaning and shaking their heads at the boredom of going through this again, for the hundredth or thousandth time, but then laughing and horsing around once they got into it, because it made them feel like rookies again). The coaches never stopped working. You'd see one on a camp stool reaching into a ball bag and then flipping up a fresh ball, over and over, into the air for a batter, just to one side of him, to swing at and whack into the soft-toss screen before them. A coach would step out from behind the cage in batting practice and, smiling in encouragement, talk earnestly to a batter while he pointed to the batter's knee, touched the point of his front shoulder, then executed a little twist of his own hips, as example, with his hands held back, while a swing was dissected and put together again. A thickset older pitching coach, with his feet oddly tilting upward on the steep back side of a practice mound, would murmur vertically up to a towering young right-hander and then take the pitcher's wrist and turn it a fraction to the left while gently gesturing with his own hand, up and down, as the kneeling catcher waited patiently at the other end, with his mitt hand resting on one thigh. In the afternoon games, the coaches, as usual, sat together, with the manager in among them, on a little row of chairs just outside the overpopulated dugout (on the home-plate side, I mean), where they could catch some rays as they followed each pitch and swing and play, and confabulated among themselves while the batters and pitchers came and went. In odd moments, whenever a coach waited for his next pupil to step into the cage, or while a couple of them were drinking soup from cardboard cups during the lunch break, I came over and asked questions—and found them, without exception, burning to talk about the work.

Dave Duncan, the quiet, much esteemed Oakland pitching coach, said that he had come to rely on his veterans to take up some of the teaching load. "I use good pitchers only," he added. "Shoot, why wouldn't I take advantage of Rick Honeycutt's ability to throw the slider? He's got a great understanding of that pitch and the mechanics of it. He can teach that better than I can."

Phil Garner, the smart, direct young manager of the Brewers, said that the talent shortage sometimes affected the way managers and coaches dealt with gifted players. "If somebody makes a mistake, or says I'm not going to do this, you can reprimand him, but you can't sit him down, because you have no one to replace him with," he said. "You can yell at him or call him into your office, but what else can you do? And there's an economic factor—with all that money he's getting, how long are you going to keep him on the bench?"

Leo Mazzone, the pitching coach for the Atlanta Braves, watches over the finest assemblage of young arms in the land—the Messrs. Glavine, Smoltz, Avery, et al., and now a brand-new partner, Greg Maddux, late of the Cubs, who is the incumbent Cy

Young Award holder in his league. Mazzone believes that staying his hand is often the best remedy for the pitching blahs, and cites in evidence John Smoltz's melodramatic adventures in 1991, a season in which the right-hander's pitching record stood at a horrific 2-11 by the first week in July. Smoltz then turned things around in electrifying fashion, finishing up at 14-13, while his team completed its rush from last place to first in a single season. "We felt the stuff was there and the talent was there, and the best thing we could do was keep giving him the ball every fifth day," Mazzone said. "Bobby Cox, our manager, kept telling Smoltzie, 'We believe in you, we have faith in you.' I think more pitchers are hurt by overcoaching than the other way. So many managers and coaches will drift this way, then that way after each performance. One day, the pitcher's great, and the next time out you go to him all upset and say he's not so good. You can't get a pitcher on an upbeat tempo that way. If they're talented and physically healthy, just let them go."

The chorus of outdoor male voices and the looks of so many squinty, brown-eared, friendly coachfaces under caps had begun to blur and blend in my mind, and, in need of synthesis, or something, I went to Walt Jocketty, who is director of baseball administration for the Athletics. He is a Minnesotan, blond and blue-eyed, and, at forty-two, has been through almost every level of the game; it's the consensus that he will be a general manager somewhere one of these days. In conversation, he has the pausing, open-ended tone that I have noticed in many experienced baseball executives, as befits a business in which success or its devastating opposite is so often determined by the weird hop, the frayed tendon, or the bloop, wrong-field double off the hands.

The talent squeeze—a decline of experienced prospects because of fewer diamonds and fewer accumulated innings, along with the unceasing present competition among the various professional sports for a handful of young genius athletes, the future superstars—afflicts baseball in particular, Jocketty pointed out, since the road to the majors in baseball is longer than it is in other sports. The Shaquille O'Neal legend—from high-school star to national megacelebrity in four years—isn't something baseball can offer as bait to a seventeen-year-old all-sport, all-state prospect. At the same time, the continuing expansion of baseball's major leagues and diminution of the minors makes the matriculation of rookies feel hurried and inadequate: suddenly they are in your big-team dugout, where they sit and don't ask questions. "I don't know if they think they know it all, or if they're afraid someone will notice that they don't know enough," Jocketty said. "It's puzzling. Just lately, I think I'm starting to see more of them talking to the veterans, after they've been around awhile. Maybe they're deciding, Look, maybe I've missed something."

Before I left Arizona this year, I made a point of paying a visit to the back diamond at Ho Ho Kam Park, the Cubs' spring-training center, in Mesa. The back field, which is notable for a tall, shaggy stand of eucalyptus trees on its third-base side, is dusty and inelegant; fans who find their way behind the left-field fence of the main diamond may think for a moment that they've stumbled on a high-school field. Then they hang around, some of them standing with their fingers looped through the chain-link fencing behind home, because the place, with its shadows and sunshine and its carpet of dried leaves in the dirt, has kept the informality and sense of ease that once characterized spring training everywhere. When I got there, I found Tom Trebelhorn rapping out ground balls to a handful of second-level Cubs players, raggedly bunched into groups behind the second-base and first-base positions on the diamond. A young second baseman and first baseman stepped forward in unison, and Trebelhorn, taking back his long, interesting-looking fungo bat, knocked a ball to the left side of the second baseman, just within reach, and he went low for the scoop, reversed his feet, and threw easily over to first.

"Good play!" Trebelhorn called out. "You knew you had time to get it right. That's experience! That's your good knowledge!"

He fielded the lobbed return toss with his bare right hand (he bats left-handed) and launched the next bouncer toward second with the same easy motion, but this time the ball caught the rim of the infield grass and darted low: a surprise for the new man out there, who flinched but then snaffled the ball in the outer part of his mitt.

"Yeah—*play* that lipper!" Trebelhorn responded. "Tough play! Atta boy, Tommy! Good field!"

Trebelhorn, an old friend, sounded the same as ever, which is to say exactly like every high-school and summer-camp baseball coach of my distant baseball past. He looked over and saw me, and called, "Same time, same place! Was it this *day* last year? I tell you one thing—this is probably the same fungo I had here then."

There was a pause while some of his students rearranged themselves, and he came over bare-armed, intense, sinewy, and with the same never-fail, ready smile. "The eternal, polite, patient routines of baseball that keep us all together," he said, burying my hand in his.

Same Treb-talk, too. He's the kind of man who makes you glad you didn't take up astronomy or the cello as a sideline. Now, at forty-five, he is in his second season as a Cubs coach, after seven seasons as a minor-league manager and then six as manager of the Milwaukee Brewers, the post he held when I first came to know him and to listen to him. His Brewer teams, a bit undermanned, were customary contenders in the American League East but were also afflicted with a phenomenal propensity for injuries to key players. When I caught up with him in 1992 as a new coach with the Cubs, here on the back diamond at Ho Ho Kam, he said that his friends had always told him he was a coach at heart. "The perfect job at last!" he said. I knew he had never made it up to the majors in his playing days (he finished at Lewiston, in the Northwest League), but that, too, he once explained, was an advantage for anyone who wanted to stay on in the game. "If my ability as a player is a little short, I'm going to have to understand this situation a half second quicker than the guy who's bigger and stronger," he said. "I'm going to have to work more. That's why you see so many coaches and managers, even at the high-school level, who were never such hot players. They were good thinkers, good at noticing, and they had imagination."

Practice went on in its old patterns: with another coach, out on the mound behind his little half screen, throwing a pitch that was lined or bounced or popped up by the batter in the cage; and then Trebelhorn, from the sideline, at once batting *his* ball to the waiting infielders. In the pauses, Treb told me the names of some of the young Cub infielders he was working; a couple of them—Jose Vizcaino and big Kevin Roberson—I recognized from my previous visit, and Treb identified another, Chuck McElroy, as a pitcher with secret hopes of being converted into an infielder one of these days. By their youthful faces and the high numbers on the back of their uniform tops, I knew that most of the Cubs here would soon be sent down to the minor-league complex and would end up in Iowa or Orlando this summer. Some would not make it back up to the big club's spring roster next year. Trebelhorn would stay on with the Cubs through the season, as bench coach and offensive coordinator, but it seemed clear to me that this sort of patient, one-ball-at-a-time work was something for which he has a particular genius. (Up until a few years ago, he was a high-school history teacher in the off-season.) He was incapable of patronizing young ballplayers, and his ridiculous, winning chatter disarmed their cool. I couldn't prove it, but I had the impression that these youngsters, for all their ambitions, were happy enough to be here today, on a lesser diamond, along with their upbeat, down-home sort of coach, and far from the awesome likes of Mark Grace and Candy Maldonado.

Treb kept the workout working. "One more shot!" he called to Roberson, at first base. "Here comes a double down the line. Feet, feet! ... Yes, *sir!*"

A moment later, he paused to watch a left-handed hitter in the cage, Dwight Smith, and called over, "When do you pull?"

"After?" Smith said tentatively.

"After is right!" Trebelhorn said. "If you start to pull and the pitcher pitches you away, you're dead! Don't die on me—*wait!*"

He picked up his fungo—a narrow wand widening to a thicker, bottle-shaped outer shaft, which was wrapped in dirty white tape. Wielding the ancient instrument, an experienced batting coach, altering the range and speed of his ground balls by excruciating increments, can reduce a powerful, full-grown infielder to a panting rag doll in a matter of minutes. Many coaches have shifted over to the aluminum bat for infield work, but Treb told me that he preferred the sound and heft of the fungo. A few years ago, he'd set about restoring an antique, dark-stained fungo that had turned up in one of the Brewers' bat bags, and when he unwrapped the tape from the barrel he'd discovered a team name, Hollywood Stars, stamped there. "From the old Pacific Coast League, if you can believe it," he said. "That fungo was at least forty years old."

The workout ended; the bats were bagged and the balls collected and tossed into a supermarket cart. Trebelhorn and the tall young Cubs walked around the low perimeter fence and through another gate, and came slowly across the outfield grass of the stadium diamond, in the warm sunshine. The fans were coming in and finding their way to their seats for the afternoon game.

We reached the dugout, and the players ducked their heads and went into the clubhouse for lunch, but Treb stopped in front of the box seats and began signing baseballs and programs for some kids there. I wondered if they knew who he was. Soon he was talking about the game again: about its appealing pace and its sense of intimacy with individual players, and about its waning in the inner cities—in the Bronx, and in Chicago's Robert Taylor Homes, where Kirby Puckett grew up, and in the parts of the Bay Area where Claudell Washington grew up—and about the absolute necessity of turning that around somehow. "There's plenty of baseball players waiting in there," he said. "And there's doctors, lawyers, teachers, judges—young women and young men. We're doing a very bad job there and we all know it." Then he was on to recreational preferences around the country—computer people hiking in the Sierras, immigrants playing soccer in Central Park. "Asians are playing basketball like crazy right now," he declared.

Suddenly, he reminded me of Bart Giamatti, another world-class talker and connector, and I felt reassured about the old game of baseball. Tom Trebelhorn could be my commissioner for a while: a private appointment. He signed another ball and said to its possessor, a startled-looking ten- or twelve-year-old girl, "It's a different world now, but I don't think we need to take baseball out of its socio-economic context. We're getting the same thinking athletes that I.B.M. gets in *its* work force. It's all one and the same."

"Thank you," she said.

Treb laughed and stopped signing, and he and I said we'd try to meet here again—same time, same place—a year from now. "Same fungo," I said.

"Same fungo," he said. "I was thinking about that just the other day, trying to figure out how long I'd been doing this. Did you ever throw up bottle caps and try to hit them with a broom when you were a kid? I sure did. It's thirty-five years I've been hitting something round with something flat. Too late to stop now."

Takes: Digging Up Willie

1991

Willie Mays, sole proprietor of the six-hundred level in the distinguished lifetime homers edifice (he has six hundred and sixty of them) still looked loose when he once again came to Scottsdale for the spring semester as some kind of coach for the Giants. (One Giants official, asked by a visiting TV reporter for Mays' job description, said, "Willie's work here is to be Willie Mays.") Some mornings, you could hear Mays' boyish, high-voiced, jabbering way of talking even before you got through the tunnel into the clubhouse, and you'd find him in there perhaps autographing boxes of team baseballs at a table while he agitated with the clubhouse man and anybody else around. Each day, he wore a faded pink polo shirt with "Say Hey" over the breast. He looked his age—he just turned sixty—but you could still see the thick muscles under the now softer skin of his forearms. He was a little impatient when I asked him to remember a favorite home run for me—I hadn't stopped to think what sort of catalogue selection this would entail—but then he said, "Home run against Claude Raymond, in the Astrodome. Somebody was on first, and it tied the game. Jim Davenport won it for us in the eleventh or twelfth inning. Raymond threw me thirteen fastballs, and I fouled them off. The ball went over the fence in left-center field. What *year*? You'd have to look that up. Ask Claude Raymond—he probably knows it better than I do. That was the only dramatic type of home run I ever hit."

Tracking this one down took a while, but the trip was worth it. Lon Simmons, a handsome, deep-voiced veteran California broadcaster, vividly remembered the confrontation and its result, and said he thought that the blow had been Mays' six-hundredth round-tripper. Not quite, it turned out. No. 600, on September 22, 1969, was in fact a game-winning pinch-hit job, down in San Diego, when Mays batted for George Foster and hit one out against a rookie pitcher named Mike Corkins.

"Why'd it have to be me?" Corkins said disconsolately to his manager, Preston Gomez, after the game. (I found the tale in Charles Einstein's book, "Willie's Time.")

"Son," Gomez said gently, "there've been five hundred and ninety-nine before you."

I continued the quest over the telephone once I got home, helped immeasurably by a bulldog Giants media person at Candlestick Park. "What about this one?" she said, evidently consulting some thick Book of Willie out there by the Bay. "August 29, 1965—a three-run homer against Jack Fisher, of the Mets, in the ninth inning. It was Willie's seventeenth of the month."

"Sorry," I said. "It's got to be in Houston."

"Hmmm. Well—Oop, how about June 13, 1967? Mays failed as a pinch-hitter in the sixth inning, in Houston, but stayed in the game and won it with a grand slam against Barry Latman. It was his first slam since '62."

"Wrong pitcher," I said. "It *sounds* exciting, but who are we to say?"

There was another pause, and then she had it. The homer, Willie's No. 501, had indeed tied up the game, just as Mays told me, in the Astrodome on September 14, 1965—a fearsome month in the National League, I recalled, when the Giants had fought off two or three closely pursuing clubs, only to fall to the Dodgers near the end. Mays, going for the fences in the ninth, had become "embroiled in a prolonged battle with reliever Claude Raymond," my faraway researcher read aloud, and had fouled off four pitches before "sending the ball soaring four hundred feet over the center-field fence." Davenport's pinch-hit single then won the game, in the twelfth.

Four foul balls? I went to Claude Raymond, just as Willie had told me to in the first place. Possibly the only Quebec-born right-hander yet to attain the majors (Denis Boucher, a *habitant* rookie twirler with the Blue Jays, throws left and *bats* right), Raymond had wound up his career, predictably enough, with the Montreal Expos in 1971, and had then stayed on as a color commentator for that club. I called him at home, and he remembered the moment at once.

"I threw Mays thirteen straight fastballs," he said, even before I could ask. "And he fouled off thirteen. Jay Alou was the base runner on first, and Mays was up there to hit a home run. All those fouls were nicks or little ticks back to the screen—nothing close to a base hit. Then I threw one more, a little inside, and Willie bailed out but opened up on the ball at the same time, the way only he could do, and it went out. I remember Paul Richards, our general manager, came up to me afterward and said how happy he was I'd gone fastball all the way. He said it was a great duel."

I told Raymond that Mays had described it as the only dramatic home run of his career.

"Well, it's a great compliment," Raymond said, in his pleasing North Gaul tones. "You can thank him for me."

Willie was right about the thirteen fouls, after all, but perhaps we can quarrel with him just the same. David Bush covers the Athletics for the San Francisco *Chronicle,* and when I asked him to remember a homer for me he came up with a long standoff game he'd listened to at home, on the radio, back when he was a freshman at U.Cal, in 1963. "That game matched up Juan Marichal, of the Giants, against Warren Spahn, and it went on interminably," Bush said. "No score after nine innings, no score after twelve. Both the starting pitchers stayed in there. I was a Giants fan, of course, but by this time I was rooting for Spahn, because of who he was and because he was just about at the end of his career. Willie beat him,

1–0, with a homer in the bottom of the fifteenth. I didn't see it, but I still feel as if I *almost* saw it. It was that kind of a hit."

David's story reminded me of something, and when I got home I dug out my files of the *SABR Bulletin,* a useful newsletter published for members of the Society for American Baseball Research. There, in the February, 1991, issue, I reconfirmed the news: Willie Mays is the only major-league ballplayer to have hit a home run in every inning from the first through the sixteenth; moreover, he leads all comers with twenty-two lifetime extra-inning home runs. (Jack Clark is second, with seventeen.) Too bad none of them were dramatic.

The scholarly search after Mays' favorite home run had a funny and corrective shirt-tail. A week or two after the story appeared in *The New Yorker,* in May of 1991—it was part of a piece about home runs, most which has since been made superfluous by Messrs. McGwire, Sosa, and Bonds—I had a cheerful letter from Charles Einstein, who is retired now and living in New Jersey. He'd been at the Mays v. Raymond meeting, and had just tracked down a tape of the game broadcast. "It was four fouls, not thirteen," he wrote. "Nothing impeaches the memory of an old ballplayer more than another old ballplayer who remembers the moment the same way."

Five springs later, again at the Giants' Scottsdale Stadium, in Arizona, Vida Blue sat cross-legged in his familiar camp chair, just in front of the stands, now and then extending a hand back over his shoulder to accept an unseen fan's pen and program; and the man indoors, sitting at the same southeast corner of the same clubhouse table, was Willie Mays. He is sixty-six now, and his seamed, heavy face hasn't much say hey left in it, but he is never without company. Visiting writers and sportscasters, stopping by to pay their respects in the morning, have found that they share a wish to grab some of the youngest and newest Giants, chattering over there in front of their lockers, and say, "Do you have any *idea* how this man played?"

Mays, in self-protection, has developed a selective memory, and conversational openers from his visitors about his celebrated overhead catch against Vic Wertz in the 1954 World Series or the four-homer game in 1961 no longer light up the Proustian hot stove. This year, though, a visiting senior writer from back East got lucky when he brought up an early Maysian catch and throw against the Dodgers—the Billy Cox play.

"Damn!" Mays cried excitedly. "You saw that? You were there?"

Yes, the writer had been there—as a fan at the Polo Grounds. "August, 1951," he said. "Cox was the base runner at third. You caught the ball running full tilt toward right, turned in midair, and threw him out at the plate. You threw before you could get turned around—let the ball go with your back to the plate. The throw went to the catcher on the fly—it must have been Westrum—and he tagged Cox out, sliding."

"You got it!" Mays said. "I've been sayin' this for a long time, and nobody here believes me." He was kidding, of course, but his voice had come up at last: almost the old, high Willie piping. "Now, tell 'em how it was."

I told it again—it was easy because I'd never seen such a play, before or since—and, as I did, it seemed to me that Willie Mays and I could still see the long, curving flight of the white ball through the afternoon light, bang into the big mitt, and the slide and the amazing out, and together remember the expanding moment when the staring players on the field and those just emerging from the dugouts, and the shouting fans, and maybe even the startled twenty-year-old rookie center fielder himself, now retrieving his fallen cap from the grass, understood that something new and electric had just begun to happen to baseball.

For Openers

1982

Spring was a little late this year. In March, as is my custom, I went south to meet the sun and watch the ball teams at early play, but what I met was warm rain in Arizona, cold rain in Florida, and many dispiriting views of players in windbreakers running muddy laps around the perimeter of their soaked and useless fields. Baseball's own weather—the lowering clouds left by last year's seven-week strike, and the persistent residual gloom of a decade or more of labor strife and public folly—also had a part in my unseasonal mopiness, I think, and when I came home I found myself eager as never before for Opening Day. The season—the real thing: the sudden new standings and fresh stats, the return of line scores and box scores and speculation and involvement—might make me well again. Even the intervention of an astounding early-April blizzard, which wiped out almost the entire first week of scheduled play east of Chicago, only sharpened my boyish expectations. Four successive Yankee games were cancelled, while the ground crew at Yankee Stadium shovelled and hosed away a foot or more of drifts, but Easter Sunday did the trick, bringing us thin sunlight, a pale but reviving outfield greensward, flags and bands, Robert Merrill (in terrific midseason anthem form), and the visiting White Sox. Chief Groundskeeper Jimmy Esposito, the Peary of the recent Bronxian expeditions, threw out the first ball, to grateful cries from the small crowd, and baseball, at very long last, was back.

Opening Day, I should add, is normally a mini-holiday in the baseball year, with approximately the same significance as Groundhog Day on the larger calendar. The only certified baseball wonder ever to befall in Game One was the inaugural-day no-hitter pitched by Bob Feller against the White Sox on April 16, 1940. Feller, the eminent Cleveland fireballer, went on to pitch two more perfectos in his distinguished career, but the first one is the one treasured by late-night barroom zealots, who always introduce it by saying, "Name the only game in which all the players on one team ended up with the same batting averages"—.000, that is—"that they started with." The point is moot, of course, since it may be argued that the hapless Pale Hose all began that afternoon with no averages at all, but this, to be sure, is what baseball talk is *for.* (Once that burning issue has been thrashed out, it may even occur to one of the advocates present to wheel out another stumper, as codicil to the Feller game: "Name two players on the field that day who each played more than twenty years for one of those teams, who each went on into the Hall of Fame, and who never played in a World Series." The White Sox are the tipoff. The two are Ted Lyons, who pitched for them from 1923 to 1946, and Luke Appling, who was the Chicago shortstop from 1930 to 1950. When I was in college, a classmate of mine—a gifted eclectic who had grown up in Chicago—once startled me by announcing, "Ted Lyons is the Mies van der Rohe of pitchers.") I myself would put forward a less well-remembered contest as the best opener ever— the game in Washington on April 13, 1926, in which the Senators' Walter Johnson pitched his seventh Opening Day shutout (a record, by a mile), beating the Philadelphia Athletics, 1–0, in fifteen innings. Vice-President Dawes attended, but the records do not reveal whether he lasted the distance, as the Big Train did.

"Happy New Year!" several baseball friends of mine exclaimed when we met and shook hands in the basement corridors of the Stadium or around the batting cage early on Easter afternoon— thus reinforcing a conviction I have that the cheerfulness of a brand-new baseball season is better founded than the dogged, vinous optimism of New Year's Eve. Seen from the veranda of Opening Day, the sunlit new season appears to stretch away almost endlessly into summer. The winners of each first game may entertain hopes, however manic, of a wholly unexpected pennant, while the losers remind themselves that there remain one hundred and sixty-one games in which to do better. The occasion also invites a view in the opposite direction—toward long-gone April afternoons and the first bands and bunting of a career. Every ballplayer remembers his own first Opening Day—the day he made the club not as a September rookie called up for a few trial at-bats or late relief innings but as one of the chosen, part of a new team. Yogi Berra, a Yankee coach of long tenure, instantly smiled—a gentle, seamed smile, like a Gladstone bag opening—when I asked if he still remembered his first spring game here at the Stadium. "Oh, yeah," he said hoarsely. "You don't forget that. We played the Athletics, and Spud Chandler pitched for us. We got beat. I'd been up for a few games in '46, but this was different. I played right field—did you know that? Aaron Robinson was our catcher then, so they stuck me out in right."

I knew. I attended that opener, on a cold April day in 1947, thirty-five years ago—can that be possible?—and sat with friends in the lower right-field grandstand, and I have a clear memory of watching Yogi fall on his face in pursuit of a drive hit toward right center. It was my first sight of him, and I knew at once he'd never make it in the majors—never in a million years.

Yankee manager Bob Lemon said, "Mine was 1946. I was a center fielder for the Indians then—I hadn't batted my way out of the lineup yet—and Bob Feller won us the game. I had butterflies, all right." This was before the long-postponed first game had begun, and I asked Lemon if he had butterflies now.

"No," he said. "I don't think you can have butterflies for a *week.*"

The Yanks and the White Sox were to play a doubleheader, with the second game tacked on at the last minute to make up for one of the snow-outs. It was not the first Opening Day double-header ever played, as some of the players and scribes on hand seemed to think. Back on April 20, 1903—if I may indulge in a little more game-dropping here—the Boston Pilgrims began their home season by splitting a morning-afternoon twin bill with the Athletics at the old Huntington Avenue Grounds, in Boston. In the morning game, the Pilgrims (they became the Red Sox in 1907) bunted nine times against the Athletics' starter, Rube Waddell, while beating him by 9–4. The strategy was devised by Boston manager Jimmy Collins, who inflamed his players with the news that Rube, a notorious night owl, had been on the town the night before and, indeed, had probably not risen before noon for many years. In the afternoon game, Chief Bender evened things up by outpitching the Pilgrims' ace, Cy Young, as the Athletics won, 10–7. It was the first victory of Bender's career.

The outcome of an Opening Day game barely matters, of course, since the winning and losing managers will each fall back on the same cliché when it's over: "Well, it's still early." The moment didn't seem worth the wait up at the Stadium, where the first game went into extra innings, tied at 6–6, and wasn't resolved until the twelfth, when Chicago shortstop Bill Almon smote a triple against Goose Gossage that hit the center-field fence on the fly— left fielder Dave Winfield, in loping pursuit, stared up at the airborne object in wonder, like a Montauk gull watcher—and was shortly scored with what became the winning counter.

Winter had returned to the Bronx by this time, bringing splashes of rain and a chilling breeze, and I did not stay for the nightcap—a pitchers' duel, it turned out, between Tommy John and the young White Sox left-hander Brit Burns, who shut out the Yanks for a 2–0 win and a Chicago sweep. Bill Almon had two more hits in that game, giving him five for the afternoon and a guaranteed best Opening Day to think about for the rest of his life.

Almon and the White Sox repaired to Fenway Park the next afternoon, and so did I. My holiday pleasure at being there for another opener (the Bosox had played three weekend games against the Orioles, down in Baltimore, but this was their home inaugural) was all the greater because the occasion marked the seventieth season for the little green wraparound palace. There had been rain again on this morning in Boston, and the temperature was barely out of the thirties when I turned up at the ballpark, a couple of hours before game time, but Lansdowne Street was already stuffed with fans, many of them in parkas and Red Sox caps and toting thermoses and blankets, who milled about cheerfully and noisily under the leafless trees while they waited for the ballpark gates to open. Fenway Park has a grimy red brick exterior, with two upper stories of narrow windows set above the main gates, and the look of the place on this gray, soggy morning reminded me of old photographs of turn-of-the-century workers filing in to work at the long red brick textile mills in Lowell and Lawrence.

Manager Ralph Houk was sitting in the Boston dugout, with his paws buried in the pockets of his warmup jacket. He gave me a damp, tobacco-brown smile in response to my poll and said, "Yankee Stadium. April of 1947. I didn't play—I was about the third-string Yankee catcher—but, my God, how exciting it all was. I'd never seen that many people at one time before in my life. I hadn't been off the farm for long, and most of the games I'd played in up to then were in the old Western Association—places like Topeka, I mean. I remember looking up at all the people in that steep upper deck at the Stadium and wondering why they didn't fall out of the stands and down onto the field."

Houk grew up in Lawrence, Kansas, but it should be added that he did not come *directly* from the farm to the big leagues: he spent four years with the 9th Armored Division Rangers in Europe during the Second World War, in extended combat, and emerged with the Silver Star, the Bronze Star, a Purple Heart, and the rank of major. He played eight years with the Yankees and then moved along to his real career, managing. In 1978, he retired after sixteen years as a major-league skipper but soon found that he couldn't stand being away from the game. Last spring, he returned to manage the Red Sox, whom he brought home only two and a half games behind the first-place Brewers in the combined split-season league standings.

I reminded the Major that Yogi Berra had been in right field on that Opening Day in the Bronx in 1947, and he said, "Yes, he had a little trouble out there, didn't he?" He laughed, perhaps struck by the same vision I had of Berra on his belly on the grass. "Poor Yog," Houk said. "All he could ever do was hit and play ball. A great, great hitter."

Peter Gammons was next—the exemplary, much-admired young baseball writer for the Boston *Globe*, elegant on this day in a flannel blazer and a blue-and-white striped sweater.

"Right here in 1971," he said. "I'd been covering high-school and college ball for two years, so coming up to the Sox was a big, big change for me. It was cold and windy. Ray Culp pitched about a six-hitter against the Yankees, and we won. Everybody was making diving catches and blocking the plate and all. It was one of those days when all of us in the park got excited about the way the team looked—instant pennant fever. After the game, Bobby Murcer said, 'The Red Sox always look great when Culp is pitching. It's the other eighty per cent of the games that they have to worry about.' I was so young and naïve that I didn't think he was serious, but of course he was absolutely right."

I was in a mood for more history here at Fenway Park, because the Red Sox had invited Smokey Joe Wood, the celebrated mound star of the World Champion 1912 Boston team, to come up and throw out the ceremonial first pitch. Mr. Wood, a small gent inside two layers of sweaters and a raincoat, is ninety-two, and he had announced early (through his younger son, Bob Wood) that he would not be available to the media on this day, but I was pretty sure that he'd talk to me. He would tell me what it had felt like here on April 20, 1912, when the Red Sox had beaten the New York Highlanders (later known as the Yankees), 7–6, with Tris Speaker driving in the winning run off Hippo Vaughn. Smugly I explained to Boston writers I knew that the previous spring Mr. Wood and I had attended a notable college game together in New Haven, at which a Yale pitcher, Ron Darling, threw no-hit ball against a St. John's nine, only to be defeated in the twelfth.

Here, an hour before game time, I found Mr. Wood eating lunch in the big, comfortable Fenway rooftop press lounge, where he was surrounded by relatives and admiring glances from the assembled writers and scouts and front-office people. We greeted each other happily, and after some inquiries about his health I whipped out my notebook and pen. "Tell me about that first game here at Fenway Park, Mr. Wood," I said. "What was it like here that day?"

"I have no idea," he said. "Can't remember a single thing about it. I didn't pitch—that's all I know. Just another ballgame."

I folded up my notebook again, but three or four months later Smokey Joe Wood's forgotten Opening Day was suddenly illuminated for me when I unwrapped a long, odd-shaped envelope with a Boston postmark, sent by a friend, and found within it a splendid photograph of the two teams, taken on that special day. I don't moon about bygone baseball, to tell the truth, but I've had this picture framed, and still have it on top of a low bookcase at home, where I can see it often in passing. The narrow elongated rectangle, some forty inches wide, depicts the Red Sox and New York Highlander players standing in a straggly, informal line moments before the first official game ever played at Fenway Park. You can pick out some of the faces in the slightly faded print—the big New York starter Hippo Vaughn, Boston manager Jake Stahl, the august Tris Speaker and his pitcher-roommate Smokey Joe Wood. Standing among the players there's a team executive or front-office man in a business suit and one of those curly derbies of the time, not far from a miniature batboy, but what you goggle at is the number of guys here: forty-seven. It was too many for the photographer to capture on a single plate. He seems to have required three exposures—you can spot the little disparities in the size of the players at the seams and the slightly altered light—which he melded into one in the darkroom. Some of the players are grinning or holding back a smile, and at last you see why. A couple of Red Sox players (including Smokey Joe Wood, in his tilted cap) have run around after posing at one end of the picture and sneaked back into the shot at the other: they're in here twice. Hey, this is Opening Day, baseball is back and anything can happen. As it turned out, 1912 was a famous year for the Boston Red Sox, who won the American League pennant and then beat John McGraw's Giants in the World Series, in eight games (one was a tie, called for darkness). Joe Wood went 34-5 for the Sox, with a 1.91 earned-run average—one of the best seasons ever, for any pitcher—and won three more games in the Series, including the finale. All that was just ahead for him on this day, but the photograph does what Mr. Wood's memory couldn't do for him, seventy years down the line. It makes him young.

Takes: Pride

2002

At Port St. Lucie early in March, Tom Seaver ran into his old White Sox manager Tony La Russa in front of the visiting-team dugout during batting practice, and pretended he had a bone to pick. Seaver, who is fifty-seven now, works with the Mets pitchers during spring training, and becomes a Mets broadcaster once the season begins. La Russa was here with his strong Cardinals team, up from Jupiter for an afternoon exhibition. But the game Seaver wanted to talk about was his maiden effort for La Russa, back on April 8, 1984, at Comiskey Park, when he fell into difficulties against the Tigers and found himself trailing by 3–2 in the top of the fifth, with two runners aboard and nobody out. The moment was socially tense for both men, who'd never expected to find themselves on the same side like this until the ChiSox coup over the winter, when they noticed that the aging star had been left unprotected on the Mets roster and snapped him up. The effect in New York, I recall, was that of a mother watching her infant snatched off the front lawn in a drive-by kidnapping.

Tom, enjoying this reunion, now imitated his earlier self standing on the mound at Comiskey Park and allowing his jaw to drop open at the vision of his approaching manager, with his hand sheepishly held out for the ball. 'I'm bringing in Agosto, who's good at fielding bunts,' Seaver said, imitating La Russa, but then shifted to himself, the famous flinger, as he pretended not to understand and made the manager repeat the message. Then he gave up the mound and tromped away.

Here in Florida, a batboy and a couple of writers were happily listening in on the moment, and La Russa kept nodding his head in agreement with the Seaver scenario.

"I don't see you again—I'm gone by the time the game ends and we've lost it," Seaver resumed. "Next day, I grab a bat and go out and stand in the outfield during B.P. No mitt. I'm like a statue out there, even when a couple of batted balls come by. I wait and then, sure enough, here you come—the manager, walking all the way out to the goddam outfield to apologize." And Tony, in vivid mime, became an Elmer Fudd manager looking up at a tall future Hall of Famer and trying to get the right words out.

"'Listen to me,'" Tom said. He was fake-stern, his voice going up. "'If I lose twenty games a year for you for the next five years, I'm still over .500, lifetime, as a pitcher. Do you think I got that way because I couldn't field *fucking bunts?*'"

Seaver went 33-28 for La Russa during his two and a quarter seasons in Chicago, and finished his career with the 1986 American League champion Red Sox, whom he joined that summer. When I got home from spring training, I checked out the Tom and Tony moment, and found that Seaver's rant was right on the money. Handing the ball over to his manager, there on the mound at Comiskey, he stood 273-172 lifetime, or one hundred and one games over .500—a nice neighborhood for an argument.

Let Go, Mets

2002

Baseball never seems serious until along about Memorial Day, but this time the early stuff has felt like a soap. Seven weeks into the season, the Yankees' newborn television network, YES, and Cablevision have contrived to block three million customers from catching any of a scheduled hundred and thirty games over their home sets, because of a fee squabble. The Red Sox, under new ownership and an amiable new manager (Grady Little), who says that he plans never to go to sleep mad at any of his players, have sailed off to a 26-9 start, the best record in either league. Earlier, baseball commissioner Bud Selig reminded owners that a million-dollar fine would be levied against the club of any official heard to utter a single word or groan about labor issues during the current negotiations with the Players Association over the sport's expired basic agreement. (He didn't mention a finder's fee if a breach should occur, but if that is in the books—well, Bud, you have my number.) The Pirates, losers of a hundred games last year, raised their ticket prices for the new season; in April they found themselves unexpectedly and briefly at the top of the National League Central Division, even as their attendance headed in the other direction. Speaking of tickets, a friend of a friend of mine called the Yankees the other day to ask about the availability of good seats for a Thursday, July 18th, game against the Tigers, and was told sure, there were some left, and did he want the order at $47 or $55 or $65 per? Maybe the fan should hop out to the Giants' Pacific Bell Park, where he might still catch Barry Bonds from a nice $28 box behind home. Hurry.

The Minnesota Twins, targeted for termination before the start of this season by Commissioner Selig, have held on to first place in the American League Central, while the Montreal Expos, the other Dead Team Walking, were for a time leading or nearly leading the frail National League East. With things as they are, this counts as great—or semi-ironic, reverse-popular great—news for the commissioner, whose own club, the Milwaukee Brewers (operated for the present by his daughter, Wendy Selig-Prieb), is in the cellar of the N.L. Central. The Brewers, who play in a new stadium, Miller Park, built at taxpayers' expense, are not on Selig's schedule for possible "contraction," as the end of franchise life is euphemistically known.

Meantime, in another part of town, John Rocker, the hyper ex-Braves, ex-Indians reliever and No. 7 line subway critic, was briefly dispatched to the minors by his latest club, the Texas Rangers, after compiling a 9.53 earned-run average. "No! He was?" exclaimed Mets manager Bobby Valentine on being told the news. Mike Cameron, an outfielder with the Seattle Mariners, hit four home runs in one game, against the White Sox, becoming the eleventh man in modern baseball to pull off this feat. Lou Gehrig was the first. The Chicago pitchers responsible for the homers—Jon Rauch and Jim Parque—who'd thrown Cameron two fat pitches apiece, were dispatched to the minors after the game. Elsewhere, another pitcher, the Reds' Jose Rijo—perhaps remembered as the M.V.P. of the 1990 World Series—won his first game in seven years (against the Cubs, on April 21st), after enduring five surgeries and a six-year absence from the majors.

Earlier in our story, Jeffrey Loria, the New York art-dealer owner of the Expos (who drew an average 7,935 spectators per home game last year), was permitted to trade up for a different low-interest (fans, not loans) club, the Florida Marlins. The Montreal front office, decimated by the transaction, is now staffed by Major League Baseball employees; this qualifies the 'Spos' new

skipper, Frank Robinson, as the first commander of a baseball pro-
tectorate. Meantime, Randy Johnson and Curt Schilling, the World
Champion Arizona Diamondbacks' stellar starting duo last year
(they went 21-6 and 22-6, respectively), started up where they left
off, and stood at a cumulative 14-2 at last count. Johnson, pitching
against the Colorado Rockies in his fifth start, gave up two hits and
struck out seventeen. Three of his last four pitches were timed at a
hundred miles an hour.

Barry Bonds, who hit a record seventy-three home runs last
year, smacked two on the Giants' Opening Day, and two more the
next afternoon. That same week, a teammate, second baseman Jeff
Kent, came off the disabled list, after nearly being fined thirty-
seven thousand dollars per missed game by the Giants for violating
a risk clause in his contract while incurring a preseason wrist injury. Kent said he'd hurt himself while washing his truck, but eye-
witnesses came forward to say they'd seen him crash while doing
wheelies on his Harley. Thirty-seven thousand multiplied by a
hundred and sixty-two games equals Kent's salary of six million
bucks—which remained intact when the Giants' front office, like
Tony Soprano the dad, lost its nerve at the last instant and forgave.

And, only recently, the *Post* contributed the tingling headline
"MR. MET VS. TALIBAN"..."*Baseball Mascot Stationed at Gitmo.*"
Mr. Met, the Mets' roving macrocephalic, had just celebrated his
fortieth year on the job, at a Sunday date against the Expos, without any announcement that his inner self, an Army reserve major
named Lee Reynolds, was no longer with us, having been called up
for duty at Guantánamo Bay. More on Mr. Met later.

My plan to spend a lot more time with the Mets this season has
been rewarded, sort of. Once again, I have come to see that uncertainty and reversal are the everyday flavor of the game—a truth
obscured or forgotten when you hang around the Yankees. Last
year, the Mets were second worst in batting in the National League,
worst in runs scored and slugging average, and first, in a close contest, in ennui. All that would end with their expensive off-season
acquisition of Mo Vaughn, the eminent ex-Angels and ex-Red Sox

first baseman-slugger, and the perennial All Star Robbie Alomar, by consensus the best second baseman of our epoch. The infield, where Edgardo Alfonzo had been shifted from second base to third, would be the Mets' best in a long time. The starting pitching, according to my winter Mets party line, was up in the air, given the three new starters Pedro Astacio, Jeff D'Amico, and Shawn Estes, who all came intriguingly decked out in accomplishment and physical frailty. The bullpen was a serious concern, given the continuing disablement of its archducal lefty, John Franco, after an elbow repair in December. Defense—well, no worry there, at least. The swift Roger Cedeño and the burgeoning (how long can you say "promising"?) Jay Payton, in center, would catch everything airborne, and perhaps even steal some bases at last.

Well, no: cancel the above. These Mets assumptions—every one of them—have turned out to be wrong. Mo Vaughn and Robbie Alomar have yet to get untracked at the plate, at this writing or waiting. (Some of Mo's missing power has been attributed to his swinging a bat that was two or three ounces heavier than he thought it was: a baseball first, to me.) Cedeño circling and staggering under a long fly ball and then missing the catch and Payton mindlessly popping up on the first pitch have gnawed their way into my Mets consciousness, like Seaver's fastball and Mookie Wilson's hopper. The infield has been grotesquely awful in stretches and presumably cannot do worse: the club's forty-six errors are the most in either league. The starting pitchers, by contrast, have been sound and can be counted—if you count the right way—among the better staffs around. In the pen, David Weathers, Grant Roberts, Scott Strickland, and Armando Benitez have proved hostile and unflappable. With a dog's breakfast of team stats like this, the Mets couldn't be expected to win—except that they won just enough to stay in first place in their division for two weeks running.

Nothing about these Mets remains true for long, which is why you watch them in action with a riveted and memorizing anxiety: Mo's glowering gaze at the pitcher from behind the parapet of his right shoulder; Mo signing autographs for the Baha Men R. & B.

group, with his low-pulled cap pushing out his ears; Al Leiter's midgame clenched jaw and clenched mind; Joe McEwing's balletic hoppings in the batter's box, where he starts and finishes his swing on tiptoe; Alomar's scary backhand flips of the ball from out of his glove; Mike Piazza's cockily tilted helmet and ticking calm when he's up at bat; Pedro Astacio waggling his drooping right hand on the mound like a fishing lure as he looks in for the sign; and Edgardo Alfonzo (the Met of Mets, to me) dropping the head of his bat on the away pitch and smoothly redirecting the ball—this time, anyway—for a single into right field. If you find all this in your mind's eye at three-forty-five in the morning, you've renewed your license as a Mets fan and can come back the next day.

A reminder that Metsball can produce moments not elsewhere known to man arrived in an early-season Saturday game against the Expos, when Leiter, fielding a little sacrifice bunt, saw his routine toss over to the covering second baseman, Alomar, disappear in mid-flight, swallowed by an alien glove. It was a low-tech magic effect—you could see Leiter's "Wha?" in the middle of it the same instant you heard your own. John Valentin, the old-pro infielder who came over from the Red Sox this year, was filling in for the day at first base, an unfamiliar corner to him. Hurrying toward the plate to field the expected bunt was absolutely the correct move for him, but, when the ball went to Leiter instead, Valentin back-pedalled uncertainly and then stuck out his mitt as the toss to first arced past him—oop! Nobody in the stands or on the field had ever seen this mini-cutoff play before, but the splendor of it was lost on Leiter, who was quickly victimized by another infield error and six unearned Montreal runs. The next miscue belonged to Rey Ordóñez, the routinely impeccable Mets shortstop, who also dropped a relay, in the fourth, and, two innings later, flubbed a little four-hop grounder, for his third error of the day. Ordóñez, amid a scattering of embarrassed boos, stared uncomprehending at the ball lying at his feet. In 1999, he committed four errors during the entire season, and began a run of a hundred and one errorless games at the position, a string unmatched by any shortstop in major-league history. After the game was over—the Mets had rallied energetically, converting an 0–7 deficit into an eventual 8–7 lead, only to lose the thing in the eleventh, on a home run by the vibrant Montreal slugger Vladimir Guerrero—I drove home in a refreshed haze of Metsian wonder.

Ordóñez had slammed his mitt—a black Wilson A2000 model—against the clubhouse wall after the game, and then snipped the laces out of it with a pair of trainer's scissors, making sure it would never clank again. This was more revenge than mojo, since he shifts to a fresh mitt every couple of weeks. Mo Vaughn and John Valentin, by contrast, have played with the same gloves for eight or nine years now—"I like things comfortable," Mo said—and the mitts feel as if there's more pine tar than leather to them by now. When Valentin let me grab hold of his for a minute, in the clubhouse, it grabbed me back.

Even in the midst of his troubles, Ordóñez continued to pull off dazzlingly difficult plays, including his patented stretching dive to the right, when he reaches across his body to backhand a scorching drive and at the same time drops to his right knee or extends the leg full-length, like a dancer flying into a split. This brings him to a skidding halt, with his body rising and turning in the same motion for the throw across the diamond; the left leg has trailed a fraction, opening his upper body enough to allow some steam on the peg. Nothing in modern baseball is prettier than this. It was the easier stuff that was giving him fits, that extra beat of time which told him and the rest of us how hard the work is after all.

I went back to Shea the day after the eleven-inning loss to the Expos, but this time sat jam-packed in the stands in short left, where patches of pale sunshine and mild booing (while Mets starter Steve Trachsel gave back an early 3–1 lead) and the shrilling of kiddie fans kept us cheerful. Fans in every style and vintage of Mets gear paraded up and down the aisles, and returning, view-blocking food-bearers, in ancient ritual, paused to ogle the field in response to the smallest hint of action. A busy dad in front of me missed Alomar's first-inning homer while on forage, and then blew Robbie's next dinger, in the third, when he'd gone down again for ice cream. Some mini-minors near me had to stand on their seats, teetering and peering—and sometimes grabbing my shirt or ear to keep balance—to catch fractional glimpses of the batter, way off to our right. Now and then one of the standees would step on the wrong part of his seat and disappear from view, like a wader taken down by a shark, but then resurface smiling, with peanut dust and bits of popcorn in his hair. The noise was amazing, and not much like the apprehensive or vengeful sounds of Yankee Stadium, where every game must be won.

These peewee fans enjoyed some between-inning gambollings by Mr. Met and a bunch of visiting mascots—the Phillie Phanatic, the Oakland white elephant, the Pirates' parrot, the Padres' tonsured friar, and others—here to help celebrate his ostensible fortieth anniversary. But I date back to the Polo Grounds era with this club, and recall Mr. Met's predecessor, a beagle named Homer—a dog, I mean, and not a parade float. (There was a vivid follow-up to the mention of Homer a few days after it ran in *The New Yorker,* in a letter from a reader named Wilson Seibert: "The reference to Homer absolutely floored me; I had thought the world had forgotten that game little beagle. Here's the inside story: It was during one of the team's first traumatic years, and the TV and radio sponsor was Rheingold beer, under the sometimes wild leadership of Philip Liebmann. I was a young copywriter at J. Walter Thompson, and we worked to fill nine innings with the likes of Miss Rheingold. Homer was Liebmann's idea. He had been trained in Hollywood by Rudd Weatherwax, the man responsible for Lassie. The premise was that, after every Mets home run, Homer would be released, round the bases, and slide into home. Honest! Casey Stengel hated the deal, to say the least, and disliked the dog intensely. He nixed the original plan to have Homer sit in the dugout with the players. In rehearsals, Homer was super. But, as we all remember, those original Mets were kind of shy about knocking the ball out of the park. Marv Throneberry was one of the leading candidates, but not often. Finally, the dog got his chance: the ball went into the bleachers, and, as the player reached home, Homer was set free. He circled first with the crowd roaring, touched second—and headed straight into center field. It took three fielders, two ushers, and the handler to capture him. End of Homer. Sent back to California on the next plane.")

I am no fan of the present-day Queens icon, holding that a stitched and grinning white ball is not the face of fun, but this time withheld complaint and even joined in speculative conversations about him in our loge sector. None of us knew as yet that the anima of Mr. Met was elsewhere, serving his country. But had not Mr. Met been known to add a tactful yarmulke to his getup in the past, on High Holy Day games? (I thought not.) And were these warm-hearted visiting mascots the real thing, flown in for the afternoon from their distant home fields around the league, or were they untrained local talent, mere walk-ons under those outsized heads? (I took the cynical second view.) I didn't know it, but the same Santa debate was being argued up in the first-base-side mezzanine at this very moment, by my Mets-fan friend Gerry and his ten-year-old son, Guy, who was shocked at his father's suggestion that the mascot co-celebrants were not on the up and up. When the game ended—the Mets won it, 6–4—and they went home, someone turned on the Dodgers-Padres game, over ESPN, and there was the Padres' Swinging Friar shaking his belly on Pacific Coast time. "Oh, Daad!" Guy said, crestfallen.

I was back among the grownups the next evening—well, back in the pressbox—for the best entertainment of the young season, an extended docudrama against the Atlanta Braves, unexpectedly captured by the Mets, 7–6, in twelve. The Braves have eaten the Mets' lunch in recent years, while on the way to their brilliant run of ten straight post-season appearances, but this year's edition has proved fallible and just now stood last in the National League East. The game, in any case, suspended speculation with its own news. Shawn Estes, the Mets lefty starter, was rocked for two homers and five runs in the second inning but permitted by Bobby Valentine to stay on through the fifth, while he recaptured his poise and his curveball. Mike Piazza had led off the Mets' second inning with a homer to dead center field, and then did it again, farther and deeper, to start off the seventh. Doubles by Edgardo Alfonzo and Jeromy Burnitz now trimmed the Atlanta lead to 6–3, and Ordóñez, ordered to bunt on the first pitch, delivered Burnitz from third base on a delicious squeeze, with the runner crossing the plate untouched and no play at any base. "LetsgoMets!" . . . "LetsgoMets!" and here came John Valentin, up to bat in place of the pitcher, with a tying two-run shot, barely over the wall and a foot or two inside the left-field foul pole: his first pinch-hit homer in a ten-years-plus career. Stuff like this should be saved for September.

The Mets bullpen flingers had matters their way by now—they combined with Estes for what became a nine-inning midgame shutout, in fact—but Braves manager Bobby Cox slipped out of a pickle in the tenth, when he ordered a startling intentional pass to the dangerous Alfonzo, moving the winning run up to third base, before Burnitz struck out to end the threat. The same situation came up again in the twelfth—you could hear the fans yammering about the coincidence—as Alfonzo again stepped in with runners at first and second. But this time Cox was down to a rookie pitcher named Gryboski, who could not be trusted to work with the bases loaded; Alfonzo rapped his third pitch to right-center for a single and the game.

Readers who infer a continuous cheering and optimism in the stands throughout this long test don't understand Mets fans. When Armando Benitez, the large fireballer, came on in the tenth, he was welcomed with the low, round noises of discontent. Benitez was the best closer in the league last year, with forty-three saves and the Rolaids Relief Man award to prove it. Standing on the mound with his head tilted back a fraction, he stares down at the batter as if through reading glasses, and then delivers serious heat. He is affable in the clubhouse, but too often (for me, at least) appears to be drawing upon a boyish optimism while at work; even when he's in serious difficulties you can see him checking out the illuminated, second-deck sign in short right field as it flashes the m.p.h. of his latest delivery. Benitez blew three saves along the way last year, two of them in critical late-season games against the Braves, hence the pitiless reminders. Here, in the unfamiliar role of holder, he held for his two innings, surrendering a bare single, and gave way to Scott Strickland, who got the win. Bobby Valentine is impatient with the Shea fans' disloyalty to Armando—"The intelligence level could be greater," he once muttered about them. On another day, he pointed out that the Giants didn't make the playoffs last year, either, and that *their* closer, Robb Nen, blew seven saves. "What would happen if he was our guy?" Bobby said, shuddering.

The baseball skyline took on a different look on May 7th, when Barry Bonds came to town, with ten homers in tow. Already this year he had overtaken Harmon Killebrew, whose five hundred and seventy-three home runs had him in sixth place on the lifetime list, and was a few weeks or so away from Mark McGwire's five hundred and eighty-three. Sometime before the summer, he will put away Frank Robinson's fourth-best five hundred and eighty-six, and when the season is done he should be well into the six hundreds, an upland terrain heretofore occupied only by his godfather, Willie Mays. Ruth and Aaron are the last two peaks.

We should not be distracted by a mere record, though. The news about Bonds is that he plays every day and still does it almost better than anyone else. Arriving at Shea, he was batting a league-leading .391, and also stood first in on-base percentage and slugging average—and walks. Bases on balls are boring, but they have become a daily reality for Bonds now, a dangling spear in his flank. Last year, he broke an ancient mark held by Babe Ruth when he walked a hundred and seventy-seven times, but with fifty free passes to date he'll surpass that and then some.

The walks were on his mind during a pre-game press conference, when he said that all those early free trips this year had made it tougher to get his early-season swing adjusted. "This is probably the hardest thing I've gone through in my career," he went on. "But I have the mentality and the focus to withstand it." He said he was happy that the Giants had been in strong contention in recent years—if they'd been in last place it would have been devastating. Team-play references are reflexive P.R. for star players these days, but Bonds here unexpectedly began talking about Curt Schilling and Randy Johnson's work in the World Series last fall, which he called the greatest pitching performance he'd ever seen. "But if Gonzalez doesn't get that hit"—in the bottom of the ninth inning of the last game—"they would have lost. Their team won that World Series. . . . There's no one person in baseball."

Pressed about the Aaron record, Bonds said, "I don't have enough games in my body to get there. I don't have enough years with a hundred and seventy walks to get there."

Bonds had his cap on backward during the press conference, above that jewelled-cross earring, and he spoke in the softly or grandly self-assured way that has irritated writers and fans throughout his career. Some baseball people I know believe that the accolade of "best player in baseball" widely bestowed upon Ken Griffey, Jr., a few years back was an intentional insult to Bonds, who has been persistently disliked and underrated. But there's been an almost tectonic shift in view about him, which arises less from his maturity than from the at last acknowledged evidence that in him we have a dedicated team player, a superior outfielder and base stealer, and a four-time Most Valuable Player who must be placed among the handful of best players who ever lived. Bobby Valentine, responding to a question about accusations of Bonds' steroid use in reaching his present strength and size, said, "Did they shoot steroids in his *eyes*?" And he brought up another tall left fielder, named Williams, and said, "If there's one of those two that's a little better than the other . . . well, my goodness."

Friends of mine who resist such talk get to hear my favorite Bonds record. When he steals fourteen more bases—he'll get around to this, for sure—he will take sole possession of the 500 Homers Plus 500 Stolen Bases Club. (It's always called a "club," for some reason; think of this one as the Porcellian.) He is already in the 400 HRs-400 SBs Club, of course: he's the only one there. You have to go back to the 300 Homers-300 Stolen Bases frat, down the

street, to find him some company. There are three other members—
Andre Dawson, Willie Mays, and Barry's father, Bobby Bonds.

Bonds, stepping up to the plate with no one aboard in the very
first inning of the Giants' three-game visit, evoked the customary
emotions. Batting left, he crowds the plate, and, with his long legs
and fashionably long pants (they now engulf his shoetops, thanks
to little elastic straps that slip over his spikes), expectant shoulders,
and slightly choked-up, forwardly thrumming black bat, vacuums
the available air from the moment. Almost visible were his records
and his seventeen years in the majors; as one baseball guy said,
"He's seen every pitch in history." Boos fell upon him—from apprehension or as character-comment—but they weren't as loud as
those that followed the one, two, three, four straight balls now
handed down by Mets starter Steve Trachsel. None of the pitches
came near the strike zone; there was no attempt by Trachsel to dis-
guise what was going on. He would take his chances with the rest
of the Giants' order, but Barry was too tough to mess with. This
was modern, high-scoring baseball, when single runs don't matter
as much as they did in Babe Ruth's day. Get used to it.

Bonds drew four more walks and a plunk on the side (another
form of free pass) across the remainder of this game and the next
two, while the Giants finished their sweep and at last knocked the
Mets out of first place. Bonds' only hit of the series was a solo
homer against Pedro Astacio in the finale—a short-stroke flick
of the bat that sent the ball over the left-center-field wall—which
began a three-run game-tying rally by the Giants. I was watching
via television, and while the Mets commentators made much of
this dinger and an earlier Mo Vaughn shot off the scoreboard, nobody said anything about a walk to Bonds in his next at-bat beyond oohing over Astacio's first fling, high and inside, which put
Barry in the dirt. None of the next three pitches came close to the
strike zone, and the walk moved up a prior base runner, Rich Au-
rilia, who soon became the winning run. Bonds was unperturbed
by the knockdown. "Who's winning?" he said to the reporters in
the clubhouse. "That's all that matters." It was the only visit to

Shea that the Giants and Bonds will make this year, but, thanks to interleague play, he will be unexpectedly on view at Yankee Stadium on June 7th, 8th, and 9th—back for the bullfight or the baseball.

John Franco, the Mets captain and famous reliever, was lounging on a dugout step just after the early Bonds press conference, and when someone repeated Barry's "I don't have enough games in my body to get there" line to him he made a dismissive little violin-playing gesture. Old pros are hard on each other, and Franco had something nearer than Hank Aaron on his mind. The next day, Mets general manager Steve Phillips broke the bad news: an MRI had disclosed that Franco's medial collateral ligament and flexor tendon had pulled loose from the bone in his elbow, and that he would require a ligament replacement (the "Tommy John" operation) and a year to fifteen months of rehabilitation if he was ever to pitch again. Franco, who is forty-one, said he was thinking it over. Meeting the writers the next afternoon, he broke down in tears when he told us that when he'd got home the previous night, after the news was out, his ten-year-old son, J.J., had asked, "Is it my fault because we played catch the day before?"

Franco's tears and toughness came as no surprise. A five-ten (at best) lefty reliever and stopper, he has compiled eighteen years in the majors and four hundred and twenty-two saves on attitude and a cutter. No fastball. He's a local guy all the way, the son of a city sanitation worker and a product of Lafayette High and St. John's University. Watching him at work all this time—he came aboard the Mets in 1990—you understood always that he would be only just good enough for the crisis at hand. Even when he closed the deal—got rid of the last batter of the day on a changeup and came down off the mound yelling and punching the air—he looked more human than triumphant: a Met like the rest of us, living out his wildest dream. Catching him again here, perhaps for the thousandth time, I saw that his snapping dark eyes, the cool little head loll, the tongue that rolls out in the middle of a laugh, the dismissive "Naah!," and the rest—clean-line haircut and a downturned dark mustache—were all New York, but of a kind we know better now than we used to. He's a firefighter.

Franco decided to have the operation, and hopes to rejoin the Mets by July or August next year. I hope he can do it, too, but I wish even more that he'd stop now and let himself up a little. Grant Roberts, a twenty-four-year-old bullpen teammate of Franco's, said, "I've loved just seeing him here every day," which is my thought exactly. My Mets friends Gerry and Barbara and Peter and Brooke and my wife, Carol, and I will talk about Franco in the stands at Shea, while things go from worse to worse. The other day, Alomar and Ordóñez pulled off a breathtaking play behind second base against the Colorado Rockies—a behind-the-back flip from Robbie to the outstretched Rey. Two innings later, Ordóñez made a throwing error, and then Alomar threw a routine double-play toss past Mo Vaughn at first. Lately, with nobody hitting, the Mets lost eight out of nine games, to reach the .500 level: official mediocrity. Then Pedro Astacio and Jeff D'Amico threw back-to-back two-hit shutouts against the Dodgers. Who needs hitting?

Baseball weirdness abounds—the Marlins drew a home crowd of 5,461 the day they took over first place in the N.L. East—and attendance is seriously down in nine big-league cities. Maybe gloomy Bud Selig is right. Everybody wants to see a winner but we only want a win. Baseball at Shea gives you a lot of between-time, and we're working on Mr. Met's love life, and our all-time team made up of players with girls' names—Pete Rose, Mark Grace, Babe Ruth, and this guy on the Brewers Mark Loretta, and the rest—and what do you suppose happens to marriages that begin with those scoreboard proposals: "Cheryl Will You Marry Me?" Let's go, Mo.

SUMMER

Early Innings

1992

I was born in 1920, and became an addicted reader at a precocious age. Peeling back the leaves of memory I discover a peculiar mulch of names: Steerforth, Tuan Jim, Moon Mullins, Colonel Sebastian Moran. Sunny Jim Bottomley, Dazzy Vance, Goose Goslin. Bob La Follette, Carter Glass, Rexford Guy Tugwell. Robert Benchley, A. E. Housman, Erich Maria Remarque. Hack Wilson, Riggs Stephenson, Senator Pat Harrison and Representative Sol Bloom. Pie Traynor and Harry Hopkins. Kenesaw Mountain Landis and Benjamin Cardozo. Pepper Martin. George F. Babbitt. The Scottsboro Boys. Franklin Delano Roosevelt. Babe Ruth. In my early teens, I knew the Detroit Tigers' batting order and F.D.R.'s first Cabinet, both by heart. Mel Ott's swing, Jimmie Foxx's upper arms, and Senator Borah's eyebrows were clear in my mind's eye. Baseball, which was late in its first golden age, meant a lot to me, but it didn't come first, because I seem to have been a fan of everything at that age—a born pain in the neck. A city kid, I read John Kieran, Walter Lippmann, Richards Vidmer, Heywood Broun, and Dan Daniel just about every day, and what I read stuck. By the time I'd turned twelve, my favorite authors included Conan Doyle, Charles Dickens, Will James on cowboys, Joseph A. Altsheler on Indians, and Dr. Raymond L. Ditmars on reptiles. Another batting order I could have run off for you would have presented some prime species among the Elapidae—a family that includes cobras, coral snakes, kraits, and mambas, and is cousin to the deadly sea snakes of the China Sea.

Back then, baseball and politics were not the strange mix that they would appear to be today, because they were both plainly where the action lay. I grew up in New York and attended Lincoln School of Teachers College (*old* Lincoln, in Manhattan parlance), a font of progressive education where we were encouraged to follow our interests with avidity; no Lincoln parent was ever known to have said, "Shut up, kid." My own parents were divorced, and I lived with my father, a lawyer of liberal proclivities who voted for Norman Thomas, the Socialist candidate, in the Presidential election of 1932 and again in 1936. He started me in baseball. He had grown up in Cleveland in the Nap Lajoie-Addie Joss era, but he was too smart to try to interpose his passion for the Indians on his son's idolatrous attachment to the Yankees and the Giants, any more than he would have allowed himself to smile at the four or five Roosevelt-Garner buttons I kept affixed to my windbreaker (above my knickers) in the weeks before Election Day in 1932.

The early to mid-nineteen-thirties were tough times in the United States, but palmy days for a boy-Democrat baseball fan in New York. Carl Hubbell, gravely bowing twice from the waist before each delivery, was throwing his magical screwball for the Giants, and Joe DiMaggio, arriving from San Francisco in '36 amid vast heraldings, took up his spread-legged stance at the Stadium, and batted .323 and .346 in his first two years in the Bronx. He was the first celebrated rookie to come up to either team after I had attained full baseball awareness: *my* Joe DiMaggio. My other team, the New Deal, also kept winning. Every week in 1933, it seemed, the White House gave birth to another progressive, society-shaking national agency (the A.A.A., the N.R.A., the C.C.C., the T.V.A.), which Congress would enact into law by a huge majority. In my city, Fiorello LaGuardia led the Fusion Party, routed the forces of Tammany Hall, and, as mayor, cleared slums, wrote a new city charter, and turned up at five-alarmers wearing a fire chief's helmet. (I interviewed the Little Flower for my high-school paper later in the decade, after sitting for seven hours in his waiting room. I can't remember anything he said, but I can still see his feet, under the mayoral swivel chair, not quite touching the floor.) Terrible things were going on in Ethiopia and Spain and Germany, to be sure, but at home almost everything I wanted to happen seemed to come to pass within a few weeks or months—most of all in baseball. The Yankees and the Giants between them captured eight pennants in the thirties, and even played against each other in a subway series in 1936 (hello, ambivalence) and again in 1937. The Yankees won both times; indeed, they captured all five of their World Series engagements in the decade, losing only three games in the process. Their 12-1 October won-lost totals against the Giants, Cubs, and Reds in '37, '38, and '39 made me sense at last that winning wasn't everything it was cracked up to be; my later defection to the Red Sox and toward the pain-pleasure principle had begun.

There are more holes than fabric in my earliest baseball recollections. My father began taking me and my four-years-older sister to games at some point in the latter twenties, but no first-ever view of Babe Ruth or of the green barn of the Polo Grounds remains in mind. We must have attended with some regularity, because I'm sure I saw the Babe and Lou Gehrig hit back-to-back home runs on more than one occasion. Mel Ott's stumpy, cow-tail swing is still before me, and so are Gehrig's thick calves and Ruth's débutante ankles. Baseball caps were different back then: smaller and flatter than today's constructions—more like the workmen's caps that one saw on every street. Some of the visiting players—the Cardinals, for instance—wore their caps cheerfully askew or tipped back on their heads, but never the Yankees. Gloves were much smaller, too, and the outfielders left theirs on the grass, in the shallow parts of the field, when their side came in to bat; I wondered why a batted ball wouldn't strike them on the fly or on the bounce someday, but it never happened. John McGraw, for one, wouldn't have permitted such a thing. He was managing the Giants, with his arms folded across his vest (he wore a suit some days and a uniform on others), and kept his tough, thick chin aimed at the umpires. I would look for him—along with Ott and Bill Terry and Travis Jackson—the minute we arrived at our seats in the Polo Grounds.

I liked it best when we came into the place from up top, rather than through the gates down at the foot of the lower-right-field stand. You reached the upper-deck turnstiles by walking down a steep, short ramp from the Speedway, the broad avenue that swept down from Coogan's Bluff and along the Harlem River, and once you got inside, the long field within the horseshoe of decked stands seemed to stretch away forever below you, toward the bleachers and the clubhouse pavilion in center. My father made me notice how often Terry, a terrific straightaway slugger, would launch an extra base hit into that bottomless countryside ("a homer in any other park" was the accompanying refrain), and, sure enough, now and then Terry would reaffirm the parable by hammering still another triple into the pigeoned distance. Everything about the Polo Grounds was special, right down to the looped iron chains that separated each sector of box seats from its neighbor and could burn your bare arm on a summer afternoon if you weren't careful. Far along each outfield wall, a sloping mini-roof projected outward, imparting a thin wedge of shadow for the bullpen crews sitting there: they looked like cows sheltering beside a pasture shed in August.

Across the river, the view when you arrived was different but equally delectable: a panorama of svelte infield and steep, filigree-topped inner battlements that was offered and then snatched away as one's straw-seat I.R.T. train rumbled into the elevated station at 161st Street. If the Polo Grounds felt pastoral, Yankee Stadium was Metropole, the big city personified. For some reason, we always walked around it along the right-field side, never the other way, and each time I would wonder about the oddly arrayed ticket kiosks (General Admission fifty-five cents; Reserved Grandstand a dollar ten) that stood off at such a distance from the gates. Something about security, I decided; one of these days, they'll demand to see passports there. Inside, up the pleasing ramps, I would stop and bend over, peering through the horizontal slot between the dark, overhanging mezzanine and the descending sweep of grandstand seats which led one's entranced eye to the sunlit green of the field and the players on it. Then I'd look for the Babe. The first Yankee manager I can remember in residence was Bob Shawkey, which means 1930. I was nine years old.

I can't seem to put my hand on any one particular game I went to with my father back then; it's strange. But I went often, and soon came to know the difference between intimate afternoon games at the Stadium (play started at 3:15 p.m.), when a handful of boys and night workers and layabouts and late-arriving business-men (with vests and straw hats) would cluster together in the stands close to home plate or down in the lower rows of the bleachers, and sold-out, roaring, seventy-thousand-plus Sunday doublehead-ers against the Tigers or the Indians or the Senators (the famous rivalry with the Bosox is missing in memory), when I would eat, cheer, and groan my way grandly toward the distant horizon of evening, while the Yankees, most of the time, would win and then win again. The handsome Wes Ferrell always started the first Sun-day game for the Indians, and proved a tough nut to crack. But why, I wonder, do I think of Bill Dickey's ears? In any case, I know I was in the Stadium on Monday, May 5, 1930, when Lefty Gomez, a twitchy rookie southpaw, pitched his very first game for the Yan-kees, and beat Red Faber and the White Sox, 4–1, striking out his first three batters in succession. I talked about the day and the game with Gomez many years later, and he told me that he had looked up in the stands before the first inning and realized that the ticket-holders there easily outnumbered the population of his home town, Rodeo, California, and perhaps his home county as well.

I attended the Gomez inaugural not with my father but with a pink-cheeked lady named Mrs. Baker, who was—well, she was my governess. Groans and derisive laughter are all very well, but Mrs. Baker (who had a very brief tenure, alas) was a companion any boy would cherish. She had proposed the trip to Yankee Stadium, and she was the one who first noticed a new name out on the mound that afternoon, and made me see how hard the kid was throwing and what he might mean for the Yanks in the future. "Remember the day," she said, and I did. Within another year, I was too old for such babysitting but still in need of late-afternoon companionship before my father got home from his Wall Street office (my sister was away at school by now); he solved the matter by hiring a Columbia undergraduate named Tex Goldschmidt, who proved to be such a genius at the job that he soon moved in with us to stay. Tex knew less about big-league ball than Mrs. Baker, but we caught him up in a hurry.

Baseball memories are seductive, tempting us always toward sweetness and undercomplexity. It should not be inferred (I remind myself) that the game was a unique bond between my father and me, or always near the top of my own distracted interests. If forced to rank the preoccupying family passions in my home at that time, I would put reading at the top of the list, closely followed by conversation and opinions, politics, loneliness (my father had not yet remarried, and I missed my mother), friends, jokes, exercises and active sports, animals (see below), theatre and the movies, professional and college sports, museums, and a very large Misc. Even before my teens, I thought of myself as a full participant, and my fair-minded old man did not patronize me at the dinner table or elsewhere. He supported my naturalist bent, for instance, which meant that a census taken on any given day at our narrow brownstone on East Ninety-third Street might have included a monkey (a Javanese macaque who was an inveterate biter); three or four snakes (including a five-foot king snake, the Mona Lisa of my collection, that sometimes lived for a day or two at a time behind the books in the library); assorted horned toads, salamanders, and tropical fish; white mice (dinner for the snakes); a wheezy Boston terrier; and two or three cats, with occasional kittens.

Baseball (to get back on track here) had the longest run each year, but other sports also got my full attention. September meant Forest Hills, with Tilden and Vines, Don Budge and Fred Perry.

Ivy League football still mattered in those times, and I saw Harvard's immortal Barry Wood and Yale's ditto Albie Booth go at each other more than once; we also caught Chick Meehan's N.Y.U. Violets, and even some City College games, up at Lewisohn Stadium. Winter brought the thrilling Rangers (Frank Boucher, Ching Johnson, and the Cook brothers) and the bespangled old Americans; there was wire netting atop the boards, instead of Plexiglas, and Madison Square Garden was blue with cigarette and cigar smoke above the painted ice. I went there on weekends, never on school nights, usually in company with my mother and stepfather, who were red-hot hockey fans. Twice a year, they took me to the six-day bicycle races at the Garden (Reggie McNamara, Alfred Letourner, Franco Georgetti, Torchy Peden), and, in midwinter, to track events there, with Glenn Cunningham and Gene Venzke trying and again failing to break the four-minute mile at the Millrose Games. Looking back, I wonder how I got through school at all. My mother, I should explain, had been a Red Sox fan while growing up in Boston, but her attachment to the game did not revive until the mid-nineteen-forties, when she fetched up at Presbyterian Hospital for a minor surgical procedure; a fellow-patient across the hall at Harkness Pavilion was Walker Cooper, the incumbent Giants catcher, drydocked for knee repairs, who kept in touch by listening to the Giants' game broadcasts every day. My mother turned her radio on, too, and was hooked.

Sports were different in my youth—a series of events to look forward to and then to turn over in memory, rather than a huge, omnipresent industry, with its own economics and politics and crushing public relations. How it felt to be a young baseball fan in the thirties can be appreciated only if I can bring back this lighter and fresher atmosphere. Attending a game meant a lot, to adults as well as to a boy, because it was the only way you could encounter athletes and watch what they did. There was no television, no instant replay, no evening highlights. We saw the players' faces in newspaper photographs, or in the pages of *Baseball,* an engrossing monthly with an invariable red cover, to which I subscribed, and here and there in an advertisement. (I think Lou Gehrig plugged Fleischmann's Yeast, a health remedy said to be good for the complexion.) We never heard athletes' voices or became aware of their "image." Bo Jackson and Joe Montana and Michael Jordan were light-years away. Baseball by radio was a rarity, confined for the most part to the World Series; the three New York teams, in fact, banned radio coverage of their regular-season games between 1934 and 1938, on the theory that daily broadcasts would damage attendance. Following baseball always required a visit to the players' place of business and, once there, you watched them with attention, undistracted by Diamond Vision or rock music or game promotions. Seeing the players in action on the field, always at a little distance, gave them a heroic tinge. (The only player I can remember encountering on the street, one day on the West Side, was the Babe, in retirement by then, swathed in his familiar camel-hair coat with matching cap.)

We kept up by reading baseball. Four daily newspapers arrived at my house every day—the *Times* and the *Herald Tribune* by breakfast time, and the *Sun* and the *World-Telegram* folded under my father's arm when he got home from the office. The games were played by daylight, and, with all sixteen teams situated inside two time zones, we never went to bed without knowledge of that day's baseball. Line scores were on the front page of the afternoon dailies, scrupulously updated edition by edition, with black squares off to the right indicating latter innings, as yet unplayed, in Wrigley Field or Sportsman's Park. I soon came to know all the bylines— John Drebinger, James P. Dawson, and Roscoe McGowen in the *Times* (John Kieran was the columnist); Rud Rennie and Richards Vidmer in the *Trib;* Dan Daniel, Joe Williams, and Tom Meany in the *World-Telly* (along with Willard Mullin's vigorous sports cartoons); Frank Graham in the *Sun;* and, now and then, Bill Corum in the *Sunday American,* a paper I sometimes acquired for its terrific comics.

Richards Vidmer, if memory is to be trusted, was my favorite scribe, but before that, back when I was nine or ten years old, what

I loved best in the sports pages were box scores and, above all, names. I knew the names of a few dozen friends and teachers at school, of course, and of family members and family friends, but only in baseball could I encounter anyone like Mel Ott. One of the Yankee pitchers was named George Pipgras, and Earle Combs played center. Connie Mack, a skinny gent, managed the Athletics and was in fact Cornelius McGillicuddy. Jimmie Foxx was his prime slugger. I had a double letter in my name, too, but it didn't match up to a Foxx or an Ott. Or to Joe Stripp. I read on, day after day, and found rafts of names that prickled or sang in one's mind. Eppa Rixey, Goose Goslin, Firpo Marberry, Jack Rothrock, Eldon Auker, Luke Appling, Mule Haas, Adolfo Luque (for years I thought it was pronounced "Lyoo-kyoo")—Dickens couldn't have done better. Paul Derringer was exciting: a man named for a pistol! I lingered over Heinie Manush (sort of like sitting on a cereal) and Van Lingle Mungo, the Dodger ace. When I exchanged baseball celebrities with pals at school, we used last names, to show a suave familiarity, but no one ever just said "Mungo," or even "Van Mungo." When he came up in conversation, it was obligatory to roll out the full name, as if it were a royal title, and everyone in the group would join in at the end, in chorus: "Van Lin-gle MUN-*go!*"

Nicknames and sobriquets came along, too, attaching themselves like pilot fish: Lon Warneke, the Arkansas Hummingbird; Travis (Stonewall) Jackson; Deacon Danny MacFayden (in sportswriterese, he was always "*bespectacled* Deacon Danny MacFayden"); Tony (Poosh 'Em Up) Lazzeri (what he pooshed up, whether fly balls or base runners, I never did learn). And then, once and always, Babe Ruth—the Bambino, the Sultan of Swat.

By every measure, this was a bewitching time for a kid to discover baseball. The rabbit ball had got loose in both leagues in 1930 (I wasn't aware of it)—a season in which Bill Terry batted .401 and the Giants batted .319 as a team. I can't say for sure that I knew about Hack Wilson's astounding hundred and ninety R.B.I.s for the Cubs, but Babe Herman's .393 for the Dodgers must have made an impression. (The *lowly* Dodgers. As I should have said before, the

Dodgers—or Robins, as they were called in tabloid headlines—
were just another team in the National League to me back then; I
don't think I set foot in Ebbets Field until the 1941 World Series.
But they became the enemy in 1934, when they knocked the Giants
out of a pennant in September.) The batters in both leagues were
reined in a bit after 1930, but the game didn't exactly become dull.
Lefty Grove had a 31-4 season for the A's in 1931, and Dizzy Dean's
30-7 helped win a pennant for the Gas House Gang Cardinals in
1934. That was Babe Ruth's last summer in the Bronx, but I think I
was paying more attention to Gehrig just then, what with his triple-
crown .363, forty-nine homers, and hundred and sixty-five runs
batted in. I became more aware of other teams as the thirties (and
my teens) wore along, and eventually came to think of them as personalities—sixteen different but familiar faces ranged around a large
dinner table, as it were. To this day, I still feel a little stir of fear inside me when I think about the Tigers, because of the mighty Detroit teams of 1934 and 1935, which two years running shouldered
the Yankees out of a pennant. I hated Charlie Gehringer's pale face
and deadly stroke. One day in '34, I read that a Yankee bench player
had taunted Gehringer, only to be silenced by Yankee manager Joe
McCarthy. "Shut up," Marse Joe said. "He's hitting .360—get him
mad and he'll bat .500." Gehringer played second in the same infield
with Hank Greenberg, Billy Rogell, and Marv Owen; that summer,
the four of them drove in four hundred and sixty-two runs.

The World Series got my attention early. I don't think I read
about Connie Mack's Ehmke strategem in 1929 (I had just turned
nine), but I heard about it somehow. Probably it was my father
who explained how the wily Philadelphia skipper had wheeled out
the veteran righty as a surprise starter in the opening game against
the Cubs, even though Howard Ehmke hadn't pitched an inning of
ball since August; he went the distance in a winning 3–1 performance, and struck out thirteen batters along the way. But I was living in the sports pages by 1932, when the mighty Yankees blew
away the Cubs in a four-game series, blasting eight home runs. It
troubled me in later years that I seemed to have no clear recollec-

tion of what came to be that Series' most famous moment, when Babe Ruth did or did not call his home run against Charlie Root in the fifth inning of the third game, out at Wrigley Field. What *I* remembered about that game was that Ruth and Gehrig had smacked two homers each. A recent investigation of the microfilm files of the times seems to have cleared up the mystery, inasmuch as John Drebinger's story for that date makes no mention of the Ruthian feat in its lead, or, indeed, until the thirty-fourth paragraph, when he hints that Ruth did gesture toward the bleachers ("in no mistaken motions the Babe notified the crowd that the nature of his retaliation would be a wallop right out of the confines of the park"), after taking some guff from the hometown rooters as he stepped up to the plate, but then Drebinger seems to veer toward the other interpretation, which is that Ruth's gesture was simply to show that he knew the count ("Ruth signalled with his fingers after each pitch to let the spectators know exactly how the situation stood. Then the mightiest blow of all fell"). The *next*-mightiest blow came on the ensuing pitch, by the way: a home run by Lou Gehrig.

I remember 1933 even better. Tex Goldschmidt and I were in the lower stands behind third base at the Stadium on Saturday, April 29th, when the Yankees lost a game to the ominous Senators on a play I have never seen duplicated—lost, as Drebinger put it, "to the utter consternation of a crowd of 36,000." With the Yanks trailing by 6–2 in the ninth, Ruth and then Gehrig singled, and Sammy Byrd (a pinch-runner for the portly Ruth) came home on a single by Dixie Walker. Tony Lazzeri now launched a drive to deep right center. Gehrig hesitated at second base, but Walker, at first, did not, and when the ball went over Goslin's head the two runners came around third in tandem, separated by a single stride. The relay—Goslin to Joe Cronin to catcher Luke Sewell—arrived at the same instant with the onrushing Gehrig, and Sewell, whirling in the dust, tagged out both runners with one sweeping gesture, each on a different side of the plate. I was aghast—and remembered the wound all summer, as the Senators went on to win the A.L. pennant, beating out the Yanks by seven games.

Startling things happened in baseball that season. The first All-Star Game was played, out at Comiskey Park, to a full-house audience; Babe Ruth won it with a two-run homer and Lefty Gomez garnered the win. On August 3rd, Lefty Grove shut out the Yankees, terminating a string (sorry: a skein) of three hundred and eight consecutive games, going back almost exactly two years, in which the Bombers had never once been held scoreless. The record stands, unbeaten and unthreatened, to this day. Later that month, Jimmie Foxx batted in nine runs in a single game, a league record at the time; and, later still, Gehrig played in his one-thousand-three-hundred-and-eighth consecutive game, thereby eclipsing the old mark established by a Yankee teammate, Everett Scott, in 1925. *That* story in the *Times,* by James P. Dawson, mentions the new record in a terse, two-graf lead, and brusquely fills in the details down at the bottom of the column, recounting how action was halted after the first inning for a brief ceremony at home plate, when league president Will Harridge presented Gehrig with a silver statuette "suitably inscribed." Then they got back to baseball: "This simple ceremony over, the Yankees went out almost immediately and played like a winning team, but only for a short time." There was no mooning over records in those days.

It's always useful to have two teams to care about, as I had already learned. My other sweethearts, the Giants, moved into first place in their league on June 13th and were never dislodged. On the weekend of the Fourth of July, they gave us something to remember. I was just back from an auto trip to the Century of Progress World's Fair, in Chicago, taken in the company of three schoolmates and a science teacher, all of us crammed into an ancient Packard, and of course I had no ticket for the big doubleheader against the Cardinals at the Polo Grounds. I'm positive I read John Drebinger the next morning, though—and then read him again: "Pitching of a superman variety that dazzled a crowd of 50,000 and bewildered the Cardinals gave the Giants two throbbing victories at the Polo Grounds yesterday over a stretch of six hours. Carl Hubbell, master lefthander of Bill Terry's amazing hurling corps, blazed the trail by firing away for eighteen scoreless innings to win the opening game from the Cards, 1 to 0....Then the broad-shouldered Roy Parmelee strode to the mound and through semi-darkness and finally a drizzling rain, blanked the St. Louisans in a nine-inning nightcap, 1 to 0. A homer in the fourth inning by Johnny Vergez decided this battle."

Trumpet arias at this glorious level require no footnotes, and I would add only that Tex Carleton, the Cardinal starter in the first game, threw sixteen scoreless innings himself before giving way to a reliever. He was pitching on two days' rest, and Dizzy Dean, the starter and eventual loser of the afterpiece, on one. The first game got its eighteen innings over with in four hours and three minutes, by the way, and the nightcap was done in an hour and twenty-five.

The Giants went the distance in 1933, as I have said, and took the World Series as well, beating the Senators by four games to one. Hubbell, who had wound up the regular season with an earned-run average of 1.66 (he was voted Most Valuable Player in his league), won two games, while Ott drove in the winning runs in the opener with a home run, and wrapped matters up with a tenth-inning shot in the finale. I had pleaded with my father to get us some seats for one of the games at the Polo Grounds, but he didn't come through. I imagine now that he didn't want to spend the money; times were tough just then. I attended the games by a different means—radio. Five different New York stations carried the Series that year, and I'm pretty sure I listened either to Ted Husing, on WABC, or to the old NBC warhorse, Graham McNamee, over at WEAF or WJZ. (Whoever it was, I recall repeated references to the "boy man-agers"—Bill Terry and the Senators' Joe Cronin, who had each lately taken the helm at the old franchises.) I knew how to keep score by this time, and I rushed home from school—for the four weekday games, that is—turned on the big Stromberg-Carlson (with its glowing Bakelite dial), and kept track, inning by inning, on scorecards I drew on one of my father's yellow legal pads.

When my father got home, I sat him down and ran through it all, almost pitch by pitch, telling him the baseball.

I was playing ball myself all this time—or trying to, despite the handicaps of living in the city and of my modestly muscled physique. But I kept my mitt in top shape with neat's-foot oil, and possessed a couple of Louisville Slugger bats and three or four baseballs, one so heavily wrapped in friction tape that making contact with it with a bat felt like hiking a frying pan. (One of the bats, as I recall, bore lifelong scars as the result of a game of one-o'-cat played with a rock.) Neat's-foot oil was a magical yellow elixir made from cattle bones and skin—and also a password, unknown to girls. "What's a *neat*?" every true American boy must have asked himself at some point or other, imagining some frightful amputation made necessary by the demands of the pastime.

What skills I owned had been coached by my father from an early age. Yes, reader: we threw the old pill around, and although it did not provide me with an instant ticket to the major leagues, as I must have expected at one time, it was endlessly pleasurable. I imagined myself a pitcher, and my old man and I put in long hours of pitch and catch, with a rickety shed (magically known as the Bull Pen) as backstop; this was at a little summer colony on the west bank of the Hudson, where we rented. My father had several gloves of his own, including an antique catcher's mitt that resembled a hatbox or a round dictionary. Wearing this, he would squat down again and again, putting up a target, and then fire the ball back (or fetch it from the weeds somewhere), gravely snapping the ball from behind his ear like Mickey Cochrane. Once in a while, there would be a satisfying pop as the ball hit the pocket, and he would nod silently and then flip the pill back again. His pitching lexicon was from his own boyhood: "inshoot," "hook," "hard one," and "drop." My own drop dropped to earth so often that I hated the pitch and began to shake him off.

I kept at it, in season and out, and, when I finally began to get some growth, developed a pleasing roundhouse curve that sometimes sailed over a corner of the plate (or a cap or newspaper), to the amazement of my school friends. Encouraged, I began to work on a screwball, and eventually could throw something that infinitesimally broke the wrong way, although always too high to invite a swing; I began walking around school corridors with my pitching hand turned palm outward, like Carl Hubbell's, but nobody noticed. Working on the screwball one cold March afternoon (I was thirteen, I think), on a covered but windy rooftop playground at Lincoln, I ruined my arm for good. I continued pitching on into high school (mine was a boarding school in northern Connecticut), but I didn't make the big team; by that time, the batters I faced were smarter and did frightful things to my trusty roundhouse. I fanned a batter here and there, but took up smoking and irony in self-defense. A short career.

When I began writing this brief memoir, I was surprised to find how often its trail circled back to my father. If I continue now with his baseball story, instead of my own, it's because the two are so different yet feel intertwined and continuous. He was born in 1889, and lost his father at the age of eight, in a maritime disaster. He had no brothers, and I think he concluded early on that it was incumbent on him to learn and excel at every sport, all on his own. Such a plan requires courage and energy, and he had both in large supply. A slim, tall, bald, brown-eyed man, of handsome demeanor (there is some Seneca Indian blood on his side of the family), he pursued all sports except golf, and avidly kept at them his whole life. He was a fierce swimmer, mountain climber, canoeist, tennis player, fly fisherman, tap dancer, figure skater, and ballplayer; he was still downhill-skiing in his middle seventies, when a stern family meeting was required to pry him from the slopes, for his own good. He was not a great natural athlete, but his spirit made him a tough adversary. My Oedipal struggles with him on the tennis court went on almost into my thirties, but we stayed cheerful; somewhere along the line, a family doctor took me aside and said, "Don't try to keep up with him. Nobody's ever going to do that."

Baseball meant a great deal to my father, and he was lucky enough to grow up in a time when there were diamonds and pickup nines in every hamlet in America. He played first base and pitched, and in his late teens joined a village team, the Tamworth Tigers, that played in the White Mountain valleys of New Hampshire, where he and his mother and sister went on their vacations. Years later, he told me about the time he and some of the other Tamworth stars—Ned Johnson, Paul Twitchell, Lincoln and Dana Steele—formed a team of their own and took a train up into Canada, where they played in a regional tournament; he pitched the only game they got to play, against a much better club (semi-pros, he suspected), and got his ears knocked off. The trip back (he said, still smiling at the pain) was a long one. Many years after this, on a car trip when he was in his seventies, my father found himself near the mountains he knew so well and made a swing over to Chocorua and Tamworth to check out the scenes of his youth. He found the Remick Bros. General Store still in business, and when he went in, the man at the counter, behind the postcards and the little birchbark canoes, was Wadsworth Remick, who had played with him on the Tigers long ago. Waddy Remick. There were no signs of recognition, however, and my old man, perhaps uncomfortable in the role of visiting big-city slicker, didn't press the matter. He bought a pack of gum or something, and was just going out the door when he heard, "Played any first base lately, Ernest?"

I think people gave up with reluctance in olden days. My father sailed through Harvard in three years, making Phi Beta Kappa, but he didn't make the varsity in baseball, and had to settle for playing on a class team. Most men would call it a day after that, but not my father. He went to law school, got married, went off to the war in France, came back and moved from Cleveland to New York and joined a law firm—and played ball. I think my very first recollection of him—I was a small child—is of standing beside him in a little downstairs bathroom of our summer place while he washed dirt off his face and arms after a ballgame. Rivers of brown earth ran into the sink. Later that same summer, I was with my mother on the sidelines when my father, pitching for some Rockland County nine, conked a batter on the top of his head with an errant fastball. The man fell over backward and lay still for a moment or two, and my mother said, "Oh, God—he's done it!" The batter recovered, he and my father shook hands, and the game went on, but the moment, like its predecessor, stayed with me. Jung would envy such tableaux.

Years passed. In the summer of 1937, I worked on a small combined ranch and farm in northern Missouri, owned by a relative who was raising purebred white-faced Herefords. I drove cattle to their water holes on horseback, cleaned chicken coops, and shot marauding evening rabbits in the vegetable garden. It was a drought year, and the temperature would go well over a hundred degrees every afternoon; white dust lay on the trees. I was sixteen. Both the Giants and the Yankees were rushing toward another pennant in New York (it was the DiMaggio, Henrich, Rolfe, Crosetti Yankees by now), but I had a hard time finding news of them in the austere, photoless columns of the Kansas City *Star*. All I could pick up on the radio was Franc Laux doing Cardinals games over KMOX.

My father arrived for a visit, and soon discovered that there would be a local ballgame the next Sunday, with some of the hands on the ranch representing our nearby town. Somehow, he cajoled his way onto the team (he was close to fifty but looked much younger); he played first base, and got a single in a losing cause. Late in the game, I was sent up to pinch-hit for somebody. The pitcher, a large and unpleasant-looking young man, must have felt distaste at the sight of a scared sixteen-year-old dude standing in, because he dismissed me with two fiery fastballs and then a curve that I waved at without hope, without a chance. I sat down again. My father said nothing at the time, but later on in the day, perhaps riding back to supper, he murmured, "What'd he throw you—two hard ones and a hook?" I nodded, my ears burning. There was a pause, and Father said, "The curveball away can be very tough." It was late afternoon, but the view from my side of the car suddenly grew brighter.

It is hard to hear stories like this now without an accompanying inner smirk. We are wary of sentiment and obsessively knowing, and we feel obliged to put a spin of psychology or economic determinism or bored contempt on all clear-color memories. I suppose someone could say that my father was a privileged Wasp, who was able to pursue some adolescent, rustic yearnings far too late in life. But that would miss the point. My father was knowing, too; he was a New York sophisticate who spurned cynicism. He had only limited financial success as a Wall Street lawyer, but that work allowed him to put in great amounts of time with the American Civil Liberties Union, which he served as a long-term chairman of its national board. Most of his life, I heard him talk about the latest issues or cases involving censorship, Jim Crow laws, voting rights, freedom of speech, racial and sexual discrimination, and threats to the Constitution; these struggles continue to this day, God knows, but the difference back then was that men and women like my father always sounded as if such battles would be won in the end. The news was always harsh, and fresh threats to freedom immediate, but every problem was capable of solution somewhere down the line. We don't hold such ideas anymore—about our freedoms or about anything else. My father looked on baseball the same way; he would never be a big-league player, or even a college player, but whenever he found a game he jumped at the chance to play and to win.

If this sounds like a romantic or foolish impulse to us today, it is because most of American life, including baseball, no longer feels feasible. We know everything about the game now, thanks to instant replay and computerized stats, and what we seem to have concluded is that almost none of us are good enough to play it. Thanks to television and sports journalism, we also know everything about the skills and financial worth and private lives of the enormous young men we have hired to play baseball for us, but we don't seem to know how to keep their salaries or their personalities within human proportions. We don't like them as much as we once did, and we don't like ourselves as much, either. Baseball becomes feasible from time to time, not much more, and we fans must make prodigious efforts to rearrange our profoundly ironic contemporary psyches in order to allow its old pleasures to reach us. My father wasn't naïve; he was lucky.

One more thing. American men don't think about baseball as much as they used to, but such thoughts once went deep. In my middle thirties, I still followed the Yankees and the Giants in the standings, but my own playing days were long forgotten; I had not yet tried writing about the sport. I was living in the suburbs, and one night I had a vivid dream, in which I arose from my bed (it was almost a movie dream), went downstairs, and walked outdoors in the dark. I continued down our little patch of lawn and crossed the tiny bridge at the foot of our property, and there, within a tangle of underbrush, discovered a single gravestone. I leaned forward (I absolutely guarantee all this) and found my own name inscribed there and, below it, the dates of my birth and of the present year, the dream time: "1920–1955." The dream scared me, needless to say, but providentially I was making periodic visits to a shrink at the time. I took the dream to our next session like a trophy but, having recounted it, had no idea what it might mean.

"What does it suggest to you?" the goodly man said, in predictable fashion.

"It's sort of like those monuments out by the flagpole in deep center field at the Stadium," I said. Then I stopped and cried, "Oh... *Oh,*" because of course it had suddenly come clear. My dreams of becoming a major-league ballplayer had died at last.

The Companions of the Game

1975

The San Francisco Giants, it seems, are about to be sold to some Japanese businessmen. The news, which appeared in the *Times* late last month, was somehow both startling and boring— instant antipodal emotions that only stories about quintuplets or the business side of sports arouse in me. The *Times'* account was a blurry, hedging affair, beginning with a denial by the Giants' front office of the reported deal, followed by several paragraphs explaining why it probably would go through. It was generally known, of course, that the club has been in financial difficulties for several years, and earlier this summer its president, Horace C. Stoneham, announced that his controlling share of the National Exhibition Company (which is the team's florid, nineteenth-century corporate handle) was up for sale. A San Francisco-based group, headed by a real-estate man named Robert A. Lurie and including the National League president, Chub Feeney, who is a nephew of Stoneham's, and Bill Rigney, a former Giant manager, had been talking with Stoneham, but the Japanese offer of seventeen million dollars—for the club, its minor-league affiliates, and some baseball and hotel properties at the Giants' spring-training headquarters in Phoenix, Arizona—is apparently a good deal higher than any other bids so far. (It was, in fact, a great deal lower, since the Japanese sportsmen never let anyone see the color of their yen, and the deal fell through.) The sale, in any case, will require the approval of the other National League owners, who will vote on the matter sometime after the World Series.

As a lifetime Giants fan whose passionate boyhood attachment had been slowly cooled by the departure of my heroes from the Polo Grounds in 1958, by the decline and eventual retirement of Willie Mays, and by the pale neutrality of middle age, I tried to summon up a semblance of outraged xenophobia at the news of the possible Toyotafication of my old team and my old pastime, but it became clear to me in the same instant that I simply didn't give a damn. Big-league baseball is a commercial enterprise, and the business of Japan, as Calvin Coolidge probably meant to tell us, is business. There was a time when the ownership of a ball team by a hometown brewer or chewing-gum family did not seem an especially important part of its public identity, but in the past twenty years eight of the original sixteen big-league clubs have been sold (and in some cases resold and re-resold) to new business interests, while eight new clubs have been born, four of which have later changed hands. As a result, the financial adventures of some teams are almost better publicized (and often a good deal more interesting) than their achievements in the pennant race. A typical modern ball team is operated coldly and from a distance, just like any other conglomerate subentity with interesting tax-depletion build-ins and excellent P.R. overtones. Their owners and operators are men whose money derives from, and whose deepest loyalties adhere to, insurance companies, broadcasting chains, oil wells, whiskey manufacture, real-estate sales, trucking and shipping lines, quick-lunch chains, and the like, and it doesn't seem to make much difference if one of the teams should now land in the portfolio of some enterprising visitors whose hero is Sadaharu Oh instead of Babe Ruth, and whose cash comes from the marketing of *sake* or electronic calculators or sushiburgers.

For all that, there is one aspect of the sale of the Giants that seems worth attention, worth caring about, and that is the departure of Horace Stoneham from baseball. The Stoneham family has owned the Giants ever since Horace's father, Charles A. Stoneham, purchased the club, in 1919, in partnership with a New York City magistrate named Francis X. McQuade and the team's famous manager, John J. McGraw. Charles Stoneham, who held the majority interest in the team, died in 1936, and Horace Stoneham, then thirty-two years old, succeeded him, thus becoming the youngest club president in baseball history. The Stoneham family has *been* the Giants for more than half a century, for it has had no other business in that time. Along with Calvin Griffith, of the Minnesota Twins (formerly the Washington Senators), Stoneham is the last of the pure baseball men, the owners who owned nothing but their team and cared for nothing but the game. (Tom Yawkey, the long-time Red Sox owner, is of the same breed, but he is also the possessor of a sizable fortune.)

In recent years, it has been the custom for men at baseball gatherings to talk about Horace Stoneham with affectionate and patronizing sadness. "*I like* Horace," the conversation always begins. "Hell, everybody likes him, but..." The sentence trails off, and the speaker shakes his head in the manner of a young lawyer who has undertaken to bring order out of his mother's checkbook. Nothing has gone right for Stoneham in recent years, but there was a time when he had his share of success. His Giants have won five pennants, a world championship, and one divisional title. He has hired winning managers. In his father's time, he recommended the selection of McGraw's successor, Bill Terry, who captured a world championship in his first year at the helm, and in 1948 he snatched Leo Durocher from the despised Brooklyn Dodgers. Stoneham was capable of risky and decisive moves, such as the house-cleaning in 1949, when he traded away the stars of a popular but nonwinning Giants club—Johnny Mize, Walker Cooper, Sid Gordon, Willard Marshall, and Buddy Kerr—to make room for Eddie Stanky and Alvin Dark and the others who would, under Durocher, fashion the marvelous winning summers of 1951 and 1954. The Giants' scouts and farms delivered up some true stars—Monte Irvin, Willie Mays, Willie McCovey, Juan Marichal, and Orlando Cepeda—and estimable front-liners like Sal Maglie, Whitey Lockman, Bobby Thomson, Larry Jansen, the Alou brothers, Gaylord Perry, and Bobby Bonds. Until quite recently, in fact, the Stoneham record has been one of the better ones in baseball, a high-risk business in which true dynasties are extremely rare.

The Dodgers, to be sure, were far more successful than Stoneham's club in the last decade of their co-tenancy of New York, and when the two clubs moved west, in 1958, the disparity widened. The Los Angeles Dodgers have won five pennants and three World Series since their relocation, and the extraordinary season-long outpouring of fans to Dodger Stadium, which regularly tops the home-attendance figures of all other clubs, has made the team the most profitable franchise in baseball. For the San Francisco Giants, it has been quite the other way. The team was idolized in its first few summers, drawing one million eight hundred thousand customers in its first season in Candlestick Park, and there was a famous pennant (and very nearly a world championship) in 1962. From the day Candlestick opened, however, it was plain that its site and its design were disastrous. Its summerlong icy winds and swirling bayside fogs, which often made the act of watching a ball game into something like an Eskimo manhood ritual, have become an old, bad local joke. These discouragements, coupled with five straight second-place finishes between 1965 and 1969, cut attendance in half by 1970, a particularly heavy falloff coming in 1968, when the A's established residency across the Bay. Since then, the proximity of the two clubs has clearly strained the limited audience and the dim baseball fealty of the area, but the A's, now three-time world champions, have had much the better of it. Last year, the A's drew 845,693, while the Giants, who finished fifth in their division, drew 519,991—the worst in either league.

The most riveting difference between the Oakland A's and the San Francisco Giants is not, however, in their comparative records or attendance figures but in their owners. Indeed, the temperament and reputation of the two men are at such utter removes that they almost seem to represent polarities of human behavior, and their presence in the same business and the same metropolis suggests nothing so much as fictional irony flung off by Ayn Rand. Charles O. Finley, the owner of the A's, is a relative newcomer to baseball, who has in a short time achieved an extraordinary success, and perhaps even greater notoriety. He is a self-made man, a millionaire insurance salesman, who has built a formidable championship club by relying almost exclusively on his own intelligence, quickness, hunches, and energetic dealing. He is a great promoter with a perfect inner instrument attuned to the heat of the crowd, the glare of the event, and he is an instinctive and embarrassing self-aggrandizer. He is an innovator who has disturbed the quiet, dim halls of baseball and altered the game irrevocably. As an executive, he takes a personal hand in all the daily details of his club, including the most minute decisions on the field, and he swiftly disposes of managers and subalterns who cannot abide his meddling. The A's headquarters, in the Oakland-Alameda County Coliseum, consists mainly of empty offices. Most of the time, Finley follows his team by telephone from an office in Chicago, either plugging into a local radio broadcast or being provided with a running play-by-play account of the action by someone on the scene. Baseball as occasion—the enjoyment and company of the game—apparently means nothing to him. Finley is generally reputed to be without friends, and his treatment of his players has been characterized by habitual suspicion, truculence, inconsistency, public abasement, impatience, flattery, parsimony, and ingratitude. He also wins.

Horace Stoneham is—well, most of all he is not Charlie Finley. He inherited his team and his position, and he does not want baseball quickly or wildly altered. Indeed, it may well be that he wishes the game to be more as it was when he first came to it as a youth. He is shy, self-effacing, and apparently incapable of public attitudinizing. He attends every home game but is seldom recognized, even by the hoariest Giants fans. His decisions are arrived at after due consideration, and the most common criticism levelled at him is that he often sticks with a losing manager or an elder player long after his usefulness to the club has been exhausted. He relies on old friends for baseball counsel and for company; most of his advisers and colleagues—men like Tom Sheehan; Garry Schumacher; Rosy Ryan; Carl Hubbell, director of player development; and Jack Schwarz, farm director—have been with the Giants for thirty or forty years. Perhaps because Stoneham grew up in a time when baseball was the only game in town and thus seemed to succeed on its own merits, he has a limited interest in vivid public relations, commercial tie-ins, and other hypes. His relations with the press have been cordial (in the words of Wells Twombly, of the San Francisco *Examiner,* he treats reporters like "beloved guests"), and his dealings with his players are marked by generosity and mutual admiration. In 1972, when his dwindling financial resources forced him at last to trade away Willie Mays, perhaps the greatest Giant of them all, he arranged a deal that permitted Mays to move along to the Mets with a salary and a subsequent retirement plan that would guarantee his comfort for the rest of his life. Horace Stoneham is convivial with his friends but instinctively private, and it is possible to guess that the only quality he may share with Charlie Finley is loneliness. He has been losing, and now he has lost, and he is thus fair game for the glum attention of writers and the secret scorn of men who understand nothing but success.

Early this summer, I began compiling information and talking to West Coast ballplayers and baseball writers with the idea of trying to interview Charlie Finley, perhaps while watching a game with him. For some reason (for *several* reasons), I kept holding off on the story, however, and then, when I read that the San Francisco Giants were up for sale, it suddenly came to me that the baseball magnate I really wanted to spend an afternoon with was Horace Stoneham. I got on the telephone to some friends of mine and his (I had never met him), and explained that I did not want to discuss attendance figures or sales prices with him but just wanted to talk baseball. Stoneham called me back in less than an hour. "Come on out," he said in a cheerful, gravelly, Polo Grounds sort of voice. "Come out, and we'll go to the game together."

I dressed all wrong for it, of course. The game that Stoneham and I had fixed upon was a midweek afternoon meeting between the Giants and the San Diego Padres in late June—a brilliant, sunshiny day at Candlestick Park, it turned out, and almost the perfect temperature for a curling match. I had flown out from New York that morning, and reported to Stoneham's office a few minutes before game time. He shook my hand and examined my airy East Coast midsummer getup and said, "Oh, no, this won't do." He went to a closet and produced a voluminous, ancient camel's-hair polo coat and helped me into it. He is a round, pink-faced man with close-cropped white hair, round horn-rimmed spectacles, and a hospitable Irish smile, and he looked much younger than I had expected. (He is seventy-two.) He was wearing tweeds, with an expensive-looking silk tie—a gambler's tie—but he, too, put on a topcoat and buttoned it up before we went out into the sunshine. Stoneham's box, on the press level, was capacious but utilitarian, with none of the Augustan appointments and Late Hefner upholsteries I have seen in some sports-owners' piazzas. There was a perfect view of the ballplayers arrayed below us on the AstroTurf, a few hundred scattered fans—most of whom seemed to be kids in variously emblazoned windbreakers—and thousands of empty orange-colored seats. The game matched up two good young right-handed fastballers—the Giants' John Montefusco and the Padres' Joe McIntosh. I kept track of things for a few minutes, but then I quickly gave it up, because an afternoon of Horace Stoneham's baseball cannot be fitted into a scorecard.

"I think the first Giants game I ever saw was the first half of a doubleheader on the Fourth of July in 1912," he told me. "The Giants' battery was Christy Mathewson and Chief Meyers. They opened with their stars in the first game, you see, because they charged separate admissions for the morning and afternoon games, and that way they got out the crowds early. I've forgotten who the other team was. I was nine years old. My father grew up in New Jersey, and his boyhood idol, his particular hero, was the great Giant left fielder Mike Tiernan, who came from Jersey City. Later, when my pop bought the club, he liked to say that he'd followed Tiernan over to the Giants.

"My father bought the team in 1919, and in 1921, as you may know, we played the first of three consecutive World Series against the Yankees, who shared the Polo Grounds with us in those days. That Series in '21 had a funny kind of ending. We were ahead by one run—I think it was 1–0—in the ninth, and Aaron Ward got on base for the Yanks. Frank Baker—Home Run Baker—came up and knocked a ball to right that looked like a sure hit, but our second baseman, Rawlings, made a great play on it, running it down almost in right field, and threw to Kelly to get him. Ward must have thought the ball had gone through, because he passed second and just kept on running. George Kelly—oh, he had the best arm in baseball—saw him, and he fired the ball across to Frisch at third, and Frisch took the throw and tagged Ward just as he slid in. I can still see that, with Ward in the dirt and Frank Frisch making the tag and then landing on his fanny, with the ball still in his glove. It was a double play and it ended it all, but it happened so fast that everybody in the stands just sat there for a minute. They couldn't believe the Series was over."

Stoneham talked in an energetic, good-humored way. He reminded me of a good standup, middle-of-the-night bar conversationalist. "I was in the stands that day. I was still in school, at Loyola School. I was a mediocre second baseman on the team there. I went to a lot of Giants games, of course. Jimmy Walker was a state assemblyman then, and he used to come to the game every day. I got to know him very well—Hey, look at *this!*"

Von Joshua, the Giant center fielder—the 1975 Giant center fielder—had singled, and a run was coming across the plate. Within another minute or two, the Giants were ahead by 3–0, still in the first inning, and McIntosh had been knocked out of the game.

Stoneham resumed, but we were in 1939 now, at a famous Polo Grounds disaster that I had seen. "You were there?" Stoneham said. "Then, of course, you remember what happened. It was early in the summer, but that game cost us the pennant. We were playing the Cincinnati Reds head and head and if we win we have a good shot at first place. Then somebody hit that ball for them—maybe it was Harry Craft—that hooked foul into the left-field upper deck, and the umpire called it fair and waved the runners around. Everybody could see it was foul, so there was a big squabble, and Billy Jurges, our shortstop, he spit right in George Magerkurth's face, and Magerkurth swung on him. Well, they were both suspended of course—the player and the umpire both together. We called up Frank Scalzi to take Jurges's place, but a few days later Lou Chiozza and Joe Moore had a collision going after a fly ball and Chiozza got a broken leg, and we never did get going again."

I asked Stoneham about his first job with the Giants, and he told me that he had gone to work in the ticket department when he was in his early twenties. "We had a lady, Miss Wilson, who ran it all then," he said. "None of this computer business. Well, bit by bit I got into the running of the ballpark, and then my father put me in charge of operations there. In those days, in the twenties, the Polo Grounds was open for events maybe two hundred days out of the year. The Coogan family owned the real estate, but the park belonged to the club. We had football—pro games and college games—we had the circus there, we had tennis and the midget automobiles. We had a skating rink in the outfield once, and even a week of outdoor opera. We had soccer—the Hakoah team came in after they won some international title, I think it was, and drew fifty-two thousand, so we knew it was a popular sport even then. We had visiting British soccer teams, and a team, I remember, that represented the Indiana Flooring Company. I think we had every sport at the Polo Grounds except polo. I did my best to arrange that, but we never could work it out.

"I came to know the ballplayers then, of course. I used to see them in the mornings. I got to be friends with some of them, like Ross Youngs, the great outfielder who died so young. Ross Youngs, from Shiner, Texas. When he first came along—before I knew him—he was signed by the Giants at a time when the team was on the road. Ross was in town and the Giants were away, and he went right over and got into a pickup baseball game over by the docks on Seventy-ninth Street, next to the railroad yards there. It's where they have the marina now. He had that intense desire to play ball.

"I was about twenty years old when Mr. McGraw asked my father to let me go to spring training. We trained in Sarasota back then. I remember that Mr. McGraw called me up to his room there and showed me a letter he had just written to my father about a young prospect named Hack Wilson, who'd been on a Class B team in Portsmouth, Virginia. He wore a red undershirt under his uniform. Mr. McGraw had written, 'If hustle counts, he's sure to make it.' Everybody called him, 'Mr. McGraw'—everybody but my father, of course. Mr. McGraw, he called my father 'Charlie' or 'C.A.'—C.A. for Charles Abraham Stoneham, named after Abraham Lincoln."

We were in the third inning, and the Padres had a base runner on second. The next Padre batter, shortstop Enzo Hernandez, is an indifferent hitter, but now he singled to left and drove in the first San Diego run. "Oh, you sucker," Stoneham said, shaking his head sadly. "That's the history of the game. The pitcher lets up on the out man, and he hurts you."

The rally died, and Stoneham cheered up quickly. "We were talking about John McGraw," he said. "Well, another time in spring training he wrote a letter back to my father that said, 'There's a young fellow down here named Ott who is the best hitter on the farm level I've ever seen.' As you know, Mr. McGraw never did let Mel Ott go out to the minors. He brought him up to the Giants when he was just seventeen years old. He didn't want anybody spoiling that funny batting style—some manager telling him, 'You can't hit that way. You've got to put that front foot down.' When Ott started out, he was a switch-hitter. He never hit righty in a game, as far as I know. Ott didn't get to play much the first couple of years and McGraw would sometimes let him go over to New Jersey on the weekends and pick up some extra cash by playing with a semipro team. He played with the Paterson Silk Sox. Later on, Ottie and Carl Hubbell were roommates. Oh, my, there were so many games that Carl won by 2–0, 1–0—something like that—where Ott knocked in the winning run. You couldn't count them all."

In the fourth inning, Stoneham took a telephone call at his seat, and I overheard him say, "We've sent flowers, and I wrote Mrs.

Gordon this morning." I had read in the newspaper that morning that Sid Gordon, a Giant infielder-outfielder in the nineteen-forties, had dropped dead while playing softball. Strangely enough, I had read a story about him and Horace Stoneham in a sports column only a few days earlier. Gordon had been a holdout in the spring of 1949, but he finally came to terms for twenty-five hundred dollars less than he had demanded. Horace Stoneham was always made uneasy by prolonged salary disputes with his players, and in December of 1949 he mailed Gordon a check for the twenty-five hundred dollars—a considerable gesture, since Gordon had been traded in the autumn and was by then a member of the Boston Braves.

Now Stoneham hung up the telephone, and I asked him about the business of trades. "Well," he said, "you always hate to see your players leave. Maybe I'm too much of a sentimentalist. You can make mistakes trading, of course, but if you never make a mistake, you're not really trying. We made that big trade with the Braves involving Sid Gordon and the others because Leo Durocher wanted his own kind of team. He always had great success with players that could maneuver the bat. With younger players he was—well, he could be a little impatient. Everything with Leo was . . . *spontaneous.*

"One of the times that really hurt was when it came time to trade Freddie Fitzsimmons, who went over to the Dodgers in the middle thirties there, after more than ten years with us. He was really upset when he left us. He cried. What a competitor he was! He had no friends when he was out there on the mound. He'd show the batter his back when he pitched—he had that big rotation—and he was a remarkable fielder, with great agility for somebody with such a bulky build. Sometimes there'd be a hard grounder or a line drive hit through the box there and he'd stick out his *foot* at it to stop it going through. Anything to win. I can still see him sticking out that foot and knocking the ball down or maybe deflecting it to some infielder.

"All those games in the Polo Grounds—well, most of the time I watched them from a window in the clubhouse, way out beyond center field. You remember what it was like there?" I did indeed. I always used to wonder about the distant figures that one could sometimes see peering out of the little screened windows set into that green, faraway wall. "There was just a table and chairs there— the same place where my pop used to sit and watch. I was out there when Bobby Thomson hit the home run in 1951 that beat the Dodgers in the last playoff game. We were down three runs in the ninth, and I was commiserating with Sal Maglie, who'd been taken out of the game, and trying to tell him what a great year it had been. We saw Lockman's hit that brought in the first run, but the side of the bleachers blocked our view so we couldn't see if Bobby's hit was going to go in, but I knew it was up the wall, so I said to Sal, 'Well, at least we've tied it up.' Some tie! The same thing with Willie's catch off Vic Wertz in the 1954 Series. I watched him come all the way out after it, and then he went out of sight behind that big black screen we had there that formed a background for the hitters. But I heard the crowd, and I knew he'd made the catch. I knew it anyway, I think, because I'd seen him make all those other impossible catches. I liked that view of things in the Polo Grounds. The last day we played there, I couldn't go to the game. I just didn't want to see it come to an end."

We were in the fourth inning and the Giants had a couple of runners on, and now the Giants' second baseman, Derrel Thomas, delivered them both with a sharp single up the middle. A thin scattering of cheers reached us, and Stoneham beamed. I ventured to ask him if he had a favorite among all the Giant clubs he watched down the years.

"Ah, I've seen so many of them," he said. "You'd have to break them down into periods. People are always asking me how the ballplayers compare now with the old-timers, and all you can say is they're at least the equal. The equipment is much better now, of course, but the competition for athletes [he gave it the old New York sound: "athaletes"] is greater, with the other sports getting so big. The best of them can play all sports, you know. We've lost some of our top draft choices to football. When I was a young fellow, all the colleges had good baseball programs, but now a lot of them have given up the game.

"You know, we have a good team right here, but we've had injuries. Gary Matthews and Von Joshua got hurt on the same day. Matthews is going to miss about a month, they say, with the broken knuckle on his left hand. But I think we're going to pick up and pull ourselves together. This is a young team, and I do like that. We have a lot of young arms."

He looked up at the scoreboard. "Those Cubbies are beating the Phils again, I see," he said. "They must have some kind of wind there—look at all those home runs. Yes, so many things can happen to a team in a year, you know. We had a lot of strange events in '33, when we ended up winning the Series. Johnny Vergez had an appendectomy, and Charlie Dressen came up and filled in— he'd been managing in the Southern Association. He told Adolfo Luque how to pitch to the final Washington batter in the Series— it was somebody he'd seen down there. Lefty O'Doul came back with us that year, too, and he got a big pinch hit in the Series, off of Alvin Crowder. I remember that Luque was limping around at the party after we'd won the last game, and when we asked him about it, it turned out he'd split his big toenail throwing those curves during the game. He bore down that hard, he broke his toe.

"When Sal Maglie was first with us, he was just an average pitcher. [Stoneham had moved along about fifteen years.] But when he jumped down to the Mexican League, in 1946, the team he played for there was managed by Dolf Luque, and when we got him back he'd mastered all those great curveballs, and nobody could touch him."

We were joined now by Garry Schumacher, the retired press director for the Giants, who was for many years a redoubtable Polo Grounds pressbox sage.

"Garry, we've been talking about Luque and Sal and some of the other old-timers," Stoneham said.

"Hey, do you remember how Maglie used to have fun with Roy Campanella?" Schumacher said. "Every now and then, in a game when it didn't mean anything, he'd plunk Roy right in the belly with one of those curveballs. You know how Roy used to look when he stood up there and crowded the plate."

Stoneham laughed. "Sure, I remember now," he said. "Oh, Campy was a good man. He was a friend of ours."

"Did you get to the time Marichal and Spahn hooked up against each other for sixteen innings?" Schumacher asked.

Stoneham nodded several times, thinking about it, and it suddenly came to me that he and Garry Schumacher and his other friends had probably talked together hundreds of times about each of these famous games and vanished companions. Old afternoons were fresh and past players stayed young, and it was the talking that kept them that way.

Now, however, the Padres had two base runners aboard, and Stoneham leaned forward in his seat. "They've been getting some strange-looking hits here," he said. "It looks like they're slapping at the ball." He called to his pitcher. "Bear down, John!"

Montefusco struck out the next batter and Stoneham said, "Boy, that fastball is the answer."

"Did you tell about that doubleheader against the Cards in '33?" Schumacher said. "The one where Hubbell won the first, 1–0, in eighteen, and Parmelee beat Dean, 1–0, in the nightcap, and we held on to first place?"

"That was a day," Stoneham said. "Hubbell sure won a lot of big ones in his time. You know, he first belonged to the Tiger organization, but he never played in the majors with them, because they thought that screwball of his would only ruin his arm. Then it happened that our scout, Dick Kinsella, was a delegate to the Democratic National Convention of 1928, down in Texas, and one day when he was there he went to a game and saw Hubbell, who was pitching for the Beaumont club. He signed him up. He saw what that pitch would do for him."

Schumacher, who was not wearing a coat, had been blowing on his hands, and now he said goodbye and went inside to warm up.

"In any list of our teams, you'd have to mention the '54 club," Stoneham went on. (The Giants met the Cleveland Indians in the World Series of 1954, and beat them in four straight games, although the Indians had been prohibitive favorites. It was the only Stoneham team to win a World Series.) "Willie and Don Mueller and Dusty Rhodes. It's funny, but the thing I remember about that club is all the double plays they got that year that ended up with a base runner caught out of position—being put out by a throw behind him, or something like that. A great heads-up team. Dusty Rhodes got all the publicity for those pinch-hit homers, but I think Henry Thompson was the key man for us in that Series. Dusty's first home run was nothing—real Chinese—but the one he hit the next day went nine miles. You know, Dusty Rhodes works on a tugboat in New York Harbor now. He belongs to the seafarers' union, or whatever they call it. I still hear from him. And Davey Williams is a deputy sheriff down in Dallas. I try to keep in touch. I got a letter from Burgess Whitehead just this week, from—let me see. From Windsor, North Carolina."

I asked Stoneham when he had first seen Willie Mays.

"Willie Mays first reported to us in New York carrying a toilet kit and three bats," Stoneham said. His face was lit up. "But the first time I saw him play was way before that. He was with Trenton, in a Class B league, and we'd just played a game in Philadelphia, and some of us rented a car and drove out to watch him play. They had a little pressbox, just about the size of this box. Bill McKechnie, Jr., was the general manager there, and Chick Genovese was manager, and Bill warned us that Mays might be a little tight because of our being there. Well, Willie got about two hits in the first few innings, and in the seventh he came up and hit a ball into a gas station that was across the street beyond the left-field fence. That's how tight he was.

"Henry Thompson had seen him play in exhibitions, and he told me how Willie sometimes ran after a ball in the outfield and caught it in his bare hand. I said, 'Oh, sure.' You know—I didn't believe it. And then, of course, he did it lots of times for us. I missed his greatest play, when he made an unbelievable catch like that in Brooklyn, just as he crashed into the outfield wall. And I remember after Willie had been with us a couple of years I was out watching our farm club at St. Cloud, Minnesota, and I saw all the young players—Willie Kirkland and Orlando Cepeda and Andre Rodgers—making those basket catches in the outfield, and I said, 'Hey, who loused up all these kids?' It was Willie, of course—they'd seen him on the television and they were all trying to imitate him. Nobody else had those reflexes, though, and nobody else could get away with what he did."

Stoneham left his seat for a few minutes to talk to some visitors who had been brought up to the box to be introduced, and then he made a couple of telephone calls. When he sat down again, we were in the eighth inning and the Giants were ahead by 6–1.

"We were talking about Juan Marichal," he said. "Well, one of the remarkable things about him was that even when he first came up he knew everything there was to know about the game of baseball. He came from the Dominican Republic, and young General Trujillo—the big man's son, I mean—he'd put Juan into the Air Force there in order to have him play on his team. There must have been some great coach or manager in that Air Force who taught Juan, because he did everything right from the beginning.

"I think we were the first club that signed players from that whole area. They'd have their winter leagues in the fall, and after the World Series we'd take a couple of scouts and go down and see our friends. I think the first time I ever saw Jose Pagan play—he came in a game to pinch-hit—he was fourteen years old. Our scout down there was Alex Pompez, who was a Cuban. He saw Fidel Castro play ball when Castro was a young fellow, and sent us a report on him. Castro was a right-handed pitcher. When he came up—you know, came into power—we checked back in our files, and it was the same Castro. A good ballplayer. I think if he'd stayed in the game he'd have made it to the majors. You know what a fan he is."

Bobby Murcer, the Giants' right fielder, doubled in a run, and a minute or two later Chris Speier drove in another. It was a Giants afternoon.

"I just hope fellows like Chris and Bobby get a break in the All-Star Game balloting," Stoneham said. "Bobby's done everything we expected when we got him from the Yankees—everything and more. He's a fine man. But the fans tend to overlook this year's play on their ballots, you know. They vote on reputation. Well, I'm not going to the All-Star Game this year anyway. They're having business meetings all day, before the game. Who wants *that?* That used to be a holiday. You'd go to the game and then you'd see your friends in the evening. It's the same way at our board meetings. When I first came on our board, all the conversation was about baseball. We'd sit and talk about the game. Now the lawyers outnumber the baseball people. In the old days, it was nothing but baseball people on the ball clubs—it was a personal thing. Even with somebody like Mr. Wrigley, it was him that owned the team, not the company."

The Padres came up in the ninth, trailing by 8–1, and Stoneham clapped his hands.

"Who would you pick on an All-Time Giants team?" he said. Then he answered his own question. "I'd have Travis Jackson at short," he said. "Travis never got in the Hall of Fame, but he came up with us and took Dave Bancroft's job away from him. Terry's the best first baseman. Can I play Frisch at second *and* at third? Mays and Ott and Ross Youngs in the outfield. But Monte Irvin's got to be out there somewhere, too. If Monte had come up from the Negro Leagues a few years sooner, he'd be known now as one of the great ballplayers of all time. And we can't leave off Irish Meusel, either. Frank Snyder is catching. But Gus Mancuso was a great defensive catcher, and so was Wes Westrum."

Montefusco, who looked tired, walked his second Padre batter of the inning, and then threw a pitch past his catcher. "He's trying to aim the ball," Stoneham said. He stood up. "Come on, John!" he pleaded. Then he turned and said, "Oh, I almost forgot Willie Mc-Covey. Where do we play him? Or Joe Moore, our best leadoff man. You'd try to bat him third and he'd hit .250. Put him back up top there and he'd hit .330."

His all-time roster was growing by the minute, but now there was a swift double play on the field, and the game ended. "All *right*," Stoneham said. The Giants had won.

We went back to Stoneham's office. I took off the polo coat, and Stoneham hung it up in the closet again. I suddenly wondered how many Giants games it had seen. Stoneham signed a couple of letters that were waiting on his desk, and buzzed his secretary on the intercom. "I'm getting a haircut in the morning," he told her, "so I'll be a little late getting in. Good night, Florence."

We went outside and walked down a ramp in the sunshine. The wind had dropped, and the low hills around the Bay were all alight. It was one of those afternoons when you felt that summer might never end. I started to say something to Stoneham about his parting with the Giants and how I felt about it, but he smiled and cut me off.

"You can't get discouraged over a few bad breaks," he said. "In this game, you're always losing sometimes. You can't let yourself complain or feel sorry for yourself."

He walked me to my car in the parking lot, and we shook hands and said goodbye.

Scout

1976

Baseball has so altered in recent years that many of the classic prototypes of the game seem on the point of disappearing altogether. The rookie pitcher called up to the parent club in midseason does not arrive with cinders in his hair and a straw suitcase in his freckled paw but strolls into the carpeted, air-conditioned big-league clubhouse with a calfskin flight bag over his shoulder (and a Kurt Vonnegut paperback in the bag), where he is greeted by some teammates who played college ball with him or against him a year or two earlier in Southern California. Over in the corner, the club's famous slugger, having just prolonged his slump by going oh for five in a nationally televised game, now abandons his attempt to find surcease in transcendental meditation and suddenly seizes his hair-dryer and bashes it to smithereens against the wall. The manager, dressing in his office, asks a writer about the commotion, smiles and shakes his head, then slaps a little cologne on his ungrizzled cheeks and steps into his fawn leisure suit. His telephone rings: the general manager wants him to stop by upstairs for a minute to hear about the latest meeting with the personal agent of the angry (and still unsigned) famous slugger. If these contemporary patterns are startling, it is probably only because they contrast so vividly with the images of baseball's dramatis personae that most of us memorized in our youth. Over the years, sometimes reluctantly, sometimes willingly, I have gradually given up my boyhood impressions of baseball stars, and of baseball veterans and owners and writers, until only one old portrait remains. In this scene, a man sits alone on a splintery plank bleacher seat, with a foot cocked up on the row in front of him and his chin resting on one hand as he gazes intently at some young ballplayers in action on a bumpy, weed-strewn country ballfield. He sits motionless in the hot sunshine, with a shapeless canvas hat cocked over his eyes. At last, responding to something on the field not perceptible to the rest of us, he takes out a little notebook and writes a few words in it, and then replaces it in his windbreaker pocket. The players steal a glance at the lone stranger as they come in from the field at the end of a half inning; the managers pretend to ignore him. Nobody knows his name, but everybody recognizes him, for he is a figure of profound, almost occult knowledge, with a great power over the future. He is a baseball scout.

I have often noticed scouts at spring-training games, where they appear in numbers and always seem to roost together, and now and then I have spotted one at a big-league park, but I never tried to penetrate their arcane company. This spring, it occurred to me that these brooding, silent birds might constitute another threatened species, and I decided to attempt some field studies. Several baseball friends advised me to look up Ray Scarborough, who is a regional and special-assignment scout for the California Angels. Scarborough, I was told, was a veteran field man, with a high reputation for his baseball knowledge and his exceptional independence of judgment. He had been a member of the outstanding scouting staff put together by Harry Dalton, who was responsible in great part for assembling the formidable Baltimore teams that dominated the American League in the late nineteen-sixties and early seventies. Dalton had moved along to the Angels in 1971 to take the pivotal general manager's position, and soon thereafter he sent for Ray Scarborough and five other stalwarts of his Baltimore G-2. Early in May, I reached Scarborough by telephone at his home in Mount Olive, North Carolina, and proposed myself as a travelling companion on his next safari. Scarborough, who talks in an attractive Tarheel legato, responded with such alacrity and friendliness that it occurred to me for the first time that the life of a baseball scout might be a lonely one. He told me that I had caught him in a rare moment at home during the busiest part of his year—the weeks just prior to organized baseball's annual June talent draft—during which he was scouting free agents: high-school and college players who appeared promising and were about to graduate or otherwise surrender their amateur athletic status. He was leaving soon to look over a young pitching prospect in Kentucky and another in Michigan, and he invited me to come scouting with him.

Two days later, as I waited by the gate in the Louisville airport where Ray Scarborough's inbound morning flight had been announced, I began to wonder how I would recognize him. I remembered him as a big, hardworking, right-handed curveball pitcher with the Washington Senators—and later the Red Sox and the Yankees—but that had been a good twenty-five years back. I needn't have worried. Scarborough is a heavy, energetic, deep-chested man, with an exuberant nose (his baseball contemporaries called him Horn), curly black hair, and a sunburst smile, and the moment I spotted him among the arriving passengers my baseball unconscious offered up some instant corroboration: a younger Ray Scarborough, in baggy old-fashioned baseball pants, wheeling and firing on the mound; Scarborough in an old-style, low-crowned baseball cap emblazoned with a big "W," staring out at me in black-and-white from some ancient sports page. We greeted each other and retrieved his bags, and in a few minutes we were in our rented wheels, rolling south through some lovely, soft-green Kentucky hill country, and Scarborough had made me feel that we were already old friends. He told me that we were headed for Elizabethtown, some forty miles away, to see a young pitcher named Tim Brandenburg, a lefty who would be starting that afternoon for his Elizabethtown High School team in a state district tournament game. I asked Ray how he had heard about Brandenburg (I had in mind a whispered midnight telephone call from a back-country baseball sleuth, or a scribbled note from some old teammate of

Scarborough's now buried in the boonies), and then I learned that scouting, like everything else in baseball, is undergoing some revolutionary changes.

The twenty-four big-league clubs are rivals in a narrow and intensely competitive business arena, and until very recently the proudest emblems of their independence were probably their enormous scouting staffs. The 1974 edition of the *Baseball Blue Book*, which is the business directory of the game, listed the names and clubs of six hundred and fifty-nine scouts—or fifty-nine more than the total number of players carried on major-league rosters. A few of these were part-timers, or "bird dogs" (who are paid a fee only when a player they have spotted is signed to a contract), but each club was carrying somewhere between twenty and thirty full-time scouts, whose rather modest salaries and rather sizable travel expenses added up to a very considerable item on the corporate books. In 1965, Branch Rickey estimated that the scouting expenses of the twenty clubs of that time came to at least five million dollars, and if the figure is extended by a decade of inflation and the addition of four expansion teams, the bottom-line scouting figure must have reached at least seven and a half million dollars. This is a high price even for top-level corporate intelligence, and, reluctantly but inevitably, the owners voted in 1974 to establish a centralized scouting force. This body, the Major League Scouting Bureau, which is now in its second year of a three-year initial contract, deploys a total of sixty-nine scouts, who work under the direction of Jim Wilson, the former general manager of the Milwaukee Brewers. Operating out of Newport Beach, California, it issues computerized scouting reports on every free-agent prospect in high-school and college ball; the reports, which are brought up to date at intervals as fresh scouting data come in, are sent to all the clubs that subscribe to the service. The Angels, who listed twenty-two scouts before the advent of the Bureau, now carry fifteen, of whom six (including Ray Scarborough) are full-timers. Most of his springtime travels, Ray told me, were for the purpose of "cross-checking"—that is, evaluating an apparently thorough but anonymous M.L.S.B. report on free-agent players, whose qualifications had also gone out to seventeen rival clubs. We were on our way to cross-check Tim Brandenburg.

"It's changed now, because I don't know who wrote the report we have on Brandenburg," Scarborough said "The Bureau scouts came from the different clubs, and they're experienced men, but in the old days you always knew the man in your organization who had written a report, and you knew if he was conservative or the other way, so you could make a pretty good evaluation. There was an intimacy to it that made for group confidence and good decisions. It's different now, and cross-checking is more important than ever, especially with the high-rated prospects, so you try to get as many people as possible in your organization to see them. As you know, in the annual June draft of free agents the club that finished last the year before gets to pick first, and the club that finished next to last picks second. That's the way it goes until six or seven hundred names are disposed of—sometimes even more. We pick sixth next month. But the real talent in free agents never runs very deep—some baseball people think it drops way off after the first seven or eight names—and you just can't make a mistake in your two top choices, because then you have to wait till next year. Those first two or three draft picks we make next month have to be *right*, and that means that the scouts who have seen them need thorough judgment. If you see a good-looking high-school player who isn't throwing well or running well on the day you happen to be there, you have to find out why. You don't want a kid knocked out of your thinking for one bad day. But if there's something wrong, if you have some kind of doubt, you'd better go back and check that doubt.

"I think almost anybody can recognize the tools. You or me or the popcorn man can see if a boy is throwing hard or making pretty good contact at the plate. The hard part about free-agent scouting is being able to project. What will this pitcher be like in five years? Will he throw faster? Will he have a better curve? You check his build, and let's say you see narrow shoulders and heavy legs. Will he develop, or will that condition prevail? Jim Kaat was a frail, skinny kid, but he grew with his ability and became a huge man. In the end, I think, size is much less important with a pitcher than a good, loose arm and that good body action. You see a Nolan Ryan, and he's jumping at you off that mound. With a seventeen- or eighteen-year-old pitcher, you hope for a good fastball rather than a first-rate curve, because the curve can be taught but the fastball may never come. Even then you can't be sure. Tom Seaver had an indifferent fastball when he was young, and now look at him! Projecting a youngster isn't easy. What you really want to know about him is how much *stomach* does he have. If you could cut a boy open and look at his heart and guts, and then go home with him and see what kind of preparations he makes for a game, why then... then..." Scarborough laughed and shook his head. "Then my job would be a whole lot easier."

Scarborough, who was driving, was wearing a plaid sports jacket, a navy-blue polo shirt, yellow twill pants, and black alligator shoes. I had entertained some fears that considerations of security might make him cautious in talking to me about his profession, but for the most part he sounded like any good travelling man talking about the special demands of his territory and the splendors of his line.

I asked him to tell me about some of the top prospects he had scouted so far this year.

"Well, let's see," he said, sitting up a little straighter at the wheel. "There's a boy in Springfield, Ohio, named Glass—Timothy Glass, a catcher. He goes about two hundred and fifteen pounds. Runs real well—gets to first in about four-two. A good, strong arm and good hands. He hits with power, but he uppercuts and swings through a lot of pitches. He wears contact lenses, and there has to be some question about his eyesight. But he's almost a complete player. I think he'll be gone by the time it comes around to us, and we're only number six. Then, we've checked a pitcher named Richard Whaley, from Jackonsville, North Carolina. I've seen him four times already, and I like what I've seen. He's a left-hander, six-two, sort of lean and willowy, with an excellent rotation on his curve.

And there's another pitcher down in Hialeah High School—Hialeah, Florida, that is. He's a big right-hander named Ben Grassbeck or Gribseck—something like that [the name is Grzybek]. He goes about six-six, and he can throw *hard*. He broke his foot a few weeks ago, and that might cost him a lot of money."

I said to Scarborough that it seemed to me he had already covered a good deal of ground in this young baseball season.

"Well, I have to see about fifty free agents in the spring," he said. "Fifty boys who can play a little. I'm flying more than I used to, so maybe it's a little less tiring. Up to a couple of years ago, I was doing about twenty-five or thirty thousand miles a year. Just the week before last I drove up to Baltimore, then to Richmond and Norfolk, and then back up to Trenton, New Jersey. About seventeen hundred miles. It takes a lot out of you, and sometimes it can be sort of a lonesome job. Once in a while, I take my wife with me, if it's a local trip—to Tidewater or someplace like that. We get these Bureau scouting reports so late that you've got to jump if you want to catch a boy. If he's not in a tourney or a playoff or something, you might miss him altogether."

As Scarborough was saying this, it came to me that he had meant twenty-five or thirty thousand miles by *automobile*—miles he had put in at the wheel in search of one summer's young ballplayers. I looked out my window for a while at some Kentucky farms and silos and tried to imagine this. Then I asked Ray which players among the current major-leaguers he had scouted or signed.

"People always ask that," he said. "The truth is, what with the draft, almost nobody in scouting can take that kind of credit anymore."

"What about bird dogs?" I asked.

Ray laughed and said, "Well, it's supposed to be sort of crude to call them that now. A few years back, they suddenly all became 'commission scouts.' I guess there are still a few of them left. They were part of a whole network of contacts that each territorial scout put together, and the moment they sent him word about some good-looking boy, he'd hustle right out and take a look himself, and then tell his regional supervisor about him. The territorial scout is what this business is all about. If the club signed up somebody he'd seen, he could always think, 'That's *my* player.' A lot of them have gone out of business since the Bureau, and it's a real shame.

"Well, as I was saying, it's a group sort of thing now, and, of course, it's just luck if your club gets to draft a particular player you're after—even some kid you've been downright enthusiastic about. The only players in the majors right now who I've had anything to do with came up in the Baltimore organization, because there hasn't been time yet for the Angels' draft choices I've seen to make it up to the top. With Baltimore, I saw Paul Mitchell, that young pitcher who just went to Oakland in the Jackson trade. He's a real live one—a regular bulldog. And there's Don Hood, who's with the Indians now. And that big kid who's doing all that good work with the Orioles now—I think he's even leading the league in earned-run average...." He paused and frowned. "Seems like I can't remember *anybody's* name some days," he murmured. "Garland! Wayne Garland, of course. Listen, I first saw him in Connie Mack ball, over in Jackson, Tennessee. He was just about to pitch, and he was drinking a Pepsi and eating the biggest hot dog you ever saw, but he pitched a good game that night. A big right-hander, and he could really hump up and throw that ball. Harry Dalton and Dee Phillips came and had a look at him, and when we got him in the draft we gave him what he wanted. I think he got about thirty thousand. You've got to sign those good ones when you can—there aren't enough good arms available.

"I'll tell you a funny thing. The finest left-handed pitcher I ever scouted in a high school is with the Angels right now—Frank Tanana. But I didn't have a single thing to do with his being with us, because I was scouting for Baltimore then, and we didn't get him. He was pitching in a high-school league in Detroit where they only gave you three balls and two strikes, and those batters were *mesmerized!* He had stuff and poise, and an outstanding change of pace, and his attitude was just about perfect. He really knew how to pitch."

Ray bent forward and peered up at the sky, which had become gray and threatening. "Now, don't tell me," he said. "Yes, it's going to rain, sure as the devil. Do you know, that's the number-one occupational hazard of this profession. You have to wait over a day, and that means you often miss another game and another prospect. It's a real problem."

Ray Scarborough is a cheerful man, and even the spattering of the first few raindrops on our windshield didn't make him gloomy for long. "At least it's easier to get to a boy than it sometimes was in the old days," he said. "Back in 1959 or 1960, when I was just starting, I found a pitcher named James Barrier, who lived way up on top of a mountain in Jonas Ridge, North Carolina. I had to walk the last couple of miles up. He lived in a little old house with his parents and a whole lot of brothers and sisters, and he walked I don't know how many miles to school every day. I saw him pitch a game on a field where it looked like they hadn't mowed the outfield for weeks, and they had a ground rule that a ball lost in the tall grass behind the outfielders was a double, but if you lost it in front of you it was a homer, because you should have kept your eye on it. That's the truth. We signed him and gave him a bonus so he could go to Appalachian State Teachers College, and he went on and won about fifteen games one year with Newton-Conover, in the Western Carolina League. He never made it into Class A ball, and he quit after about four years, but I imagine he was always a kind of an example to a lot of kids he played with. The last I heard of him, he'd got a Ph.D. from Clemson and was head of biology at Baptist College, down in Charleston, South Carolina. I always thought that was one of the best signings I ever made."

We came to Elizabethtown and found the high school, but it was still raining lightly when we pulled into the parking lot next to the wet green ballfield, and it had begun to look like a wasted journey. There was nobody in sight but a little group of middle-aged men in golf caps and assorted rain gear who were standing together and glumly looking up at the sky—more baseball scouts, it turned out. They greeted Ray warmly, and he introduced them to me: Floyd Baker, of the Twins; Ray Holton, of the Scouting Bureau; Joe Bowen, the director of scouting for the Reds; and Nick Kamzic, who is one of the Angels' supervisors of scouting. All of them had come to see Tim Brandenburg. Kamzic and Scarborough moved a few steps away from the others and compared notes on their recent travels and discoveries (Kamzic was optimistic about Steve Trout, a young left-handed pitcher from South Holland, Illinois, who is the son of the old Tiger hurler Dizzy Trout), but soon the rain began to come down harder, and we all ran for shelter. Back in our car, Ray opened a briefcase and handed me his copy of the Bureau's scouting report on Brandenburg—a single mimeographed sheet, with Brandenburg's vital statistics printed out in drab computeresque capitals, and then two parallel columns of figures under the headings "PRES" and "FUT." On the left-hand side of the page, there was a rating key with figures ranging from eight ("OUTSTANDING") down to two ("POOR"), and then a column of categories marked "FASTBALL," "CURVE," "CONTROL," "CHANGE OF PACE," and (bracketed together) "SLIDER, KNUCKLEBALL, OTHER," followed by "POISE," "BB INSTINCTS," "AGGRESSIVENESS." Brandenburg's "PRES" ratings were all fours and fives, except for a zero in the bracketed entry; in the "FUT" column the ratings had all gone up to five, and his curveball had become a six ("ABOVE AVE."). Down at the bottom of the page I read: "AVE. MAJOR LEAGUE CURVEBALL AT THIS TIME & CAN THROW IT FOR A STRIKE WHEN HE WANTS TO. GOOD FIELDER. HAS FULL ARM ACTION. FOLLOWS THROUGH GOOD & USES BODY TO ITS FULLEST. ONLY WEAKNESS I CAN SEE IS BELOW-AVE. MAJOR LEAGUE FASTBALL. HOWEVER, I DO PROJECT A MAJOR LEAGUE FASTBALL IN FUTURE." Then, under "SUMMATION & SIGNABILITY," I saw "HAS THE TOOLS TO BECOME A

GOOD MAJOR LEAGUE PITCHER. . . . MUST ALSO COMBAT COLLEGE OFFERS." The report depressed me; I felt as if I had accidentally glanced into a brightly lit window across the street and then had secretly begun to watch the activities of a stranger there.

The rain was letting up, but a fresh wind was buffeting the trees beyond the outfield fence. Scarborough wiped the inside of our foggy windshield with his handkerchief. "Golly Pete," he said. "If I was young Mr. Brandenburg, I'd be a little nervous right now, waiting all this time. There's more pressure than you can hardly imagine on a young player in a situation like this. Usually, there aren't too many folks in the stands at a high-school game, and he can see those scouts all sitting there, with their little hats on. Come *on*, rain—just quit, now."

The rain did stop, and half an hour later we were sitting on some damp bright-yellow aluminum bleacher seats, and the stands had suddenly filled up with spectators: high-school kids, most of them, in jeans and overalls and emblazoned T-shirts and floppy far-out hats and shiny rain jackets and big boots—high-school kids anywhere. Everyone was clapping for the game to begin. Directly in front of me, an older man wearing a camouflage-spotted hunting cap turned around and said, "If Brandenburg wasn't pitching, I'd be off fishin' right now." Then the players for the visiting team—North Hardin High, from Radcliff, Kentucky—ran out on the wet field, wearing electric-blue shirts and white pants (the teams had drawn for the home-team last-up privilege, and the visitors had won), and the game began at last—not much of a game, at that, because the Elizabethtown Panthers (gold shirts with a gigantic purple ventral "E" and striped white pants) immediately batted around, scoring five runs, thanks in part to a bases-loaded single by Tim Brandenburg. Ray watched all this with considerable impatience, casting glances from time to time at the low, hurrying clouds just above us. The teams changed sides, and Brandenburg sauntered very slowly out to the mound. Some of the girls in the stands called "Tim! Tim! *Tim!*" in unison. Brandenburg had curly hair and a Roman nose; he didn't look heavily muscled, but he had the sloping shoulders and long arms of a pitcher. I could not remember how long it had been since I had seen a ballplayer who looked so young. Throwing left-handed, and pitching, for some reason, with no windup at all, he ran up a full count on the first batter and then struck him out with a sharp-breaking curve.

"Look at that," Ray murmured in a puzzled way. "Why is he pitching like that, I wonder. Why doesn't he wind up? It's like he's playing catch out there.... Well, I see he's bowlegged—there aren't many real athletes who aren't, they tell me."

Brandenburg struck out the second batter and retired the third on an easy grounder.

"Yes, that's a pretty good curveball," Ray said to me. "It has a good, tight spin on it. I think if he'd push off the mound he'd get more action on it. But it's hard to see a guy with his build getting much faster. He can pitch in the minors, that's for sure."

Elizabethtown kept scoring runs, and Tim Brandenburg kept dismissing the enemy batters without effort, and after three innings the score had gone to 8–0. Nick Kamzic climbed up the stands and squeezed in next to Ray, and after Brandenburg surrendered a single—the first hit of the day for North Hardin—he said, "He seems to have more drive when he pitches off the stretch. He drops down and pushes off better."

"Yes, but he may have trouble holding men on," Ray said. "I mean, the way he rocks back instead of coming straight on down. But that's correctable."

Brandenburg gave up a foul and then rubbed up the new ball with great deliberation. He looked around at the crowd in rather imperious fashion.

"Hey, now!" Ray said, grinning. "He's a showman. He's a candidate for *New York*. I'll tell you, if I had an eight-run lead and it looked like rain, I'd be firin' that ball. But this kid has a pretty good arm. You want to make him throw harder, but you can't. His best stuff is up out of the strike zone. When he comes down with it, he loses velocity. If he could get some mustard on it, on top of his breaking stuff, he'd be in pretty good shape. I think it's that no-windup. You want to teach a kid like this to drive that lead shoulder toward the catcher's mitt. That makes the ball come in low, and we have a low strike zone now."

All this was perfectly evident to me as soon as Ray pointed it out. I had the curious feeling that I was listening to a brilliant English instructor explicating some famous novel or play. I thought I had known some of the passages by heart—known them almost too well—but now I began to hear different rhythms and truths. An old text had become fresh and exciting again.

"This kid is pretty advanced in most areas," Ray went on, "but you always look for places where a boy can be improved." He paused, and then, almost to himself, he murmured, "You always want them to be better."

The game ended—it was a seven-inning affair—with Elizabethtown on top by 9–0, and some of the young people in the stands ran out on the field and stood around Tim Brandenburg in a happy circle. He had given up two hits and struck out seventeen batters. I had begun to play scout, of course, and had become hard to please, and it was not until Scarborough and I were in our car and on the way back to Louisville that it came to me that Tim Brandenburg was almost surely the best high-school pitcher I had ever seen.

I asked Ray what he thought, and he remained silent for some time. "I'm thinking what I'll write on my report," he said at last. "Overall, the boy has a chance to pitch. He's not an outstanding prospect, but he has a good opportunity. Off what I saw today, I'd say he might go in the fourth or fifth round of the draft. If you had to, you might take him in the third round. He looks sort of like the kind of pitcher that tops out at about the AA level because of his lack of velocity. That curve is a good one, but he might have to develop another pitch—a slip pitch or something—if he's going to make it to the majors. In the end, it will probably depend on his intelligence and how much he wants to make it to the top."

I asked Scarborough what was meant by the word "signability," which I had seen on the Bureau's report, and he pointed out that although each club had exclusive rights to a player it acquired in the draft, it still had to negotiate financial terms with that player. If they couldn't agree, the player would once more become a free agent and might be drafted all over again—usually in a redraw that forms part of another draft each year, in January—by a different club, or even by the same club. "If you think a boy is worth fifteen thousand dollars and he and his parents and his coach think he's worth fifty, *that's* a signability problem," Scarborough said. "More players than you'd think don't get signed—especially the high-school kids, because they can always choose to go off to college instead. Sometimes, if you're lucky, you can sign half of them. Your main effort is always to sign your top five or six draft picks. It seems unusual, but a good college player is always more signable than a high-school boy, because he has no place else to go after he graduates. He's got to come to you.

"Of course, signing a player you want real bad is absolutely different from what it was back before the clubs pushed through the draft system, about ten or twelve years ago, after they'd all spent so much money on those bonus babies. If this was back then, and we wanted this boy, I'd have made it a point to get to know his parents on this trip, so that when the time came we might get in there ahead of the other clubs. That used to be about the liveliest part of it all, especially with a really and truly top prospect, and it was downright enjoyable sometimes what you had to do."

Scarborough grinned and slapped the steering wheel with one hand. "I'll never forget signing a fellow named Cotton Clayton, way back in the early sixties," he said. "He was an outfielder, and he could do it *all*. He was a valuable piece of property. Harry Dalton wanted him, and Lee MacPhail, who was our G.M. at Baltimore then—he wanted him. I made an appointment to see Clayton down in his hometown of Henderson, North Carolina, and I checked into the local motel. You had to make an appointment, because just about every other club was anxious to get him, too, but especially the Cardinals. I made damn sure to get him to come up to my motel room, and I swore to myself he'd never get out until I'd signed him. I also made sure that Harry and Lee, up in Baltimore, were ready on the other end of the phone. This was in the bonus days, you understand, and I had about fifty thousand dollars at my disposal, but when Clayton came in and sat down I just didn't know how to get around to the subject at hand."

Ray laughed delightedly. "Well, sir, we talked about rabbits and about farming and about basketball—everything but money. He was one tough bargainer. When we finally got to it, we began around twenty-five thousand, and every time he'd tilt the pot a little I'd shake my head and say, 'Well, let me talk to Harry,' and I'd go off and make a telephone call. We talked and talked, and we got awful tired in that room, and finally he said, 'Well, I can't take one penny less than fifty thousand.' I pulled back—sort of recoiled—and said, 'You just knocked me out of the box,' but I said that we needed a left-hand-hitting outfielder so bad that I'd make one last call to Lee MacPhail and see if I could talk him into it. I said, 'If I can somehow do that, will you sign for ten thousand a year for five years, with a starting salary of a thousand dollars a month, and will you sign *before you leave this room?*'

"Well, he squirmed and squirmed, because, of course, he'd promised the Cardinals and some of the other scouts he'd never sign anything without talking to them first. But he finally said yes, and I called Lee, and Lee whispered 'Sign him!' and I pulled out the contract—which I'd had ready all along, of course—and he signed, and I shook his hand and checked *out* of the motel and went home. And do you know that the next man who checked into that exact room that day was Eddie Lyons, of the Cardinals? He wanted Clayton just as bad as we did, only he'd stopped off on the way to sign a third baseman down there he'd liked. He got my room, but I'd got his outfielder!"

I couldn't remember having heard of Cotton Clayton in big-league ball, and I asked Ray what had happened to him.

"Cotton Clayton ended up playing in the International League for about four or five years," he said. "He had some bad breaks along the way—that's the way it is sometimes—and he never did get to the majors. Now he has a tire business down in Henderson—along with the farm that I bought with that fifty thousand."

The next morning, Ray Scarborough and I caught an early flight to Detroit, where we would pick up another car and drive to Ypsilanti to scout a highly celebrated pitching prospect named Bob Owchinko, who played for Eastern Michigan University. During the flight, I asked Ray if he could remember when he himself had first been scouted. He told me he had grown up on a small farm in Mount Gilead, in central North Carolina. He was the fourth of six brothers (there was one sister), and all the Scarboroughs loved to play ball. Work on the farm was long and hard, but their father made a little diamond out behind the house, and there was time for some family baseball there in the evenings. Sometimes Ray and his next-older brother, Steve, would walk five miles in to town to play in a pickup game. Eventually, Ray was given an athletic scholarship to Rutherford Junior College, in the Carolina Piedmont section, where another brother, Bill, was doing some coaching.

In the summer when Ray turned seventeen, a shiny black Cadillac rolled up to the Scarborough farm one day, and a man wearing a suit and tie stepped out. "It was a Cardinal scout named Pat Crawford," Ray said, "and he'd come to look me over. He was a real Dapper Dan, and I was *impressed.* 'Can you th'ow for me?' he asked, and I said yes, sir. But there wasn't anybody else at home right then, so we didn't know who I could throw to. I offered to throw to him, but he declined. Well, finally he pointed to a red clay bank off across the road and said, 'Son, how would you like to th'ow into that bank?' We paced off the distance and he took a white handkerchief out of his pocket and stuck it up in place on that bank with a little rock. Then he got some baseballs out of the trunk of the Cadillac, and I threw for about ten minutes at his old hanky. He must have liked what he saw, because he invited me to a Cardinals tryout camp in Charlotte. Mr. Rickey was there, and some others, and they picked three of us out of about a hundred or more, so I knew they thought I could play. But they only offered me sixty dollars a month, so I decided I wasn't ready to go into baseball yet."

Ray wanted to continue with college after his two years at Rutherford, but he knew he had to earn his way. He hoped to pick up some cash by playing in the semipro Coastal Plain League but was told that he was too small. "I only weighed about a hundred and twenty-eight, which wasn't big enough even for mumblety-peg," he said to me. "I finally hooked on with a town team in Aberdeen, North Carolina, in the Sand Hill League. We played ball two days and picked peaches the rest of the time. I got twelve dollars and fifty cents a week for playin' and pickin'. No bonus, no Social Security."

He stayed out of school that winter and worked as a carhop in a drive-in, but he had begun to grow, and the next spring—the spring of 1938—he was given a tryout with a team in Hickory, North Carolina, in the Carolina League.

"That was an outlaw league," Ray said. "You know—outside of regular organized baseball. It was just a string of teams from little cities like Concord and Gastonia and Kannapolis. Strictly semipro, but there were a lot of players I'd heard of—Art Shires and Packy Rogers and Prince Henry Oana—and we all got paid. Well, I won myself a job and, do you know, I actually pitched the opening game of the season for the Hickory Rebels, against Lenoir. I was just a squirt with a curve and a fastball, but I thought I was the biggest dog in town."

Ray's route to the big time was not quite arrowlike. Pitching with the Rebels won him an athletic scholarship to Wake Forest, and there he began to receive some attention from big-league scouts—famous men like Gene McCann, of the Yankees, and Paul Florence, of the Reds. He was treated to a special courtesy trip to Philadelphia, where he visited Shibe Park and shook hands with

Connie Mack. Money and celebrity seemed to be in the offing, but Scarborough injured his arm while pitching in the fifth game of his senior year at Wake Forest, and the scouts suddenly disappeared. He took his degree and taught high school for a year, at Tabor City, North Carolina, while he waited for his arm to come around, and then signed on with Chattanooga, in the Class A Southern League, for a fifteen-hundred-dollar bonus—a fraction of the sum the scouts had been talking about before his injury. He was sent down to Selma, Alabama, in Class B, and there, at last, he began to win. He broke the league strikeout record there, came back to Chattanooga, and joined the Washington Senators in June, 1942, just a month before his twenty-fifth birthday. "I'd finally made it off the farm," Ray said. He pitched in the majors until 1953.

Eastern Michigan is a rising power in college baseball, and the trim diamond and attractive little roofed grandstand that Ray Scarborough and I found in Ypsilanti that day were much more inviting than a lot of spring-training ball parks I could recall. We were there for a Mid-American Conference doubleheader between the Eastern Michigan Hurons and the Falcons, from Bowling Green State University, in Ohio. The home team was just finishing infield practice under a cloudy sky, and the Huron squad members, in white uniforms with green lettering, were ranged along the third-base line, where they gave some noisy cheers for each of their starting infielders as he whipped his last peg in to the catcher and trotted off the field. Football stuff. Ray Scarborough greeted some scouting friends and then sat down with a California colleague, Al Hollingsworth, who is also a special-assignment scout for the Angels, operating out of Texas. Hollingsworth has thick white hair, blue eyes, and a tanned, classic old-ballplayer's face, with crinkly lines around the eyes and mouth. If you were casting for the part of a veteran scout in a baseball movie, you would pick Al Hollingsworth.

"Hey, I hear we won last night!" he said to Ray. "Somebody told me. It was about 7–5."

Scarborough had been complaining that morning that it was often impossible on the road to pick up the results of Angels games from the West Coast, and he brightened at the news. (Angels victories had been rare in recent weeks; in fact, the club was dead last in the American League West.) "That's more like it," he said. "Who pitched?"

"All I heard was Alvarez hit a home run," Hollingsworth said. He told Ray he had just flown in from Denison, Texas, where he had seen a young pitcher named Darwin the day before. "He's about twenty years old, and he's comin' on," he said. "He threw about eighty-six, eighty-seven on the speed gun. He got ripped pretty good yesterday, though. He reminds you a little of a Granger or a Perzanowski. His arm's way over here, and his ball don't tail."

"I hear there's a catcher on this Bowling Green team," Ray said. "I don't recall his name, though."

"You got anything on a kid named Brown, in Indiana?" Hollingsworth said. "All I have on him is a phone number."

And then the game began, and we all began to watch Bob Owchinko, who had brought us there. The Bureau scouting report on him had rated him a premium choice, with an above-average fastball, a curveball with a tight spin, a screwball, and a loose overhead arm action. He was a tall, solidly built left-hander, and he was using a full windup, with a high-kicking delivery and a long stride. He was hiding the ball well between pitches. He fanned the first two Bowling Green hitters, gave up a single to the catcher (whose name, it turned out, was Larry Owen), walked a batter, and then got the side out with another strikeout.

"A nice big boy," Ray murmured. "He's got heavy legs and sort of a big tail, but that never hurt Lolich, did it? Pitchers can get away with that better than others. I like the way this boy comes at the batter."

The stands were filling up, and Ray kept getting up to exchange greetings with more scouts as they took seats around us, in a companionable cluster directly behind home plate—Dick Teed and Brandy Davis, of the Phillies; Pat Gillick and Dave Yoakum, of the

Yankees; Howie Haak (a famous name in scouting), of the Pirates; Syd Thrift, of the A's; Joe Bowen, of the Reds, who had been with us the day before in Elizabethtown. (If you were writing a baseball movie or a baseball novel, you would give your scouts names like these.) The scouts sat back quietly, some with their arms folded or a knee cocked up, and watched the field with motionless intensity. They looked like businessmen at a staff conference. Nobody seemed to be taking any notes.

I remarked that Owchinko appeared to be a good drawing card, and Ray said, "In the old days, you'd have had a *drove* of scouts at a game like this. They tell me the Bureau tries to discourage their men from being too close with any of the rest of us, because they're supposed to represent their clubs impartially, but I can't see how that's going to work. You just can't keep friendship out of scouting, because so many of these fellows have been buddies for years. A lot of us have played with each other or against each other, and we go back a long way together. It's a fraternity."

The teams changed sides, and the home-plate umpire—a short, dark-haired man, whose black suit was already stained with sweat and dust—walked back to the stands with his mask in one hand and chatted with the scouts. He poked a forefinger through the wire of the foul screen and gravely shook fingers with Ray Scarborough.

"That's Tom Ravashiere," Ray said after the umpire had gone back to work. "He was a good ump in the International League for years and years. He's out of baseball now, but I guess he still does games like this. He lives around here someplace."

Both the teams on the field looked well trained and extremely combative, and the young players made up for their occasional mistakes with some eye-popping plays. At one point, Owchinko hustled off the mound, snatched up an attempted sacrifice bunt, and whirled and threw the Falcon base runner out at second with a fiery peg. In the bottom of the same inning—the fourth—a Bowling Green outfielder made a diving, sliding catch on his belly in short center field, and then Owen, the catcher, threw out a base runner trying to steal second—threw him out a mile. Ray and the other scouts shook their heads and exchanged little smiles, enjoying it. The clouds had begun to break up, and the green of the outfield grass had turned light and glistening. Good game.

Owchinko had been striking out enemy batters in considerable numbers, but now, in the sixth, he seemed to lose his concentration, walking the first two men. Then there was an error behind him on an easy double-play grounder, and a moment later a Bowling Green outfielder named Jeff Groth whacked a long drive over the left-field fence for a grand-slam home run. Silence in the stands—a very brief silence, it turned out, for in the home half the Eastern Michigan hitters came alive, with a walk, a ground-rule double, and a two-run single, and then, after a couple of mistakes by the visitors, a culminating three-run homer to center by the Eastern Michigan right fielder, Thom Boutin. The whole Huron team came out to the third-base foul line to welcome him home, and the student fans around us screeched ecstatically. Owchinko walked the leadoff man in the top of the seventh and seemed to be struggling ("Come *on*, Chink!" the fans pleaded), but the tying run died at second, and the Hurons had won it, 5–4.

"I don't know if he got tired, or what, but his velocity wasn't good at the end," Ray said. "I'd like to have seen if he could get two strikes on a man and then break off the curveball. When he gave up that homer, he'd got in the position of trying to throw strikes past the batter, instead of trying to get the man out. He threw that pitch sort of easy—a mistake pitch. But that's normal. I try never to notice if a pitcher gives up a hit. It's his motion I'm watching. Same thing with a hitter—I don't care if he hits, as long as he's making contact and swings well. But this was a good performance by Owchinko. You could make a few mechanical changes with his delivery. Being sort of big-assed, he stops his right leg sometimes, so his body can't open up, and he has to throw from over *here*. But he's got a chance to make a pretty good pitcher. I think this boy might go in the first round. I'd love for us to get him along about the second round, but he won't be around that long."

Most of the scouts had disappeared, but we waited for the second game of the doubleheader, because Ray wanted to have a look at the next Eastern Michigan pitcher—a junior named Bob Welch. During the interval, I wandered out beyond the left-field stands and found Bob Owchinko lying on his stomach on the grass, with a towel around his neck. His face was red and he was streaming perspiration. I asked him if he had noticed the scouts behind home during the game.

"Yeah, I saw them there, staring me in the face," he said. "They don't bother me—I know what they're here for."

"Do you care about which club will draft you next month?" I said.

"I've been waiting for a career in major-league ball since I was eleven, and now it's here," he said. "It's about time. I don't care where I go, but I do like hot weather."

The second game began, and after Bob Welch—yes, that Bob Welch—had thrown about six pitches Ray Scarborough exclaimed, "There's a good-looking body! He's almost got these boys over-matched already."

Welch, a right-hander, looked even taller and stronger than Bob Owchinko, and he threw with a kind of explosive elegance. There was something commanding about him.

"See out there?" Ray said. "See him cocking his wrist like that behind his back? That can strain your elbow. It could hurt him. He's cutting the ball a little—turning his hand—which takes off some velocity. If he did it a little more, it would be a slider. I wish he'd turn loose—he's got a real good arm."

Welch fired two fastballs, fanning the batter.

"*There!*" Ray said. "I like that! He comes off that mound like he means business." He stood up, smiling with pleasure. "I believe I'll be making a trip back here a year from now. Maybe we better go quick, before I get dissatisfied with the whole 1976 draft."

Ray Scarborough and I parted in Detroit that evening. I went home to New York, and he flew to Madison, Wisconsin, where he planned to watch a prospect from the University of Michigan in a game the next day. What he met there, however, was rain. Early in June, Ray went out to Anaheim and, in company with Harry

Dalton and Walter Shannon (the Angels' director of scouting) and Nick Kamzic and Al Hollingsworth and nine other Angel scouts and executives, participated in four days of intensive discussions and appraisal of all the high-school and college free agents that they had scouted and cross-checked and talked about. The draft, which came on June 8, was conducted in the baseball commissioner's office, in New York, over an open telephone hookup to all twenty-four clubs. The Houston Astros, with first pick, chose a much admired left-handed pitching star from Arizona State University named Floyd Bannister. The Angels' first choice, on the sixth pick, was a power-hitting outfielder named Kenny Landreaux, also from Arizona State. Tim Brandenburg went to the Kansas City Royals in the second round—the forty-second player in the country to be drafted. The Angels did not bid on him. As for Bob Owchinko, he went to the San Diego Padres on the fifth pick in the first round. A little later in June, at the National Collegiate Athletic Association championships in Omaha, the Eastern Michigan ball team went all the way into the finals before losing to the University of Arizona. On the way, they upset the favorites, Arizona State, thanks to a seven-hitter thrown by Owchinko.

I thought about Ray Scarborough while the draft was going on, and later I looked up the names of some of the players he had scouted. Timothy Glass, the catcher from Springfield, Ohio, went to the Indians in the first round. Ben Grzybek, the pitcher from Hialeah, was the first-round choice of the Royals—thus becoming a potential future teammate of Brandenburg's. Richard Whaley, the willowy left-hander from Jacksonville, North Carolina, had developed a sore arm late in the spring, which probably dropped him in the draft; he was picked by the Phillies in the third round—No. 65 nationally. None of the free agents Ray had talked to me about with such enthusiasm went to the Angels. Larry Owen, the Bowling Green catcher we had seen in Ypsilanti, was chosen by the Angels in the eighteenth round. Seven hundred and eighty-six players were drafted in all, most of whom would perform only briefly in professional ball, if at all.

I caught up with Ray Scarborough again on the evening of July 5th, in another baseball setting: we were part of a crowd of 60,942 spectators at a holiday game between the Phillies and the Dodgers, in Philadelphia's Veterans Stadium. Scarborough was there in a different scouting capacity—evaluating players on both clubs (but especially the Phillies) as potential material for post-season trades with the Angels. Ray looked younger and more rested than he had during our trip in May, and he told me that he had been taking it easy since the draft, putting in a lot of time working in his vegetable garden at home in Mount Olive. He had also caught up on his own business interests, which include real estate, a small tobacco farm, a bank directorship, and a share in a musical-instrument-and-records business.

I asked him how he felt about the Angels' draft, and he said, "Well, you always want to be associated with your club's top man, of course. I did see Bob Ferris, who we picked in the second round, and a fellow named Porter we took a little farther down, but otherwise we didn't get any of the boys I'd checked. The only fruits of your work are the boys who end up with your own organization, and the luck of the draft can sure knock you down. You work like hell all year, and then... Sure, I felt bad—I felt *punctured*—but on the other hand, when I listened to what our people had to say about Ken Landreaux at our meeting in Anaheim, I had confidence that he was a better first choice for us than Glass or Owchinko, or the others I'd seen. Next year, it might be the other way around. You know, a scout can go for years and years and never get in on a top pick. You take Mace Brown, of the Red Sox. Mace is a real fine scout, and he went for I don't know how many years without much luck, and I remember once he said, 'All this work for nothing,' or something like that. But he hung on, and then he came up with Jim Rice, who was a first-round pick."

I said that this sounded like more patience and optimism than most men could be expected to bring to their work, and Ray nodded. We were sitting behind home plate at Veterans Stadium, and he looked slowly around at the glittering, brightly lit field and the noisy throng filling every seat in the circular, triple-decked park. "I think it has to be a private thing," he said at last. "You don't go around saying it, but I'm *devoted* to the club I work for. It was downright satisfying being connected with that winning Baltimore outfit, and I do like working for a man like Harry Dalton. I'm interested in being with him and Walter Shannon and the rest, trying to make California the same kind of organization. But first of all it's the baseball. Those airports and motels and cars are pretty taxing on a man, and I keep thinking I'm going to ease off one of these years, but I never quite do it. It's love of the game of baseball that keeps me at it. I still feel there's no greater reward a young man can achieve than attaining the major leagues as a player. I truly mean that. I don't care what the price is, I think it's worth it. Nothing can beat it."

Distance

1980

On the afternoon of October 2, 1968—a warm, sunshiny day in St. Louis—Mickey Stanley, the Detroit Tiger shortstop, singled to center field to lead off the top of the ninth inning of the opening game of the 1968 World Series. It was only the fifth hit of the game for the Tigers, who by this time were trailing the National League Champion St. Louis Cardinals by a score of 4–0, so there were only minimal sounds of anxiety among the 54,692 spectators—hometown rooters, for the most part—in the stands at Busch Stadium. The next batter, the dangerous Al Kaline, worked the count to two and two and then fanned, swinging away at a fastball, to an accompanying roar from the crowd. A moment later, there was a second enormous cheer, louder and more sustained than the first. The Cardinal catcher, Tim McCarver, who had straightened up to throw the ball back to his pitcher, now hesitated. The pitcher, Bob Gibson, a notoriously swift worker on the mound, motioned to his battery mate to return the ball. Instead, McCarver pointed with his gloved hand at something behind Gibson's head. Gibson, staring uncomprehendingly at his catcher, yelled, "Throw the goddam ball back, will you! C'mon, c'mon, let's go!" Still holding the ball, McCarver pointed again, and Gibson, turning around, read the illuminated message on the center-field scoreboard, which perhaps only he in the ballpark had not seen until that moment: "Gibson's fifteenth strikeout in one game ties the all-time World Series record held by Sandy Koufax." Gibson, at the center of a great tureen of noise, dug at the dirt of the mound with his spikes and then uneasily doffed his cap. ("I *hate* that sort of thing," he said later.) With the ball retrieved at last, he went to work on the next Tiger, Norm Cash, a left-handed batter, who ran the count to two and two, fouled off several pitches, and then struck out, swinging at a slider. Gibson, a long-legged, powerfully built right-hander, whose habitual aura of glowering intensity on the mound seemed to deepen toward rancor whenever his club was ahead in the late stages of a game, now swiftly attacked the next Detroit hitter, Willie Horton. Again the count went to two and two and stuck there while Horton fouled off two or three pitches. Gibson stretched and threw again, and Horton, a righty batter, flinched away from the pitch, which seemed headed for his rib cage, but the ball, another slider, broke abruptly away under his fists and caught the inside corner of the plate. Tom Gorman, the home-plate umpire, threw up his right hand, and the game was over. McCarver, talking about this moment not long ago (he is now a radio and television broadcaster with the Phillies), said, "I can still see that last pitch, and I'll bet Willie Horton thinks to this day that the ball hit him—that's how much it broke. Talk about a batter *shuddering!*"

Bob Gibson's one-game World Series record of seventeen strikeouts stands intact, and so do my memories of that famous afternoon. In recent weeks, I have firmed up my recollections by consulting the box score and the inning-by-inning recapitulations of the game, by watching filmed highlights of the play, and by talking to a number of participants, including Gibson himself. (He had had no idea, he told me, that he was close to a record that afternoon. "You're concentrating so hard out there that you don't think of those things," he said.) Gibson seemed to take absolute charge of that game in the second inning, when he struck out the side on eleven pitches. By the end of four innings, he had run off eight strikeouts. Not until I reexamined the box score, however, did I realize that there had been only two ground-ball outs by the Tigers in the course of nine innings. This, too, must be a record (baseball statistics, for once, don't tell us), but the phenomenally low figure, when taken along with the seventeen strikeouts, suggests what kind of pitching the Tiger batters were up against that afternoon. Most National League batters in the nineteen-sixties believed that Gibson's fastball compared only with the blazers thrown by the Dodgers' Sandy Koufax (who retired in 1966 with an arthritic elbow) and by the Reds' Jim Maloney. Gibson's pitch flashed through the strike zone with a unique, upward-moving, right-to-left sail that snatched it away from a right-handed batter or caused it to jump up and in at a left-handed swinger—a natural break of six to eight inches—and hitters who didn't miss the ball altogether usually fouled it off or nudged it harmlessly into the air. The pitch, which was delivered with a driving, downward flick of Gibson's long forefinger and middle finger (what pitchers call "cutting the ball"), very much resembled an inhumanly fast slider, and was often taken for such by batters who were unfamiliar with his stuff. Joe Pepitone, of the Yankees, concluded the All-Star Game of 1965 by fanning on three successive Gibson fastballs and then shook his head and called out to the pitcher, "Throw me that slider one more time!" Gibson, to be sure, did have a slider—a superior breaking pitch that arrived, disconcertingly, at about three-quarters of the speed of the fastball and, most of the time, with exquisite control. Tim McCarver, who caught Gibson longer than anyone else, says that Gibson became a great pitcher during the summer of 1966 (his sixth full season in the majors), when he achieved absolute mastery of the outside corner of the plate while pitching to right-handed batters and—it was the same pitch, of course—the inside corner to left-handed batters. He could hit this sliver of air with his fastball or his slider with equal consistency, and he worked the opposite edge of the plate as well. "He *lived* on the corners," McCarver said. A third Gibson delivery was a fastball that broke downward instead of up and away; for this pitch, he held the ball with his fingers parallel to the seams (instead of across the seams, as was the case with the sailer), and he twisted his wrist counterclockwise as he threw—"turning it over," in mound parlance. He also had a curveball, adequate but unextraordinary, that he threw mostly to left-handers and mostly for balls, to set up an ensuing fastball. But it was the combination of the devastating slider and the famous fastball (plus some other, less tangible assets that we shall get to in time) that made Gibson almost untouchable at his best, just as Sandy Koufax's down-diving curveball worked in such terrible (to hitters) concert with his illustrious upriding fastball.

"Hitting is rhythm," McCarver said to me, "and if you allow major-league hitters to see only one pitch—to swing repeatedly through a certain area of the plate—eventually they'll get to you and begin to hit it, even if it's a great fastball. But anybody who can control and switch off between two first-class pitches will make the hitters start reaching, either in or out, and then the game belongs to the pitcher. Besides all that, Bob had such great stuff and was so intimidating out there that he'd make the batter open up his front shoulder just a fraction too fast, no matter what the count was. The other key to good hitting, of course, is keeping that shoulder—the left shoulder for a right-handed batter, I mean, and vice versa—in place, and the most common flaw is pulling it back. Gibson had guys pulling back that shoulder who normally wouldn't be caught dead doing it. Their ass was in the dugout, as we say."

Mike Shannon, who played third base behind Gibson in the 1968 Series opening game (he didn't handle the ball once), remembers feeling pity for the Detroit batters that afternoon. "Most of them had never seen Gibby before," he said, "and they had no *idea* what they were up against." Shannon, who is now a television game announcer with the Cards, told me that he encounters some of the 1968 Tigers from time to time in the course of his baseball travels, and that they almost compulsively want to talk about the game. "It's as if they can't believe it to this day," he said. "But neither can I. I've never seen major-league hitters overmatched that way. It was like watching a big-league pitcher against Little League batters. It was frightening."

Gibson, of course, was already a celebrated winning pitcher by 1968. Like many other fans, I had first become aware of his fastball and his unique pitching mannerisms and his burning intensity on the mound when he won two out of the three games he pitched against the Yankees in the 1964 World Series, including a tense, exhausting victory in the clinching seventh game. Then, in 1967, I had watched him capture three of the Cardinals' four October victories over the Red Sox, again including the seventh game—a feat that won him the Most Valuable Player award for that Series. I had also seen him work eight or ten regular-season games over the previous five years or more. Although he was of only moderate size for a pitcher—six feet one and about a hundred and eighty-five pounds—Gibson always appeared to take up a lot of space on the mound, and the sense of intimidation that McCarver mentioned had something to do with his sombre, almost funereal demeanor as he stared in at his catcher, with his cap pulled low over his black face and strong jaw, and with the ball held behind his right hip (he always wore a sweatshirt under his uniform, with the long, Cardinals-red sleeves extending all the way down to his wrists), and with his glove cocked on his left hip, parallel to the ground. Everything about him looked mean and loose—arms, elbows, shoulders, even his legs—as, with a quick little shrug, he launched into his delivery. When there was no one on base, he had an old-fashioned full crank-up, with the right foot turning in midmotion to slip into its slot in front of the mound and his long arms coming together over his head before his backward lean, which was deep enough to require him to peer over his left shoulder at his catcher while his upraised left leg crooked and kicked. The ensuing sustained forward drive was made up of a medium-sized stride of that leg and a blurrily fast, slinglike motion of the right arm, which came over at about three-quarters height and then snapped down and (with the fastball and the slider) across his left knee. It was not a long drop-down delivery like Tom Seaver's (for contrast), or a tight, brisk, body-opening motion like Whitey Ford's.

The pitch, as I have said, shot across the plate with a notable amount of right-to-left (from Gibson's vantage point) action, and his catchers sometimes gave the curious impression that they were cutting off a ball that was headed on a much longer journey—a one-hundred-foot fastball. But with Gibson pitching you were always a little distracted from the plate and the batter, because his delivery continued so extravagantly after the ball was released that you almost felt that the pitch was incidental to the whole affair. The follow-through sometimes suggested a far-out basketball move—a fast downcourt feint. His right leg, which was up and twisted to the right in the air as the ball was let go (all normal enough for a right-handed pitcher), now continued forward in a sudden sidewise rush, crossing his planted left leg, actually stepping over it, and he finished with a full running step toward the right-field foul line, which wrenched his body in the same direction, so that he now had to follow the flight of the ball by peering over his right shoulder. Both his arms whirled in the air to help him keep his balance during this acrobatic maneuver, but the key to his overpowering speed and stuff was not the strength of his pitching arm—it was the powerful, driving thrust of his legs, culminating in that final extra step, which brought his right foot clomping down on the sloping left-hand side of the mound, with the full weight of his body slamming and twisting behind it. (Gibson's arm never gave him undue trouble, but he had serious difficulties with his knees in the latter stages of his career, and eventually had to have a torn cartilage removed from the right knee, which had pushed off to start all the tens of thousands of his pitches over the years and had then had to withstand the punishing force of the last stage of his unique delivery.) All in all, the pitch and its extended amplifications made it look as if Gibson were leaping at the batter, with hostile intent. He always looked much closer to the plate at the end than any other pitcher; he made pitching seem unfair.

The players in the Detroit clubhouse after Gibson's seventeen-strikeout game had none of the aggrieved, blustery manner of batters on a losing team who wish to suggest that only bad luck or their own bad play kept them from putting away a pitcher who has just beaten them. Denny McLain, the starting Tiger pitcher, who had won thirty-one games that summer but had lasted only five innings in the Series opener, said, "I was awed. I was *awed*," and

Dick McAuliffe, the Detroit second baseman, said that he could think of no one he had ever faced with whom Gibson could be compared. "He doesn't remind me of anybody," he said. "He's all by himself."

I was awed, too, of course, but nothing I had seen on the field at Busch Stadium that afternoon startled me as much as Gibson's postgame comportment in the clubhouse. In October of 1964 and again in 1967, I had noticed that Bob Gibson often appeared to be less elated than his teammates in the noisy, jam-packed, overexuberant World Series locker rooms—a man at a little distance from the crowd. But somehow I must have expected that his astounding performance here in the 1968 opener would change him—that his record-breaking turn on the mound would make him more lighthearted and accommodating; he would be smiling and modest and self-deprecating, but also joyful about his feat, and this would diminish that almost immeasurable distance he had just established, out on the field, between himself and the rest of us. He would seem boyish, in short, and we, the grown-up watchers of the game, would then be able to call him by his first name (even if we didn't know him), and forgive him for what he had done, and thus to love him, as is the ancient custom in these high sporting dramas. But Gibson was unchanged. Talking to the sportswriters gathered in a thick, uncomfortable crowd around his locker, he looked at each reporter who asked him a question (Gibson is an exceptionally handsome man, with small ears, very dark skin, and a strikingly direct gaze) and then answered it gravely and briefly. When one writer asked him if he had always been as competitive as he had seemed on this day, he said yes, and he added that he had played several hundred games of ticktacktoe against one of his young daughters and that she had yet to win a game from him. He said this with a little smile, but it seemed to me that he meant it: he couldn't let himself lose to anyone. Then someone asked him if he had been surprised by what he had just done on the field, and Gibson said, "I'm never surprised by anything I do."

The shock of this went out across the ten-deep bank of writer faces like a seismic wave, and the returning, murmurous counter-waves of reaction were made up of uneasy laughter and whispers of "*What* did he say?" and some ripples of disbelieving silence and (it seemed to me) a considerable, almost visible wave of dislike, or perhaps hatred. This occasion, it should be remembered, was before the time when players' enormous salaries and their accompanying television-bred notoriety had given birth to a kind of athlete who could choose to become famous for his sullenness and foul temper, just as another might be identified by his gentle smile and unvarying sweetness of disposition. In 1968, ballplayers, particularly black ballplayers in near-Southern cities like St. Louis, did not talk outrageously to the press. Bob Gibson, however, was not projecting an image but telling us a fact about himself. He was beyond us, it seemed, but the truth of the matter is that no one at Busch Stadium should have been much surprised by his achievement that afternoon, for it was only a continuation of the kind of pitching he had sustained all through that summer of 1968—a season in which he won twenty-two games for the Cardinals while losing nine, and also compiled an earned-run average of 1.12 runs per game: the best pitching performance, by that measurement, in the history of modern baseball.

When Bob Gibson retired, at the age of thirty-nine, at the end of the 1975 season, after seventeen summers with the Cardinals, he had won two hundred and fifty-one games, and his record of 3,117 strikeouts was second only to Walter Johnson's 3,508. Last year. however, Gaylord Perry, who is still going strong at the age of forty-two, passed Gibson on the lifetime-strikeout list (Perry is now with the Yankees and has 3,267 whiffs to his credit at this writing), while three other active pitchers—Nolan Ryan, Tom Seaver, and Steve Carlton—may surpass Gibson's mark next summer. (By the end of the 1981 season, Gaylord Perry had accounted for 3,336 lifetime strikeouts, while Ryan stood at 3,249, Carlton at 3,148, and Seaver at 3,075. Steve Carlton's total is a new National League record, eclipsing Gibson's old mark, because, unlike Perry and Ryan, he has pitched only in that league.) This kind of erosion of the game's most famous fixed numbers—the landmarks of the pastime—by swirling tides of newcomers is always happening, of course; it is the process that makes baseball statistics seem alive and urgent to the true fan. But Gibson's displacement unsettled me, and when I read in the sports pages last spring that he was among the players who would become eligible for election to baseball's Hall of Fame at the end of this season, after the obligatory five-year post-retirement waiting period (the qualifications for official immortality are established by the Baseball Writers Association of America, whose three hundred-odd members conduct a Hall of Fame balloting in the off-season each year), I sensed that Gibson might be about to slip away into the quiet corridors of baseball history. It is always a discomfiting moment for a long-term follower of the game when a favorite player, whose every feat and gesture on the field still retain clarity and color, is declared safe for embronzement, but the possibility of Bob Gibson's imminent apotheosis at Cooperstown came as a shock to me. He seemed too impatient, too large, and too restless a figure to be stilled and put away in this particular fashion; somehow, he would shrug off the speeches and honorifics when they came, just as he had busied himself unhappily on the mound when the crowd stopped the rush of the game to cheer him at Busch Stadium that afternoon in 1968. For me, at least, Bob Gibson was still burning to pitch to the next batter. But in another, oddly opposite sense it seemed wrong to think of Gibson as a participant in the soft, sweet rituals with which newly elected baseball immortals are inducted into the Hall of Fame at the ceremonial in Cooperstown each August—the reading of the players' records and their official citations; their speeches of acceptance and gratitude; the obligatory picture-taking, with the still-young heroes, in civilian clothes, holding up their plaques and standing among the smaller, white-haired, earlier great figures who have come back for the occasion: old gents at a reunion, blinking in the hot upstate sunlight—because baseball up to now has never quite known what to make of Bob Gibson, and has slightly but persistently failed to pay him his full due as a player and as a man.

With this conviction in mind, I determined early this summer to look up Gibson and try to get to know him a little better. I wanted to see how he was faring now that he could no longer stare down at the batters of the world from the height of the pitcher's mound. I knew that he was still living in Omaha, his home town, and when I reached him there by telephone he told me to come on out if I wanted to. Not a warm invitation, but not a wary one, either. In the next week or two, I mentioned my forthcoming trip to some friends of mine—good baseball fans, all of them—and noticed that many of them seemed to have forgotten Bob Gibson's eminence and élan, if, indeed, they had ever been aware of them. In the history of the game, it seemed, as in his playing days, he already stood at a little distance from the crowd, a little beyond us all. But then I talked about Gibson with some players—old teammates or opponents of his—and they responded more warmly.

Pete Rose, who talks in the same runaway-taxi style in which he runs bases, said, "I'm always afraid I'll forget some pitcher when I start rating them, because I've faced so many of them. I started out against people like Warren Spahn, you know. But the best pitcher I ever batted against was Juan Marichal, because he threw so many goddam different kinds of good pitches against you. The hardest thrower of them all was Sandy Koufax, and the greatest competitor was Bob Gibson. He worked so fast out there, and he always had the hood up. He always wanted to close his own deal. He wasn't no badman, but he never talked to you, because he was battling you so hard. I sure as hell don't miss batting against him, but I miss him in the game."

Billy Williams, now a coach for the Cubs, who hit four hundred and twenty-six home runs during his sixteen years with that team and two years with the Oakland A's, told me, "Bob Gibson always got *on* with it. He didn't stand around out there and look around the park, you know. You always got the same message from him: 'Look, I'm goin' to throw this pitch and either you hit it or I get your ass out.' You like a guy like that. The infielders were never on their heels out there behind him. Everyone's on their toes, and it's a better game for everybody. I used to love the afternoon games at Wrigley Field when Gibby pitched against our Fergie Jenkins, because you could always plan something early for that evening. They *hurried.* Gibby was as serious as anybody you ever saw, and you had to be ready at all times. There was hitters that tried to step out on him, to break his pace, but if you did that too often he'd knock you down. He let you know who was out there on the mound. Made himself felt. He never let up, even on the hottest days there in St. Louis, which is the hottest place in the world. Just walked out there in the heat and threw the ball past people."

Tim McCarver said, "He was an intimidating, arrogant-looking athlete. The arrogance he projected toward batters was fearsome. There was no guile to his pitching, just him glaring down at that batter. He wanted the game played on his own terms. He worked very fast, and that pace was part of his personality on the mound, part of the way he dominated the game. One of the things he couldn't stand was a catcher coming out there to talk to him. In my first full year with the Cardinals, when I was only twenty-one years old, our manager was Johnny Keane, who was a fanatic about having a catcher establish communications with his pitcher. So I'd get a signal from Keane that meant 'Go on out there and settle him down,' but then I'd look out and see Hoot glaring in at me." McCarver laughed, and shook his head. "Well, sometimes I'd walk out halfway, to try to appease both parties!"

McCarver is an intimate friend of Bob Gibson's, and he told me that Gibson was much the same off the field as on the mound. "Bob is relatively shy," he said. "He's a nice man, but he's quiet. He doesn't enjoy small talk. He doesn't like to waste his time with anything that's weak or offhand. He wants to deal from strength all the time. That's why he projects this uppity-black-man figure that so many people in baseball seem to hate. He's very proud, you know, and he had a ghetto upbringing, so you could understand why he was so sensitive to bigotry—up to a point. But we have a great relationship—me, a kid from Memphis, Tennessee, and him an elegant black man from Omaha. Any relationship you get into with Bob is going to be intense. He's a strong man, with strong feelings."

Joe Torre, the manager of the New York Mets, who played with Gibson from 1969 to 1974, is also a close friend. When I called on him late in June, in the clubhouse at Shea Stadium, and told him I was about to go west to visit Gibson, he beckoned me over to a framed photograph on one wall of his office. The picture shows the three friends posing beside a batting cage in their Cardinals uniforms. Torre, a heavy-faced man with dark eyebrows and a falsely menacing appearance, and McCarver, who has a cheerful, snub-nosed Irish look to him, are both grinning at the photographer, with their arms around the shoulders of Bob Gibson, who is between them; it's impossible to tell if Gibson is smiling, though, because his back is turned to the camera. "That says it all," Torre said. "He alienated a lot of people—most of all the press, who didn't always know what to make of him. He has this great confidence in himself: 'Hey, I'm me. Take me or leave me.' There was never any selling of Bob Gibson. He's an admirable man. On the mound, he had very tangible intangibles. He had that hunger, that killer instinct. He threw at a lot of batters but not nearly as many as you've heard. But he'd never deny it if you asked him. I think this is great. There's no other sport except boxing that has such a hard one-on-one confrontation as you get when a pitcher and a hitter go up against each other. Any edge you can get on the hitter, any doubt you can put in his mind, you use. And Bob Gibson would never give up that edge. He was your enemy out there. I try to teach this to our pitchers. The more coldness, the more mystery about you, the more chance you have of getting them out.

"I played against him before I played with him, and either way he never talked to you. Never. I was on some All-Star teams with him, and even then he didn't talk to you. There was the one in Minnesota, when I was catching him and we were ahead 6–5, I think, in the ninth. I'm catching, and Tony Oliva, a great hitter, is leading off, and Gibby goes strike one, strike two. Now I want a fastball up and in, I think to myself, and maybe I should go out there and tell him this—tell him, whatever he does, not to throw it down and in to Oliva. So I go out and tell him, and Gibby just gives me that look of his. Doesn't say a word. I go back and squat down and give him the signal—fastball up and in—and he throws it *down* and in, and Oliva hits it for a double to left center. To this day, I think Gibby did it on purpose. He didn't want to be told *anything*. So then there's an infield out, and then he strikes out the last two batters, of course, and we win. In the shower, I say, 'Nice pitching,' and he still doesn't say anything to me. Ask him about it."

Torre lit a long cigar, and said, "Quite a man. He can seem distant and uncaring to some people, but he's not the cold person he's been described as. There are no areas between us where he's withdrawn. Things go deep with him. I miss talking to him during the season, and it's my fault, because I'm always so damn busy. He doesn't call me, because he never wants to make himself a pain in the ass to a friend. But he is my friend. The other day, I got a photograph of himself he'd sent me, and he'd signed it 'Love, Bob.' How many other ballplayers are going to do that? How many other friends?"

Most ballplayers who are discussing a past rival or a teammate go directly to the man's craft—what pitches he could hit, his arm, his range afield, or (with pitchers) his stuff and what he threw when the count was against him. But I had begun to notice that the baseball people talking about Bob Gibson all seemed anxious to get at something deeper; Gibson the man was even more vivid and interesting to them than Gibson the great pitcher. Bill White, the well-known TV and radio announcer with the Yankees, played first base behind Gibson with the Cards for seven years, and was then traded to the Phillies and had to play against him. "He was tough and uncompromising," White told me. "Koufax and Don Drysdale were just the same, with variations for their personalities—they had that same hard state of mind. But I think a great black athlete is sometimes tougher in a game, because every black has had it tough on the way up. Any black player who has a sense of himself, who wants to make something of himself, has something of Bob Gibson's attitude. Gibson had a chip on his shoulder out there—which was good. He was mean enough. He had no remorse. I remember when he hit Jim Ray Hart on the shoulder—he was bending away from a pitch—and broke his collarbone. Bob didn't say anything to him. I'd been his roomie for a while on the Cards, but the first time I batted against him, when I went over to the Phillies, he hit me in the arm. It didn't surprise me at all."

And, once again, Mike Shannon: "I think every superior athlete has some special motivation. With Bob Gibson, it wasn't that he wanted to win so much as that he didn't want to lose. He *hated* to lose. He just wouldn't accept it."

It was ninety-seven degrees at the Omaha airport when I landed there early one evening in July, and when I called Bob Gibson from my motel he invited me to come on out and cool off with a dip in his pool. He picked me up in his car—a black 1972 Mercedes SEL, lovingly kept up, with CB equipment (his call signal is Redbird) and terse "BG" license plates. Gibson looked well kept up himself, in tailored jeans, a white polo shirt, thin gold spectacles, a gold bracelet on his left wrist, a World Series ring, and a necklace with a pendant "45" in gold—his old uniform number. He is forty-four years old, but only his glasses spoiled the impression that he was perfectly capable of working nine tough innings the next afternoon. I asked him what he did for exercise these days, and he said, "Nothing." I expressed surprise, and he said, "I played sports hard for thirty years, which is enough. Now I'm tired of all that." No apology, no accompanying smile or joke: no small talk. He spoke pleasantly enough, though, in a light, almost boyish voice, and when he did laugh—a little later, after we were more used to each other—the sound of it made me realize that only in the world of sports would he be considered anything but a young man. There were some quiet spells in the car during our longish drive out to his house, in Bellevue, a comfortable suburban district on the south side of town, but by the time we got there I had lost any sense of foreboding that I might have had about imposing myself on such a famously private man.

Bob Gibson has done well for himself in Omaha. He was born and grew up there in the black North Side ghetto; his mother was a laundress, and his father died before he was born. He was the youngest of seven children—his three sisters and three brothers are all still living—and at the time of his birth the family lived in a four-room shack. When he was an infant there, he was bitten on the ear by a rat. By the end of his playing days, Gibson was earning more than a hundred and fifty thousand dollars a year, which made him one of the two or three best-paid players of his time, and he invested his money with care. Today, he is the chairman of the board—an interracial board—of the Community Bank of Nebraska, which he helped get started seven years ago, and which does most of its business in the black community of Omaha. He is also the co-owner and the active, day-to-day manager of a new and successful medium-sized bar-restaurant called Gibby's, a couple of blocks away from Creighton University, which Gibson entered as a freshman on a basketball scholarship in 1954. Much of Gibson's life these days seems new. Gibby's opened in late 1978, and last November he was married to Wendy Nelson, whom I met at their home, to the accompaniment of frenzied barking from their four-month-old miniature schnauzer, Mia. ("Kill, Mia!" Gibson said delightedly. "Kill, girl!") Wendy Gibson, a composed, striking-looking blond woman in her late twenties, is in the financial division of the local telephone company, where she works, by preference, on the very early shift, driving to work each day shortly after dawn in the family's *other* Mercedes. (Gibson's previous marriage, to Charline Johnson, ended in divorce some years ago; their children, Renee and Annette, are grown up and have moved away from Omaha. A captivating oil portrait of the two girls and their father—all of them much younger then—hangs in Gibson's study in his new house; the artist is an old friend and teammate, Curt Flood.) Wendy and Bob Gibson moved into their house last May.

It is a spacious, comfortably furnished and carpeted three-story contemporary wooden structure, with a sundeck that looks over a steep hillside and a thick green growth of oaks and cottonwoods. A flight of steps leads down from the deck to a big swimming pool, which had had its inaugural only a week before my arrival. Bob Gibson is handy. He helped design the new house, and he put in the deck stairs and built a raised wooden patio beside the pool, and also did most of the landscape work on the grounds, laying in some old railroad ties to form a rose garden and planting shrubs and young trees everywhere. The pool was built to Gibson's design; its sides and bottom are painted black—a da Vinci-like idea of his, meant to help the water hold the heat of the sun in the spring and fall. Somehow, though, he had not remembered the warmish mid-summer Nebraska sunshine, and when he and I slipped into the inky waves, the water temperature stood at ninety-two degrees—only a fraction cooler than the steamy, locust-loud night air. "Another mistake," Gibson said mildly. Swimming was a bit like sloshing through black-bean soup, but after a couple of turns up and down the pool he and I settled ourselves comfortably enough on the top steps at the shallow end, with our legs dangling in the water, and while Mia sniffed and circled me warily we talked a little baseball.

I asked Gibson if he recalled the low-and-inside pitch he had thrown to Tony Oliva in that All-Star Game, against Joe Torre's signals.

"Well, I never really liked being on the All-Star team," he said. "I liked the honor of it, being voted one of the best, but I couldn't get used to the idea of playing with people from other teams in the league—guys who I'd have to go out and try to beat just a couple of days later. I didn't even like having Joe catch me—he was with the Braves then—because I figured he'd learn how to hit me. In that same game, he came out and told me not to throw the high fastball to Harmon Killebrew, because the word was that he ate up that pitch." Gibson's voice was almost incredulous as he said this. "Well, hell. I struck him out with three high fastballs. But in any of the All-Star games where I got to pitch early"—Gibson was voted onto the National League All-Star squad eight times—"I'd always dress right away and get out of there in a hurry, before the other players got done and came into the clubhouse. I didn't want to hang around and make friends. I don't think there's any place in the game for a pitcher smiling and joking with the hitters. I was all business on the mound—it is a business, isn't it?—and I think some of the writers used to call me cold or arrogant because of that. I didn't want to be friends with anybody on the other side, except perhaps with Willie Stargell—how could you not talk to that guy? None of this was meant to scare guys, or anything. It was just the way I felt. When Orlando Cepeda was with us, I used to watch him and Marichal laughing and fooling around before a game. They'd been on the Giants together, you know. But then Cepeda would go out and *kill* Marichal at the plate—one of the best pitchers I ever saw—and when it was over they'd go to dinner together and laugh some more. It just made me shake my head. I didn't understand it."

I had been wondering how to bring up the business of his knocking down his old roommate Bill White, but now Gibson offered the story of his own accord. "Even before Bill was traded, I used to tell him that if he ever dived across the plate to swing at an outside pitch, the way he liked to, I'd have to hit him," he said. "And then, the very first time, he went for a pitch that was *this* far outside and swung at it, and so I hit him on the elbow with the next pitch. [Some years earlier, Gibson hit Duke Snider after similar provocation, and broke his elbow.] Bill saw it coming, and he yelled 'Yaah!' even before it got him. And I yelled over to him, 'You son of a bitch, you went for that outside ball! That pitch, that part of the plate, belongs to me! If I make a mistake inside, all right, but the outside is mine and don't you forget it.' He said, 'You're crazy,' but he understood me."

I mentioned a famous moment when Gibson had hit Tommie Agee, of the Mets, on the batting helmet with the very first pitch of the first inning of the first Cardinals spring-training game in 1968. Agee had come over from the Chicago White Sox and the American

League in the previous winter, and when Gibson's first swallow of the spring conked him, several Gibson students among the Mets and Cardinals baseball writers in the press box at Al Lang Field called out, "Welcome to the National League, Tommie!" (Agee went to the hospital for observation, but was found not to have suffered serious injury.)

Gibson was silent for a moment, and then he said, "It's very easy to hit a batter in the body with a pitch. There's nothing to it. It's a lot harder to hit him in the head. Any time you hit him in the head, it's really his own fault. Anyway, that was just spring training."

Joe Torre had told me that the Agee-plunking was an accident, but I noted now that Gibson had not quite denied intention in the affair. He had put doubt in my mind, just as Torre had told me he would. He still wanted that edge.

"I did throw at John Milner in spring training once," Gibson went on, paddling his legs in the water. "Because of that swing of his—that dive at the ball." Milner, an outfielder then with the Mets and now with the Pirates, invariably takes a full-scale, left-handed downtown swing at the ball, as if he meant to pull every pitch into the right-field stands. "I don't like batters taking that big cut, with their hats falling off and their buttons popping and every goddam thing like that. It doesn't show any respect for the pitcher. That batter's not doing any thinking up there, so I'm going to *make* him think. The next time, he won't look so fancy out there. He'll be a better-looking hitter. So I got Milner that once, and then, months later, at Shea Stadium, Tom Seaver began to pitch me up and inside, knocking me down, and it took me a minute to realize that it must have been to pay me back for something *in spring training*. I couldn't believe that."

There was a little silence at poolside while I digested this. Gibson sounded almost like a veteran samurai warrior recalling an ancient code of pain and honor. I suggested that there must be days when he still badly missed being out there on the mound, back in the thick of things.

"No, I have no desire to get out and throw the fastball again," he said quietly. "Even if I wanted to, I couldn't."

I had noticed that Gibson limped slightly as he walked around the pool, and the accounts of some of his baseball injuries and how he had reacted to them at the time came back to me. In July of 1967, while pitching against the Pirates in St. Louis, he was struck just above his right ankle by a line drive off the bat of Roberto Clemente. He went down in a heap, but after the Cardinals trainer had treated the injury with a pain-deadening spray, Gibson insisted on staying in the game. He walked Willie Stargell, retired Bill Mazeroski on a pop-up, and then, firing a three-two pitch to Donn Clendenon, came down hard on the right leg with his characteristic spinning follow-through and snapped the already cracked bone. Dal Maxvill, then a Cardinals shortstop and now a Cardinals coach, said to me recently, "That was the most extraordinary thing I ever saw in baseball—Gibby pitching to those batters with a broken leg. Everyone who was there that day remembered it afterward, for always, and every young pitcher who came onto our club while Gibson was still with us was told about it. We didn't have too many pitchers turning up with upset stomachs or hangnails on our team after that."

Gibson came back to win three games against the Red Sox in the World Series that fall, but his next serious injury, in midseason of 1973, took a heavier toll. Leading off first base in a game against the Mets at Shea Stadium, he made a sudden dive back toward the base after an infield line drive was caught, but collapsed when his right knee buckled. The trainer and the team doctor came out to succor him, but Gibson cried "Don't touch it! Don't touch it!" and again refused to be taken out of the game. When the inning ended, he walked to the mound and began his warmup tosses and fell heavily to the ground. The surgeon—Dr. Stan London—who performed the cartilage operation the next day said afterward that Gibson had the knees of an eighty-year-old man. Gibson recovered in time to pitch and win a game that September, and he continued for two more full seasons on the mound, although, as he told me now, he sometimes had to sit in the clubhouse for two hours after a game before he felt able to head for the showers. "I'd had the left knee drained about seventeen times, too," he said. "I'd sit like this"—he hung his head and arms like a broken puppet— "and I'd think, *Why do I put up with this? Why, why?*" He laughed now, mocking himself. "I just couldn't give it up," he said. "Couldn't let go."

I asked if he'd become a different kind of pitcher then, using changeups and slip pitches, the way many older hurlers do in their final seasons.

"No, I always threw hard," he said. "They didn't use me much in my final season, after I'd announced I was going to retire—I never did understand that. But once, when I hadn't pitched in three weeks, they brought me into a game against Houston in extra innings—I was the last pitcher we had—and I struck out the side on nine pitches that were nothing but fastballs. So I still had something left, even at the end. I always had pretty good control, you know, so it wasn't like I didn't know what I was doing out there. But later that season I gave up a grand-slam home run to Pete La-Cock, of the Cubs, and that told me it was about time for me to get off the mound for good." Gibson spoke lightly enough, but at the time this home run was an almost insupportable blow to his pride. A pitcher who was with the Cubs that year told me that as LaCock (who is not exactly famous as a slugger) circled the bases, Gibson stalked after him around the base paths, reviling him for what he had done.

"Pitching is about ninety per cent thinking," Gibson went on. "I threw hard when I was younger, but I didn't know how to get people out. I don't care how hard you throw, somebody's going to hit it if you don't think out there. It's not all that detailed—you don't think three or four pitches ahead. But one pitch might set up the next two you throw—it depends what the guy does with it. You know. If he misses a fastball by a foot, then he'll see another one. If he fouls it off or *just* misses it, he'll probably get a breaking ball next. It isn't exactly scientific, or anything."

Gibson suddenly laughed in the darkness beside me. "But not everybody understands what a pitcher *does*," he said. "About his control, I mean. I remember when Mike Shannon was moved in from the outfield and began playing third base for us—back in the middle sixties, it was. He was really nervous over there. He kept asking me where I wanted him to play—up or back, near the line or away. He wanted instructions. I always told him I didn't give a damn where he played unless there was a right-handed batter coming up with a man on first and less than two out, but then he should be ready, because he'd be getting a ground ball, right to him or around his area. And I'd throw a sinker down and in, and the batter would hit it on the ground to Mike, to start the double play, and when we came in off the field Mike would look at me with his mouth open, and he'd say, 'But how did you *know?*' He didn't have the faintest idea that when I threw that pitch to the batter he *had* to hit it to him there! He didn't know what pitching was all about."

To go back a little, Gibson also won his second start in the 1968 Cardinals-Tigers World Series—a 10–1 decision in the fourth game, during which he fanned ten batters and whacked a home run. It was Gibson's seventh straight World Series victory—an all-time record. The Tigers, however, captured the Series, rallying in stimulating fashion after trailing by three games to one, and beating Gibson in the memorable finale, when Detroit outfielder Jim Northrup, batting with two out and two on in the seventh inning of the scoreless game, smashed a long drive that was misjudged by Curt Flood in center field, who then slipped on the turf and allowed the ball to go over his head for a triple. The Tigers won the game by 4–1, and the Most Valuable Player award for the Series went to Mickey Lolich, a portly left-handed sinkerball specialist, who won the second, fifth, and seventh games. Gibson, however, had established a Series record of thirty-five strikeouts (still standing), and a few weeks later he was named the Most Valuable Player of the National League for 1968 and became the unanimous winner of the Cy Young Award as the league's best pitcher. The following year, 1969, Gibson compiled a 20-13 record, with an earned-run average of 2.18, and in 1970 his 23-7 won-lost mark and 3.12 E.R.A. won him the Cy Young again. Injuries began to gnaw him after that, but he declined only stubbornly, throwing a no-hitter against the Pirates in 1971 and running off eleven straight victories in the course of a 19-11 season in 1972. His lifetime earned-run average of 2.91 runs per game is the ninth-best in baseball history. (Walter Johnson's 2.37 leads all comers, while Tom Seaver, at 2.62, and Jim Palmer, at 2.73, stand third and fourth on the all-time list at this writing.)

Many observers (including this one) believe that Gibson's 1.12 earned-run average in 1968 is one of the Everests of the game, ranking with Joe DiMaggio's fifty-six-consecutive-game hitting streak in 1941 and Hack Wilson's hundred and ninety runs batted in in 1930. Gibson's record, however, was not much noted or celebrated in its time, partly because it was achieved in a summer during which the pitchers in both leagues established a mesmerizing dominance over the batters. The leagues' combined batting average fell to an all-time low of .237, and twenty-one per cent of all games played were shutouts. Many pitchers came up with startling performances that summer. Gaylord Perry, of the Giants, and Ray Washburn, of the Cardinals, threw no-hit games on successive days at Candlestick Park; Jerry Koosman, a rookie, won nineteen games for the Mets; Denny McLain, as I have noted, won thirty-one games for the Tigers; and Don Drysdale, of the Dodgers, ran off fifty-eight and two-thirds consecutive shutout innings—a record that still stands. At the end of the year, the baseball fathers studied these figures and determined to rebalance the game by shaving five inches off the height of the mound (reducing it to ten inches), and by closing up the upper and lower limits of the strike zone. Gibson's golden season may always appear a mite tarnished by these circumstances, but even a brief rundown of his 1968 summer outings suggests that in that single season he came as close to some ideal of pitching as most of us are ever likely to witness or wish for.

Younger fans may argue for Ron Guidry's marvellous 25-3 season for the Yankees in 1978, when he threw nine shutouts and wound up with a 1.74 earned-run average. Others will cite Steve Carlton's one-man-band performance in 1972, when he finished with an earned-run average of 1.97 and a record of 27-10—all this for a frightful last-place Phillies team that won only fifty-nine games in all—while geezers may bring up Carl Hubbell's 23-12 and 1.66 earned-run mark for the Giants in 1933. But no matter: these great case studies of the game are forever moot.

On May 28, 1968, Bob Gibson lost to the Giants, 3–1, and saw his record for the year decline to three victories and five defeats. Surprisingly, however, his earned-run average of 1.52 for the young season was fifth in the National League at this point—an oddity explicable by the fact that his teammates had supplied him with a total of four runs in the five games he lost: starvation fare. On June 2nd, Gibson pitched the Cardinals into first place (this was before the leagues had been subdivided into East and West sectors) with a 6-3 victory over the Mets; the final Mets run—a homer by Ed Charles—came in the seventh inning. It was also the final run that Gibson surrendered in the month of June, for he threw shutout games in his next five outings. Only the last of these brought him much attention from the national press, and that came because reporters had noticed that his next appearance, on July 1st, would be against the Dodgers in Los Angeles, and that his mound opponent there would be Don Drysdale, whose record shutout skein of fifty-eight and two-thirds innings had been set over a span of six games in late May and early June. A matchup between the two seemed exciting indeed, for Drysdale, who was six feet five and threw almost sidearm, had a hostile scowl, a devastating fastball, and a reputation for knocking down batters he didn't care for: another intimidator. Gibson by now had forty-eight scoreless innings to his credit, but the tension of the famous confrontation vanished in the very first inning, when two Dodgers singled and Gibson, while pitching to Ron Fairly, let go a wild pitch that allowed Len Gabrielson to score from third base. Gibson had lost the duel with Drysdale and a shot at his record, but he won the game, by 5–1. He then pitched a shutout against the Giants, beat Houston by 8–1, and afterward shut out the Mets and the Phillies in succession. On July 30th, once again facing the Mets, Gibson surrendered a run with two out in the fourth inning, when Ed Charles scored on a double by Eddie Kranepool—the same Ed Charles who had homered against him on June 2nd. In that span—from June 2nd to July 30th—Gibson had given up two earned runs (and two runs in toto) in ninety-six and two-thirds innings.

Gibson won that Mets game, and he did not lose a game, in fact, until August 24th, when he fanned fifteen Pirates but lost, 6–4, after giving up a three-run homer to Willie Stargell. Between May 28th and August 24th, Gibson had won fifteen straight games, ten of them shutouts. He threw two more shutouts in his next two outings, and somebody figured out that in the course of three straight games in August, Gibson's infielders had to make only eight assists. (His shortstop, Dal Maxvill, told a reporter, "It's like having a night off out there when he's pitching.") Possibly tired by now—or perhaps a bit understimulated, since his club had run away with the league by this point, having established a fourteen-and-a-half-game lead over the second-place Reds by August 1st—Gibson lost three games in September, one of them to the no-hitter by Gaylord Perry. His final victory, on September 27th, was a 1–0 decision over the Astros—his thirteenth shutout. His season was over; the World Series and the Tigers were just ahead.

A further thin cement of statistics will finish the monument. Gibson completed twenty-eight of the thirty-four games he started in 1968, and was never removed in the middle of an inning—never knocked out of the box. His 1.12 earned-run average is second only to the all-time low of 1.01, established by the Red Sox' Hub Leonard in 1914, and it eclipsed the old National League mark of 1.22, set by Grover Cleveland Alexander in 1915. Gibson's thirteen shutouts are second only to the sixteen that Alexander achieved the following summer. But those very low early figures, it should be understood, must be slightly discounted, for they were established in the sludgy, Pleistocene era of the game, when aces like Leonard and Alexander and Walter Johnson and the White Sox' Red Faber regularly ran off season-long earned-run averages of two runs or less per game, thanks to the dead ball then in use. The lively ball, which came into the game in 1921, when the owners began to notice how much the fans seemed to enjoy watching a young outfielder (and former pitcher) named George Herman Ruth hit towering drives into the bleachers, put an end to the pitchers' hold over the game, and none of the four worthies I have cited ever pitched consistently in the less-than-three-runs-per-game level after 1922. Bob Gibson, we may conclude, was the man most responsible for the *next* major change in the dimensions of the sport—the lowering of the mound and the shrinkage of the strike zone that came along in 1969. Gibson, like all pitchers, complained bitterly when these new rules were announced, but Bob Broeg, the sports editor of the St. Louis *Post-Dispatch* and the dean of Cardinals sportswriters, told him he had only himself to blame. "I said, 'Goddam it, Gib, you're changing the game!'" Broeg told me not long ago. "'It isn't fun anymore. You're making it like hockey.'"

On another day, Omaha slowly came to a broil under a lazy white sun while Gibson and I ran some early-morning errands in his car—a visit to his bank, a stop at the drive-in window of another bank, where he picked up the payroll checks for Gibby's—and wound up at the restaurant, where the daytime help greeted the boss cheerfully. Gibson seemed in an easy frame of mind, and he looked younger than ever. I recalled that many of his teammates had told me what good company he was in the dugout and on road trips— on days when he wasn't pitching. He was a comical, shrill-voiced bench jockey, and a grouchy but lighthearted clubhouse agitator, who was sometimes known to bang a bat repeatedly and horribly on the metal locker of a teammate who was seen to be suffering the aftereffects of too many ice-cream sodas the previous evening. While he drove, Gibson, with a little urging, recalled how he had pitched to some of the prime hitters of his day—inside fastballs to

Willie Mays (who feasted on breaking pitches), belt-high inside deliveries to Eddie Mathews, low and away to Roberto Clemente, and so on. He said that Frank Robinson used to deceive pitchers with his plate-crowding (Robinson was a right-handed slugger of fearsome power, whose customary stance at the plate was that of an impatient subway traveller leaning over the edge of the platform and peering down the tracks for the D train), because they took it to mean that he was eager for an inside pitch. "Besides," he said, "they'd be afraid of hitting him and putting him on base. So they'd work him outside, and he'd hit the shit out of the ball. I always tried him inside, and I got him out there—sometimes. He was like Willie Mays—if you got the ball outside to Willie at all, he'd just *kill* you. The same with Clemente. I could throw him a fastball knee-high on the outside corner seventeen times in a row, but if I ever got it two inches up, he'd hit it out of sight. That's the mark of a good hitter—the tiniest mistake and he'll punish you. Other batters—well, somebody like Joe Adcock was just a guess hitter. You'd pitch him up and in, and he'd swing and miss every time. He just didn't give a damn. I don't know what's the matter with so many hitters—it's like their brains small up." He shook his head and laughed softly. "Me, too. I got beat by Tommy Davis twice the same way. In one game, I'd struck him out three times on sliders away. But I saw that he'd been inching up and inching up toward that part of the plate, so I decided to fool him and come inside, and he hit a homer and beat me, one-oh. And then, in another game, I did exactly the same thing. I tried to outthink him, and he hit the inside pitch for a homer, and it was one-oh all over again. So I could get dumb, too."

I said that he didn't seem to have made too many mistakes in the summer of '68. Gibson thought for a moment or two and said, "You can't say it was a fluke, although some people *have* said that. Just say it was totally unusual. Everything I threw that year seemed to go where I wanted it. Everything was down, all year. I was never that good again, because they went and changed the rules on me. The next year was a terrific struggle. I had a good season, but I never worked so hard in my life, because so many of my breaking pitches were up. I'll never know, but I doubt very seriously I'd have had another one-point-one-two E.R.A., even if they'd left the mound where it was. I'd like to think I'd really perfected my pitching to that point, but I'll never know."

The talk shifted to pitchers, and Gibson (echoing Pete Rose) said he thought that Juan Marichal had been the best hurler of their time, because of his absolute control. "I had a better fastball and a better slider, but he was a better pitcher than me or Koufax," he said. Among contemporary pitchers, he had warm things to say about the Phillies' Steve Carlton, once a young teammate of his on the Cards. "He's always had a great arm," he said. "And if you have a good arm and you're in the game long enough, you're going to learn how to pitch. He sure knows how now. What makes a player great to me is longevity."

I named some other mound stars of the sixties and seventies, and Gibson shrugged and shook his head. "I guess I was never much in awe of anybody," he said. "I think you have to have that attitude if you're going to go far in this game. People have always said that I was too confident, but I think you'll find that most guys who can play are pretty cocky." The locution "He can play"—as in "Carl Yastrzemski can play a little"—is a throwaway line, the professionals' designation for star-quality athletes. "They're not sitting around worrying about who they're going to pitch against or bat against the next day. You hear a lot of talk about the pressure of the game, but I think most of that comes from the media. Most guys don't let things worry them. Pressure comes when you're not doing well. I've always thought that you only really enjoy baseball when you're good at it. For someone who isn't at the top of the game—who's just hanging on somewhere on down the totem pole—it's a real tough job, every day. But when I was playing I never wished I was doing anything else. I think being a professional athlete is the finest thing a man can do."

I asked about the source of his great confidence in himself, and he said, "I've always been that way. After all, I was playing basketball with grown men when I was thirteen years old. I always thought I was good enough to play with anyone. I don't know where that came from."

When Gibson was playing baseball, he was considered one of the two or three very best athletes in the game. His early basketball experience had come when he was a water boy with an itinerant black basketball team, the Y Travellers (named for Omaha's North Branch Y.M.C.A.), which was coached by his grown-up oldest brother, Josh; whenever the Travellers ran up a comfortable lead over some local Nebraska or Iowa all-star club, Josh would send his kid brother into the game, just to rub things in a little. Bob Gibson won city and statewide basketball honors at Technical High School, in Omaha, and a few in baseball, too (he was a catcher in the beginning), and he broke every basketball record at Creighton, where he was the first black student to be given a basketball scholarship—and, for that matter, to play on the team. After leaving Creighton, he played for the Harlem Globetrotters during the 1957–58 season, after he had signed on as a pitcher with the Cardinals organization. "It was all right being with the Trotters," Gibson told me, "but I hated that clowning around. I wanted to play all the time—I mean, I wanted to play to win."

In spite of Gibson's spinning, staggering pitching motion, which certainly did not leave him in the squared-away, weight-on-both-feet attitude that coaches recommend as the proper post-delivery fielding stance for the position, he was agile enough out there to win the Gold Glove award as the best defensive pitcher in his league every season from 1965 through 1973. Fans and writers and players still talk about some of his fielding plays in the same awestruck tones they use for the seventeen-strikeout Series game. In one play (I can still see it) in the 1964 World Series, he scampered over and plucked up a hard-hit ball struck by Joe Pepitone that had nailed him on the hip and caromed halfway to third base; Gibson leaped and turned one hundred and eighty degrees in midair and made an overhead throw to first—a basketball one-handed fall-away jumper—that nipped Pepitone at the bag. There was also a nationally televised game in which he ran down a ball that a Giants batter had bounced over his head out on the mound; Gibson caught up with it while running full tilt away from the plate and toward second base, and he flipped it, underhand and right-handed and away from his body (try it), to first for the out. Tim McCarver, who weighs a solid hundred and ninety pounds, told me that one day when he and Gibson were horsing around on the field, Bob had suddenly seized him and lifted him above his head at arm's length, holding him aloft like some Olympic weight lifter at the end of a clean and jerk. "The man is somewhat startling," McCarver said.

Gibby's is a welcoming sort of place—a squared-off, three-sided bar downstairs, with strips of stained-glass decoration on the far wall and a short flight of steps up to the sun-filled upper level, where there are some comfortable wooden-backed dining booths and hanging plants everywhere. On a busy night—on Saturdays, for instance, when a jazz group comes in to play—Gibby's has room for about a hundred and thirty diners and twenty more customers at the bar. I was not surprised to learn that Gibson had had a hand in the restaurant's design and construction. He is there every day, starting at eight in the morning, when he turns up to check the books for the previous night's business, to inspect the incoming meat and produce (the menu is modest, and is built around steaks and shrimp and delicious hamburgers), and generally to keep an eye on things. "I want to make sure nobody is throwing out the forks with the garbage," he said lightly. He went to bartenders' school for three months before Gibby's opened—not so much to learn how to mix cocktails, although he can now whip up eighty different drinks, as to learn how veteran waiters and bartenders can fleece a rookie owner. "What I *should* have done was to become an accountant," he said. "About ninety per cent of the job is damned paperwork." Gibby's clientele is an interesting mixture of races and ages and sexes—a "neat crowd," according to the owner ("neat" is a favorite word), and perhaps the only such cosmopolitan mixture in Omaha. The waiters are mostly young black men, and the bartenders mostly young black women. Gibson is a calm and approachable boss; the staff seems to care about him, and vice versa. When a small, very young waitress began putting coins into a cigarette machine near us, Bob said reprovingly, "Those aren't for you, are they?" (They weren't.) Later on, he let slip that the previous week he had taken the four-year-old daughter of one of his female bartenders out to his new pool for the afternoon when her mother couldn't find a babysitter. At the last moment, he also asked the daughter of one of his regular customers to come along, too. "I used to have little girls myself," he said to me. A lot of the arriving diners and drinkers at Gibby's say hello to him in an easy, friendly way, but there isn't much hearty bar chatter with the host. Not many people would feel impelled to buddy up to Bob Gibson. I suggested that he must be exposed to a good deal of barside baseball expertise at his place of work, and he said, "Who wants to talk to fans? They always know so much, to hear them tell it, and they always think baseball is so easy. You hear them say, 'Oh, I was a pretty good ballplayer myself back when I was in school, but then I got this injury....' Some cabdriver gave me that one day, and I said, 'Oh, really? That's funny, because when 1 was young I really wanted to be a cabdriver, only I had this little problem with my eyes, so I never made it.' He thought I was serious. It went right over his head."

Gibson's impatience with trifling or intrusive strangers accounted for considerable coolness between him and the media during his playing days—a mistrust that may even keep him out of the Hall of Fame for a year or two, since some members of the Baseball Writers Association have been known to allow personal pique to influence their judgment. (Each writer selects up to ten names of eligible former players he thinks worthy of the Hall of Fame, and a player must be named on seventy-five per cent of the ballots in order to be immortalized.) A couple of years ago, when Willie Mays first came up for election, twenty-three members of the

B.W.A. resolutely omitted him from their ballots. A good many St. Louis reporters still recall when in 1967 Gibson had the cast removed from his broken leg and then, annoyed by their clubhouse importunings and questions, taped a sheet of paper to his shirtfront on which he had written "1. Yes, it's off; 2. No, it doesn't hurt; 3. I don't know how much longer"; and so on. The club was in a pennant race, of course, and Gibson's condition was a matter of daily concern to Cardinals fans everywhere, so his broadside was not taken in good part.

"I don't like all this personal contact with the press," Gibson told me. "The press expects everyone to be congenial. Everyone's *not* congenial! They want to put every athlete in the same category as every other athlete. It's as if they thought they owned you." I had been told of a St. Louis television reporter who had once done something to offend one of Gibson's teammates and had then tried to reassure Gibson about their relationship. "You know I'll never do anything to hurt you, Bob," he said. Gibson looked at him incredulously and said, "Why, hell, the only way you could ever hurt me is if you happened to be a pretty good fastball hitter!" One longtime Cardinals writer said to me, "Bob was a thorny, obdurate personality, and there weren't too many people who were crazy about him. If he'd had a little more give to him, he could have owned this city. If he'd had Lou Brock's personality, he'd still be working for the Cardinals somewhere."

There is a standoff here. The price of Bob Gibson's owning St. Louis seems to be his agreeing—in his mind, at least—to let the press own him. I have considerable sympathy for any writer who had to ask Bob Gibson some sharp, news-producing questions two or three times a week over the span of a decade or more, but wanting Gibson with a sunny, less obdurate temperament would be to want him a less difficult, less dangerous man on the mound—not quite a Bob Gibson, not quite a great pitcher. The man is indivisible, and it is the wonder of him. It is my own suspicion that both sportswriters and fans are increasingly resentful of the fame and adulation and immense wealth that are now bestowed so swiftly upon so many young professional athletes, and are envious of their privileged and apparently carefree style of living. The resentment is a half-conscious appreciation of the fact that they themselves—the fans and the media people, that is—have to a great degree created these golden youths, and because of that there is indeed a wish to own them; to demand ceaseless, inhumanly repeated dazzling performances from them on the field, and to require absolute access to their private lives as well. Most athletes, who are very young when they first come to prominence and, for the most part, have a very limited experience of the world, respond to these demands either with a convulsive, wholly artificial public "image" of affability, or (more often, of late) with surliness or angry silence. Bob Gibson did neither. Somehow, he has always kept his distance and his strangeness, and there is something upright and old-fashioned about such stubborn propriety. He is there if anyone really wants to close that space—the whole man, and not a piece of him or an image of him—but many of us may prefer not to do so, because at a distance (from sixty feet six inches away, perhaps) he stands whole and undiminished, and beyond our envy: the athlete incarnate, the player.

Gibson had allowed me to close this space a little by his willingness to talk about himself, and I had begun to sense the intensity of relationships with him that Tim McCarver had told me about, and the absence of any withdrawn places in him that Joe Torre had mentioned. There is reason to believe that he has allowed himself to become more approachable since he left the game. Bob Broeg, who covered Gibson from his first day in spring training as a rookie, in 1958, to his retirement, at the end of the 1975 season, said to me, "Bob didn't know how his personality worked against him. I don't think I wrote many things about him over the years that weren't appreciative of his great skills—he and Dizzy Dean were the two best pitchers I ever saw here—but he was always indifferent to me. One day, late in his career, I was in the clubhouse with him, and he was as closed off as ever, and I finally said, 'You've never said a kind or personal word to me in the years I've known you.' I walked away, and he chased me all the way across the room to ask what I meant. I'd pinked him, and he was extremely upset. He just didn't realize how cold he could be in everyday relationships."

But other intimates of Gibson's from his Cardinals days have a very different view of him. Gene Gieselmann, the team's trainer—he is thirty-three years old but looks much younger—counts Gibson among his closest and warmest friends. "My memories of baseball are all shiny where he's concerned," he said. "I cherish him. I think his problems with people go back to his never having had a father. He never knew him, you know. He dearly loved his mother, but I don't think he was very close to anyone else in his family. So when somebody, especially a white person"—Gieselmann is white—"showed him over a long period of time that he could be more than just a trainer or more than just another ballplayer, and that there could be something deeper in their relationship—well, that meant a lot to him, and then he showed how sensitive and generous he really was."

Gibson is a compulsive truthteller, and he appears to have a wry understanding of the burdens of that self-imposed role. At one point, he was talking with me about the difference between himself and Joe Torre when it came to dealing with writers and other strangers, and he said, "Joe knows everybody, and he recognizes them right away. I don't. I always had a hard time remembering people's names and recognizing their faces." There was a moment of silence, and then he added, "That's only half of it. I didn't *care*. And if I think somebody's wrong I'm going to say it."

I suddenly recalled an incident some years ago involving Gibson and another player, a well-known American League infielder, who were members of a small troupe of ballplayers making a postseason tour of military bases in the Pacific. Gibson's roommate on the trip was a public-relations man with one of the major-league teams, who was acting as an escort and travel agent for the group. Early in the trip, the infielder let drop some plainly anti-Semitic remarks about the P.R. man, who was Jewish, and Gibson stopped him in midsentence and advised him to keep his distance and not to talk to him for the remainder of the trip. "And if I ever pitch against you," Gibson said levelly, "I'm going to hit you on the coconut with my first pitch." Fortunately (or perhaps unfortunately), the two never did play against each other.

Gibson told me that racism had been easy to find when he came into baseball. When he first reported to the Cards' spring-training camp, in St. Petersburg, in 1958, he presented himself at the Bainbridge Hotel, where the club was quartered, and asked for his room, but he was guided out a side door, where a taxi picked him up and drove him to the house of a black family on the other side of town; the same arrangement had been made for all the team's black players. (Three years later, the entire club moved to a different, unsegregated hotel in St. Pete.) Earlier, when he was an eighteen-year-old sophomore at Creighton, Gibson and the rest of the college's basketball team had gone to Oklahoma by train for a game against the University of Tulsa, and on the way Gibson was told that he wouldn't be able to eat or sleep with his teammates there. "I cried when I was told that," Gibson said to me. "I wouldn't have gone if I'd known. I wasn't ready for that."

At one point, I said to Gibson that when I had seen him play I had always been very much aware of the fact that he was a black athlete; somehow, his race had always appeared to be a considerable part of what he brought to the mound when he went to work out there.

He didn't respond—he simply said nothing at all—and I understood that my remark was not a question that anyone could easily respond to; it was not a question at all. But a little later he mentioned the many times he had been harassed by semi-official white people—hotel clerks and traffic cops and the like—who later began fawning on him when they learned that he was *the* Bob Gibson, the famous pitcher. "It's nice to get attention and favors," he said, "but I can never forget the fact that if I were an ordinary black person I'd be in the shithouse, like millions of others." He paused a moment, and then added, "I'm happy I'm *not* ordinary, though."

All this was said without surface bitterness or cynicism but with an intensity that went beyond his words. Some days later, Bill

White, who is also black, commented on this tone of Gibson's. "He was always so proud," he said to me. "You could see it in his face and in the way he met people and talked to them. He never dropped it. I used to tell him, 'You can't be as tough on people as you are—it hurts you.' And he would say, 'You can do that, take all that, but I can't.' We didn't agree. But, of course, you never know what it's been like for another person. Some people have the ability to forget these things, but Bob Gibson always had the ability to make everybody remember what he had been through."

Gibson and I spent the afternoon at the restaurant, and he and Wendy had me to dinner at their house that night: steaks and mustard greens, prepared by the Gibsons together, and a Cabernet Sauvignon. (He is a demanding, accomplished cook; when he was playing, he invariably got his own meals at home when he returned from road trips and road cooking.) It was our last evening. Bob showed me some of the nineteenth-century American antiques he collects—a delicate bevelled-glass-front walnut secretary, an immense Barbary Coast-style sideboard, and so on—and took me into a basement room where he keeps his HO-gauge model-railroad set: an entire railhead in miniature, with yards and sidings and a downtown terminal, complete with surrounding streets and buildings. He said he didn't use the trains much anymore. The three of us took another swim in the pool, and Bob and I played a little noisy one-o'-cat with Mia in the living room with an old tennis ball. Gibson was relaxed and playful, but, as always, there was a silence about him: an air not of something held back but of a space within him that is not quite filled. At one point, I asked him if he liked Omaha, and he said, "Not all that much. It's all right. It's what I know." Then I asked if he liked the restaurant business, and in the same brusque way he said, "It isn't much, but it sure is better than doing nothing."

I knew that Gibson had had a brief career in sports television with the American Broadcasting Company, shortly after his retirement as a player. He was a "color man" with ABC's "Monday Night Baseball," and on one occasion he conducted an impromptu, nationally televised interview with the Pittsburgh Pirates' John Candelaria, just after Candelaria had pitched a no-hit game. Gibson's questions centered on the future financial rewards of Candelaria's gem, but this insidey banter between co-professionals was evidently not a line of sports talk that the network brass approved of, and Gibson's media career declined after that, although he has since done some baseball broadcasts with the HBO cable network. It was a disappointment to him.

When Gibson was out of the room for a moment, I said to Wendy that I sensed something missing or incomplete in Bob, and she said, "Yes, he's still looking for something, and I don't know if the right thing for him will ever come along. It's sad."

Last winter, Gibson made inquiries with the Cardinals and the Royals and the Mets and the Giants in the hope of landing a job as a pitching coach; interest was expressed, but nothing quite worked out. One difficulty may be the very modest salaries of big-league coaches, but when I talked to Bob about his joining some team in this capacity I got the feeling that he might be willing to make a considerable financial sacrifice in order to get back into the game. Several of Gibson's old friends and teammates told me later that they had heard of his wish to get back into baseball, and without exception they hoped he would. They said that the game would be better off with a man of Gibson's character back in uniform. But some of them went on to express their doubt that he would be satisfied with a job of such limited rewards as that of a pitching coach. "It won't be enough for him," one man said. "Nothing will ever be enough for him now."

"I don't miss pitching," Gibson said to me on that last evening, "but I can't say that I don't miss the game. I miss it a *little*. There's a lot I don't want to get back to. I don't want the fame or the money or all that attention. I always hated all the waiting around a pitcher has to do. I used to wish I could press a button the minute I'd finished a game and make the next four days just disappear. I sure as hell don't miss the travelling. I think it's the life I miss—all the activity that's around baseball. I don't miss playing baseball but I miss...baseball. *Baseball.* Does that sound like a crazy man?"

For the first time in our long talks, he seemed a bit uncertain. He did not sound crazy but only like a man who could no longer find work or a challenge that was nearly difficult enough to nurture his extraordinarily demanding inner requirements. Maybe there was no such work, outside of pitching. Baseball is the most individual and the most difficult of all team sports, and the handful of young men who can play it superbly must sense, however glimmeringly, that there will be some long-lasting future payment exacted for the privileges and satisfactions they have won for themselves. Like other team sports, baseball cannot be played in middle age; there is no cheerful, companionable afternoon to the game, as there is for old golfers and tennis players and the like. A lot of ex-ballplayers become sentimental, self-pitying, garrulous bores when they are cut off from the game. Some of them, including some great stars, go to pieces.

Thinking of what Wendy had said, I told Bob Gibson that I was sometimes aware of a sadness in him.

"Sad?" he said uncomprehendingly. "No, I'm not sad. I just think I've been spoiled. When you've been an athlete, there's no place for you to go. You're much harder to please. But where I am right now is where the average person has been all along. I'm like millions of others now, and I'm finding out what that's like. I don't think the ordinary person ever gets to do anything they enjoy nearly as much as I enjoyed playing ball. I haven't found my niche now that that's over—or maybe I have found it and I don't know it. Maybe I'll still find something I like as much as I liked pitching, but I don't know if I will. I sure hope so."

Maybe he will. Athletes illuminate our imagination and raise our hopes for ourselves to such an extent that we often want the best of them to become models for us in every area of life—an unfair and childish expectation. But Bob Gibson is a tough and resolute man, and the unique blend of independence and pride and self-imposed isolation in his character—the distance again—will continue to serve him in the new and even more difficult contest he is engaged in. Those who know him best will look to him for something brilliant and special now, just as they have always done. Even those of us who have not been spoiled by any athletic triumphs of our own and the fulfillment of the wild expectations of our early youth are aware of a humdrum, twilight quality to all our doings of middle life, however successful they may prove to be. There is a loss of light and ease and early joy, and we look to other exemplars—mentors and philosophers: grown men—to sustain us in that loss. A few athletes, a rare handful, have gone on, once their day out on the field was done, to join that number, and it is possible—the expectation will not quite go away—that Bob Gibson may be among them someday. Nothing he ever does will surprise me.

The Web of the Game

1981

An afternoon in mid-May, and we are waiting for the game to begin. We are in shadow, and the sunlit field before us is a thick, springy green—an old diamond, beautifully kept up. The grass continues beyond the low chain-link fence that encloses the out-field, extending itself on the right-field side into a rougher, feature-less sward that terminates in a low line of distant trees, still showing a pale, early-summer green. We are almost in the country. Our seats are in the seventh row of the grandstand, on the home side of the diamond, about halfway between third base and home plate. The seats themselves are more comforting to spirit than to body, being a surviving variant example of the pure late-Doric Polo Grounds mode: the backs made of a continuous running row of wood slats, divided off by pairs of narrow cast-iron arms, within which are slatted let-down seats, grown arthritic with rust and countless layers of gray paint. The rows are stacked so closely upon each other (one discovers) that a happening on the field of suffi-cient interest to warrant a rise or half-rise to one's feet is often made more memorable by a sharp crack to the kneecaps delivered by the backs of the seats just forward; in time, one finds that a dan-druff of gray paint flakes from the same source has fallen on one's lap and scorecard. None of this matters, for this view and these stands and this park—it is Yale Field, in New Haven—are renowned for their felicity. The grandstand is a low, penumbrous steel-post shed that holds the infield in a pleasant horseshoe-curved embrace.

The back wall of the grandstand, behind the uppermost row of seats, is broken by an arcade of open arches, admitting a soft back light that silhouettes the upper audience and also discloses an overhead bonework of struts and beams supporting the roof—the pigeonland of all the ballparks of our youth. The game we are waiting for—Yale vs. St. John's University—is a considerable event, for it is part of the National Collegiate Athletic Association's northeast regional tournament, the winner of which will qualify for a berth at the national collegiate championships in Omaha in June, the World Series of college baseball. Another pair of teams, Maine and Central Michigan—the Black Bears and the Chippewas—have just finished their game here, the first of a doubleheader. Maine won it, 10–2, but the ultimate winner will not be picked here for three more days, when the four teams will have completed a difficult double-elimination tournament. Good, hard competition, but the stands at Yale Field are half empty today. Call them half full, because everyone on hand—some twenty-five hundred fans—must know something about the quality of the teams here, or at least enough to qualify either as a partisan or as an expert, which would explain the hum of talk and expectation that runs through the grandstand even while the Yale team, in pinstriped home whites, is still taking infield practice.

I am seated in a little sector of senior New Haven men—Townies rather than Old Elis. One of them a couple of rows in front of me says, "They used to fill this place in the old days, before there was all the baseball on TV."

His neighbor, a small man in a tweed cap, says, "The biggest crowd I ever saw in here—the biggest ever, I bet—was for a high-school game. Shelton and Naugatuck, about twenty years ago."

An old gent with a cane, seated just to my left, says, "They filled it up that day the Yankees came here, with Ruth and Gehrig and the rest of them. An exhibition game."

A fan just beyond the old gentleman—a good-looking man in his sixties, with an open, friendly face, a large smile, and a thick stand of gray hair—leans toward my neighbor and says, "When *was* that game, Joe? 1930? 1932?"

"Oh, I can't remember," the old man says. "Somewhere in there. My youngest son was mascot for the Yankees that day, so I could figure it out, I suppose." He is not much interested. His eyes are on the field. "Say, look at these fellows throw!" he says. "Did you see that outfielder peg in the ball?"

"That was the day Babe Ruth said this was about the best-looking ballpark he'd ever seen," the man beyond says. "You remember that."

"I can remember long before this park was built," the old man says. "It was already the Yale ballfield when I got here, but they put in these stands later— Who is this shortstop? He's a hefty-looking bird."

"How many Yale games do you think you've seen, Joe?" the smiling man asks.

"Oh, I couldn't begin to count them. But I haven't seen a Yale team play in—I don't know how long. Not for years. These fellows today, they play in the Cape Cod League in the summers. They let the freshmen play here now, too. They recruit them more, I suppose. They're athletes—you can see that."

The Yale team finishes its warmup ritual, and St. John's—light-gray uniforms with scarlet cap bills and scarlet socks—replaces it on the field.

"St. John's has always had a good club," the old man tells me. "Even back when my sons were playing ball, it was a good ball team. But not as good as this one. Oh, my! Did you see this catcher throw down to second? Did you see that! I bet you in all the years I was here I didn't have twenty fellows who could throw."

"Your sons played here?" I ask him. "For Yale?"

"My son Joe was captain in '41," he says. "He was a pitcher. He pitched against my son Steve here one day. Steve was pitching for Colgate, and my other son, Bob—my youngest—was on the same Colgate team. A good little left-handed first baseman."

I am about to ask how that game turned out, but the old man has taken out a small gold pocket watch, with a hunting case, which he snaps open. Three-fourteen. "Can't they get this *started*?" he says impatiently.

I say something admiring about the watch, and he hands it to me carefully. "I've had that watch for sixty-eight years," he says. "I always carried it in my vest pocket, back when we wore vests."

The little watch has a considerable heft to it: a weight of authority. I turn it over and find an inscription on the back. It is in script and a bit worn, but I can still make it out:

PRESENTED TO JOE WOOD

BY HIS FRIEND A. E. SMITH

IN APPRECIATION OF HIS SPLENDID

PITCHING WHICH BROUGHT THE

WORLD'S CHAMPIONSHIP

TO BOSTON IN 1912.

"Who was A. E. Smith, Mr. Wood?" I ask.

"He was a manufacturer."

I know the rest. Joe Wood, the old gentleman on my left, was the baseball coach at Yale for twenty years—from 1923 to 1942. Before that, he was a sometime outfielder for the Cleveland Indians, who batted .366 in 1921. Before *that*, he was a celebrated right-handed pitcher for the Boston Red Sox—Smokey Joe Wood, who won thirty-four games for the Bosox in 1912, when he finished up with a record of 34-5, pitching ten shutouts and sixteen consecutive victories along the way. In the World Series that fall—one of the two or three finest ever played—he won three of the four games he pitched, including the famous finale: the game of Hooper's catch and Snodgrass's muff and Tris Speaker's killing tenth-inning single. Next to Walter Johnson, Smokey Joe Wood was the most famous fastballer of his era. Still is, no doubt, in the minds of the few surviving fans who saw him at his best. He is ninety-one years old.

None of this, I should explain—neither my presence at the game nor my companions in the stands—was an accident. I had been a fervent admirer of Smokey Joe Wood ever since I read his account of his baseball beginnings and his subsequent career in

Lawrence Ritter's "The Glory of Their Times," a cherished, classic volume of oral history of the early days of the pastime. Mr. Wood was in his seventies when that book was published, in 1966, and I was startled and pleased a few weeks ago when I ran across an article by Joan Whaley, in *Baseball Digest,* which informed me that he was still hale and still talking baseball in stimulating fashion. He was living with a married daughter in New Haven, and my first impulse was to jump in my car and drive up to press a call. But something held me back; it did not seem quite right to present myself uninvited at his door, even as a pilgrim. Then Ron Darling and Frank Viola gave me my chance. Darling, who was a junior at Yale this past year, is the best pitcher ever to take the mound for the Blue. He is better than Johnny Broaca, who went on to pitch for the Yankees and the Indians for five seasons in the mid-nineteen-thirties; he is better than Frank Quinn, who compiled a 1.57 career earned-run average at Yale in 1946, '47, and '48. (He is also a better all-around ballplayer than George Bush, who played first base and captained the Elis in 1948, and then somehow drifted off into politics instead of baseball.) Darling, a right-handed fastball thrower, won eleven games and lost two as a sophomore, with an earned-run average of 1.31, and this year he was 9-3 and 2.42, with eighty-nine strikeouts in his ninety-three innings of work—the finest college pitcher in the Northeast, according to major-league scouts, with the possible exception of Frank Viola, a junior left-handed curveball ace at St. John's, who was undefeated this year, 9–0, and had a neat earned-run average of 1.00. St. John's, a Catholic university in Queens, is almost a baseball powerhouse—not quite in the same class, perhaps, as such perennial national champions or challengers as Arizona, Arizona State, Texas, and Southern California, whose teams play Sun Belt schedules of close to sixty games, but good enough to have gone as the Northeast's representative to the national tournament in Omaha in 1980, where Viola defeated the eventual winner, Arizona, in the first round. St. John's, by the way, does not recruit high-school stars from faraway states, as do most of these rival college powers; all but one player on this year's thirty-three-man Redmen squad grew up and went to school in New York City or in nearby suburbs. This 1981 St. John's team ran off an awesome 31-2 record, capturing the Eastern College Metro (Greater New York, that is) elimination, while Yale, winning its last nine games in a row, concluded its regular season with a record of 24-12-1, which was good enough to win its first Eastern Intercollegiate League championship since 1956. (That tie in Yale's record was a game against the University of Central Florida, played during the Elis' spring-training tour in March, and was called because of darkness after seven innings, with the score tied at 21–21. Darling did not pitch that day.) The two teams, along with Central Michigan (Mid-America Conference) and Maine (New England Conference), qualified for the tournament at New Haven, and the luck of the draw pitted Yale (and Darling) against St. John's (and Viola) in the second game of the opening doubleheader. Perfect. Darling, by the way, had indicated that he might be willing to turn professional this summer if he were to be picked in an early round of the annual amateur draft conducted by the major leagues in mid-June, and Viola had been talked about as a potential big-leaguer ever since his freshman year, so their matchup suddenly became an obligatory reunion for every front-rank baseball scout east of the Ohio River. (About fifty of them turned up, with their speed guns and clipboards, and their glowing reports of the game, I learned later, altered the draft priorities of several clubs.)

Perfect, but who would get in touch with Mr. Wood and persuade him to come out to Yale Field with me for the game? Why, Dick Lee would—Dick Lee, *of course.* Richard C. Lee (he was the smiling man sitting just beyond Smokey Joe in our row) is a former Democratic mayor of New Haven, an extremely popular (eight consecutive terms, sixteen years in office), innovative officeholder who, among other things, presided over the widely admired urban renewal of his city during the nineteen-sixties and, before that, thought up and pushed through the first Operation Head Start program (for minority-group preschoolers) in the country. Dick Lee knows everybody in New Haven, including Smokey Joe

Wood and several friends of mine there, one of whom provided me with his telephone number. I called Lee at his office (he is assistant to the chairman of the Union Trust Company, in New Haven) and proposed our party. "Wonderful!" he cried at once. "You have come to the right man. I'll bring Joe. Count on me!" Even over the telephone, I could see him smiling.

Dick Lee did not play baseball for Yale, but the nature of his partisanship became clear in the very early moments of the Yale-St. John's game. "Yay! " he shouted in a stentorian baritone as Ron Darling set down three St. John's batters in order in the first. "Yay, Ron *baby!*" he boomed out as Darling dismissed three more batters in the second, fanning the last two. "Now *c'mon*, Yale! Let's get something started, gang! Yay!" Lee had told me that he pitched for some lesser-known New Haven teams—the Dixwell Community House sandlot team and the Jewish Home for Children nine (the Utopians), among others—while he was growing up in the ivyless Newhallville neighborhood. Some years later, having passed up college altogether, he went to work for Yale as its public-relations officer. By the time he became mayor, in 1953, the university was his own—another precinct to be worried about and looked after. A born politician, he appears to draw on some inner deep-water reservoir of concern that enables him to preside effortlessly and affectionately over each encounter of his day; he was the host at our game, and at intervals he primed Joe Wood with questions about his baseball past, which he seemed to know almost by heart.

"Yes, that's right, I did play for the Bloomer Girls a few games," Mr. Wood said in response to one such cue. "I was about sixteen, and I was pitching for our town team in Ness City, Kansas. The Bloomer Girls were a barnstorming team, but they used to pick up a few young local fellows on the sly to play along with them if they needed to fill out their lineup. I was one of those. I never wore a wig, though—I wouldn't have done that. I guess I looked young enough to pass for a girl anyway. Bill Stern, the old radio broadcaster, must have used that story about forty times, but he always got it wrong about the wig."

There was a yell around us, and an instantly ensuing groan, as Yale's big freshman catcher, Tony Paterno, leading off the bottom of the second, lined sharply to the St. John's shortstop, who made a fine play on the ball. Joe Wood peered intently out at the field through his thickish horn-rimmed spectacles. He shook his head a little. "You know, I can't hardly follow the damned ball now," he said. "It's better for me if I'm someplace where I can get up high behind the plate. I was up to Fenway Park for two games last year, and they let me sit in the pressbox there at that beautiful park. I could see it all from there. The groundskeeper has got that field just like a living room."

I asked him if he still rooted for the Red Sox.

"Oh, yes," he said. "All my life. A couple of years ago, when they had that big lead in the middle of the summer, they asked me if I'd come up and throw out the first ball at one of their World Series games or playoff games. But then they dropped out of it, of course. Now it looks like it'll never happen."

He spoke in a quiet, almost measured tone, but there was no tinge of disappointment or self-pity in it. It was the voice of age. He was wearing a blue windbreaker over a buttoned-up plaid shirt, made formal with a small dark-red bow tie. There was a brown straw hat on his bald head. The years had imparted a delicate thinness to the skin on his cheeks and neck, but his face had a determined look to it, with a strong chin and a broad, unsmiling mouth. Watching him, I recalled one of the pictures in "The Glory of Their Times"—a team photograph taken in 1906, in which he is sitting cross-legged down in front of a row of men in baggy baseball pants and lace-up, collared baseball shirts with "NESS CITY" across the front in block letters. The men are standing in attitudes of cheerful assurance, with their arms folded, and their mushy little baseball gloves are hanging from their belts. Joe Wood, the smallest player in the picture, is wearing a dark warmup shirt, with the sleeves rolled halfway up his forearms, and his striped baseball cap is pushed back a little, revealing a part in the middle of his hair. There is an intent, unsmiling look on his boyish face—the same grave demeanor you can spot in a subsequent photograph, taken in 1912, in which he is standing beside his Red Sox manager, Jake Stahl, and wearing a heavy woollen three-button suit, a stiff collar, a narrow necktie with a stickpin, and a stylish black porkpie hat pulled low over his handsome, famous face: Smokey Joe Wood at twenty-two. (The moniker, by the way, was given him by Paul Shannon, a sportswriter for the Boston *Post;* before that, he was sometimes called Ozone Wood—"ozone" for the air cleaved by the hapless batters who faced him.) The young man in the photographs and the old man beside me at the ballpark had the same broad, sloping shoulders, but there was nothing burly or physically imposing about him then or now.

"What kind of a pitcher were you, Mr. Wood?" I asked him.

"I had a curve and a fastball," he said. "That's all. I didn't even have brains enough to slow up on the batters. The fastball had a hop on it. You had to be *fast* to have that happen to the ball."

I said that I vividly recalled Sandy Koufax's fastball, which sometimes seemed to jump so violently as it crossed the plate that his catcher had to shoot up his mitt to intercept it.

"Mine didn't go up that far. Just enough for them to miss it." He half turned to me as he said this, and gave me a little glance and an infinitesimal smile. A twinkle. "I don't know where my speed came from," he went on. "I wasn't any bigger or stronger-looking then than I am now. I always could throw hard, and once I saw I was able to get batters out, I figured I was crazy enough to play ball for a living. My father was a criminal lawyer in Kansas, and before that out in Ouray, Colorado, where I first played ball, and my brother went to law school and got a degree, but I didn't even graduate from high school. I ate and slept baseball all my life."

The flow of recollection from Joe Wood was perhaps not as smooth and rivery as I have suggested here. For one thing, he spoke slowly and with care—not unlike the way he walked to the grandstand at Yale Field from the parking lot beyond left field, making his way along the grass firmly enough but looking where he was going, too, and helping himself a bit with his cane. Nothing infirm about him, but nothing hurrying or sprightly, either. For another, the game was well in progress by now, and its principals and sudden events kept interrupting our colloquy. Ron Darling, a poised, impressive figure on the mound, alternated his popping fastballs with just enough down-breaking sliders and an occasional curveball to keep the St. John's batters unhappy. Everything was thrown with heat—his strikeout pitch is a Seaver-high fastball, but his slider, which slides at the last possible instant, is an even deadlier weapon—but without any signs of strain or anxiety. He threw over the top, smoothly driving his front (left) shoulder at the batter in picturebook style, and by the third or fourth inning he had imposed his will and his pace on the game. He was rolling. He is a dark-haired, olive-skinned young man (he lives in Millbury, Massachusetts, near Worcester, but he was born in Hawaii; his mother is Chinese-Hawaiian by birth) with long, powerful legs, but his pitcherlike proportions tend to conceal, rather than emphasize, his six feet two inches and his hundred and ninety-five pounds. He also swings the bat well enough (.331 this year) to play right field for Yale when he isn't pitching; in our game he was the designated hitter as well as the pitcher for the Elis.

"That's a nice build for a pitcher, isn't it?" Joe Wood murmured during the St. John's fifth. Almost as he spoke, Darling executed a twisting dive to his right to snaffle a hard-hit grounder up the middle by Brian Miller, the St. John's shortstop, and threw him out at first. ("Hey-*hey!*" Dick Lee cried. "Yay, Ronnie!") "*And* he's an athlete out there," Wood added. "The scouts like that, you know. Oh, this fellow's a lot better than Broaca ever was."

Frank Viola, for his part, was as imperturbable as Darling on the mound, if not quite as awesome. A lanky, sharp-shouldered lefty, he threw an assortment of speeds and spins, mostly sinkers and down-darting sliders, that had the Yale batters swinging from their shoe tops and, for the most part, hammering the ball into the dirt. He had the stuff and poise of a veteran relief pitcher, and the St. John's infield—especially Brian Miller and a stubby, ebullient second baseman named Steve Scafa—performed behind him with the swift, almost haughty confidence that imparts an elegance and calm and sense of ease to baseball at its best. It was a scoreless game after five, and a beauty.

"What was the score of that game you beat Walter Johnson in, in your big year?" Dick Lee asked our guest between innings.

We all knew the answer, I think. In September of 1912, Walter Johnson came to Fenway Park (it was brand-new that year) with the Senators and pitched against young Joe Wood, who then had a string of thirteen consecutive victories to his credit. That summer, Johnson had established a league record of sixteen straight wins, so the matchup was not merely an overflow, sellout affair but perhaps the most anticipated, most discussed non-championship game in the American League up to that time.

"We won it, 1–0," Joe Wood said quietly, "but it wasn't his fault I beat him that day. If he'd had the team behind him that I did, he'd have set every kind of record in baseball. You have to remember that Walter Johnson played for a second-division team almost all through his career. All those years, and he had to work from the bottom every time he pitched."

"Were you faster than he was?" I asked.

"Oh, I don't think there was ever anybody faster than Walter," he murmured.

"But Johnson said just the opposite!" Dick Lee cried. "He said no one was faster than *you!*"

"He was just that kind of fellow, to say something like that," Wood said. "That was just like the man. Walter Johnson was a great big sort of a pitcher, with hands that came clear down to his knees. Why, the way he threw the ball, the only reason anybody ever got even a foul off him was because everybody in the league knew he'd never come inside to a batter. Walter Johnson was a prince of men—a gentleman first, last, and always."

It came to me that this was the first time I had ever heard anybody use the phrase "a prince of men" in a non-satiric fashion. In any case, the Johnson-Wood argument did not really need settling, then or now. Smokey Joe went on to tie Johnson with sixteen straight victories that season, an American League record, subsequently tied by Lefty Grove and Schoolboy Rowe [and, in 2001, by Roger Clemens]. (Over in the National League that year, Rube Marquard won *nineteen* straight for the Giants—a single-season mark first set by Tim Keefe of the Giants in 1888 and untouched as yet by anyone else.) Johnson and Wood pretty well divided up the A.L. mound honors that summer, when Johnson won thirty-two games and lost twelve, posting the best earned-run average (1.39) and the most strikeouts (three hundred and three), while Wood won the most games and established the best winning percentage with his 34-5 mark (not including his three World Series wins, of course).

These last figures are firmly emplaced in the baseball crannies of my mind, and in the minds of most students of the game, because, it turned out, they represent the autumn of Joe Wood's pitching career as well as its first full flowering. Early in the spring of 1913, he was injured in a fielding play, and he was never near to being the same pitcher again. One of the game's sad speculations over the years has been what Joe Wood's status in the pantheon of great pitchers would be if he had remained sound. I did not need any reminder of his accident, but I had been given one just the same when Dick Lee introduced me to him, shortly before the game. We had stopped to pick up Mr. Wood at his small, red-shuttered white house on Marvel Road, and when he came down the concrete path to join us I got out of Lee's Cadillac to shake the hand that once shook the baseball world.

"Mr. Wood," I said, "this is a great honor."

"Ow—*ow!*" he cried, cringing before me and attempting to extricate his paw.

"Oh, oh... I'm *terribly* sorry," I said, appalled. "Is it—is this because of your fall off the roof?" Three years ago, at the age of eighty-eight, he had fallen off a ladder while investigating a leak, and had cracked several ribs.

"Hell, no!" he said indignantly. "This is the arm I threw out in 1913!"

I felt awful. I had touched history—and almost brought it to its knees.

Now, at the game, he told me how it all happened. "I can't remember now if it was on the road or at Fenway Park," he said. "Anyway, it was against Detroit. There was a swinging bunt down the line, and I went to field it and slipped on the wet grass and went down and landed on my hand. I broke it right here." He pointed to a spot just below his wrist, on the back of his freckled, slightly gnarled right hand. "It's what they call a subperiosteal fracture. They put it in a cast, and I had to sit out awhile. Well, this was in 1913, right after we'd won the championship, and every team was out to get us, of course. So as soon as the cast came off, the manager would come up to me every now and then and want to know how soon I was going to get back to pitching. Well, maybe I got back to it too soon and maybe I didn't, but the arm never felt right again. The shoulder went bad. I still went on pitching, but the fastball had lost that hop. I never threw a day after that when I wasn't in pain. Most of the time, I'd pitch and then it would hurt so bad that I wasn't able to raise my hand again for days afterward. So I was about a halftime pitcher after that. You have to understand that in those days if you didn't work you didn't get paid. Now they lay out as long as they need to and get a shot of that cortisone. But we had to play, ready or not. I was a married man, just starting a family, and in order to get my check I had to be in there. So I pitched."

He pitched less, but not much less well. In 1915, he was 15-5 for the Red Sox, with an earned-run average of 1.49, which was the best in the league. But the pain was so persistent that he sat out the entire 1916 season, on his farm, near Shohala, Pennsylvania, hoping that the rest would restore his arm. It did not. He pitched in eight more games after that—all of them for the Cleveland Indians, to whom he was sold in 1917—but he never won again.

"Did you become a different kind of pitcher after you hurt your arm?" I asked. "More off-speed stuff, I mean?"

"No, I still pitched the fastball."

"But all that pain—"

"I tried not to think about that." He gave me the same small smile and bright glance. "I just loved to be out there," he said. "It was as simple as that."

Our afternoon slid by in a distraction of baseball and memory, and I almost felt myself at some dreamlike doubleheader involving the then and the now, the semi-anonymous strong young men waging their close, marvellous game on the sunlit green field before us while bygone players and heroes of baseball history—long gone now, most of them—replayed their vivid, famous innings for me in the words and recollections of my companion. Yale kept putting men aboard against Viola and failing to move them along; Rich Diana, the husky center fielder (he is also an All-Ivy League half-back), whacked a long double to left but then died on second—the sixth stranded Eli base runner in five innings. Darling appeared to be struggling a little, walking two successive batters in the sixth, but he saved himself with a whirling pickoff to second base—a timed play brilliantly completed by his shortstop, Bob Brooke—and then struck out St. John's big first baseman, Karl Komyathy, for the last out. St. John's had yet to manage a hit against him.

In the home half of the sixth, Yale put its leadoff batter aboard with a single but could not bunt him along. Joe Wood was distressed. "I could teach these fellows to bunt in one minute," he said. "Nobody can't hardly bunt anymore. You've got to get your weight more forward than he did, so you're not reaching for the ball. And he should have his right hand higher up on the bat."

The inning ended, and we reversed directions once again. "Ty Cobb was the greatest bat-handler you ever saw," Wood said. "He used to go out to the ballpark early in the morning with a pitcher and work on hitting the ball to all fields, over and over. He batted that strange way, with his fists apart, you know, but he could have hit just as well no matter how he held it. He just knew what to do with a bat in hand. And baserunning—why, I saw him get on base and steal second, steal third, and then steal home. *The* best. A lot of fellows in my time shortened up on the bat when they had to—

that's what the St. John's boys should try against this good pitcher. Next to Cobb, Shoeless Joe Jackson was the best left-handed hitter I ever saw, and he was always down at the end of the bat until there were two strikes on him. Then he'd shorten up a little, to give himself a better chance."

Dick Lee said, "That's what you've been telling Charlie Polka, isn't it, Joe? "

"Yes, sir, and it's helped him," Wood said. "He's tried it, and now he knows that all you have to do is make contact and the ball will fly a long way."

Both men saw my look of bewilderment, and they laughed together.

"Charlie Polka is a Little League player," Dick Lee explained. "He's about eleven years old."

"He lives right across the street from me," Wood said. "He plays for the 500 Blake team—that's named for a restaurant here in town. I've got him shortened up on the bat, and now he's a hitter. Charlie Polka is a natural."

"Is that how you batted?" I asked.

"Not at first," he said. "But after I went over to Cleveland in 1917 to join my old roommate, Tris Speaker, I started to play the outfield, and I began to take up on the bat, because I knew I'd have to hit a little better if I was going to make the team. I never was any wonder at the plate, but I was good enough to last six more years, playing with Spoke."

Tris Speaker (Wood had called him by his old nickname, Spoke) was the Joe DiMaggio or Willie Mays of the first two decades of this century—the nonpareil center fielder of his day. "He had a beautiful left-handed arm," Joe Wood said. "He always played very shallow in center—you could do that in those days, because of the dead ball. I saw him make a lot of plays to second base from there—pick up what looked like a clean single and fire the ball to second in time to force the base runner coming down from first. Or he could throw the ball behind a runner and pick him off that way. And just as fine a man as he was a ballplayer. He was a Southern gentleman—well, he was from Hubbard, Texas. Back in the early days, when we were living together on the beach at Winthrop during the season, out beyond Revere, Spoke would sometimes cook up a mess of fried chicken in the evening. He'd cook, and then I'd do the dishes."

Listening to this, I sensed the web of baseball about me. Tris Speaker had driven in the tying run in the tenth inning of the last game of the 1912 World Series, at Fenway Park, after Fred Merkle and Chief Meyers, of the Giants, had let his easy foul pop fall untouched between them. A moment or two later, Joe Wood had won his third game of the Series and the Red Sox were champions. My father saw that game—he was at Harvard Law School at the time, and got a ticket somehow—and he told me about it many times. He was terrifically excited to be there, but I think my mother must have relished the famous victory even more. She grew up in Boston and was a true Red Sox fan, even though young women didn't go to many games then. My father grew up in Cleveland, so he was an Indians rooter, of course. In 1915, my parents got married and went to live in Cleveland, where my father began to practice law. Tris Speaker was traded to the Indians in 1916—a terrible shock to Red Sox fans—and Joe Wood came out of his brief retirement to join him on the club a year later. My parents' first child, my older sister, was born in Cleveland late in 1916, and the next year my father went off to Europe—off to the war. My mother once told me that in the summer afternoons of 1917 she would often push a baby carriage past League Park, the Indians' home field, out on Linwood Avenue, which was a block or two away from my parents' house. Sometimes there was a game going on, and if she heard a roar of pleasure from the fans inside she would tell herself that probably Tris Speaker had just done something special. She was lonely in Cleveland, she told me, and it made her feel good to know that Tris Speaker was there in the same town with her. "Tris Speaker and I were traded to Cleveland in the same year," she said.

A yell and an explosion of cheering brought me back to Yale Field. We were in the top of the seventh, and the Yale second baseman and captain, Gerry Harrington, had just leaped high to snatch down a burning line drive—the force of it almost knocked him over backward in midair. Then he flipped the ball to second to double off a St. John's base runner and end the inning. "These fellows came to *play!*" Dick Lee said.

Most no-hitters produce at least one such heaven-sent gift somewhere along the line, and I began to believe that Ron Darling, who was still untouched on the mound, might be pitching the game of his young life. I turned to ask Mr. Wood how many no-hitters he recalled—he had seen Mathewson and Marquard and Babe Ruth (Ruth, the pitcher, that is) and Coveleski and the rest of them, after all—but he seemed transfixed by something on the field. "Look at *that!*" he said, in a harsh, disbelieving way. "This Yale coach has his own coaches out there on the lines, by God! They're professionals—not just players, the way I always had it when I was here. The coach has his own coaches...I never knew that."

"Did you have special coaches when you were coming up with the Red Sox?" I said, hoping to change his mood. "A pitching coach, I mean, or a batting coach?"

He didn't catch the question, and I repeated it.

"No, no," he said, a little impatiently. "We talked about the other players and the pitchers among ourselves in those days. We players. We didn't need anybody to help us."

He was staring straight ahead at the field. I thought he looked a bit chilly. It was well past five o'clock now, and a skim of clouds had covered the sun.

Dick Lee stole a glance at him, too. "Hey, Joe, doesn't this Darling remind you a little of Carl Hubbell on the mound?" he said in a cheerful, distracting sort of voice. "The way he picks up his front leg, I mean. You remember how Hubbell would go way up on the stretch and then drop his hands down by his ankles before he threw the ball?"

"Hubbell?" Joe Wood said. He shook his head, making an effort. "Well, to me this pitcher's a little like that fellow Eckersley," he said slowly. "The way he moves forward there."

He was right. Ron Darling had exactly the same float and glide that the Red Sox' Dennis Eckersley conveys when he is pitching well.

"How do today's players compare with the men you played with, Mr. Wood?" l asked.

"I'd rather not answer that question," he said. He had taken out his watch again. He studied it and then tucked it away carefully, and then he glanced over at me, perhaps wondering if he had been impolite. "That Pete Rose plays hard," he added. "Him and a few more. I don't *like* Pete Rose, exactly, but he looks like he plays the game the way we did. He'd play for the fun of it if he had to."

He resumed his study of the field, and now and then I saw him stare again at the heavyset Yale third-base coach on our side of the diamond. Scoreless games make for a long day at the ballpark, and Joe Wood's day had probably been longer than ours. More than once, I had seen him struggle to his feet to catch some exciting play or moment on the field, only to have it end before he was quite up. Then he would sit down again, leaning on his cane while he lowered himself. I had more questions for Mr. Wood, but now I tried to put them out of my mind. Earlier in the afternoon, he had remarked that several old Yale players had dropped in at his house before the game to say hello and to talk about the old days. "People come by and see me all the time," he had said. "People I don't even know, from as far away as Colorado. Why, I had a fellow come in all the way from Canada the other day, who just wanted to talk about the old days. They all want that, somehow. It's gone on too long."

It had gone on for him, I realized, for as long as most lifetimes. He had played ball for fourteen years, all told, and people had been asking him to talk about it for nearly sixty years. For him, the last juice and sweetness must have been squeezed out of these ancient games years ago, but he was still expected to respond to our amateur expertise, our insatiable vicariousness. Old men are patronized in much the same fashion as athletes; because we take pride in them, we expect their intimacy in return. I had intruded after all.

We were in the eighth now...and then in the ninth. Still no score, and each new batter, each pitch was greeted with clappings and deepening cries of encouragement and anxiety from the stands and the players alike. The close-packed rows hummed with ceaseless, nervous sounds of conversation and speculation—and impatience for the dénouement, and a fear of it, too. All around me in our section I could see the same look of resignation and boredom and pleasure that now showed on my own face, I knew—the look of longtime fans who understand that one can never leave a very long close game, no matter how much inconvenience and exasperation it imposes on us. The difficulty of baseball is imperious.

"Yay! Yay!" Dick Lee cried when Yale left fielder Joe Dufek led off the eighth with a single. "Now come *on,* you guys! I gotta get home for dinner." But the next Yale batter bunted into a force play at second, and the chance was gone. "Well, all right—for *breakfast!*" Lee said, slumping back in his seat.

The two pitchers held us—each as intent and calm and purposeful as the other. Ron Darling, never deviating from the purity of his stylish body-lean and leg-crook and his riding, downthrusting delivery, poured fastballs through the diminishing daylight. He looked as fast as ever now, or faster, and in both the ninth and the tenth he dismissed the side in order and with four more strikeouts. Viola was dominant in his own fashion, also setting down the Yale hitters one, two, three in the ninth and tenth, with a handful of pitches. His rhythm—the constant variety of speeds and location on his pitches—had the enemy batters leaning and swaying with his motion, and, as antistrophe, was almost as exciting to watch as Darling's flair and flame. With two out in the top of the eleventh, a St. John's batter nudged a soft little roller up the first-base line—such an easy, waiting, schoolboy sort of chance that the

Yale first baseman, O'Connor, allowed the ball to carom off his mitt: a miserable little butchery, except that the second baseman, seeing his pitcher sprinting for the bag, now snatched up the ball and flipped it toward him almost despairingly. Darling took the toss while diving full-length at the bag and, rolling in the dirt, beat the runner by a hair.

"Oh, my!" said Joe Wood. "Oh, my, oh, my!"

Then in the bottom of the inning Yale suddenly loaded the bases—a hit, a walk, another walk (Viola was just missing the corners now)—and we all came to our feet, yelling and pleading. The tilted stands and the low roof deepened the cheers and sent them rolling across the field. There were two out, and the Yale batter, Dan Costello, swung at the first pitch and bounced it gently to short, for a force that ended the rally. Somehow, I think, we knew that we had seen Yale's last chance.

"I would have taken that pitch," I said, entering the out in my scorecard. "To keep the pressure on him."

"I don't know," Joe Wood said at once. "He's just walked two. You might get the cripple on the first pitch and then see nothing but hooks. Hit away."

He was back in the game.

Steve Scafa, leading off the twelfth, got a little piece of Darling's first pitch on the handle of his bat, and the ball looped softly over the shortstop's head and into left: a hit. The loudspeakers told us that Ron Darling's eleven innings of no-hit pitching had set a new N.C.A.A. tournament record. Everyone at Yale Field stood up— the St. John's players, too, coming off their bench and out onto the field—and applauded Darling's masterpiece. We were scarcely seated again before Scafa stole second as the Yale catcher, Paterno, bobbled the pitch. Scafa, who is blurrily quick, had stolen thirty-five bases during the season. Now he stole third as well. With one out and runners at the corners (the other St. John's man had reached first on an error), Darling ran the count to three and two and fanned the next batter—his fifteenth strikeout of the game. Two out. Darling sighed and stared in, and then stepped off the mound while the St. John's coach put in a pinch-runner at first—who took off for second on the very next pitch. Paterno fired the ball quickly this time, and Darling, staggering off the mound with his follow-through, did not cut it off. Scafa came ten feet down the third-base line and stopped there, while the pinch-runner suddenly jammed on the brakes, stranding himself between first and second: a play, clearly—an inserted crisis. The Yale second baseman glanced twice at Scafa, freezing him, and then made a little run at the hung-up base runner to his left and threw to first. With that, Scafa instantly broke for the plate. Lured by the vision of the third out just a few feet away from him on the base path, the Yale first baseman hesitated, fractionally and fatally, before he spun and threw home, where Scafa slid past the tag and came up, leaping and clapping, into the arms of his teammates. That was the game. Darling struck out his last man, but a new St. John's pitcher, a right-handed fireballer named Eric Stampfl, walked on and blew the Elis away in their half.

"Well, that's a shame," Joe Wood said, getting up for the last time. It was close to six-thirty, but he looked fine now. "If that man scores before the third out, it counts, you know," he said. "That's why it worked. I never saw a better-played game anyplace—college or big-league. That's a swell ballgame."

Several things happened afterward. Neither Yale nor St. John's qualified for the college World Series, it turned out; the University of Maine defeated St. John's in the final game of the playoffs at New Haven (neither Viola nor Darling was sufficiently recovered from his ordeal to pitch again) and made the trip to Omaha, where it, too, was eliminated. Arizona State won the national title. On June 9th, Ron Darling was selected by the Texas Rangers at the major-league amateur-player draft in New York. He was the ninth player in the country to be chosen. Frank Viola, the thirty-seventh pick, went to the Minnesota Twins. (The Seattle Mariners, who had the first pick this year, had been ready to take Darling, which would have made him the coveted No. 1 selection in the draft, but the club backed off at the last moment because of Darling's considerable salary demands. As it was, he signed with the Rangers for a hundred-thousand-dollar bonus.) On June 12th, the major-league players unanimously struck the twenty-six big-league teams. The strike has brought major-league ball to a halt, and no one can predict when play will resume. Because of this sudden silence, the St. John's-Yale struggle has become the best and most vivid game of the year for me, so far. It may stay that way even after the strike ends. "I think that game will always be on my mind," Ron Darling said after it was over. I feel the same way. I think I will remember it all my life. So will Joe Wood. Somebody will probably tell Ron Darling that Smokey Joe Wood was at the game that afternoon and saw him pitch eleven scoreless no-hit innings against St. John's, and someday—perhaps years from now, when he, too, may possibly be a celebrated major-league strikeout artist—it may occur to him that his heartbreaking 0–1 loss in May 1981 and Walter Johnson's 0–1 loss at Fenway Park in September 1912 are now woven together into the fabric of baseball. Pitch by pitch, inning by inning, Ron Darling had made that happen. He stitched us together.

Takes: Penmen

2002

Fans and writers expect a lot of the players—we're looking for the exceptional, every day, and great quotes after—and we're in need of baseball archetypes, as well. The eccentric reliever has almost held his own here, while other familiar figures—the wise, white-haired manager; the back-country coach (a Kansas City Royals old-timer, talking to me one day about George Brett's line drives, said, "Everything he hits goes through the infield like a stream of milk"), and the boy-phenom slugger or strikeout artist—have been slipping from sight, smoothed into nullity by ESPN, Just for Men, the Bible, and tattoos. Modern-day closers scare you with their heat and size—the storky Robb Nen, the pale and musing Troy Percival, or the camp-trailer-wide Rich Garces—but oddball isn't in their repertory. None of them have startled their teammates in the fashion of Dick Hall, a sidearming righty reliever with Earl Weaver's Orioles in the sixties (and a graduate of Swarthmore), who once whipped out a slide rule during a rain delay and quickly produced a close estimate of the number of raindrops falling within the foul lines at Memorial Stadium. Dennis Eckersley, soon to matriculate at the Hall of Fame, had a unique vocabulary—money was "iron" and booze was "oil," while his "walk-off piece" for the sudden game-ending home run has already gone into the language of baseball—to match his flying hair and flowing, excitable delivery. Roger MacDowell, a prime bullpen prankster and cheerer-upper with the terrific, mid-eighties Mets, once came onto the field at Dodger Stadium with his uniform pants over his head and upper body, his uniform shirt buttoned in place around his legs, his mitt on one foot, his laced-up spikes on his hands, and a stuffed, smiley-face pillow-case head, complete with Mets cap, dangling below: an upside-down ballplayer, ready for action.

The "Nasty Boys" bullpen trio who helped the Cincinnati Reds achieve a World Championship in 1990 featured a cumulative strangeness that could have toured the hard-rock band circuit: Norm Charlton, a strong-jawed, thick-shouldered, silver-blond lefty fastball-forkball-slider dominator (with a degree in Political Science and Religion and Physical Education from Rice University); Rob Dibble, a sullen fastballer whose heater regularly exceeded a hundred miles an hour on the gun (his 12.8 strikeouts-per-nine-innings ratio in 1990 was the highest in baseball history); and closer Randy Myers, the ex-Met longterm subscriber to *Soldier of Fortune* magazine who had only lately stopped wearing camouflage underwear under his uniform.

Dibble was sore about something that October of 1990—I think he felt unrecognized, if that's possible—and talked unceasingly throughout the playoffs (when the Reds eliminated the Pirates, in six games) and the Series sweep over the Oakland Athletics. At those noisy autumn games, it was as if he had been magically piped into some vast underground source of gas, and any reporter whose notebook was running low could pull in at the pump and fill up. When I found him in the clubhouse one night, he was in his customary Mario Lemieux Pittsburgh Penguins game shirt, and ready to spout: "I never ice. I take painkillers—Darvon when I get up, and then Medipren and that Canadian stuff, 2-2-2's. They're all legal. I take them during the day and then I never have to worry about my arm. I come to the park and my arm never hurts at all. I know you're supposed to take food with painkillers, but I never eat breakfast. I throw up blood a lot and then I take a Pepto-Bismol." (Dibble pitched on for five more years, with or without breakfast, and is now visible on summer evenings as a baseball analyst with ESPN. He seems fine—healthy but somehow less interesting.)

Dan Quisenberry, the splendid Kansas City Royals submariner, was eccentric only in his delivery—a swallowlike, harmless-looking thing that rose abruptly from a few inches above dirt-level on the mound, then changed its mind in mid-passage and crossed the plate in a downward glide, just catching a corner of the strike zone as it passed the batter's knees. It was fun to watch and to write about, I found: "His ball in flight suggests the kiddie-ride concession at a country fairgrounds—all swoops and swerves but nothing there to make a mother nervous; standing close to it, your first response is a smile." Batters found him more irritating than amusing: the four-hop ground ball or measly, squirming single was about all they could manage against him, and Quis rode the pitch (and an extremely tough-minded approach to his work) to an eleven-year career, with a 2.76 earned-run average and two hundred and forty-four saves.

Off the field, he was gentle and curious, with signs of a smile always hovering under his pinkish mustache. Plus funny. I still want to commission an embroiderer to make me a wall-sampler out of his "I have seen the future and it's very much like the present, only longer." I wrote a piece about Quis, and then tried to hang around him some more as a friend. When he was getting ready to retire—he finished up with the Cardinals and briefly with the 1990 Giants—he asked me if I thought he could become a poet some day. I was a New York editor and he wanted to know his chances. I said sure, Quis, anything you try will come out great, but in my heart I thought no, never. I didn't want him to run into disappointment.

I was wrong about this, it turned out. Quisenberry stayed on in Kansas City after he'd hung them up—he and his wife and two kids had a nice house in the suburb of Leawood—and his accumulating poems, a hundred of them, came out in a book, "On Days Like This," which was published in 1998, the same year as his unexpected death from a brain tumor. The surprise of his writings was overtaken but not surpassed by the surprise of his departure. As one would expect, there are some good baseball poems in the book, including "Ode to Ben Oglivie," which is addressed to his old Red Sox and Brewers nemesis, who doted on lowball stuff. My favorite Quis poem, though, finds him finished with baseball but not sorry about it. Absolutely himself:

Breakfast of Champions

sat down with the old-timers
the 80-year-old hall-of-famer
tellin a story about a dinner
honoring black kids and
him bein the only goddam rebel around

and the other fella who hit that
homerun forty years ago
that everyone heard about
he said the park wasn't
no bigger than this café

and the guy chewin on bacon
a three-sport letterman at LSU
played big league ball 18 years
managed another seven
spoke of sharpening his cleats
and fightin in the clubhouse
talked with his mouth full

i listened, stared at their gnarled hands
ate my granola
carved the cantaloupe
drank skim milk
and ordered some more decaf
told no stories

Takes: Payback

2002

Jack Buck, the veteran Cardinals announcer, died the other day, and when the news came I instantly flashed back to a summer evening in 1988, when he nailed me to the mast. We'd run into each other at Shea Stadium before a Cardinals-Mets game, and he asked if I'd mind doing five minutes on the radio with him, just before the first pitch. I agreed, of course—we were friends of long standing—and once the interview began I was gratified when he quickly mentioned that I had a new baseball book out. He went on a bit about my baseball smarts and my deft ways in turning the midsentence pivot, and I thanked him.

Then he said, "Roger, I enjoyed your writing, as always, but I thought there were places in this book where you got sort of long."

Excellent, I thought: the man isn't just strewing roses here. What a pro! I laughed and said well, perhaps I did sometimes get caught up in a game story and let it run on a bit.

"Yes, I know," Buck said, "but this was different. Sometimes your book seemed really, really long to me."

Puzzled, I tried to keep the smile in my voice (we were on the air), but looked at him with fresh attention. Interesting, I said carefully. Maybe I did need to go back and look at some of these chapters again.

"Yes, maybe, you should," he said, glistening with delight. "A good book, of course, but a real long one."

What was this? A famous broadcaster and a so-called friend knifing me out in the open like this? Skewering a pal, laying him bare before an audience of millions? My mouth opened but only a strangled sound came out. Then the light went on. I fell back in my chair, while Jack aimed a silent "Gotcha!" pistol at my head and pulled the trigger. He wrapped up the interview in friendly fashion, and told his Cardinals fans he'd be right back. They would never know what this had been about, but we did.

The previous summer, I had written a *New Yorker* piece about the Baseball Hall of Fame, at Cooperstown, which had ended with a description of the 1987 Induction Day ceremonies. Catfish Hunter, Billy Williams, and the great Negro Leagues infielder Ray Dandridge were admitted, and Jack Lang, of the New York *Daily News,* had been voted in as the winner of the J.G. Taylor Spink Award for old scribes. "The sun shone," I wrote "and the speeches and encomiums were sweet and boring and almost not too long. The Commissioner reminded us that Catfish Hunter had played for both Charles Finley and George Steinbrenner (they were both there, down front with the V.I.P.s), which was enough in itself, he said, to put a man into the Hall of Fame. Jack Lang was teary, and Jack Buck (the voice of the Cardinals, who received the Ford C. Frick Award for his long career in baseball broadcasting) was lengthily grateful...."

Jack Buck's pleasure in the baseball instant—the sudden chance perceived—was unsurpassed, and once on the air, of course, he was just right. Never long.

Wings of Fire

1998

Pity the pitchers. Fences in the new ballparks have crept closer; weight work and nutritional supplements and steroids are beefing up the batters to Schwarzeneggerian proportions, while the strike zone, as called by umpires bending low to follow the down-dropping split-finger pitch, has shrivelled to doily size, with its bottom hem almost at ankle level, exactly where the hitters want it. Mark McGwire, the Cardinals' pink-bearded basher, may have struck the tonal chord for this young 1998 season when he rapped a home run in each of his team's first four games. (Only Willie Mays had ever done this before.) Or was it Junior Griffey hitting a pair of two-run homers in two successive games against the Red Sox?

If the sport has needed a balancing figure to represent the other side of things—the sweating, embattled view from the mound, that is—it has found him, cast in bronze, in the person of Bret Saberhagen, a fourteen-year veteran right-hander who began this season for the Red Sox in brisk fashion, rushing off to a 4-0 record in his first four starts, with a league-leading 1.96 earned-run average. Saberhagen has been a known high-quality performer, to be sure, winning two Cy Young Awards while with the Royals in the eighties, but all this appeared to have ended for him three years ago, when, pitching for the Colorado Rockies, he blew out his shoulder in devastating fashion, severing a group of ligaments collectively known as the capsule—a horrific pitching injury never previously encountered in the profession. David Altchek, a distinguished New

York orthopedist who also serves as team physician to the Mets, performed a complex two-hour restorative surgery but warned Saberhagen, who is thirty-four, not to expect to resume his career. Saberhagen would have none of that, and now, after two years of almost unimaginable rehabilitation, he has come back all the way, and then some. His triumph makes a point not only about athletic perseverance but about the hazards and chronic anxieties that afflict all pitchers these days—their rising numbers on the disabled list, an across-the-board increase in arm and shoulder breakdowns and surgeries, the postponed or cancelled careers of some once-promising rookie flingers, and the departure of so many worn-down older mound stars from their accustomed place in the middle of things. The list of high-priced surgical patients restored to action this season also includes Hideo Nomo, the Dodger fireballer, who was pitching again after an off-season elbow operation; David Cone, who had shoulder repairs for the second time in two years; and John Smoltz, of the famously durable Braves rotation, who had bone chips and calcium deposits removed from his elbow. Others were not so lucky. On almost every morning during spring training, those little agate lines in the back columns of the sports pages would carry pitching news that made you wince or sigh. Bryan Harvey, a nine-year relief ace with the Angels and the Marlins, threw one pitch, felt something pop in his surgically repaired shoulder, and ended his comeback on the spot. Roger McDowell, a redoubtable reliever and charmer, once of the Mets, announced his retirement after undergoing three shoulder surgeries in the past two years, while the towering Ben McDonald, once a local hero in Baltimore, was released by the Brewers after a nine-year career replete with injuries and rehabs. And Jose Rijo, a fiery M.V.P. in the 1990 World Series, who has endured five arm and shoulder operations in the past three years, got an O.K. from the Reds to start throwing again, but carefully. When Opening Day came along, there were forty-four officially disabled pitchers on the team rosters, with most of them in various degrees of recovery from elbow or shoulder invasions.

Pitchers everywhere were talking about their arms this spring. Jeff Brantley, an exuberant reliever whom I encountered just after he had thrown in a little B-game for the Cardinals at their new camp, in Jupiter, Florida, happily waggled his ice-bagged arm for me, because last year he could barely use it. His forty-four saves for the Reds tied for most in the National League in 1996, but he hurt too much after that to keep up. When Dr. James Andrews, a celebrated orthopedic surgeon in Birmingham, Alabama, opened his shoulder last June, he determined that Brantley had been pitching with a torn labrum (a shoulder cartilage) for at least the past five years. "When you go out to pitch, you pitch," Brantley told me. "You can throw through soreness—I pitched great. There's a certain amount of uncomfortability that you're going to have to overcome. The amount of damage you do depends on how long you're going to get the money and how much money you're going to get. When the ninth inning comes along, you just go out there and suck it up. My arm was sore, it hurt front and back, and when the time came when I couldn't throw anymore I knew it was time to go for surgery. I couldn't move it at all. It would get out to here"—he pointed in midair, as if hailing a cab—"and just stop." He laughed.

Al Leiter, the dashing thirty-two-year-old lefty starter who came over to the Mets this year, told me that there was pain and then there was normal soreness. He should know: he is a hard thrower who runs up a lot of strikeouts and bases on balls. Last fall, he started the seventh game of the World Series for the Florida Marlins and fanned seven batters while holding the Indians to two runs; the Marlins won the classic in eleven innings.

"There are times now that I'm older when I feel a twinge or two," Leiter said, "but you just block that out. You've gotta get that man out, you know. You can't walk off the mound."

What was normal soreness, I wanted to know.

"Normal soreness comes the day you pitch and the day after. It's achy-sore. It feels like somebody punched you in the arm about fifty times."

I had to talk to Rick Honeycutt by phone: he was home in Tennessee this spring—out of baseball, after twenty years in the majors. He is a left-hander, with a ducking screwball, and for the past decade he had been a highly respected late-innings specialist; he appeared in eighteen post-season games for the successful 1988–92 Oakland Athletics. With the Cardinals last year, he was sidelined for the entire season, and after he decided to hang up his spikes he underwent surgery to prepare him for everyday life: a ligament transplant in his left elbow that would free him up to open doors, drive a car, and play a little golf again.

Honeycutt paused when I asked how many operations he had required in all. "Let's see," he said. "Maybe it's four—you sort of lose track. Most shoulder surgeries are only for wear and tear. But I was a sinker-slider guy and I threw it both ways." He meant that he rotated his wrist clockwise in mid-pitch, which is natural for lefties, and also rotated it to the left—the screwball delivery, which is not. "I was torquing it from the inside out and also from the outside in, and that's hard on your arm."

As I pressed Honey for details—I was beginning to feel like another resident on "E.R."—he seemed anxious to assure me that he hadn't been hurting every day. "I lived on medication pretty much," he said. "I took anti-inflammatories like Indocin and Volteran—you can't mix those with Advil, you know—and maybe some cortisone now and then. One year I think I had seven or eight cortisone shots." Honeycutt spoke without bitterness or irony; none of the pitchers I talked to sounded surprised about their travails. He was missing the game a great deal—"having my withdrawal," as he put it—and Brantley, as I have noted, had been ecstatic to be back throwing again. When I suggested to Al Leiter that his was one of the few million-dollar professions that could end without warning, in the space of a single pitch, he agreed. "The only parallel," he offered, "would be going down in a corporate helicopter crash."

The rap on present-day pitchers is that they don't work often enough, don't stay out there very long, can't throw strikes, and won't cut loose with the fastball; they also break down, get too much money, listen only to their agents, and aren't anything like our memories of Ol' (fill in blank), who threw eight or nine innings every fourth day, and lasted with the home club for twenty years. Those were the days.

Well, maybe. Baseball is never as simple as we think it has been, and the present arms crisis is stuffed with more than the usual paradoxes and contradictions. One general manager told me that he wonders whether the pitchers aren't throwing the same number of pitches over their lifetimes that they used to but in a different pattern: far fewer while they're growing up, and a lot more later, when better conditioning and high salaries keep them on in the game. Yes, pitchers pitch in a five-man rotation now, and expect to go five or maybe six innings per start; and relievers have specialties, which include long and middle relief, setup man, and closer. They are not failed or second-level starters, as they were in the old days, I mean; most of them have been working at their own quirky line since high school. Everyone in baseball is aware of Greg Maddux and Tom Glavine and Smoltz and the rest of that fabulously successful Braves rotation, but it was the 1996 World Champion Yankees who established once again that a deep and various relief corps can be as important as the guys you start with. What this means in psychic terms is that all the pitchers—starters, relievers, closers—expect to go at top gear all the time.

What you notice on the tube in so many games nowadays is that the mild old situations of baseball have become claustrophobic, and that the pitchers appear to be working in a condition of prolonged semi-crisis. They attack that little strike zone with fastballs—sometimes up in the nineties on the clock—and also lean heavily upon the high-risk slider (high risk for arms, that is) and a variety of other pitches as well, which they try not to throw for strikes, in the hope that the batter will make an out on a pitch he should have left alone. The split-finger fastball and the circle change—so called because it's thrown with the pitcher's forefinger and thumb making a circle (the traditional "O.K." sign)—are the current flings du jour. Many of these diving, pausing sorts of pitches will be taken for a ball, or nubbed or bonked for a foul, running up the count, slowing the game, and making the middle-aged fan long for Tom Seaver's or Vida Blue's old high-riding fastball through the upper story of the strike zone.

Those days won't come back. David Cone, the Yankee ace, told me that he'd been watching videos of old-time games and had been amazed by the way pitchers looked then. "That real high leg kick, the fluid motion, the higher mounds, the higher strike zone—why, Yogi Berra was almost standing up, it looked like," he said. "All that had such an impact on how pitchers pitched."

The mound was lowered from its official fifteen inches to ten after the 1968 season, in order to cheer up the hitters: that was the year Bob Gibson put together an earned-run average of 1.12 in the National League and only one hitter, Carl Yastrzemski, reached the .300 level in the American. Cone describes the present strike zone as being side-to-side, when it used to be up-and-down, and believes that the lower mound requires pitchers to risk arm damage as they stride out and reach out farther in their deliveries in order to move the ball within its low target area. "That's got to be more stress on your joints," he said. Other pitchers agree, including Rick Honeycutt, who also believes that many contemporary mounds aren't properly kept up or given the ideal front slope, with the same detrimental result that Cone mentioned. Honeycutt's solution to the aching-arm syndrome is to have the leagues appoint Nolan Ryan to the post of official mound supervisor. "Wherever Nolan went, the mounds were great," he said.

The typical young pitcher (call him Tip) out there right now is bigger than Tom Seaver or Vida Blue, and is possibly in better shape than they were; he works all year round at his isometrics and stretching exercises, his light-weights regimen and elastic-tube repetitions (which will build up the rotator cuff to resist injury). He is looked after by a corps of professional trainers, dietitians, and orthopedists unimagined twenty years ago, who have recourse to a battery of expensive weight machines, digitalized images of Tip in action (a stick figure pitching on the screen, seen from above, from in front, from the side), and the magnetic-resonance-imaging machine, which is the critical resource of contemporary sports medicine. Tip is a valuable property, and he knows it. He wants nothing to do with the good old days; he has heard those horror stories, even from some of the older pitchers on his own team, and he has seen the zipperlike monster scars on the shoulders and chests and elbows of some of his team's immortals as they were changing into their uniforms before Old Timers' Day.

I know the stories, too; I heard them everywhere this spring. Ben McDonald, pitching at the age of seventeen for his Louisiana high-school team in a state semifinal, threw two hundred and ten pitches in a fourteen-inning game; the next afternoon, he was summoned back in relief in the third inning. In 1989, Al Leiter, then a Yankee, threw a hundred and sixty-two pitches at the Stadium against the Twins on a cold April night; Leiter says his manager, Dallas Green, told him that he'd wanted to "stretch him out" a little. Leiter broke down in his second start after that, and underwent rotator-cuff surgery in early September. "He stretched me out, all right," Leiter said to me in Florida. Doc Gooden, no longer the free-throwing Lochinvar of that glorious 24-4 season in 1985, was kept in a chilly afternoon Mets game against the Expos in April of 1991 (I was there) for more than a hundred and forty pitches; the Mets' manager, Bud Harrelson, explained that he had kept Gooden in the game because he was still at full velocity. Doc required labrum and rotator-cuff repairs early in September, and did not pitch again that year. There is darker stuff as well—whispers of gothic hurts which skim about the clubhouse like wraiths. Gil Patterson, a legendary fast-balling prospect with the Yankees in the mid-seventies, had eight operations on his pitching arm, then turned around and learned to throw left-handed; in the tale, he got it up to 85 m.p.h. on the gun from that side but unaccountably had trouble with his control.

Tip is lucky, because his manager and general manager certainly aren't going to risk his future on a single big-game stretch-out (except, just possibly, with some club, late in September or early in October, in a set of innings that his team really needs to win to stay in this particular playoff chase or championship playoff or—wow!—the World Series at last). And if Tip should run into hard times and feel something sharp and nasty chewing at his shoulder or his elbow—an insult confirmed and clarified by the M.R.I.—the surgery he receives will be swift and expert and, in all likelihood, arthroscopic: a little window-hole fix-up or clean-out to ward off more serious trouble down the line.

Good, but why does Tip break down at all? Why, just two years ago, did all three of the Mets' arriving prodigy pitchers—Jason Isringhausen, Paul Wilson, and Bill Pulsipher—come crashing down with disabling injuries? Why did an equally spectacular rookie foursome of the early nineties—the Athletics' Todd Van Poppel, Don Peters, Kirk Dressendorfer, and David Zancanaro, first-round draft choices all—come to so little in the majors? Where are the Bob Fellers and Warren Spahns and Bob Gibsons of this generation? Where's the next Roger Clemens or Nolan Ryan coming from? How do they differ from Tip, over there, icing his arm in front of his locker?

They were older, for one thing—in years or in bodies, or both—when they made it up to the show. Feller, it's true, was only seventeen when he joined the Indians, in 1936, and began vaporizing American League batters, but he had come straight off his father's farm in Van Meter, Iowa, and already had the physique of a field hand. Bob Gibson, a great athlete, played for the Harlem Globetrotters before he got to the Cardinals. Spahn went off to the Army in 1943 and didn't pitch his first full year for the Boston Braves until he was twenty-six. Nolan Ryan had put in more than five hundred innings, over five seasons, by the time he turned twenty-five, but it was late in the day before he got that powerful and elegant motion put together—"beautiful mechanics," in the parlance—and began striking out three hundred batters a year (and walking two hundred more) for the Angels. Roger Clemens—well, Roger is a tree. (Just stand next to him: you'd need to count rings.)

All these past and imminent Hall of Famers had powerful legs as well as powerful arms—legs you wouldn't believe if you'd grown up in a mall, like today's strong, frail athletes.

I have heard gruff old scouts complain that today's young pitchers would never be capable of the brutal self-punishment of a Clemens, who rebuilt himself in amazing fashion before the 1997 season, his fourteenth in the majors, in preparation for his 21-7 year with the Blue Jays and a fourth Cy Young, or of a Steve Carlton, the dominating recent Phillies left-hander, who used to twist his arm repeatedly in a container filled with uncooked rice as a means of keeping his forearm tuned up to the demands of his killer slider, but this charge feels unfair. No, where the newcomers fall short, through no fault of their own, is in athletic ability. There simply aren't enough prime arms to go around: thanks to expansion, there are at least a hundred and fifty pitchers now on big-league rosters who would otherwise be toiling in the semi-obscurity of the minors. Meantime, the always limited number of teen-age genius athletes—the same Superbods who once went only into professional baseball—can contemplate a vastly expanded sports market, where fabulous careers in football, basketball, hockey, tennis, golf, track and field, and, yes, soccer are also available to them. Only a handful of them still pick the old pastime.

Both the Athletics and the Mets have given intense thought to the multiple setbacks of their celebrated young hopefuls, and although the soul-searchings continue, neither club has been able to find a flaw in its overall program. Rather, each came to the conclusion that some of these great prospects had arrived with prior damage to their arms, or were at deep risk because of inbred awkwardnesses in their deliveries—poor mechanics. These young men were treated with extravagant care, but, like so many of their contemporaries, they missed the standard five or six years' seasoning in the minors that they could have expected a few decades ago. Most players who make it to the majors now get there after two or three years in minor-league ball at best, where, if they are pitchers, they have been handled with particular tenderness. When they reach the majors, they find themselves under the gun, with unpredictable results. The A's president, Sandy Alderson, pointed out to me that the risk actually goes up if they are extremely talented, because great young pitchers who get to throw a lot of major-league innings when they are in their early twenties are the ones most likely to suffer a career-ending or altering serious injury—Doc Gooden and Fernando Valenzuela, for instance. Indeed, he said, projecting the fate of brilliant young pitchers, who are scouted everywhere while they're still in high school, has become so chancy that more and more clubs are passing them up in the early rounds of the draft, because of the breakdowns and the money wasted in their signing and development. Those three young Mets suffered different turns of ill fortune, for reasons beyond anyone's control. Isringhausen, who throws (or threw) a high-risk knuckle-curve, had suffered prior damage to his medial collateral ligament, and it was operated on in January; he also broke his pitching hand while irritably smashing a trash container after a bad performance last April. Then he was found to have tuberculosis. Still on the Mets' long-term D.L., he is back home in Illinois and is undergoing rehab. Paul Wilson, a composed, strikingly handsome right-hander, had an uncommon reaction to minor arthroscopic shoulder surgery two years ago, which began to limit his ability to throw. He had a bad scare in early March this year, in a B-game down at Port St. Lucie, when severe pain kicked up in the same place in his shoulder. Everyone there was struck dumb, suspecting the worst, an end to his career, but an M.R.I., up in New York, revealed that some adhesions around his scar had torn loose, and that he would be all right, after all. I was on hand the morning he came back into camp, and the clubhouse hugs and yells and the look on the clubhouse faces—from the batboys to the coaches and managers and even the writers—made it like Christmas.

Dr. Altchek, who is forty-one and has the long chest and eager look of a young reliever, told me that the incidence of surgery-inducing injuries is greater among young pitchers than among professional football players, and also that pitching is a more violent activity for the elbow and the shoulder than anything experienced in football. "The minor-league-to-major-league structure is a pyramid, and what's involved for the players within it is a real Darwinian process," he said. "A lot of kids I get to see are enormously talented, but they can't hold up. It isn't their talent that breaks down—it's their bodies. It takes a unique combination of talent and body-fibre type to make it all the way." Pulse—Bill Pulsipher—broke down: I saw it happen two years ago at Port St. Lucie, when he came out of a game in mid-inning, holding his left arm to one side in an awkward way, and with a mixed look of pain and anger and disbelief on his face. I can't say I was surprised, for I had first seen his cavalry-charge pitching style in Pittsfield, in the Class A New York-Penn League, in 1992, when he was eighteen. Lanky and glowering, he threw left-handed heat with a flurrying sidearm rush of arms and legs that blew away the batters and made you laugh and gasp at the same time. You looked forward to seeing him again, up the line in baseball, but rather thought it wouldn't happen. Moving along in the minors, he ran into elbow damage—a partial medial-collateral-ligament tear that had begun at some earlier point. He rested the elbow over the 1995–96 off-season, but completed the injury when he impetuously decided to air out his arm in that spring game. Dr. Andrews, the Birmingham specialist who did the Brantley procedure, performed a replacement operation on Pulsipher (a Tommy John innovation pioneered by Dr. Frank Jobe, of Los Angeles), removing a tendon from his forearm and stitching it into place inside the elbow. Pulse went into rehabilitation for a full year, and suffered a difficult sort of season last summer. Pitching in games at four minor-league levels, from Rookie League to Class AAA, he encountered inordinate, baffling problems with his control—thirty-eight bases on balls in twenty-four innings at Norfolk, for instance. Cautiously, the Mets' coaches were trying to calm down his delivery a little, hoping to save a potentially great career by easing his explosive ways out there. He also consulted Dr. Allan Lans, a psychiatrist who directs the Mets Employee Assistance Program.

It came out that Pulsipher was suffering from anxiety brought about by his lack of control and by the odd way his new arm was performing. Nothing felt right to him. He couldn't grip the ball right, he couldn't find where to release it, he couldn't pick up the catcher. Lans put him on Prozac. Pulse had a terrific spring this time, giving up only two runs over the sixteen innings he worked, and when I talked to him once again in Port St. Lucie he was energetic in speech, as before—eager to get on with it, man. He has reddish, narrow features, and an almost theatrical burning gaze. "My control problems weren't all in my arm," he said at once. "I had something going on in my head at the same time. Now I'm taking Prozac. I've changed my motion—I'm not slinging it so much from the side. It feels normal now, and the way I used to throw doesn't. When I got hurt, it wasn't because I was overexcited. I just had an injury. If I'd had better mechanics, it might not have happened. Anyway, I'm still a young man."

Pulse was sent back to Norfolk when the spring season ended. He was upset about it, of course, but the Mets had laid on a new fifth starter, from Japan, Masato Yoshii, and there wasn't another starter's slot available. The coaches assured Pulsipher that this was the right step for him; they wanted to "get Norfolk out of his biography," as they put it. He is expected back, perhaps late this summer, and everyone on the Mets is pulling for him.

Eager young pitchers need a lot of luck just now—most of all in the people who are in charge of their careers. Bob Apodaca, the Mets' pitching coach, may be just the right fit for Pulsipher, not only because he is unblustery in manner—he has a dark, thoughtful gaze and speaks with a teacher's precision—but because he specializes in slowing things down. Last year, when the Mets surprised themselves and everyone else with their strong third-place finish in the powerful National League East, Apodaca turned around several careers among the Mets' hurlers, often by urging a little less heat, a little more patience. He taught a changeup to the fastballer Dave Mlicki, and now he is working on the same thing with Al Leiter. "Farters and grunters" is his term for full-bore, maximum effort pitchers like these, and now the two can even laugh at themselves a little.

"You try to educate pitchers, but you also observe," Apodaca told me. Describing the proper, elbow-saving delivery for a slider, he said, "You don't want to pare it like an orange, you want to slice it," and it came to me later that every Mets pitcher probably carries this poster-clear image in his mind now. Apodaca seemed calm about the Isringhausen-Wilson-Pulsipher debacle. "The list of these injuries goes on everywhere," he said. "It's nothing that we're teaching. It's an industry-wide problem."

Speaking of Pulse, he said, "You don't tinker with natural ability. Pulsipher doesn't land with a nice, closed foot, he lands on an open foot. We're not going to change that, but we've got a better handle on the pacing of his delivery and the calmness of it. He had that quick, violent delivery that almost forced his fastball into a slider, pitch after pitch. He was getting around the ball, which puts such a strain on the elbow. Now he can do everything with a baseball, because we're not interested in where it's going when it crosses the plate but how he delivers it. Stay within your strength. Be sound mechanically."

Apodaca sounded so reasonable that I said something about how these pitching problems—all these pains and breakdowns—looked like a dark cloud that might go away someday, but he wasn't optimistic.

"I don't think we're going to see any end to it, because these kids are so strong and so violent," he said. "The combative strain is always there. It's such a violent act to throw a baseball. There isn't a machine invented by man that can duplicate the G-force that's initiated by the arm action of a throw. We're asking their bodies to absorb this, but it's in their genes to throw hard. We're always going to see shoulder injuries and elbow injuries, as long as there is baseball, and we're going to go right on making the surgeons rich."

The Bard in the Booth

1999

There are baseball fans, it must be admitted, who don't like
Tim McCarver's stuff. After they've listened to the celebrated baseball analyst working another World Series game, say, or a Fox
Saturday Baseball Game of the Week, or a WNYW Yankees game,
with Bobby Murcer, or, before that for many years, a Mets yawner
or triumph with Ralph Kiner as sidekick, certain friends of mine
have found fault. A few of them sound apologetic about it, as if
they have failed Tim somehow; others plain can't stand him. Because I don't understand any of this, I have been at pains to listen
to their whinings, which can be easily summarized: Tim McCarver
likes to talk. He laughs and enjoys himself at ballgames. He makes
jokes—puns, even. He uses fancy words. He's excitable—he gets
carried away by the baseball. He's always going on and on about
some little thing. He thinks he knows how the game should be
played. He knows too much.

Well, yes. Tim McCarver loves to talk. He is the only person I
know who says "albeit" out loud ("That drive also reached the left-
field stands, albeit about a hundred feet lower"). He also says
"ergo" and "to reiterate" quite a lot, and is a master of the sub-
junctive mid-sentence tense-switch: "Had he broken for the ball
immediately, he makes the play." Quotes from Milton or Shake-
speare arrive without preamble—not just easy sporting tropes like
"tomorrow and tomorrow and tomorrow" or "Cry 'Havoc!' and
let slip the dogs of war" but a mid-game "Love's Labor's Lost"

dredging, "Mirth cannot move a soul in agony," which he once produced, extempore, to describe Cubs players during a losing streak.

The answer to another, more abstract rap on Tim—"He's so smart, who does he think he is, anyway?"—isn't as easy, but, if pressed, the man himself might murmur that he's a pretty fair noticer.

"The last thing Hank Aaron always did before he stepped into the batter's box was to clear his throat," McCarver said to me not long ago. "He went 'h'cch…h'mm'—a little double cough that only the umpire and catcher could pick up. You heard it every time. The only other player who did that was Mike Schmidt, the great Phillies third baseman, and he made exactly the same sound. Two Hall of Fame sluggers with the same trademark. Isn't that remarkable?"

McCarver caught his first major-league game for the Cardinals in 1959, at the age of seventeen, and played his last with the Phillies in 1980, but contemporary fans can be forgiven if they sometimes view his intervening nineteen-hundred-odd games with the Cards and Phillies (with brief stopovers at the Expos and Red Sox) as no more than a useful warmup for his real career. During the countless TV hours I have spent in his company over the past sixteen or seventeen years of regular (I was going to say "non-stop") Mets and Yankees listening, I have rarely heard him mention his own appearances in a couple of All-Star Games, his participation in three League Championship series, or the three World Series he played in (he batted .478 for the winning Cardinals in the 1964 Series, against the Yankees, and won the fifth game with a tenth-inning three-run homer); when he does bring back some particular two-and-two Bob Gibson slider he called for or an ancient, still chewable bases-loaded contretemps, it is only to elucidate the game at hand, the one he is talking about. Aaron's little cough came up in a conversation this spring, when he was extolling the catcher's front-row view of things. "For a catcher, you know, everything is so crystal clear," he said. "As a broadcaster, you see the game the same way he does, only a couple of stories higher."

The catcher-commentator hookup pleased him, and his voice went up a notch or two, sliding into the alto as he went on about his job. "Where else do you get the opportunity to talk about what your mind has preserved?" he said. "Every little thing you've seen or noticed—you have no idea how much you're storing. It's instinct for me to watch where the center fielder is playing, depending on the count on the batter. Curt Flood, our center fielder on the Cardinals, used to quiz me about our pitchers and the signs I'd put down and where I'd set up behind the batter with each count and situation. I can see myself looking out at Curt Simmons"—a veteran left-handed pitcher on the same club—"and there in the background is Flood in motion, slipping toward the right-center-field gap with the pitch. He did this every time, he moved with every pitch. You know, I haven't said this yet"—said it on the air, he meant—"but the center fielder is the only defensive player who never sets up straight away. He puts himself off one shoulder or the other of the pitcher, in order to get that jump. The only exception is Ken Griffey, Jr.—the only one I've ever seen who gets away with that." Later on, in the telecast of a Mariners-Yankees game I caught a few days after this conversation, McCarver made this exact point about Griffey.

The little colloquy is pure Tim. A subject, the catcher's view of things, yields a theme—catchers and pitchers and center fielders—with illustrative variations, followed by a refurbished baseball truth that one somehow hasn't quite noticed before (center fielders don't set up straight away), and a closing vivid exception or lesson (Griffey is unique). The narrator's happiness in pursuing the point has enticed you along, and you feel wiser and somehow younger as a result. McCarver, trim at fifty-seven, has a catcher's classic strong jaw and thick hands, and looks to be in good enough shape to catch a late inning or two in an emergency, but it is his voice that slips into uniform in mid-game. He is affable and charming, but his youthful, excitable tone, which still shows touches of his native

Tennessee—"Lahn drahve!"—when he is running down a play or an idea, is one of the star turns of modern sport.

Baseball is the ultimate one-thing-then-another-thing diversion, and what you want for a companion in its meanderings is a man who enjoys the slow parts as much as the rapids. I can still bring back McCarver's thrilled, precise reportings from the Astrodome during the agonizing Mets-Astros National League Championship's sixth game there in 1986, and when I dropped this lure before him the other day he sprang after it in characteristic fashion. But then, shifting, he brought up another kind of game— a Mets-Braves night meeting in Atlanta, on July 4, 1985—which remains his own favorite Mets disorder. "July 4th and 5th, actually," he said.

"Gooden started. Double rain delay. Keith Hernandez batted for the cycle. Their pitcher, Rick Camp, ties it with a home run in the bottom of the eighteenth—his only major-league home run. Then the Mets win with five runs—they still hold the record for most runs scored in the top of the nineteenth inning. Ted Turner shot off the fireworks at three-fifty-eight in the morning. There was a Shriners' convention in Atlanta that day, and when we get back to the hotel at something like four-forty in the morning their motor scooters were parked in the lobby. Bizarre!"

Only later did it come to me that Tim and his fellow Mets broadcasters had to have kept talking for the better part of eight hours that night—a trek he had brought back for me all in italics.

Early each year, in this recurring winter dream, I find myself strapped down on a table in the Baseball Laboratory, with an iron cap affixed to my head and electrodes hooked up to my toes and torso, while Dr. Pretorius, the mad scientist, bustles about in his white coat, pushing buttons and pulling levers that will deliver the most recent shocks and jolts of baseball news to my quivering psyche. "Shall ve begin?" he said in the latest episode, back last March, as he consulted his giant clipboard and punched in the latest horrid

data. "Ready? Herr Mo Vaughn has left the Red Sox. He is ein Anaheim Angel now."

He flipped a giant switch, completing the circuit into my fan-
brain. Bells clanged, blinding bolts of static crackled upward, and
an array of instrument needles swung into the red. A thin curl of
smoke arose from my left ear, but I didn't blink or stir. "Hmm,"
murmured Dr. P., regarding me contemptuously. "Is this lab animal
kaput?" Further spirit-sapping trials were zapped into me—David
Wells had left the Yankees; the umpires were filing a labor grievance
to protest a proposed alteration in the strike zone—but brought
forth barely a groan.

"Vun more," the doctor said, an Ernest Thesiger sneer of disappointment twisting his face. He twiddled again, then read out the
final experiment. "After sixteen years, the Mets haff dropped Tim
McCarver as their television analyst. He is McGone."

"No, no!" I shouted, kicking and flailing under my bonds.
"Not that! It can't be! Aaaarghh!!" A long scream shattered the
night.

The Mets have never quite explained their decision, which was
delivered to McCarver by telephone. Rumors remain that it was
Mets manager Bobby Valentine who pulled the trigger, because of
McCarver's persistent and terrifyingly clear presentations, over the
air, of some awaiting pickle or tactical miasma that the smiling
skipper might have just brought upon himself with his latest pitching or pinch-hitting move. McCarver's mental swiftness and situational foresight are legendary; he is a congenital first-guesser.
During a Reds-Pirates league-championship game in 1990, he cor-
rectly foresaw an awaiting disaster a full inning away, after Reds
manager Lou Piniella, late in the day, had inserted a new catcher
and new pitcher into the lineup in what Tim believed to be the
wrong order. Lou didn't exactly appreciate the call, which played
out exactly the way McCarver had foreseen, but when he learned
that Tim had made the point before the event, not after, he calmed
down. It isn't surprising that McCarver has had overtures to man-

age or to become a general manager (from the Expos, the Twins, and the Cardinals), nor that he passed them up.

The Mets replaced McCarver in the booth with their most famous family member, Tom Seaver, and Tim, accepting an offer from George Steinbrenner, moved along to the Yankees, where he has teamed up smoothly with the reliable, low-key incumbent, Bobby Murcer, for forty-seven games over Channel 5. Understandably, the two have not yet attained the Zen-like pauses and meshings of the long Kiner connection. The real mystery about Tim's firing, of course, is how the Mets management could have failed to sense that in an era of fluctuating rosters, expanding franchises, and perpetually decamping high-priced stars it is the resident radio and TV broadcasters who preserve the sense of familiarity and stability and character which we once attached to our favorite players, and to their team. The voices of Red Barber and Mel Allen, Curt Gowdy, Phil Rizzuto, Vin Scully, and Ernie Harwell are sewn into memory not just to the teams and heroes and games they talked into life but to the exact places and times of day and time of life in which we heard them, year after year. I need only think of the murmurous, unhopeful Ned Martin ("There's a foul, carved to right") to bring back my own summer sufferings over the Red Sox through the sixties and seventies, sometimes with a glimpse of me, in my bunk below decks, tilting my little portable to one side or the other in the dark to hold the signal from Fenway Park or far Comiskey, while the sloop I was aboard swung slowly at its anchor. Television shuts us indoors, to be sure, but the men and women in the booth—more expert now than ever before— keep their hold on the fan and the sport. Harry Caray died last year, and was mourned by many people who had never been to Wrigley Field; his son Skip is a play-by-play fixture in Atlanta, and his grandson Chip does the same work for the Cubs; Jack Buck's son Joe now teams with McCarver on Fox network games. The daily coverage of Braves games over the TBS Superstation, and Cubs and White Sox games over WGN, along with ESPN's Sunday-night games and Wednesday doubleheaders, have brought platoons of fresh announcers and game analysts into every sports-alert American home. The iron-tonsilled Ernie Harwell and Vin Scully are still at it, and if I list some other favorites of mine—Ralph Kiner, the retired Hank Greenwald, Jim Kaat (another Yankee Stadium fixture), the classically calm Joe Morgan, and Tim McCarver—it is not to dismiss dozens of others across the land, each of whom means all the game to somebody.

For young Tim McCarver, growing up in Memphis, it was Harry Caray, then chortling and braying for the Cardinals over KMOX, who was the model. "There was such a frivolity all the time," he recalls. "One of the things that's enjoyable about a broadcaster is the very fact that he prepares and then lets it go. There was something unbridled about Harry's passion."

McCarver, in turn, sometimes sounds like an unbridled twelve-year-old—a bright kid lit up not just by baseball but by his own vocabulary and the rush of his thoughts. This spring, pointing out that the head groundskeeper at Tiger Stadium is a woman, Heather Nabozny, he suggested that the often traditional anthem for the fifth-inning infield sweep might be called "Y.W.C.A." if played there. Lately, I haven't heard him roll out the classic nicknames he has sometimes affixed to certain pitches—"Sir Charles," for the masterful curve of a Doc Gooden or Darryl Kile; the "Dewdrop Inn," for a late-breaking curve; and "Linda Ronstadt," for a super fastball (after her "Blue Bayou," which, uh, well, it just blew by you, the batter)—but they'll be back. On the other hand, Tim also once managed a triumphant "Cone burned the Candaele at both ends" (faintings in the booth) when David Cone easily struck out the Astros' infielder Casey Candaele in 1992. Not bad, but not close to the moment in a Giants-Cubs game, back in the late eighties, when a Giants catcher, Kirt Manwaring, barely avoided a pick-off throw at first base with a leap back to the bag. "One Giant step for Manwaring," as Tim smoothly offered. On a Saturday this May, after the young White Sox third baseman Greg Norton ripped a two-run homer against the Yankees' Ramiro Mendoza, Tim discussed the pitch and the flaw in Mendoza's delivery with Bobby Murcer, and then cried "Noh-ton! Noh-ton!" in mock pain. Ralph Kramden had entered the booth.

The son of a Memphis police officer, and the fourth of five children, McCarver became a multi-letter local football and baseball star. He attributes his athletic and intellectual persistence to his father, and his affinity for classical texts to a couple of teachers, Brother William and Kevin Gavin, at the Christian Brothers High School. On the point of accepting a football scholarship to Notre Dame or the University of Tennessee, Tim became a Cardinal instead, accepting a signing bonus of seventy-five thousand dollars. (He came within a whisker of signing with the Yankees.) Once in the majors, he continued his studies over seven post-seasons at Memphis State and the University of Oklahoma, from which his wife, Anne, had graduated. (The McCarvers, who have recently separated, are the parents of two grown daughters.) A regular with the Cardinals at twenty-one, in time he attached himself instinctively to grandees like Bob Gibson and Joe Torre, who were implacable in the field and suavely at home with sommeliers around the league. "Of course, Tim was a favorite," Torre said not long ago. "He had that intelligence and a great outlook. He was always teaching us ways to win." He recalls McCarver, his road roomie, coming in after a vinous night and climbing into bed with "The Gulag Archipelago."

Another friend, Steve Hirdt, the executive vice-president of the Elias Sports Bureau, the official statistician for Major League Baseball, says, "Tim is unapologetic about bringing an intellectual perspective to the game. He won't dumb down. Better than anyone, he understands that baseball has this great capacity that allows fans to play along in their minds. He has also stayed current with the players of the day, and connects his opinion about the specific play—whether to bunt or not bunt, that sort of thing—with the abilities of the batter and the infielders he's looking at. He's as well prepared as anyone I've ever dealt with."

On McCarver's pre-game warmups, he stops off at visiting-team locker rooms, where, more often than not, he finds a manager he has played alongside of or batted against, or a coach who was a clubhouse bridge partner. He may be working up a little riff on the actual value of Frank Thomas's on-base percentage, or the pickoff move of a Toronto left-hander he doesn't know well, and the old-boy network always helps out. "Getting ready is preparation by immersion," Tim said, "but only about ten per cent of what you get is used. If you have something ready, it'll come out in a natural way. You can't be waiting to bring it up."

He had told me earlier about a moment in a 1996 Yankees-Braves World Series game at Atlanta-Fulton County Stadium, when he noticed Braves bench coach Jim Beauchamp gesturing from the dugout to shift his outfielders into proper position. "I wondered how Jim could be sure when he had got them placed right," McCarver said. "That's a deep dugout—how did he know?" Seeking out Beauchamp—they'd been Cardinals teammates—Tim learned that he'd waved directions to his left fielder until the player stood on an invisible surveyor's line extending out to a point between the headlights of an automobile depicted on a Chevron billboard above the left-field wall; then he placed his right fielder in the same fashion, perching him between the double "O" of a Hooters ad out beyond. Now they were straight away.

"It's such great stuff—you'd love to Telestrate it," Tim said (the Telestrator is an electronic gizmo that allows announcers to draw helpful arrows and underlinings on the screen image), "but it ended up on the cutting-room floor. It never came up. Now that whole ballpark is gone."

What McCarver is most alert to, however, is the game itself. Since his presence on the scene is nuanced and unaggressive—he has avoided the macho flaunting of statistics which afflicts some of the younger practitioners—we don't always pick up on the life-time database of playing and remembering which he can bring to bear within a little conversational reminder of what's up, how the count on the batter has suddenly altered the situation, how a defensive shift has been executed or blunted. Working with Joe Buck and Bob Brenly, he was in remarkable form during the latter stages of the Yankees-Padres World Series last fall, when every late deployment of the doomed and worn-down San Diego pitchers and batters by their manager, Bruce Bochy, appeared to run into the exact disaster that McCarver had seen lurking around a corner just ahead. "No game analyst ever had a better World Series," Steve Wulf, the executive editor of ESPN: The Magazine, said to me after it was over. McCarver, in any case, has incorporated some of this deep-dish knowledge and intuition into three baseball books, "Oh, Baby, I Love It!" (1987, with Ray Robinson); "Tim McCarver's Baseball for Brain Surgeons and Other Fans" (1998, with Danny Peary); and "The Perfect Season" (1999, also with Peary), in which the fibre, as in breakfast food, comes cunningly packaged with flavor.

Keeping close tabs on Tim McCarver, as I've been doing this year, I have come to realize that though the prime stuff is always there he never needs to force it. For him, instinctively, the game outweighs awe for the celebrity star or puff for the awaited, overtouted new record—a condition which permits critical distance and enthusiasm in equal measure. Late in July, he was unmerciful with the Indians' celebrated second baseman Robbie Alomar when he unexpectedly attempted a two-out bunt, with a base runner on first—bunting for himself, that is, and not the team. "I don't care who you are," McCarver said. "That's a terrible play by a great player." But two innings later, when Alomar began a double play in which he flipped the ball out of his glove to his shortstop, Omar Vizquel, who took it bare-handed and got off the throw to first in the same gesture, Tim was reduced to an exclamatory torrent that lasted right through the replays: "Unbelievable. That was unbelievable! ... Watch: Throws with gloved hand, catches with bare hand. Unbelievable!"

During the Yankees' unexpected late-summer hitting drought, McCarver and Murcer (and director Bill Webb) provided illustrations of the bad habits that reliable batters like Derek Jeter and Tino Martinez can fall into when things aren't going their way—in particular, dropping their hands when at the plate, out of over-eagerness. Watching Scott Brosius doing the same thing against the Royals one afternoon, Tim said, "Hitters have to trust their hands just like guys who blow the trumpet." The criticism was offered in McCarver's familiar upbeat manner, with the same alertness of tone in an unimportant inning that he had brought to bear during the final chords of the World Series.

A 12–4 drubbing of the Yanks by the White Sox, back in May, has stayed with me. Early on in the small debacle, McCarver lightly confected a "Rhode Island leaguer" (after the Texas leaguer, which drops in front of an outfielder) out of a tiny infield pop, though Bobby Murcer took him to task for it. When the Yanks, who were in a losing streak, again fell behind and a few fans began to boo, Tim reminded us that the amazing 1998 champions had never encountered hard times—they were "struggle-proof." Still, he said, we should not have allowed ourselves to expect that this year's Yanks would be a continuation of last year's: "Like that 101 Journalism course which I never took: 'Never assume.'" He was not much impressed with Chili Davis's leadoff solo home run in the fourth—"a tourniquet to a big inning"—and somewhere worked in the startling statistic that American League hitters last year had batted a collective .386 on the 2–0 count.

He was almost affectionate with the floundering Yankees ("Nothing ever eats at Paul O'Neill inside: it's all outside!") until Tino Martinez got himself thrown out at home plate in the seventh, while trying to score from second base. "They shouldn't have done it!" McCarver said, shocked. "You cannot be thrown out at home, trailing 9–4." As usual, he was aggrieved by a bad play but not by a bad game. He never blames baseball.

A few days after this, I said to McCarver that this had felt like an old Mets game, back in one of their dreary stretches in the early nineties, and that I'd stayed with it to the end, as I so often did then, perhaps only because he was there.

"So much of a game comes from how it's told," McCarver said. "Rhythm and cadence are the key. Just in talking to your partner, you're telling your audience, 'I know what you're thinking.' You're saying this, and they're drawn in and complimented at the same time. You want to keep things simple for the ordinary listener and not annoy the hardened fan. If we're getting more sophisticated in delivering the game, it should become easier to understand." He paused, considering. "Sophisticated is simple," he said.

Style

2000

David Cone, the veteran Yankee right-hander, had a miserable time of it in 2000, his fifteenth season in the majors. Only the year before, he had pitched a perfect game against the Montreal Expos in late July, but he performed indifferently after that. This season, his bread-and-butter pitch, the slider, mysteriously deserted him, and he absorbed some uncharacteristic poundings and early departures. Manager Joe Torre kept him in the starting rotation, however, and at times he appeared on the verge of recapturing his old form. Then bad luck or the long ball would disappoint him once again. Late in July, at a time when the team had solidified its hold on first place in the American League East after the late acquisition of the veteran sluggers Jose Canseco and David Justice, the Yanks sent Cone down to their training facility in Tampa, to work on some fundamentals with a coach, Billy Connors. Cone's record by this time stood at 1-10, with a 6.88 earned-run average. He was thirty-eight years old.

The refurbished Yankees had been winning in July, even while Cone had gone south (in both ways), and they maintained a cruise-control pace now as the midsummer weeks went by, holding a divisional lead over the Red Sox that stayed stuck between three and five games. More S.U.V. than juggernaut, they rarely won more than three in a row and never lost more, but you could look out the windows, so to speak, and begin to enjoy the ride. Shortly after David got back from Tampa—he was there for a little over a week—the clubhouse was delighted by the arrival of the amiable all-purpose infielder Luis Sojo, an old friend and teammate who had been in temporary residence with the Pirates. He'd been let go after the 1999 campaign—according to one story because George Steinbrenner didn't like his habit of leaving the top button of his uniform unbuttoned. Sojo, a Venezuelan, is thirty-four but looks as if he'd put on a much older guy's body that morning by mistake. Seamed and saggy, forever smiling, he could sit uncomplaining on the bench by the hour or day or week, then deliver solid innings at almost any infield position, plus (as the Mets will not forget) the big base hit. Later in this season, there was speculation that Sojo might actually be older than his announced age, but the players liked the idea that he'd *added* a year or two to his data somewhere along the line, the better to fit his face.

The Yankee tone—no hangers-on, no TV in the main part of the clubhouse, no blasting CD portables—was working on the new personnel. Canseco, a grownup Bash Brother with a lifetime four hundred and forty homers, became a part-timer or d.h. without a murmur, and Justice, never known for his immodesty when he played with the Indians and Braves, was finding that attitude was not a requirement here. Playing every day in left or right or as a left-handed d.h., uncoiling on the inside pitch from his upright, shoulder-pointing stance and lacing it long, he led the Yankee offense for the rest of the distance, with twenty homers by the end and sixty runs batted in. He had a couple of two-homer days, and supplied the afterpiece in the team's most electrifying finish of the year, at the Stadium on August 8th—a lead-off, first-pitch ninth-inning homer by Bernie Williams, against the Oakland closer Jason Isringhausen, which tied the game at 3–3, and then Justice's shot into the right-center-field bleachers on the very next delivery, which won it. You could see it again via the late-night replays, or, almost better, on Isringhausen's line in the box score the next day: "(L)" for loser, "0" for innings or parts of innings pitched, and the same "2" five times over—hits, runs, earned runs, home runs, and pitches delivered and disbelieved.

Almost as unlikely for Bronxian fans was the arrival onstage of Glenallen Hill. If you were writing a baseball novel or musical you'd throw away a passage like this, while congratulating yourself for your characters' vibrant names. *David Justice,* tah-dah!... *Glenallen Hill,* sounds like a single malt! Hill, who joined the Yankees after service with five different teams in his twelve-year career, startled his teammates with the shortest batting stroke since Mike Tyson. A righty hitter, he took an almost open stance, with the bat poised somewhat forward, then completed his brusque business with a cut that used no more than a third of the available distance. It was like someone idly banging shut a closet door while walking down the hall. "I've never seen anyone hit like Glenallen," Joe Torre said. Hill announced himself with a first-at-bat homer, then a pinch-hit, ninth-inning grand slam against the Twins, at the Metrodome, and later sent a poke into the rarely visited center-field black seats at the Stadium. His .411 and ten dingers made him the American League Player of the Month for August, and toward the end of that run you'd see his teammates edging up toward the front of the dugout for each of his plate appearances, and then whooping and falling about with laughter whenever another shot—*Bonkk: elsewhere!*—went out.

Indoors, Hill would return from shower to locker with a towel enfolding his middle in the style of an Egyptian pharaoh and a modish pigskin ditty bag slung from one shoulder. His torso cuts down dramatically from his enormous shoulders to a mini-waist and tyke's tokus—a nice top-level sample, in an era of player bods unimaginable to Babe Ruth or Johnny Mize. Hill affected short tangerine-colored dreadlocks when he first arrived with the Yanks, but after a conversation with the manager quickly converted to the low-upkeep David Justice-Yul Brynner pate mode. Joe admitted later that this was his first do-consultation.

Justice is high-style, too. Leaving work one afternoon after a day game, he wore yellowish mini-shades, a round canvas hat pulled down to his ears, knee-length baggy shorts, and a silky outer shirt, untucked and unbuttoned, of a sensational orange. Outstanding, but when Glenallen walked out, a few minutes later, he was less dramatic in similarly oversized shorts and shirt, but ahead, I'd say, by 3.7 points in the critical Not Really Trying division. This battle, like the R.B.I. and dinger stats, went on all summer.

Stuff like this reminds you how young the players really are. Weekends now, there were little kids rocketing around in the clubhouse—Jason Grimsley's three towheaded sons always led the pack—and the fathers, dropping a soft word or gesture into the action, became playground dads, a role for them that we writers never imagine. I got the same reminder whenever I came by a couple of players heading off for the weight room or the batting cage, hours before game time, in their gym shorts and sneakers and cutoff tops—Jorge Posada with a bat, Mike Stanton with a weight bar in one hand. "Morning," they offered, going by, fresher and more hopeful than they'd looked late last night: inbound commuters now. Another day, Derek Jeter brought over a letter from his thick daily stack and asked Scott Brosius for help with the handwriting. Then Chris Turner read it, too—there's a lot of interest in Derek's mail. "I am a sixty-eight-year-old widow," they made out, line by line, "and I would like you to accompany my eighteen-year-old great-niece to her graduation dance. She is a good person and so are you." And Brosius recalled a letter he'd had, maybe last year, from a woman who'd wanted him to fix up a date for her daughter with Derek. "Who am I in there, the grandpa?" he said indignantly.

Later on, a batboy, Luigi Castillo, stopped by Cone's locker for a minute, to talk about his cut fastball—Luigi's, not David's. He's seventeen but looks younger—a five-foot-something pitcher in the Jaws Division of the Bronx Little League, who plays at Roberto Clemente Field, in Crotona Park. When I asked what "Jaws" stood for, he said he didn't know. Before this, he pitched on a team called Lola's All Stars. The last time I heard, Luigi's E.R.A. was 2.38. A year ago, after he and Cone began to throw together in the outfield, David showed him how to hold his curveball loosely, with a little gap showing between the thumb and forefinger. When

Luigi took it into a game, the first batter said, "Jesus, where did *that* come from?" On that hot Sunday last year when David had to sit out a rain delay in the middle of his perfect game, he grabbed Luigi the moment the sky began to lighten and threw with him, out beside the tarps, to stay loose. "He's my idol and my role model," Castillo said to me. "He's given me a little of his talent to go with my talent."

Another day, and the writers—George King of the *Post*; Larry Rocca, of *Newsday*; Ken Davidoff, of the *Record*; Anthony Mc-Carron, of the *News*; the *Post*'s Ursula Reel; Bill Madden, the *News* columnist, among others—are standing around in the middle of the clubhouse once again, facing in different directions like gulls on a beach. They know this place better than their own living rooms, and their eyes roam across the ranged player cubicles in search of an unwary occupant—or, worse, a player talking to another writer. But this is midsummer, and there isn't enough news to keep the mutual nuclear deterrence on full alert. Most of the players hang in their lounge or the training room, which are off limits, but we all know their slots here: Cone and Chuck Knoblauch on opposite sides of the short hallway that leads to Joe's office and the coaches' room beyond, and the agreeable Mike Stanton and the useful Jorge Posada farther up on the right-hand side. (Cone's locker faces a column, affording an illusory sense of privacy, and it feels as if much of my summer has been spent there, with my back against the fake-stucco column-façade, while Cone sits and talks and I stand and write.) Bernie Williams has the élite corner space, back near the front door—the suite once occupied by Mattingly—and Paul O'Neill supervises us all from the head of the room, on the same flank with Roger Clemens and Mariano Rivera. To the left side, near the showers, is El Duque country, while Derek Jeter's spot, farther up, is getting so crowded after games that he'll probably be moved next year.

Just now I overhear Michael Kay, the broadcaster, discussing the stock market with a clubhouse attendant named Joe Lee and Jason Zillo, the assistant director of media relations and publicity.

Lee, who has a terrific smile, is a senior at Fordham majoring in finance. "Give me two million at a quarter below prime and I'll—" he says, but I turn away, swooning.

Don Zimmer is in the big leather chair just inside the door of Joe's office, an upright bat in his pink hands. The top button of his uniform pants is comfortably unbuttoned. He's been talking about the dog tracks, as usual, and about friends of his in cities all around the country. "St. Pete?" he says at one point. "I'm *huge* in St. Pete." Then he gets back to baseball, where he's got fifty-three years in. We've been wondering whether David Cone's problems come down to his age in the end, and Zim says, "Age is a crazy thing—I never paid no attention to it. If you're twenty-two and can't pitch you're no use to me. If you're forty and can't pitch it's the same. I've seen pitchers who were done at thirty-two and others just getting going. Some get a little age and they start changing what they do every time out, but that don't mean anything. Yaz and Cal Ripken changed their swings every week for their whole career, and Will Clark's never changed his. Don't worry about it—show me what you got."

Up in the press box, every night ends the same way. Herb Steier, a retired *Times* sports copy editor, comes to every game and sits motionless in the third row, his hands in front of him on the long table. He doesn't keep score but watches the action intently, with bright, dark eyes. When the ninth inning comes, he gets up and stands by the railing behind the last row of writers, near the exit, and after the potential final batter of the game has been announced, Bob Sheppard, the ancient and elegant Hall of Fame announcer, comes out of his booth and stands next to him, with a book under his arm. (He reads novels or works of history between announcements.) Eddie Layton, the Stadium organist, is there, too, wearing a little skipper's cap. Eddie has a private yacht—well, it's a mini-tug, called Impulse—that he keeps on the Hudson, up near Tarrytown. He gets a limo ride to the Stadium most days from his apartment in Queens—it's in his contract—and a nice lift home with Bob Sheppard and Herb Steier at night. Eddie and Bob

Sheppard make a bet on every single Yankee game—the time of the game, the total number of base runners, number of pitches by bullpen pitchers, whatever—but won't tell you which one of them is ahead. The stakes are steady: a penny a game.

Steier is Sheppard's neighbor, out in Baldwin, Long Island, and he drives him to work every day and home again at its end; they're old friends. Sheppard, a stylish fellow, is wearing an Argyle sweater and espadrilles tonight. This is his fiftieth year on the job at Yankee Stadium, and once in a while I ask him to enunciate a player's name for me, just for the thrill of it. " 'Shige-to-shi Ha-se-ga-wa,' " he'll respond, ringing the vowels. It sounds like an airport.

The instant the last batter strikes out or pops up or grounds out Sheppard and Steier and Layton do an about-face and depart at a slow sprint. Out the door they go and turn right in the loge-level corridor, still running. A few kids out there are already rocketing down the tilted runways. "Start spreadin' the noooss..." comes blaring out from everywhere (the Yanks have won again), but Bob and Herb and Eddie have turned right again, into the quiet elevator lobby, where the nearer car awaits them, its door open. Down they go and out at street level, still at a careful run. Herb's car, a beige 1995 Maxima, is in its regular slot in the team parking lot, just across the alley—the second car on the right. They're in, they're out, a left turn up the street, where they grab a right, jumping onto the Deegan, heading home. The cops there have the eastbound traffic stopped dead, waiting for Bob Sheppard: no one else in New York is allowed to make this turn. Two minutes, maybe two-twenty, after the game has ended and they're gone, home free, the first of fifty thousand out of the building, every night.

Cone's first start after Tampa—Saturday afternoon, August 5th, against the Mariners—came in two parts. Working with a pared-down, tauter motion, he threw early strikes to the tough Seattle batters but kept running up his pitch counts thereafter, straining for the K. At one stretch he went to the full count against eight straight batters. Much was at stake, and there was something like a groan or a sigh in the press rows when Alex Rodriguez pounced on a fastball that had drifted over the plate and drove it into the right-field stands for the second and third runs of the inning.

Down by 3–2, Cone now persevered, perhaps recalling the look on Joe Torre's face when he'd taken him up the tunnel between innings for a talk about body language. But Torre kept him in the game for a full six—no more runs, six strikeouts, and a startling hundred and thirty-seven pitches. When Cone fanned Mike Cameron in the fifth, the announcement came that it had been his twenty-five-hundredth career strikeout—a level he shares only with Clemens and Randy Johnson, among all active pitchers—and the fans delivered a sustained full minute of applause: an ovation, of all things. They'd been waiting weeks for the chance. The Yanks lost the game in the end, going down in the ninth, 6–5 (Doc Gooden took the loss), and leaving David's horrible W-L record intact. "It's frustrating," he said. "I feel as if I'm this far from locking in a good groove." He held up his fingers, barely apart.

Cone looked thinner than he had in the spring, and I suspected that his season was getting to him away from the park now, too. Always an insomniac, he'd been short of sleep for weeks. It wasn't like the old days, when pain in his arm or shoulder woke him up every night, and when painkillers bothered his stomach, and sleeping pills left him down and dopey. He had no pain at all this year— he felt great—and that, in turn, added to his broodings in the dark. Maybe he needed pain in order to throw right...Some nights now, he'd pop an Ambien, which was good for four hours' sleep, but then he'd find himself awake again at dawn and still thinking about this year and his record. His mind would go over the places where a couple of Yankee runs would have turned things his way and made his miserable season look a bit more respectable; he knew these games and innings and pitches by heart. On a similar performance record that I'd been keeping, I found nine games, out of his twenty-two starts from April 12th to August 20th, in which fortune had dealt him a chilly hand. He'd lost two of those games, departing behind by one and two runs. The Yanks won three games and lost two in which he'd also pitched well but did not gain the decision, and, more painfully, they'd lost two in which he left with a lead that was then squandered. In these nine selected games—which do not include far worse outings of his, let's be clear—Cone was an official 0-2 over fifty-seven innings, with fifty-four hits surrendered and an earned-run average of 3.15. In that spell, the Yanks had scored nineteen runs on his behalf, or 3.0 per game. This built-in unfairness is a commonplace in baseball, to be sure, brooded over by guys who are becalmed in a season or only suffering through brief slumps. Bert Blyleven, talking to David in July, reminded him that it wasn't how you pitched but which games you pitched that mattered. This is Nembutal backward: a guaranteed formula for sleeplessness.

Luck turns bad for hitters, too, of course. Paul O'Neill, battling a midsummer hip injury and a Gobi-like aridity at the plate, hit some predictable scorchers straight into the glove of a waiting infielder. "Never mind, Paulie," David said in the dugout after one such setback. "Next time, that's a chinker that falls in." But the following day he came by O'Neill's locker and said, "Remember what I said last night? Well, fuck that—you're never going to get that hit back again."

David told me now that he'd return next year, no matter what. He didn't know where—probably it wouldn't be with the Yankees—but he wasn't going to go out on this note. But Lynn Cone, David's wife, said that he was considering retirement: it was on his mind all the time. "He's a basket case," she said one day. "I tell him he's got to put stuff like this away until the end of the season. Nobody can deal with everything at the same time this way, night after night. But you know David. "

Lynn had been there through the hard games. I couldn't count the times I'd found her, well after midnight, standing amid a scattering of relatives and cops and Stadium attendants just inside the press gate looking thin and beautiful in a stylish leather jacket, with perfect makeup and her shining hair slicked back—as she waited for her husband to appear at the top of the stairs after another horrible day at the plant. One night there, she waved me over to say that she'd called his old teammate Chili Davis and asked him to call David back—he needed a lift. Chili came through, but when David asked where he was headed next he said, "Maui—living the life." When David got off the phone he said, "Why am I doing this? Why am I still killing myself like this?"

Cone asked me now and then what I thought about retirement, and I'd said I just hoped he wasn't going to be one of those guys who go through life after baseball with the conviction that they can still strike out the side. The great Steve Carlton, who is fifty-six now, was famously rumored to believe this, and Jim Palmer, when we'd talked at Shea, said that only a little hamstring injury had kept him from a longer career. He had retired in 1984 but later changed his mind, and when he started up again in spring training, seven years later, he'd found that he still had his great stuff. "I could still get batters out, except that I got hurt," he said. But guys who'd been at the Orioles' camp in Sarasota that spring—Tom Boswell, the Washington *Post* columnist, was one of them—said this wasn't true at all: Palmer had been atrocious.

Mark Gubicza, David's long-term friend and teammate with the Royals, quit baseball in 1998, and is a budding sports TV star, making regular appearances on Fox's "Baseball Today" show, on the West Coast. He believes that David would find the transition tougher than he can imagine. "Maybe you never get over it," Gubie told me. "If somebody came to me tomorrow and said, 'Listen, we need you to pitch this one big game on Sunday,' I'd be there in a heartbeat. It's in your blood."

I kept trying to think of something useful to say to David, to help him make up his mind, but I couldn't come up with the right examples. Dreams and pride suffused the field. Jim Bouton, still pitching in a semi-amateur circuit at the age of fifty-eight, had told me that he'd stopped just lately when batters at that level began to take him deep. One doofus who'd just hit a home run off a knuckler of his actually produced the ball after the game and asked for a certifying autograph. Bouton obliged but felt compelled to add "aluminum bat" in parentheses under his name.

It must be torture to give up something tough and demanding that you once did extremely well, I finally said to David. If butchers and lawyers and schoolteachers felt this way, how could pitchers and tenors and Presidents be expected to pull it off—people who lived off the crowds and thrilling repeated challenges, and weren't old yet except within their professions? How would you ever get used to that? I said I could remember Dennis Eckersley talking about this, at the moment after he'd hung them up at the close of a twenty-four-year career. When I went back to some old notes of mine to hunt out Eck's lines, I could almost see his long legs propped up on his locker in the grottolike clubhouse at Fenway Park that Sunday, and his eyes burning like flashlights as he spoke: "I've thought about it a lot—I mean a lot. There's no getting around the fact that it's going to be devastating. It's like dying—you know it's inevitable but no matter how you get ready for it you're not ready."

But Cone surprised me once again. He didn't believe that illusions about his strikeouts or sliders would haunt him, once he decided to retire. It was the other way around. "I've always been a super-realist," he said. "I go over things in my mind—I can't let them alone. It's how bad I've been that gets me. I could use a little fantasy right now. Guys who can kid themselves are much better off."

David had been smoking more. He smoked Marlboro Lights. I almost never saw him light up, even when he was at home, but Lynn said he'd stopped inviting me to drive up to the Stadium with him or back home after a game, as he sometimes had, because he smoked in the car and didn't want me to know. When I asked him how many cigarettes a day he smoked, he said more lately but less than a pack; Lynn said he was way up over that by now. Cone did tell me that his doctor, John Olichney, had recently prescribed Zyban, a mild anti-depressant that would help you get off nicotine when you were ready. One of its side effects was powerful dreams, and then, here in August, David said that only the night before he'd found himself pitching for the Red Sox, in a dream. It was all perfectly clear—the green wall behind him and the red letters on the uniform. "It wouldn't be bad there, at that," he said musingly. "*That* would be a change—pitching with those fans on my side. And I like Jimy Williams as a manager. I've always wondered what living in New England would be like..." The dream had become an option for him. He was there already, pitching with better luck in a year when he could win.

And then he won. Next time out, handed a welcome seven-run lead against the A's, he gave up two runs over six innings, with eight strikeouts. He had tempo, he had poise. With two on in the fifth, he fanned the side. The 12–6 victory took him off the schneid—his first win in sixteen starts. On the road after this, he beat the Texas Rangers, 10–2, on a sweltering night in Arlington—with strikeouts of Rafael Palmeiro, on a first-class slider, and Frank Catalanotto, on the split, as Whiffs of the Day.

On the phone—I was in Maine, writing and worrying—he no longer sounded puzzled or haunted. Lynn had come along on this trip. They'd gotten in some nice pool time at Anaheim, and they were looking forward to a family dinner with an uncle of hers who lived in San Dimas.

Great, I said, but what was going on? How come he suddenly looked so workmanlike, so suave? What kind of body language was this?

"I'm national news," he said. "'Cone Ends Slump!' It's been one hell of a dry spell."

He said that what excited him right now was the fastball, which had more life to it, even though the numbers were still mostly in the eighties. It didn't show on the gun but there was late movement to it at last.

Did Billy Connors do all this? I asked.

"He was certainly part of it," David said. "He'd asked me to visualize the way it felt back when I was throwing good and winning games. He particularly wanted me to keep my hands farther away from my body in the middle of the delivery."

I said this sounded like the opposite of what his old friend Tony Ferreira had been telling him, a million years ago in Florida, and David laughed and said, "Yeah, this always happens." The new, trimmed-down delivery wasn't quite second nature to him so far, he went on. It was almost as if he'd had to learn a whole new muscle memory.

His father, Ed Cone, had come to New York before this swing west, and the two of them had gone over some videos from 1986 and 1987 which reminded them how deliberate he'd once been on the rubber, and how vital it was for him not to rush things when he was ahead in the count. This was going to become part of his new pattern now, too, he hoped.

While his dad was still in the city, he and Ed had gone up to Columbia-Presbyterian to visit Darryl Strawberry, who'd had to come up from Tampa for more cancer surgery. This time, a tumor near one of his kidneys had been taken out. Straw's room, in McKeen Pavilion, was just down the hall from the room where David had been after his aneurysm operation, and where he'd listened to Doc Gooden pitch his no-hitter. Charisse Strawberry was there with her husband; it was like a Mets family reunion. Darryl kept talking about David's problems.

Sunday, August 20th, Yankee Stadium

Whitey Ford, my favorite Yankee alumnus, came back to the Stadium this afternoon for a Day in his honor and told George Steinbrenner that it was really nice of him to have one of these affairs for a guy who wasn't Italian. The occasion felt like a rain check for an Old Timers' Day, but without the geezers to embarrass us by creaking through the motions of a game. Whitey was a bit pale—he's seventy-one and had recently undergone chemotherapy for recurring skin cancer—but hadn't lost his sparkle. His celebrated smile hangs around the corners of his mouth, always at the ready, and his wife, Joan, looks like someone who's heard laughter every day for forty years.

"I've been a Yankee for fifty years, and I'll be a Yankee forever," Whitey told the enchanted crowd, but I thought he summed himself up better at a pre-game mini press conference, when he said, "I was never nervous out there"—out there pitching, he meant. His sixteen-year, 236-106 won-lost record comes out at .690, which is the best percentage in baseball for pitchers with more than two hundred wins. He's the winningest Yankee pitcher of all. Answering our then-vs.-now questions, Ford agreed that the smaller modern ballparks and shrunken millennial strike zone would have raised his 2.75 lifetime E.R.A. but—one-beat pause— "but I'd have won as many."

Whitey was born in Manhattan and grew up on the sandlots of Astoria, and witnessed his first major-league game from the Stadium bleachers in 1938, at the age of nine. "You had to come to the park to see the players then," he reminded us. One of his boyhood teams was called the 34th Avenue Boys, and I remember his telling me one day that playing unsupervised, parent-free ball in those summers he often got in fifty innings over the course of a Friday-to-Sunday weekend—twenty or so as a pitcher and the rest wherever he could jump in. Equally dated and flavorful, I realized during this reunion, is Ford's accent—the pure I.R.T., which has almost gone out of earshot nowadays, thanks to the flattening and duhing of television.

Cone pitched against the Anaheim Angels on Whitey Day, and I wasn't the only writer there who sensed a connection. Ford agreed. "I've thought that sometimes, watching him," he said. "He's from the other side"—a righty, that is—"but he has a good curveball and fastball like I did, and he comes from all different angles. He stays on top, the same way, and brings his shoulder out over his front foot."

Cone, told about the compliment, was flattered but wary. "I'm no Whitey Ford, that's for sure," he said. He told me that he'd consulted with Ford during the difficult days before the aneurysm operation, because Ford in his day had also suffered puzzling vascular problems in his shoulder, and had undergone corrective surgery. When Whitey resumed pitching he noticed that he'd stopped sweating on his left, or soupbone, side. Explaining the medical oddity to the press back then, he cited a popular toiletry of the day and said, "With me, a 5-Day Deodorant Pad lasts ten days."

Cone, at six-one, and Ford, at five-ten, share a graceful, put-together look that makes them appear a little smaller than their size, and they have both been famously businesslike at their place of work. Comparisons stop there, I guess. Prodigal with his pitch counts, Cone strikes out more batters per game than Ford did—he's averaged close to one K per inning in his career—and walks more, too. This takes time, while with Whitey you'd look up from your scorecard or peanut and find that the inning was already over. On this day, though, Coney got on with it. The Ford press conference overlapped a bit with the first inning, and I missed him striking out the side, after going to three-and-two on all three batters. I was back when he wrapped up the second by fanning Troy Glaus on the slider away—the genuine sailer, which left the batter tilting awkwardly to starboard and Cone already headed toward the dugout. He pitched six shutout innings, striking out six—it was nice to see the ice-cream-cone "K" symbols flapping from the upper-deck facings again—and departed the scene most reluctantly, ahead by 3–0. Only the bullpen, which had lately taken on the texture of a damp hot-dog roll, could spoil the day: five runs in, and the game and Cone's win gone.

Three in a row would have been nice, but, never mind, Cone was back, and this game against the Angels on Whitey's Day was of a higher order. In full form, he'd pitched like a house afire, suddenly performing in relation to nothing but the last pitch and the one that came next. Fastball, slider in, sinker, fastball up, curveball down, fastball inside—he called on each without musing, picking up the sign and swinging into his motion in almost the same breath, and correcting a pitch away from the plate or too low with something sharper and better that kept him level in the count or ahead.

There were no pauses for forehead-wiping with his glove-tip, no ir-ritated shakeoffs of his catcher's signs, and none of the puzzled, slack-jawed starings that had accompanied his unaccountable ear-lier efforts. Watching him at work like this, you could compare him to nobody but himself, and wonder why it had taken him so long to find the model that had once been so reliably at hand. Pitching is style, and when you have it it appears innate and un-touchable: yes, this is me. When it's gone, you must think and grope—it's more a psychic loss than something mechanical—and you feel bereft and clunky even before you've been punished by another defeat. Now the key had been turned, and style, from wherever it had been, came whispering back, perhaps to stay a bit and to make it all feel so easy.

Takes: Three Petes

Spring, 1981: On a frigid, wind-torn gray morning in Clearwater, I asked Pete Rose what he did about slumps.

"Well, I don't think there's anybody's going to get me out for long," he said. "Nobody's got a book on me. I switch-hit and I hit the ball everywhere. I can hit the fastball and the breaking ball, and I might hit you down the right-field line one time and up the other way the next time. If some pitcher's been getting me out, I'll do one of six things. I might move up in the box or move back. I might move away from the plate or come closer. I might choke up more or choke up less. I can usually tell what I'm doing wrong by the flight of the ball. I've seen guys play major-league ball for ten, twelve years, and if they go oh-for-fifteen they want to change their stance, like it's the end of the world. That's ridiculous. The only thing that's rough about this game is that you can't turn it on and off like a faucet. If I'm swinging good, I'll come to the park even on an off day, just to keep it going. This game is mental. There's a lot of thinking in it. You watch the pitcher from the batter's box and see what's going good for him. You watch the ball and it's sending you messages—the knuckleball don't spin, screwball's got backspin, slider's got that dot. It's easy. I like to watch the ball leave the pitcher's hand, and I like to watch the catcher catch it and throw it back to him. It's a habit I got into. I like the umpire to tell me where the ball is. He says, 'Strike one,' and I say, 'O.K., you missed one. Now give me one.'" Rose had a bat in his hands and had taken up his exaggerated, crouching at-bat posture (he was batting lefty, perhaps because I was taking notes right-handed), and was staring back in disbelief at some imaginary umpire behind him. A little crowd of writers and Phillies laughed at the pantomime. Pete Rose could draw a crowd in a cemetery.

"It never changes," he went on. "The pitchers don't change. Tom Seaver don't change. If you're a good hitter, hitting in the majors is easier, 'cause you're facing the same pitchers all the time. I'm particular about that. I have to know the way a guy throws. If you don't believe me, look at my Championship Series record, where I got more hits than anybody in the game, and then look at my World Series average. I don't know the pitchers in the World Series, unless they were in my league once, but look at what happens in the fifth and sixth and seventh games, when I begin to see the same guys out there pitching. Look that up."

I looked it up. In the five World Series in which Rose has played (in 1970, 1972, 1975, 1976, and 1980), he has gone hitless at the plate—0 for 16—in the opening games. His second-game average is .157. His third-game average is .285. His fourth-game average is .285. His fifth-game average—he has been in four of them—is .375. His sixth-game average, for three games, is .416. He is 4 for 9 in his two seventh World Series games—.444. Nothing about Pete Rose surprises me anymore, but still...

Fall, 1985: At 8:01 p.m. E.D.T. on Wednesday, September 11, in the first inning of a game with the San Diego Padres in Riverfront Stadium, Pete Rose stroked a soft single off the Padres' right-hander Eric Show. It was Hit No. 4,192 for Rose, at last putting him one ahead of Ty Cobb's life total on the all-time hit parade, and by the time it struck the ground in short left-center field there were some of us in the land who had the impression that we had already witnessed and counted each of Pete's 3,161 other singles, and even his 3,767 previous at-bats in the majors. I was delighted for many reasons, most of all for Rose himself, whose stroke and style and fervor and ebullient good cheer I have written about for more than two decades now, but I think I was almost more pleased by Pete's next hit—a triple to left, in the seventh—which broke the new record (as will every hit of his from now on) and suggested that baseball as we know it would now be permitted to resume, and that games, not monuments, are its purpose and reward. The "Cobb Countdown" had been a daily feature of the sports pages for better than two years, appearing even on the many mornings when it was dutifully noted that Pete hadn't played the previous evening, or that he'd gone oh-for-three in the game. The slowly oncoming Blessed Bingle had given rise to a whole cottage industry of Rosean artifacts, including 4,192 autographed Pete Rose ceramic plates ($25 to $125 apiece), 4,192 numbered Pete Rose color prints ($175 apiece), fifty silk-screened Pete Rose prints by Andy Warhol ($3,000 apiece), and much more, of course—possibly including a four-thousand-one-hundred-and-ninety-two-percent rise in the national riboflavin intake, thanks to those Pete Rose Wheaties commercials. I did not attend the game, however, being of the impression that I would probably not spot anything there that was invisible to the three hundred and seventy-five reporters and cameramen who were on hand that evening. I'm sorry I missed Pete's company and his jokes and one-liners (there were fifteen mass press conferences in the ten days prior to and including Der Tag), and even his tears when he broke the record. I also treasure some of the footnotes and substats that were turned up by the press moles digging back through Rose's 3,475 prior box-score appearances: for instance, his twenty-nine hits against future dentists (Jim Lonborg is one of them); his hundred and thirty-one hits against Hall of Famers (Warren Spahn, Sandy Koufax, Robin Roberts, Bob Gibson, Juan Marichal, Don Drysdale, and Hoyt Wilhelm); his hundred and three hits against the Niekro brothers ("I wish they'd been triplets," Pete said); and his six hits to date against Dwight Gooden, who wasn't born until after Rose had already rapped out three hundred and nine major-league blows.

Pete is great, but Cobb was better, having achieved his famous total (in 1928, when he retired) in four hundred and forty-two fewer games and in 2,339 fewer at-bats; Pete is a lifetime .305 batter, but Cobb, at .367, was the best hitter the game has ever seen. I feel like an old crab in pointing out these obvious discrepancies, but they exist, and the obdurate fact of them makes you wonder about our apparent wish for guaranteed present greatness or historic certification, or whatever it is that has driven us to make so much of this particular milestone. Late in the summer, I began to wonder who it was Cobb had supplanted in the lifetime lists, and after spending a happy half hour with my nose in the Baseball Encyclopedia I decided that it must have been Honus Wagner (3,430), whom Cobb motored past in 1923, six years after the Dutchman's retirement. But what happened on that September day in 1923? How had the local scribes and fans and historians celebrated the end of the "Wagner Watch," I wondered. (Subsequent archaeology shows that Cobb surpassed Wagner's lifetime hits record on September 20, 1923, in the course of a four-for-four afternoon against the Red Sox at Fenway Park.) Finding no mention of the moment in several histories of the pastime, I called up Seymour Siwoff, the grand sachem of the Elias Sports Bureau, a Fort Knox of stats, which keeps track of every jot and tittle in the books, not quite including Sunday foul tips in the Federal League.

"Nothing happened!" Siwoff said instantly when I put the question to him. "Just the other day, we tried to come up with some mention of the event. We looked and looked, but there was nothing there. The hype wasn't in. This Rose thing was a sitting target all the way. There was much more of a challenge for Pete in 1978, when he was going after Joe DiMaggio's consecutive-game hitting streak, winding up in a tie with Willie Keeler at forty-four, which is still the best in the National League. Any single-season record has a finite ending, so it means something."

Fall, 1999: The introductions of Major League Baseball's All-Century Team on the brightly lighted field in Atlanta before the second game of the World Series were affecting, but the ovation and sustained applause for Pete Rose was news. Pete, raising his scarlet Reds cap and turning his thick, familiar face upward toward his vehement supporters, drew more attention than Babe Ruth or Lou Gehrig or Jackie Robinson when those names were announced, and more than Sandy Koufax or Willie Mays or Yogi Berra or, say, Mark McGwire, who were up on the mid-diamond dais in company with the fourteen other living electees. Rose, of course, has been absent from the game since 1989, when he signed an agreement to a lifetime banishment from the sport because of his gambling on ballgames. His reappearance on the MasterCard fan ballots, which circulated all summer, and his presence here at Turner Field were at the sufferance of Commissioner Bud Selig, who had decided it would be unfair to keep Pete away, just this once.

Rose was the only man on the platform who could be said to be working, and he did himself some more good a bit later, when Jim Gray, a field interviewer for NBC Sports, pressed him vehemently in a pre-game one-on-one, wanting to know if he was "willing to show contrition, admit that you bet on baseball, and make some sort of apology." Pete, who has never admitted to the gambling charges, in spite of a detailed and devastating body of evidence against him, seemed genuinely startled at Gray's invitation to step into the confessional. "I'm surprised you're bombarding me like this," he said. "This is a prosecutor's brief, not an interview." The earnest and pale-faced Gray wouldn't drop it, and the interview lit up telephone call-boards at talk shows and NBC stations all around the country that evening, as indignant fans weighed in on behalf of Charlie Hustle.

Being at the park, I caught this Q. and A. only in replay, and, while I felt that Jim Gray might have shifted ground once he saw that Pete wasn't going to do a Jimmy Swaggert for us, I shared his apparent wish to grab Pete by the throat (figuratively—a *little* figuratively) and shake a morsel of candor out of him about the moldering aspersion. It isn't about to happen. Rose, an inveterate card-show and call-in-radio Dreyfus, has stiffed the nation on this issue for a decade, as he did when he refused the late Commissioner

Bart Giamatti's repeated invitations to defend himself in an open hearing. He claims never to have seen the published evidence—pages of betting logs in his handwriting, including bets on his own team, and records of phone calls from bookies to the clubhouse (he was the manager) at the Reds' Riverfront Stadium. These could be produced and tested in court, were Rose ever to mount an attempt to clear his name. But this is not Pete's way. He has become Nixonian, clothed in humility and splendor as he barges down Denial. He is Shoeless Joe coming out of the cornfield in "Field of Dreams," and America loves him for it.

What Rose is campaigning for isn't exoneration but admission to the Hall of Fame, from which he was officially debarred by the commissioner's office as part of his exile. If the gate were to be lifted, Pete would pop into the temple in an instant—for his four thousand two hundred and fifty-six hits, his thirty-five hundred games played and fourteen thousand at-bats (the most for any player, all of them), and his vividly remembered style of play, which showed us how a player with limited abilities could make it all the way, just on desire. Fans, in any case, are all for this outcome—every poll shows it, by a wide margin—but Commissioner Selig remains obdurate: no reconsideration will be offered, nothing has changed in the landscape. His old Cincinnati players and teammates are not part of the chorus pleading for Rose's readmission to baseball. Johnny Bench, asked once how soon Rose should be admitted to the Hall of Fame, said, "As soon as he's innocent."

At the jam-packed Pete Rose press conference staged by Major League Baseball an hour or so before the field ceremonies, Pete, his oddly orange hair shining in the lights, was cheerful and unconscionable, addressing old writer friends and columnists by name, and scanning the house (which included some strong supporters of his) to see how he was getting over. He was sorry about the whole thing, he told us—or said, rather, that he would do "anything in my power to change what has happened to me in the last ten years." He told us he had never met Bud Selig but that he might arm-wrestle him when he did. He evoked Bart Giamatti—"Wouldn't it be nice if Bart could be here tonight?"—and said he believed that Bart would have given him a second chance. He wondered about the ovation he would perhaps receive here tonight—would it last as long as the cheers and applause he got in Cincinnati the night he broke Ty Cobb's record? He was a teacher, he told us, and knew what was required to help a team that was down. "It's tough to turn an attitude around," he said.

Baffled, I stuck my own hand up at last and asked how his plaque at Cooperstown might read, should he be reinstated and admitted to the Hall.

"Well, first of all it would be as long as this table here," Rose said, and reminded us that he had played on the winning team more often than anybody in the history of sports. "When I went to the ballpark, I thought I was going to win."

Not what I'd meant, as we both knew.

Part of me, the Jim Gray part, believes, against all odds, that Pete Rose will get into the Hall—on the Commissioner's terms, not his. If he does, the line "Suspended from baseball in 1989 for betting on games; reinstated 20—" won't take up all that much room on the crowded, ringing bronze. Do it, Pete, and we will come.

FALL

Takes: Jacksonian

1977

With the Yankees leading the 1977 World Series by three games to two, we came back to New York for the extraordinary conclusion. In this game, the Dodgers took an early 3–2 lead on Reggie Smith's home run off Mike Torrez; it was the third round-tripper for Smith, who was beginning to look like the dominant figure in the Series. The other Reggie came up to bat in the fourth inning (he had walked in the second) and instantly pulled Burt Hooton's first delivery into the right-field stands on a low, long parabola, scoring Munson ahead of him and putting the Yankees ahead for the rest of the game and the rest of the year. Jackson stepped up to the plate again in the next inning (Elias Sosa was now pitching for the Dodgers), with two out and Willie Randolph on first, and this time I called the shot. "He's going to hit it out of here on the first pitch," I announced to my neighbors in the press rows, and so he did. It was a lower drive than the first and carried only four or five rows into the same right-field sector, but it was much more resoundingly hit; at first it looked like a double, or even a loud single, but it stayed up there—a swift white message flying out on an invisible wire—and vanished into the turbulent darkness of the crowd.

My call was not pure divination. With the strange insect gaze of his shining eyeglasses, with his ominous Boche-like helmet pulled low, with his massive shoulders, his gauntleted wrists, his high-held bat, and his enormously muscled legs spread wide, Reggie Jackson makes a frightening figure at bat. But he is not a great hitter. Perhaps he is not even a good one. A chronic overstrider and overswinger, he swings through a lot of pitches, and the unchecked flailing power of his immense cut causes his whole body to drop down a foot or more. He often concludes a trip to the plate (and a Yankee inning) with his legs grotesquely twisted and his batting helmet falling over his eyes—and with the ball, flipped underhand by the departing catcher, rolling gently out to the mound. It is this image, taken in conjunction with his salary and his unending publicity in the sports pages, that seems to enrage so many fans. "Munson!" they cry, like classicists citing Aeschylus. "Now, you take Munson—*there's* a hitter!" And they are right. But Reggie Jackson is streaky and excitable. I have an inexpungeable memory of the two violent doubles he hit for the Oakland A's against Tom Seaver in the sixth game of the 1973 World Series, and of the homer he hit the next day against Jon Matlack to destroy the Mets. I remember the gargantuan, into-the-lights home run he hit in the All-Star Game of 1971 in Detroit. And so on. Reggie Jackson is the most emotional slugger I have ever seen. Late in a close big game—and with the deep, baying cries from the stands rolling across the field: "Reg-gie! Reg-gie! Reg-gie!"—he strides to the plate and taps it with his bat and settles his batting helmet and gets his feet right and turns his glittery regard toward the pitcher, and we suddenly know that it is a different hitter we are watching now, and a different man. Get *ready*, everybody—it's show time. And, besides, Reggie had been crushing the ball in batting practice and he had hit a homer in each of the last two games against the Dodgers. Hence (to sound very much like Howard Cosell) my call.

I did not call the third homer. One does not predict miracles. This one also came on the first ball pitched—a low and much more difficult pitch, I thought, from knuckleballer Charlie Hough. The ball flew out on a higher and slower trajectory—inviting wonder and incredulity—this time toward the unoccupied sector in far-away center field that forms the black background for the hitters at the plate, and even before it struck and caromed once out there and before the showers of paper and the explosions of shouting came out of the crowd, one could almost begin to realize how many things Reggie Jackson had altered on this night. The game was won, of course (it was 8–4 in the end), and the Yankees were world champions once again. It was their first championship since 1962, and their twenty-first in all. Jackson's five homers for the Series was a new record, and so were his ten runs and twenty-five total bases. The three home runs in a single Series game had been done before—by Babe Ruth, in 1926 and again in 1928, but neither of Ruth's splurges had come on consecutive at-bats, and neither had been conclusive. Reggie Jackson's homer in the previous game had been hit on his last trip to the plate, and his base on balls in the second inning had been on four straight pitches. This meant that he had hit four home runs on four consecutive swings of the bat—a deed apparently unique in the annals of the game. But Jackson's achievement, to be sure, cannot properly be measured against any of the famous *sustained* one-man performances in World Series history—by Brooks Robinson in 1970, for instance, or by Roberto Clemente in 1971. Reggie's night—a thunderclap—was both less and more. It was *hors concours.* Jackson, in any case, had won this game and this World Series, and he had also, in some extraordinary confirming fashion, won this entire season, reminding us all of its multiple themes and moods and pleasures, which were now culminated in one resounding and unimaginable final chord.

Beyond this—or to one side of it, perhaps—Reggie had at last secured his own fame. He had justified his gigantic salary, if it *could* be justified, and in all probability he had suddenly increased the number of players who will now decide to seek their fortunes as free agents in the next few years. More than that, he had arranged for them all to receive a great deal more money for their services. Even the flintiest traditionalists among the owners—and among the fans, too—must sense that a new time has arrived in baseball. We are in the Jacksonian Era.

This World Series was famous at the very end, but it was notorious all the time. Even while they were winning, the Yankees continued their off-the-field bickerings and grudges and complaints. During the Series, clubhouse reporters wrote that Thurman Munson hoped to play for Cleveland next year, that Mickey Rivers and Graig Nettles were also eager to be traded, that Ed Figueroa had almost jumped the team, and that Reggie Jackson was bitterly critical of Martin's use of Catfish Hunter in the second game. A newsmagazine story claimed that in the middle of the season two Yankee players had asked George Steinbrenner to fire Billy Martin; Thurman Munson said that the story was a lie. A press conference was convened by the Yankees at which it was announced that the club was giving Billy Martin a new car and a bonus. Reggie Jackson, who is never at a loss for words, continued to grant startling interviews to great masses of media people. "I couldn't quit this summer, because of all the kids and the blacks and the little people who are pulling for me," he said at one point. "I represent both the underdog and the overdog in our society."

In the Dodger camp, the tone of the news, at least, was different. Manager Tom Lasorda, who did a remarkable job on the field this summer and this fall, attracted hundreds of reporters to pregame interviews, during which he told a lot of Vegas-style standup-comic jokes, and also declared his love for his country and his family and the Dodger organization. "During the national anthem," he said at one point, "a tear came to my eye—I'm not ashamed to admit that. It's the kind of guy I *am*." He made frequent mention of the Big Dodger in the Sky. One day, he confirmed to reporters that he and his wife had had dinner the night before with his good friend Frank Sinatra and *his* wife. Lasorda said that his friend Don Rickles had come to the clubhouse before the fourth game to invigorate his players with insults. "Our team is a big family," he said. "I *love* my players. They've got manners, they've got morals. They're outstanding human beings." The Dodger players, who are clean-shaven and neatly dressed and youthful in appearance, were friendly and cheerful with the press. (The Dodgers are instructed in public relations during spring training, and many of them who live in and around Los Angeles appear at community dinners and other Dodger-boosting functions during the off-season.) Steve Garvey, asked by a reporter what he thought about the Yankee Stadium fans, paused for a moment and then said, "Well, throwing things on the field is not my idea of a well-rounded human being."

I think I prefer the sour Yankee style to the Dodgers' sweetness, since it may bear a closer resemblance to the true state of morale on a professional ball team during the interminable season. It probably doesn't matter much either way. The outcome of this World Series suggests that neither of these contrasting public images had anything to do with what happened on the field. What we can be certain of is that none of this will go away. We live in an unprivate time, and the roar of personality and celebrity has almost drowned out the cheering in the stands. The ironic and most remarkable aspect of Reggie Jackson's feat is that for a moment there, on that littered, brilliant field, he—he, of all people—almost made us forget this. Suddenly he confirmed all our old, secret hopes. He reminded us why we had come there in the first place—for the game and not the news of the game, for the feat and not the feature. What he had done was so difficult and yet was done so well that it was inexplicable. He had become a hero.

Blue Collar

1982

I. STREAKY

The St. Louis Cardinals' spirited comeback victory over the Milwaukee Brewers in a seven-game World Series was in many ways a simulacrum of the season itself, where around the leagues the quality of the games often did not quite match our hopes, but the closeness of the competition and the size of the crowds and the accompanying sense of occasion and adventure made for a kind of baseball that seemed, from first to last, inspiriting and involving and endlessly talkable. No other recent season, I believe, has pleased so many home-town baseball fans or left them with such warm feelings for their game. We know how it all came out in the end, of course, but I think we should remind ourselves about how many different teams were involved in the long, close races this year. At the All-Star Game break, which is the traditional, if not actual, mid-point of the season, thirteen clubs were bunched within four games of the top in the four divisions, with some surprising and refreshing names—the Braves, the Padres, the White Sox, and the Mariners—among them. Five weeks later, on August 16th, thirteen teams remained in the hunt, and another five weeks along, on September 20th, there were still ten of them—at least two in each division—with an excellent shot at the playoffs. The Cardinals captured their demi-crown first, six days before the end; in retrospect, their sudden certainty, their lack of crises, should have told us more about the quality of this club than it seemed to show at the time.

This was the streakiest season in baseball history. The Braves startled their new manager, Joe Torre, with a record-breaking opening sprint of thirteen straight wins, and the Padres followed with an eleven-game winning string of their own, also in the very early going. Other market gainers included the Cardinals, the Orioles, and the Brewers, who won twelve, ten, and eight in a row, respectively. Downside competition was equally vigorous. The fitful Braves suddenly dropped eleven straight games in August, and the Cubs, the Twins, and the Mets lost thirteen, fourteen, and fifteen games in a row.

The great one-man performance of the year was by Milwaukee shortstop Robin Yount, who finished first in his league in hits, total bases, doubles (a tie), and slugging percentage. He also batted .331 (one point below the top mark in the league), hit twenty-nine homers, and drove in a hundred and fourteen runs. Most shortstops, of course, hold down their jobs because they are quick and lithe and can cover the ground, and Yount's offensive performance has been equalled in the past only by Hall of Fame shortstops Ernie Banks and Honus Wagner. Yount was voted Most Valuable Player in the American League, and the choice has never been easier. Other Brewers did well, too: first baseman Cecil Cooper, third baseman Paul Molitor, and Yount were the only three American Leaguers to finish with more than two hundred hits, and Molitor led the league in runs.

Rickey Henderson's new record of a hundred and thirty stolen bases is a strange business, for he is so far ahead of his nearest competitors, past or present, that comparisons become meaningless. In the first half of the season, he was stealing bases at a rate of almost one per game, which is unheard of, and he sailed past Lou Brock's old mark of a hundred and eighteen on August 27th. A shoulder injury kept him out of action through most of September, and cost him an even more startling final figure. Henderson, who leads off the Oakland order, bats out of a deep crouch and draws a great many bases on balls; he had the third-best on-base average in his league this year. Once there, he *ran*. He stole second base ninety-four times, third base thirty-four times, and home twice. Three times, he stole four bases in one game. He was picked off or caught stealing forty-two times, which is also a record, but conservatives who are impelled to linger on this figure must also count in the number of errors caused by his speed—wild pick-off throws, and so on—and notice the distorted infield defenses he imposed on the other team whenever he took a lead off first. Close observers of the team tell me that Henderson is at last beginning to study the pitchers' moves out there—Brock's record, which he set at the age of thirty-five, was more a matter of wile than of celerity—but his secret still lies in his ability to fly instantly into high gear on the base paths, with two pumping strides of his powerfully muscled legs. He is also an extraordinarily talented defensive outfielder—"the best left fielder I've ever seen," in Earl Weaver's judgment. Henderson is twenty-three years old, and we must assume that he will do better in the years ahead.

A day or two before Rickey broke the old record, Tiger manager Sparky Anderson kicked up a monumental fuss when he accused Billy Martin of ordering Fred Stanley, the Oakland shortstop, to allow himself to be picked off second by the Tiger pitcher so that Henderson, then parked at first, would be free to motor. Sparky has the highest indignation quota in modern skipperdom, but in this landmark case I come down on Billy's side. Back in June, while attending an A's–White Sox game in Oakland, I had observed the same situation—Stanley on second, Henderson on first, nobody out—and the same brilliant move sprang into my mind: burn Stanley, perhaps in a double steal, and then watch Rickey steal third and fly away home any old way he wants. I forget what did happen, but it was something quite different, and nobody scored, and I shook my head sadly—a thinker ahead of my time.

All through this summer of slipshod, enthusiastic competition, I kept reading about some faraway game or far-out series in one city or another that I badly wished I had seen. There was, for instance, the lengthy mid-August meeting between the Cards and the Giants in St. Louis, which the Cardinals captured when their wholly anonymous third-string catcher, Glenn Brummer, stole home in the twelfth inning—stole it all on his own, on a brainstorm, really, with no signal or invitation from his manager or coach: *Hey, what if...* It was his second career stolen base. I also recall a mad moment, glimpsed by me on television, in the midst of a game in Atlanta, when Dodger catcher Mike Scioscia snatched up a bunt and threw wildly past third in an attempt to cut down a base runner there. The ball went squiggling and bouncing out along the base of the grandstand fence in short left field while several base runners tore happily around the base paths; when a few dozen hometown fans out there leaned over, as fans will do, to cheer the ball on its way, a section of the fence collapsed under their weight and spilled them, fans and fence and all, onto the field and on top of the ball. No damage, except perhaps to the psyches of the umpires, who then conferred at length in a miserable-looking *now-what?* sort of huddle, and eventually took a run down off the board and ordered an Atlanta base runner back a notch or two. Thunderous booing, but, as it turned out, the event made hardly a ripple in a game in which the two clubs whanged out seven home runs and thirty-five hits between them, with the Braves winning at last by 12–11.

I was in Atlanta in late July for a six-hour steambath doubleheader between Joe Torre's league-leading Braves—"America's Team," in their relentless promotions—and the second-place Padres, during which I gained a startled new sense of this, my own, my native team and its unbridled ways. The Braves won the opener by 9–2, on an uncharacteristic complete-game outing by a starting pitcher, Bob Walk, and then took the nightcap, 8–6, in their more customary recent style, coming from behind three times and rapping out four home runs, the last of which, struck by the bearded minuscule second baseman, Glenn Hubbard, sent us home happy in the tenth. Their star slugger, the six-foot-five Dale Murphy, came up with two singles, a double, two homers, and four runs batted in in the games, along with a leaping catch, in the deepest part of the park, that robbed Ruppert Jones of a two-run homer in the top of that same tenth.

What I kept from this visit, and played over in my head for many nights afterward, was a moment in the first game of the doubleheader when a surefire third-to-home-to-first triple play suddenly wasn't. With the bases loaded in the third, and nobody out, Bruce Benedict hit a sharp ground ball to the Padres' Luis Salazar, at third, who stepped on the bag and fired to catcher Terry Kennedy at home. Kennedy, standing on the plate, took the throw well before the front base runner (it was Bob Horner) arrived and in the same motion threw to first in plenty of time to retire the batter. Almost at the same instant Kennedy could be seen stomping the dirt around home and attempting to tear his ears off, because of his Little League mistake: the out at third had nullified the force at home, where the catcher now needed to tag Horner before finishing the odd, counterclockwise play at first. Well, tough, we wise-guys said, smiling at each other in the pressbox; too bad Terry got excited down there, but it's a rock for him to let the run score that way. But we were wrong, too, it turned out. After the game, home-plate umpire Paul Runge approached a couple of writers outside the Braves clubhouse, and asked what they'd thought of the Kennedy play at home. They shook their heads smugly and talked about the nullified force, but Runge didn't join in. "Didn't anybody see Horner's slide?" he said. "He missed home plate by two feet. He hasn't touched it yet. I took a little time to clean off the plate, waiting to see if anybody'd noticed." But nobody had—all eyes except Runge's had reflexively followed the relay to first and then switched back to enjoy Kennedy's embarrassment. If anyone had come out of the San Diego dugout before the next pitch was delivered and asked to have the ball thrown back to the catcher again, Horner would have been out after all, and the first appealed triple play in history would be in the books. I ran into Terry Kennedy in Arizona the following March, and learned that he'd never been told about Horner's wide slide. "So now I'm dumb twice on the same play," he said cheerfully. "Do they keep records for that?" (I found Paul Runge by telephone in July, 2002—he's retired and living in Southern California—and ran the twenty-year-old play past him, just to check my old notes. At first, he denied memory of the moment, but when I brought up the players and the situation again, he said, "Yes, that's right! Horner slid way wide of the plate on the right side—I can see it now." He also reconfirmed the unappealed third out, but umpires—I realized, listening to him—aren't much into the might-have-been.)

America's Team ran into frightful luck in the first game of the National League championship Series, when a drenching downpour interrupted the proceedings at Busch Stadium with one out in the bottom of the fifth inning. At the time, the Braves were leading the home-team Cardinals by 1–0, with the ancient knuckleballer Phil Niekro in imperturbable good form on the mound, and two more outs would have brought them a truncated but legal victory. The next night, starting over, Atlanta had to face the Cards' veteran righty Bob Forsch, who shut them out on three hits, while his teammates were offering instructive lessons in their distinctive killer-gnat style of attack. Redbird left fielder Lonnie Smith led off the sixth with a difficult little bouncer to right that he beat out with his sprinter's speed, and five ensuing and distracting singles broke open the game, which the Cardinals took by 7–0. Twelve of the fourteen Cardinal hits were singles, poked or looped or bounced about on the stadium's patchy lettuce-green pitch-and-putt Astro-Turf carpet. "The Cardinals are always going from first to damn third," Joe Torre muttered.

Another rain postponement allowed Torre to bring back Niekro, on minimal rest, for Game Two—an improvisation that showed us once and for all the frailness of the Atlanta staff. "We never had a rotation—not really," Torre said in a candid moment. The Braves' pitching roster included no left-handers at all, and every hurler except Niekro had done duty in the bullpen at some time or other during the summer. This game, in any case, was a little beauty, with Niekro serving up his dying-moth deliveries through six innings and helping himself with a run-scoring sacrifice fly; he departed in the seventh, ahead by 3–2, but the Cardinals caught up in the eighth—again on speed, when center fielder Willie McGee barely beat out an inning-ending double-play relay at first while the tying run came in—and won it in the ninth on two singles and a sac. Bruce Sutter, the Cardinal bullpen ace, collected the last six Atlanta outs with his patented down-darting, split-finger fastball. That was all, really. The Braves' pitcher in Game Three, in Atlanta on Sunday, was Rick Camp, who had lost his last six decisions. He was gone again in a twinkling, surrendering four runs in the second inning, as the home of the Braves fell into miserable silence, and the Cardinals won the game, 6–2, and the pennant with it.

The end of the season, followed by the quick, deadly-short playoffs, eliminates so many familiar and praiseworthy teams—intimates of ours by now—in such a short time that the autumn air seems to bring a sweet, sharp smell of disappointment and loss, even as we look forward to the excitement of a resolution. I felt this tang more acutely than ever in Milwaukee, where the Angels, who had jumped away to a two-game lead over the Brewers out in Anaheim, with two wonderfully pitched games by Tommy John and Bruce Kison, now suddenly and shockingly expired in three successive losses to the Brewers. You could see the likelihood of such an end growing, day by day—inning by inning, I imagine—on the faces of the California veterans and, most of all, in the frozen, closed-off stare of their crusty skipper, Gene Mauch, who had managed for twenty-two prior seasons in the majors without attaining a World Series and now saw the prize snatched away once again.

2. MIDLANDS

The seven-game Series, which was captured at very long last by the Cardinals, lacked for nothing but restraint and consistency, and its motto might have been "Both Things Are True." Both teams proved themselves capable of the gallant comeback victory (the Brewers in the fourth game, the Cardinals in the second and seventh) and of the abysmal collapse (the Cardinals lost the first game by 10–0, and the Brewers lost the sixth by 13–1). By far the best pitching performances of the Series came during these blowouts— Mike Caldwell's three-hit shutout in the opener, and John Stuper's rainy-night four-hit masterpiece in the interminably delayed Game Six—and thus lost most of their lustre, while the worst of all pitching possibilities, a walk with the bases loaded, miserably settled Game Two. The feared and famous Brewer batters sometimes awed us (Molitor had a record five hits in one game, and Yount a record four hits in each of two games), while the Cards' speed and defense were super in patches, yet it was the *Milwaukee* defense that won Game Five, in which the Cardinals rapped out fifteen base hits. The big boppers in the middle of the Brewer lineup—Ted Simmons, Ben Oglivie, and Gorman Thomas—together batted in a meagre seven runs, with a cumulative .171 average, in the seven games; while a Cardinal rookie, Willie McGee, hit two homers and batted in four runs in one.

Between them, the two teams committed eighteen errors and stranded ninety-three base runners in the gawky quadrille. And so it went, up and down, forward and sidewise, through this entertaining and dishevelled pageant, which once again conclusively proved the truth of the grand baseball adage: good pitching will always beat good hitting, and vice versa. And even here we should append a demurrer: it probably *was* the Cardinals' pitching—Stuper, Joaquin Andujar (whose 1.35 earned-run average was the best on view), and, at the very end, Bruce Sutter—that made the difference, barely, and won (or maybe just ended) this particular fall unclassic.

The rival clubs were wonderfully different in abilities and philosophy. The quick Cardinals were a team of movement, tension, opportunism, and defense—a team born to play on artificial turf— and the ticking, intimidating Brewers, who play at home on grass, were always willing to wait to beat you with their bats. Some baseball writers said that the Brewer batting order presented the most menacing nine swingers in a row since the 1939 Yankees; others claimed that the Cardinals' outfield of Lonnie Smith, George Hendrick, and Willie McGee was the fastest picket line the sport had ever seen. Then there was the business of the two shortstops—the incomparable Robin Yount being repeatedly compared to the incomparable (for other reasons, primarily his magical playmaking) Ozzie Smith; and, above it all, the more comical and symbolic matter of appearance and style, with some wonderfully hirsute and raggedyass Brewer veterans (Gorman Thomas, Pete Vuckovich, Mike Caldwell) always seeming to present themselves in opposition to the younger and thinner, neatly combed Cardinals—Keith Hernandez, Tommy Herr, Joaquin Andujar, John Stuper. The frowsy, hard-playing Gorman Thomas is a walking strip mine. He has worn the same pair of uniform stockings—now as threadbare as the Shroud of Turin—in every game since Opening Day of 1978. During the Series, a group of us in the Brewer clubhouse were chatting with Thomas's father—he is the retired postmaster of Charleston, S.C.—and some genius reporter asked what Gorman's room had looked like back when he was a teen-ager. "Turrible!" Thomas *père* cried, wincing at the thought. "Why, I could hardly make myself look in theah!")

Nor were the managers much alike, with the thick-bodied, self-assured, experienced Herzog—this was his tenth season as a major-league skipper—sometimes seeming at an antipodal remove from the silent, slow-moving Harvey Kuenn, a Milwaukee native who took over the team reins only this past June, after eleven seasons as a coach. A great hitter in his day—he batted .353 for the Tigers one year—Kuenn had experienced serious illness in recent times, and two years ago he lost a leg to surgery. All such preliminary postures and ironies tend to fade in our minds once the World Series teams actually take the field, but they are there just the same, and we hope against hope that the fortunes of play and the crowning of a champion will bring them flooding back again and give them deeper and clearer ultimate meaning. Foolishly, we want our games turned into some kind of moral drama, and this time, once again, we were disappointed.

The Cardinals, who had suffered that embarrassing 10–0 whitewashing in the Series opener, got themselves out of a pickle the next night when they rallied in the sixth to tie up Game Two at 4–4; the key blow was Darrell Porter's two-run, wrong-field double against Don Sutton. The game's untidy clarification came in the bottom of the eighth when, with two Cards aboard, young Peter Ladd threw a three-and-two fastball to Lonnie Smith that home-plate ump Bill Haller called ball four. Disagreeing—shaking his head and staring about angrily—Ladd now delivered four more balls in rapid succession to Steve Braun, and the winning tally strolled home. After the game, the reporters kept asking Ted Simmons whether that last pitch to Smith had indeed been a strike, and Simmons—like most catchers, a realist—kept saying, "Ball four to Smith had nothing to do with it. Those things happen sometimes. It was ball four to Braun that beat us."

We repaired to Milwaukee, where, on a cold and blustery evening in the old steel-post park, County Stadium, Willie McGee staged his party. There were a few other happenings in the game, to be sure, including the frightening one-hop smash by Ted Simmons that caromed off Andujar's knee, retiring him for the rest of the evening and perhaps for the rest of the going, but McGee kept our attention. He opened with a very fine first-inning catch against Molitor, in the deepest part of center field. With two mates aboard in the fifth, he smashed a Pete Vuckovich changeup pitch into the right-field bleachers. In the seventh, he leaned away from a message-bearing greeting up under his chin and then drove Vuckovich's next delivery over the wall in right center. In the ninth, with the Cards now up by 6–2, he sprinted lengthily to his right and leaped up onto the left-center-field wall to pull down a mighty poke by Gorman Thomas. McGee, a skinny, thin-necked switch-hitter, was called up from the Cards' Louisville farm last May to fill in for an injured player in center field, but he made himself so much at home out there, batting .296 for the rest of the year, that he could never be returned to the bench. He is twenty-four and still has the evasive, sweetly shy look of a rookie. When he was acquired from the Yankees in a minor-league-level swap last year, no one in either club thought to tell him about the deal, which he first learned of in a buried sports-page item, and he still wears the anonymously high uniform number—51—that he was given in spring training. The wish to protect or patronize someone so young and gentle is hard to avoid, but McGee seems able to handle things as they come. He has thrived with the Cardinals, and found a more literal home with Ozzie Smith, who invited the young rookie to come and live with him this first season. During the summer, a few players and broadcasters around the league perhaps inescapably began referring to McGee as "E.T.," but here, surrounded at his clubhouse locker by fifty or sixty big-city sportswriters, he murmured, "I'd appreciate it if you'd call me by my name. Nobody should be able to change your name. That's almost like changing your life."

He is, in any case, at ease in the game. "Once you're to goin', you're O.K.," he says. His power is startling—he'd hit two triples and one homer in the playoffs, and had missed another, an inside-the-park job, only because of a baserunning lapse—but I think his deeper talent (and his chances for a much lower uniform number) lies in his fielding. "I like to time the ball out there," he said at one point, and he had already shown us what he meant. In the ninth-inning play against Gorman Thomas, he had gone at full tilt from mid-center field into deep left center and then to the top of the wall there all in one flowing, waterlike motion—a cat up a tree—with no pause or acceleration near the end to adjust for the catch; at the top of his leap, with his back to the field, he put his glove up and a bit to his left, and the ball, in the same instant, arrived. Only the Willie Mayses of this world can do that.

The Brewers' big two-out, six-run rally in the seventh inning of Game Four was made up of some very small fragments indeed, including a tiny, foolish error by Cardinal pitcher Dave LaPoint, who bobbled an easy toss at first base and gave the runner, Ben Oglivie, a life; a couple of bases on balls; a checked-swing, accidental single by Yount; a wild pitch; and—most of all, perhaps—a bluffed bunt by Cecil Cooper, which caused Cardinal third baseman Ken Oberkfell to station himself a step or two closer to the plate in response. Cooper now mashed a low liner that barely nubbed off the heel of Oberkfell's glove, as the tying run came in; Gorman Thomas's single then drove in the two runs that won the breathlessly exciting game, 7–5. Three St. Louis relief pitchers tried to stem the winning Milwaukee rally—none of them named Sutter, who had worked two innings and a bit in each of the two previous games and thus used up his quota of effective pitches for the next game or two. Fans sometimes wonder how a pitcher can be worn down by such brief exercise, but the question does not take into account the effort involved in throwing the Sutter version of the split-finger fastball. For this delivery, he holds the ball between his separated forefinger and middle finger, with his thumb tucked up underneath, almost in marble-shooting position, and throws the pitch hard. It is the quirk of the thumb that causes the Sutter special to dive downward at the moment it approaches the strike zone.

Waiting for a six-run rally is an edgy business, but the Brewer fans, all fifty-six thousand of them, kept up their good spirits there in Game Four, even when they were behind by 5–1. It was a sensationally beautiful afternoon—Indian summer, you felt—with a brisk, in-blowing breeze, and the ruffled grass a very dark green out there, and, now and then, the startling fat shadow of the Goodyear blimp sailing across the diamond. "Here we go, Brewers! Here we go!" the jam-packed family crowd sang out again and again, and then the old-style ballpark organ would chip in with an odd little tinkling refrain (the opening bars of Elton John's "Bennie and the Jets"), which began a rhythmic clap-clapping that swept up one side of the low, deep stands and then down the other—a breeze of clapping and hope. There was nothing new or fancy about this, but fanciness is not Milwaukee's style. The huge pre-game tailgate parties in the parking lot before each home game feature beer and bratwurst (the smell of the cooking fires is almost unbearably delicious), though, to tell the truth, there aren't all that many tailgates, because the cars are mostly campers, not station wagons. I couldn't help comparing these rites and noises with the crowd-stuff back in St. Louis, at the Cardinals' circular downtown park, where the fans clap and cheer in dutiful response to a different tune, endlessly repeated—the Budweiser jingle—and are further belabored by the undeviating glottal enthusiasm of the game announcer: "Now coming up to bat for your Cardinals—OZ-ZEEE...*Smith!!!*" Busch-league stuff.

I belonged to the Brewers by now, in short, and my affection for the team and the town had been secured, if that was needed, by a noontime visit I had made the previous day to Cesar's Inn, the West Milwaukee tavern owned and operated by Audrey Kuenn— Mrs. Manager. The place is only a few blocks from County Stadium—you can see the banks of lights from the front door—so it's convenient for Harvey; the Kuenns live in the back of Cesar's, with their rooms separated from the bar by a Dutch door, the top half of which seems to be open at all times. The bar is a low, smoky, exceedingly cheerful room, with cardboard cartoon cutouts of Harvey's Wallbangers stuck up behind the bottles, and the roar of Brewer talk among the patrons competing with the big, eclectic jukebox—a *good* jukebox: the J. Geils Band's "Angel in Blue," Alabama's "Mountain Music," Eddy Duchin's old "Time on My Hands," Smokey Robinson, the Andrews Sisters. There is a pool table jammed into one half of the lounge, and the lights on the wall are imitation baseballs, with little crossed bats underneath. Photos and paintings of Harv everywhere, of course. When I was there, the folks at the bar were youngish men in T-shirts and mustaches and old high-school-team windbreakers and emblazoned industrial caps; they mostly drank Miller's, but one man near me at the bar was working on Hennessy's cognac with Pabst chasers. The clientele at Cesar's Inn turns up in bunches after the shifts change at the big manufacturing plants in nearby West Allis—Harnischfeger (overhead cranes) and Rexnord (chain belts) and Allis-Chalmers.

The late shift sometimes includes men from another neighborhood plant—Gorman Thomas or Jim Gantner or Pete Vuckovich—in for a brew after a night game. On busy nights, Bob McClure and Mike Caldwell have been known to slip behind the bar to help out.

I introduced myself to Audrey Kuenn, a trim, extremely pleasant woman in blue slacks and a tan blouse, who told me that she had experienced a few moments of doubt when Harvey was named manager, back in June, because she didn't want to lose her close friendship with the Brewer wives, who call her Mom. But it didn't change; they all went on sitting together in Section 3, just as before, and screamed the team home. The Kuenns have been married for eight years (each was married previously), and now I asked Audrey if she'd ever seen Harvey play ball. "No, I didn't," she said. "It used to be the old Braves who played in this park, you know, Eddie Mathews and Joe Adcock and the rest"—the Braves won a World Championship in 1957 but abandoned Milwaukee in 1966, moving to Atlanta and leaving a very bitter feeling among local fans for their perfidy—"and I never got to see any American League players."

"He was *something*," I said, and she said, "I'll bet. But I don't think I could have stood it, watching Harv—I get so excited."

Our conversation was conducted in fragments, because Audrey Kuenn had bar business to look after, and the phone kept ringing (the Kuenns are in the book, and one of the callers that morning was a man who told Audrey to tell Harvey to tell Gorman Thomas to keep his eye on the ball; "I sure will," she said), and the Kuenns' three dogs—Nicky and Jingles, the boxers, and Ugsly, the pug—seemed a bit restless, too, and no wonder. Then the bar talk and Series talk went up a notch or two when a young man and his girlfriend came in, bringing along *their* boxer, name of Harley, who had a half-embarrassed, dog-in-a-paper-hat look, because he had been painted Brewer blue from head to foot and nose to tail (blue hair spray, it turned out), with a tan "1" on his back and the Brewer baseball-mitt logo in tan on his forehead and a wiggly tan "Go Brewers" in script on each flank. "It's better on his other side," Harley's owner told me, pointing to the message. "I got better at it the second time." Audrey Kuenn went out back to tell Harvey to finish getting dressed, because it was time for him to get to the park, and when she returned, just before Harvey came out and said hello to everyone in the place, and then goodbye to everyone in the place, she said to me, "When we got to the hotel in St. Louis the other day, I said to Harv, 'Can you *believe* we're here?' and he said, 'Never in a million years.'"

Brewer fans had to endure a different and much more painful sort of waiting game the next day—Game Five and the last baseball of the year at County Stadium—when they watched the Cardinals come thundering up from astern and almost snatch back a game they seemed to have safely lost from the outset. In the ninth, down by four runs, the visitors slammed out two doubles and two singles, all in succession, to close to 6–4, with the tying runs on base. Harvey Kuenn, again the undermanager, at last came out to the mound to get his tottering starter, Caldwell, who had been cuffed about all day and barely reprieved again and again by some unlikely fielding gem by his teammates. McClure, in relief, got the last two outs. Back in the early going, Yount and then Molitor and then Charlie Moore had made marvellous plays in successive innings—Moore's a skidding full-length dive on his chest to rob Lonnie Smith of at least a double—and Cooper and then Molitor did more of the same late in the game: five runs saved, by my count. ("God *damn,* they made some great plays out there," Herzog said later, shaking his head.) Robin Yount hit two singles, a double, and a home run ("M.V.P.!" the home hordes shouted. "M.V.P.!"), but the hits that mattered most were probably the two little singles struck by Moore and Gantner in the eighth, against Bruce Sutter, each of which scored a run—the runs that won the game.

The exulting homeward-bound Brewer rooters whooping down the stadium ramps and the TV lights and ten-deep crowds around Robin Yount in the clubhouse made it look as if this Series had already been won and its hero chosen, but when I glanced through my scorebook I realized that the Cards had racked up nine runs on twenty-three hits in the past two games. They had fallen back and now trailed in the Series, to be sure, but somehow they felt like the oncoming team. I was reminded of some cautionary words I had heard from Ted Simmons a bit earlier in the week. "Emotions die down after we get out of here," he had said. "There are no edges—only games. People who look for edges set themselves up for a big disappointment." Down at the other end of the Milwaukee clubhouse, away from the lights and the noise, the Brewer clubhouse rats—Thomas and Fingers and Vuckovich and Money— were deep in their regular gin games, with their beers set about them in a cluster on the table. The season had a little longer to go.

I missed the rest. Laid low by a virus, I had to go home instead of to St. Louis, and thus watched from a distance, by television, the runaway, rain-flooded Game Six (actually, I was sensibly in bed and asleep when it ended, well into the next day), which the Cardinals won by 13–1; and then, the next night, Game Seven—the riveting, marvellous finale, in which the fiery Andujar, recently off his crutches, pitched so well early on and Sutter pitched so well at the very end, getting the last six outs in succession when it most mattered. The Brewers rallied in the middle innings, to lead at 3–1, but the resourceful Cards responded instantly with three runs of their own, doing in the exhausted Pete Vuckovich. The last big blow of the year was Keith Hernandez' two-run single up the middle, hit off a fine pitch by Bob McClure, who—ah, baseball!—had played on the same team with Hernandez back in junior high school in California. The final score was 6–3. All the teams I really cared about this year—the Braves, the Orioles, the Angels, and now the Brewers—had lost, one by one, and had broken my heart a little in the process. But, after all, I am a Red Sox fan. Wait till next year.

Takes: The Confines

1984

Early on the day of the first Cubs-Padres playoff game, Cubs Manager Jim Frey went to his bedroom window to check the wind—*too* early, it turned out, for it was four-thirty in the morning and still pitch-black out there. He went back to bed. He got what he wanted, though, for there was a lovely Cubs wind at Wrigley Field by game time that afternoon—blowing straight out, that is, at a good twenty miles an hour—and throughout the day you could hear the shuffle and pop of the flags snapping in the breeze. The scoops of bunting set around the gray-blue facing of the steep upper deck were also astir, and, farther out, the tall center-field flagpole above the great gray-green scoreboard and the rising pyramid of bleachers flew a double row of pennants (team flags, in the order of finish, top to bottom, of the National League divisions), which kept up a gala, regattalike flutter all through the shining afternoon. The famous ivy, thickly overgrowing the outfield walls from pole to pole, showed October tints, and the graceful old brickwork of the inner-field façade suggested football weather as well. There were treetops swaying out along Waveland Avenue, beyond left field, and Sheffield Avenue, beyond right, and other flags were aloft on the rooftops of the low neighborhood houses there, with a fine range of colors and loyalties to choose among: Old Glory, Israel, Ireland, Puerto Rico, and, of course, the Cubs. In among the flags, a couple of big tethered balloons shifted and shouldered in the moving air, and the parapets and extemporaneous stands on the roofs were jammed with unticketed, opportunistic fans, who counted themselves lucky to be close enough to pick up glimpses of the game along with the sounds and sense of it. The angling, early-autumn sunlight illuminated white-and-blue Cubs pennants in the stands around the park and silhouetted a long, sweeping line of heads and shoulders of the spectators in the topmost row of the lower deck, and when the Cubs' center fielder, Bob Dernier, sprinted to his left and abruptly bent low to pull in a line drive, early on, there was a sudden gleam, a dart of light, from his dark glasses as he made the grab. Even the noises of the day—the deep, happy roaring of the fans; the ancient, carny-show strains of the Wrigley Field organ (sometimes playing upbeat old airs like Cole Porter's "From This Moment On")—seemed to reach us with a washed and wonderful clarity, and in my seat in the airy, down-sloping lower left-field stands (an overflow press sector), I kept tight hold on my rustling scorecard and stat sheets, and felt at one with the weather and the world. It was as if the entire baseball season—all those hundreds of games and thousands of innings—had happened, just this one time, in order to bring this afternoon to pass: a championship game, and the Cubs, for once, in it. Only one possibility could spoil things on a day like this—and I could almost see the same thought on the faces of the holiday throngs pushing along under the stands before game time: the unexpected, awful shadow of a doubt—and even that was taken care of in the quickest possible way. Dernier, leading off against the Padres' Eric Show in the bottom of the first, rocketed the second pitch to him into the screen above the left-field bleachers, and a bare moment or two later Gary Matthews got another shot up into the wind, which landed above and beyond the ivy in left center, a good four hundred feet away. Rick Sutcliffe came up to bat in the third, and *his* homer—a low, hurrying, near line drive over the right-side bleachers: a *shot*—didn't need the wind at all, and it told us, if any doubt remained, what kind of day this was meant to be. Chicago won, 13–0.

Before we say goodbye to the Cubs, who are about to make their sudden departure from this season and this account (they won again the next afternoon, this time playing shortball—speed and defense and the extra base—for a neat 4–2 decision, then they were wiped out in three straight losses out in San Diego), another lingering look at the Friendly Confines and its team may be forgiven. The Cubs' great success in 1984 and abrupt termination in the championships can best be appreciated if we remind ourselves about the team's unique place in the sport. The Cubs are the Smithsonian of baseball, a caucus of institutions, many of which were on view during the playoff festivities. "Mr. Cub," Ernie Banks, who put in nineteen years' distinguished service at shortstop and first base, reappeared in uniform as an honorary member of the 1984 team and threw out the first ball (a trick flip from behind his back on the mound) before the first game. The next day, the ritual was performed by Jack Brickhouse, who had broadcast thirty-four years of Cub games before his retirement, in 1982; his successor in the booth, the incumbent Harry Caray, is a *transferred* institution, who had previously put in eleven years' work with the White Sox. Steve Trout, the southpaw who pitched and won the second playoff game against the Padres, is a son of Dizzy Trout, who pitched and won a game against the Cubs in their last previous post-season adventure, the 1945 World Series, against Detroit. And so on.

I spotted Bill Veeck, who sat in the centerfield bleachers throughout the season and the playoffs, through my binoculars, with a Vincent van Gogh straw hat on his bean, a beer in his hand, and his pegleg comfortably out in the aisle, while a stream of friends and writers and well-wishers came by to shake his hand and spoil his view. I almost walked out there to pay my respects to Veeck, a favorite old friend of mine, but then I decided that I didn't want to add to the distracting crush of admirers around him. So many reporters wanted to interview him during the playoffs that he was forced to set up a schedule of incoming telephone interviews at his house; one writer told me he had got his story at seven-twenty in the morning. Veeck died fifteen months later, but I treasure this distant last glimpse of him at home in his favorite old ballpark and relishing a game. Baseball, he always said, should be *savored.*

Veeck was most recently in baseball as the owner and chief executive of the White Sox, but his father, William Veeck, Sr., was president of the Cubs from 1919 to 1933, and Veeck the Younger grew up in Wrigley Field and had his first job in the business with the team thereafter. It was Bill Veeck, in fact, who persuaded the Wrigleys to plant ivy out along the outfield walls, in 1938. I was having dinner with Veeck and the peerless Hank Greenberg in Arizona a few years ago, when during the first cocktail he began talking about the old Wrigley Field days, and described a bygone Cubs program vendor as being "a great duker."

"What's a duker, Bill?" I asked.

"You don't know what a duker is?" he said happily. "O.K.—get up and go over there and then walk by our table."

"What?" I said.

"Just go over and walk on by me, here at the table," he ordered. "You'll see."

I got up and followed his directions, and as I strolled past Veeck in his chair I suddenly found myself holding his menu.

"That's a scorecard," he said. "It's in your duke, in your hand—he just put it there—and now you owe him a quarter. The man was also a genius with those paper tweety-birds on a stick. No little boy or girl got by him without getting one, and now if his daddy doesn't want to pay for it he has to take it away from his own kid and give it back to our vendor. A great man."

The only trouble with the great duker was that he was a crook, Veeck went on. "We had to put one of our people up on on a higher level with a pair of binoculars to keep tabs on him and make sure we got our end. Do you know the name of that vendor?"

I didn't know but Hank Greenberg must have, because he was nodding his big head up and down in anticipation of my reaction.

"Jack Ruby," Veeck said.

The best-known Cub fixture, of course—almost an honored institution—is defeat. No other club has had a manager who described his team's home fans as unemployables, as did a recent incumbent named Lee Elia, and no other franchise has taken so mild a view of its own fortunes as to allow its team to amble along with no manager at all, as the Cubs did from 1961 to 1965, when the day-to-day direction was handled by a rotating board of coaches. Leo Durocher took over after that and whipped the team up into second place a couple of times, but the last pennant, in '45, is still so vivid in the memory of the fans that this year in Chicago I kept hearing references to Hank Borowy, the pitcher who won the first and sixth games of that World Series, and lost the fifth and seventh.

We won't know for some time where the 1984 Cubs will fit into this sweet, dismal history, but I think we can already do honor to the principals—Dallas Green and Jim Frey, and the newborn or new-bought stars on the field—for reversing this deep-running tide so precipitately. There was no preparation for this at the beginning of the year, when the Cubs, fifth-place finishers the year before, lost eleven straight games in spring training, but some late trades suddenly filled the team's needs—a lead-off man, a center fielder, more speed (Bob Dernier, who came from the Phillies on March 27th, took care of all three), more and then still more pitching—and they began to win and began to be noticed. On June 23rd, before a national television audience, the Cubs beat the Cardinals, 12–11, in eleven innings, in a game in which Ryne Sandberg, their remarkable young star, hit two home runs against Bruce Sutter—one in the ninth and another in the tenth (with two out and a man aboard), each time retying the score. "Sandberg is the best player I have ever seen," Cardinal manager Whitey Herzog said afterward.

It is the Cub fans who will have to sort out this season—most of all, the unshirted, violently partisan multitudes in the Wrigley Field bleachers, who sustain the closest fan-to-player attachment anywhere in baseball—and I will not patronize them by claiming a share of their happiness during the summer or pretending to understand their pain and shock at its end. Baseball, as I have sometimes suggested, is above all a matter of belonging, and belonging to the Cubs takes a lifetime. But to Chicago the Cubs are something more than just a team. Wrigley Field is almost the last of the old neighborhood ballparks, and the antiquity of the place (it was built in 1914, two years after Fenway Park opened for business in Boston) and the absence of night ball there (the Wrigley family believed that the crowds and the noise would be an affront to the nearby residents) remind us what the game once felt like and how it fitted into the patterns of city life. I took a little stroll around the blocks off to the north and east of Wrigley Field one morning before game time and fell into conversation with a short, cheerful young woman named Debra Price, who was out jogging. She was wearing a sweatshirt with huge Cubs emblazoning, and was accompanied by her black cat, Dufus, who runs with her. She told me she had lived just around the corner, on Kenmore Avenue, until August, when she took a job in Denver (she is in labor relations), but had come back for the games because her old roommate, Karen Miller, had been lucky enough to get hold of a pair of tickets. "I was going through a bad Cubs withdrawal out there," she said. "It used to be incredibly convenient living so close to the park here. You could walk over at nine in the morning and pick up your seats for that afternoon. It was always easy to get seats, because the team wasn't going anywhere. I can't quite believe this whole year, or understand it. I'm a little young to be a real Cubs fan, but I think I qualify. I was there two years ago the day Bill Buckner got his two-hundredth hit of the season, and Jody Davis has been sort of a constant for me. There's a lot of character and sentimentality in what the Cubs are. They've always seemed older than the White Sox in this town—I don't know why. They have this kind of *humor* about them. The Cubs are outside the realm."

On Grace Street, I paid an impromptu visit to the House of the Good Shepherd, a convent whose sizable, unmarked back-yard parking lot has been a public secret shared by suburban Cubs fans for forty years or more. The parking revenue now accounts for more than a third of the annual budget for the convent, which does its main work in family care. I was told about this by a pleasant, impressive nun named Sister Patricia, who said she respected and admired the Cubs for sticking to daytime ball. She wouldn't quite declare her own feelings about this year's team, but I thought I could tell that she was—well, *pleased.* I asked about a vendor I had seen out on Grace Street who was selling wonderful T-shirts with the message "THE CUBS — A TICKET TO HEAVEN," but Sister Patricia shook her head. "Not ours," she said. "That's outside the walls." When I took my leave, I noticed that the sister who let me out was wearing a little paper Cubs logo—the red letter "C" inside a circle of blue—over her heart on her white habit.

Ninety Feet

1991

Pennant baseball would have a different address this year—
something I sensed along about seven-thirty on a mid-September
Saturday evening, in steamy, stuffed Atlanta Fulton County Stadium, at a point where the game between the first-place Dodgers
and second-place (just barely) Braves in the National League West
division was heading into its ninth inning of deep uninterest. The
Braves, whom I'd seen knocked out of first place the night before,
had here surrendered a pair of first-inning runs on a misplay by
their center fielder, Ron Gant, but then crawled back to even
things, 2–2, at which point the game seemed to stall, panting in the
miasmal heat. An early, game-halting cloudburst and the ensuing
mud moppings felt like the highlight of the day, all things considered, unless you counted the war whoops and imploring cheers
and carryings on of the 44,773 Atlanta supporters, who had been
cleaving the air with cherry-red foam-rubber tomahawks for better
than three and a half hours now, to no avail. Making inquiry, I
learned that the weaponry was new—the tomahawks were a tie-in
freebie issued at the park that day, plugging both the Braves and a
local rock station—but the armchops and woo-woos had been in
fashion since early summer. It was still another secondhand spon-
taneity, probably begun in spring training this year, when a little
band of Florida State grads had turned up at the Braves camp in
West Palm Beach one day to cheer on a fellow Seminole, Deion
Sanders (then trying out for a slot on the Atlanta roster), with

some old-school football-style chops and chants. When the Braves moved north, the custom tagged along. This was interesting, as socio-anthropology goes, but plainly ineffectual. Players came up to bat, took or swung at or fouled off various pitches, backed away to rub their sweaty palms, and stepped in for further fatuity. Nothing happened. Up in the pressbox, writers were reading the news sections of the papers. Desperate for action, I reexamined my scorecard, vainly hoping for some pitch or bounce or stratagem that had escaped my notice. Zip. Then I picked up my game binoculars and panned slowly around the circling upper-deck façade, jotting down in my notebook some of the painted fan-banner messages: "Captain Justice and the American Bream," "The Mother of All Series," "The Last Shall Be First," "Lower Beer Prices." The cheers and war cries had gone away, and over behind third base some first-row fans had hung up their tomahawks in a neat row on the back edge of the visiting-team dugout. I sighed and rubbed my eyes, and my neighbor to the left leaned over and said, "What are the rules? Does somebody have to win this thing?"

I can't account for what came next, but in some fashion the tie and the failure of the players to break it, the weight of the zeros, the fading of the day, and the weary wishings of the great crowd now seized the game and shook it awake, and what had been tedious and endless became edged and dangerous and terrific fun. I had seen this same shift in some long games before: nothing happens but everything changes. The Braves' Otis Nixon beat out a little chop in the bottom of the ninth and was bunted along. John Candelaria came in from the Dodger bullpen and walked Pendleton intentionally, and then, to enormous cries, struck out David Justice, swinging. Then McDowell came in and retired Gant. On we went into extra innings, but we were finished with groans and sighs. This game, in fact—with its etiolated innings and its swollen cast of pinch-hitters, pinch-runners, double switches, and relief-relievers—was a precursor, had we known it, of some of those stretched, austere, and difficult games that caught up the whole country in October. Even its solution held an omen. Jerry Willard, an obscure catcher called up from Richmond earlier in the month, came in to pinch-hit for the Braves in the eleventh, battled McDowell lengthily, and worked a splendid base on balls. Pendleton's mis-hit bloop fell into short left for a double, sending the pinch-runner, Mitchell, to third, and Gant lined a sudden shot into the left-field corner, to win at last. Baseball was back in business and the Braves were back in first. "A strange day," said Atlanta manager Bobby Cox, shaking his head. "There's still a long way to go, but you would have hated to lose this one." He looked at his watch—it was getting on for nine. "I don't suppose dinner reservations are going to work," he said.

I flew home the next morning, and began learning the Braves better on the tube that afternoon, when Sid Bream hit a grand slam in the very first inning, and the strange, screen-filling, twenty-one-year-old Steve Avery worked his way effortlessly through the Dodger order, closing them down, 9–1, while throwing his fastball and masterful curves downhill, it seemed, from his high and easy windup. I wanted to go back to Atlanta—Atlanta later, with bunting up, I mean—but the two teams led me (and a lot more fans, by now) a difficult chase down the next three weeks. The Dodgers, far from being done, took over first once again, but lost it at the end of the week, on Avery's next outing, at Chavez Ravine, when he blanked them, 3–0. I had begun to pick up on the teams at odd hours and on esoteric parts of my TV or radio dials. The Braves, and their long-term announcer, Skip Caray, were on good old TBS, of course—a spot up in the upper tier of my television dial, where I had for years given them no more than a passing glance on my way to the Battle of Stalingrad yet again, in riveting black and-white, or to the mating habits of ptarmigans. Now I stayed longer. The Dodgers, three time zones away, were much tougher for me, and the Saturday-night game of the Braves series out there somehow escaped me altogether. I found a box score but no game account in a Monday paper: the Dodgers had won, 2–1, with a run in the eighth and another in the ninth—but *how?* I had the little rows of totals and the various extra-base hits, and the pitchers' account books as well, but an exact script was beyond my powers of reconstruction.

(This catch-up cryptography has become an essential art for Eastern fans, when so many night games on the opposite coast go unreported in the morning dailies.) When I did sort it out at last, there was no consolation: two Atlanta infield errors in the eighth, and then a Juan Samuel game-winning triple in the ninth. The Dodgers won again the next day, when Ramon Martinez pitched a shutout and hit the first home run of his life. My wife noticed along in here that I had begun groaning or cursing by my set, or with my ear glued to the sports-phone number in the middle of the night. I was hooked.

The Dodgers stayed in front, by a little, as the days ran down, and I did not believe they would lose. They had led all summer, after all—they were nine and a half up on the third-place Braves at the All-Star break—and their powerful, store-bought lineup (Eddie Murray, Juan Samuel, Darryl Strawberry, Brett Butler, Kal Daniels, Gary Carter) knew the way home, if any team did. I did not change my mind late on the following Sunday night—it was a week before the end now—when, over ESPN, I saw them catch up with the Giants on a fluke play, an all-timer, after Sharperson broke his bat while hitting a hard infield bouncer, and a bat fragment went whirring out between third and short, distracting third baseman Matt Williams as he tried to make the play, and then *struck the ball once again,* in midair, as the tying run came home. Strawberry singled in the winner, and the Dodger lead was still one game. This sort of luck, if anybody needs to be told, is an absolute sign of a pennant to come—but so, too, was the kind of game, two nights later at Cincinnati, that the Braves pulled out with a Dave Justice home run after they had spotted the Reds a six-run lead in the first inning. The competition was brutal by now, east and west: Hershiser threw a two-hitter for seven innings, and Smoltz a two-hitter for eight, with ten strikeouts, on the very same night. The Dodgers were winning at home and the Braves on the road, but then I realized that the Atlanta wins, night after night—five of them now, then six—were going up on the scoreboard at Dodger Stadium (and on the clubhouse television set) before the Dodgers had begun, or at least finished, their games. The time zones would settle this, and now, sure enough, the Dodgers dropped a game to the Padres after the Braves had won still again. It was all tied up, with three games to go. What the Dodgers had not wanted—had dreaded down the last weeks—was just ahead: a three-game weekend series against the Giants at Candlestick Park, with the pennant at stake.

I made the trip, and what surprised me about the games was not the competitive fire of the fifth-place Giants but some shrill sounds of whining from the Dodger side. "The guy that wins—nobody likes him," said manager Lasorda on the field before the Friday-night meeting. "If we had a bad year, our team wouldn't feel good if we beat the Giants now. This is unique." A bit before, Brett Butler had said, "The Braves want to win but the Giants want to spoil. They are motivated by hatred and spoiling," and Darryl Strawberry joined the whimpers with "If they want to beat us so bad, why didn't they beat us earlier, when it counted?"

The fans wanted it this way, that's why. "Beat L.A.! Beat L.A.!" the well-wrapped Candlestick hordes chanted. "If We're Not Going, They're Not" proclaimed a banner in left field, while old true hearts in the stands, I don't doubt, reminded each other happily of the Joe Morgan home run that had knocked the Dodgers out of a pennant here in 1982. The Braves were leading the Astros once again, up on the scoreboard, when the teams ran out on the field. The Giants took charge of things very quickly, when Will Clark hit a whistling two-run homer over the left-field fence in the bottom of the first, and Matt Williams, a few pitches later, flew another one even deeper into the same sector. The visitors hung on miserably, and brought the go-ahead run to the plate with two on in the seventh, against Giant reliever Jeff Brantley. But the batter—it was Strawberry—took strike three, motionless, and the chance was gone. The next afternoon, the now second-place Dodgers ran into the fine young Giant left-hander Trevor Wilson on a good day (there are two Trevor Wilsons: one a Koufax and the other Charlie Brown), and he threw a two-hitter, closing down their season. In his clubhouse, Roger Craig said, "I'm glad the way it happened, but you have to have some compassion for the Dodgers." Someone asked Will Clark if he felt the same way. "Am I sorry for the Dodgers?" he replied. He burst out laughing.

The seven-game National League Championship Series, a classic dimmed only by the accident of a remarkable ensuing World Series, feels doomed and painful even at this distance, because of the elimination of the Pirates at its end, and because of the way they lost. Their inability to score any runs at all against the puissant Atlanta pitching in the last two games of their year (and, indeed, over their final three games at Three Rivers Stadium) weirdly prefigured the fate of the Braves, in turn, at the end of the World Series, and formed part of an almost mystical pattern of mirrorings and connections between the two events. The Pirates were the only surviving semifinalists from the 1990 pennant championships, in which they had lost to the Reds in six briskly contested games, and were the best-balanced and most consistent club in the majors this year. They won the most games, and they were never seriously challenged in their division after the middle of May. Everyone, I think, was happy to welcome them back to the playoffs and now wanted to see them—in particular, their famous outfield trio of Barry Bonds, Andy Van Slyke, and Bobby Bonilla—strut their stuff in a World Series.

"If we win this, experience will have been a big factor," Van Slyke said at Three Rivers Stadium before the playoff opener. "If we don't, it wasn't." Van Slyke is the heart of this Pittsburgh club, and he got them off winging with an exuberant home run and then an R.B.I. double in his first two at-bats of the evening—more than enough in a winning 5–1 Pirate effort. But nothing was easy for long in these games. Steve Avery fanned the side in the bottom of the first inning the following night, and continued in similar implacable style—half smiling out there, blowing out a deep breath just before the delivery, and firing one elegant pitch after another—as he shut down the Pirates, 1–0. Another youngster, Mark

Lemke, also introduced himself to America when he drove in the lone run with an oddly bounced double past third base, and then made the lead stand up when he snatched an infield single on his knees behind second in the eighth, to hold the tying base runner in check. "Too much Avery," said Pirate manager Leyland after this game was over. "He was the best I've seen all year. We could have played another two hours against him and still not scored."

I had my date with the American League in Toronto (where the Minnesota Twins won three straight from the Blue Jays, and moved along into the World Series) and so missed a firsthand view of the tortuous twists and writhings these games now took in the other park, in a series that kept promising to go in one direction and then rushing to its opposite—doubling back on itself, so to speak, to surprise and silence us all. The Braves fans and then the Braves themselves (three consecutive doubles and then a home run) administered a fearful tomahawking to the visiting Pittsburghs in the early part of their carefree 10–3 win in Game Three. But here they dropped two grudging, difficult games—3–2 (in ten innings) and 1–0—in each case on a critical mistake by their young right fielder, Justice: a late and useless peg of his that got loose behind third and allowed a Pittsburgh run to come home; and then, on the next night, his failure to touch third base as he came flying in with a thrilling but then nullified counter. (Watching on television, I thought he'd just grazed the bag with his spikes, but the umpire did not agree.) Other gruesome misadventures around the inner segment of the diamond befell the Atlantas in this one—a blown bases-loaded squeeze play in the second, and then a rare interference-call out when Brian Hunter tangled with the catcher in front of the plate while running out his tapped ground ball. Inexperience in big games was killing the young Braves, I could see. The Pirates would win.

They never scored again, and that slow expiration felt draining and miserable even to those of us watching from a distance, because this was the last go-around for this particular crew of Pirates, who will lose Bobby Bonilla to free agency this winter (the have-not Pittsburgh franchise can't afford to stay in an extended high-priced bidding war for his services), and may also have seen Bonds' future as a great star go glimmering after his collapse at the plate in two successive playoffs. Confined to three meaningless singles by the Reds last fall (after an M.V.P. season), he batted .148 this time, with no runs driven in; twice in the fifth game, manager Bobby Cox elected to have Bonilla walked intentionally in order to pitch to Bonds with a run in scoring position—an astounding turn of events—and twice Bonds failed to deliver. The agony of these losses could be seen in Van Slyke's grimaces and kicks at the turf as one after another of his at-bats came to nothing, but all the Pirates were suffering on the bench as the final game slipped away. (The Braves won it, 4–0.) Their wholesale failure at the plate, you could sense, had taken them not just out of the games but out of the luck of the games: the eluding, seeing-eye grounder; the peg and the slide and the right call at a crucial base; the crazy bounce or the odd, never-before play somewhere that brings in an unexpected run and turns the week around.

In a series with so few easy pleasures, we learned how to treasure the other kind of ball—in particular, the stirring duel in the sixth game between Steve Avery and the Pirates' tough and grizzled right-hander Doug Drabek, the Cy Young incumbent, who together put up sixteen consecutive zeros on the scoreboard before the Braves' lone run came home in the ninth. The contrast in pitching styles and ideas was riveting. Drabek, all craft and experience, was making the hitters swing at his best stuff, and even when he sometimes fell behind he kept the ball away or served up drooping inside sinkers and curveballs that could only be hit foul, if they were hit at all. His look of worn, mustachioed resolution was a perfect movie touch, just as Avery's untroubled phiz suited him—a dangerous kid, not yet old enough to doubt his strength or his power to make things come out his way. He was brusque on the mound, and threw an outstanding assortment of curveballs in addition to his flashing fastball: an impressive repertoire for a youngster. Steve Buechele, the Pirates' third baseman, said, "I don't believe he's twenty-one—he's lying." As I watched Avery in this game and in his other outings over these two weeks, it came to me more than once how much he reminded me of the handful of true athletes I'd encountered back in school, when I was a teen-ager trying to play sports. Nothing shook those gilded young men or seemed to touch their deep-water composure, even in extremity. It didn't even occur to them that they could make a mistake out there, mess up in plain sight, and as a result they never looked anxious or hurried. They had more time than the rest of us. When somebody mentioned this inviolable youthful composure of Avery's to Bobby Cox, he smiled and said, "Yes, I'd rather he was the manager and I was the pitcher."

That sixth game was played on a chilly night at Three Rivers, with the temperature touching forty by the time it was over. The place was a winter heath, appropriate to the event and the drawing down of another season. The Pirates were still ahead in the series until the ninth inning, it might be remembered, but the bundled-up players on both benches, hugging themselves for comfort, looked aged and apprehensive. No one would win tonight. The spell was broken by Greg Olson, the Atlanta catcher, who waited for a sinking inside fastball from Drabek—he'd grounded out on the same pitch in the seventh—and drove the ball into left for a double that brought Ron Gant home with the ember, the searched-for fire, in his grasp.

The hankie hordes were in full cry at the Metrodome, where the World Series began. Kent Hrbek, who's played with the Twins for a decade, said he thought the fan screaming was lower by a decibel or two from 1987, but I couldn't hear it. Tom Boswell, the Washington *Post* columnist, who sat a few seats down from me in the upper press rows behind home, had forehandedly brought along some chainsaw earplugs, and after one Twins uprising I spotted a couple of other writers communicating with handwritten notes. The same sort of thing went on down in Atlanta, where the tomahawking—joined, in a front box, by Ted Turner and his wife, Jane

Fonda, and by their guests, Jimmy and Rosalynn Carter (who sometimes deployed a sophisticated rubato in their down chop)—had been noticed nationwide during the playoffs.

I saw the first tomahawk protesters outside the Metrodome before the Series opener, and when I got there again the next afternoon the gathering of Native Americans—and some photographers and onlooking fans—was larger: perhaps thirty or forty of them by now. They were Ojibwas and Lakotas, some of whom had come down from the White Earth Reservation, north of Detroit Lakes. A group of male singers and drummers had gathered on a sloping triangle of lawn just to the right of the main gate. It was twilight, and the deep tomtom noises and strange (and not so strange) sounds of the Indian songs seemed almost visible in the air. Most of the demonstrators wore jeans or work clothes, brightened here and there by a red bandanna or a red cotton ribbon plaiting the hair. Some of the men and women wore paper stickers showing a red bar across two tomahawks, and there were a lot of "AIM" buttons as well—for the American Indian Movement. Others were carrying signs: "HAVE RESPECT / STOP THE CHOP," "INDIANS ARE PEOPLE / NOT MASCOTS," "DRUMS: THE MUSIC OF AMERICA," and a plain "RESPECT." One small child, in the arms of his mother, wore a handwritten sign pinned to his sweater which said, "I am an Anishinabe." The Twins fans coming in seemed curious and polite about the demonstration, and a few of them stopped to ask questions.

I talked to a round-faced woman from the reservation, Andrea Bonga, who had brought along her ten-year-old son, Patrick. "There's nothing new about this," Ms. Bonga said. "Being a stereotype has been a problem for us for a long time. Nothing has changed for the Indian people in my lifetime." I noticed that Patrick Bonga was carrying a homer hankie, and when I asked him if he was a Twins fan, he nodded shyly. "I like Chili Davis," he said.

The same sort of demonstrations went on outside Atlanta Fulton County Stadium when the games moved along; this time, the drummers and singers were Cherokees, for the most part. The

crowd feeling was different there, I thought—more impatient—
and there were louder, conflicting sounds of drumming and chanting from a group of imitation Indians nearby, rooting for the
Braves. In the crowd around the demonstrators I saw a man wearing a huge plastic tomahawk on his head, with the message "Station
Z93—Classic Rock & Roll."

I didn't know what to make of all this—I doubt if anyone did.
It has been suggested that the Braves should change their name to
the Brave, or perhaps the Raves, but I don't think anything of the
sort is going to happen. I don't think the tomahawk chop, which is
part of the growing, almost Japanese ritualization of sport in this
country, is going to go away quickly, either. The team name and
the chants and the chops may be cheerful in intention, but they're
injuries as well: little cuts that stand for something a good deal
worse. When I listened to the rock-blaring speakers and the roaring, hankie-brandishing hordes around me at the game in Minneapolis that night, I felt as if we were children in there, and that
the adults were all outside the Dome, up on that triangle of grass.

I went home and watched the terrific last two games on television. I wanted to see the pitching up close and, to tell the truth, I
didn't want to watch the resolution of a Series like this one with my
fingers in my ears. The ending wrung us once again: 4–3 in eleven
innings the first night, and then 1–0 in ten, with the Twins bringing home the late last run each time, to seize their great prize. They
are a fine club, and what impressed me most about them here at
the end was their bottomless, almost casual confidence; they knew
themselves, and they seemed to sense that no uncharacteristic, astounding effort would be required to bring them safely home, even
in such straits. The Braves, it felt to me, weren't absolutely at this
level; they had been underdogs right along and had surprised themselves again and again through the late season and after, and privately they may have been still counting on something like youth
or luck or some unimaginable stroke to make up the difference
once again. But this may not be the case. The temptation to draw

large conclusions about winners and losers is very strong, but coming up one run short at the end of sixteen hundred innings probably can't be called a failure of character.

Even from a distance, the baseball in these games seemed close to pain. "I can't *take* much more of this," I'd say, getting up from my seat and walking off into another room. "Come *on!*" The cry wasn't directed at the next batter or as a plea to the incoming new pitcher: it was against baseball fate. Then I would rush back and join the game once again.

The Braves kept hitting into loud outs in Game Six—hard shots that flew directly at some fielder, near-homers (by Pendleton and then Justice) that flew foul at the last instant, a line-drive double play—but luck is beside the point at such times: winners must seize the day. The winner on this night was Kirby Puckett, the ebullient and all-round-talented Minnesota medicine ball, who had himself quite an evening: a marvel of a catch, up against the left-field Plexiglas, that took a home run away from Ron Gant, a triple that drove in one run and soon became a second; a run-scoring sacrifice fly; and the home run, leading off the bottom of the eleventh, that won it, 4–3. "Unbelievable," he said after the game, speaking for millions. "I feel as if I've been in a fifteen-round fight."

The television was almost up to the baseball. The veteran announcers, Tim McCarver and Jack Buck, were into the game in all senses—prescient and useful, but also clearly knocked over by the kind of action we were seeing. In the middle of the final game, McCarver pointed out that Pendleton, the third baseman, was playing miles off the bag against a right-handed batter, Brian Harper, because Harper would never be able to pull the kind of fastballs that Smoltz was throwing; a bare instant later, Harper bounced a grounder directly into Pendleton's glove. The cameras, in turn, found other news to convey: the fatigue now shadowing the faces of the tough young starters, Avery and Erickson (somewhere in this final weekend Avery had said, "Every game I've pitched since August has been the game of my life"); the imperious concentra-

tion of Peña; the careworn, ever more downcast mien of Bobby
Cox, in the dugout, as the game began to slip through his fingers;
and the anguish of Charlie Leibrandt—in a rare relief appearance—squeezing his eyes shut in disbelief after giving up the Puckett home run; four players in a row on the Braves bench, gnawing
their nails; Tom Kelly, expressionless in the shadows, waiting and
waiting; a woman in the stands biting her lips, with her homer hankie crushed in her palm.

Lonnie Smith, stepping in for the lead-off at-bat of the final
game, leaned over and shook hands with the catcher, Brian Harper.
Nobody had ever seen such a thing, but its meaning was eloquent:
This has been *something,* hasn't it? The game was clear and unclut-
tered, with John Smoltz and Jack Morris, the two starters, almost
bustling their way through the enemy order, inning after inning—
out of my way, you. Smoltz, with his long face and smoothie mustache, had a lidded, impenetrable look to him: the hood was down,
as players used to say. He often started off a fresh batter with another fastball, up in the nineties somewhere, while Morris, the old
battler, was perhaps more saving and surprising with his hard stuff.
Four times, he struck out the last batter of an inning: a specialty
of his.

Games like this have rigid proprieties. There should be a hero,
but someone must fail as well. This doesn't always happen, and we
mourn its absence then. The Braves had a clear chance to win this
game before they lost it, and Lonnie Smith's baserunning mistake, in
the top of the eighth inning, will always be there now, in our minds
and in the books, inexplicable and implacable. On first base with no
outs, after a broken-bat single, he took off as Pendleton smashed a
double over Puckett's head and to the wall in deep left-center, but
paused on the base path just beyond second—a fatal indecision that
cost him the chance to score. The run was a sure thing, but then it
wasn't, and Lonnie wound up at third. Morris, with surgical care,
now elicited two little topped ground balls, the second of which became a first-to-home-to-first bases-loaded double play that extin-
guished the crisis. Just after Pendleton launched his double (to go

back a bit), Knoblauch and his keystone partner, Gagne, feinted a force-play peg to second—the trifling everyday deke maneuver, without the ball, that once or twice in a month will make a careless base runner pause, or even go into a slide out there, because he hasn't been paying attention. The crestfallen Smith admitted after the game that he had indeed failed to pick up the ball in its flight, but claimed that the mimed stuff around second had nothing to do with it. He has since changed his mind about this, it seems, which must mean that he took a later look at the replays. The tape shows him off and running, with his head down, then clearly turning his gaze to the right at the moment Knoblauch fields and then starts to throw the phantom ball. Lonnie scurries unchecked around the corner and is then apparently struck by a late and awful moment of doubt: *What was that?* He stops, turns, and looks about, and then— too late—continues. Whatever happened, whatever the cause, its meaning was clear. The Braves, who had fought a Series-long succession of battles up and down the narrow salient between third and home, came up ninety feet short for the year.

The Twins, after moving a runner up to the same base in the eighth and again in the ninth, all without result, turned the trick in the tenth, when Gladden doubled against Peña (a ball that took a high bounce in left-center and was fractionally misplayed by Brian Hunter), moved to third on a sacrifice, and, after some final maneuverings, came home with the Series-winning run on a pinch-hit single by Gene Larkin.

The casting of Lonnie Smith and Jack Morris as antagonists in the final scene was somebody's masterstroke. Morris was thirty-six and Smith thirty-five, and each was in his fifteenth year in the majors, with extensive post-season experience accumulated along the way; Lonnie, in fact, had played in three prior World Series—with the Phillies, Cardinals, and Royals—never before on the losing side. Both he and Morris, moreover, had been almost last-minute additions to their club rosters this year—Smith winning a job in spring training as pinch-hitter and outfield fill-in, and Morris as a late free agent. Smith, it will be recalled, came to prominence for the

Braves only after becoming the replacement for Otis Nixon, the team's efficient lead-off batter and left fielder, who was suspended in the middle of September for a drug infraction. Lonnie had performed staunchly in this difficult role (he'd hit three home runs in the Series), and only his misfortune in the final game might make some of us notice that the Braves had been a little short in run-making capacity in all the late going.

Morris has been a durable and ferocious competitor throughout his career, without ever drawing the awards and accolades that have gone to contemporaries like Nolan Ryan, Roger Clemens, and Orel Hershiser. He won more games in the nineteen-eighties (a hundred and sixty-two) than any other pitcher in baseball, and he is the current—and counting—American League leader in consecutive starts (four hundred and thirty-one). Batters know that he comes into a game armed with a 90-m.p.h.-plus fastball (he can turn it over on a right-handed hitter), a breaking ball, a changeup, and a killing split-finger delivery—and with a sixth pitch, so to speak, which is his thirst for battle. He is not a famous finisher at this point in his career, except when he has to be. After he has emerged on top in still another big game (I remember this from the 1984 Tigers-Padres World Series, but more particularly from an eye-to-eye duel he fought for nine innings with Mike Flanagan, of the Blue Jays, in the closing days of the 1987 pennant race), he always looks more excited and appreciative about the event than anyone else in the clubhouse, and his big, horsy, nineteenth-century football-player's face (with that middle part to his long hair, and his soup-strainer mustache) remains alight with the joy of combat. "I made him hit my pitch right there!" he will say about a critical out. During the playoffs this year, Tom Kelly told me that he couldn't think of any other pitcher with Morris's ability to come up with the big strikeout when he most needed it in a game. "Quite an athlete," he said. "He knows where the finish line is, and how to get there."

Morris, it might be pointed out, was considered to be on the downside of his career with the Tigers after sustaining a fractured elbow in 1989. He wound up with a losing record that year (for the first time since 1978) and again last year. The Tigers and Twins played a couple of series against each other toward the end of the 1990 campaign, however, and Tom Kelly got the impression that the old Jack Morris had somehow reappeared. He checked with his pitching coach, Dick Such, who had noticed the same thing, and their recommendation to general manager Andy MacPhail helped bring Jack aboard the Twins as a free agent over the winter.

It was still 0–0 after nine innings of the last game of this World Series, by which time Morris, who was working on three days' rest, had given up seven hits but had thrown a hundred and eighteen pitches. Enough. Kelly walked down the Twins dugout and told Morris he'd done a great job, more than anyone could imagine, and he was taking him out. Morris protested—he felt fine. He couldn't possibly come out of a game like this. Dick Such unexpectedly sided with the pitcher. Kelly looked at them, shrugged, and said, "What the heck, it's just another game." Jack went back out there, still throwing in the nineties, and won.

Now he has departed. A free agent once again when the games were over, Morris, together with his agent, told the Twins that he would venture into the market in search of a contract at the topmost levels: something on the order of four and a half million a year. The Minnesota organization, which will not compete financially at such levels, even as World Champions, has wished him well. It's sad, but I think we should not mourn too much. Pennants are very hard to come by in baseball these days, and repeating as World Champions seems to be beyond rational expectation. This World Series is over, and we can watch its departure only with gratitude—a great ocean liner, brilliant with lights and the sounds of celebration, slipping off down the dark waters, not soon to come this way again.

One for the Good Guys

1996

Baseball, a sneaky quick-change artist, sometimes arranges a dramatic shift in the look and feel of a game in the middle innings, even from one pitch to the next, but more often it is orderliness and the apparent stability of things—what we knew about these teams and these two pitchers, what we sensed about them in the first couple of innings—that is confirmed in the end. Now that the pastime has brought down the curtain on another season in customary fashion, with a storm of confetti and shouting and (it's hard to believe) the promise of another owner-induced labor crisis, it's a treat to think back on the post-season just departed, not only for the sparkle and grinding tension of the 1996 games but because they represented the most astounding shift in a baseball reputation since Pete Rose. The upset victory—well, almost an upset—pulled off by the Yankees over the defending Atlanta Braves, who were playing in their fourth World Series in the nineties, was the first championship for the Pinstripes since 1978, but this was almost less of an achievement than their apotheosis and captivating stroll down the runway in the role of Miss America. For a third of the century, the Yankees have presented themselves as the sports equivalent of imperial Rome. For them, bygone emperors and Praetorians can never die, and bewreathed shades of Ruth and Gehrig; DiMaggio, Berra, and Ford; Casey and Billy; Reggie and the Mick still shuffle about the Bronxian temple, rearranging their togas and clearing their throats during every losing streak. The Yanks' twenty-two prior World Championships, their thirty-three pennants, their thirty-eight plaques in the Hall of Fame, those thirteen "retired" uniform numbers, the weepy pre-game encomiums on the center-field video screen to the recent or not so recent dead—Mickey Mantle, Mel Allen, Thurman Munson—have been made inescapable ingredients of each fan's visit to the Stadium. Visitors are also enjoined by the management to visit Monument Park, out by the bullpens: a Kremlin wall of the sport where twelve panegyrical monuments or embronzements have been added to the piquant scattering of stones and tablets that once looked in at us from deep center field.

The burden of this relentless and irrelevant P.R. during the Yankees' long struggles to regain their October form can at last be thrown aside—what a load it was!—and we are free to celebrate the new champions not for what they represented but for what they were: a competent though far from overpowering amalgam of engaging young stars and gritty hired guns who absolutely enjoyed themselves and each other during a succession of hairbreadth escapes in the late going, and were almost as entranced as the rest of us when they won. The Yankees—who'd have thought it—had become lovable.

How did we love them? Let us count the ways. Because they didn't spit. Because they didn't just hit home runs. Because of their fans (including one hooky-playing twelve-year-old from Old Tappan, N.J.). Because of their luck—oh, man, were they ever lucky! Because of Cecil's forearms—and his hands. Because of Derek and Bernie. Because Paul (it turned out) could still run, and Straw (it turned out) could still field. Because of Doc's no-hitter. Because of Macarena Night. Because of Mo Rivera in the seventh and eighth, and John Wetteland in the ninth. Because of John's cap. Because of George—no, scratch that; this is about love. Because of Zimm. Because of some umps (let's face it). Because of Joe Torre, yes.

Enamored rooters for other freshly crowned major-league champions have been known to come up with stuff like this in the days and nights just after a World Series, but rarely in recent baseball times has the doting run so deep. One would have to go back to the 1979 rival Pittsburgh and Baltimore clubs to find a similar affection, and fans of those Willie Stargell "We Are Family" Pirates, as I recall, did not include many new converts like—well, like me. I mean, sophisticated old baseball cognoscenti with a fully developed, long-standing coolness toward the club in question, who this time were absolutely turned around by six weeks' worth of terrific hometown ball. Not every New Yorker came over to these Yanks in the end, but the holdouts were rare and flinty of heart. Encountered in the elevator on the morning after Bernie Williams's eleventh-inning homer had beaten the Orioles in the first A.L. Championship playoff game, an upstairs neighbor of mine held up a warning hand when he saw my face and announced, "I hate the Yankees."

"But this Yankee team is different," I insisted. "Last night—"

"Fuck 'em," he said, and we finished the journey in silence.

Charlie and a few others aside, this was a local baseball autumn to savor, not so much because the Yankees won a World Championship as because so many of them seemed to be involved in the process. In spite of the club's sixty-six-million-dollar payroll; its blue-chip tenured stars like David Cone, Wade Boggs, Paul O'Neill, and John Wetteland; its between-season acquisitions of old pros Joe Girardi, Mariano Duncan, Tino Martinez, and Kenny Rogers; its midsummer trade for the weighty Cecil Fielder; and its brilliant revival of Darryl Strawberry, picked up by Mr. Steinbrenner from the Northern League St. Paul Saints, these Yankees habitually presented and appeared to relish a scuffling, low-rent, anxiety-prone form of ball, in which the club, by defense or pitching, or even by moving up an occasional base runner, attempted to scratch out a lead until it was Rivera time, with Wetteland waiting to turn out the lights. The team won twenty-nine of the thirty-one regular-season games in which the pair appeared—most often, it felt, inch by excruciating inch. This sort of effort requires a deep and busy roster. Everyone gets to play, because there aren't enough outs left to wait for the power hitters to come up again, and fans learn to expect the brief contributions of a middle-inning pitcher like the bankerish sinkerballer David Weathers or the trooper-erect Jeff Nelson; to notice that Tim Raines, back in the lead-off spot once again, has just rapped his third single of the day; to realize afterward that it was Bernie Williams's tag-up at first base that led to a critical late-inning run; and, in their mind's eye, still see the looped single to right by young Ruben Rivera that beat the Orioles in the tenth inning that September night.

Watching the home side battle back on the scoreboard feels familiar to us only because of baseball movies, where the Mammoths or the Titans slowly but routinely make up lost ground against the bad guys, up in those little boxes. Real-life games may shift in tone, but the true turnaround doesn't come along very often—especially in the majors, where the first team to score in a game wins about seventy per cent of the time. Except this fall. Trailing in the eighth inning, in the ninth, in the fifth, in the eighth, in the eighth, in the fifth (by six runs), and then again in the eighth (by three), the Yankees won all six of those October games—and five more. Who cares about the 1927 immortals? Who needs the 1961 champs? These '96 Yanks wore us out.

The Yankees slipped into first place in their division on April 30th and stayed there (despite some late lurches), but their new era of good feeling almost predated their success. For me, their spring clubhouse in Tampa felt different because of Dwight Gooden. In recovery from a year and a half of baseball exile, imposed after repeated drug-code violations, he looked like a soul released: a look that sports fans—and non-sports people, too, of course—have come to recognize and perhaps at last think about a little. His early struggles on the mound were almost pitiful, but everybody on the roster seemed to stop by his locker each day to bump fists with him or say a word, and his gratitude and excitement over the club's patience with this double rehab were touching. Owner Steinbrenner gets full marks here, and so do Manager Torre and his staff.

Gooden's no-hitter against the Mariners on May 14th felt like a deserved miracle. I came home from the movies or someplace that night and turned on the set in time to see him reeling and struggling toward the finish line. He threw a wild pitch, a grunting fastball to an outer corner, and a slew of careful, dipping sliders. There was a scary play out behind first, where Tino Martinez scuttled on hands and knees toward the bag, too late for the out: an error, the scorer said. Doc's motions—the sudden swipe across his forehead with his glove tip, the storklike leg-lift—were familiar but no longer magical. In the closeups, he had lost the sphinxlike impassivity that he wore during his lengthy declining run with the Mets; now he was a sweating, workaday pitcher, battling like anyone else to hold things together. When it was over (it was Gooden's first no-hitter), my eyes were damp. Then the phone began to ring—old Mets friends, yelling and carrying on.

Other good stuff showed itself early, as three young home-grown stars stepped forward. Derek Jeter, a twenty-two-year-old rookie, imperturbably took over at shortstop and outperformed the more breathtaking Mets phenom across town, Rey Ordóñez, at least at the plate. Mariano Rivera, a great young arm, a smoothie, was suddenly untouchable after 10 p.m. The stringbean Bernie Williams—scratching that surveyor's line in the dirt with his bat, boyishly jumping in the air over a big ball-four call, and turning on tough inside pitches like a young Yastrzemski—at last became the charismatic, middle-of-the-order, middle-of-the-field leader that scouts and prior managers had foreseen and had almost begun to despair of. And so on. When David Cone went down with an aneurysm in his pitching arm, early in May—a shocking blow—Andy Pettitte and Gooden (he went ten-and-two before wearing out, understandably, in late summer) and the restored Jimmy Key firmed up almost visibly, as did the middle-inning relievers. And when Cone, back from surgery, reappeared on Labor Day his seven no-hit innings delivered an E-mail message to the rest of the league about the Yankees' plans for themselves in the remainder of the going. Stopping by the clubhouse late in the summer, you'd spot Tino Martinez and Joe Girardi, say, visiting or eating with Paul

O'Neill or Mariano Duncan or Tim Raines or Wade Boggs, and sense something about the team that was rarer than mere winning: the Yankees were grownups.

Joe Torre, the familiar onetime National League Gold Glove catcher and M.V.P., and ex-Mets, ex-Braves, and ex-Cardinals skipper, and just lately the All Greater Metropolitan, Italian-descended, Marine Park-born, St. Francis Prep-educated Manager, Father, Brother, Husband, and Everything Else of the Year, felt like a perfect fit for this mature bunch when he arrived this year, making it clear from the outset that the only Yankee business at hand was to win. No one—well, no one since Casey Stengel—had moved into the manager's office at the Stadium with more aplomb and fewer glances upstairs. Eighteen years as a major-league player and fourteen as a major-league manager had produced in him a calm tension that appeared impervious to ego or job anxiety. Perhaps because his Yankees did so well so quickly, his looks and managerial accoutrements, taken together, became an essential part of the mix. His saggy, dark-eyed gaze and rumpled face, with those late-game streakings of his lucky red candy around the mouth ("You look like you're wearing lipstick," observed the umpire Jim Evans during the Series); his prairie mortician's gait and glumness when he headed for the mound to remove a pitcher; his Don-like (Calabria, not Oxford) sidewise tilt and cocked ear for the ceaseless dugout gerbillings and counsellings of his bench coach Don (it's his name) Zimmer; his refusal to explain away strategic late-game moves that had gone sour; and his instinctive support for a young infielder or rival manager suddenly in the soup were job qualifications of a high order in his impossible post. He got along famously with the implacable New York media pack, partly from prior acquaintance during his five years of managing the Mets, but more because his instincts were toward openness and information, and away from the more common managerial traits of concealment and blather. "I try to avoid situations where you want to save your ass," he murmured at one point. More than just quotable, his responses took the dialogue to the right place. Asked after the game if he had seen a television replay of the hotly disputed home run (or fly-ball out) against the Orioles which was intercepted by the twelve-year-old Jeffrey Maier in right field, Torre said, "Did anyone see a replay of Bernie's home run?"—the Yankee homer that had indisputably won the thing. Prodded about another ump's call in another hard game, he said, "The umps weren't very good, but we were worse." Asked if he was happy about Strawberry's at-bats during a 1-for-10 slump, he said, "Straw isn't happy about his at-bats."

Other managers pick up this stuff, to be sure, but Torre is a natural, whether as a fan ("I can't sleep after we win and after we don't win") or as the weary older father (he's fifty-six) of an eight-month-old daughter: "We're both up three times every night. We're on the same schedule." When the whole Torre family was catapulted into tabloid and local-channel immortality after Joe's older brother Frank's replacement heart was stitched into place at Columbia-Presbyterian Medical Center, late in the week of the World Series, the worn-down manager (by now he looked like a Beckett character) appeared to accept this ferocious assault on his privacy and patience as another part of the job. Facing the massed TV cameras, he answered all the reporters' questions (and then answered them again for the latecomers): he told how, just back from Atlanta in the middle of the night, he'd found the telephone message indicating that Frank's long-awaited heart had turned up at last; told what he'd said to Frank and what Frank had said to him before he went into the operating room; repeated what the doctors had said and what his super-fan sister, the Ursuline nun Sister Marguerite, had prayed and had said; discussed his pitching and his batting order and his dinner plans. Just another day at the office. The next evening, he was back uptown managing another tough game—the one that ended with the tying Braves runner still at third base and with Torre, pinned on the bench in an armlock, enduring a lingering kiss from Don Zimmer.

An umpire died on the field on opening day in Cincinnati; Roger Clemens struck out twenty batters in a September game against the Tigers, just ten years after he first performed the feat (he walked no batters in either game); Tom Lasorda at last stepped down as Dodger manager; and the Mariners displayed their new, six-foot-three shortstop, Alex Rodriguez, who batted .358, with thirty-six home runs, in the first flowering of what looks like a remarkable career. Nothing further will be offered here in summation of the 1996 season and its divisional-level playoffs—there it goes: bye-bye!—except a numerical footnote to mark the 4,962 home runs smacked this year (five hundred and four more than the old record), and the seventeen hitters who attained the once sacrosanct forty-homer level. I was there, in any case, for the most famous round-tripper of the year, which was hit by Derek Jeter and caught (in slipshod fashion) by Jeffrey Maier, a foot or two above the upstretched glove of Oriole outfielder Tony Tarasco at the foot of the right-field porch at the Stadium. My seat for the notorious event was deep in the auxiliary press rows behind third base, and for a time I had no more idea about what had happened (our pressbox TV monitors were down) than Rich Garcia, the right-field-line ump, who amazingly only saw the ball disappear into the stands. Then I realized that Tarasco, pointing upward and shooting out his other arm like a cash-register drawer, was reenacting the caper à la Marcel Marceau. (He was lighthearted about it in the clubhouse later on, repeatedly describing the kid's swipe as a magic trick. "Merlin must be in the house," he said.) The homer stood, after an epochal beef, the Yanks won, and Jeff Maier got to come back to the Stadium the next day and sit in the *News* box behind the Yankee dugout. His fame, it is certain, will last a bit more than fifteen minutes. Whatever his fate or future, every year or couple of years or five years for the rest of his life he can expect a telephone call on the date—perhaps to the site of his archeological dig in far Uzbekistan, or his dental clinic in the Paramus Mall—and the voice of some scrounging faraway feature writer, saying, "Hello, Dr. Maier? Jeffrey? Aren't you the Jeff Maier who—" Jeff, say hello to Ralph Branca.

The Orioles didn't play very well in the League Championships, which the Yankees walked away with after three stifling wins at Oriole Park, thus sustaining their deep-voodoo 9-0 winning spell over the O's at home. The critical truth that came over me (and the Orioles' home rooters, too, I imagine) as play unfolded was the insufficiency or unreliability of air power—the home run, that is—as a reliable strategic force. From my seat in the second row of the left-field upper deck, the cramped Camden Yards playing field, with its tight foul lines and short, quirkily angled outfield fences, felt like a subdivided suburban plot. You could go out and play here, but watch out! I could easily see how the O's had whacked their record two hundred and fifty-seven homers here this year, but even as the variously arcing or streaking or ricocheting dingers now began to fly about the place—some suddenly disappearing below my feet—they seemed to become less interesting as the games progressed, if only because the Orioles offered so little else in their own behalf. Thirteen of their nineteen runs in the series were scored on homers, but they never stole a base, rarely moved a runner, and left ten men to die on second or third base in the late innings. The celebrated center of their defense showed startling flaws—a weakness in Cal Ripken's throwing, and even some uncertainty by Robbie Alomar, an infield star of the first magnitude, whose between-the-wickets error in the final game opened the floodgates for a six-run Yankee inning. Nothing is gained by replaying here the infamous earlier moment when Alomar, in a late-September game, spat in the face of umpire John Hirschbeck after a disputed call at home plate. It might be noted, though, that the ultimate victim of the league's insufficient response to this offense (a five-day suspension, to be served when play resumes next April) wasn't the fans or the umpires but Alomar himself. Unshriven by the more obvious and appropriate penalty of immediate dismissal from all further games this year, he will now always be remembered, I believe, not just for his incomparable skills but for a guttersnipe moment that he cannot retract or repay.

"How come baseball makes everybody feel so happy?" a New Jersey-woman (a daughter of mine, if truth be told) asked me over the phone the morning after David Cone's critical and steely 5–2 win over the Braves in the third game of the World Series. I can't remember what I said, but part of the answer could have been that the game, often at the very last instant, allows half the fans to feel the excruciating relief of not being on the other side. As parable, let's cut to the fourth Series game, down in Atlanta, where the Braves, the defending World Champions and familiar October-baseball habitués, had matters well in hand after five innings, leading by 6–0 and heading smoothly toward a 3–1 lead in this Series, which they'd begun by simply trampling the Yankees in the Bronx, winning by 12–1 and 4–0—and thus sustaining a post-season outburst of unmatched offensive ferocity in which they'd outscored their opponents by forty-eight runs to two. (Perhaps understandably, a dangerous smugness had begun to infect the Atlanta sports philosophes, with one local columnist suggesting that it was scarcely worth the bother of playing out such a one-sided Series, and another murmuring of the Braves, "Theirs is a higher standard.")

Now, to be sure, the visitors scored three comeback runs in the sixth inning, on some singles, a walk, and a little Braves error out in right field, but the home-side reliever, Mike Bielecki, quickly struck out three Yanks in a row, ending the threat. Not to worry. Hanging around for the seventh-inning stretch, the happy Atlantans root-root-rooted for the home team, essayed a bit of farewell woo-wooing and forearm chopping, here and there flaunting those foam-rubber tomahawks, and then, in considerable numbers, began to file down the aisles, headed for home. You couldn't blame them: it was after eleven, and tomorrow was a school day. This Series was a lock, and they'd catch the rest of the Braves' win on the car radio. In one respect, at least, Yankee fans now suddenly had the better of it, for the vast majority of them were already at home, eight hundred and fifty miles to the north, where they were following the gloomy proceedings via Fox TV. Well, maybe one more batter, most were thinking—you couldn't blame them, either; it was another one of those late, overstuffed games—and they waited while Charlie Hayes's little lead-off nubber in the eighth rolled gently up the third-base line like a windup toy and died there, still two inches fair: an eighty-five-foot single. Laughing and shaking their heads—isn't baseball weird—they hung on a bit longer, waiting for the next thing.

All sports are eventful, but baseball, unlike the others, sometimes becomes situational as well, suddenly presenting its participants—the players and the fans together—with as many interconnections and possibilities and opportunities for interesting disaster as a Cheever Thanksgiving dinner. More and more relatives turn up and crowd in around the table, some of whom you didn't expect to see here at all, somebody is pouring another round of drinks, and suddenly there doesn't appear to be enough silverware or stuffing to go around. Nerves and certainties are fraying, cousins are eying each other apprehensively, voices are raised in the kitchen. Something awful is about to happen. How hot it is in here. How fraught.

Three batters along, with Mariano Duncan on first and Hayes now on third, Jim Leyritz, a late replacement, stood in to face the Braves' fireballing relief stopper, Mark Wohlers—a right-hander-vs.-right-handed-batter setup, and thus comforting for the Braves. Wohlers threw a fastball—a ninety-eight-mile-an-hour streak that Leyritz swung at smoothly and fouled back. Leyritz, a backup catcher, has a quirky style at the plate. After each pitch, he spins his bat forward in his right hand like a baton twirler, and when he steps back in, ready to swing, he stiffens his left leg and delicately points the foot forward in an almost feminine balletic gesture. On this at-bat, he also wore on his left elbow a thick, clunky-looking brace that looked like Japanese armor: protection for a painful bruise he'd sustained when struck on the biceps by a pitch in a playoff game against the Orioles.

Leyritz took a ball, then another, and, still putting a good swing on the ball, fouled off two more pitches. The home crowd had gone quiet, and up in the pressbox behind the plate you could hear the Yankee players, on the top step of their dugout, barking encouragement to Leyritz. Another pitch arrived—a slider this time, a slider that didn't slide—and Leyritz hit the ball over the left-field fence, tying the game and changing this World Series for good.

Although altered, the game situation persisted, thickening in detail and possibilities as the pitchers and batters came and went for both sides. We were in Atlanta, which meant National League rules: no designated hitter. Under these classic conditions, a tie game in late innings becomes a crisis in slow motion, with each manager glancing at his bullpen and his dwindling list of pinch-hitters, which he must match up, of course, against the right-handed or left-handed remaining pitchers on the other side, while also focussing on the possibilities from the point of view of his op-posing skipper. Fans, happily surveying the field and studying their filling-up scorecards, in fancy begin to enter the minds of the rival managers:

Joe Torre (top of the ninth; two on and two out): Look at Cecil out there, leading off second again. I sure don't want to lose his bat if this goes another inning, but he's no Road Runner, and how will I feel if we get a safe knock here and he gets thrown out at the plate? Damn... To run for him or not to run, that is the question. Well, O.K.—get Andy Fox out there. Sorry, Cec. Now we'll get a hit and go ahead in this thing, for sure.

It didn't happen.

Bobby Cox (top of the tenth, two out, with Yankee base run-ners Tim Raines on second base and Jeter on first): Well, here comes Bernie Williams up, wouldn't you know it? This guy killed the Rangers and killed the Orioles, and I'm not going to let him kill us here. I'll never hear the end of it if I put him on and the front guy scores, but it's sure as hell the right thing to do this time. (He signals for the intentional base on balls to Williams.) Who will they bat here—it's gonna be Boggs, bet your butt on it.

Joe Torre: Yes. Now. Finally it's Boggs time. All we need is ball four, Wade baby!

Torre had already wheeled in five pinch-hitters or runners, and six pitchers (forty-one players got into this game before it was done, including thirteen pitchers and five different third basemen),

and for him to have Wade Boggs, a five-time American League batting champion with a deadly eye for the strike zone, still available
to pinch-hit in this extremity was a miracle of conservation. Steve
Avery, the incumbent Braves pitcher, worked manfully at the task,
throwing a one-and-two strike or near-strike that Boggs let go by
and that ump Steve Rippley called a ball instead. Wincing, Avery
delivered another ball and then ball four, forcing in the go-ahead
run.

The thunderstruck Bobby Cox (we will skip a further visit to
his noggin here, out of respect), beckoning in a fresh pitcher named
Brad Clontz, also took care of the suddenly imperative need to
play his last offensive card by simultanously inserting his left-
handed slugger, Ryan Klesko, in the game, routinely switching the
two names on his lineup card so that Klesko would lead off the
Braves' half of the inning. Nothing, however, can be routine about
a tenth-inning contretemps in the World Series. Idly regarding the
Troy-like panorama below, the baseball gods noticed that Klesko,
an indifferent fielder who had to take the field somewhere on this
no-d.h. diamond, was playing first base, and arranged for the next
Yankee batter, Charlie Hayes, to send up a soft little pop fly that
Klesko somehow lost in the lights as the Yankees' insurance run
came barrelling home. Later on—after Joe Torre and Don Zimmer
had finished pounding and yelling at each other ("Wow! Wasn't
that—!" "Shut up—who's pitching next?") and Klesko had struck
out and Wetteland had come on to finish up and the reporters had
cranked out their comparisons between this epic and the Mookie
Wilson-Bill Buckner sixth game in the 1986 series—Torre said,
"That was the best game I've been involved with, ever. Nothing else
comes close."

Baseball anxiety, which is to say baseball happiness, came in a
different flavor the next night, when Andy Pettitte, matched
against the Braves' John Smoltz in a face-off of this year's potential
Cy Young Award winners, fired an edgy, hold-your-breath shutout
that the Yanks won, 1–0, thanks to a fly ball that Marquis Grissom

dropped in center field for a two-base error, and a Fielder double. Pettitte, who numbed the Atlanta batters with his tailing fastball, also contributed a pair of breathtaking defensive plays in the sixth, nervily barehanding a bunt and firing to third base for a force, and then, on the very next pitch, pouncing on a comebacker to begin the game's backbreaking double play. Sudden events like this can make careers, and for Pettitte—David Cone said it—this game was a defining moment. The win, nailed down when O'Neill caught up with Luis Polonia's drive to deep right center, wrapped up the Yanks' unlikely sweep down in Atlanta. They had won all eight of their post-season road games this year, which is unheard of, and that 8–6 comeback, the longest post-season game ever played, was the second-biggest turnabout in World Series history.

We know the rest. The Yankees, back before their home hordes, scored all three of their runs in a third-inning flareup against the near-invincible Greg Maddux, with Joe Girardi contributing that rarest and most thrilling sight in baseball's catalogue, a triple over the center fielder's head. Jimmy Key, the Yankee starter, had inordinate trouble throwing strikes but never gave in, refusing to deliver the inviting, problem-solving, game-risking pitch up over the plate. Wetteland wrapped up, after practically inducing mass heart failure when he gave up three singles and the Braves' second run in the ninth, and the Yanks went into their pigpile. They had conquered a proud and powerful and (I heard this everywhere) unlikable team, after beating their unmatched trio of starters: Tom Glavine, Smoltz, and Maddux. They beat them in the toughest, most grudging competition imaginable, because the three did not exactly fold up: their combined earned-run average in these games, as they probably won't forget, was 1.23. Maddux, a four-time winner of the Cy Young Award, went out in style, saying, "Obviously, it hurts losing, but the atmosphere here is matched nowhere. It's exciting to be out there on the mound in front of people going freaky. It's wild. Even though we lost, in a while we're going to appreciate being in this place."

As always happens, I wanted the baseball back, even at the moment of its ending. Watching Wade Boggs up on that police horse, with his hat off and his fist in the air, and the field full of cops and debris, I kept turning back in my mind to the pleasures of Yankee baseball as it had been at this game's beginning, with the crowd, a mass somehow more tightly packed into a single body than at any other park, weaving and writhing together, rocking and boogying along between innings, to the enormous music from the videotron and sound system blasting out "Cotton Eye Joe" and "Rock and Roll (Part II)." It was better, of course, during the action, when everyone was jumping up for the play or the third strike, with their arms raised, and with that motion turning into a front-to-back moving wave, as its leaders—rows of friends together in their gear and their high spirits, all hand-slapping and high-fiving—began making those everybody-up gestures that drove me bananas even while they made me smile and got me up, too. There was the crowd sound, too—that many-thousands roar around you and above and below you, a curving, enveloping noise so deep and thick that you felt it inside your head and your stomach and lower inside you as well; sometimes the noise was so loud that the Stadium became a part of the instrument, trembling and thrumming with it, the way it has always done and was meant to do. The fans' joyfulness was there as well, along with their apprehension, with the crowd feeding on its own noise and its brash energy, and laughing at the power of its familiar deafening yells: "Oooh-oh! Oooh-oh! Oooh-oh!" and "Let's go, Yank-ees! Let's go, Yank-ees!" or, quicker, "Le'sgoYank-ees! Le'sgoYank-ees!" or the ancient, brisk clap-clap clapclapclap staccato—a one, two, threefourfive beat that zinged around the stands and lifted us with a quicker insistence.

This Yankee crowd is quick and dead sure of itself, and proud of its harsh, vulgar, big-city reputation as the most demanding and judgmental body in sports: the La Scala of the pastime. It knows baseball, it misses nothing, and it makes up its mind in an instant: that sudden deep "Booo!" or the irredeemable "Aaaah-sole! Aaaah-sssole!" Plus it's funny. When the estimable Bobby Cox, his world in pieces around him, headed back to his dugout after protesting a terrible ump's call out at second base, and then got himself thrown out of the game by third-base umpire Tim Welke—they'd been wrangling all week—the bleachers and back-rows chorus did a triumphant parody of that gruesome Atlanta tomahawk chant, with its own fresh lyrics: "Fuck the Braaaves! Fuck thuh Braa-aves!" and then had to stop; it had broken itself up. Yes, we had the nice victory parade and the ticker tape, with the Mayor and the Governor in their Yankee caps, and our guys, the smiling players, up on the trucks, but never mind all that now. This other stuff is what we'll want to hold on to, with winter coming along. Never mind the monuments.

Legends of the Fens

September, 2001

Make mine Boston, just for a while again, after all baseball news went glimmering last Tuesday morning. This was before, back when we could still take pleasure in our games. The Red Sox, as I was saying, have blown another season, this time falling on their faces with a thirteen-out-of-fourteen-game string of losses. They've lost a manager, the quirkily oblique Jimy Williams, who perhaps found his fungo bat the most enjoyable attribute of the job, and once, responding to a query about the team's lack of speed on the base paths, offered the Zenlike "You can't get a ticket riding a bicycle on a freeway, can you?" The bleacher fans chant "Yankees suck!" on a day when the team is playing the Atlanta Braves. (I was there and can swear to this.) The Sox' everyday catcher, Scott Hatteberg, has thrown out ten of a hundred and nine enemy base stealers, the worst such average in memory. On the other hand, he is the only man ever to bat into a triple play (on August 6th, against the Texas Rangers) and then smack a grand-slam home run in his very next at-bat. Boston loyalists can spray the Yankees' incomparable thirty-nine-year-old Roger Clemens with unspeakable invective when he warms up in the bullpen just in front of the Fenway Park bleachers but more or less applaud him when he goes on to beat them, 3–1, as he did on August 31st, striking out ten batters and lifting his won-lost totals to 18-1 for the season—this because they take bitter pleasure in the knowledge that their mistrusted general manager, Dan Duquette, let Roger depart the Sox in 1996, declaring him to be in the "twilight of his career." The Red Sox are also the only team whose favorite slugger, the gently ferocious d.h. Manny Ramirez, wears the outsized uniform pants of the fattest player on the squad, reliever Rich (El Guapo) Garces, for style's sake. And the Red Sox are the only team with a curse.

I confess that I've made light of the "Curse of the Bambino"— a neat tagline and title used by the *Globe* columnist Dan Shaughnessy, when he wrote a book about the home team's extensive and eloquent failures to nail down another World Championship after they last did it, in 1918, and stuck needles into the club's owner, Harry Frazee, for his decision, a year later, to sell Babe Ruth, then a star pitcher for the Bostons, to the Yankees because, it was said, he needed cash as a backer of a Broadway musical. Kitschy kid stuff to me—right up to the moment at the end of May this year when the Red Sox' double-incumbent Cy Young Award starter, Pedro Martínez, mouthing off a bit after beating the Yanks by 3–0, laughingly offered, "I don't believe in damn curses. Wake up the damn Bambino and have me face him. Maybe I'll drill him in the ass." As every grandmother, tavernkeeper, and six-year-old in New England knows by now, Pedro has not won a game since. Struck down almost on the instant by a shoulder ailment, he sat out two months, then pitched valiantly on his return but without picking up another win. Now doctors have found that he is suffering from a slight tear in the rotator cuff, and he may be through for the season. Only in Boston.

Writers waiting to gain postgame admission to the Red Sox manager's office at Fenway Park line up outside the clubhouse, separated by a metal rail from the jammed-together, slowly departing right-field-side patrons, who are headed home in the opposite direction. If the Sox have won, the crowd is noisy and uninteresting, but when they have lost again, as they do by habit in late summer, this year and every year, the tableau becomes weighty and shadowed, with more irony and history and atmosphere to take in than any mere game can account for. It's dark down here under the stands, for one thing, and the shuffling, oppressed humanity, the dingy lighting, the food smells, the bunched strands of wires and cables running haphazard overhead, and the damp, oddly tilting stone floor cast a spell of F Deck aboard the Titanic. Fenway Park floods a visitor with more images than a dozen other ballparks put together, every image apt. The joint opened on April 20, 1912, less than a week after John Jacob Astor and Leonardo DiCaprio gallantly left the lifeboats to the ladies. The Sox beat the New York Highlanders (the pre-Yanks), 7–6, that first Fenway afternoon, beginning a season that would feature Smokey Joe Wood's 34-5 pitching record for the Bostons, and a World Championship over John McGraw's Giants.

Not many of the faces facing me now, on a more recent date, appear comforted by the memory. Many of the men have thick upper bodies, partly concealed behind loose shirts or sweats, but with boyish-looking shorts and big sneakers below. Here comes a large, dignified-looking gent with well-tended white hair, a bankerish demeanor, and a white T-shirt emblazoned with, yes, "Yankees suck," in blue block letters. There are more kids than you see at Yankee Stadium; fewer Latinos but perhaps more families. Some of the nine- and ten- and eleven-year-old boys, with their big mitts and Red Sox wristbands and summer buzz cuts, carry an unmistakable Fenian bloom—a look that is confirmed in the faces of their dads. I know what they know, and it comes to me once again—forget the Titanic—that these lads could be from Armagh or Roscommon instead of Melrose or Walpole or West Newton, and their heads already full of the Battle of the Boyne and the Easter uprising and Cuchulainn the Hound of Ulster. These local heirs have been handed a similar burden of oppression and unfairness from their earliest breakfast memories, which have the old man groaning over still another bleeding headline in the Globe sports pages ("Boggs slapped with palimony suit," "Sox postseason loss skein at 13," "Pedro falls to Bombers"), and you can almost envision the kids exchanging miserable glances as they try to fit the fresh stuff in with the troubles they were born into and the long tales imparted during their first trips to Mass at the Fens. There's 1975 to remember, and Why Did We Take Out Willoughby?

and Bucky Dent's dying screen shot on a haunted October afternoon in '78, and black Billy Buckner slowly straightening up behind first base at Shea Stadium in '86, with the easy ground ball
skittering off behind him, and, farther away, Pesky holding on to
the ball in St. Louis while the Cardinals' World Series-winning run
comes in: throw the ball, Johnny, for the love of God. There's
Pudge leaving us, and Roger and Mo as well.

We haven't won since before Grandpa's time, Timmy my boy,
when we let Babe Ruth go—yes, he was ours, a thug of a lefty
pitcher then, and he got away. It doesn't mean anything, this Curse
of the Bambino, but some day, maybe in your lifetime...Don't
you go worrying about it.

While I stood in line outside manager Joe Kerrigan's office,
moments after the Sox had lost to the Yankees in familiar but heartbreaking fashion, to run their losing streak to six, a teen-age boy,
mournful under his backward-facing Sox cap, was nudged closer to
me by the outflowing crowd. Spotting the credential hung around
my neck and my clutched tape recorder and notebook, he leaned
close, tilted his head, and murmured, "Ask him what's going on."

Good question. This year's promising Red Sox saw their vibrant shortstop Nomar Garciaparra, a two-time defending batting
champion, go down early with wrist surgery, and in June lost
Pedro, the best pitcher in baseball, to that aching shoulder. Against
all expectations, the Sox hung in, mounting an offense around the
electrifying Ramirez, a free-agent slugger who fired a home run
into the left-field screen off his first Fenway pitch. They also sent a
succession of tough elder non-Pedros to the mound—the knuckleballer Tim Wakefield, the thirty-eight-year-old ex-Yankee David
Cone, and the erstwhile Dodger (and Met and Brewer and Tiger)
strikeout machine Hideo Nomo, who threw a no-hitter against the
Orioles in the second game of the year. The Sox grabbed first place
in their division, at times leading the pack by as much as four
games, and then, yielding to the inevitable, fell behind the Yankees
in early July, but hung close as they waited for their missing icons

to get better—Nomar by August; Pedro, with luck, in September—and help win a shot at the wild-card opening in the playoffs.

But rosiness never lingers long around the Red Sox. Despite the team's success, a cranky dislike festered between some of the regulars and their semi-silent manager, Jimy Williams, who rarely visited the clubhouse, posted late and mystifying lineups, and responded to press queries with a gnomic and infuriating "Manager's decision." Irritability became a clubhouse refrain. Why am I sitting out again? Why the hell am I coming out of the bullpen so often in no-win games? Manny Ramirez smiled through it all, with CD earphones clapped on to blank out the sounds of bickering. Somewhere in my notes is a reminder about the flaplet that began when Trot Nixon let drop that the ailing Carl Everett might be "waiting around and not rehabbing or anything"—and attempted to take it back the next day with "I am not trying to piss off Carl by any means because that is not my job."

The clubhouse hostility was benign, a heat rash, compared with relations between Williams and his boss, the executive vice-president and general manager, Dan Duquette; the two parted so vividly a year ago (perhaps when Duquette refused to back the manager in a dispute with the ill-tempered and scary Everett) that it was not expected that Williams would be back this spring. Duquette, stiff and cautious by temperament, is not above tossing the occasional player or manager to the writers, in the manner of a fox loin to the hounds. Asked on the Red Sox radio show why Pedro Martínez had been removed after the sixth inning of a strong effort against the Yankees in June (the Yanks rallied against the Boston relievers and won the game), he said, "I think Jimy needs to talk to the fans about his thinking on that, because it caused a lot of controversy in the market here throughout New England." Martínez, it turned out, was already suffering from the shoulder inflammation that would put him on the disabled list, but neither the manager nor the G.M. could find a way to be straight with the media about the news.

It all came apart on August 16th, when the consonantally challenged Jimy was axed, after the team, in slow decline, had slipped
behind the onrushing Oakland Athletics on the wild-card sideline.
Managers always get canned during bad news, and the Sox' hopes
had long since turned sour. Jason Varitek, an essential catcher and
pitch-caller, broke his elbow making a diving catch in foul territory; Everett sat out too many games with a sore knee and swung
at too many up pitches when he did play; Manny fell into a de-
pressing slump; and, worse, Garciaparra's return to action was cut
short when his wrist blew up again, finishing him for the year. The
emotional high-water mark at the Fens, it turned out, had come
with a 4–3 win over the White Sox on July 29th, Nomar's first day
back, when he tied the game with a homer in the sixth and won it
with a single in his next at-bat.

The burdened inheritor of these woes was Joe Kerrigan, the
lean and furrowed pitching coach, who was named manager only
when Duquette, by his own unhelpful admission, failed to persuade Felipe Alou, the revered ex-Montreal skipper, to accept the
post. Kerrigan, a computer apostolic, was widely credited for the
Sox' astounding conversion from their long tradition of Wall-
bashing into a pitching-and-defense club, with the lowest earned-
run average in the league over the previous two years. He also
served as advance scout, scouring game tapes from around the
league and disseminating them in daily printouts of pitcher proclivities and situational batting scenarios. Hardworking and intellectual, he was handicapped—in the minds of his players, if not his
own—by having never previously managed a game, at any level.

Quickly it became clear that Kerrigan lacked another essential
managerial attribute: luck. The departed Jimy, for all his veterans'
injuries and whinings, had put a respectable, fiercely contending
lineup on the field every day that could coax out wins under unlikely circumstances, but on Saturday night, August 25th, ten days
into the Kerrigan regime, the Bostons ran into an abutment in
Texas: a ghastly eighteen-inning, six-hour-and-thirty-five-minute
standoff against the Rangers, played in soaking ninety-degree

weather, which was lost, 8–7, at two-forty in the morning. Only a bit earlier, the schedule had twice forced the Sox to play a game a continent away from one completed the previous day (this happened within a span of ten days, in fact), and the psychic toll of those post-dawn arrivals and screwed-up body clocks, taken with the nine pitchers wasted in Texas, finished the club just as it was about to enter the critical stretch of the season—thirteen successive games against the Indians and the Yankees, away and at home and away again. Every player and fan and sportswriter had stuck a Post-it on these couple of weeks in his mind and looked forward to them since spring training. Too late. The Sox, down to the Yankees by four games after the eighteen-inning debacle, were six behind by the time the two met at last, at Fenway Park, less than a week later, and in the toils of the free-fall streak that would push their season into nullity and despond.

The Yankee games, it turned out, were high entertainment, stuffed with old-fashioned low-score baseball and great pitching, and played out in front of a gallant, beaten-down audience that half expected loss and irrelevance and could handle irony with the flair of a Nomar plucking up a low line drive behind second. Baseball news was piling up elsewhere, to be sure—Barry Bonds in avid pursuit of Mark McGwire's home-run record; the embarrassments of the Atlanta Braves; the inexorable successes of the Mariners and their skinny new star, Ichiro; and the recent moment, undreamed of in "Field of Dreams" or "Casey at the Bat," when Omar Vizquel, the Indians shortstop, complained to an ump about the distracting earrings sported by Seattle reliever Arthur Rhodes, and won an on-the-spot disjewelment—but these bonbons would have to wait.

The outsized Clemens, riding the wave of his fourth or fifth or fiftieth career reinvention, filled the Friday-night game with himself, throwing ninety-two-mile-an-hour splitters that had the Sox batters waving at his stuff in the dirt (Dante Bichette even reached first after fanning on a wild pitch), coughing up doubles off the wall, shouting at himself for a mistake or another great pitch, and drawing sustenance from the low, baiting cries of "Ro-ger!

Rohhhhh-ger!" rolling in from the bleacher wolfpack. The Rocket will pick up his sixth Cy Young Award this winter, and he has pitched so well for so long—eighteen years now, with active-career leading marks in wins, innings pitched, complete games, and strikeouts—that seeing him work is like watching Monet at his easel or F.D.R. lighting a Camel. Almost every game he gets into produces another historical voice-over. His strikeout of Chris Stynes to close the Boston seventh became his ninety-eighth outing with ten or more K's, and moved him (we were told) past Sandy Koufax and into third place in the annals in this category. It was an effort to notice that Clemens was actually trailing in the game, 1–0, at this juncture, having been clearly outpitched by the Boston starter, the veteran Frank Castillo, whose exquisite in-and-out, fast-and-slow stuff had the Yankee batters swaying at the plate like cobras to a flageolet.

The fans had noticed, though, and their cries of disbelief when a different pitcher, the deeply fallible Derek Lowe, came out in Castillo's place to start the eighth were followed by noises of shock and outrage when the infield misplayed a grounder, putting the lead-off Yankee batter on base, and Jorge Posada swiftly deposited another Lowe offering into the center-field stands—the game-winning poke, as it turned out. Boston baseball had once again proved confirmatory: Roger can't lose this year, and the abiding tradition in this traditional rivalry is Yanks win.

Kerrigan, in his office, was rational. This had been only Castillo's fourth effort since a stint in rehab, he pointed out, and Lowe was well rested—the kind of humane considerations that most September managers of contending teams keep safely stuffed away with their New Year's resolutions. Cruelly, I preferred Lowe's summation, which he delivered from beneath his clubhouse sun visor: "Every little bad thing has turned into a big bad thing for me lately. The booing has been going on for months. We've had a good year and now it seems like we've faded in the last couple of weeks. I'd boo, too."

Saturday morning put the Kerrigan decision into perspective: it was madness. Up in the pressbox, Dan Shaughnessy, the amiable, pink-haired Globe master, said, "It's a legend every day around here. The whole scene of Kerrigan taking out Castillo after two hits and fourteen straight outs—why, it's a fable already. It'll never be forgotten."

"It's like the other manager getting the can with his team only four games out of first place," said a New York columnist. "The story of Jimy is improving every day. It's just a matter of time before he's beloved."

Pleasure in bad news is an old reporters' game, but one perhaps played best here in Boston. I'd heard the raw anger of the fans the night before, and the resident writers told me that general wrath over the Sox' recent failings was deeper than it had ever been. The other local obsessions, the Bruins and the Celtics, have fallen from the heights of late, and in May and June expectations about the Sox were almost off the charts. Manny Ramirez, leading the league in batting and home runs, was living at the Ritz for a thousand dollars a day. Eddie Andelman, the veteran sports announcer on Boston's WEEI, announced a "Yankee Elimination" party on his show, and the call-ins went wild. The Sox had spent a hundred and ten million dollars in salaries this time around, the second-highest total in baseball. The Sox had Nomar and Pedro. The Sox had to win.

Why, amid such blighted memories, do I find Fenway such a benign baseball setting, and baseball happiness closer at hand here than anywhere else? It can't just be the postcard setting: that dinky red peanut-and-cashew wagon plunk in the middle of Yawkey Way, or the patio street signs for sale inside the souvenir shop across the street (a Palazzo of Memorabilia) that say "Hideo Nomo Drive" (forty smackers), or the stunning not-for-sale poster in there depicting a skinny young Yaz, in those pinkish striped stockings, just finishing his swing. Inside the doomed park, an older souvenir stand by the front gate bears a "Red Sox Apparel" sign, and outdoors again, down by the players' parking lot, on Van Ness Street, the kid autograph hunters lie face down on the pavement, peering under the canvased-off chain-link fence, where they can pick up no more than an inch or two of the shoes of their arriving heroes or the make of the tires on their swollen S.U.V.s. "Mr.

Ramirez!" the kids cry out, shoving pens and baseball cards and pennants under the barrier. "Mr. Everett, Mr. Everett!" Fenway Park will be torn down before long—as soon as the sale of the club to one or another of the six current bidding consortiums is completed, in the next few months, and the new management gets its act and its political connections (and its new general manager) together and finds a spot to put up a nice modern five-hundred-million-dollar park with luxury suites and limo parking. One fan I know has begun a last-minute "muttering campaign," to persuade Jack Welch, the retired G.E. genius, to snap up the club. "Self-made Salem boy, fanatic fan, practitioner of tough love," his E-mail runs. "God knows they need something."

I don't care that much. I will sign no petitions to save Fenway (I've been asked), and I don't believe that it's simply habit and an old green-walled brick ball yard and my faded memories of Yaz and the Kid and El Tiante that make Fenway work. I think it's pain and anger, and all the gruesome, farcical losses as well. Yankee Stadium sells you winning and nothing much else, but Fenway offers the full range—rage and sweetness and ridiculous remembering—and makes games here matter, however you groan or curse.

The Saturday disappointment differed only in the barest details from its predecessor. There was bright and blowy September weather this time, and a quicker insufficient lead for the home side: a solo homer by Trot Nixon, the first Boston batter of the day. You could almost hear the "uh-oh"s as the ball went out. Pedro Martínez and Orlando Hernández held it right there for the next hour or so, while a nice little flow of K's and mannerisms accumulated in the sunshine. In the fifth, El Duque shouted "I got it!" while fielding a mini-pop by Mike Lansing—a magical tipoff, on the order of Patty Duke at the water pump, that he is bilingual at last.

The convalescent Pedro took his leave after six, and the Sox unravelment built itself around a modest eighth-inning fly ball that was lost in the sun glare or the gusting breeze in short right field, good for the tying run in time, and Bernie Williams's ninth-inning homer, which reached the first row of seats in center. In two games, the starters had nothing to show for their thirteen goose-egg innings, and the Sox trailed by eight in the East instead of a coulda-been four. Over. Sunday promised little more than a spicy pitchers' pairing—David Cone versus his Yankee replacement, Mike Mussina, who had signed on with the Bombers for $88.5 million over six years—but the quality of the game quickly put secondary distractions to one side. Mussina had pitched so well this year that a little more run support could have found him at Clemens's level, instead of his entering 13-11. Cone, for his part, had rediscovered himself at the Fens, bouncing back from his horrific, injury-marred 4-14 record and that 6.91 earned-run blot last year. Adopting a mini-windup fashioned by Kerrigan, and waiting out a two months' sidelining with a shoulder inflammation, he found better results even while working within pitch limitations on his thirty-eight-year-old arm. He stood at 8-3 on this day, with the Boston rooters and interloper Yankee fans perhaps finding equal pleasure from the Sox' run of a dozen consecutive wins in starts of his this summer. As Cone said last year when things were going the other way for him, "Sometimes it's not how you pitch but which games you pitch that matter."

This game—which would end up 1–0, Yankees, with the losing pitcher more or less in triumph and the winner in near-despair—will go straight into the Boston family storybook. Indeed, you can already savor the bitter, flushed-faced joy of future Back Bay grandpas and barflies when they come to the good part—the ninth-inning pinch-hit, two-out, two-strike single sailed into left center by Carl Everett for the first and only Sox hit of the evening, and the ruination of Mussina's masterpiece. "Sure, the Yankees won it, lad—what did you expect—but oh, my!"

Mussina and Cone pitch with intensity and with the same leaning stillness while they take in the catcher's sign and begin their little back step. Mussina had such stuff and command this time that he rarely threw the knuckle curve that has been his signature. Nor, of course, did we see the deep courtier's bow of his that inaugurates a pitch with base runners aboard. He was brooding and hunched—a man who wanted no news at all this day and almost got that wish. Nine of his eventual thirteen strikeouts went into the books in the first five innings—he struck out the side in the second—with most of the victims standing immobile as the dismissing ninety-plus fastball or the downflared two-seamer flicked by.

Cone's work provided greater amusement, but mostly he avoided the high counts, bases on balls, or crisis innings that we have come to know so well. He throws more curves than sliders these days, and as always on a good Cone day you enjoyed his thinking almost more than the speed or slant of a given pitch—the wisdom of his four pitches just out of the strike zone to Tino Martinez in the fourth, say, before he fanned Posada to end the inning. The game was going by in a rush, with the accruing edginess of the Mussina no-hitter and possible perfecto matched now by anxiety about Cone's pitch count and potential removal by attrition. Still no score. The Yankees, in fact, brought in no runs at all in the first seven innings of any game of their three-game sweep—another first, for any pair of teams, in the annals.

Cone, visibly less by now, worked through an eighth inning of lowering troubles, with the quick Soriano on first after a lead-off single. Knoblauch went down with a fly ball and Jeter on a strikeout; Derek said later that his tottering wave at Cone's sidearmer was the worst swing of his professional career. With Soriano on second now, Bernie Williams stroked a high drive that was pulled in by Nixon a step in front of the center-field wall. The end—the first ending, that is—arrived predictably enough in the Yankee ninth, when the fill-in Boston second baseman, Lou Merloni, botched a hard-hit double-play grounder that would have closed the inning. Enrique Wilson's double brought in the run at last, and finished Coney for the day. At least he got the shot, having talked his manager into letting him go back out there and take what came: death by the bullet, not the bullpen.

The building, no-hit, nobody-on melodrama by Mussina had been buzzed about and gabbled over in the stands all evening, because it was Cone, of course, who had last turned the trick, two years ago this past July, when he shut down the Montreal Expos on Yogi Berra Day at the Stadium, for the sixteenth such marvel on record. The coincidence added a flair of moral drama to the proceedings, and now in the ninth Everett's two-out, 1-and-2-count single, struck off a third successive high fastball, was greeted by pathetically exulting Fenwayian cries. Mussina had got within two outs of a perfect game four years ago in Baltimore, but he had to come up here to be inaugurated into the Hall of Pain.

No gleam of light has showed itself for the Red Sox since that day, and their season has trailed off into scandal and bottomless loss. A pitching coach (Kerrigan's successor) was fired moments after a losing game, more or less in full sight of the media, causing Garciaparra to mutter, "That's why nobody wants to fucking play here." The whine was delivered to a teammate but overheard and disclosed by a hovering writer, as has happened before in the players' slummy little tenement. Pedro has continued to pitch, despite his subpar shoulder; he was taken out of his start in New York ten days ago, down by 3–2, after fifty-four pitches. No one in baseball—well, no one outside of the Boston management—can understand how a franchise arm could have been put at such risk.

After winning a game at last, against Cleveland, the Red Sox dropped four more—"Again, a Crushing Defeat for Region" was the headline over a prior Shaughnessy column in the Globe—and trailed the Yankees by thirteen games before the Trade Center tragedy intervened. David Cone lost to Mussina once again, with the teams in New York, in a suspense-free 9-2 renewal. Coming off the field in the sixth after throwing a second home run of the day to Martinez (Tino drove in five runs, all told), David received a handsome, non-ironic standing O from the fans. He was gracious in the clubhouse: "It was very, very appreciated. I can't remember the last time I tipped my hat after giving up five runs." But his season and his hopes of pitching in Fenway in the post-season had gone south, along with everyone else's, and it came out in time that he'd gone wild in the clubhouse after the accolade, throwing chairs and food around—a "snappage," in his lexicon.

Cone will be back next year—his great game up in Boston as-
sures it*—but I don't think it will be with the Red Sox. Losing him
will be sad for the Fenwayites, but it fits nicely within the legend.
He is bitterly disappointed about the collapse of the Red Sox, but
loss, of course, is something these pros encounter almost every
day. When Cone learned that the dour and inward Mike Mussina
was still feeling the shock of Everett's killer single, he arranged to
meet him at the Stadium, where he comforted him with a longer
view. "It's not so bad to talk about a game like that after it's over,"
he explained to me. "You don't want to turn a masterpiece into a
negative. It feels pretty good to be told that you were part of the
best game played this year."

*It didn't happen. Cone received no offers in the spring of 2002, and has begun a
career as baseball broadcaster.

Can You Believe It?

2001

Come back, Shane Spencer. Baseball, taking its late leave after
an astounding run of post-season games and a World Series captured by the Arizona Diamondbacks in the last inning of the seventh and final game, is missed now like the passing of Christmas or
a kid's hero in fadeout over the hill. Gone are the games and, this
time, the telling of the games, as well. For a week or more while the
Series was going on, friends encountered on the street here in New
York or urgently heard from by telephone or E-mail began with
"Wasn't that—" or "Could you believe it when—" and they'd tell
you where they were when Tino Martinez tied up Game Four with
his two-run homer, with two out in the ninth, or how they were
still watching but had actually—can you believe it!—gone to bed
and were almost asleep when Scott Brosius did exactly the same
thing the next night: hit a two-out, two-run, game-tying shot off
the same Diamondbacks closer. Then we were ready to jump back
to Game Four again and Derek Jeter's tenth-inning mini-dinger,
just into the right-field stands, which came in an at-bat that began
just before midnight on October 31st, and won the thing four minutes later, in November. And did you catch that TV shot of the guy
in the stands, in the middle of all that screaming and jumping, holding up a sign that said "Mr. November"? Wasn't that something?
Can you believe it?

Baseball as melodrama, with the winning or tying runs arriving
in sudden reversal in the bottom of the ninth inning, is the way

children or non-fans expect the games to go, but when it happened three times in this World Series, including the finale, it was the hardened fans and the players and coaches, and even the writers, who were dumbfounded, exchanging excited glances and shaking their heads after the latest stroke of the unlikely. Reggie Jackson, murmuring mostly to himself late in the Yankee clubhouse after Game Five, said, "I don't understand it. It's unbelievable. I'm amazed." Winners' disbelief became endemic in the Series, at first afflicting the suave defending-champion Yankees, after they had swept their three games at the Stadium in adventure-comix fashion, and then the upstart Diamondbacks, at their resortlike Bank One Ballpark, in Phoenix, when they turned around Game Seven in its final instants. Their pair of runs against Mariano Rivera, the best closer in history, produced a 3–2 win and snatched away a fourth successive World Championship from the sovereign Yankees. In a different autumn, the defeat of the Yankees would have been the cause for fierce, exulting cries around the country, but this time, thanks to the events of September 11th, these joys were tempered and orderly, and the Arizona turnabout became a continuation of the other two late-game miracles, back in New York, and a gift to fans and Americans everywhere.

The last part of the story, still being told in exclamatory fashion by Arizona friends meeting in downtown Phoenix or Flagstaff or Tucson or Tempe, or at the mall or pool or corral, is the one that matters, of course. Trailing by 2–1, at the end of an improbable string of innings that had matched up two twenty-game winners— Roger Clemens and the D'Backs' ace or co-ace, Curt Schilling— and facing the imminent arrival of a Yankee hug-up on the field and another autumn-sunlight parade up Broadway, the newcomers pieced together three hits and a pair of bunts to topple the fabled and nearly untouchable Mariano. Yankee defense and Yankee pitching, the pillars of their recent empire, both failed in plain sight here, brought down by the Diamondbacks' courage and opportunism. A lead-off Arizona single by the thirty-seven-year-old classicist Mark Grace, and the expected sacrifice bunt from Damian

Miller, which was thrown wild past second base by Rivera, brought the first pausing "Uh-oh"s up and down the Eastern time zone. Another bunt became a force-out at third, but the tying run was delivered on a broken-bat double stroked to right by shortstop Tony Womack. A different Rivera pitch, which barely brushed the hand of the new batter, Craig Counsell, may have been the killing mistake, in retrospect. With the bases loaded now and only one out, Joe Torre chose to have his infield play in, and the championship poke—a softly looped single by Luis Gonzalez onto the grass in short left-center, catchable by Jeter in the other configuration— brought Jay Bell flying in from third and sent the pompom-waving multitudes into frenzies of happiness. Home players, boiling out of the dugout, threw themselves into pigpiles around the infield, with the Yankees, for once, looking on in wintry silence.

A word must be said here for Fox Sports' Tim McCarver, the stay-at-homes' seatmate at these big games, who looked at the left-hitting Gonzalez as he stood in against Rivera in this last at-bat of the year and expressed concern about Mariano's habit of pitching inside. "Left-handers get a lot of broken-bat hits into the shallow part of the outfield," he observed. "That's the danger of bringing the infield in with a guy like Rivera on the mound." No sooner said: Gonzalez, on his second swing, broke his bat and delivered the flare.

Arizona fans are a little short on baseball lore—the franchise is four years old, and their World Championship is the quickest to arrive for any expansion team—but they did a lot of catching up in this game. The principals—the Yankee starter Roger Clemens; the averted-gaze, sleekly firing Rivera; the blond and long-chested Curt Schilling; and the six-foot-ten Randy Johnson, back in action as a late reliever and ultimate winner (he took three games in the Series, all told) a day after his smothering seven innings and hundred and one pitches in Game Six—had been in the news and on our minds throughout these games. Their presence, together here in the last act, gave them a mythic substantiality; they were like those gigantic Bread and Puppet Theatre heads you saw bobbing along in protest parades in the sixties.

Clemens, sweating ferociously in the eighty-seven-degree heat, with his minuscule, bunched-together features squinched into a knot of concentration, stared down every difficulty (he had men on base in every inning), struck out ten, and turned over a six-and-a-third-inning 1–1 tie on his departure. He had already delivered the dodgy, essential third game, back at Yankee Stadium, with a 2–1 outing, pitched despite a strained and sore right hamstring, which brought the Yanks back from their early two-game deficit, and he looked like the hero here, and a strong choice as Most Valuable Player. The ancient knock on Clemens has been that he doesn't do well in big games, but the canard should now expire. As manager Joe Torre put it, "I don't think he will have to defend himself again."

Schilling (at 22-6 this year for the Diamondbacks) and Clemens (with his 20-3) were the first twenty-game winners to face off in a final Series game since 1985. Schilling's arrival in Arizona, in July of last year, after a massive trade with the Phillies, was a grand coup for the free-spending owner, Jerry Colangelo, a Phoenix developer, who had arrived in baseball on his own terms—"kicked in the door," as Schilling put it—and was determined to deliver a championship without the customary period of hangdog smiling and losing that most new owners endure. Randy Johnson, the left-handed Ionic column, had arrived as a free agent two seasons before, signing on for $52.4 million over four years. He and Schilling simply panzered the National League this summer, accounting for forty-seven per cent of the team's wins, and winning nine of the pair's eleven starts in the playoffs. Johnson, who is thirty-eight, struck out three hundred and seventy-two batters in the course of his 21-6 summer, and has just picked up a third successive Cy Young Award; his opposite number is Clemens, who took the honor for the sixth time.

Schilling, with that dominating jaw and rock-star pack of hair, is attractive and smart and—well, we can no longer say "over-assured," can we? Asked by a reporter about the "mystique and aura" of the Yankees, he said they sounded like a pair of strippers to him. Back in September, he wrote a moving, widely distributed essay about America after the Trade Center attack. I retain a vivid picture of the complete-game 2–0 shutout that Schilling delivered for the Phillies against Toronto in the 1993 World Series, when he pitched on pure character in the late going, and betweentimes lay back on the bench like an expiring emir, his head hidden beneath a towel. He came into this Series announcing his availability as the starter for the first, fourth, and seventh games, and the efforts of his manager, Bob Brenly, to bring this about encouraged a rush of double-thinking and position-taking by the media. Benefitted by a 9–1 Arizona waltz in the opener, Schilling did return on three days' rest for Game Four. Ahead by 3–1, in a strong performance, he was taken out after seven innings: a defensible logic, perhaps, right up to the moment when the Arizona closer Byung-Hyun Kim suffered that sudden incandescence at the hands of Tino Martinez. Brenly, staring down a roomful of second-guessers, admitted in a postgame interview that one of his reasons for the removal had been to save Schilling for a start in Game Seven, when and if.

This did come to pass, as we know, but now the beleaguered skipper faced a trip on his knees to the top of one of the nearby peaks (a favorite Apache way of saying "I'm sorry") for permitting Curt to bat for himself in the seventh inning in the tied-up, 1–1 final—and to cough up Alfonso Soriano's eighth-inning go-ahead homer. Brenly's last move of the year was Randy Johnson, whom he had kept in action in Game Six, the previous evening, for all those pitches, despite a 15–2 home-team lead. Dead wrong, said the writers to each other, except that the reappearing Randy—a spectre and a half to the Yankees' left-handed batters by now—delivered four outs, and turned the proceedings over to his teammates in the ninth, who won it. No wonder managers hug everybody when the champagne begins to flow. What Brenly knew, of course, was that Johnson, a hard nut, had pulled off the same feat while pitching for the Seattle Mariners in the American League divisional championships of 1995, when he came back on one day's rest after capturing the third game and stubbornly tacked on three more innings for the win that eliminated the Yankees, of all people. Since then, the Yankees had emerged as winners in fourteen post-season series, including the last eleven in a row (a stretch of seventy-two games, all told) before they ran into Randy again in a significant game—but he had become a bad habit for them after all.

The Diamondbacks showed confidence and fortitude in this Series (and some terrific plays around second base), and their deserved trophy, the first for any professional team in the Valley of the Sun, is being carried about to banquets and football games there, where it's touched and rubbed like a holy relic. Mark Grace and Matt Williams, the venerated infield corners, may feel the same way about their Series rings, when they arrive: the first for either one after their combined twenty-nine seasons in the show.

In a less shadowed baseball autumn, there might be more time to think about a flurry of feats and farewells that turned up before the close of regular play. The celebrations of Cal Ripken Day in Baltimore were fervent. The pale-eyed god, retiring after twenty-one seasons, which had included that 2,632-consecutive-games wonder, 3,184 lifetime base hits, and nineteen consecutive All-Star Game appearances, waved to the fans from a slowly circling convertible, out beyond where Camden Yards groundskeepers had mowed his No. 8 into the outfield grass. There were gifts and tears and "whereas"es. When the Orioles ran out onto the field to begin the game against the Red Sox, first baseman Jeff Conine tossed the infield warmup ball toward Ripken, as usual, but this time threw it over by the stands—so that Cal had to run it down in foul territory. When he turned around, there was no sign of his teammates. A different batch of Orioles—the lineup from August 12, 1981, his very first start in the majors—had appeared from the third-base dugout: Rick Dempsey behind the plate, Eddie Murray at first, Rich Dauer at second, and Gary Roenicke, Al Bumbry, and Ken Singleton heading toward their positions around the outfield. There were empty places at shortstop, where the late Mark Belanger had held forth, and at third, where Ripken played back then. The middle-aged O's were in their ancient uniforms, and wore caps displaying that long-gone grinning-bird logo. And here came Earl Weaver, tiny and snowy-haired, walking up to the home-plate ump with his lineup card. Sensation.

In San Diego, Tony Gwynn, the perennial Padre batting champion, hung them up after twenty seasons and a lifetime .338. In San Francisco, the Giants' Barry Bonds, largely underappreciated as the best player of his time, took care of the slur with his seventy-three home runs, eclipsing Mark McGwire's once epochal seventy. (McGwire has just retired, unexpectedly departing at the age of thirty-eight because of chronic knee problems.) Bonds's season-long assault on the McGwire mark was almost quietly waged, because he was so clearly and admirably engrossed in trying to help his team win, which used to be the main idea. Almost more impressive to his fellow-pros was Barry's .863 slugging average (total bases per at-bat) this year, which is tops in the books, ever.

Attention must be paid also to Rickey Henderson, whose final hit of the year for the Padres put him into the three-thousand-lifetime-hits coterie. Henderson, of course, is the forever stolen-base champ: his 1,395 swipes puts him four hundred and fifty-seven ahead of the nearest pursuer, Lou Brock. This year, Rickey also went past Ty Cobb for most lifetime runs scored and Babe Ruth for most walks, but I prefer his all-time seventy-nine lead-off home runs, because each of them, if you think about it, so depressed and pissed off some pitcher. In his prime, with the vivid Oakland teams of the eighties, Henderson leading off first base was a twitchy, squinting packet of energy—you laughed at the sight—that drove the pitcher and the infielders to distraction. He became such a threat to the outcome of close games that more than one manager made the decision to walk the batter just ahead of him (with the bases empty, I mean) in order to clog his progress. Irritation became Henderson's life work, afflicting even his teammates along the way. After Rickey won a protracted argument with the Oakland management over the payment of a million-dollar bonus clause in his contract in 1989, Athletics general manager Sandy Alderson heard that the transaction didn't seem to have cleared a bank.

Rickey, legend has it, had framed the check instead of cashing it, and had it up on a wall at home.

Baseball's story this year will always turn back to Yankee Stadium, where the games for a time felt diminished and trivial after the September 11th attack on the World Trade Center. Ceremonials and long minutes of silence, players in Fire and Police Department caps (and the "PAPD" version, for the Port Authority's cops), plus attending groups of policemen and firemen, vociferously cheered, greeted the resumption of play after a week's suspension, but the altered thoughts and fractured attention that each of us now bore didn't allow much fun to come through. When the Yanks dropped the first two games of the divisional playoffs to the headlong young Oakland A's, at the Stadium, I bade goodbye to them and their eminent departing seniors in my heart, perhaps almost with relief that I wouldn't soon again be hearing "God Bless America" in these emotional settings. (How many other New Yorkers there, I'd asked myself, could remember breakfast times in the late sixties, an epoch away, when Larry Josephson, a host with the left-leaning radio station WBAI, would do a little fund-raising by playing Kate Smith's "God Bless America" over and over again, non-stop, until his listeners had phoned in fifty bucks' worth of pledges, in self-defense?)

And then, with the Yankees away in Oakland for the weekend games, pessimism took a sudden kick in the pants from Derek Jeter and his play up the first-base line in Game Three. With the Yanks clinging to a parlous 1–0 lead in the seventh (these series are three losses and out) and an Athletics base runner, Jeremy Giambi, leading off first, Terrence Long drove a smash into the right-field corner, where the ball was grabbed and flung plateward by Shane Spencer. His throw airmailed both cutoff men, Soriano and Martinez, and was skipping aimlessly along when Jeter arrived from the middle of the diamond, snatched up the ball backhand, and in the same motion flipped it sidewise to catcher Jorge Posada, who tagged the flying Giambi on the back of his right leg a fraction before his foot touched the plate. The feat takes longer in the telling than the playing, but what was clear on the instant was that Giambi was out, that the Yankees would win, and that nobody at Network Associates Coliseum or anyplace else had ever seen this done before. Electrifying and liberating, the play blew loose a gust of change and baseball happiness back in New York. Anything was possible now, even a couple of seconds of pure good news.

The play has been memorized everywhere. When you rerun the footage, Jeter's presence on the right side of the diamond still startles, but Derek is at ease in this strange place. With his body bent double for the backhand grab, he starts the play running full tilt into foul ground, thirty feet from home, and finishes it like a tricky touch-football lateral. (One friend of mine saw a bucket-brigade shift and lean to Jeter's hand-along.) The flip, in any case, perfectly leads Posada, putting the ball into his mitt with his arms extended, at a juncture where he can complete the sweep and tag in the same motion. If the throw arrives a few inches closer to his body, the play becomes a catch and a lunge, and the runner is already past him. Giambi should have slid—he would have been safe if he had—but he didn't.

The play unsettled or even undid the Athletics, who did not distinguish themselves in their swiftly following run of losses: a 9–2 beating the next day (in which their cleanup batter, Jermaine Dye, weirdly suffered a broken left tibia with his own tipped foul); and, back at Yankee Stadium again the very next day, their error-strewn 5–3 elimination. Jeter delivered two hits in this game, and fell on his back into a front-row box beyond third base in the eighth while completing an outlandish catch. The bleacher fans had not been on hand in Oakland, but now they gave him their all— the full "Der-ek JEET-AH!" over and over. With the next stage for the Yanks assured, the first sense of a different text or script for New York was in the air.

Jeter keeps rearriving. He is twenty-seven, with six full seasons and one base hit short of twelve hundred to his credit—the most for anyone in baseball since 1996. Casting back to decide which of his rivals among the great current generation of shortstops might also have been capable of the relay play out in Oakland, I come up with the Indians' Omar Vizquel, but I don't think he would have imagined it.

Joe Torre said, "This kid, with that play the other day, thinks cool in hot situations. And making that play, he never has any regard for putting his body in peril or being embarrassed with a bad swing. We have a number of them, but he's a true leader at a very early age."

The Seattle Mariners, who will have but a cameo role in this account, tied a record with their hundred and sixteen wins this summer but contrived to turn up at the Stadium two down in the American League Championship Series, after strong performances by Andy Pettitte, Mike Mussina, and Rivera out at Safeco Field. The clubs now exchanged lopsided wins in the third and fifth games, the last a 12–3 elimination party by the Yankees. What deserves remembrance is the middle, fourth game, an austere classic that has been dimmed a bit by the World Series. The gimpy Clemens and his successor, Ramiro Mendoza, had between them given up only a lone single when Bret Boone delivered a homer with two out in the eighth, for the first run of the game. This was the evening when the Yankees' extreme debility at the plate— which was to finish them off in the end—fully showed itself, as they found themselves unable to bring home any of the eight batters walked by the Mariners' Paul Abbott. But heigh-ho, no matter: here came Bernie Williams, with his one-out, full-count homer against Arthur Rhodes, to tie things up again in the eighth, and then Alfonso Soriano, the rookie second baseman, to win it with a two-run walk-off job in the ninth. Magical.

Bronx fans had a party the next night, when their guys blew out the visitors, with some old Yankee icons—Paul O'Neill, Bernie Williams, and Tino Martinez—each contributing a home run. The Mariners' celebrity star Ichiro Suzuki was a bust in these games, repeatedly driven off the plate by inside pitching, and the Seattle express, gone now without much of a struggle, would not threaten the famous hundred and twenty-five total wins (regular-season plus post-season victories) rung up by these same Yankees in 1998. "Hey-hey-hey, goodbye!" sang the top-deck fans, to the old "Sha-na-na" strains, while the lower stands, for no reason, fell to chanting "Hip hip Jor-hay! Hip hip Jor-hay!" during a Posada at-bat, throwing their arms up like cheerleaders. With the World Series gained once again and an extra week or more of New York baseball guaranteed, the bleacherites stayed on after the game ended, pointing and cheering when Joe Torre went over to Rudy Giuliani's box, next to the home dugout, and escorted the Mayor—a devout Yankee fan, a guy who stays on until the end of the game—onto the field with the other heroes.

Seattle manager Lou Piniella, a classy gent, told the writers how he'd looked around at the yowling and stomping fans as they disported themselves after the Yankees' horrid bat-around sixth, even taunting his club with "Overrated! Overrated!" and almost wanted to cheer a little, too. "I thought, Boy, this city has suffered a lot, and tonight they let out a lot of emotions," he said. "I felt good for them, I really did—and that's a strange thought to come from a manager who's getting his ass kicked."

What Piniella felt about New York was shared, I believe, by fans and casual baseball watchers everywhere this fall, and perhaps even by some who have but a passing awareness of baseball. The Yankees are famous symbols for the city, of course, but only in a Steinbrennerian, overdog sort of way. This particular Yankee team, however, is very well known, thanks to its continuity of players— the center core of Paul O'Neill, Tino Martinez, Scott Brosius, Derek Jeter, Bernie Williams, Chuck Knoblauch, Andy Pettitte, and Mariano Rivera, who go back nearly half a decade together— and to their hundreds of accumulated hours on national television. Their smallest mannerisms are familiar to countless Americans, who this year may have been seeing them, even without knowing it, as home folks—the only New York family on their radar. The Yankee players had been on the scene, so to speak, on the morning of September 11th, when the bad news for the country arrived, and how they felt and how they would fare now mattered. And millions here in the city felt the connection: the Yanks were us.

President Bush threw the ceremonial first pitch of Game Three for a strike, from the full distance, and the Yankees and the weather seemed to take it from there. Arizona's veteran-loaded assemblage had been assuring themselves that the clamor and history of the old ballpark wouldn't bother them, but the chilly, swirling Bronx breezes felt unfair. Foul balls sailed sidewise out of reach, back by the screen, while Diamondback infielders bumped into each other on routine pops, and their discomfited pitchers let fly with three wild pitches. *Our* wind, the fans felt, pumping their fists into it. Clemens, defending a 1–1 score, pitched on undistracted, and Yankee defense produced a diving grab by Soriano in the sixth that saved a run, and, just afterward, a skidding backhand catch by Spencer in left field, as he collared Matt Williams's rocket. The Yankees' go-ahead run in the bottom half, delivered by Brosius, was hailed by cowbells and flying bits of paper, and soon came Rivera to nail things down. Almost a great game.

It was Halloween the next night, when Game Four produced the first of Byung-Hyun Kim's bitter disappointments. Spencer this time threw a runner out at home, on a super play, but the indomitable Arizonas were ahead, by 3–1, in the ninth when Tino Martinez, with Paul O'Neill on base after a single, hit Kim's first offering over the wall in center. Kim is a submariner, but Tino had gone into the clubhouse video room here to study his slants against the earlier batters. He looked for a rising fastball on the first pitch, and jumped on it. Derek Jeter, by contrast, took an outside Kim offering into the short-right-field seats for that winning blow in the tenth, and flew into home plate like a descending parachutist.

The "Wow"s and "No way"s echoing down the Stadium ramps and around the clubhouse as well were so loud that it was a while before I remembered that Orlando Hernández, who had started the game and pitched eloquently in his six and a third innings, had held out a philosopher's promise of an ending like this. Talking via an interpreter on Tuesday afternoon, a day before his start, he declined to discuss his previous autumn triumphs and adventures with the Yankees. "It doesn't really do anything," El Duque said, "but on Thursday, God willing"—Thursday had just arrived—"we'll be able to speak about tomorrow's game."

Diamondback rooters will have to make do with a tinged and perhaps parochial closing view of these proceedings, which now takes us aboard the No. 4 Lexington Avenue Express one last time, headed uptown for Game Five. Late autumn and the imminent end of baseball bring a particular blackness and sense of foreboding to the Stadium, with its dark backgrounds and blue facings. The fans are bundled in their winter gear, and the serried rows of faces have a mushroomy hue. Not much optimism had carried over from the midnight events that tied up the Series, and the Diamondbacks' fresh 2–0 advantage—two solo home runs in their fifth, against Mussina—felt insurmountable. The Yankee batters couldn't do much against Miguel Batista, a determined journeyman righty, and the fans fell into souvenir bouts of cries and applause for Paul O'Neill, who was retiring when the Series ended, and for Martinez and Brosius and Knoblauch and perhaps even El Duque, who might not be back again, either. When the ninth arrived, I said goodbye to colleagues in the auxiliary press box (I wasn't going to Phoenix) and moved a few yards along to the main box, where I could stand behind the back row and then make a quick jump along to the elevators and the clubhouses when the last out arrived. I was still there when Brosius, coming up to bat against the selfsame Kim (what was he doing here, anyway?) with two outs and Posada on second, swung his bat and insistently threw both hands into the air. Jumping a little myself, I saw more than a hundred writers and columnists look up from their computer screens and game stories, and then down again as they unanimously and professionally punched in "Del" or "Cancel" or "Shit." We were tied again, lightning had struck twice, and Kim, who had cringed down to his knees as the

Brosius shot went out, was being comforted by his infielders, with Mark Grace hugging him like a dad.

The mini-game that now transpired required an extra graf or two from the writers for Soriano's horizontal dive and catch, with the bases loaded in the eleventh, when he snaffled Reggie Sanders's low drive in the webbing of his mitt to save a couple of runs. But Brenly was down to the bottom of his bullpen, and Soriano's single to right in the twelfth brought in Knoblauch, with the winning run and the amazing three-night sweep.

"It's 'Groundhog Day,'" Joe Torre said. "I don't know what's going on."

This replica last-gasp Yankee win and their brief but doomed lead in the Series weren't the only things to take home at the end. From the eighth inning on, the bleacher fans and then the entire right side of the Stadium delivered an extended homage to their dour and departing neighbor, Paul O'Neill. Nothing started this, not a catch or a play—they'd saved up for the moment. "Paulie!" came the deep chant. "Paulie!" It went on for long minutes, with a spontaneous "clap-clap, clapclapclap" echo thrown in after each proclamation, and the name coming in booming, incised block letters now: "PAUL OH NEILL!" ... "PAUL OH NEILL!"

He looked up at the fans from the field, twisting his head to one side as if to acknowledge what was going on but without throwing out anything as blatant as a wave. When the half-inning ended, he tipped his cap from in front of the dugout. "I'm thinking, What's the right thing to do here?" he said later. "We were still losing the game."

I've written often and at length about O'Neill's line drives and flung helmets and scarifying at-bats—scarifying to him, of course—and it sometimes startled me that people I knew continued to misread him, and to find his self-absorption annoying or egocentric. But those grimacing scowls, I always felt, came from a sense of rigor and duty he had imposed upon himself. Shy and driven, and privately religious, he believed he'd been given a tremendous gift, which he had to repay with each game and inning and at-bat. His teammates and his family sometimes tried to kid him about the doom and gloom, but he never let himself up. One of his four brothers, Robert, called his sister Molly (the oldest sibling) last summer in the middle of a 1-for-17 drought of Paul's, and said, "I just heard from Happy—calling from the George Washington Bridge. He said the jump was looking better and better." In his self-flagellating desire, O'Neill reminded me of Carl Yastrzemski, who never gave himself a day off, either. Yaz had more talent than Paul and could carry his Red Sox team for days on end, but for me and those folks around right field O'Neill summed up this particular Yankee club, which made such a serious business out of winning, and did it for so long.

Standing in front of his locker when the game was over—and for once looking younger than his years—O'Neill said, "We've done all we can possibly do in this Stadium. We left it all on the field."

I'm not sure whether another bunch of players will come along whom we can follow with the unstinting interest and affection that we gave to this élite group, or even whether baseball, when spring comes back, will seem worth caring about again. I doubt that it will offer the balm that these Yankee games did, but, as Fats Waller used to say, "One never knows, do one?"

Takes: The Purist

2002

Ted Williams has been gone for a couple of months now, but he remains in mind, unchanged by his final stat. He'd played his last game with the Red Sox more than forty years ago, but generations of fans too young to have seen him play attached themselves avidly to the legends—his over-.400 batting average in 1941, which he risked by disdaining to sit out a doubleheader on the final day, and collected six hits, for a triumphant .406; his capering dance around the bases after his walk-off home run in the All-Star Game that same year; his extended tours of duty as a Navy fighter pilot in the Second World War and then with the Marines in Korea, where he flew some of his missions as wingman to John Glenn; the home run into the stands at Fenway Park on his last career at-bat, in 1960, which became the centerpiece of a Homeric account of the event by John Updike, "Hub Fans Bid Kid Adieu."

Great feats become fixed and bronzed in the aura of many old sports heroes—Joe DiMaggio was a walking effigy by the time he'd reached his fifties—but Ted stayed in the present tense, even in old age, and became something like a family connection, a wild old in-law or famous cousin, to countless New Englanders, not all of them baseball fans. Modern-day players felt the same way. At the ceremonies before the 1999 All-Star Game, in Fenway Park, Williams threw out the first pitch from the front of the mound (at eighty, and enfeebled by a stroke, he was in a golf cart), and was detained out there afterward, surrounded by present and recent superstars—Tony Gwynn, Nomar Garciaparra, Mark McGwire, Sammy Sosa, Larry Walker—who'd clustered forward to shake his hand and stand near him. The P.A. announcer begged the celebrities to take their seats, but they were like kids who'd waited all morning for an autograph; they didn't want the moment to end.

Wanting to know him and waiting to extend the visit was something I knew about. When he talked about hitting it was as if you and he were equals in the exciting debate. He was never lofty about it, despite his lifetime .344 batting average, five hundred and twenty-one homers, and .482 lifetime on-base percentage (the best ever), plus the ghostly speculative numbers that could be tacked onto his totals had he not missed the better part of five seasons while in the service. He appeared to remember baseball first-hand, without sadness or sentimentality, and he became young again when he talked about it. (More on Ted Williams—continuing the visit, so to speak—appears in the next chapter.)

Williams and I became friends when we discovered that each of us had a son named John Henry, and we always asked about the opposite J.H. whenever we hadn't seen each other for a while. We'd just gotten this over with once again at the Red Sox spring camp in Winter Haven—this was in 1985, and we were sitting on a bench in right field—when Ted said, "You remember how I'm down here working with our young guys in the system, trying to get something going in their heads about hitting?"

I said yes, I'd written about this a few springs ago, and Williams said, "Well, I don't live too far from here, so it's no big deal for me to come back again in July or August and see the kids playing with our team here. I know which ones are worth checking back on. I know the ones that should be hitting up around .280 or .300, now they've got their feet wet, and which you look to to begin driving the ball, but you know what I find? They're all down around .245 or .260 and they've forgotten everything we ever talked about. You know why?"

He was indignant, his chin in the air.

"Why, Ted?" I asked.

"They're fucking their brains out," he said. "They're just kids but they're all married, and the ones that aren't have got somebody living in with them, so it's like they're married. They're just thinking of that one thing. Roger, do you remember the kind of year I had the year before I came up with the Red Sox. I didn't do too bad that summer, did I?"

"No, Ted," I said, wondering where this was going. "You had a super year, there in Minneapolis. Everybody'd heard about you, even before you arrived." (He'd batted .366 with the Millers in 1938, the best in the American Association, and also led the league in home runs, runs batted in, and runs scored.)

"And I didn't have too bad of a year that first year with the Red Sox, did I?"

"No, it was a great year." (Williams batted .327 in 1939, his opening summer at Fenway Park, and led the league with 145 runs batted in.)

"Roger," the Splinter said, "I didn't get laid for the first time until the All-Star Game break of my second year in the majors. I was thinking about hitting."

Kiss Kiss, Bang Bang

2002

Before the Anaheim Angels ran onto the field for home ball-games this fall, you heard the loudspeakers at Edison Field putting out "Back in the Saddle Again," but the hokey touch may not fit them much longer. The Angels, who went forty-one years without qualifying for a single inning of World Series play, unexpectedly stand as World Champions, and the shade of Gene Autry should be allowed to dismount at last. The founding owner of the 1961 expansion club became known throughout the sport as "the Cowboy," and the brave smile he sustained through the endless back trails of baseball fatuity (he died in 1998, at ninety-one) made everyone hope for a pennant for him someday. Now it's happened. Jackie Autry, his widow, produced his white cowboy hat at the on-field award ceremonials after the team put down the San Francisco Giants, 4–1, in the seventh and deciding World Series game, and waved it for the exulting scarlet-clad home crowd. It was like George Steinbrenner brandishing Babe Ruth's bow tie, only sweeter. The team has belonged to Disney since 1996, but it's up for sale, at a suddenly improved price. Michael Eisner, there on the same stand with the commissioner and the rest of the brass, wore an Angels cap, but appeared stunned under its curved brim; a year ago, the Angels finished forty-one games back in their division.

This was the noisiest World Series to date, with the California fans endlessly whacking those scarlet or black-and-orange plastic ThunderStix together (the sound is like a shipment of tin pails falling downstairs), and the teams knocking out a hundred and forty-two hits and a record twenty-one homers and eighty-five runs. Although the rivals tied or reversed the lead six times during the Series, and four of the games were settled by one run—the Angels took the last two, at home, to grab the title—the humiliation of both sets of starting pitchers (their combined 7.82 earned-run average set another Series record) deprived the games of the anxious silences and sense of foreboding that accompany a classic. This was another action movie, all bangs and blasts, with the Angels' affinity for the retributive big inning providing one main plotline, and Barry Bonds, a monstrous Vaderish force looming up again and again in the middle of the Giants' batting order, the other. Terrific entertainment, and undemanding.

This was not much like last year's Series, one of the best of all, in which the Yankees produced those two last-gasp home runs at the Stadium, and led the Arizona Diamondbacks in the bottom of the ninth inning of the seventh game, out in Phoenix—of course, America was thinking—before the defense and Mariano Rivera came unglued and cost the Yanks a fourth straight championship. This year's Yankees, again easy winners in the American League East, disappeared quickly, going down to the wild-card Angels in the divisional playoffs, in four games. Back-to-back eighth-inning home runs by Garret Anderson and Troy Glaus took away a game in the Bronx that El Duque had seemed to have safely in hand; out west, where the even-up elimination was resumed, a 6–1 Yankee lead dissolved while the batters were swinging feebly at the fiery sliders of a twenty-year-old rookie reliever named Francisco Rodriguez. The next day, Doomsday, the Angels ran off ten hits and eight runs in the fifth: the biggest one-inning October outburst in seventy-three years. Adios, empire.

When the debacle was picked over, much blame fell upon the losing Yankee starters—Andy Pettitte had lasted three innings, Mike Mussina four, and David Wells departed after a seven-hit barrage in the fifth—but the Angels batters did similar heavy damage to the Twins' pitchers in the next post-season stage, and to the Giants after that. All three celebrity pitchers are in their thirties, while Roger Clemens, who started the first game and departed in the sixth, long before the Yankees' winning rally, is forty. Age may not have been the only problem, though. Patience, stout pitching, and a strong defense have been the cinder blocks of the splendid Yankee edifice, but they were rarely in evidence this time around. The 2002 Yankees hit a lot of home runs—more than any other team in the American League except the Texas Rangers—but also struck out the most. It was the Angels, you began to see, who kept showing a useful aversion to the K.

As the Yankees began to slip behind in the games out west, it seemed to me that they had taken on a weird resemblance to their remarkable second baseman, Alfonso Soriano, who set all sorts of franchise records this year as a lead-off man but lost his stroke in the late-September going while he lunged and flailed after a fortieth home run, to go with his forty-one stolen bases. Soriano is stubbornly impulsive—he managed only twenty-three bases on balls in seven hundred and forty-one plate appearances—and it's time someone convinced him that the home run and the free pass are part of the same idea. Barry Bonds, for instance. When Bonds' season ended, someone noticed that his all-time hundred and ninety-eight bases on balls plus nine plunkings by the pitchers taken alone gave him a higher on-base percentage than Soriano's entire offensive output. Or maybe Alfonso will have noticed the smaller, much less talented Angels lead-off guy, David Eckstein, who said during the Series, "I enjoy fouling off pitches. I definitely like to have at least a six-pitch at-bat. I hate the first-pitch strike, second-pitch groundout." Paul O'Neill used to work on the pitchers this way— you loved watching him—but this year it was the other guys who remembered the knack.

Old fans and columnists, not all of them in Boston, have been whining about the recent domination of the Yankees and the Atlanta Braves (who have made it into post-season play for eleven straight seasons) and that tilted playing field which is said to favor the oversalaried big-market clubs—except maybe in Queens.

Friends of mine were crowing when the Yankees and the Braves and the wealthy, defending-champion Diamondbacks all went down together in the first round of post-season play, and there was a wider delight when the Minnesota Twins, who had once been scheduled for "contraction"—a euphemism for corporate death— by Commissioner Bud Selig, easily won their Central division and then upset the Oakland Athletics in the divisionals. But these same purists, handed a World Series that unexpectedly matched up two vivid wild-card teams with a combined salary total that equals the Yankees' hundred-and-seventy-million-dollar top, showed a sudden affinity for "The West Wing" or wrestling or an early bedtime.

What the snoozers missed was a jamboree of offense, sustained by semi-familiar combatants—barring Barry—who quickly impinged on the imagination. Tens of thousands of grownup Californians brandished stuffed monkeys, screaming for another rally, and surrendered themselves blissfully to a new, Nipponized style of rooting. The Angels played only three games at the Stadium this summer, thanks to the unfortunate new unbalanced schedule, but it didn't take much effort now for me to begin sorting them out: the slashing, overeager Eckstein—a "gnat," to his manager, Mike Scioscia—who requires a full-body, Little League sort of heave to get the ball over from short to first; the pink-bearded Darin Erstad holding out his vertical bat at the pitcher like an artist measuring perspective on his brush; Tim Salmon settling into his lounge-chair posture at the plate; and the suave Garret Anderson, a superstar in hiding (everyone says this, but the epithet sticks), with a late, calm, left-handed swing that makes you squirm with pleasure. These and other Angels regulars—the young third-baseman slugger Troy Glaus, second baseman Adam Kennedy, and first baseman Scott Spiezio—sometimes projected the large, earnest blandness of a suburban high-school football team, and you had to look into the bullpen to find the bristly or creepy antidote: right-hander Brendan Donnelly staring at his catcher through his grasshopper-eye spectacles; Ben Weber's windup-toy, Tik-Tok of Oz delivery; the pallid and squinting closer, Troy Percival; and the Olmec-visaged phenom Francisco Rodriguez.

On the Giants' side, the recurrent Barry at times appeared to blot out the rest of the lineup on presence alone, but when his at-bats were over, one way or another, here came the banged-up thirty-seven-year-old catcher, Benito Santiago, once again burdened with insult after another intentional base on balls to Bonds, or with anticlimax after another Bonds homer. Benito has pizzazz—his shar-pei face is framed by diamond earrings, and columns of tattooed Japanese ideographs crawl down his right arm—and his winning two-run homer in the eighth inning of the fourth National League Championship game, against the Cardinals, which followed a well-booed pass to Bonds, was the populist dinger of the year in San Francisco.

Another rookie pitcher for the Angels was twenty-four-year-old John Lackey, who was allowed to start the critical seventh game of the World Series, and won it after delivering five innings of heavy-breathing, furiously concentrated effort, in which he gave up four hits and a lone run. Excellent work, but I found almost more satisfaction in the luck of Chad Zerbe, a thirty-year-old left-handed reliever, who happened to be the pitcher of record for the Giants in the sixth inning of Game Five, just before they blew open a 16–4 laugher, to go ahead in the Series for the last time. Five years ago, he was pitching for the Sonoma County Crushers, in the independent Western League, a back hallway of baseball, and sometimes rode the team bus on a twelve-hour run north to play against the Tri-City Posse, in Pasco, Washington. Neither Nolan Ryan nor Juan Marichal nor Pedro Martínez has a World Series "W" attached to his name, but now Chad Zerbe does.

Before we get on with this California Series—think of it as Stanford vs. U.C.L.A.—a U-turn can swing us back to the regular season and quickly out again. It will go down as a dreary one in most fans' recollections. The death of the thirty-three-year-old Cardinals starter Darryl Kile, on June 22nd, who died in his sleep from an undiagnosed heart disorder while the team was in Chicago, threw a shadow across the games. Somehow these Tony La Russa Cards kept themselves together, capturing the National League

Central Division, and when they brushed past the Diamondbacks in the Divisional playoffs, with astounding successive victories over Randy Johnson and Curt Schilling, the coming reward of the World Series felt—to me and to most fans, I believe—like no less than their due. But what is due is often not done, and it was the Giants who got there instead, after a seven-game playoff. Bright expectations also hung about the Oakland Athletics (and their shortstop and coming M.V.P., Miguel Tejada), who ran off a thrilling record streak of twenty straight wins in August and September, and won the tough American League West, only to fall before the Twins, of all people, in the pennant elimination. It was the third straight year in which the A's, a tender birch, had shrivelled and cast their leaves in the first cold of October.

Locally, the last-place Mets outdid themselves in futility by not winning a single home game in August. They will go on from here without manager Bobby Valentine, who was fired after the season ended; his successor, Art Howe, the recent and successful skipper of the Oakland Athletics, has been greeted with extreme coolness by croakers in the Greek-chorus media swarm. This was also a summer of apprehensions and ironies surrounding the ancient labor dispute. Boredom and irritation became the prime baseball currency, right up to the morning of August 30th, when a surprise settlement was announced. The strike was averted by some minimal give-and-take between the same old parties, in the face of widespread fan protests and editorial rumblings over the spectacle of an overexpanded but cable-enriched three-and-a-half-billion-dollar monopoly and an élite labor force that averaged just under two and a half million dollars in salary headed for their ninth work stoppage in three decades. The new agreement will require all clubs to share thirty-four per cent of their net local revenues in an evenly divided pool, and increases a luxury tax on the highest-spending clubs, but the ceasefire left an empty taste, more Diet Coke than Mumm's. Some of the blame for this derives, I think, from Major League Baseball's gooey glorifications of bygone heroes, and its lack of imagination in publicizing the vigor and unpredictability of the game itself.

Ted Williams, who died in July at the age of eighty-three, went out with almost a liberating rush of national affection, a joyful sadness. There was also a distracting—well, astounding—Page Six sort of sidebar to the obituaries, when it came out that his son John Henry had arranged to have his body cryogenically frozen, to preserve Ted's DNA or batting eye for possible resurrection or something. Later on, I saw a newspaper piece about a psychic who was trying to reach Ted out there, to discuss the bizarreness. But Ted Williams is beyond this, in every sense. His electric energy when batting or talking about batting is its own preservative. No one else took such lively interest in the work, or carried it off with such flair, and fans who got to see him up at the plate a few times sensed in some degree that they had been admitted to an inner circle of difficulty and pleasure. The picture of Ted batting is burned deep into the collective New England memory: the youthful, intelligent gaze switching from his bat to the pitcher and back again; the loosening shrug he gave his limbs and shoulders as he stepped in; the lightly bent knees and tilted head; and the bat held well up behind, completing a tall vertical line at plate-side—from foot to knee to elbow to chin to bat tip—that defined for the pitcher the dimensions of the chilling task at hand. His right-front shoulder drooped as the pitcher's motion began (he batted left, of course), putting the bat still farther back, but your attention now swerved to his lead hip, which had cocked and turned even as he strode forward, so that his body, now moving swiftly toward the pitch, simultaneously coiled and twisted away. The extended swing (if he chose to swing) would start a fraction late but then catch up, reaching full power as his hands and arms drove through the ball. But that hip-cock was the whole trick: it made you smile even as you drew in your breath. It kept him loose—there was a touch of cha-cha-cha there—and it provided that extra beat of time which hitters call the prime ingredient of a sound swing. He'd given himself a chance.

Williams had a great eye for the strike zone—he famously wouldn't offer at a pitch that was a millimeter in or away—and when his book "My Turn at Bat"(written with John Underwood), came out in 1969, we fans studied its mesmerizing cover: a color photograph of Ted at the plate, with a diagram before him that showed seventy-seven baseballs exactly filling the rectangle of the strike zone. The balls were in different colors, ranging from gray to yellow to ochre to green, and then to deep red for three stacked baseballs in the middle of the zone. Each of the balls in the photograph also had a batting average of likelihood printed on it, from .230 on the whitish gray pitch farthest down and away, to a purple bottom inside-corner sphere at .250, and then ranging on up to .400 for those three crimson gophers. Williams himself had conceived the diagram and presided over its printing, and everyone believed that it represented a chart inside his head that he consulted each time he stepped in. "Get a good pitch to hit" was his mantra and he repeated it all his life.

Each year, we fans hold on to the vision of a few plays or pitches, to keep us warm in the winter, and for me these include Jason Giambi's rainy fourteenth-inning grand-slam home run against the Twins at the Stadium, which ended the game with a 13–12 victory; and a catch at Fenway Park by the Athletics' Terrence Long, who reached deep into the right-center-field bullpen in full stride to snatch back a shot by Manny Ramirez. In July, the Minnesota center fielder Torii Hunter was struck in the side by a pitch thrown by the Indians' Danys Baez during a Twins-Indians game in Cleveland. Writhing, Hunter spotted the ball still in the dirt, and unexpectedly grabbed it up and fired back, nailing Baez in the groin. The play, even the thought, was new to me, and I looked for it as one of the entries in baseball's "Memorable Moments," a much touted M.L.B.-MasterCard promotion that took up thirty minutes of prime time before the fourth game of the World Series, in San Francisco, but in vain. The No. 1 memorable moment, it turned out, was Cal Ripken's consecutive-games streak, which was never exactly a moment, if you think about it. Nor was Lou Gehrig's teary farewell speech, nor Jackie Robinson's breaking baseball's ancient color bar, the fifth- and third-rated entries, respectively, in the contest. Oddly, the ten finalists did not include Bobby Thomson's pennant-winning Polo Grounds home run in 1951, or

Carlton Fisk's killer twelfth-inning blow against the Reds in 1975, or the moment when someone on the promotional side of things first decided that what the pastime really needed was more on-the-field pageantry and honorings, to break baseball's old habit of slow but remorseless action. George Frazier, a fabled style-setting columnist for the Boston *Globe*, once observed that the warm-weather sport does not include a half-hour pause in which people march out onto the field and throw sticks in the air, but now Bud Selig has taken away that joke, among others.

Barry Bonds, of course, was the central event of this season, just as he was last year, when his seventy-three home runs wiped out Mark McGwire's briefly epochal seventy. Bonds' forty-six round-trippers this time elevated him to a lifetime six hundred and thirteen; he trails only his godfather Willie Mays, Babe Ruth, and Hank Aaron on this list. Bonds is thirty-eight years old, and perhaps three outstanding seasons away from Hank's all-time seven hundred and fifty-five. It will be a stretch for him, but Bonds has been startling us for some time now. For me, his latest achievement, a .370 batting average, which won him the National League batting title by more than thirty points, ranks among his rarer feats. Those bases on balls, taken with his hits, not only gave him the new one-season on-base-percentage mark, of .582, but meant that he did his damage while being allowed fewer than three official at-bats per game. His Most Valuable Player award, announced last week, is his fifth—two more than anyone else has up on the mantel.

Bonds—with his shortened-up black bat twitching behind his ear, and that short-arc slash at the ball ticking within—stands in the middle of the Giants' batting order like an aneurysm. Pitchers think about him before, during, and after each appearance: in the lingo, he keeps turning over the order. He is not much liked—he is not about us, he has always made clear—but I've noticed that his home runs now invite a higher laughter. The Giants' batting coach, Gene Clines, runs up the dugout steps, eyes agoggle, after each Barry blast, shouting "Oh, my Godd!" Bonds' opening-game homer, against the Angels' Jarrod Washburn, came on his first World Series at-bat, after a seventeen-year wait, and replays on the TV monitors picked up an inadvertent little grin on Washburn's face: Wow, and off me! Next night, still in Anaheim, Tim Salmon hit two home runs for the Angels in the course of their long come-back win, but Bonds' ninth-inning, four-hundred-and-eighty-five-foot monster, which brought the Giants up to 11–10, was observed by an eager row of Angels from the front railing of their dugout, and you could lip-read Salmon's "That's the farthest ball I've ever seen!" Bonds' fourth and final Series homer, in the sixth inning of Game Six, which put the Giants ahead by 4–0 for the nonce, re-versed an inside ninety-seven-mile-an-hour fastball by Frankie Rodriguez—everyone on both teams had been waiting for this face-off—and this time Barry allowed himself a little smile, too.

Murmurings about Bonds' possible use of steroids—he has de-nied the charge—fade when you watch him play for a few games, because his true strength is so obviously mental. There were no reservations in what you heard about him at Series time. "It's un-canny for a guy to be this locked in for three years now," said Gary Matthews—yes, Ted Williams's old tutee, who was the batting coach for the Milwaukee Brewers this year. "To do it time after time this way—nobody's ever been there before, man." Tom Glavine, the cold-faced Atlanta left-hander, said, "I don't know if you'd pitch to Barry even if Babe Ruth was hitting behind him right now. He's that good a player." In the Giants clubhouse after the fourth Series game, the distinguished ESPN analyst Joe Morgan said, "Every time Bonds walks onto the field, he knows he's the best player there. I saw Willie Mays play and I played against Aaron, but I've never seen anyone as feared in a game as Barry Bonds."

I will take a pass on Bonds' eventual niche in the pantheon—though it's hard to disagree with the *Chronicle* columnist Ray Ratto, who rates him perhaps the third-best player ever, behind only Ruth and Mays. Ratto said that Barry could never expect to climb higher, and Bonds was burned about the restriction as soon as he read it. My useful friend Charles Einstein took a longer view, in a letter he sent along a week or so after his piece ran in *The New Yorker*. "I think I would agree about Bonds being third to Ruth and Mays," he wrote. "Presumably this would give us a second-string all-time outfield of Aaron, DiMaggio, and Ted Williams (!). And thus a third string of Clemente, Mantle, and Ty Cobb (!!). But who among us wants to be the one to inform Stan Musial that he couldn't even make the third team?"

The place to appreciate Bonds is at Pacific Bell Park, which was put up three years ago in the China Basin area of downtown San Francisco by the Giants' owner, Peter A. Magowan, at a cost of three hundred and sixty million dollars. It's the first privately financed park since Dodger Stadium, forty years ago, and the pressing load of debt on Magowan and a consortium of local banks and businesses is one of the reasons that a players' strike wasn't allowed to happen this time around. Unlike some owners who never come to the games, Magowan is a passionate and knowledgeable fan, and his godlike eye can be perceived in the Pac Bell details. Out in front, a statue of Willie Mays in late full swing is better art and better baseball than the Hank Aaron effigy in Atlanta or the Stan Musial icon in St. Louis. More significantly, Magowan was smart enough to understand that making home runs easier for Bonds and future Giants sluggers would be less fun for the ticket-buyers in the end than making sure they'd be rare. Pac Bell is the second most difficult park in the majors for home-run hitters, and the common wisdom around the league last year was that, given a different home venue, Bonds would have hit ninety.

Ticket-holders in Pac Bell's topmost right-field deck, called the View Level, can see a sweep of water, with the far end of the Bay Bridge angling away toward Oakland, and during afternoon games fans all around the park can watch the sail peaks of tall sloops gliding past the twenty-five-foot-high right-field wall. An all-time Giants' "Splash Hits" notice board posted on the wall bears a current "23"—twenty-one of them by Bonds. The bleacher stands in left and center have been kept low, and what you get from behind home plate is a sweep of sky—very few parks do this anymore—and an exhilarating sense of the invisible Bay nearby. When Bonds drove a three-run homer over the wall to tie up the Cardinals, 4–4, in the fifth inning of the third National League Championship game, Fox TV picked up a guy in a yellow kayak out there in McCovey Cove, who fished out the ball with a net. Funny, but what we saw from inside was better. Barry put a tremendous drive on the ball, which sailed and flickered through the soft afternoon air and disappeared into another realm.

The World Series games went on forever, thanks to all those runs, but also zipped by, faster and faster, as the lead changed hands and the ominous end came nearer. This always happens. The Angels edged ahead in the Series, at Pac Bell, after Game Three, in which they batted around in the third inning and again in the fourth, putting up four runs each time, but the Giants pulled level with a 4–3 win in Game Four, the next day. Then they won again, in the 16–4 blowout, and the lads (as old-time San Francisco fans think of them) headed back to Anaheim needing but one more win to take their first World Series since 1954.

I had my hopes way up, too—my loyalty to the Giants goes back to Carl Hubbell and Bill Terry—but I couldn't help noticing that even when the Angels lost they kept right on hitting. Back in that 11–10 win, in Game Two, none of their batters—not one in the forty they sent up to the plate—struck out. When I mentioned this to the Anaheim batting coach, Mickey Hatcher, he said, "Yes, and did you see that most of our home runs have been solos, with nobody on base?" He said this approvingly. "We like each of our hitters to be his own batting coach. Our guys aren't thinking home runs; they're thinking on-base percentage, runs scored, and R.B.I.s. Getting those three in mind is the big thing we try to accomplish in spring training." Hatcher has a pink, rowdy-looking face—he will be remembered as the Dodger batter who helped sink the Oakland A's with two numbing first-inning home runs in the 1988 World

Series—but here he sounded like a free swinger who'd found holy redemption.

The house of baseball contains many ways, and the Giants' own comeback win, in the chilly winds of Game Four, started with a ten-foot single squirted off home plate by pitcher Kirk Rueter (allowed to bat for himself because skipper Dusty Baker desperately needed to rest his bullpen) in the fifth, and a bunt by lead-off man Kenny Lofton that meandered up the foul line like a six-year-old bicyclist's first solo: fair, fair, foul—oop, fair—foul, then miraculously fair again. It was watched from close range by the hovering third baseman, Troy Glaus, whose late grab plucked it up from the white of the foul line: base hit. A couple of singles and a sacrifice tied up the game at 3–3, and David Bell's whistling drive to center in the eighth, struck against Frankie Rodriguez, of all people, won the essential game. The screechings and leapings and back-poundings of the bundled-up Giants rooters next to me in the left-field bleachers (where I was sitting, amid the frozen flower of American sporting media) were being repeated pretty much all around the Bay. During the second act of the San Francisco Opera's production of Mozart's "Die Entführung aus dem Serail," the tenor Paul Groves stepped forward during the recitative that precedes Belmonte's celestial aria to interpolate "Tree-oomph! Tree-oomph! In base-ball, Giants vier, Angels drei!" Tumult.

The next evening's excessive events—this was the Giants' 16–4 runaway—brought cacophonous Pac Bell celebrations as well, and a pure Dada flash when J. T. Snow, rushing in with the Giants' ninth run, on a triple by Lofton, saw out of the corner of his eye the tiny three-and-a-half-year-old batboy, Darren Baker, weirdly collecting Lofton's bat from beside home plate. This was a digitalized startler: baby Forrest Gump in the fall classic. Scary, too, because the Angels catcher Bengie Molina was bracing himself for the imminent arrival of another base runner, David Bell, but Snow, like an old-style railroad man bending for a mailbag, leaned back as he crossed the plate and grabbed Darren by the front of his jacket, snatching him to safety. The replays, which ran on television all the next day, ended with a reaction shot of Darren's dad, Dusty Baker, clutching his ears in embarrassment. If the Giants had won the championship, J.T.'s save would have been their Christmas card.

All week long, I'd been trying to decide which of these two lively clubs deserved to win the World Series, on history and mojo. I'd seen the Giants fail in four different post-season playoffs and two World Series, going back to 1962, my first year on this beat. I recalled their collapse in 1987, when the team went back to St. Louis, ahead by three games to two in the league championships, and dropped the closing two to the Cardinals. Also, this was Dusty Baker's last hurrah, after a successful decade at the helm; he and Magowan have had a falling out, and he has just stepped down. (His successor will be Felipe Alou, who must be ravished to find a Barry Bonds in his lineup, after his ten lean years with the Montreal Expos.) Jeff Kent will not be re-signed, in all likelihood, and free agents David Bell and Reggie Sanders may not return, either. This was a last stand for the sprightly old bunch. On the other hand, I still held a clear memory of the shocked faces of Gene Autry and Angels manager Gene Mauch when, in 1986, an almost certain series-clinching win against the Red Sox evanesced after a four-run Sox rally capped by Dave Henderson's homer in the ninth. Two more games were required to complete the debacle, but the two Genes never did get to a World Series, and the reliever Donnie Moore, who surrendered the Henderson blow, couldn't stop brooding about his failure; three years later, he committed suicide. Your turn to win now, Angels.

The expert I wanted to consult in this dilemma was my departed friend Bill Rigney, who managed the Giants for their first three years out in San Francisco and again in 1976, and also managed the Angels for a decade, from their inception. I needed Rig, because I know he would have put his hand up to his mouth and whispered, "Giants!"

Baseball is fun until it suddenly isn't, and even now the shock of the Giants' two losses in Anaheim awaits me, a beast in the bed, when I wake up in the night. Back at Pac Bell, Mike Scioscia, talking about his rotation, had said, "Kevin Appier is going to start Game Six, unforeseeing anything that might happen tonight." The participle, a fresh depiction of baseball's uncertainty, stuck in my mind, and perfectly fits the Giants' and the Giants fans' condition late in Game Six. Everything had gone their way so far in the evening, with Appier swiftly dismissed and joy accumulating from thirty-nine-year-old Shawon Dunston's two-run homer in the fifth (Dunston kissed his son, Shawon, Jr., another member of Dusty's Boys Town, on the way back to the dugout) and Bonds' solo job an inning later. Barry kissed his son Nikolai, too, and then Dusty Baker, out on the mound to relieve his starter, Russ Ortiz, with one out in the seventh and the Giants up by 5–0, unexpectedly handed him the game ball, as a keepsake and memorial. Kiss, kiss—it was Christmas in October.

The Giants reliever Felix Rodriguez—the other F. Rodriguez, in our thinking—arriving in this happy scene, found runners at first and second base, with one out. A bare eight outs were required for the party, starting perhaps with the familiar awaiting batter, first baseman Scott Spiezio. A switch-hitter, Spiezio took up a left-handed stance against the righty Rodriguez. Spiezio crowds the plate, but Rodriguez has a rising four-seam fastball that he can deliver reliably to the outer corner against lefties, away from their power. He did this seven times, with Spiezio smoothly fouling off four of the pitches with late swings. With the count full, Rodriguez tried a fresh plan, down and in, just above the batter's knees, and Spiezio hit it into the right-field stands for a three-run homer.

It required three more Angels runs, which came in the eighth, and one more Angels comeback the next day—a pitchers' battle, of all things, in which all the runs in the 4–1 victory had arrived by the third inning—to settle this World Series, but I think everyone up in the Bay part of California knows that it was the Spiezio at-bat that ruined the festival. What I said—what we all said at the moment—was "Uh-oh," and we were right. The Angels' comeback from a 5–0 deficit was the best ever by a Series team facing elimination.

Now the Anaheim rooters, perhaps leaving their ThunderStix home in the closet, will have a fresh season in which to discover whether their Angels are the real deal or a bunch of hardworking, doubt-free swingers who stayed hot for five late weeks of baseball in 2002.

Spiezio, who is thirty, was prepared for his moment, if we weren't. He'd been practicing for it for more than a quarter century. His father, Ed Spiezio, a former third baseman who played in two World Series with the Cardinals, began pitching to Scott when he was three or four years old, and already a boy switch-hitter. Ed built two mounds in the back yard—one at the regular distance, and a forty-foot one to speed him up against fastballs—and had Scott situational hitting almost from the beginning. At the end of the day, every day, the situation was always Game Seven of the World Series, with the tying and winning runs aboard. The Spiezios did this all summer long, and in cold weather—this was in Morris, Illinois, where Ed Spiezio has a furniture store—they'd move into the basement and do it some more.

"He'd imitate different pitchers—sometimes special guys like Kent Tekulve, throwing from off to the side," Spiezio fils said in the clubhouse. "He'd even act like he was a left-hander, which was sort of impossible. But he was getting me ready to be a major-league ballplayer. It was my whole life."

Spiezio, who has a youthful look and a cool little mustache and beard, is a rock singer in his spare time, with a group called Sandfrog, but he'd made baseball sound like the more exotic line of work: something that kids might really want to look into one of these days. "Listen," he said, "I enjoy it. The time I put in was pure enjoyment."

Robert Menasse

Die Hauptstadt

Roman

Suhrkamp

Die Arbeit an diesem Buch wurde gefördert
vom Deutschen Literaturfonds e.V.

6. Auflage 2017

Erste Auflage 2017
© Suhrkamp Verlag Berlin 2017
Satz: Satz-Offizin Hümmer GmbH, Waldbüttelbrunn
Druck: CPI – Ebner & Spiegel, Ulm
Printed in Germany
ISBN 978-3-518-42758-3

»Rêver, c'est le bonheur;
attendre, c'est la vie.«

Victor Hugo

Prolog

Da läuft ein Schwein! David de Vriend sah es, als er ein Fenster des Wohnzimmers öffnete, um noch ein letztes Mal den Blick über den Platz schweifen zu lassen, bevor er diese Wohnung für immer verließ. Er war kein sentimentaler Mensch. Er hatte sechzig Jahre hier gewohnt, sechzig Jahre lang auf diesen Platz geschaut, und jetzt schloss er damit ab. Das war alles. Das war sein Lieblingssatz – wann immer er etwas erzählen, berichten, bezeugen sollte, sagte er zwei oder drei Sätze und dann: »Das war alles.« Dieser Satz war für ihn die einzig legitime Zusammenfassung von jedem Moment oder Abschnitt seines Lebens. Die Umzugsfirma hatte die paar Habseligkeiten abgeholt, die er an die neue Adresse mitnahm. Habseligkeiten – ein merkwürdiges Wort, das aber keine Wirkung auf ihn hatte. Dann sind die Männer von der Entrümpelungsfirma gekommen, um alles Übrige wegzuschaffen, nicht nur was nicht niet- und nagelfest war, sondern auch die Nieten und Nägel, sie rissen heraus, zerlegten, transportierten ab, bis die Wohnung »besenrein« war, wie man das nannte. De Vriend hatte sich einen Kaffee gemacht, solange der Herd noch da war und seine Espressomaschine da stand, den Männern zugeschaut, darauf achtend, ihnen nicht im Weg zu stehen, noch lange hatte er die leere Kaffeetasse in der Hand gehalten, sie schließlich in einen Müllsack fallen lassen. Dann waren die Männer fort, die Wohnung leer. Besenrein. Das war alles. Noch ein letzter Blick aus dem Fenster. Es gab da unten nichts, was er nicht kannte, und nun musste er ausziehen, weil eine andere Zeit gekommen war – und jetzt sah er ... tatsächlich: Da unten war ein Schwein! Mitten in Brüssel, in Sainte-Catherine. Es musste von der Rue de la Braie gekommen sein, lief den Bauzaun vor dem Haus entlang, de Vriend beugte sich aus dem Fenster und sah, wie das Schwein nun rechts an der Ecke zur Rue du Vieux Marché aux Grains, einigen Passanten ausweichend, beinahe vor ein Taxi lief.

Kai-Uwe Frigge, von der Notbremsung nach vorn geworfen, fiel in den Sitz zurück. Er verzog das Gesicht. Er kam zu spät. Er war genervt. Was war jetzt wieder los? Er war nicht wirklich zu spät, es war nur so, dass er bei einem Treffen immer Wert darauf legte, zehn Minuten vor der vereinbarten Zeit da zu sein, vor allem an Regentagen, um sich auf der Toilette noch schnell wieder in Ordnung zu bringen, das regennasse Haar, die beschlagene Brille, bevor die Person kam, mit der er verabredet war –

Ein Schwein! Haben Sie das gesehen, Monsieur?, rief der Taxifahrer. Springt mir fast vor den Wagen! Er beugte sich weit über das Lenkrad: Da! Da! Sehen Sie es?

Jetzt sah es Kai-Uwe Frigge. Er wischte mit dem Handrücken über die Scheibe, das Schwein lief seitlich weg, schmutzig rosa glänzte der nasse Leib des Tiers im Licht der Laternen.

Wir sind da, Monsieur! Näher kann ich nicht ranfahren. Also so was! Läuft mir ein Schwein fast in den Wagen! Schwein gehabt, kann ich da nur sagen!

Fenia Xenopoulou saß im Restaurant Menelas am ersten Tisch neben dem großen Fenster mit Blick über den Platz. Sie ärgerte sich, dass sie viel zu früh gekommen war. Das war nicht souverän, wenn sie schon wartend dasaß, wenn er kam. Sie war nervös. Sie hatte befürchtet, dass es wegen des Regens einen Stau geben würde, sie hatte zu viel Wegzeit einkalkuliert. Nun saß sie bereits beim zweiten Ouzo. Der Kellner umschwirrte sie wie eine lästige Wespe. Sie starrte das Glas an und befahl sich, es nicht anzurühren. Der Kellner brachte eine Karaffe mit frischem Wasser. Dann brachte er einen kleinen Teller mit Oliven – und sagte: Ein Schwein!

Wie bitte? Fenia blickte auf, sah, dass der Kellner gebannt auf den Platz hinausschaute, und nun sah sie es: Das Schwein lief auf das Restaurant zu, in einem lächerlichen Galopp, diese kurzen vor und zurück schwingenden Beinchen unter dem runden schweren Körper. Sie dachte zuerst, das sei ein Hund, eines von diesen abstoßenden Biestern, die von Witwen gemästet werden, aber – nein, es war tatsächlich ein Schwein! Fast wie aus einem Bilderbuch, sie sah den Rüssel, die Ohren als Linien, als Konturen, so zeichnet man für Kinder ein Schwein, aber dieses schien aus einem Horrorkinderbuch entsprungen. Es war kein Wildschwein, es war ein verdrecktes, aber eindeutig rosa Hausschwein, das etwas Irres hatte, etwas Bedrohliches. Am Fenster lief das Regenwasser herunter, verschwommen sah Fenia Xenopoulou, wie das Schwein plötzlich vor einigen Passanten abbremste, die Beinchen durchgestreckt, es rutschte, warf sich zur Seite, knickte ein, gewann wieder Boden und galoppierte zurück, nun in Richtung Hotel Atlas. In diesem Moment verließ Ryszard Oswiecki das Hotel. Schon beim Verlassen des Lifts, während er das Hotelfoyer durchquerte, hatte er sich die Kapuze seiner Jacke über den Kopf gezogen, nun trat er hinaus in den Regen, eilig, aber nicht zu schnell, er wollte nicht auffallen. Der Regen war ein Glück: Kapuze, eiliger Schritt, das war unter diesen Gegebenheiten völlig normal und unauffällig. Niemand sollte später aussagen können, er habe einen Mann flüchten sehen, etwa so alt, schätzungsweise so groß, und die Farbe der Jacke – natürlich, die wisse er auch noch … Rasch wandte er sich nach rechts, da hörte er aufgeregte Rufe, einen Schrei und ein seltsam quietschendes Keuchen. Er hielt kurz inne, schaute zurück. Jetzt bemerkte er das Schwein. Er konnte nicht glauben, was er sah. Da stand ein Schwein zwischen zwei dieser schmiedeeisernen Pfosten, die den Vorplatz des Hotels säumten, es stand da mit gesenktem Kopf, in der Haltung eines Stiers, bevor er zum Angriff übergeht, es hatte etwas Lächerliches, zugleich doch Bedrohliches. Es war völlig rätselhaft: Woher kam dieses Schwein, wieso stand es da? Ryszard Oswiecki hatte den Eindruck, dass alles Leben auf diesem Platz, zumindest soweit er ihn nun überblickte, erstarrt und eingefroren war, die kleinen Augen des Tiers reflektierten schimmernd das Neonlicht der Hotelfassade – da begann Ryszard Oswiecki zu laufen! Er lief nach rechts weg, blickte nochmals zurück, das Schwein riss schnaufend den Schädel hoch, machte ein paar kleine Schritte rückwärts, drehte sich um und rannte quer über den Platz, hinüber zu der Baumreihe vor dem Flämischen Kulturzentrum De Markten. Die Passanten, die die Szene beobachtet hatten, sahen dem Schwein nach und nicht dem Mann mit der Kapuze – und jetzt sah Martin Susman das Tier. Er wohnte in dem Haus neben dem Hotel Atlas, öffnete just in diesem Moment das Fenster, um zu lüften, und traute seinen Augen nicht: Das sah aus wie ein Schwein! Er hatte gerade über sein Leben nachgedacht, über die Zufälle, die dazu geführt hatten, dass er, ein Kind österreichischer Bauern, nun in Brüssel lebte und arbeitete, er war in einer Stimmung, in der ihm alles verrückt und fremd erschien, aber ein frei laufendes Schwein da unten auf dem Platz, das war allzu verrückt, das konnte nur ein Streich seiner Phantasie sein, eine Projektion seiner Erinnerungen! Er schaute, aber er sah das Schwein nicht mehr.

Das Schwein lief auf die Kirche Sainte-Catherine zu, querte die Rue Sainte-Catherine, hielt sich links, den Touristen ausweichend, die aus der Kirche kamen, lief an der Kirche vorbei zum Quai aux Briques, die Touristen lachten, sie hielten wohl das gestresste, fast schon kollabierende Tier für Folklore, für irgendein lokales Phänomen. Manche würden später im Reiseführer suchen, ob es dazu eine Erklärung gab. Werden nicht im spanischen Pamplona an irgendeinem Feiertag Stiere durch die Straßen der Stadt getrieben? Vielleicht macht man das in Brüssel mit Schweinen? Wenn man das Unbegreifliche dort erlebt, wo man gar nicht erwartet, alles zu verstehen – wie heiter ist dann das Leben.

In diesem Moment bog Gouda Mustafa um die Ecke und stieß fast mit dem Schwein zusammen. Fast? Hatte es ihn nicht doch berührt, sein Bein gestreift? Ein Schwein? Gouda Mustafa sprang in Panik zur Seite, verlor das Gleichgewicht und fiel. Nun lag er in einer Pfütze, wälzte sich herum, was die Sache noch schlimmer machte, aber es war nicht der Dreck der Gosse, es war die Berührung, wenn es denn überhaupt eine gewesen war, mit dem unreinen Tier, durch die er sich beschmutzt fühlte.

Da sah er eine Hand, die sich zu ihm hinunterstreckte, er sah das Gesicht eines älteren Herrn, ein trauriges, besorgtes Gesicht, regennass, der alte Mann schien zu weinen. Das war Professor Alois Erhart. Gouda Mustafa verstand nicht, was er sagte, er verstand nur das Wort »okay«.

Okay! Okay!, sagte Gouda Mustafa.

Professor Erhart redete weiter, auf Englisch, er sagte, dass auch er heute schon gestürzt sei, aber er war so konfus, dass er »failed« sagte statt »fell«. Gouda Mustafa verstand ihn nicht, sagte noch einmal: Okay!

Da kam schon das Blaulicht. Die Rettung. Polizei. Der ganze Platz rotierte, flackerte, zuckte im Blaulicht. Die Einsatzfahrzeuge rasten heulend zum Hotel Atlas. Der Himmel über Brüssel tat seine Schuldigkeit: Es regnete. Jetzt schien es blau blitzende Tropfen zu regnen. Dazu nun ein starker Windstoß – der manchem Passanten den Regenschirm hochriss und umstülpte. Gouda Mustafa nahm die Hand von Professor Erhart, ließ sich aufhelfen. Sein Vater hatte ihn vor Europa gewarnt.

Erstes Kapitel

Zusammenhänge müssen
nicht wirklich bestehen, aber ohne sie
würde alles zerfallen.

Wer hat den Senf erfunden? Das ist kein guter Anfang für einen Roman. Andererseits: Es kann keinen guten Anfang geben, weil es, ob gut oder weniger gut, gar keinen Anfang gibt. Denn jeder denkbare erste Satz ist bereits ein Ende – auch wenn es danach weitergeht. Er steht am Ende von Abertausenden von Seiten, die nie geschrieben wurden: der Vorgeschichte.

Eigentlich müsste man, wenn man einen Roman zu lesen beginnt, gleich nach dem ersten Satz zurückblättern können. Das war der Traum von Martin Susman, das hatte er eigentlich werden wollen: ein Vorgeschichtenerzähler. Er hatte ein Archäologiestudium abgebrochen und dann erst – egal, das tut hier nichts zur Sache, es gehört zur Vorgeschichte, die jeder Romananfang ausblenden muss, weil es sonst am Ende nie zu einem Anfang kommt.

Martin Susman saß am Schreibtisch, den Laptop hatte er zur Seite geschoben, und drückte aus zwei verschiedenen Tuben Senf auf einen Teller, einen scharfen englischen und einen süßen deutschen, und fragte sich, wer den Senf erfunden hat. Wer ist auf diese schrullige Idee gekommen, eine Paste zu produzieren, die den Eigengeschmack einer Speise völlig überdeckt, ohne selbst gut zu schmecken? Und wie war es möglich, dass sich dies als Massenartikel durchsetzen konnte? Es ist, dachte er, ein Produkt wie Coca-Cola. Ein Produkt, das niemandem fehlen würde, wenn es nicht da wäre.

Martin Susman hatte auf dem Heimweg in der Delhaize-Filiale auf dem Boulevard Anspach zwei Flaschen Wein, einen Bund gelbe Tulpen, eine Bratwurst und dazu ganz selbstverständlich auch Senf gekauft, gleich zwei Tuben,

weil er sich zwischen süß und scharf nicht entscheiden
konnte.

Die Bratwurst hüpfte und zischte nun in der Pfanne, die
Flamme war zu stark aufgedreht, das Fett verbrannte, die
Wurst verkohlte, aber Martin schenkte dem keine Beach-
tung. Er saß da und starrte den etwas helleren gelblichen
und daneben den dunkelbraunen Senfkringel auf dem weißen Teller an, Miniatur-Skulpturen von Hundekot. Das Anstarren von Senf auf einem Teller, während in der Pfanne
eine Wurst verbrennt, ist in der Fachliteratur noch nicht als
eindeutiges und typisches Symptom für eine Depression beschrieben worden – dennoch können wir es als solches interpretieren.

Der Senf auf dem Teller. Das offene Fenster, der Regenvor-
hang. Die modrige Luft, der Gestank von verkohlendem
Fleisch, das Knistern des platzenden Darms und brennenden
Fetts, die Kotskulpturen auf dem Porzellanteller – da hörte
Martin Susman den Schuss.

Er erschrak nicht. Es hatte sich angehört, als wäre in der Nach-
barwohnung eine Champagnerflasche geöffnet worden. Hinter der eigentümlich dünnen Wand befand sich allerdings
keine Wohnung, sondern ein Hotelzimmer. Nebenan war
das Hotel Atlas – was für ein euphemistischer Name für dieses schmächtige Haus, in dem vor allem gebeugte, Trolley-
Koffer hinter sich herziehende Lobbyisten abstiegen. Immer
wieder hörte Martin Susman, ohne dass es ihn weiter kümmerte, durch die Wand Dinge, die er nicht unbedingt hören
wollte. Reality-TV oder, wer weiß, bloß Reality, Schnarchen
oder Stöhnen.

Der Regen wurde stärker. Martin hatte den Wunsch, das
Haus zu verlassen. Er war auf Brüssel gut vorbereitet. Er hatte bei seinem Abschiedsfest in Wien bemüht sinnige Ge-
schenke als Ausstattung für Brüssel bekommen, darunter

neun Regenschirme, vom klassischen britischen »Long« über den deutschen »Knirps« bis zum italienischen »Mini« in drei Benetton-Farben, dazu noch zwei Regenponchos für Radfahrer.

Er saß reglos vor seinem Teller und starrte den Senf an. Dass er später der Polizei genau sagen konnte, zu welcher Uhrzeit der Schuss gefallen war, verdankte sich der Tatsache, dass ihn das vermeintliche Knallen eines Champagnerkorkens dazu animiert hatte, selbst eine Flasche Wein zu öffnen. Er schob das Trinken jeden Tag möglichst weit hinaus, er trank auf keinen Fall vor 19 Uhr. Er sah auf die Uhr: Es war 19 Uhr 35. Er ging zum Kühlschrank, holte den Wein heraus, drehte die Herdflamme ab, kippte die Wurst in den Mülleimer, stellte die Pfanne in den Abwasch, öffnete den Wasserhahn. Das Wasser zischte auf der heißen Pfanne. Schau nicht schon wieder ins Narrenkastl!, hatte seine Mutter gezischt, wenn er vor einem Buch gesessen und mit verlorenem Blick vor sich hin gestarrt hatte, statt im Stall beim Füttern der Schweine und beim Ausmisten mitzuhelfen.

Doktor Martin Susman saß da, vor sich einen Teller mit Senf, schenkte sich ein Glas Wein ein, dann noch eins, das Fenster war offen, ab und zu stand er auf, stellte sich an das Fenster, sah kurz hinaus, dann setzte er sich wieder an den Tisch. Beim dritten Glas wischte Blaulicht durch das Fenster über die Wände seines Zimmers. Rhythmisch blinkten die Tulpen bläulich in der Vase auf dem Kamin. Das Telefon läutete. Er hob nicht ab. Es sollte noch ein paar Mal läuten. Martin Susman sah auf dem Display, wer der Anrufer war. Er hob nicht ab.

Vorgeschichte. Sie ist so bedeutsam und zugleich unscheinbar flackernd wie das ewige Licht in der Kirche von Sainte-Catherine, am anderen Ende des Platzes Vieux Marché aux Grains, an dem Martin Susman wohnte.

Einige wenige Passanten waren vor dem Regen in die Kirche geflüchtet, sie standen unschlüssig herum oder wanderten durch das Kirchenschiff, die Touristen blätterten in ihren Reiseführern und folgten dem Stationenweg der Sehenswürdigkeiten: »Schwarze Madonna, 14. Jahrhundert«, »Porträt der heiligen Katharina«, »Typisch flämische Kanzel, wahrscheinlich aus Mechelen«, »Grabsteine von Gilles-Lambert Godecharle« …

Ab und zu ein Blitz.

Der Mann, der alleine in einer Kirchenbank saß, schien zu beten. Die Ellenbogen aufgestützt, das Kinn auf die verschränkten Hände gelegt, der Rücken rund. Er trug eine schwarze Jacke mit Kapuze, die Kapuze hatte er über den Kopf gezogen, und wäre auf dem Rücken seiner Jacke nicht »Guinness« gestanden, man hätte ihn auf den ersten Blick für einen Mönch in einer Kutte halten können.

Die Jacke mit der Kapuze war wohl dem Brüsseler Regen geschuldet, aber der Eindruck, den er damit machte, verriet doch auch etwas Grundsätzliches über diesen Mann. Er war auf seine Art tatsächlich ein Mönch: Er hielt das Mönchische oder was er sich darunter vorstellte, Askese, Meditation und Exerzitien, für die Rettung in einem Leben, das unausgesetzt von Chaos und Zerstreuung bedroht war. Das war für ihn nicht an einen Orden oder ein Kloster, nicht an Weltabgewandtheit gebunden: Jeder Mann konnte, ja musste, egal was sein Beruf oder seine Funktion war, in seinem Feld ein Mönch sein, der auf seine Aufgabe konzentrierte Knecht eines höheren Willens.

Er liebte es, den gefolterten Mann am Kreuz zu betrachten und an den Tod zu denken. Das war für ihn jedes Mal eine Reinigung der Gefühle, Bündelung des Denkens und Stärkung seiner Energie.

Das war Mateusz Oswiecki. Sein Taufname, der auch in seinem Pass stand, war allerdings Ryszard. Zu Mateusz ist Oswiecki erst als Schüler im Seminar der Lubranski-Akademie in Poznań geworden, wo jeder »erleuchtete Zögling« einen von elf Apostel-Namen als Beinamen erhielt. Er war wiedergetauft und gesalbt worden zu »Matthäus, der Zöllner«. Obwohl er aus dem Seminar ausschied, behielt er den Namen bei, als seinen Nom de guerre. Die Grenzen, an denen er seinen Pass zeigen musste, passierte er als Ryszard. Geheimdienstlich war er, auf Grund der Aussagen einiger ehemaliger Kontaktpersonen, als »Matek« bekannt, die Koseform von Mateusz. So ließ er sich von Mitstreitern nennen. Als Mateusz erfüllte er seine Mission, als Matek wurde er gesucht, als Ryszard schlüpfte er durch die Maschen.

Oswiecki betete nicht. Er formulierte nicht still Sätze, die mit »Herr« begannen und immer nur Wünsche waren, »Gib mir die Kraft –«, dies oder jenes zu tun, »Segne –« dies oder jenes … Man hatte sich nichts zu wünschen von einem absoluten Geist, der schwieg. Er betrachtete den ans Kreuz genagelten Mann. Die Erfahrung, die dieser Mensch beispielhaft für die Menschheit gemacht und am Ende auch ausgesprochen hatte, war die des völligen Verlassen-Seins im Moment der Konfrontation mit dem Absoluten: wenn die Hülle aufgeritzt, aufgeschlagen, aufgeschnitten, durchstochen und aufgerissen wird, wenn die Schmerzensschreie des Lebens in ein Wimmern und endlich in das Schweigen übergehen. Nur im Schweigen ist das Leben dem allmächtigen Geist nahe, der in einer unfassbaren Laune das Gegenteil seines Seins aus sich selbst entlassen hat: die Zeit. Der Mensch kann vom Zeitpunkt seiner Geburt zurück und zurück und weiter zurück denken, ewig, ewig zurück, er wird zu keinem Anfang kommen und mit seinem läppischen Begriff von Zeit nur eines begreifen: Er ist, bevor er war, ewig nicht gewesen. Und er kann vorausdenken, vom Moment seines Todes an in alle

Zukunft, er wird zu keinem Ende kommen, nur zu dieser Einsicht: Er wird ewig nicht mehr sein. Und das Zwischenspiel zwischen Ewigkeit und Ewigkeit ist die Zeit – das Lärmen, das Stimmengewirr, das Maschinengestampfe, das Dröhnen von Motoren, das Knallen und Krachen der Waffen, das Schmerzensgeschrei und die verzweifelten Lustschreie, die Choräle der wütenden und der freudig betrogenen Massen, das Donnergrollen und Angstkeuchen im mikroskopischen Terrarium der Erde.

Mateusz Oswiecki betrachtete den gefolterten Mann.

Er hatte die Hände nicht gefaltet. Er drückte mit verschränkten Händen die Fingernägel in die Handrücken, bis die Knöchel krachten und die Haut brannte. Er spürte einen Schmerz, der älter war als er selbst. Er konnte diesen Schmerz jederzeit händeringend abrufen. Sein Großvater Ryszard war Anfang 1940 in den Untergrund gegangen, um unter General Stefan Rowecki im polnischen Widerstand gegen die Deutschen zu kämpfen. Er wurde schon im April desselben Jahres verraten, verhaftet, gefoltert und schließlich in Lublin als Partisan öffentlich erschossen. Damals war die Großmutter im achten Monat schwanger, das Kind kam im Mai 1940 in Kielce zur Welt und erhielt den Namen seines Vaters. Es wurde, um etwaiger Sippenhaftung zu entgehen, nach Poznań zur Familie eines Großonkels gebracht, der die deutsche Volksliste unterschrieben hatte. Dort wuchs er auf und erlebte mit sechzehn Jahren den Aufstand. Der junge Gymnasiast schloss sich der Gruppe von Major Franczak an, um im antikommunistischen Widerstand zu kämpfen. Er wurde bei Sabotageaktionen, später bei Entführungen von Spitzeln der Sicherheitspolizei eingesetzt – und im Jahr 1964 von einem Kameraden für 6000 Zloty verraten. Er wurde in einer konspirativen Wohnung verhaftet und in einem Keller der SB zu Tode gefoltert. Damals war seine Braut Marija bereits schwanger, das Kind kam im Februar 1965 im Dorf Kozice Gorne zur Welt und wurde auf den Namen seines Großvaters und seines Vaters getauft. Wieder ein Sohn, der seinen Vater nicht kennenlernen konnte. Die Mutter erzählte wenig. Einmal: »Wir trafen uns in den Feldern oder im Wald. Zu unseren Rendezvous kam er mit einer Pistole und mit Granaten.«

Ein ewig schweigender Großvater. Ein ewig schweigender Vater. Die Polen, das war Mateks Lehre, hatten immer für die Freiheit Europas gekämpft, jeder, der in den Kampf eintrat, war im Schweigen aufgewachsen und kämpfte, bis er ins Schweigen einging.

Seine Mutter fuhr mit ihm zu den Priestern, suchte Fürsprecher, kaufte Empfehlungsschreiben, sie vertraute auf den Schutz, den die Kirche gewähren konnte. Schließlich brachte sie ihn bei den Schulbrüdern in Poznań unter. Dort erfuhr er selbst die Verletzlichkeit des menschlichen Körpers: Das Blut ist ein Schmier- und Gleitmittel beim Eindringen in die Hülle, die Haut nur feuchtes Pergament, auf das ein Messer Landkarten zeichnet, der Mund und der Schreihals ein schwarzes Loch, das gestopft wird, bis der letzte Laut abstirbt und es stumm nur noch aufsaugt, was Leben spenden sollte. Und dort bekam er auch eine völlig neue Vorstellung von »Untergrund«. Als die Zöglinge ihre apostolischen Schutznamen erhielten, wurden sie in die Katakomben des gewaltig herrlichen Doms von Poznań geführt, in die geheimen unterirdischen Gewölbe und Grabkammern, über Steintreppen, die im Licht der Fackeln schimmerten und blitzten, hinunter in den tiefsten Untergrund, durch einen letzten rohen Stollen in eine Kammer, die sich als versunkene Kapelle des Todes und des ewigen Lebens erwies: ein Tonnengewölbe, im 10. christlichen Jahrhundert hundert Fuß unter der blutgetränkten Erde Polens in den Stein hineingetrieben. An der Stirnseite dieses Raums befand sich ein monumentales Kreuz mit einer erschreckend naturalistischen Christusgestalt, dahinter Reliefs von Engeln, die aus dem Stein hervortraten oder in ihn hinein- und durch ihn hindurchzugehen schienen, schrecklich lebendig im Flackern der Flammen. Davor eine Madonna – wie sie der junge Ryszard noch nie gesehen hatte, in keiner Kirche, auf keiner Abbildung in seinen Büchern: Sie war völlig vermummt! Die Madonna trug einen Umhang, den sie so über Stirn, Nase und Mund geschlagen hatte, dass durch einen schmalen Spalt in all dem Tuch nur ihre Augen zu sehen waren, Augenhöhlen so tief und so tot, wie sie es nach tausend Jahren der Tränen nur sein konnten. Dies alles, wie auch der Altar, gemeißelt und geformt aus dem Stein und dem Tonmergel der hier durchbrochenen geologischen Schicht. Bänke aus kaltem Gestein, auf denen, mit dem Rücken zu Ryszard und den anderen eintretenden Zöglingen, elf Mönche in schwarzen Kutten saßen, die gesenkten Köpfe von ihren Kapuzen bedeckt.

Die Zöglinge wurden durch den Mittelgang zwischen den betenden Mönchen nach vorne zu Christus geführt, wo sie sich bekreuzigten und dann angewiesen wurden, sich umzudrehen. Ryszard schaute zurück, und nun sah er: Unter den Kapuzen schimmerten Totenschädel, die Rosenkränze in den Händen der Mönche hingen an Fingerknochen – diese Mönche waren Skelette.

Man ist Gott unter der Erde näher als auf den Gipfeln der Berge.

Mateusz Oswiecki schlug die Fingerkuppen mehrmals gegen die Stirn. Er fühlte sich schwer vom Fleisch und modrig. Und in seiner Bauchhöhle, links etwas unterhalb des Nabels, spürte er ein Brennen. Er wusste: Da brennt der Tod. Er machte ihm keine Angst. Er nahm ihm die Angst.

Diese Skelette in Kutten waren die Gebeine von Missionsbischof Jordanes und den Mitgliedern des Gründungskollegiums des Bistums Posen. Seit fast tausend Jahren verharrten sie hier im ewig schweigenden Gebet. Vor diesen elf Skeletten wurde jedem Zögling einer von elf Apostel-Namen zugesprochen. Elf? Kein Judas? Doch. Aber einem Schüler den Namen Petrus', des ersten Stellvertreters Gottes auf Erden, zu geben, wäre eine Anmaßung gewesen. Wer auserwählt ist, wird auch als Johannes oder Paulus zum Petrus.

Mateusz Oswiecki presste die Handflächen an seine Ohren. So viele Stimmen in seinem Kopf. Er schloss die Augen. Zu viele Bilder. Das war nicht Erinnerung, nicht Vorgeschichte. Das war jetzt da, jetzt, so wie er da saß vor dem Gekreuzigten. Und wie das Brennen im Bauch. Er hatte keine Angst, nur das klamme Gefühl, wie man es vor einer großen Prüfung hat, vor einer schweren Aufgabe. Eine Prüfung, die man nur ein einziges Mal ablegen kann, ist die schwerste. Er öffnete die Augen wieder, sah auf und blickte auf das Wundmal in der Seite des Erlösten.

Im Grunde beneidete Mateusz Oswiecki seine Opfer. Sie hatten es hinter sich.

Er stand auf, trat aus dem Stein der Kirche, blickte kurz hinüber zum Blaulicht, das vor dem Hotel Atlas tanzte, und ging langsam mit gesenktem Kopf, die Kapuze tief in die Stirn gezogen, durch den Regen zur Metro-Station Sainte-Catherine.

Als Alois Erhart zum Hotel Atlas zurückkam, wurde ihm zunächst der Zutritt verwehrt. Zumindest interpretierte er die Hand, die ein Polizist ihm vor dem Hoteleingang entgegenstreckte, als Aufforderung, stehen zu bleiben. Was der Polizist sagte, verstand er nicht. Er konnte nicht gut Französisch.

Er hatte schon von weitem das rotierende Blaulicht der Polizei und des Rettungswagens gesehen – und an einen Selbstmörder gedacht. Langsam war er auf das Hotel zugegangen, und sofort war wieder dieses Gefühl da gewesen, das ihn schon zu Mittag erfasst hatte: als würde sich das Nichts, in das jeder Mensch früher oder später stürzt, plötzlich, wie eine Ankündigung oder gar Aufforderung, in Brustkorb und Bauchhöhle ausbreiten. Klamm und atemlos hatte er es gespürt: dieses Wunder, dass sich in der begrenzten Hülle des Körpers eine wachsende Leere unendlich ausdehnen kann. Die Seele als schwarzes Loch, das alle Erfahrungen, die er ein ganzes Leben lang gemacht hatte, aufsaugte und verschwinden ließ, bis sich nur noch das Nichts ausdehnte, absolute Leere, ganz schwarz, aber ohne die Milde einer sternlosen Nacht.

Nun stand er da, vor den Stufen zum Eingang des Hotels, mit schmerzenden Knochen und vor Müdigkeit brennenden Muskeln, hinter ihm einige wenige Schaulustige, und sagte auf Englisch: Er sei Gast in diesem Hotel, habe hier ein Zimmer – was nichts am ausgestreckten Arm änderte. Die Situation kam ihm so surreal vor, dass er sich nicht gewundert hätte, wenn er nun verhaftet worden wäre. Aber er war nicht nur der alte Mann, dessen Körper ihm unwiderruflich den Dienst zu versagen begann, er war auch der Professor Emeritus DDr. Erhart, der ein halbes Leben Autorität dargestellt hatte. Tourist, sagte er bestimmt, er sei Tourist. Hier! In diesem Hotel. Und er wünsche in sein Zimmer zu gehen. Darauf begleitete der Beamte ihn in die Lobby und führte ihn zu einem fast zwei Meter großen Mann, etwa Mitte fünfzig, in einem viel zu engen grauen Anzug, der ihn aufforderte, sich auszuweisen.

Warum stand der Professor mit gesenktem Kopf da? Er sah den prallen Gasbauch dieses riesigen Mannes – und empfand plötzlich Mitleid. Es gibt Menschen, die in ihrer massigen physischen Präsenz ewig stark scheinen, immer fit, nie kränkelnd, bis sie plötzlich wie vom Blitz getroffen daliegen, tot in einem Alter, von dem man sagt: Das ist doch kein

Alter. Immer stolz auf ihre Konstitution, hielten sie sich für
unsterblich, solange sie ihren Körper vor anderen aufbauen,
anderen entgegenschieben konnten. Diese Menschen wurden nie mit der Frage konfrontiert, welche Entscheidung
sie treffen würden, wenn sie alt und chronisch krank wären,
in absehbarer Zeit ein Pflegefall. Dieser Mann war im Innersten verfault und morsch, er würde demnächst fallen, er wusste es nur nicht.

Professor Erhart reichte ihm den Pass.

Wann er angekommen sei? Parlez-vous français? No? English? Wann er das Hotel verlassen habe. Ob er zwischen neunzehn und zwanzig Uhr im Hotel gewesen sei?

Warum diese Fragen?

Mordkommission. Ein Mann sei in einem Zimmer dieses
Hotels erschossen worden.

Sein rechter Unterarm schmerzte. Professor Erhart dachte,
dass es vielleicht schon auffällig wurde, wie er immer wieder
über den Arm strich, ihn drückte, knetete.

Er holte seine Digitalkamera aus der Seitentasche seiner Re-
genjacke, schaltete sie ein. Er konnte zeigen, wo er gewesen
war: Auf jedem Foto stand, wann er es aufgenommen hatte.

Der Mann lächelte. Sah die Fotos durch. Nachmittag im Europa-Viertel, Schuman-Platz. Das Berlaymont-, das Justus-
Lipsius-Gebäude. Das Straßenschild »Rue Joseph II«. Warum dieses Straßenschild?

Ich bin Österreicher!

Ach ja.

Die Skulptur »Der Traum Europa« in der Rue de la Loi. Die
Bronzefigur eines blinden (oder schlafwandelnden?) Mannes,
der von einem Sockel aus einen Schritt ins Leere macht. Was
die Touristen alles fotografieren! Da. Neunzehn Uhr fünfzehn: Grand Place. Mehrere Fotos dort bis neunzehn Uhr

achtundzwanzig. Dann das letzte Foto: zwanzig Uhr vier, Sainte-Catherine, das Kirchenschiff. Der Mann drückte weiter, da war wieder das erste Foto. Er drückte zurück. Der Christus, der Altar, davor in einer Bank ein Mann, auf dessen Rücken »Guinness« stand.

Er grinste und gab ihm den Fotoapparat zurück.

Als Alois Erhart in sein Zimmer kam, ging er zum Fenster, er sah durch die Scheibe hinaus auf den Regen, strich sich durch das nasse Haar, hörte in sich hinein. Er hörte nichts. Als er gegen Mittag angekommen war, hatte er gleich das Fenster geöffnet, sich schließlich weit hinausgelehnt, um einen besseren Überblick über den Platz zu bekommen, zu weit hatte er sich hinausgebeugt, fast hätte er das Gleichgewicht verloren, er hatte keinen Boden mehr unter den Füßen, sah schon den Asphalt auf sich zukommen, das ging so schnell, er stieß sich zurück, fiel vor dem Fenster zu Boden, wobei er mit dem rechten Unterarm am Heizkörper anschlug, saß in einer lächerlichen Verrenkung auf dem Fußboden – und hatte das Gefühl, als befände er sich im freien Fall, den er doch gerade noch vermieden hatte, ein Gefühl, das man vielleicht spürt in der Sekunde vor dem Tod. Dann hatte er sich hochgezogen, auf das Bett gesetzt, keuchend, und plötzlich war diese Euphorie da: Er war frei. Noch. Er konnte souverän entscheiden. Und er würde die Entscheidung treffen. Jetzt noch nicht. Aber rechtzeitig. Selbstmörder – blöder Begriff! Selbstbestimmter, freier Mensch! Er wusste, dass er musste – und plötzlich wusste er auch, dass er konnte. Der Tod, das war ihm nun klar, war so banal und nichtig und unvermeidlich wie der Punkt »Allfälliges« am Ende einer Tagesordnung. Das war der Moment, wo nichts mehr kam. Das Sterben musste er überspringen. Springen.

Er wollte nicht so sterben wie seine Frau. So hilflos am Ende, darauf angewiesen, dass er ihr –

Er nahm die Fernbedienung, schaltete den Fernsehapparat ein. Zog das Hemd aus, sah, dass er einen Bluterguss am rechten Arm hatte. Er drückte auf die Fernbedienung: weiter! Er zog die Hose aus, weiter! Die Socken, weiter! Die Unterhose, weiter! Da landete er beim Sender Arte. Hier begann gerade ein Spielfilm, ein Klassiker: »Verdammt in alle Ewigkeit«. Es war Jahrzehnte her, dass er diesen Film gesehen hatte. Er legte sich auf das Bett. Eine Stimme sagte: »Dieser Film wird Ihnen präsentiert von parship.de, der führenden Partneragentur.«

Es war kein Zufall, dass Fenia Xenopoulou just in dem Moment, als der Rettungswagen auf den Platz einbog und die Sirene zu hören war, an Rettung gedacht hatte. Sie hatte seit Tagen an nichts anderes gedacht, es war ihr geradezu zur fixen Idee geworden, und darum dachte sie es auch jetzt: Rettung! Er muss mich retten!

Sie saß beim Abendessen im Restaurant Menelas, das sich genau gegenüber vom Hotel Atlas befand, zusammen mit Kai-Uwe Frigge, den sie, seit einer kurzen Affäre vor zwei Jahren, privat Fridsch nannte, wobei kokett offenblieb, ob sie seinen Namen zu »Fritz« verballhornte, weil er ein Deutscher war, oder ob sie auf »Fridge«, den Kühlschrank, anspielte, weil er in seiner sachlich korrekten Art so kalt wirkte. Frigge, ein schlaksiger, wendiger Mann Mitte vierzig, aus Hamburg stammend, seit zehn Jahren in Brüssel, hatte bei den Grabenkämpfen, Intrigen und Tauschgeschäften, die der Konstituierung eines neuen Kabinetts der Europäischen Kommission naturgemäß vorangehen, Glück gehabt (oder sich eben nicht auf sein Glück verlassen) und einen beeindruckenden Karrieresprung gemacht: Nun war er Kabinettschef in der Generaldirektion für Handel, damit der einflussreiche Büroleiter von einem der mächtigsten Kommissare der Union.

Dass sich die beiden in dieser Stadt voll von erstklassigen Restaurants ausgerechnet bei einem Griechen trafen, der sich dann als eher mittelmäßig erwies, war nicht der Wunsch von Fenia Xenopoulou gewesen, sie hatte kein Heimweh und keine Sehnsucht nach dem Geschmack und den Aromen der heimatlichen Küche. Kai-Uwe Frigge hatte das vorgeschlagen: Er wollte seiner griechischen Kollegin ein Zeichen von Solidarität geben, jetzt, da nach dem Beinahe-Staatsbankrott Griechenlands und dem vierten sündteuren EU-Rettungspaket, »die Griechen« bei den Kollegen und in der Öffentlichkeit völlig unten durch waren. Er war sich eines Pluspunkts sicher, als er per Mail »Menelas? Am Vieux Marché aux Grains, Sainte-Catherine, angeblich sehr guter Grieche!« als Treffpunkt vorschlug, und sie hatte »Okay« geantwortet. Ihr war das egal gewesen. Sie lebte und arbeitete schon zu lange in Brüssel, um sich noch mit Patriotismus zu beschäftigen. Was sie wollte, war: Rettung. Ihre eigene.

Den Fonds, der den Bankrott Griechenlands verhindern sollte, Rettungsschirm zu nennen, war schon unfreiwillig komisch, sagte Frigge. Na ja, Metaphern sind bei uns im Haus Glückssache!

Es belustigte Fenia Xenopoulou nicht im Geringsten, sie verstand gar nicht, was er meinte, aber sie lachte strahlend. Es wirkte maskenhaft, und sie war sich nicht sicher, ob man es merkte, das Gekünstelte, oder ob es noch funktionierte, worauf sie sich früher immer hatte verlassen können: dass der meisterhafte Einsatz von Gesichtsmuskeln, Timing, blendend weißen Zähnen und einem warmen Blick ein Bild unwiderstehlicher Natürlichkeit ergaben. Man muss auch für das Artifizielle ein natürliches Talent haben, aber Fenia war auf Grund ihres Karriereknicks – in ihrem Alter! Sie wurde vierzig! – so verstört, dass sie sich selbst ihres natürlichen Talents, nämlich wissentlich zu gefallen, nicht mehr sicher war. Der

Selbstzweifel, so empfand sie es, überzog wie eine Schuppenflechte ihre Erscheinung.

Kai-Uwe hatte nur einen Bauernsalat bestellt, Fenias erster Impuls war es zu sagen: Den nehme ich auch. Aber dann hörte sie sich Giouvetsi bestellen! Es war lauwarm und triefte vor Fett. Warum hatte sie sich nicht mehr unter Kontrolle? Sie begann aus dem Leim zu gehen. Sie musste aufpassen. Der Kellner schenkte Wein nach. Sie sah das Weinglas an und dachte: noch einmal achtzig Kalorien. Sie nippte am Wasser, nahm all ihre Kraft zusammen und sah Kai-Uwe an, sie versuchte, das Wasserglas mit beiden Händen an ihre Unterlippe drückend, komplizenhaft und zugleich verführerisch zu schauen. Innerlich fluchte sie. Was war mit ihr los?

Rettungsschirm!, sagte Kai-Uwe. Auf Deutsch kann man solche Neologismen bilden, und sie müssen nur dreimal in der Frankfurter Allgemeinen gestanden haben, und schon kommen sie jedem Gebildeten völlig normal vor. Und dann ist das nicht mehr wegzubringen. Die Chefin sagt das in jede Kamera. Die Übersetzer sind ganz schön ins Schwitzen gekommen. Das Englische und das Französische kennen den Rettungsring und den Regenschirm. Aber was, wurden wir gefragt, ist bitte ein »Rettungsschirm«? Die Franzosen übersetzten ihn zunächst mit »parachute«. Dann kam Protest aus dem Élysée-Palast: Ein Fallschirm verhindere keinen Absturz, er verlangsame ihn nur, das sei das falsche Signal, die Deutschen mögen bitte –

Wenn er eine Olive aß, den Kern auf den Teller legte, dann kam es Fenia so vor, als würde er nur den Geschmack der Olive zu sich nehmen, die Kalorien aber in die Küche zurückschicken.

Da begann das Jaulen der Sirene, dann das Blaulicht, blau blau blau blau …

Fridsch?

Ja?

Du musst – sie wollte es schon aussprechen: mich retten. Aber das war unmöglich. Sie korrigierte sich: mir helfen! Nein, sie musste kompetent, nicht hilfsbedürftig auftreten.

Ja? Er schaute durch das Fenster des Restaurants hinüber zum Hotel Atlas. Er sah, wie eine Tragbahre aus dem Rettungswagen gezogen wurde, wie Männer damit ins Hotel hineinliefen. So nahe das Menelas dem Hotel auch war, die Distanz war doch zu groß, als dass er an den Tod gedacht hätte. Es war für ihn bloß eine Choreographie, Menschen bewegten sich zu Licht und Ton.

Du musst – hatte sie schon gesagt, nun wollte sie die Worte ungesagt machen, aber das ging nicht mehr – … verstehen … aber das tust du ja! Ich weiß es, du verstehst, dass ich –

Ja? Er sah sie an.

Die Sirenen der Polizeiautos.

Fenia Xenopoulou hatte zunächst in der Generaldirektion für Wettbewerb gearbeitet. Der Kommissar, ein Spanier, war ahnungslos gewesen. Aber jeder Kommissar ist so gut wie sein Büro, und sie war als ein hervorragender Teil eines perfekt funktionierenden Büros aufgefallen. Sie ließ sich scheiden. Sie hatte weder Zeit noch Lust, jedes zweite oder später jedes dritte oder vierte Wochenende einen Mann in ihrem Brüsseler Apartment sitzen zu haben oder in Athen zu besuchen, der über irgendwelche Intimitäten der Athener Society plauderte und dabei Zigarren paffte wie die Karikatur eines Neureichen. Sie hatte einen Staranwalt geheiratet und warf einen Provinzadvokaten aus der Wohnung! Dann kletterte sie eine Sprosse höher und kam ins Kabinett des Kommissars für Handel. Im Handel erwirbt man Meriten, wenn man Handelsbeschränkungen zertrümmert. Es gab für sie kein Privatleben mehr, keine Fesseln, es gab nur den freien Welthandel. Sie glaubte wirklich, dass die Karriere, die sie vor sich sah, ihr

Lohn dafür sein werde, dass sie an einer Verbesserung der Welt Anteil hatte. Fair Trade war für sie eine Tautologie. Trade war doch die Voraussetzung für globale Fairness. Der Kommissar, ein Holländer, hatte Skrupel. Er war so unglaublich korrekt. Fenia arbeitete hart, um auszurechnen, wie viel Gulden seine Skrupel kosteten. Der Mann rechnete tatsächlich immer noch in Gulden! Der Lorbeer, den er erhielt, wenn Fenia ihn überzeugt hatte, war Goldes wert! Nun sollte der nächste Sprung kommen. Sie erwartete, nach den europäischen Wahlen bei der Neukonstituierung der Kommission weiter aufzusteigen. Und tatsächlich: Sie wurde befördert. Sie bekam eine Abteilung. Was war das Problem? Sie empfand diese Beförderung als Rückstufung, als Karriereknick, als Abschiebung: Sie wurde Leiterin der Direktion C (»Kommunikation«) in der Generaldirektion für Kultur!

Kultur!

Sie hatte Wirtschaft studiert, London School of Economics, Postgraduate an der Stanford University, den Concours bestanden, und jetzt saß sie in der Kultur – das war nicht einmal so sinnvoll wie Monopoly-Spielen! Die Kultur war ein bedeutungsloses Ressort, ohne Budget, ohne Gewicht in der Kommission, ohne Einfluss und Macht. Kollegen nannten die Kultur ein Alibi-Ressort – wenn es das wenigstens wäre! Ein Alibi ist wichtig, jede Tat braucht ein Alibi! Aber die Kultur war nicht einmal Augenwischerei, weil es kein Auge gab, das hinschaute, was die Kultur machte. Wenn der Kommissar für Handel oder für Energie, ja sogar wenn die Kommissarin für Fischfang während einer Sitzung der Kommission auf die Toilette musste, wurde die Diskussion unterbrochen und gewartet, bis er oder sie zurückkam. Aber wenn die Kultur-Kommissarin rausmusste, wurde unbeeindruckt weiterverhandelt, ja es fiel gar nicht auf, ob sie am Verhandlungstisch oder auf der Toilette saß.

Fenia Xenopoulou war in einen Aufzug eingestiegen, der zwar hochgefahren, aber dann unbemerkt zwischen zwei Stockwerken stecken geblieben war.

Ich muss raus!, sagte sie. Als sie von der Toilette zurückkam, sah sie, dass er telefonierte. Er hatte nicht gewartet.

Fridsch und Fenia schauten durch das große Fenster hinüber zum Hotel, schweigend wie ein altes Ehepaar, das froh war, dass etwas passierte, worüber man dann ein paar Sätze sagen konnte.

Was ist da los?

Keine Ahnung! Vielleicht hatte einer im Hotel einen Herzinfarkt?, sagte Fridsch.

Aber wegen eines Herzinfarkts kommt doch nicht gleich die Polizei!

Richtig, sagte er. Und nach einer kleinen Pause – hätte er fast gesagt: apropos Herz. Was macht dein Liebesleben? Aber er verkniff sich diese Frage.

Du hast doch etwas auf dem Herzen!, sagte er.

Ja!

Du kannst mir alles erzählen!

Er hörte zu und nickte und nickte, von Zeit zu Zeit sagte er gedehnt »okay«, um ihr zu zeigen, dass er ihr folgte, und schließlich sagte er: Was kann ich für dich tun?

Du musst mich anfordern. Kannst du mich – ja: anfordern? Ich will zurück zum Handel. Oder kannst du mit Queneau reden? Du verstehst dich doch gut mit ihm. Er hört auf dich. Vielleicht kann er etwas tun. Ich muss weg von der Kultur. Ich ersticke dort!

Ja, sagte er. Plötzlich hatte er Angst. Das ist vielleicht ein zu großes Wort. Er spürte eine Beklemmung, die er sich nicht erklären konnte. Er dachte nie über sein Leben nach. Er hatte irgendwann früher über sein Leben nachgedacht – sehr viel früher, damals, als er noch keine Lebenserfahrung gehabt hatte. Es waren Phantasien, Träume gewesen, er hatte Träumen mit Nachdenklichkeit verwechselt. Man konnte nicht sagen, dass er seinen Träumen nachgegangen war. Er war, so wie man zu einem bestimmten Bahnsteig geht, dorthin gegangen, wo die Reise zu einem bestimmten Ziel eben beginnt. Seither befand er sich auf Schienen. Er wusste in seinem Innersten, dass es oft auch bloßes Glück war, wenn man nicht entgleiste. Aber es gab, solange man auf den Schienen war, nichts, worüber man weiter nachdenken musste. Leben. Es funktioniert oder es funktioniert nicht. Wenn es funktioniert, dann wird »es« durch »man« ersetzt. Man funktioniert. Er dachte das alles nicht. Das war ihm einfach klar. Er verwechselte diese Klarheit mit einem sicheren Grund, auf dem er ging, ohne bei jedem einzelnen Schritt nachdenken zu müssen. Aber da war jetzt ein leichtes Schwanken auf diesem Grund. Warum? Er fragte sich das nicht. Er spürte nur diese leichte Beklemmung. Jetzt muss ich kurz auf die Toilette! Er wusch sich die Hände, betrachtete sich im Spiegel. Er war sich nicht fremd. Nicht fremd ist allerdings auch nicht vertraut. Er nahm aus seinem Portemonnaie eine Viagra-Tablette. Er hatte immer eine bei sich. Er zerbiss sie, nahm einen Schluck Wasser, dann wusch er sich noch einmal die Hände. Er wusste, dass Fenia, genauso wie er, morgen sehr früh rausmusste. Dass sie also bald ins Bett mussten. Sie mussten funktionieren.

Sie nahmen ein Taxi nach Ixelles, zu seinem Apartment. Er täuschte Begehren vor, sie täuschte einen Orgasmus vor. Die Chemie stimmte. Durch das Fenster blinkte blau das Licht der Leuchtreklame von der Bar Le Cerf Bleu, auf der anderen Straßenseite. Kai-Uwe Frigge stand noch einmal auf und zog den Vorhang zu.

Stand da ein Mann am Fenster? Der schwarze Rächer. Das Phantom. Der Schattenmann. Es sah aus wie eine Comicfigur, die an die Wand des verlassenen Hauses gemalt worden war: Alle Fenster dieses Hauses schräg gegenüber vom Hotel Atlas, an der Ecke zur Rue de la Braie, waren dunkel, die Auslage des Geschäftslokals war mit Brettern vernagelt, auf den Brettern flatterten die Fetzen halb heruntergerissener Plakate. Daneben an der Hauswand Graffiti, hingesprayte Wörter, unlesbar – Ornamente, Geheimschrift, Symbole? Vor dem Haus ein Bauzaun, darauf ein Schild der Abbruchfirma De Meuter. Natürlich wusste Kommissar Brunfaut, dass diese schwarze Gestalt, eingerahmt von einem Fenstergeviert in der ersten Etage des toten Hauses, kein Graffito war. Aber sie machte diesen Eindruck. An allen Ecken und Enden dieser Stadt waren ja Häuserwände und Brandmauern bis hinauf zu den Dachfirsten mit Comicbildern bemalt, mit Kopien und Variationen der Zeichnungen von Hergé oder Morris, den Tieren von Bonom oder Werken von den Jungen, die sich für die Nachfolger dieser Künstler hielten. Wenn Brüssel ein offenes Buch war, dann war es ein Comicband.

Kommissar Brunfaut war aus dem Hotel Atlas herausgekommen, um den Kollegen im Einsatzfahrzeug die Anweisung zu geben, die Nachbarhäuser abzuklappern und nachzufragen, ob jemand vielleicht zufällig zur fraglichen Zeit aus dem Fenster geschaut und etwas gesehen hatte.

Das Jahr fängt ja gut an, Kommissar!

Jeder Tag fängt ja gut an, sagte Brunfaut. Der Regen hatte nachgelassen, der Kommissar stand breitbeinig da, zog den Hosenbund hoch und ließ, während er mit den Männern redete, den Blick über die Fassaden der gegenüberliegenden Häuser wandern. Und da sah er sie: die fenstergerahmte Schattenfigur.

Da stand tatsächlich ein Mann am Fenster. Eines Abbruchhauses. Der Kommissar schaute hinauf, fixierte ihn. Der Mann bewegte sich nicht. War das wirklich ein Mensch? Oder eine Puppe? Warum sollte dort hinter dem Fenster eine Puppe stehen? Oder war das ein Schatten, dessen Kontur ihn täuschte? Oder doch ein Graffito? Der Kommissar grinste. Nicht wirklich natürlich. Innerlich. Nein, da stand ein Mann! Schaute er herunter? Sah er, dass der Kommissar zu ihm hinaufschaute? Was hatte er gesehen?

Los!, sagte Kommissar Brunfaut. An die Arbeit! Du nimmst dieses Haus, du das dort! Und du –

Die Bruchbude auch? Die steht doch leer!

Ja, die auch – schau einmal da hinauf!

In diesem Moment war der Schattenmann verschwunden.

Er trat vom Fenster zurück. Wo hatte er seine Zigaretten? Vielleicht im Mantel. Der Mantel lag auf dem Küchenstuhl, dem einzigen Möbel, das es in dieser Wohnung noch gab. David de Vriend ging in die Küche, nahm den Mantel. Was wollte er? Den Mantel. Warum? Unschlüssig stand er da, schaute den Mantel an. Es war Zeit zu gehen. Ja. Hier war nichts mehr. Zu tun. Die Wohnung war vollständig ausgeräumt. Er schaute auf einen rechteckigen Fleck an der Wand. Da hatte ein Bild gehangen. »Wald bei Boortmeerbeek«, ein idyllisches Landschaftsbild. Daran konnte er sich noch erinnern: wie er es hier aufgehängt hatte. Dann hatte er es ein Leben lang vor Augen gehabt, bis er es gar nicht mehr gesehen hatte. Und jetzt: eine Leerstelle. Nur noch zu sehen, dass da etwas gewesen ist, was nicht mehr da war. Lebensgeschichte: ein leerer Umriss auf einer Tapete, die auch schon über eine Vorgeschichte geklebt worden war. Darunter war die Kontur des Schranks zu sehen, der hier gestanden hatte. Was hatte er darin aufbewahrt? Was sich in einem Leben ansammelt. Der Dreck dahinter! Der kommt dann zum Vorschein. Verklumpter Staub, Schlieren von fettigem, rußigem, schimmelndem Schmutz. Du kannst dein ganzes Leben lang putzen, ja putze nur dein Leben, am Ende aber, wenn ausgeräumt wird, bleibt ein Dreck über! Hinter jeder Fläche, die du putzt, hinter jeder Fassade, die du polierst. Wenn du jung bist, glaub nicht, dass da noch nichts verrottet, verschimmelt und verfault wäre, wenn dein Leben plötzlich weggeräumt wird. Du bist jung und glaubst, dass du noch nichts oder zu wenig gehabt hast vom Leben? Aber der Dreck dahinter ist immer der Dreck eines ganzen Lebens. Es bleibt nur der Dreck, weil du Dreck bist und im Dreck landest. Wenn du aber alt wirst: Glück gehabt. Aber du hast dich getäuscht, auch wenn du dein ganzes geschenktes Leben lang geputzt hast – am Ende wird ausgeräumt, und was sieht man? Dreck. Er ist hinter allem, unter allem, er ist die Grundlage von allem, was du geputzt hast. Ein sauberes Leben. Das hast du gehabt. Bis der Dreck zum Vorschein kommt. Dort war die Spüle gewesen. Ununterbrochen hatte er abgewaschen. Einen Geschirrspüler hatte er nie besessen. Jeden Teller, jede Tasse hatte er nach Gebrauch sofort abgewaschen. Wenn er alleine einen Kaffee getrunken hatte, und er war ja alleine, fast immer ist er alleine gewesen, dann hatte er den Kaffee im Stehen getrunken, gleich neben der Spüle, damit er die Tasse sofort waschen konnte, den letzten Schluck vom Kaffee nehmen und den Wasserhahn aufdrehen, das war immer eins gewesen, ausspülen, abtrocknen und glänzend wischen und die Tasse zurückstellen, damit alles sauber ist, das ist ihm immer wichtig gewesen, ein sauberes Leben, und dann: Was sieht man jetzt, da, wo die Spüle gewesen ist? Moder, Schimmelpilz, Schlieren, Dreck. Sogar im Dunkeln oder Halbdunkeln sah man den Dreck. Es war nichts mehr da, alles ausgeräumt, aber das war noch da, das war zu sehen: die Dreckschlieren hinter dem geputzten Leben.

Er warf den Mantel wieder über den Stuhl. Er wollte – was?

Er sah sich um. Warum ging er nicht? Er sollte gehen. Davon-
laufen. Das war nicht mehr die Wohnung, in der er gelebt
hatte. Das waren nur noch die Räume, in denen es ein Vor-
leben gegeben hatte. Noch ein Rundgang. Wozu? Leere Räume anstarren? Er ging ins Schlafzimmer. Wo das Bett gestanden hatte, war der Holzboden heller, das Rechteck, das sich
da abzeichnete, sah im Halbdunkel aus wie eine große Fall-
tür. Er ging daran vorbei zum Fenster, warum ging er nicht
darüber hinweg, warum machte er in diesem leeren Zimmer
einen Bogen, als hätte er Angst, dass dieses Rechteck sich
wirklich öffnen und ihn verschlingen könnte? Er hatte keine
Angst. Hier hatte immer das Bett gestanden, er ging von der
Tür zum Fenster, so wie er ein Leben lang um das Bett herum
zum Fenster gegangen war. Er sah hinaus: fast in Griffweite
die Feuerstiege des Nachbargebäudes, einer Schule. Einmal
im Jahr gab es einen Probealarm, es heulte eine Sirene und
die Schüler übten, rasch und geordnet die Feuerleiter hinun-
terzusteigen. Wie oft David de Vriend an diesem Fenster gestanden und zugeschaut hatte. Die Flucht. Eine Übung. In
Griffweite – das sagt sich so. Die Stiege war in Griffweite gewesen, als er hier eingezogen war. Sie ist damals für ihn auch
ein Argument gewesen, diese Wohnung zu nehmen. Die
Wohnung hat eine sehr gute Lage, hatte der Verkäufer gesagt,
und de Vriend hatte aus diesem Fenster auf die Feuerstiege
geschaut und zugestimmt: Ja, die Lage ist gut! Er hatte gedacht, dass er, wenn es sein musste, aus diesem Fenster mit
einem Satz auf der Feuerstiege wäre und verschwinden konnte, während vorn an der Wohnungstür noch geklopft würde.
Das hatte er sich zugetraut, kein Zweifel, das hätte er geschafft.
Aber heute – wäre nicht daran zu denken. Nun war die Stiege
außer Griffweite, unerreichbar. Seit einem halben Jahrhundert waren die Kinder, die hier die Flucht übten, immer
gleich alt geblieben, immer Kinder, nur er war älter gewor-

den, zu alt schließlich, schwach und gebrechlich, und aus der Übung gekommen. Er sah aus dem Fenster und sah – keine Griffweite mehr. Ihm fiel ein, dass er rauchen wollte. Er sollte endlich gehen, verschwinden – er ging durch den Flur, aber nicht in die Küche, wo sein Mantel mit den Zigaretten war, sondern ins Wohnzimmer. Unschlüssig blieb er stehen, sah sich suchend um. Ein leerer Raum. Er wollte – was wollte er hier noch? Er ging zum Fenster, ja: noch einmal diesen Blick haben, über den Platz, an dem er ein ganzes geschenktes Leben verbracht und versucht hatte, seinen »Platz im Leben« zu finden.

Er schaute hinunter auf das Blaulicht. Er dachte nichts. Er fror. Er wusste warum. Er dachte nicht einmal, dass er es wusste und dass dies keinen weiteren Gedanken wert war. Es steckte in ihm, altes Wissen. Das musste sich nicht im Kopf formulieren. Er sah unbeweglich hinunter auf die Polizeiautos, sein Herz zog sich zusammen, dehnte sich wieder aus, ein Achselzucken der Seele.

Als er noch Lehrer war, hatte er dies den Schülern bei ihren Aufsätzen immer austreiben wollen: die Blablabla-Komma-dachte-er-Sätze.

Es war ihnen nicht auszutreiben. Kinder, sie glaubten wirklich, dass Menschen, wenn sie alleine sind, ununterbrochen Dachte-er- oder Dachte-sie-Sätze im Kopf haben. Und dann stießen diese Dachte-er- und Dachte-sie-Köpfe zusammen und produzierten Sagte-er- und Sagte-sie-Sätze. Die Wahrheit ist, dass es bis in die Köpfe hinein so unglaublich still ist unter dem gottlosen Firmament. Unser Geschwätz ist nur das Echo dieser Stille. Kalt zog sich sein Herz zusammen, dehnte sich aus. Zog sich zusammen, dehnte sich aus. Er atmete ein, er atmete aus. Wie das blaue Licht pulsierte!

Da hörte er die Klingel. Dann das Schlagen einer Faust an die Wohnungstür. Er ging in die Küche, zog den Mantel an.

Er ging ins Schlafzimmer. Immer wieder schlug jemand draußen an die Tür. David de Vriend machte wieder den kleinen Bogen, als er zum Fenster ging. Er sah hinaus. Nicht in Griffweite. Er setzte sich auf den Boden, zündete sich eine Zigarette an. Das Klopfen. Das Pochen.

Zweites Kapitel

Ideen stören, was es ohne sie
gar nicht gäbe.

Eine Depression muss man sich leisten können. Martin Susman konnte überleben: Er arbeitete auf der »Arche Noah«. Er war Beamter der Europäischen Kommission, Generaldirektion »Kultur und Bildung«, zugeteilt der Direktion C »Kommunikation«, und leitete die Abteilung EAC-C-2 »Programm und Maßnahmen Kultur«.

Intern nannten die Mitarbeiter ihr Ressort nur die »Arche Noah« oder kurz »die Arche«. Warum? Eine Arche hat kein Ziel. Sie schlingert über die Strömungen, schaukelt auf den Wogen, trotzt den Stürmen und will nur eines: sich selbst und das, was sie an Bord führt, retten.

Es hatte nicht lange gedauert, bis Martin Susman dies begriffen hatte. Er war zunächst so glücklich und stolz darauf gewesen, dass er diesen Job ergattern konnte, zumal er nicht als »END« (Expert National Détaché) von einer österreichischen Partei oder Behörde nach Brüssel geschickt worden war, sondern sich direkt bei der Kommission beworben und den Concours bestanden hatte – er war also wirklich ein europäischer Beamter, ohne nationale Verpflichtung! Und dann musste er feststellen, dass das Ressort »Bildung und Kultur« innerhalb der Europäischen Kommission kein Ansehen hatte und nur milde belächelt wurde. Im Apparat sagte man einfach »die Kultur«, wenn man von dieser Generaldirektion sprach, die »Bildung« wurde unterschlagen, obwohl im Bildungsbereich bemerkenswerte Erfolge erzielt worden waren, etwa die Entwicklung und Durchsetzung des Erasmus-Programms. Und wenn »die Kultur« gesagt wurde, dann hatte das einen Unterton, es klang so, als würden Wall-Street-Broker »Numismatik« sagen, das Hobby eines verschrobenen

Verwandten. Aber auch in der Öffentlichkeit, soweit sie sich überhaupt interessierte, war das Image der »europäischen Kultur« schlecht. Martin Susman war erst kurz im Amt gewesen, und er las noch die heimischen Zeitungen – ein typischer Anfängerfehler –, als Empörung in Österreich ausbrach, weil, wie in den Blättern zu lesen war, den Österreichern mit der Kultur »gedroht« wurde: Jeder Mitgliedstaat der EU hatte das Anrecht auf einen Kommissar-Posten, die Regierung nominierte eine Person, und der Kommissionspräsident wies ihr ein Ressort zu. Als nach den damaligen Europawahlen die Ressorts neu besetzt wurden, kam das Gerücht auf, dass der von Österreich nominierte Kommissar »die Kultur« bekommen solle. Die österreichische Koalitionsregierung zerstritt sich, weil die Partei des designierten Kommissars eine Intrige des Koalitionspartners witterte, man protestierte, die österreichischen Zeitungen machten Stimmung und sie konnten sich auf die Entrüstungsbereitschaft ihrer Leser verlassen: »Uns droht die Kultur!« Oder: »Österreich soll mit Kultur abgespeist werden!«

Das scheint als Reaktion sehr erstaunlich, wenn man bedenkt, dass sich dieses Land als »Kulturnation« – nun, vielleicht nicht »begriff«, aber doch gerne bezeichnete. Allerdings entsprach diese Reaktion dem Image und der Bedeutung, die »die Kultur« im europäischen Machtgefüge eben hatte. Image und Bedeutung hingen von der Höhe des Budgets, das ein Ressort verteilen konnte, und vom Einfluss auf politische und wirtschaftliche Eliten ab. Und mit beidem war es im Falle der »Kultur« schlecht bestellt. Schließlich bekam der österreichische Kommissar doch nicht das Kultur-Ressort, sondern die »Regionalpolitik«, was zu Jubel in der Kulturnation führte: »Wir«, so meldeten die österreichischen Blätter nun, »haben ein Budget von 337 Milliarden!«

Die »Kultur« bekam Griechenland. Das schien durchaus

stimmig, wenn man an die griechische Antike als Fundament
der europäischen Kultur denkt, oder aber auf sinnige Weise
zynisch, wenn man den Demokratieabbau in Europa in Beziehung zur Sklavenhaltergesellschaft der griechischen Antike setzen wollte – dabei war es ganz simpel: Griechenland
war wegen seiner nun schon endlosen Finanz- und Budget-
krise unten durch, deshalb wehrlos, und musste nehmen, was
es bekam. Das geringgeschätzte Ressort. Es war keine Aufgabe, es war eine Strafe: Wer mit Geld nicht umgehen kann,
der bekommt auch besser kein Geld in die Hand, bekommt
also das Ressort ohne Budget. Die griechische Kommissarin,
eine engagierte Frau, kämpfte um ein starkes Team, dem sie
vertrauen und das ihr in der Kommission doch etwas politisches Gewicht geben konnte. Es gelang ihr, einige Landsleute
anzufordern, die im Apparat der Kommission bereits über
Erfahrung verfügten, gut vernetzt mit anderen Generaldirektionen waren und einen exzellenten Ruf hatten, um mit ihnen die Schlüsselpositionen ihrer Generaldirektion zu besetzen. So war Fenia Xenopoulou vom »Handel« abgezogen und
zur Leiterin jener Direktion in der »Arche« befördert worden,
in der Martin Susman arbeitete.
Fenia hatte diese Beförderung nicht ablehnen können. Wer
im Apparat der Europäischen Kommission Karriere machen
wollte, musste Mobilité beweisen. Wer die Bereitschaft dazu
nicht demonstrierte und ein Angebot, den Aufgabenbereich
zu wechseln, ausschlug, war weg vom Fenster. Also war sie in
die Arche übersiedelt, mit dem Plan, hier erst recht ihre Mobilité unter Beweis zu stellen: indem sie sofort daranging,
den nächsten Wechsel anzustreben, unter besonderer Berück-
sichtigung der Visibilité. Dies war für den Aufstieg im Apparat ebenso entscheidend: sichtbar zu sein, so zu arbeiten, dass
man immer wieder auffiel.
Fenia wusste, was Elend war. Sie hatte es kennengelernt. Sie

hatte diese glühende Energie, die oft jenen Menschen eigen ist, denen die Misere ihrer Herkunft ewig in der Seele brennt und die nie Abstand dazu finden können, so weit sie auch kommen, weil sie ihre Seele ja immer mitnehmen. Von der ersten Lebenschance an hatte sie immer wieder bewiesen, dass sie bereit war zuzugreifen. Wenn man ihr eine Tür zeigte und sagte: Wenn du den Schlüssel findest, dann kommst du durch diese Tür ins Freie – dann suchte sie akribisch den Schlüssel, sie war auch bereit, an allen möglichen Schlüsseln sehr lange geduldig zu feilen, damit endlich einer passte, aber irgendwann kam der Moment, wo sie eine Axt nahm und die Tür zertrümmerte. Die Axt wurde schließlich zu ihrem Universalschlüssel.

Martin Susman konnte Fenia nicht ausstehen. Das Arbeitsklima war seit ihrem Eintritt in die Arche schlechter geworden. Es war deutlich, dass sie die Arbeit verachtete, die hier geleistet werden musste, zugleich machte sie unerträglichen Druck, sie deutlicher in die Auslage zu stellen.

Fenia Xenopoulou schlief gut. Für sie war Schlaf ein Teil der Körperbeherrschung, der Selbstdisziplin. Sie dockte sich an den Schlaf an wie an ein Ladegerät. Sie zog Arme und Beine an, machte den Rücken rund, drückte das Kinn gegen die Brust. Und schon lud sie Kraft für den Kampf des nächsten Tages auf. Nur wenn sie schlief, hatte sie keine Träume.

Habe ich geschnarcht?, hatte Fridsch sie in der Früh gefragt.

Nein. Ich habe gut geschlafen!

Wie ein Kind.

Ja.

Nein, eigentlich wie ein Embryo.

Embryo?

Ja. Wie du dagelegen bist. Hat mich an Fotos von Embryos erinnert! Willst du Kaffee?

Nein danke! Ich muss gleich los! Sie wollte ihn zum Abschied küssen und sagen »Denk an mich!«, aber sie tat es nicht, nickte nur und sagte: Ich muss …

Martin Susman hatte auf dem Weg zum Büro die neuesten Informationen erhalten. Er fuhr, wann immer das Wetter es erlaubte, das hieß: wenn es nicht regnete, mit dem Rad zur Arbeit. Dadurch hatte er etwas Bewegung, aber das war nicht der Hauptgrund. Die Metro machte ihn traurig. Die müden, grauen Gesichter schon am frühen Morgen. Die aufgesetzte Bereitschaft der Menschen mit ihren Trolleys und Aktenkoffern, immer dynamisch und kompetent und wettbewerbsfähig zu wirken, schlecht sitzende Masken, unter denen die wahren Gesichter verfaulten. Die Blicke ins Leere, wenn die Bettler mit den Akkordeons zustiegen, eine Nummer spielten und mit einem Joghurt-Becher um ein paar Münzen baten. Was waren das für Lieder? Martin hätte es nicht sagen können, vielleicht Schlager aus den zwanziger und dreißiger Jahren des vorigen Jahrhunderts, Vorkriegszeit. Aussteigen. Die mechanisch sich bewegenden Menschenströme, die über Rolltreppen stapften, die außer Betrieb waren, sich weiterschoben durch die mit Sperrholz verschalten, verdreckten Korridore der ewigen Baustellen des Untergrunds, vorbei an den Pizzaschnitten- und Kebab-Verschlägen, dem Geruch von Körperausscheidungen und Verwesung, schließlich der Windkanal des Aufstiegs zur Straße, hinauf in ein Tageslicht, das nicht mehr vordringt in die trübe Seele. Martin fuhr lieber mit dem Rad. Er war sehr bald Mitglied der EU-Cycling-Group geworden. Diese Gruppe stellte jedem EU-Beamten, der beitrat, zunächst einen Personal Trainer zur Verfügung, der ihm die Basics beibringt, zum Beispiel lebend mit dem Rad über die Montgomery zu kommen, der Trainer erkundet den sichersten Weg von der Wohnung zum Arbeitsplatz, der dann einige Tage gemeinsam eingeübt wird, und man lernte auch, beim Vorbeifahren die Klebeetiketten »Sie stehen im Weg!« auf Autos zu klatschen, die auf einem Radweg parkten. Die Aufkleber beschädigten die Autos nicht, sie ließen sich leicht wieder abziehen. Die EU-Cycling-Group war ein großer Erfolg, der Anteil der Radfahrer am Brüsseler Verkehr hatte sich durch die EU-Beamten in wenigen Jahren verdoppelt.

Am besten gefiel Martin, dass sich auf dem Weg von der Wohnung zum Amt spontan Gemeinschaften bildeten. Wenn er morgens von zu Hause losfuhr, stieß er spätestens auf dem Boulevard Anspach auf den ersten Kollegen, dann auf den zweiten, bis sie am Ende zu einem Pulk von oft acht oder zehn Radfahrern angewachsen waren. Die deutschen Beamten zogen auf Rennrädern am Pulk vorbei, sie radelten in Funktionskleidung zur Arbeit, als müssten sie ein Kriterium gewinnen, es waren daher fast nur Deutsche, die vor Arbeitsbeginn die Büroduschen im Keller des Amtsgebäudes benutzten. Entspannt waren die Niederländer mit ihren »Omafietsen« oder die Kollegen aus den romanischen Ländern, sie radelten gemächlich im Anzug, ohne zu schwitzen, man fuhr nebeneinander her und redete und erfuhr dabei mehr als in der Kantine – alle neuen Gerüchte, Intrigen, Karrieresprünge. Diese Radweg-Gespräche waren wichtiger als die Lektüre der European Voice und zumindest so wichtig wie das Studium der Financial Times, um auf dem Laufenden zu sein.

Auf der Rue de l'Écuyer war Bohumil Szmekal, sein Freund und Kollege von der C-1 (»Kulturpolitik und interkultureller Dialog«), zum Pulk gestoßen, keine zweihundert Meter weiter auf der Rue d'Arenberg hörten sie die Rufe von Kassándra Mercouri, der Büroleiterin von Fenia Xenopoulou. Bohumil und Martin bremsten ab und warteten, bis Kassándra zu ihnen aufgeschlossen hatte, ließen den Pulk ziehen und radelten zu dritt weiter.

Hast du schon eine Idee?, fragte Bohumil. Dann rief er aufgeregt »Pass auf!« und zeigte auf ein Auto, das vor ihnen auf dem Radweg parkte. Er holte blitzschnell einen Aufkleber aus seiner Umhängetasche, löste, freihändig weiterfahrend, die Folie ab, und schlug vorbeikurvend den Aufkleber an das Seitenfenster des Wagens. Es gab ein Hupkonzert.

Peng! Der hat gesessen!, sagte er triumphierend.

Du mit deinen Stickern bist eine größere Gefahr als die Autos, sagte Kassándra. Sie war eine mollige, stets besorgt oder gütig blickende Frau Mitte dreißig, neben der der kleine, zarte Bohumil, obwohl einige Jahre älter, wie ein schlimmer Junge wirkte. Er grinste. Jetzt sag schon: Hast du die erlösende Idee gehabt? Die Arbeit der ganzen Direktion ist völlig blockiert, weil noch immer keiner –

Was für eine Idee? Ich weiß nicht, was du meinst!

Das Big Jubilee Project! Du hast die Rundmail noch nicht beantwortet. Ich übrigens auch nicht.

Das Big Jubilee Project? Ich dachte, das muss man nicht kommentieren!

Ja. Alle stellen sich tot. Da kommt nichts. Findet keiner wichtig. Kein Wunder, wenn ich an den Reinfall von vor fünf Jahren denke!

Da war ich noch nicht da.

Wieso Reinfall? Die Zeremonie im Parlament mit den Kinderbotschaftern war doch sehr berührend! Kinder aus ganz Europa! Wie sie ihre Wünsche an die Zukunft, Friede und –

Sándra, bitte! Kinderbotschafter! Das war Kindesmissbrauch! Zum Glück hat die Öffentlichkeit nichts bemerkt! Also meine Idee ist: – Achtung! Er verriss das Rad, drängte Martin in die Mitte der Straße, schon hatte er wieder einen Sticker in der Hand, den er aber fallen ließ, Martin drängte ihn auf den Fahrradweg zurück, schrie: Du bist verrückt!

Ja. Also meine Meinung ist: Aus der Geschichte lernen heißt bekanntlich: Nie wieder! Das darf sich nicht wiederholen. Kein Jubilee mehr! Es ist teuer und peinlich! Ich kann nicht verstehen, warum Xeno das so wichtig nimmt!

Es sind alle Generaldirektionen eingebunden. Wenn sie sich da engagiert, kann sie sich hervortun, sagte Kassándra.

Sie macht jetzt richtig Druck. Heute um elf die Sitzung. Sie will unsere Ideen hören.

Ich habe das ganz anders verstanden, sagte Martin. Ich dachte –

Die Sitzung wird vielleicht verschoben! Es ist noch nicht konfirmiert, aber die Chefin will heute einen kurzfristigen Termin beim Präsidenten. Übrigens: Wisst ihr, was sie gerade liest?

Interessiert mich herzlich wenig!

Du meinst: ein Buch? Xeno liest? Komm, Sándra, du phantasierst!

Ein Buch, ja. Und ich phantasiere nicht. Ich musste es ihr express besorgen. Ihr werdet es nicht glauben!

Sag schon!

Achtung!

Pass auf!

Also. Die Chefin bereitet sich ja seit Tagen generalstabsmäßig auf das Gespräch mit dem Präsidenten vor. Sie will alles von ihm wissen, von seinen Seilschaften bis zu seinem Lieblingsessen, alles, sogar sein Lieblingsbuch. Kann man im Smalltalk vielleicht brauchen. Sie ist da extrem pingelig.

Der Präsident hat ein Lieblingsbuch?

Wahrscheinlich »Der Mann ohne Eigenschaften«!, sagte Martin.

»Der Mann ohne Eigenschaften«? Das wäre ein guter Titel für seine Autobiographie!

Kinder, bitte! Hört zu! Sie hat das über private Kanäle herausgefunden. Der Präsident hat wirklich ein Lieblingsbuch! Einen Roman! Das ist nicht öffentlich bekannt! Und er hat davon offenbar mehrere Exemplare, weil er immer wieder darin liest. Eines liegt neben seinem Bett. Eines liegt auf seinem Schreibtisch im Büro. Wahrscheinlich liegt noch eines im Apartment seiner Freundin! Kassándras Gesicht glänzte. Ein leichter Schweißfilm? Vergnügen? Wie auch immer, sagte sie, ich musste das Buch besorgen, und die Chefin liest es jetzt! Xeno liest Literatur, dachte Martin verwundert, einen Roman! Für ihre Karriere ist sie sogar bereit, einen Roman zu lesen.

Fenia Xenopoulou saß an ihrem Schreibtisch und las. Was sie las, machte sie fassungslos. Sie konnte sehr schnell lesen, sie hatte gelernt, die Seiten geradezu zu scannen, die Informationen sofort in ihrem Kopf in Schubladen zu ordnen, aus denen sie sie bei Bedarf blitzschnell hervorholen konnte. Aber das war ein Roman. Dafür hatte sie kein Raster, worum ging es da? Was waren die Informationen, die sich als brauchbar erweisen könnten, was in Gottes Namen sollte sie sich merken? Da wurde das Leben eines Mannes erzählt, gut und schön, aber: Was ging sie dieser wildfremde Mensch an? Noch dazu hatte er in einer ganz anderen Zeit gelebt, so denkt und handelt ja heute niemand mehr. Überhaupt: Hatte er wirklich gelebt, oder war das alles nur erfunden? Laut Google hatte es diesen Mann tatsächlich gegeben, er soll zu seiner Zeit eine bedeutsame Rolle gespielt haben, mit Auswirkungen auf die politische Ordnung des Kontinents und letztlich der ganzen Welt. Aber ganz so bedeutend konnte er auch nicht gewesen sein, denn sonst hätte sie doch von ihm in der Schule gehört. Er war wohl eher ein Fall für Spezialisten, und selbst die waren sich nicht einig, wie die Rolle, die dieser Mann gespielt hatte, letztlich einzuschätzen war.

Sie blätterte ungeduldig weiter, übersprang ein Kapitel. Sie verstand das nicht: Da ging es – zumindest bis jetzt – gar nicht um politische Entscheidungen. Sondern um Liebe. Das Ganze war aus dem Blickwinkel einer Frau geschrieben, die diesen Mann liebte. Aber der Name der Frau kam in dem Wikipedia-Eintrag dieses Mannes nicht vor. Und es war auch nicht klar, ob sie ihn wirklich liebte, also bis jetzt war das noch nicht klar. Sie fühlte sich jedenfalls herausgefordert, seine Aufmerksamkeit zu erobern, Einfluss auf ihn zu bekommen. Aber wenn diese Frau eine Erfindung der Romanautorin war, welchen Sinn sollte es haben, zu lesen, wie sie, eine Fiktion, Macht über einen Mann zu erlangen versuchte, der in historischen Zeiten tatsächlich Macht gehabt hatte? Wenn die Autorin zeigen wollte, wie eine Frau Macht über mächtige Männer gewinnen kann, warum hat sie nicht einen Ratgeber geschrieben? Es kamen Intrigen vor und neckische Spielchen, Kämpfe mit politischen Konkurrenten, aber letztlich – Fenia blätterte weiter, las, immer ungeduldiger, las eine Seite, blätterte zehn Seiten weiter – letztlich lief es auf die Liebe hinaus beziehungsweise darauf, wie bedeutungslos politische Macht wurde, wenn es um die Macht der Liebe ging. Konnte man das so sagen? Das war doch verrückt. Romane sind verrückt!

Fenia lehnte sich zurück. Das war das Lieblingsbuch des Präsidenten? Der Präsident war verrückt! Diese vielen Gedanken! Was sie dachte, was er dachte, woher wollte die Autorin das wissen? Wenn es diesen Mann wirklich gegeben hatte, dann gab es zweifellos Quellen in Archiven, Dokumente, Verträge, Urkunden, aber Gedanken? Gedanken werden und wurden doch nie auf Urkunden festgehalten. Wer bei Sinnen ist, vermeidet doch alles, was dazu führen könnte, dass seine Gedanken gelesen werden können.

Sie schloss die Augen, dachte plötzlich an den gestrigen Abend mit Fridsch, die Nacht. Hatte sie wirklich gedacht, dass er – hatte er gedacht, dass sie –

Sie saß starr da, aber sie meinte zu schwanken. Sie riss die Augen auf, gab sich einen Ruck – und in diesem Moment sah sie auf dem Bildschirm des Computers: Neue Nachricht von Kassándra Mercouri. »Termin beim Präsidenten heute leider doch nicht möglich. Büro des Präsidenten macht Terminvorschläge in den nächsten Tagen.«

Sie schlug das Buch zu, schob es weg.

An: B. Szmekal (»Interkultureller Dialog«), M. Susman (»Maßnahmen Kultur«), H. Athanasiadis (»Valorisierung«), C. Pinheiro da Silva (»Sprachenvielfalt«), A. Klein (»Medienkompetenz«)

– Fenia hielt kurz inne, dann löschte sie Helene Athanasiadis –

Betreff: Jubilee Project

Terminbestätigung: 11 Uhr Besprechungszimmer. Ich erwarte Vorschläge.

Das Telefon läutete, Martin Susman sah auf das Display, es war eine lokale, eine Brüsseler Nummer, die er nicht kannte, er hob ab und bereute es augenblicklich. Es war sein Bruder.

Ich bin's!

Ja. Hallo Florian!

Du weißt doch, dass ich nach Brüssel komme.

Ja.

Ich habe seit Tagen versucht, dich zu erreichen. Du hebst nicht ab.

–

Gestern Abend habe ich mindestens zehn Mal angerufen. Warum hebst du nie ab? Oder rufst zurück?

Gestern Abend? Da gab es ein Problem.

Du hast immer Probleme. Ich habe auch Probleme, deshalb –

Da war –

Ich bin jedenfalls angekommen. Bin schon im Hotel. Im Marriott. Ich habe jetzt gleich meinen ersten Termin. Treffen wir uns zum Abendessen? Wie lange wirst du arbeiten?

Bis sieben, halb acht.

Gut. Hol mich um halb neun ab.

Im Hotel?

Natürlich im Hotel. Und dann zeigst du mir ein Lokal, wo man rauchen kann.

Man kann nirgends rauchen.

Das gibt es nicht. Also halb neun. Und sei pünktlich, kleiner Bruder!

Das Big Jubilee Project. Eigentlich ist es Mrs Atkinson gewesen, die diese Idee gehabt hatte. Sie war die neue Generaldirektorin der DG KOMM, des Kommunikationsdiensts der Europäischen Kommission, verantwortlich auch für deren Corporate Image – und dieses war, wie die letzte Eurobarometer-Umfrage zeigte, in den Keller gerasselt. Das war ihr augenblicklich klar: Sie musste die Generaldirektion anders führen als ihre Vorgänger. Brave Pressearbeit, routinierter Spokesman-Service und die formale Koordination der verschnarchten Infobüros in den Mitgliedstaaten werden nicht genügen. Es gab nicht nur die schlechtesten Werte seit 1973, dem Beginn der regelmäßigen Meinungsumfragen in den Ländern der EU, die aktuellen Umfrage-Ergebnisse musste man als Super-GAU bezeichnen: Ein halbes Jahr zuvor hatten noch rund 49 Prozent der EU-Bürger die Arbeit der Kommission grundsätzlich positiv bewertet, und schon dieses Ergebnis war als »historischer Tiefststand« bezeichnet worden, unvorstellbar, dass er noch unterschritten werden konnte. Nun lag die Zahl

– unter Ausnützung aller Möglichkeiten der Schönfärberei –
bei knapp 40 Prozent, der größte Absturz in der Geschichte
des Eurobarometers, größer noch als der Einbruch der Zu-
stimmungsrate im Jahr 1999, als die Kommission wegen eines
Korruptionsskandals geschlossen zurücktreten musste. Damals
war der Sinkflug von 67 Prozent auf 59 Prozent als Katastrophe erlebt worden – aber was war das jetzt? Und warum?

Mrs Atkinson studierte die Papiere, Tabellen, Prozentrech-
nungen, Graphiken, Statistiken, und sie fragte sich, wie
es zu diesem dramatischen Vertrauensverlust in die Institution hatte kommen können. Der neue Kommissionspräsident
war mit großen Vorschusslorbeeren in den europäischen Leit-
medien bedacht worden, aber profitiert hat davon nicht die
Kommission, sondern das Europäische Parlament, dessen
Ansehen um fast fünf Prozentpunkte gestiegen war. Der Präsident hat es erstmals in der Geschichte geschafft, die Frauenquote zu erfüllen, und zwar nicht nur bei den Mitgliedern
der Kommission – zwölf von achtundzwanzig waren nun Frau-
en –, sondern auch auf der Leitungsebene der Generaldirektionen: Der Frauenanteil lag nun bei knapp 40 Prozent. Sie
selbst hatte davon profitiert, was sie, wie sie sagte, zugeben
konnte, ohne ihre Qualifikation in Frage zu stellen – im Gegenteil, es war der konsequenten Umsetzung der Quote zu
verdanken, dass Mrs Atkinson nicht dem völlig unqualifi-
zierten Karrieristen George Morland unterlegen ist, diesem
Schwein, das für diese Position zunächst im Gespräch gewesen war und das nun herumrennt und ein karikaturhaftes Bild
von ihr zeichnet, als typisches Beispiel für die Idiotie der
Quote. Ihr ist zu Ohren gekommen, dass er herumerzählt, dass
sie so eiskalt sei, dass sie selbst unter ihren kalten Händen leide und deshalb immer mit einem riesigen Muff am Schreibtisch sitze – na ja, Frauen!

Eine solche Phantasie sagte wohl alles über diesen Intriganten aus: dass er sie mit einem riesigen Muff assoziierte, zeigte eindeutig seinen typisch britischen männlichen Oberschicht-Horror vor der Vagina.

Mrs Atkinson hatte Marketing und Management an der European Business School in London studiert und mit einer Arbeit »über kontrainduktives Marketing« bravourös abgeschlossen. Sie überlegte, ob sie, um Mr Morlands Intrigen den Wind aus den Segeln zu nehmen, die Geschichte nicht offensiv wenden und den Muff zu ihrem Markenzeichen machen sollte, einen riesigen, überdimensionierten Muff, wodurch Morlands Karikatur geistlos, zugleich aber als Verstärkung der Marke wirken würde. Aber das war es nicht, was sie jetzt beschäftigte. Sie fragte sich, warum auch dieser Erfolg der Kommission, die Frauenquote, dieses deutliche Signal für die Chancen der Frauen auf diesem Kontinent, das Image der Kommission nicht verbessert hatte. Der Anteil der Frauen im Europäischen Parlament lag bloß bei 35 Prozent, aber das Ansehen des Parlaments wuchs, auch bei weiblichen Wählern aller Altersstufen, was ja in Ordnung war, aber das der Kommission stürzte ab, und das war rätselhaft, das war das Problem – diesen Trend zu stoppen und umzudrehen war nun ihre Aufgabe. Was waren die Kritikpunkte, was war der Grund für das schlechte Image der Kommission? Klischees. Vorurteile. Immer dasselbe. Mangelnde demokratische Legitimation, wuchernde Bürokratie, Regulierungswahn. Bezeichnend fand sie, dass es keine Kritik an den eigentlichen Aufgaben der Kommission gab, offenbar waren diese den Menschen gar nicht bekannt. »Mischt sich in Belange ein, die besser national geregelt werden sollten« 59 Prozent, aber »Erfüllt ihre Aufgaben schlecht« oder »sehr schlecht« bekam zusammen nur knapp 5 Prozent Zustimmung. Diesen Wiederspruch musste man sich klarmachen. Sie fragte sich, warum keiner ihrer Vorgänger die Methode der Eurobarometer-

Umfrage kritisiert und eine Änderung durchgesetzt hatte. Wenn man den Menschen anbietet, den Satz »Mischt sich in Belange ein, die besser national geregelt werden sollten« anzukreuzen, dann wird ein bestimmter Prozentsatz das tun. Diese Ist-ja-wahr-Typen, die Sage-ich-ja-immer-Idioten! Würde man aber formulieren, dass die Kommission die Bürger vor Ungerechtigkeiten schützt, die durch Unterschiede zwischen nationalen Rechtssystemen entstehen – dann wäre das Ergebnis doch gleich ein ganz anderes.

Das war ihr jetzt klar: Ihre Aufgabe konnte es nicht sein, das Image »der EU« zu verbessern, sie musste sich gezielt um das Image der Europäischen Kommission kümmern. Und die Idee, wie ihr das gelingen könnte, hatte sie eine Stunde später, beschwingt von Champagner Charlemagne Brut. Denn in diesem Moment sprang die Tür zu ihrem Zimmer auf, sie sah Catherine, ihre Sekretärin, mit einer Torte, auf der Wunderkerzen brannten, hereinkommen, hinter dem Rauch und den Sternchenfunken sah sie – tatsächlich: Das war der Präsident, und hinter ihm drängten immer mehr Menschen in den Raum, ihr Kommissar, Direktoren, Referenten, ihr ganzes Büro, und sangen »Happy Birthday«.

Sie hatte einen runden Geburtstag. Ach ja. Sie hatte dem keine Bedeutung beigemessen. Ihr Mann war in London. Ihre Tochter in New York. Beide hatten kurz angerufen. Und Freunde, mit denen sie hätte feiern wollen – hatte sie noch keine, hier in Brüssel. Und jetzt stand sie im Mittelpunkt. Überraschung. Der Präsident sprach. Einige Worte. Nicht förmlich, sehr persönlich, auch eine kleine Anspielung auf ihr Image – die sich in allgemeinem Gelächter auflöste. Menschen, die sie nur vom Grüßen kannte, zweiter dritter vierter Stock, lachten ihr zu, Champagnergläser schäumten, klirrten beim Anstoßen, sie wurde auf die Wangen geküsst, man drückte ihr den Arm, klopfte ihr auf die Schulter, Menschen, die nichts oder nur wenig von ihr wussten, zeigten ihr Sympathie oder Bereitschaft zu Sympathie, der Kommissar hob das Glas, sagte, wie sehr er sich freue, diese kompetente und überhaupt so wunderbare Mitarbeiterin in seinem Team zu haben, in dieser wichtigen Funktion, wie gut, dass es die Quote gebe, er persönlich sei ja für eine Frauenquote von 99 Prozent, selbst wolle er seinen Job natürlich nicht verlieren, aber sonst wäre er froh, wenn er nur Frauen … – Pfiffe der Männer, Macho!-Macho!-Rufe der Frauen, alles ging in Gelächter über, und Mrs Atkinson schnitt die Torte an, die nun auf der Eurobarometer-Akte auf ihrem Schreibtisch stand, Brösel und Creme auf den Statistiken, Asche von den Wunderkerzen auf dem Grab der europäischen Stimmung.

Und dann war sie wieder allein, alle waren an die Arbeit zurückgekehrt, und sie stand am großen Fenster ihres Büros, sah hinunter auf die Rue de la Loi, auf das Band der vorbeikriechenden dunklen Autos, die im leichten Regen glänzten, sie rieb sich die Hände, strich abwechselnd mit der einen Hand über den Rücken der anderen, massierte und knetete ihre Finger, die sehr lang und zart waren und dazu neigten, plötzlich die Farbe zu verlieren und weiß und gefühllos zu werden. Dann setzte sie sich wieder an den Schreibtisch, irgendetwas arbeitete in ihr, sie wartete darauf, dass es ihr klarer wurde, da stand noch ein halbvolles Glas Champagner, sie nippte daran, dachte nach, trank das Glas aus. Sie knetete ihre Finger, dann googelte sie: »Europäische Kommission Gründung«. Wann hatte die Kommission eigentlich Geburtstag? Gab es so etwas wie einen Geburtstag der Kommission? Der Tag der Gründung? Das war die Idee: Es genügte nicht, die tägliche Arbeit der Kommission möglichst gut zu verkaufen, man musste sie hochleben lassen, man musste die Menschen dazu bringen, ihr zu gratulieren, dass es sie gab, man musste sie feiern, statt bloß um Akzeptanz zu betteln, Klischees richtigzustellen und Gerüchten und Legenden zu widersprechen. Man musste die Kommission ins Zentrum stellen und nicht immer abstrakt und allgemein »die EU«. Was ist schon die EU? Verschiedene Institutionen, die ihr je eigenes Süppchen kochten und unterschiedliche Interessen vertraten, aber wenn das Ganze einen Sinn hatte, dann deshalb, weil es die Kommission gab, die doch für das Ganze stand. So sah sie das. Man musste eine Situation herstellen, in der die Kommission fröhlich im Mittelpunkt stand, als Geburtstagskind, dem man gratulierte. Hatte die Kommission also einen Geburtstag? Das war nicht so einfach zu entscheiden. War es der Tag der Gründung der EWG-Kommission oder das Datum der Gründung der Europäischen Kommission in ihrer heutigen Form nach dem EG-Fusionsvertrag? In dem einen Fall wurde die Kommission in drei Jahren sechzig, in dem anderen Fall in zwei Jahren fünfzig. Fünfzig gefiel ihr besser. Ein halbes Jahrhundert. Das war besser zu verkaufen. Und umgelegt auf ein Menschenalter: voll im Saft, erfahren, noch nicht im Übergang zu Alteisen. Außerdem waren zwei Jahre eine vernünftige Zeitspanne für eine perfekte Vorbereitung, während drei Jahre unter Umständen zu lang wären, da konnte zu viel noch aus dem Ruder laufen.

Sie recherchierte weiter. Hatte es bereits Jubiläen gegeben? Ja. Hilflose, halbherzige Feiern mit Sonntagsreden, Würdigungen von Vorgängern, ein bisschen Weihrauch für die Vorstufen der EU, fünfzig Jahre Römische Verträge, sechzig Jahre Gründung der Montanunion – wen hatte das interessiert? Niemand. Und was hat man sich davon versprochen, den EU-Skeptikern und Gegnern zu erzählen, wie schön die Gründung der Montanunion war? Als würde man einem Opa, der an Demenz litt, dazu gratulieren, dass es eine Zeit gab, in der er bei Sinnen war – während die Enkel unbeeindruckt längst alles ganz anders machten.

Grace Atkinson sah auf dem Glastisch vor der Sitzgruppe eine offene Flasche Champagner. Da war noch ein kleiner Rest in der Flasche, sie schenkte sich ein, trank. Sie war beschwingt, als sie beschloss, eine Mail an einige Abteilungen zu schicken, von denen sie glaubte, Interesse an ihrem Plan, Unterstützung und Ideen erwarten zu können. Sie musste zunächst informell Mitstreiter gewinnen, bevor sie die formelle Prozedur beginnen konnte. Ein großes Geburtstagsfest anlässlich des kommenden 50-Jahr-Jubiläums der Gründung der Europäischen Kommission, so schrieb sie, erscheine ihr als Möglichkeit, die Aufgaben und Leistungen dieser Institution in den Mittelpunkt der öffentlichen Aufmerksamkeit zu stellen, ihre Corporate Identity zu stärken, ihr Image zu verbessern, sie fröhlich zu feiern und somit aus der Defensive zu kommen.

Sie löschte das Wort »fröhlich«, dann setzte sie es wieder ein, nickte, darum ging es doch, sie rieb sich die Hände und ging aufs Ganze. In die Betreff-Zeile schrieb sie: »Big Jubilee Project – Ende der Weinerlichkeit«.

Es war Mrs Atkinsons Idee gewesen. Fenia Xenopoulou war die Erste, die darauf reagierte – und das Projekt rasch an sich zog. Das gehörte ins Kulturressort, fand Fenia, keine Frage. Das war die Chance, auf die sie gewartet hatte, um Visibilité zu zeigen. Und sie machte Martin Susman zu ihrem Sherpa, der die Last des Projekts schleppen sollte.

Grace Atkinson war zunächst froh, dass sie so schnell eine so begeisterte Mitstreiterin gefunden hatte. Und am Ende war sie heilfroh, denn durch das überdeutliche Engagement der unglückseligen Kultur geriet in Vergessenheit, dass sie es gewesen war, die diese letztlich katastrophale Idee gehabt hatte.

Ich erwarte Vorschläge, hatte Fenia Xenopoulou mit aufgeregtem Tonfall gesagt, es ist von größter Bedeutung, und ich weiß, dass ihr – Sie sah in die Runde und sagte viel zu laut einige Sätze mit großen und dramatischen Adjektiven, sie hielt das wohl für animierend, diese Korporalsprache zur Truppe, und Martin hatte den Blick gesenkt, um ihrem Blick auszuweichen, weshalb er Fenia jetzt kopflos sah, er sah jetzt nur ihr hautenges Top, den straffen, enganliegenden Rock, die Beine in der blickdichten Strumpfhose, und er dachte: Diese Frau steckt in einem Korsett, in einer Rüstung, die sie zusammenhält. Der Rock war aus feinstem Tuch, aber Martin hatte den Eindruck, der Rock würde in Scherben zerspringen, wenn man draufschlüge. Man konnte ihn nicht ausziehen, man müsste ihn aufbrechen und –

Also was sollen wir tun?

Bohumil war wieder einmal ironisch destruktiv. Zunächst einmal, sagte er, was sollten wir nicht tun? Unbedingt alles vermeiden, was bisher bei Jubiläen gemacht wurde: Peinlichkeiten, gemildert durch weitgehenden Ausschluss der Öffentlichkeit. Hochglanzbroschüren für die Altpapiercontainer. Sonntagsreden an Arbeitstagen.

Martin?

Er hatte Fenias Reaktion auf Bohumils Statement nicht gesehen, er starrte auf ihre Füße, auf die kleinen Wülste über dem Ausschnitt ihrer engen Schuhe.

Martin?

Mich interessiert die Sache nicht, hätte Martin am liebsten gesagt. Er beschloss, ganz einfach allen recht zu geben, um sich nicht zu exponieren.

In Anbetracht der Bedeutung dieser Angelegenheit, sagte er in Richtung Fenia, sei klar, dass – und nun in Richtung Bohumil: – die Fehler der Vergangenheit nicht wiederholt werden dürfen. Bohumil habe recht, wenn er daran erinnere, dass – aber Fenia habe natürlich absolut recht, wenn sie erwarte, dass. Was seien die Fehler bei bisherigen Jubiläen gewesen? Es habe keine andere Idee gegeben, als diese: anlassbedingt ein Jubiläum zu feiern. Aber der Anlass allein sei eben noch keine Idee. Dass eine Institution so und so viele Jahre existiere – gut und schön, aber was ist die Idee, welche Idee stellt man in den Mittelpunkt? Sie muss überzeugend sein, sie muss die Menschen so begeistern, dass sie zu diesem Anlass wirklich feiern wollen.

So war Martin Susman in die Falle getappt. Nach einigem Hin und Her sagte Fenia Xenopoulou: Schluss jetzt, der Einzige, der sich offenbar Gedanken gemacht habe, sei Martin. Es sei absolut logisch, was er gesagt habe. Das Um und Auf sei eine zentrale Idee. Sie beauftragte Martin, die Idee zu entwickeln und ein entsprechendes Papier zu schreiben. Wie viel Zeit er dafür veranschlage?

Zwei Monate!? Das müsse gründlich überlegt, mit Kollegen auch anderer Generaldirektionen diskutiert werden.

Eine Woche, sagte Fenia.

Unmöglich. Nächste Woche habe er die Dienstreise, die auch einige Vorbereitung erfordere und –

Also gut, zwei Wochen, einige Bullet-Points, das wirst du doch schaffen! Und mit den Kollegen werden wir erst diskutieren, wenn wir das Papier vorgelegt haben. Alles klar? Wir legen vor!

Martin Susman war wütend und gereizt, als er um sechs nach Hause fuhr, nachdem er den wichtigsten Tageskram erledigt hatte. Auf halber Strecke begann es zu regnen, den Regenponcho hatte er in der Fahrradtasche, die Fahrradtasche aber hatte er im Büro vergessen. Er kam völlig durchnässt und frierend zu Hause an und ging sofort unter die Dusche. Allerdings wurde das Wasser nicht richtig heiß, und der Duschvorhang, wie magnetisch angezogen, schmiegte sich kalt an seinen Rücken. Wütend schlug er ihn weg, wodurch er ihn halb von der Stange riss. Sofort am nächsten Tag musste er veranlassen, diesen blöden Vorhang durch eine Duschkabinentür zu ersetzen, und er wusste, dass dies nur wieder eine der Ideen war, die er nie in die Tat umsetzen würde. Er schlüpfte in den Bademantel, holte eine Flasche Jupiler aus dem Kühlschrank und setzte sich in den Fauteuil vor dem offenen Kamin. Er musste sich beruhigen, einatmen ausatmen, entspannen. Er starrte auf die Bücher im offenen Kamin.

Als Martin Susman hier eingezogen war, hatte er zunächst seinen Augen nicht getraut. Der Kamin war nicht mehr in Betrieb, seit die Wohnung mit einer Zentralheizung ausgestattet worden war. Der Vermieter hatte zwei Bretter in den Kamin montiert und Bücher daraufgestellt. Fand er wahrscheinlich nett und heimelig. Martin hatte das später auch bei Freunden und Bekannten in anderen Brüsseler Altbauwohnungen gesehen: Bücher in den nicht mehr benutzten Kaminen.

In Martins Kamin standen verschiedene Brüsseler Stadtführer, alte, zerfledderte Ausgaben, wahrscheinlich von Vormietern zurückgelassen, ein paar Bände eines Konversationslexikons aus dem Jahr 1914, drei Atlanten, einer von 1910, einer von 1943, der dritte von 1955, und ein gutes Dutzend Bände aus der Reihe »Klassiker der Weltliteratur« vom Flämischen Buchclub: »In jedem Band vier klassische Werke in zeitgemäßer Kürzung«, erschienen in den sechziger Jahren. Als Martin die Wohnung bezogen und eines Abends die Bücher durchgesehen hatte, war er schockiert gewesen, nein, das ist ein zu großes Wort, unangenehm berührt: Sollte das der Fortschritt sein – Bücher nicht mehr zu verbrennen, sondern bloß »zeitgemäß gekürzt« in einen kalten Kamin zu stellen?

Jetzt starrte er auf die Buchrücken, trank sein Bier, rauchte ein paar Zigaretten. Das Papier für das Jubiläumsprojekt – das war eine Zumutung. Als wäre er ein Werbetexter, der das Produkt EU-Kommission verkaufen soll. Er sah hinüber zu seinem Schreibtisch, da stand immer noch der Teller mit dem eingetrockneten und verkrusteten Senf. Was ist die Idee von Senf? Wir geben ihn dazu. Genial. Überzeugende Fernsehwerbung: Junge schöne Menschen drücken selig lachend Senf auf Teller, singen verzückt: Juhu, Juhu, wir geben ihn dazu! Und können sich nicht einkriegen vor Glück. Und die Senfkringel auf den Tellern schrauben sich rhythmisch in die Höhe, beginnen zu tanzen, wie zu den Flötentönen eines Schlangenbeschwörers: Juhu, Juhu, wir gehören dazu! Das war doch – er gab sich einen Ruck, zog sich an und machte sich auf den Weg ins Marriott. Er nahm den klassischen »Long«, der bot im Regen auch Schutz für zwei.

Es hatte zu regnen aufgehört. Der nasse Asphalt, die Hausfassaden und die Passanten schimmerten im Licht der Laternen und der Leuchtröhren der Frittenbude, als hätte ein flämischer Meister soeben den Firnis auf dieses Bild aufgetragen. Martin hatte diese Abendstimmung nach Regentagen in Brüssel mittlerweile schon so oft erlebt, dass sie ihm bereits eine Art Heimatgefühl gab. Ja, hier war er zu Hause. Er kaufte Zigaretten beim Inder im Night-Shop Ecke Rue Sainte-Catherine. Nach dem Bezahlen sagte der Inder immer »Dank u wel«, wenn Martin Französisch sprach, und »Merci, Monsieur«, wenn Martin auf Flämisch um seine Zigarettenmarke gebeten hatte. Das könnte man interpretieren, aber vielleicht gab es da auch nichts zu interpretieren, es war so, und irgendwann gehörte es, wie viele andere Kleinigkeiten, einfach dazu: zu Martins Gefühl, hier irgendwie zwischen vielen Welten zu Hause zu sein.

Der Wind war zwar nicht stark, aber kalt, Martin ging sehr schnell und kam natürlich viel zu früh am Marriott an. Sein

Bruder aber wartete bereits in der Hotel-Lobby, mit einem Gesichtsausdruck – so streng und selbstgerecht, ein Gesicht, das sagte: Ich habe immer die Gebote Gottes befolgt, da kann ich doch erwarten, dass.

Martin kannte dieses Gesicht nur zu gut. Immer wenn er seinen Bruder traf, sah er in ihm den Vater.

Sie begrüßten sich mit einer Umarmung, die noch sperriger ausfiel als sonst, weil Florian dabei eine Mappe an sich drückte.

Nehmen wir ein Taxi?

Nein. Ich habe im Belga Queen reserviert. Fünf Minuten zu Fuß.

Sie gingen schweigend. Schließlich fragte Martin:

Wie geht es Renate?

Gut.

Und den Kindern?

Sie sind fleißig. Gott sei Dank!

Nicht dass Martin sich seiner Herkunft schämte. Er wusste bloß nicht, ob er ein Problem damit hatte, dass sie ihm so fremd geworden war, oder damit, dass sie ihn, obwohl sie ihm so fremd geworden war, immer wieder einholte. Der Vater war vor achtzehn Jahren am 2. November gestorben, also just am Allerseelentag. Viel zu früh und so entsetzlich tragisch. Solange Martin in Österreich gelebt hatte, musste er das Trauma an jedem 2. November aufs Neue durchleben. Wenn er Zeitung las, fernsah oder auch nur das Haus verließ, wurde er schon Tage vor jedem 2. November daran erinnert: Es kommt Allerseelen. Und damit: Vaters Todestag. Und es war klar, dass er nach Hause fahren musste, da gab es keine Ausrede, weil es ein staatlicher Feiertag war, ein allgemeiner morbider Gedenktag. In Brüssel gab es am 2. November keinen Feiertag. Die eigene, die private Geschichte konnte hier absinken oder könnte, aber wenn sein Bruder kam, war augenblicklich Allerseelentag. Unausgesprochen. Der Vater war in die Maschine gekommen. Immer wieder hieß es, er sei in die Maschine gekommen. Als hätten sie nur eine Maschine gehabt. Es war der Feinbrecher. Wie immer es geschehen konnte, er ist mit dem Arm in das Mahlwerk gekommen, die Maschine hat ihn regelrecht gefressen, und er ist verblutet. Er hat geschrien wie ein Schwein. Das war der Satz: Er hat geschrien wie ein Schwein. Später gab es Stimmen, die sagten, ja, sie hätten es gehört. Aber warum war keiner zu Hilfe gekommen? Weil es das Natürlichste, das Normalste, das Gewohnte auf diesem Hof war: die Schreie der Schweine. Bei rund eintausendzweihundert Schweinen und täglichen Schlachtungen auf diesem Hof, da interpretiert man doch einen einzelnen Schrei nicht mehr heraus. Das hatte der Felber gesagt, der Schlachtmeister. »Herausinterpretieren« hat er gesagt. Aber wieso weiß man dann, dass er geschrien hat wie ein Schwein? Er muss doch geschrien haben – das haben alle gesagt. Da waren sich alle einig. Er muss unglaublich geschrien haben. Aber nur kurz. Man verliert da ja sehr schnell das Bewusstsein. Das war es eben. Es geht so schnell. Natürlich begreifen die Schweine etwas, wenn sie – aber ruck, zuck sind sie betäubt. Und schon frisst sie die Maschine. So fleißig ist der Vater gewesen, hat zwischendurch noch liegengebliebene Tierabfälle zermahlen wollen. Der Betrieb war damals zwar schon unglaublich gewachsen, aber noch nicht so logistisch perfekt durchorganisiert wie heute. Die Mutter hat den Arzt angerufen, aber sie war natürlich völlig von Sinnen – und hat den Dr. Schafzahl angerufen, den Tierarzt. Aber es war ohnehin schon alles zu spät. Einige Tage später hat der sechzehnjährige Martin in der Schule lachend erzählt, dass die Mutter den Dr. Schafzahl gerufen hat, und als keiner gelacht hatte, noch einmal: den Schafzahl zum Schweinebauern. Dann ist er tagelang still gewesen und schließlich zum Pfarrer beichten gegangen, um für die Sünde, nach dem Tod seines Vaters einen Witz gemacht zu haben, Absolution zu erhalten.

Der vier Jahre ältere Bruder hat dann den Hof übernommen, der Kronprinz, das war ohnehin immer so ausgemacht und geplant gewesen, nur eben nicht so bald, und er, Martin, der Zweitgeborene, der »Narrische«, der Ungeschickte (»Kein Wunder, wenn er immer nur liest!«), durfte studieren, das war auch immer klar gewesen: Er durfte studieren, was er wollte, und »was er wollte« bedeutete, dass der Familie egal war, was er machte, solange er keine Ansprüche stellte und nicht zur Last fiel. Archäologie.

Als die Susman-Brüder das Restaurant Belga Queen betraten, ging Florian langsam in die Mitte des Saals, ignorierte den Kellner, der sich ihm in den Weg stellte, und rief: He! Was ist das denn? Eine Kathedrale?

Martin sagte dem Kellner, sie hätten reserviert, Dr. Susman, und zu Florian: Nein, eine ehemalige Bank. Schönstes Art déco. Wir essen hier im ehemaligen Kassensaal, und dann gehen wir in den Keller, in den Tresorraum, das ist jetzt die Raucherlounge.

Martin war abgefunden worden, als Florian den Hof ganz übernommen hatte und die Mutter in Pension gegangen war, ausbezahlt mit einer Summe, die bis zu seiner Volljährigkeit treuhänderisch verwaltet worden war und die er nie in Frage gestellt und über die er nie diskutiert hatte. Dieses Geld hatte ihm ermöglicht, bequem zu studieren und sich dann auch noch ohne Druck umzuschauen, was er beruflich machen wollte. Es ist, wenn man vom Betriebswert ausging, sicherlich nicht gerecht zugegangen, aber Martin ist das egal gewesen, es hatte gereicht, Möglichkeiten zu eröffnen, und er hatte sie nutzen können. Aber jetzt wurde so getan, als hätte die Familie Martin studieren lassen und ihm diesen Superjob in der Europäischen Kommission verschafft, damit er in dieser Position Lobbyismus für die wirtschaftlichen Interessen seines Bruders betreiben konnte. Das war der Grund, warum Martin sich immer davor fürchtete, wenn Florian sich ansagte und ihn in Brüssel treffen wollte. Florian hatte den Hof, der schon zu Lebzeiten des Vaters sehr stattlich war, zum größten österreichischen Schweineproduktionsbetrieb, zu einem der größten in Europa ausgebaut, schon längst sagte er nicht mehr »Hof«, wie noch der Vater, sondern »Betrieb« – und er war der Meinung, dass es nichts Absurderes gab als die Politik der EU in Hinblick auf Schweineproduktion und -handel. Seiner Meinung nach waren da lauter Ahnungslose oder Verrückte am Werk, bestochen oder erpresst oder ideologisch verblendet von der Tierschützer-Mafia und der Vegetarier-Lobby. Es hatte keinen Sinn, mit ihm darüber zu diskutieren, er meinte das ernst, er sah ja, wie es lief, er kannte die Praxis. Er hatte seine Erfahrungen. Er begann sich politisch zu engagieren, eroberte hohe Ämter in Interessenvertretungen und kam so immer wieder zu Verhandlungen nach Brüssel. Vor kurzem wurde er zum Präsidenten von »The European Pig Producers« gewählt, einem Netzwerk der führenden Schweineproduzenten des Kontinents. In dieser Funktion und zugleich als Bundesinnungsmeister der österreichischen Schweinezüchter hatte er an diesem Tag mehrere Termine mit Abgeordneten des Europäischen Parlaments und mit Beamten der Europäischen Kommission gehabt.

Da schau her!, sagte Florian, als er die Speisekarte studierte, Schweinegulasch in Kirschenbier. Interessant. Wenn das schmeckt, lasse ich mir das Rezept geben. Stelle ich dann auf die Homepage.

Martin bestellte Moules et Frites. Und eine Flasche Wein. Dann sagte er: Wie war dein Tag? Es war eine blöde Phrase, und er versuchte gar nicht, die Frage so zu stellen, als wäre er wirklich interessiert. Er wusste, dass er damit eine Lawine lostrat, aber darum ging es ja, und Martin wollte es hinter sich bringen.

Wie wird mein Tag schon gewesen sein? Was glaubst du denn? Ich hatte mit Idioten zu tun. So ist mein Tag gewesen! Sie begreifen nichts. Sind nicht imstande, ihre Politik zu ändern, aber fordern heute von mir eine Namensänderung!

Namensänderung? Warum sollst du deinen Namen ändern?

»Nicht ich. Erkläre ich dir gleich. Du musst zuerst Folgendes wissen: Jeder Schweineproduzent will natürlich auf den chinesischen Markt. China ist der weltweit größte Importeur von Schweinefleisch. Die Nachfrage aus China ist enorm, das ist der Wachstumsmarkt.

Ist doch gut. Oder?

Ja. Wäre gut. Aber die EU ist unfähig, ein entsprechendes Handelsabkommen mit China zu verhandeln. Die Chinesen verhandeln nicht mit der EU, sondern nur mit jedem Staat einzeln. Und jeder Staat glaubt, er kann für sich allein einen super bilateralen Vertrag abschließen, die anderen ausstechen und alleine größeren Profit machen, aber in Wirklichkeit spielt China nur alle gegeneinander aus. Dabei kann kein einziges Land allein die Größenordnungen stemmen, um die es da geht. Auch in Jahren nicht. Ich gebe dir ein Beispiel: Unlängst in der Innung bekomme ich einen Anruf. Wie viele Schweinsohren kann Österreich liefern? –

Schweinsohren?

Ja, Schweinsohren. Das war jemand vom chinesischen Handelsministerium. Sage ich: Wir schlachten in Österreich jährlich fünf Millionen Schweine. Also zehn Millionen Ohren. Sagt er: zu wenig. Verabschiedet sich höflich und legt auf. Verstehst du: Wenn China sagen wir hundert Millionen Schweinsohren braucht, und es gäbe einen EU-Vertrag mit China, dann könnten wir zehn Prozent der Menge liefern. Aber wie ist die Situation? Österreich hat noch keinen bilateralen Vertrag mit China, ein gemeinsamer Vertrag der EU-Staaten wird nicht verhandelt – und ich kann meine Schweinsohren wegwerfen, in Österreich ist das Schlachtabfall. Dabei sind Schweinsohren in China eine Spezialität, es gibt eine irrsinnige Nachfrage danach, aber wir werfen sie weg oder sind froh, wenn ein Katzenfutterfabrikant sie kostenfrei bei uns abholt.

Aber selbst wenn es Verträge gäbe – man kann ja nicht nur Schweinsohren produzieren, man braucht doch das ganze Schwein dazu. Man kann ja nicht wegen der chinesischen Nachfrage nach Schweinsohren solche Mengen von ganzen Schweinen züchten und füttern und – und was machst du mit dem Rest?

Bist du blöd oder was? Es gibt dann keinen Rest mehr. Den Rest haben wir jetzt. Schlachtabfall. Schweinsohren sind nur ein Beispiel. Die Chinesen nehmen ja nicht nur Schinken, Filet, Speck, Schulter, das sowieso, sondern eben auch die Ohren, Köpfe, Schwänze, die essen alles, die nehmen alles. Was bei uns Schlachtabfall ist, kaufen die auch noch zum Filetpreis. Mit anderen Worten, ein Abkommen für Schweinehandel mit China würde bedeuten: 20 Prozent mehr Umsatz pro Schwein, und auf Grund der Nachfrage mittelfristig ein Wachstum von hundert Prozent, also eine Verdopplung der europäischen Schweineproduktion. Das, verstehst du, das wäre der Wachstumsmarkt. Es gibt keinen Industriezweig, der solche Prognosen hat.

Ich verstehe, sagte Martin, und das war nicht gut, dieses gelangweilte, bemüht geduldige, schlecht gespielt höfliche »Ich verstehe!« Sein Bruder sah ihn auf eine Weise an, dass er erschrak. Schnell sagte er: Ich verstehe nicht. Wenn es diese Möglichkeit gibt und aus China diese Nachfrage, warum –

Weil deine Kollegen verrückt sind. Völlig ahnungslos. Statt die Mitgliedstaaten zu zwingen, der Kommission die Kompetenz zu übertragen, einen EU-Handelsvertrag mit China zu machen, und zugleich mit Förderungen den Ausbau der Schweineproduktion zu finanzieren, schauen sie zu, wie China Teile und Herrsche spielt, und sie treffen Maßnahmen, um die Schweineproduktion in Europa zu reduzieren. Die Kommission ist der Meinung, es gibt in Europa zu viele Schweine. Das führt zu Preisverfall und so weiter. Also was machen sie? Weniger Förderung. Sogar Stilllegungsprämien. So, und jetzt haben wir in Europa folgende Situation: eine Überproduktion für den Binnenmarkt, die zu Preisverfall führt, und zugleich eine Blockade gegenüber einem Markt, für den wir zu wenig produzieren. Maßnahmen, die die Produktion weiter einschränken, gleichzeitig keine Maßnahmen, um auf den Markt zu kommen, auf dem wir doppelt so viel absetzen könnten.

Inzwischen war das Essen gekommen.

Wie schmeckt dein Schwein in Kirschenbier?

Wie? Ach so. Ja, geht. Jedenfalls: Was jetzt also nötig wäre, sind Investitionen, in einer Größenordnung, die kein Betrieb alleine leisten kann. Also Förderungen. Nicht Reduktion. Förderungen, offensive Wachstumspolitik. Verstehst du? Stattdessen bekommen wir Auflagen. Tierschutz. Kastenhaltung wird verboten, Zuluftboxen mit Diffusoren werden verpflichtend. Hdt-System –

Ich will gar nicht fragen, was das ist.

Es ist teuer. Es frisst den Gewinn auf. Hier, ich zeige dir etwas. Er öffnete die Mappe, die er mitgebracht hatte, blätterte, zog ein Blatt heraus.

Hier: EU-Schweinepreis-Statistik des letzten Halbjahres. 15.7.: Preisverfall in Europa: Minus von 18 Prozent. 22.7.: Talsohle erreicht. – Denkste! 19.8.: Wenig Bewegung auf den

Märkten. 9.9.: Schweinepreis um 21 Prozent gefallen. 16.9.: Notierungen stark rückläufig. 21.10.: Schweinepreis gibt 14 Prozent nach – soll ich weiterlesen?

Nein.

Rückläufig, Preisverfall, Talsohle, wieder Preisverfall. Und keine Reaktion von Seiten der EU. Seit Jahresbeginn – schau her! Da! Hier steht es! – seit Jahresbeginn schließen europaweit im Schnitt täglich 48 Schweinebauern die Stalltür für immer. Und Tausende, die versucht haben durchzuhalten, haben ein Verfahren wegen Konkursverschleppung am Hals. Dabei könnten wir doppelt so viel produzieren bei 20 Prozent höheren Abnehmerpreisen für das Schwein als Ganzes – man müsste nur einmal koordiniert in die Infrastruktur investieren und mit China reden. Aber erkläre das einmal dem Herrn Frigge. Der sagt mir, die EU habe in der Schweineproduktion leider eine andere Agenda. Zugleich verbieten sie den Mitgliedstaaten Subventionen, denn das wäre Verzerrung des Wettbewerbs. Kennst du diesen Frigge?

Nein.

Gibt es nicht. Ist ein Kollege von dir. Ich durchschaue sein Spiel nicht. Hör zu: Du musst einmal mit ihm ein Wörtchen reden, du musst ihm so ganz unter euch klarmachen, dass –

Florian! Die Kommission funktioniert nicht wie der österreichische Bauernbund!

Komm mir nicht so! Wozu haben wir dich da drinnen sitzen? Ich verstehe jetzt eines nicht: Du sagtest etwas von einer Namensänderung …? Was wollte Herr Frigge, welchen Namen sollst du ändern?

Nein, das war nicht der Frigge. Das waren die Herren Abgeordneten vom Parlament. Keine Frau dabei. Da hätte ich vielleicht ein bisschen charmieren können, aber nur Männer, und die waren in ihrer Blödheit knallhart. Die waren von der Fraktion der Europäischen Volkspartei. Verstehst du?

Nein.

Europäische Volkspartei. Ich habe erwartet, das wird ein Heimspiel für mich, ich bin ja von der Österreichischen Volkspartei. Hier im Europäischen Parlament heißt die Fraktion EPP, European People's Party.

Und?

Na ja, ich komme hierher als Präsident der European Pig Producers, also auch EPP – verstehst du? Ich hatte das Mandat, zwei Punkte zu verhandeln: Subventionen für den Ausbau der Schweineproduktion und Koordinierung des europäischen Schweineexports. Wir haben keine Minute darüber geredet. Die Abgeordneten sagten, wir müssten zuallererst unseren Namen und unser Logo ändern. Es geht nicht an, dass auf Google, wenn man die Europäische Volkspartei sucht, EPP, sofort nur Schweine auftauchen. Lach nicht! Ich sagte, das ist schwierig. Wir sind eine transnationale Organisation, vereinspolizeilich registriert in jedem einzelnen Mitgliedstaat. Das ist ein enormer Aufwand. Weißt du, was sie vorgeschlagen haben? Wir heißen ja The European Pig Producers, und wir sollen also auch das The ins Kürzel aufnehmen – dann hießen wir TEPP. Unfassbar, diese Zyniker!

Ihr habt aber nicht auf Deutsch verhandelt?

Nein, es war kein Deutscher dabei.

Dann war das nicht zynisch. Die wissen nicht, was TEPP bedeutet.

Florian wischte mit Brot den letzten Rest Gulaschsaft auf, so hatte er es schon als Kind gemacht. Den Teller vom Florian muss man nach dem Essen gar nicht mehr abwaschen, hatte die Mutter immer gesagt.

Ein bisschen süß, diese Kirschenbiersoße. Hast du nicht gesagt, man kann da im Tresor rauchen? Zeig mir das! Ich brauche jetzt dringend eine Zigarette.

Heim gingen sie wie Brüder, Arm in Arm, harmonisch über das Brüsseler Pflaster wankend und schwankend. Sie hatten noch Gin Tonics getrunken und, verführt vom Angebot, Zigarren geraucht. Das zeigte Wirkung, als sie aus den Clubfauteuils aufstanden, und noch heftiger, als sie an die frische Luft kamen. Nachdem Martin seinen Bruder im Hotel abgeliefert hatte, begann es wieder zu regnen und er merkte, dass er den Schirm im Belga Queen vergessen hatte. Er kam völlig durchnässt zu Hause an, zog Jacke und Hose aus, öffnete den Kühlschrank, zögerte kurz, holte dann doch ein Jupiler heraus und setzte sich an den Kamin. Sein Bruder hatte ihm eine Zeitschrift mitgegeben (»Schau, was ich dir mitgebracht habe: Ich bin auf dem Cover!«), die er nun – nicht las, anschaute: »THINK PIG! Das Informationsbulletin der EPP«

Drittes Kapitel

Letztlich ist der Tod auch nur der Beginn
von Folgeerscheinungen.

Auf dem Weg von der Gare Centrale zum Hauptkommissariat in der Rue Marché au Charbon blieb Émile Brunfaut immer wieder stehen, schaute um sich, ließ den Blick über die Fassaden der Häuser gleiten, beobachtete die Menschen, die eine Aufgabe oder ein Ziel hatten und die Stadt gleichsam in Betrieb nahmen. Er liebte Brüssel am frühen Morgen, wenn die Stadt erwachte. Er atmete ein paar Mal tief durch, seufzte, aber er registrierte dies mit Beklemmung, es waren keine Seufzer des Glücks. Als er die Grand Place überquerte, blieb er wieder stehen, schaute: diese Pracht! Dieser Platz zeigte seine Schönheit wahrhaftig nur zu dieser frühen Stunde, bevor ihn die Touristenmassen okkupierten. Er hasste Touristen, diese Jäger nach der Bestätigung von Klischees, die sie in ihren Köpfen mitbrachten, Menschen, die ihre Augen durch Tablets und Fotoapparate ersetzt hatten, im Weg standen und aus der lebendigen Stadt ein Museum machten und aus den Menschen, die hier arbeiteten, Statisten des Stadtbilds, Museumsdiener und Lakaien. Brüssel war schon eine polyglotte und multikulturelle Stadt, bevor diese Massen aus aller Herren Länder kamen, die hier nichts zu suchen hatten. Er atmete tief durch, drückte seine Aktentasche gegen den Bauch und versuchte, seinen Brustkorb so weit wie möglich zu dehnen. Er glotzte. Wie ein Tourist. Wie schön! Wie schön dieser Platz war! Er war nicht beglückt, er empfand eine besorgniserregende Wehmut, ein Gefühl der Trauer. Im Jahr Neunzehnhundertvierzehn, hatte sein Großvater erzählt, sei Brüssel die schönste und reichste Stadt der Welt gewesen – dann sind sie dreimal gekommen, zweimal mit Stiefeln und Gewehren, dann mit Turnschuhen und Fotoapparaten. Wir sind in ein Gefängnis gestoßen und als Diener entlassen worden. Émile Brunfaut hatte seinen Großvater nicht gemocht, respektiert ja, letztlich auch bewundert, aber lieben hatte er ihn zu Lebzeiten nicht können, diesen verbitterten alten Mann. Nun wurde er selbst alt. Viel zu früh. Er liebte Brüssel am frühen Morgen – diesen Gedanken hatte er früher doch nie gehabt. Da war er einfach über diesen Platz zur Arbeit gegangen. Jetzt sah er Brüssel – wie einer, der Abschied nehmen sollte. Warum? Er hatte nicht vor … – er ging weiter, hastig, er wollte vor dem Acht-Uhr-Briefing noch seinen Kaffee trinken und sich vorbereiten. Er wusste nicht, dass es das wirklich gab: Vorahnungen. Er war Kommissar. Er gab nichts auf Ahnungen, Mutmaßungen, Träumereien. Sein Großvater hat immer gesagt: Von einem Bier zu träumen löscht keinen Durst. Und der Kommissar hielt es so, und das wäre nicht anders, wenn er einen anderen Beruf ergriffen hätte.

Es sollte tatsächlich der Tag werden, an dem er Abschied nehmen musste. Er dachte, es wäre der Bauch. Sein großer Blähbauch drückte gegen seine Lunge und presste sie zusammen, so empfand er es und er meinte, dass das der Grund für seine Atemnot wäre, die immer wieder wie ein Seufzen klang.

Es war ein eiskalter Januartag unter einem tiefen, stahlgrauen Himmel. Die Erde, die ein Totengräber heute brechen musste, war so hart wie das Pflaster dieses prächtigen Platzes.

Beim Acht-Uhr-Briefing musste Brunfaut berichten, dass sie im Fall »Atlas-Mord« nichts in der Hand hatten, absolut nichts. Er wischte sich immer wieder mit der Hand über seinen Bauch, er hatte zuvor zum Kaffee ein Croissant gegessen, dessen fettige Brösel auf seinem Hemd klebten, er sprach und wischte, sprach weiter und wischte wieder, es wirkte wie ein Tick. Sie hatten eine männliche Leiche, Identität unbekannt. Der Mann war unter falschem Namen im Hotel abgestiegen, angeblich ein Ungar aus Budapest, aber sein Pass war gefälscht. Die Rezeptionistin habe ausgesagt, er habe Englisch mit starkem Akzent gesprochen, aber ob der Akzent ungarisch gewesen sei, könne sie nicht beurteilen. Die Männer vom Labor hatten rasch und gründlich gearbeitet, aber weder die Daktyloskopie noch die forensische Odontologie und Serologie führten zu Hinweisen, es gab keine Entsprechungen in der Datenbank der Police Fédérale. Ebenso ergebnislos war die ballistische Analyse der tödlichen Kugel. Vielleicht kommt ja noch etwas von der Europol. Der Obduktionsbericht bestätigte lediglich die Evidenz: Es war eine Hinrichtung, ein Schuss aus nächster Nähe, ins Genick. Der Täter hatte allem Anschein nach im Zimmer nichts gesucht, nichts geraubt. Die vorgefundene persönliche Habe des Opfers lieferte keinen Hinweis auf dessen wahre Identität oder gar auf ein mögliches Motiv. Es gab keine Auffälligkeiten, ausgenommen ein Schwein. Ja, ein Schwein. Mehrere befragte Personen, die sich etwa zur Tatzeit in der Nähe des Hotel Atlas aufgehalten hatten, so wie einige Anrainer, gaben an, dass ihnen ein frei herumlaufendes Schwein vor dem Hotel aufgefallen sei. Völlig mysteriös, sagte Kommissar Brunfaut, wir haben nach allen bisherigen Untersuchungen und Befragungen bei diesem Fall einen einzigen konkreten Anhaltspunkt: ein Schwein – und wir wissen nicht einmal, ob dieses Schwein überhaupt etwas mit dem Fall zu tun hat. Er wischte nochmals über seine Brust, dann legte er beide Hände auf seinen Bauch, drückte ihn hinunter und atmete dabei tief ein. Meine Herren! Keiner der Offiziere sagte etwas. Émile Brunfaut dachte nicht, dass sie vielleicht etwas verheimlichten, das er noch nicht wusste, oder dass sie einen Gedanken verschwiegen, auf den er nicht gekommen war, er stand auf und bat die Männer seines Stabs in das kleine Besprechungszimmer.

Am Stand der Dinge können wir nichts machen, nur Folgendes, sagte er. Erstens warten, ob wir von der Europol eine

Antwort auf die Daten bekommen, die wir übermittelt haben. Zweitens das Schwein. Wir kennen die Identität des Opfers nicht, aber vielleicht können wir die Identität des Schweins herausfinden. Er lachte bemüht. So ein Schwein kommt ja nicht als Tourist nach Brüssel, mit dem Flugzeug, und geht dann im Zentrum spazieren. Es muss einen Eigentümer haben, dem es entlaufen ist oder der es ausgesetzt hat. Wir überprüfen also alle Schweinebauern in der Umgebung Brüssel-Region. Und vor allem drittens: Ich will wissen, wer der Mann am Fenster des Abbruchhauses war. Möglich, dass er etwas gesehen hat. Vielleicht war es der Wohnungseigentümer, vielleicht der Hauseigentümer. Das kann man schnell herausfinden. Ich will das um 13 Uhr wissen, wenn ich zurück bin. Ich muss jetzt zum Friedhof.

Höflich sind nur noch die Friedhöfe.
Das Zimmer war überheizt, und David de Vriend ging sofort zum Fenster, um es zu öffnen. Er stellte fest, dass es sich nur kippen ließ, der Spalt so klein, dass man nicht einmal eine Hand hinausstrecken konnte. Er sah hinunter auf die stramm in Reih und Glied stehenden Grabsteine unter dem tiefen grauen Himmel und fragte, ob man diese Fensterverriegelung ändern könne, besser gesagt: entfernen.
Frau Joséphine stellte klar, dass de Vriend sie nicht »Schwester« nennen dürfe, denn das sei ja hier kein Spital, sondern eine Seniorenresidenz, nicht wahr, Herr de Vriend?
Sie sprach viel zu laut, sie schrie geradezu, das war ihr durch den jahrelangen Umgang mit den zumeist schwerhörigen alten Menschen zur zweiten Natur geworden. David de Vriend schloss die Augen, als könnte er dadurch auch die Ohren verschließen. Das Fenster – »... zu Ihrer eigenen Sicherheit ...«, hörte er sie rufen oder brüllen, er wollte nur noch, dass diese Frau verschwand. Er ertrug ihren Appellplatz-Ton so wenig

wie ihre maskenhafte Freundlichkeit, ihren unausgesetzt zu einem Lächeln gespannten Mund. Er wusste, dass er ungerecht war, aber wenn es Gerechtigkeit im Leben gäbe, dann wäre ihm dies hier erspart geblieben. Nun stand sie neben ihm, rief ihm ins Ohr: wie schön das sei, das viele Grün vor dem Fenster, nicht wahr. Er wandte sich ab, zog seine Jacke aus, warf sie auf das Bett. Sie und ihr Team seien immer für ihn da, nicht wahr, sagte sie. Wenn er Hilfe benötige oder ein Problem habe, er müsse nur rufen, hier durch das Haustelefon oder da, neben dem Bett, mit der Klingel, nicht wahr, Herr de Vriend? Sie sah sich um, mit einem Ausdruck von Begeisterung, als wäre dieses winzige Apartment eine Luxussuite, öffnete ihre Arme und schrie: Das ist jetzt also Ihr kleines Reich! Hier werden Sie sich wohlfühlen!

Das war ein Befehl. Verblüfft sah er, dass sie ihm nun die Hand entgegenstreckte. Es dauerte, bis er reagierte. Sie wollte ihre Hand schon wieder zurückziehen, als er ihr endlich seine reichte. Es gab ein kurzes Hin und Her, bis der Handschlag gelang. Also alles Gute, da sah sie seine tätowierte Nummer am Unterarm, nicht wahr, sagte sie leise. Dann trat sie ab. Und de Vriend sah sich um in seinem kleinen Reich und wunderte sich, dass ihm das nicht schon damals aufgefallen war, als er diverse Altersheime besichtigt und sich für dieses entschieden hatte: Alles in diesem Zimmer war fixiert und festgeschraubt. Es gab kein Möbelstück, das man verrücken und umstellen konnte. Nicht nur das Bett mit dem Nachtkästchen, der Schrank, halb Kleiderschrank mit weißen Schleiflacktüren, halb Vitrine mit Glastüren, auch der kleine Tisch und die L-förmig um den Tisch gehende Sitzbank waren eingebaut, der Fernsehapparat war an die Wand geschraubt, sogar das Bild über dem Bett – Venedig im Regen, in pseudoimpressionistischem Stil – war so angebracht, dass man es nicht abnehmen konnte. Warum Venedig? Und warum im Regen? Sollten Brüsseler an ihrem Lebensabend damit getröstet werden, dass es auch an den schönsten Orten der Welt regnete? Eine kleine eingebaute Küchenzeile. Es gab nichts, was man hätte verschieben, ändern, anders stellen können. Nicht einmal einen Stuhl. Alles war unabänderlich und endgültig. Er ging zum Schrank, da waren hinter Glas die paar Bücher, die er mitgenommen hatte, eingeklemmt zwischen zwei Buchstützen aus Keramik, die lesende Schweine darstellten. Ein Geschenk seiner letzten Abiturientenklasse, bevor er in Pension gegangen war. Er wollte Bücher herausnehmen, sie da und dort hinlegen, auf den Tisch, auf das Bett, sie wären dann in diesem Zimmer das einzige bewegliche Gut. Er öffnete die Schranktür, ließ den Blick über die Buchrücken gleiten, noch einmal, wurde unschlüssig – was wollte er? Lesen? Hatte er lesen wollen? Nein. Er stand da und starrte die Buchrücken an, schloss den Schrank wieder. Er wollte – was? Raus? Er wollte raus. Er trat ans Fenster. Der städtische Friedhof von Brüssel. Er hatte nichts in Griffweite. Aber in Aussicht. Er zog sich warm an.

Es waren nur wenige Schritte vom Altersheim Maison Hanssens in der Rue de l'Arbre Unique zum Haupttor des Friedhofs. Die eisige Kälte. Der graue Himmel. Das schmiedeeiserne Tor. Es beruhigte ihn, Vögel zu sehen, Krähen und Spatzen. Und so viele Maulwurfshügel zwischen den Gräbern, er konnte sich nicht erinnern, jemals auf einem Friedhof so viele Maulwurfshügel gesehen zu haben, ja dass ihm überhaupt schon einmal ein Maulwurfshügel auf einem Friedhof aufgefallen wäre. Und überall wuchsen hier Pilze zwischen dem Kriechefeu, Unmengen von Pilzen, das waren – das waren – ihm fiel der Name nicht ein. Er kannte sie, egal, sie waren ungenießbar. Das war alles. Da war ein buchstäblich verkehrtes Grab, umgestülpt durch die dicken Wurzeln eines riesigen Baumes. Daneben Grabplatten, die durch gestürzte Bäume oder herabgefallene Äste zerbrochen worden waren. Moos auf den zerstörten Steinen. Junge, neu gepflanzte Bäume neben alten, die gefallen oder gefällt worden waren und zwischen den Gräbern lagen und verrotteten. Auf diesem Todesacker starben auch die Bäume und sanken in die Erde. Auf alten Grabsteinen hingen kleine Kränze aus Gips. Manchmal zwei oder drei, einige dieser Kränze lagen auch vor den Grabsteinen oder neben den Gräbern. Als hätten morbide Kinder Reifen-Werfen gespielt.

Immer wieder blieb er vor einem Grab stehen, las die Namen, betrachtete die emaillierten Fotos. Er ging gern auf Friedhöfe, er fand es schön, dass Menschen Gräber hatten, auf denen ihr Name stand. Menschen, die gestorben waren und die man dann besuchen konnte. Er sah Gräber von Kindern, von Menschen, die sehr jung gestorben waren, an Krankheiten, Unfällen oder ermordet worden waren, tragische Schicksale, aber sie hatten ein Grab. Solange es Friedhöfe gab, gab es das Versprechen von Zivilisation. Seine Eltern, sein Bruder, seine Großeltern hatten Gräber in der Luft. Keinen Ort, den man besuchen, den man pflegen, wo man einen Stein hinlegen konnte. Keine Ruhestätte. Nur eine bleibende Unruhe, die keinen Ort des Friedens finden konnte. In der Erinnerung, die mit ihm sterben würde, gab es nur ein letztes Bild seiner Familie, aufgenommen mit dem letzten Blick – und der war bloß eine Behauptung. Er hatte nicht das Gesicht seiner Mutter gesehen, sondern nur ihre Hand, die ihn am Ärmel festhielt, bis er sich losriss, er hatte kein letztes Bild vom Vater, sondern nur eine Erinnerung an seinen Schrei »Bleib!«, den Schrei »Bleib da! Du stürzt uns ins Unglück!« – und sein kleiner Bruder: gesichtslos, nur der Rücken eines Kindes, das sich an die Mutter presste. Und sonst? Erinnerungen, die wie gestohlen wirkten aus dem Fundus der Erinnerungen anderer: Vater-Mutter-Kind-Erinnerungen, Allerwelts-Erinnerungen, die glücklichsten. So schwarz wie die Asche verbrannter Fotos.

Sein Vater hatte Tarte au Riz geliebt. Das war eine Erinnerung. Zugleich keine. Er hatte kein Bild dazu. Wie die Familie um den Tisch saß und der Vater mit vergnügt glänzendem Gesicht sagte: »Mmmh, heute gibt es endlich wieder einmal Tarte au Riz!«, und wie die Mutter die Tarte auf den Tisch stellte und der Vater die Kinder zur Räson rief: »Halt! Nicht so wild!«, und die Mutter sagte: »Zuerst bekommt der Vater ein schönes Stück!«, und – so falsch! Es gab kein Erinnerungsbild, keinen Erinnerungsfilm daran, er sah sich nicht mit der Familie am Tisch sitzen, mit Tarte au Riz, es gab nur den Satz: »Vater liebte Tarte au Riz«! Aber warum? Warum dieser Satz? Und woher kam dieser Satz? Ausgerechnet dieser Satz? Als Erinnerung an ein Leben? Zugleich ein toter Satz, begraben in seinem Kopf. Da sah er einen Grabstein, in den eingemeißelt war:

TOUT PASSE
TOUT S'EFFACE
HORS DU SOUVENIR

Er hielt inne, betrachte lange diese Inschrift, bückte sich, hob einen Kieselstein auf und legte ihn auf dieses Grab.

So viele zerstörte Gräber. Der Vandalismus der Natur. Von Baumwurzeln ausgehebelte Grabplatten, von brechenden Ästen und stürzenden Bäumen zerschmetterte Grüfte, von wuchernden Pflanzen verschluckte Steine. Die verwesenden Denkmäler des menschlichen Konkurrenzkampfes, der Gier nach Repräsentation: Baufällige, von Schimmel befallene Mausoleen, die von Macht und Reichtum einer Familie monumentales Zeugnis ablegen sollten, nun verfielen und nur noch dies zeigten: Vergänglichkeit. Davor Schilder, von der

Friedhofsverwaltung angebracht: Die Pacht für diesen Grabplatz sei mit Ende des Jahres abgelaufen.

Ohne Geld sterben selbst die Gräber.

Er war müde, überlegte kurz, ob er nicht besser zurückgehen
sollte. Nein, er wollte die Nachbarschaft ganz erkunden, in
der er nun lebte.

Er bog nach links ab, ohne auf die Wegweiser zu achten,
»Deutscher Soldatenfriedhof«, »Commonwealth War Graves«,
»Nederlandse Oorlogsgraven«, und da begannen schon die
korrekt ausgerichteten Reihen immer gleicher Grabsteine,
die in ihrer unendlichen Gleichförmigkeit, nach dem lebendigen und geradezu schreienden Chaos des zivilen Teils des
Friedhofs, eine dramatische Ruhe und Schönheit vermittel-
ten, die perfekte Erlösung von Lebensraub in einer Ästhetik
der Würde.

Im Alter von 24 Jahren – gestorben für das Vaterland.

Im Alter von 20 Jahren – gestorben für das Vaterland.

Im Alter von 26 Jahren – gestorben für das Vaterland.

Im Alter von 19 Jahren – gestorben für das Vaterland.

Im Alter von 23 Jahren – gestorben für das Vaterland.

Im Alter von 23 Jahren – gestorben für das Vaterland.

Im Alter von 22 Jahren – gestorben für das Vaterland.

Im Alter von 31 Jahren – gestorben für das Vaterland.

Im Alter von 24 Jahren – gestorben für das Vaterland.

Im Alter von 39 Jahren – gestorben für das Vaterland.

Im Alter von 21 Jahren – gestorben für das Vaterland.

Mort pour la patrie, for the glory of the nation, slachtoffers
van den plicht.

Wer hier entlangging, schritt die Reihen ab wie ein General
eine Armee der Toten, wie ein Präsident die militärische For-
mation bei einem Staatsempfang im Hades. Er schloss die
Augen. Und just in diesem Moment wurde er angesprochen.
Ein Herr, der ihn fragte, ob er Deutsch oder Englisch spreche.

Etwas Deutsch.

Ob er wisse, wo das Mausoleum der bedingungslosen Liebe sei.

Wie bitte?

Der Mann sagte, er habe im Reiseführer davon gelesen, ob er ihn verstehe? Ja? Gut. Also im Reiseführer. Das müsse hier irgendwo sein. Mausoleum der bedingungslosen Liebe. Sie wissen nicht –?

Er wisse nicht, sagte de Vriend.

Professor Erhart bedankte sich und ging weiter. Er sah am Ende der Allee ein Gebäude, vor dem einige Menschen standen, vielleicht würde man ihm dort Auskunft geben können. Er hatte noch etwas Zeit. Die meisten Teilnehmer der Reflection Group »New pact for Europe« reisten erst im Lauf dieses Vormittags an, weshalb das erste Treffen an diesem Tag für 13 Uhr angesetzt war. Er aber war zwei Tage früher gekommen, um, wenn er schon nach Brüssel eingeladen war, auch etwas von der Stadt zu sehen und nicht nur die ganze Zeit in einem geschlossenen und klimatisierten Raum zu sitzen. Er hatte in Wien keine Verpflichtungen und keine Familie. Er war in dieser Hinsicht in der schrecklichsten Situation, in der man sich in seinem Alter befinden konnte: Er war frei. Es war seinem exzellenten akademischen Ruf zu verdanken, dass er noch ab und zu Einladungen wie diese erhielt, er nahm sie stets an und bereitete sich akribisch vor, obwohl oder vielleicht weil er zunehmend das Gefühl hatte, nicht mehr Diskussionsbeiträge zu liefern, sondern mit seinen Papers im Grunde Lesungen aus seinem Testament zu halten. Aber dann sollte es eben so sein: den Erben mitzuteilen, dass es das gab, jenseits des Zeitgeists ein Erbe, das anzutreten sie herausgefordert waren.

Zunächst hatte Alois Erhart an diesem Tag das Grab von Armand Moens besucht, des einst vieldiskutierten und heute vergessenen Ökonomen, seinerzeit Professor an der Universiteit Leuven, der bereits in den sechziger Jahren des vorigen Jahrhunderts eine Theorie der nachnationalen Volkswirtschaftslehre entwickelt und davon die Notwendigkeit abgeleitet hatte, eine Vereinte Europäische Republik zu gründen. Die wachsende Verflechtung von Volkswirtschaften, die daraus folgenden wechselseitigen Abhängigkeiten, die immer größer werdende Macht multinationaler Konzerne und die wachsende Bedeutung der internationalen Finanzmärkte werden es nationalen Demokratien nicht mehr ermöglichen, ihre wesentliche Aufgabe zu erfüllen, nämlich gestaltend in die Bedingungen einzugreifen, unter denen die Menschen ihr Leben machen müssen, und tendenziell Verteilungsgerechtigkeit zu gewährleisten. »Schließt die nationalen Parlamente!« – das war der Schlachtruf eines echten Demokraten – der die Demokratie in Hinblick auf die geschichtliche Situation neu erfinden wollte. Dass seine These vom notwendigen Absterben der nationalen Demokratien damals nicht als Skandal oder als verrückte Utopie abgetan wurde, lag an der Narrenfreiheit dieser Zeit, und dass sich Moens schließlich gegen die Nationalökonomen, »die Wiederkäuer« (wie er sie nannte), nicht durchsetzen konnte, hatte denselben Grund: »Die akademische Narrenfreiheit hat uns zunächst geholfen, aber am Ende die Macht der wirklichen Narren gefestigt«, schrieb er in seinen Erinnerungen.

Erhart hatte vor fünfundvierzig Jahren als blutjunger Student einen Gastvortrag von Armand Moens in Alpbach gehört und sich seither als dessen Schüler verstanden. Getreulich hatte er all seine Publikationen gelesen. Als er selbst zum ersten Mal publizierte und diese Arbeit seinem Lehrer schickte, war dieser bereits todkrank. Moens hatte noch mit einem Brief geantwortet, aber es kam zu keinem weiteren Austausch,

weil Moens wenige Tage später starb. Nun stand Erhart gerührt vor dem Grab:

Armand Joseph Moens 1910-1972

Seitlich vor dem Grabstein befand sich ein kleines emaillier-
tes Schild, auf dem stand:

>»Toen hij het meest nodig was,
werd hij vergeten«
Studenten werkgroep »Moens eed«
aan de Katholieke Universiteit Leuven

Auf dem Grab lagen frische Blumen und eine Flasche Schnaps.
Und Glücksschweinchen. In verschiedenen Größen und aus
verschiedenen Materialien, aus Plastik, Plüsch, Holz, Keramik – die Schweine konnte sich Alois Erhart nicht erklären.
Er machte ein Foto. Dann ein zweites, nun vom Grabstein
und dem Schild, ohne die Schweinchen.

Als er recherchiert hatte, wo sich das Grab von Professor
Moens befand, war er auf den Hinweis gestoßen, dass sich
auf dem städtischen Friedhof von Brüssel auch diese Touris-
tenattraktion befand: das Mausoleum der bedingungslosen
Liebe. Das suchte er nun. Ein Brüsseler Baron, den Namen
hatte Alois Erhart vergessen, der ein Vermögen mit Beteili-
gungen an Bergwerken in Belgisch-Kongo gemacht hatte,
hatte sich bei einer Reise in die Kolonie unsterblich in eine
Frau verliebt, die er mit zurück nach Brüssel nahm, um sie
zu heiraten – »Eine Negerin!« Das führte nicht bloß zu seiner
Ächtung in der guten Brüsseler Gesellschaft, sondern vor allem zu einigen juristischen Problemen, die er nach langem
Kampf, teils durch die Hilfe bester Anwälte, teils durch Zah-
lung beträchtlicher Summen, schließlich überwand. Die Liebe des Barons trotzte allen Stürmen. »Ich bin lieber mit
dieser Frau geächtet als ohne sie geachtet!« Bei der endlich

erlaubten Hochzeit erschien niemand der geladenen Gäste, ausgenommen die alte verrückte Gräfin Adolphine Marat, die nach der Trauung zu einem Tee in ihr Palais bat. Als Trauzeugen fungierten zwei Arbeiter, die auf der Straße vor dem Standesamt einen Kanaldeckel reparierten und die bereit waren, für jeweils fünfzig Franc ihre Arbeit für eine Viertelstunde zu unterbrechen. Gräfin Marat, angefeindet dafür, dass sie zu einem Empfang für dieses Brautpaar geladen hatte, rechtfertigte sich mit den legendären Worten: »Wenn er bereit ist, dieser Frau seinen Namen zu geben, dann werde ich ihr doch einen Tee geben können!«

Diese Frau, die Libelulle hieß (das hatte sich Professor Erhart gemerkt: kleine Libelle), starb kurz darauf, im Jahr 1910, im Kindbett, nach der Totgeburt ihres Sohnes, der von der Nabelschnur stranguliert worden war. Der Baron, ach ja: Er hieß Caspers, Victor Caspers, rasend vor Schmerz, beauftragte einen französischen Architekten, ein prächtiges Mausoleum auf dem Cimetière de la Ville für seine Liebe zu errichten, einen Andachtsraum, in dessen Dach sich ein Loch befand, so geformt und berechnet, dass jedes Jahr am Tag und zur Stunde ihres Todes ein Lichtfleck in Form eines Herzens auf den Sarkophag der Geliebten fiel.

Das wollte Professor Erhart sehen. Er hatte erwartet, dass es bei einer solchen Attraktion Hinweisschilder und Wegweiser geben würde, aber nichts dergleichen. Gab es mehrere Brüsseler Friedhöfe? War er auf dem falschen?

Nun war er bei dem Gebäude angekommen, das er schon von Weitem gesehen und vor dem sich mittlerweile eine größere Gruppe von Menschen angesammelt hatte.

Er war verblüfft, als er unter den Anwesenden nun ihn sah, unverkennbar, riesig und gewichtig stand er da – das war doch der Polizist, der ihn im Hotel verhört hatte, kein Zweifel, das war dieser riesige Kommissar. Er blieb stehen, starrte zu ihm hinüber, da kreuzten sich ihre Blicke. Erhart war nicht sicher, ob der Kommissar ihn erkannte – der jetzt auch abgelenkt wurde: Zwei Männer, die raschen Schritts auf ihn zugekommen waren, begrüßten ihn, wechselten einige Worte, dann betraten sie das Gebäude, das, wie Erhart nun sah, das Krematorium war.

Es gehörte nicht zu Kommissar Brunfauts Aufgaben, bei der Kremierung eines Mordopfers anwesend zu sein. Und es gab auch keinen ermittlungstechnischen Grund. Nach einem Mord wird die Leiche beschlagnahmt und gerichtsmedizinisch obduziert. Danach wird sie zur Bestattung freigegeben. Ist die Identität des Opfers bekannt und gibt es Angehörige, wird die Bestattung von diesen organisiert. Ist die Identität nicht bekannt, wird innerhalb von 48 Stunden nach der Obduktion eine Kremierung im Auftrag der Stadt durchgeführt. Dazu erscheint ein städtischer Beamter, kontrolliert die Papiere, bestätigt, dass es sich bei dem Toten um Aktenzeichen sowieso handelt, verliest einen etwa fünfminütigen Text über die Vergänglichkeit des Lebens und den ewigen Frieden, um EU-Richtlinien-konform das Minimum einer würdigen menschlichen Bestattung zu gewährleisten, dann sinkt der Sarg in die Brennkammer ab. Später wird die Asche auf der Grünfläche neben dem Krematorium verstreut, im Grunde hingekippt, und auf einer Stele eine Plakette mit dem Namen oder, falls dieser eben nicht bekannt ist, mit dem polizeilichen Aktenzeichen des Toten angebracht. Es war nicht zu erwarten, dass ein Verdächtiger, gar der Täter selbst, zu dieser Zeremonie kam, von der, außer den damit befassten Beamten, niemand Ort und Stunde wusste. Allerdings gab es immer Publikum, Leute, die regelmäßig auf dem Friedhof spazieren gingen, Rentner, Witwen, Kinderwägen schiebende Mütter aus der Nachbarschaft, die dann aus Respekt oder Neugier stehenblieben.

Kommissar Brunfaut war allerdings nicht wegen seines Falls hierhergekommen, sondern weil dieser Tag der Todestag seines Großvaters war. Vor vielen Jahren hatte sich zu diesem Anlass noch eine beeindruckende, schließlich immer kleiner werdende Anzahl von Menschen am Grab des Großvaters versammelt, dieses Helden des belgischen Widerstands. Es wurden Geschichten erzählt, es wurde Schnaps getrunken, es wurden Lieder gesungen. Am Ende dann die Brabançonne. Bei »Les peuples libres sont amis!« wirkten die emphatisch singenden, ja brüllenden Greise wie eine Bande von Verrückten. Bei der Zeile »Le Roi, la Loi, la Liberté!« gab es immer einen, der wie ein Dirigent mit einer Handbewegung den Chor plötzlich stoppte und rief: Wir können nicht alles haben! Worauf können wir verzichten? Und alle: Auf den König! Und worauf können wir nicht verzichten? Alle: Recht und Freiheit!

Émile Brunfaut war durch diese Rituale als Jugendlicher noch ziemlich eingeschüchtert worden, hatte die Ekstase an einem Grab als peinlich empfunden, und den Mottenkugelgeruch der Anzüge der alten Männer für Schießpulvergeruch gehalten. Später, nach dem Tod der Eltern, begann er Respekt und Bewunderung für den Mann zu empfinden, der ihn, als er ein Kind war, so verängstigt hatte, und, ja, auch Stolz! Und später, als die Tränen bereit waren, aus seinen immer größer werdenden Tränensäcken zu quellen, und er die Menschen hätte umarmen mögen, die sich hier an diesem Grab Jahr für Jahr versammelt hatten, war keiner mehr da, kein Lebender, der sich an seinen Großvater und seine Heldentaten erinnern konnte. Dennoch, jedes Jahr an diesem Tag, kam er hierher und verbrachte in einsamer Kontemplation eine Stunde am Grab. Und weil es sich diesmal so ergab, ging er dann weiter zum Krematorium, wo gerade »sein Fall« eingeäschert wurde. Er hatte nicht erwartet, dass ihn dies in seinen Ermittlungen weiterbringen würde – umso erstaunter war er, als er dort einen Mann sah, mit dem er im Zuge der Erstvernehmungen am Tatort gesprochen hatte. Zunächst war ihm der Mann nur auf unklare Weise bekannt vorgekommen, und es hatte gut zehn Minuten gedauert, bis ihm klar wurde, woher er ihn kannte. Sofort lief er aus der Halle des Krematoriums, aber der Mann war nicht mehr da. Brunfaut lief noch einige Alleen des Friedhofs ab, konnte ihn aber nicht mehr finden.

Er verließ den Friedhof. Genau gegenüber vom Friedhofstor befand sich das Le Rustique, eine Kneipe, in der er jedes Mal einkehrte, wenn er das Grab des Großvaters besuchte. Brunfaut fragte sich, warum die Fenster in der Etage über dem Lokal zugemauert waren. Unvorstellbar, dass hier jemand wohnte, der den Blick auf den Friedhof nicht ertrug. Es mauert sich doch kein Mensch ein, nur weil ihn der Blick aus dem Fenster depressiv macht. So jemand wäre doch hier gar nicht erst eingezogen. Welches Rätsel verbarg sich hinter diesen zugemauerten Fenstern?

Wie immer bestellte Brunfaut einen Stoemp, das Lieblingsgericht des Großvaters und für ihn selbst ein sentimentaler Kindheitsgeschmack. Stoemp is Stoemp, hatte der Großvater immer gesagt, das Entscheidende dabei sei natürlich die Qualität der Wurst: sie müsse platzen, wenn man mit der Gabel hineinsticht. Dafür müsse die Wursthaut aber aus echtem Darm sein und nicht so ein künstlicher Plastikstrumpf, wie er immer mehr in Verwendung kommt, dramatisches Symptom des Sterbens belgischer Arbeiterkultur. Hier im Le Rustique war der Stoemp noch authentisch. Simpel, echt, perfekt. Dazu ein einfaches Stella Artois vom Fass und zum Abschluss ein kleiner Genever. Émile Brunfaut seufzte. Dann fuhr er zurück ins Kommissariat.

Als Émile Brunfaut in die »mine de charbon« zurückkam, sagte ihm der Beamte, der Journaldienst machte, dass der Hauptkommissar bereits auf ihn warte, er möge unverzüglich zu ihm in sein Zimmer kommen.

Brunfaut hatte angekündigt, dass er zum Friedhof fahren und um 13 Uhr zurück sein werde. Und alle hatten genickt. Nun war es fünf Minuten nach eins. Und jetzt musste sich der Chef wieder einmal wichtigmachen? Brunfaut erwartete eine Rüge, weil es keine begründete Veranlassung gab, dass er auf dem Friedhof spazieren ging und dann auch noch zu spät zurückkam. Er zuckte mit den Achseln, nicht wirklich natürlich, sondern in Gedanken, wartete geduldig auf den Lift, ging dann bedächtig den Korridor entlang bis zum Zimmer des Chefs, klopfte an die Tür und trat sofort ein.

Verkehrte Welt, dachte er augenblicklich: Er kam gerade vom Friedhof – aber das Begräbnis, so war sein Eindruck, fand hier statt. Links vom Hauptkommissar saß der Untersuchungsrichter, rechts von ihm der Staatsanwalt, alle mit todernsten Mienen.

Nehmen Sie Platz, Kollege Brunfaut!

Dass der Untersuchungsrichter dem Hauptkommissar im Nacken saß, verwunderte Brunfaut nicht allzu sehr: Schließlich war er der eigentliche Chef, der immer wieder Anweisungen gab und regelmäßig informiert werden wollte, wie die Ermittlungen liefen. Aber die Anwesenheit des Staatsanwalts versetzte Brunfaut sofort in Alarmbereitschaft. Denn das bedeutete: Hier gab es eine politische Intervention.

Was nützt Alarmbereitschaft, wenn der Alarm erst schrillt, wenn die Konsequenzen der Gefahr bereits ein unwiderrufliches Faktum sind?

Ja, es war ein Begräbnis, das in diesem Zimmer stattfand. Das Begräbnis des »Falls Atlas«.

Nun, sagte Hauptkommissar Maigret und schwieg. Brunfaut war überzeugt davon, dass dieser Idiot seine Karriere nur dem Zufall zu verdanken hatte, dass er diesen Namen trug, ein für die Stadt höchst unglücklicher Zufall. Er sagte nichts, schaute ungerührt zu, wie dieser Maigret nach Worten suchte. Brunfaut sah Maigret abwartend an, dieser blickte hilfesuchend zum Untersuchungsrichter, und der Untersuchungsrichter zum Staatsanwalt, der schließlich sagte: Vielen Dank, Herr Kommissar, für Ihre Zeit. Wir haben uns gerade mit dem Mordfall im Hotel Atlas befasst, bei dem Sie, wenn ich richtig informiert bin –

Ja, sagte Brunfaut.

Nun, sagte Hauptkommissar Maigret.

Es gibt neue Erkenntnisse, sagte der Untersuchungsrichter, Monsieur de Rohan. Das Einzige, was Brunfaut an dem eitlen Rohan interessant fand, war dessen Frau. Er hatte sie einmal auf einem Weihnachtsfest kennengelernt, eine junge, sehr zarte Person mit großen, schwarz umrandeten Augen, die jedes Mal, wenn sie etwas sagen wollte, von de Rohan lächelnd mit den Worten ruhiggestellt wurde: »Und du, ma biche, musst ruhig jetzt sein!« – Brunfaut hatte sofort den Wunsch gehabt, mit ihr zu schlafen. Er wusste nicht, ob es wirklich Begehren nach ihr war oder bloß die Gier, ihren Mann zu demütigen. Er war betrunken genug gewesen, es ihr ins Ohr zu sagen – sehr direkt, sehr dumm. Sie sah ihn groß an, er schämte sich augenblicklich, und sie antwortete: Heute geht das nicht. Ruf mich morgen an!

Rohan tastete mit einem selbstverliebten Handgriff seine perfekt gefönte Frisur ab und bat Hauptkommissar Maigret, den Stand der Erkenntnisse für Kommissar Brunfaut zu erläutern.

Brunfaut spürte, wie den Staatsanwalt die Hilflosigkeit der Polizisten hier anwiderte und er nur noch darauf wartete, dass endlich Klartext gesprochen werde und er gehen und sich wieder wichtigeren Dingen zuwenden konnte.

Nun, sagte Hauptkommissar Maigret. Die Sache sei die: Es gebe triftige Gründe, in diesem Fall nicht weiter zu ermitteln.

Verstehen Sie?

Nein, sagte Brunfaut, ich verstehe nicht. Heißt das: Wir ermitteln nicht weiter, oder, ich ermittle nicht weiter, oder, es wird nicht weiter ermittelt?

Es war das dritte Mal in den letzten fünf Jahren, dass er an einen Tatort gerufen worden war und vor einer Leiche gestanden hatte – die am nächsten Tag nicht mehr existierte. Sind das die triftigen Gründe: dass Brüssel die Stadt des Jüngsten Gerichts ist? Der Auferstehung der Toten? Hat sich die Seele des Ermordeten wieder mit seinem Leib vereint, und wo kein Toter, da kein Fall? Hat das die Gerichtsmedizin bestätigt?

Nun, sagte Maigret, ich verstehe –

Brunfaut sah diesen Idioten wütend an. Seine blöde Igelfrisur. Mit Haargel gezwirbelt. Als ließe der viel zu eng gezurrte Krawattenknoten ihm die Haare zu Berge stehen.

Ich verstehe, dass Sie, nun, dass Sie das jetzt nicht verstehen, aber –

Die Sache ist ganz einfach, schaltete sich nun de Rohan ein, ganz leicht zu verstehen. Wir haben mit diesem Fall nichts mehr zu tun, Sie nicht, wir nicht, keiner hier. Und was ich Ihnen jetzt zur Erklärung sage, ist streng vertraulich, Sie hören das, aber es wurde nie gesagt, alles klar? Also: Es gibt eine einzige Institution, die die Macht hat, uns einen solchen Fall zu entziehen, die ihn verschwinden lassen und auf ihre Art aufklären kann. Und diese Institution ist deshalb so mächtig, weil sie in Wirklichkeit, das heißt offiziell, gar nicht existiert. Sie ist nicht greifbar, verstehen Sie, sie greift sich solche Fälle, aber sie ist selbst nicht greifbar. Es geht da um Interessen, die –

Interessen, sagte Brunfaut.

Genau. Wir verstehen uns.

Der Staatsanwalt blickte schweigend von einem zum anderen, nickte.

Es bleibt unter uns, sagte Brunfaut, und wieder nickte der Staatsanwalt. Ja, sagte Brunfaut, es bleibt unter uns, so wie in einem Fernseh-Krimi.

Wie bitte?

Weisung von höchster Stelle, sagte Brunfaut, politische Intervention zur Behinderung der Ermittlungsarbeit, geheimnisvolle Andeutungen, ansonsten Schweigen, das ist doch unerträglich klischeehaft, aber das Klischee muss natürlich ergänzt werden: durch einen Kommissar, der sich gezwungen sieht, auf eigene Faust –

Sie werden jetzt sicher nicht –

Und der am Ende als Held –

Sie werden jetzt sicher nichts auf eigene Faust unternehmen, sagte der Staatsanwalt. Das ist eine Weisung. Und wie ich vorhin gerade erfuhr, wurde Ihrem Ansuchen auf Urlaub stattgegeben.

Aber ich habe kein Ansuchen auf Urlaub gestellt!

Nun, das ist ein kleines Missverständnis, sagte Maigret, ich hatte gesagt, dass Herr Kommissar Brunfaut noch sehr viele unverbrauchte Urlaubstage hat.

Brunfaut spürte heftige Beklemmungen, atmete tief durch.

Na wunderbar, sagte Rohan, dann verbrauchen Sie jetzt Ihre Urlaubstage, entspannen Sie sich, Sie hatten extrem viel Stress, wie ich weiß, und –

Der Staatsanwalt erhob sich, Maigret und Rohan schnellten aus ihren Stühlen, langsam stand Brunfaut auf, dieser Zwei-Meter-Mann, der die anderen hier überragte, da spürte er einen Stich in der Brust und er fiel auf den Stuhl zurück. Der Staatsanwalt blickte auf ihn hinab, sagte: Meine Herren!

Émile Brunfaut ging in sein Arbeitszimmer und stellte fest, dass der »Atlas«-Ordner mit dem Einsatzbericht, den ersten Vernehmungsprotokollen, den Tatort-Fotos und dem Obduktionsbefund von seinem Schreibtisch verschwunden war. Er hatte das allerdings auch alles in seinem Computer abgespeichert. Er gab sein Passwort ein – aber auch auf dem virtuellen Schreibtisch des Computerbildschirms war der betreffende Ordner verschwunden. Er öffnete den virtuellen Papierkorb: auch unter den gelöschten Dokumenten war die Akte nicht mehr zu finden. Das Aktivitätenprotokoll, alles, was diesen Fall betraf, war gelöscht – wann der Einsatzbefehl zum Hotel Atlas gekommen war, welche Einsatzwagen wann am Tatort eingetroffen waren, welche Beamten Dienst hatten, der erste Bericht der Spurensicherung, alles fort, der Fall hatte sich in Luft aufgelöst.

Er schnaufte, drückte seinen Bauch nach unten, um die Lunge zu entlasten, atmete tief ein, öffnete den Gürtel und den Knopf am Hosenbund. Er starrte auf den Bildschirm. Wie lange? Eine Minute? Zehn Minuten? Er merkte, dass er nicht mehr auf den Bildschirm schaute, sondern sich selbst beobachtete: Wie würde er reagieren? Er wusste es nicht. Er sah sich selbst dasitzen wie eine auf dem Stuhl zusammengesunkene Leiche. Da trommelten seine Finger wieder auf die Tastatur, er googelte: Was hatten die Medien vom Mord im Hotel Atlas berichtet? Nichts. Welches Stichwort auch immer er eingab, nichts, kein Resultat. In keiner Zeitung hatte es einen Artikel gegeben. Der Mord hatte nicht stattgefunden.

Er sah auf und bemerkte erst jetzt, dass auch sein Flipchart gesäubert worden war: Das Blatt, auf dem er bei der letzten Besprechung mit großen Buchstaben HOTEL ATLAS Pfeil SCHWEIN und fünf Fragezeichen geschrieben hatte, war abgerissen worden.

Er hatte einen seltsamen Gedanken: War das jetzt der Moment, wo er endlich zum Enkel werden musste?

Zum Enkel des berühmten Widerstandskämpfers.

Er nahm den Telefonhörer und rief die Männer seines Stabs zu sich. Er war, das spürte er, wild entschlossen.

Der Hauptinspektor, der Assistenzkommissar, die drei Inspektoren kamen herein, Kommissar Brunfaut schaltete den Computer aus, sah auf, schaute in die Gesichter dieser Männer und begriff augenblicklich: Sie wussten Bescheid und sie hatten sich längst arrangiert. Es war aussichtslos. Er stand auf, sagte, er wolle sich verabschieden, weil er Urlaub – da merkte er, dass ihm die Hose hinunterrutschte, schnell hielt er sie fest –, weil er auf Urlaub gehe und … vor den Männern wollte er nicht die Hose zuknöpfen und den Gürtel schließen, er rief: Raus mit euch!

Nun würden sich diese angepassten, braven Opportunisten das Maul darüber zerreißen, was für eine lächerliche Figur er sei. Er bekam feuchte Augen, ging zur Flipchart, nahm einen Filzstift und schrieb: La Loi, la Liberté! Dann erinnerte er sich an eine Grabinschrift, die er heute im Vorbeigehen auf dem Friedhof gesehen hatte, und schrieb darunter, in Blockbuchstaben:

TOUT PASSE

TOUT S'EFFACE

HORS DU SOUVENIR

Dann nahm er seine Aktentasche – sie war leer – und ging.

Der Algorithmus, der alles Mögliche filtert und auch das bisher Erzählte geordnet hat, ist natürlich verrückt – vor allem aber ist er beruhigend: Die Welt ist Konfetti, aber durch ihn erleben wir sie als Mosaik.

War es wegen Brunfauts Besuch des Krematoriums, dass nun folgende Verknüpfung hergestellt wurde?

Neue Mail: »Betreff: Auschwitz – Ihr Besuch«.

Martin Susman fror. Es regnete, und er war daher nicht mit dem Rad, sondern mit der Metro zur Arbeit gefahren. Der unterirdische Wind in den Schächten und Stollen war etwas anderes, härter und aggressiver als der Fahrtwind beim Radfahren. Und die dampfende Herdenwärme in den überfüllten Waggons war keine Erleichterung, sie machte ihm Angst, vor ansteckenden Krankheiten, vor allem aber fürchtete er sich davor, dass ihn diese Apathie und Ergebenheit ansteckte, die die Menschen in den Zügen stets erfasste.

»Sehr geehrter Herr Susman, ich freue mich, Sie schon bald in Auschwitz begrüßen zu dürfen!«

Er hatte sich einen Becher Tee aus der Kantine geholt und saß nun vor dem Computer, um seine Mails zu checken.

»Ich werde Sie selbstverständlich abholen von Flughafen Krakau und Sie persönlich mit dem Auto ins Lager bringen. Sie erkennen mich an dem Schild, das ich hochhalte mit Ihrem Namen.«

Angewidert stellte Susman den Tee ab. Er hatte das Gefühl, krank zu werden, nur weil er aus Angst vor Krankheit diesen Tee trank.

Die Dienstreise. Im Grunde waren alle Vorbereitungen getroffen. Der wissenschaftliche Dienst und das Museum des deutschen Vernichtungslagers Auschwitz-Birkenau wurden von der EU subventioniert, Vertreter der Europäischen Kommission nahmen jedes Jahr am 27. Januar an der Feier zur Befreiung des Lagers teil. Für die DG Kultur wurde in diesem Jahr Martin Susman entsandt, der auch mit der Bearbeitung der Förderung und der Kontrolle der eingesetzten Mittel betraut war.

»Ich möchte noch, wenn Sie erlauben, einen guten Rat Ihnen mitgeben auf den Weg. Wichtig ist warme Unterwäsche. Auschwitz-Birkenau bitter kalt ist in dieser Zeit. Wir wollen auf keinen Fall, dass sie krank werden in Auschwitz!

Ich habe bei letzten Besuch in Berlin in einem Kaufhaus Unterwäsche gekauft, die beste, die ich jemals hatte. Ich weiß nicht, wie heißt die Marke, aber bitte, gehen Sie in Geschäft, verlangen Sie deutsche Unterwäsche! Ich sage immer deutsche Unterwäsche, weil ich habe sie gekauft in Berlin, und ist sicher made in Germany. Das wird in Brüssel bekannt sein. Deutsche Unterwäsche! Ich rate Ihnen zu kaufen. Deutsche Unterwäsche ist das Beste für Auschwitz!«

Martin Susman klickte auf Antworten, schrieb drei freundliche Sätze, öffnete die nächste Mail, stand auf und ging aus dem Zimmer, schaute bei Bohumil Szmekal hinein, der gerade hastig tippte – und hielt ein Päckchen Zigaretten in die Höhe, Szmekal nickte, und sie gingen hinaus auf die Feuerleiter, um eine Zigarette zu rauchen.

Mrzne jak v ruským filmu, sagte Bohumil. Martin hatte das natürlich nicht verstanden, aber er gab ihm recht: Ja, wir bräuchten deutsche Unterwäsche!

David de Vriend verließ den Friedhof. Er fror. Er nahm das hin, er hatte schon ärgere Kälte erlebt, ohne so einen Mantel, wie er ihn jetzt trug. Er beschloss im Le Rustique einzukehren, diesem Lokal da gegenüber, eine Kleinigkeit zu essen und etwas Wärmendes zu trinken, ein Glas Rotwein. Er trat ein, fand einen Platz gleich links am Fenster. Die Kellnerin brachte die Karte, fragte: Sind Sie von der Maison Hanssens, vom Altersheim? Dann müssen Sie mir Ihre Marken zeigen, bevor ich bonniere.

Marken?

Für die Ermäßigung!

Nein, nein, sagte de Vriend – er wusste nichts von solchen Marken, zumindest hatte Schwester Joséphine ihm heute nichts davon gesagt –, ich bin normal, ich meine, normaler Gast.

Sehr gut, sagte sie und legte ihm die Speisekarte hin, er bestellte ein Glas Rotwein, ja den Hauswein. Und fragte: Zum Essen, eine Kleinigkeit, was können Sie empfehlen?

Wir haben da die normalen Sachen, sagte sie und tippte auf die Karte, und täglich ein Menu Anti-Crise.

Menu Anti-Crise?

Ja. Zuerst etwas sehr Deftiges, dann etwas sehr Süßes. Ist sehr beliebt bei uns hier. Heute Choucroute à l'Ancienne, dann Mousse au Chocolat. Achtzehn Euro ohne Marken. Und wenn Sie davor noch ein Duo de Fondue wollen, Fromages et Crevettes, dann fünfundzwanzig Euro.

Er sah diese heitere Person an und fragte sich, was das mit einem Menschen machte: Jeden Tag mit Trauergästen zu tun zu haben, nicht mit Toten, aber mit den Hinterbliebenen.

Also ein Menu Anti-Crise, sagte er, ohne Fondue.

Und ohne Marken. D'accord!

Er wartete und sah aus dem Fenster. Hinüber zum Friedhofseingang. Jetzt erst, aus der Distanz, von hier hinübersehend, fiel ihm auf, dass das Friedhofsportal eine gewisse Ähnlichkeit mit dem Tor von Birkenau hatte.

Da kam sein Rotwein.

Ein schmiedeeisernes Tor hat immer eine Ähnlichkeit mit einem schmiedeeisernen Tor. Und die Türme rechts und links? Was sollte sonst sein rechts und links von einem schmiedeeisernen Tor? Wie die Menschen im Lager – es waren Menschen, was sollten sie sonst sein? Dennoch ist der Eindruck, es gäbe eine Ähnlichkeit, verrückt. Es gibt sie nicht. Das war alles.

Viertes Kapitel

Wenn wir in die Zukunft reisen könnten,
hätten wir noch mehr Distanz.

Martin Susman wollte die Dienstreise nach Polen möglichst unbeschadet an Leib und Seele hinter sich bringen. Nie hätte er sich vorstellen können, dass ausgerechnet diese Reise ihm die Idee, mehr noch: die fixe Idee für das »Big Jubilee Project« geben und letztlich sein Leben fast auf den Kopf stellen sollte.

Aber zunächst litt er unter den Reisevorbereitungen.

Er war verblüfft, als die Verkäuferin sein Gestammel sofort unterbrach: Bien sûr, natürlich sei ihr deutsche Unterwäsche ein Begriff, sie nannte einen Markennamen, und selbstverständlich würden sie dieses – sie lächelte – deutsche Qualitätsprodukt führen.

Martin hatte Kassándra Mercouri gefragt, ob sie ein Fachgeschäft für Unterwäsche kenne, und sie hatte ihm empfohlen, nach Ixelles zu fahren, in die Galerie Toison d'Or, da gebe es einen Laden, der eine große Auswahl habe, der Laden heiße Tollé, nein, er heiße Fronde, ja, ganz sicher: Fronde. Jedenfalls stehe ja auch ganz groß »Unterwäsche« auf dem Ladenschild, »Underwear«, sagte sie, außerdem werde er das Geschäft ja gleich an der Auslage erkennen. Die hätten alles. Sie selbst kaufe ihre Unterwäsche nur dort.

Als Martin den Laden gefunden hatte – »Fronde Dessous« – und in die Auslage schaute, sah er plötzlich die mütterliche Kassándra mit anderen Augen. Hier kaufte sie ihre Unterwäsche? Kassándra? Er dachte, dass er sich offenbar nicht klar genug ausgedrückt hatte, das war jetzt zweifellos ein Missverständnis. Er sah wunderschöne, nun ja, Unterwäsche, edle, wirklich reizende Dessous, aber für ihn? Und – für Auschwitz?

Er sah sich um, sah gegenüber einen »Adventure Shop«, da bekam man alles, was man brauchte, um den Mount Everest zu besteigen ... vielleicht sollte er dort nach seiner Frostschutzausrüstung suchen, hatte er jetzt wirklich gedacht: Frostschutzausrüstung? Es war so lächerlich. Er konnte nicht entscheiden, was ihn jetzt mehr überforderte: mit seinem schlaffen, schwammigen Körper zu den gegerbten Abenteurer-Machos da hinüberzugehen oder – nein, Kassándra hatte ihm den »Fronde«-Laden empfohlen und so trat er kurzentschlossen ein.

Er fühlte sich wie ein Siebzehnjähriger aus der Provinz, der zum ersten Mal in einer Großstadtdisco ein Mädchen anspricht, als er der Verkäuferin zu erklären versuchte, was er wollte. Als er »deutsche Unterwäsche«, sagte: »Ich meine, es gibt eine speziell warme Unterwäsche, ich glaube von einer deutschen Firma, ich weiß nicht, ob Sie verstehen, was ich meine, jedenfalls besonders warm –«, schloss er die Augen, als fürchtete er, diese Frau könnte an seinen Augen ablesen, dass er sie in seiner Phantasie in ebenden Dessous sah, die die Puppen in der Auslage trugen.

Bien sûr! Da war ein Schrank mit vielen Schubladen, wie er ihn von Apotheken kannte, sie öffnete eine Lade, ließ sie wieder zugleiten, öffnete eine andere und entnahm ihr einige Cellophanpäckchen, die sie auf dem Verkaufstisch vor ihm ausbreitete. Bitte sehr, sagte sie, meinten Sie das? Unterhemd, lange Unterhose, Strümpfe, und das hier sind Pulswärmer. Hundert Prozent Angora. Und sehen Sie hier, da steht es: Deutsche Qualität. Ich sage Ihnen, diese Dinger sind heißer als die Hölle.

Sie lachte. Oder sagen wir: Sauna! Sie verreisen?

Ja, sagte er, nach – Polen.

Oh. Ich kenne Polen nicht. Aber ich stelle mir vor, das kann man dort brauchen, ist ja fast schon Sibirien. Sie lachte, riss eine Packung auf, breitete eine lange Unterhose vor ihm aus, strich über den Stoff, sagte: Bitte! Fassen Sie mal hin! Spüren Sie, wie weich und warm das ist? Das ist aus dem Fell von diesen Kaninchen gemacht, Angora, verstehen Sie? Aber aus Deutschland, das heißt: garantiert ohne Tierquälerei. Und sehen Sie hier, das Zertifikat: Die Wäsche entspricht auch schon der neuen EU-Richtlinie für Unterwäsche.

Wie bitte?

Ja, Monsieur. Hat mich auch gewundert. Unlängst war der Vertreter da, hat uns das erklärt. Es geht um das Brennverhalten der Unterwäsche, das ist jetzt geregelt.

Sie meinen – Martin lachte gekünstelt –, die Unterwäsche ist so heiß, dass Gefahr besteht, dass sie sich entzündet?

Das Mädchen lächelte. Nein, aber irgendwie geht es darum: Sie darf nicht brennbar sein. Ich weiß auch nicht warum. Und Angora ist eigentlich, ist ja Kaninchenfell. Das ist natürlich extrem brennbar. Aber jetzt nicht mehr. Das muss jetzt irgendwie imprägniert werden. EU, verstehen Sie? Vielleicht weil vor allem Raucher diese Unterwäsche kaufen, die müssen ja immer im Freien stehen, in der Kälte. Und da gibt es jetzt diese EU-Richtlinie: damit sich die Raucher nicht selbst anzünden! Sie lachte. Oder im Bett.

Im Bett?

Ja, wenn Raucher mit einer Zigarette ins Bett gehen und einschlafen –

Dann brennt das Bett –

Ja, aber diese Unterwäsche nicht. Das ist geregelt! Sehen Sie, hier: »Brennverhalten von Unterwäsche gemäß EU-Richtlinie ...«

Ich glaube es nicht, Mademoiselle.

Ich auch nicht, sagte sie.

Das Erste, was Kai-Uwe Frigge an diesem Montag machte, war, die Liste »Valise Voyage à Doha« zu überfliegen, die ihm Madeleine, seine Sekretärin, zum Unterschreiben auf den Schreibtisch gelegt hat. Das hatte Frigge hier eingeführt: Jeden Montag legte ihm Madeleine eine Liste vor, auf der für jeden Tag, von Dienstag bis Montag, gemäß seinen Terminen und Verpflichtungen, sein Dresscode festgelegt wurde. In der Regel unterschrieb Frigge die Liste, die daraufhin von Madeleine an Dubravka, seine Haushälterin, gemailt wurde. Dubravka legte dann täglich in der Früh seine Kleidung, so wie es in der Liste stand, bereit oder packte sie vor Reisen entsprechend in seinen Koffer.

Das war im Haus bekannt, und es gab einige, die darüber lächelten oder ironische Bemerkungen machten, aber das schadete Frigges Ruf nicht, im Gegenteil: Diese Schrulle zeigte, dass er bis ins Detail ein knallharter Pragmatiker war, der über die Gabe verfügte, originelle Lösungen zu finden, um beim Mitlaufen etwas weniger zu schwitzen oder beim Mitschwimmen weniger nass zu werden. In Bürokratien kommt ein solcher Ruf dem höchsten Adelsschlag gleich.

Es gibt eine bezeichnende Anekdote aus Frigges Studententagen, die Frauke Diestel von der DG Energie erzählt hatte. Sie war seinerzeit Frigges Kommilitonin an der Universität Hamburg gewesen und eine Zeitlang seine Mitbewohnerin in einer WG. Kai-Uwe, erzählte sie, habe damals eines Tages alle seine farbigen und gemusterten Hemden verschenkt und im Shopping Center Hamburger Meile bei einem Abverkauf günstig zehn identische weiße Hemden gekauft. Er habe das damals folgendermaßen erklärt: er spare jetzt täglich in der Früh Zeit, weil er nicht mehr darüber nachdenken müsse, welches Hemd zu welchem Jackett oder Pullover passe, ein weißes Hemd passe immer, egal was er darüber anziehe. Er könne jetzt, ohne lange nachzudenken, in der Früh einfach das oberste Hemd vom Stapel aus dem Schrank nehmen und anziehen, und wenn er das achte Hemd nehme, dann wisse er, dass er die schmutzigen Hemden in die Wäscherei bringen müsse, die er, wenn er das zehnte Hemd anziehe, abholen könne, so dass er am nächsten Tag wieder mit dem ersten Hemd beginnen könne. Es war irgendwie verrückt, erzählte Frauke, aber es hatte Logik. Die weißen Hemden hatte er deshalb so günstig bekommen, weil sie unverkäufliche altmodische Dinger waren, bei denen man noch Stäbchen in die Kragenspitzen stecken musste. Aber ihn hat das entzückt: Das ist noch Kultur, hatte er gesagt. Die Ärmel waren zu lang, aber er fand auf dem Flohmarkt alte Ärmelhalter, die er am Oberarm trug, um die Ärmellänge zu adjustieren. Auch das fiel für ihn unter »alte Kultur«. Männeraccessoires, das liebte er. Damals kamen diese amerikanischen Gangster- und Mafia-Filme auf, in denen die Männer alle solche Ärmelhalter trugen, das wurde Mode – und plötzlich war Kai-Uwe mit seiner schrullig pragmatischen Art und seinem völligen Desinteresse an Modetorheiten so etwas wie ein Trendsetter! Auch wenn Kai-Uwe missverstanden wird, sagte Frauke, könne man davon ausgehen, dass es seinem Ruf nützt.

Kai-Uwe Frigge war nach Durchsicht der Liste verärgert. Madeleine hatte wieder vergessen, was er ihr doch schon so oft gesagt hatte: Bei einer Reise in ein heißes Land brauchte er nicht luftige und dünne Wäsche, im Gegenteil, gerade in heißen Ländern musste er warme Kleidungsstücke mithaben, durchaus leichte, aber eben doch warme Kleidung, feine Kaschmir-Westen zum Beispiel, und auf jeden Fall Unterhemden. Man sitzt ja bei den Verhandlungen und Meetings und bei den Mahlzeiten ununterbrochen in klimatisierten, brutal runtergekühlten Räumen herum, nirgendwo friert man mehr als bei diesen Wüstenscheichs, wo Kälte als Luxus gilt und Luxus als Lebensinhalt. Wenn man in Doha nicht gerade auf einer Straße herumspaziert – aber wer macht das schon, und warum sollte man das tun? –, dann ist es dort kälter als auf einer Parkbank in Nordfinnland.

Er rief Madeleine zu sich, wies sie an, die Liste neu zu machen. Vergessen Sie alle diese Leinen- und Seiden-Dinger, das geht in Straßburg im Sommer, aber nie in Doha. Wolle, Kaschmir, ja? Westen und Unterhemden. Und Halstuch, Schal. Und setzen Sie bitte unter Diverses auch das Ladekabel für Telefon und Tablet auf die Liste, und Schuhcreme. Damit Dubra das auch einpackt.

Madeleine nickte, ging zur Tür.

Madeleine!

Ja, Monsieur?

Noch etwas. Setzen Sie bitte auch den blauen Schesch auf die Liste.

Nein.

Doch. Man kann nie wissen. Womöglich müssen wir doch einmal – er hüstelte – ins Freie.

Kai-Uwe Frigge sah auf die Uhr. Jetzt musste er sich noch um die »Schweinerei« kümmern, wie er es nannte.

Mateusz Oswiecki wollte vor seinem Abflug noch beten. Er musste sich sammeln. Es quälte ihn, dass er den falschen Mann exekutiert hatte.

Vor dem Durchgang zum Security-Check sah er Aktivisten, die Flugblätter verteilten, ein gutes Dutzend junger Frauen und Männer, die alle das gleiche gelbe T-Shirt trugen, mit einem Slogan auf der Brust, den er allerdings nicht lesen konnte. Drei Polizisten standen unschlüssig an der Seite, während ein anderer Polizist mit einem der Aktivisten redete, ein weiterer sprach in ein Funkgerät.

Mateusz verlangsamte seinen Schritt, um erst einmal die Szene zu überblicken, beschleunigte dann, ganz eiliger Passagier, der seinen Flug nicht versäumen wollte, versuchte mit demonstrativer Ungeduld, sich da durchzuschlängeln. Er war schon fast an der Durchgangssperre angekommen, da stellte sich ihm eine Aktivistin in den Weg. Excuse me, Sir, may I – er reagierte nicht, versuchte an ihr vorbeizugehen. Do you speak English, Sir? Sir? Er sah sie nicht an, manövrierte seinen Trolley an ihr vorbei. Parlez-vouz français? Volez-vous vers la Pologne? Are you going to Poland? Sir? It is important, een vraag, mijnheer – Er senkte den Kopf, sah aus dem Augenwinkel, dass ein Polizist zu ihm herüberblickte, und er fühlte sich sicher. Das war fast komisch: Er würde entkommen mit Hilfe eines Polizisten, der einschreiten müsste, wenn ein Passagier belästigt wird. Aber Mateusz wollte es nicht darauf ankommen lassen, wollte nicht in etwas verwickelt werden, das die Polizei hier auf den Plan gerufen hatte. Die Frau hielt ihm ein Flugblatt hin, er sah, dass ein Mann darauf abgebildet war, es sah aus wie ein Fahndungsfoto. War das ein Steckbrief? Mateusz legte das Ticket auf das Display der Durchgangsschranke, es leuchtete rot auf, was war da los? Sir, please, fliegen Sie mit Polish Airlines? Flug LO 236? Wir haben eine wichtige Information – Er wusste, dass es sinnlos war, ja dass es alles noch komplizierter machen würde, wenn er jetzt sagen würde: Sorry, ich habe es eilig! Denn dann wäre ein Gespräch eröffnet, sie würde sagen, dass sie seine Zeit nur ganz kurz in Anspruch nehmen wolle, er müsste darauf wieder etwas antworten – nein, er legte wortlos das Ticket noch einmal auf das Display, wieder leuchtete es rot, er rieb das Ticket ein paar Mal hin und her, warum verdammt funktionierte es nicht? Da kam das grüne Licht, die Glasflügel klappten auf, und er war durch. Er stellte sich in die Schlange, die langsam zum Security-Check vorrückte. Er sah ein paar Passagiere, die das Flugblatt lasen. Als er den Scanner passiert hatte, suchte er nach dem Wegweiser zu den Andachtsräumen.

Er hatte noch mehr als eine Stunde Zeit bis zum Boarding. Er lief mit seinem Trolley an den Shops vorbei, lief immer schneller, da waren schon die Gates – wo war die Flughafenkapelle? Er lief zurück, fand keinen Hinweis. Er wollte beten. Er hatte den falschen Mann erschossen. Das war ihm nach den letzten Anweisungen, die er erhalten hatte, klar geworden. Schließlich entdeckte er ein Schild mit einem Piktogramm, das wohl einen auf Knien betenden Menschen darstellte, daneben ein Pfeil, der in einen Seitengang wies. Dort wieder das betende Männchen mit dem Pfeil, der zu einem Treppenaufgang zeigte.

Er folgte den Pfeilen, musste an den heiligen Sebastian denken, an dessen von Pfeilen durchbohrte Brust. Noch vor wenigen Tagen, am 20. Januar, dem Gedenktag dieses Heiligen, des Schutzpatrons der Soldaten und Kämpfer gegen die Feinde der Kirche, hatte er dessen Schutz erfleht und um Gelingen seiner Aufgabe in Brüssel gebetet, aber irgendetwas war schiefgelaufen, und er konnte sich nicht erklären, was. Die Pfeile führten in einen von Videokameras überwachten Gang. Er ging weiter, mit gesenktem Kopf, strich sich mit dem Taschentuch über die Stirn, als würde er Schweiß abwischen, damit die Kameras sein Gesicht nicht erfassten – er wusste, dass er übertrieben vorsichtig war: Diese Überwachungskameras hier waren veraltet. Schneite es in diesem Gang? Natürlich nicht. Aber 48 Stunden lang würden von diesen Kameras Bilder in so grober Auflösung gespeichert werden, dass darauf nur ein schemenhafter Mann zu sehen wäre, der durch ein Schneetreiben zu gehen schien. Rechts und links Topfpflanzen. Aus Plastik. Hanf. Kein Zweifel, das waren Hanfpflanzen aus Plastik. Wer hatte die Idee gehabt, im Korridor zu den Kapellen Hanfpflanzen aus Plastik aufzustellen? Und was hatte derjenige sich dabei gedacht? Nun erreichte er die Andachtsräume. Es gab für jede große Religionsgemeinschaft einen eigenen Raum. Katholisch, protestantisch, jüdisch, islamisch und orthodox. Sie alle waren leer, mehr als das: so leer, als hätte keiner sie jemals betreten.

Mateusz spürte einen starken Schmerz, als er den katholischen Andachtsraum betrat. Dieser Raum war von einer unglaublichen Hässlichkeit. Unglaublich – das war schon wieder grotesk an einem Ort des Glaubens. Er spürte ein stechendes Brennen unterhalb seines Nabels, kalten Schweiß auf der Stirn, er ging ein paar Schritte nach vorn, ließ den Trolley los, zog sein Taschentuch aus der Hosentasche und wischte sich den Schweiß ab, während er die andere Hand gegen seinen Bauch drückte. Da kippte der Trolley um, es machte einen Knall, als Mateusz mit dem Schweißtuch in der Hand vor Jesus Christus stand. Die Stirnseite des Raums war mit einigen Holzlatten vertäfelt, darauf hing der Gekreuzigte – aber ohne Kreuz. Als wäre der Sohn Gottes nicht an ein Kreuz, sondern an einen Zaun genagelt worden. Von der Decke hing ein Spot, der einen harten weißen Lichtstrahl auf Jesus Christus warf, als müsste er sich, nachdem er an den Zaun genagelt worden war, noch einem letzten Verhör unterziehen. Davor stand ein kleiner hölzerner Altar, der aber eher aussah wie eine dieser Musiktruhen, wie sie viele Polen in den späten siebziger Jahren des vorigen Jahrhunderts von Reisen in den Westen mitgebracht hatten und die dann bis zur Wende als ewiges Memento ersehnter Modernität in polnischen Wohnzimmern standen. An der Seitenwand hing ein Triptychon, Öl auf Leinwand, seltsam unentschlossen zwischen abstrakt und gegenständlich. Auf dem linken Bild war eine untergehende Sonne zu erkennen, zumindest ein roter Ball, der auf eine Menschenmenge herabstürzte oder über dieser schwebte, die Menschen waren vielleicht Kardinäle in Purpur, aber vielleicht waren es auch keine Kardinäle, sondern nur Lichtspiegelungen der rot untergehenden Sonne oder Flammen oder Gewächse. Der

Mittelteil zeigte etwas, das aussah wie ein aufgespießtes UFO, vielleicht war es aber auch eine Müllverbrennungsanlage. Am klarsten war das rechte Bild des Triptychons: eine Blutlache unter gleißend weißem Licht, aus dem sich ein weißes Kreuz hervorhob. Neben dem Kreuz war ein Satz aufgemalt: »UBI LUX IBI BLUT«. Er konnte Latein, hatte es natürlich im Seminar gelernt, aber das verstand er nicht: Was bedeutete »BLUT«? Was war das für ein Wort? »Wo Licht ist, ist –« Er ging näher, schaute, ob er sich verlesen hatte, versuchte dieses rätselhafte Wort zu entziffern, »BLUT« – diese Vokabel kannte er nicht. Jetzt erst sah er, dass es wahrscheinlich, nein, ganz sicher »DEUS« hieß, so kraftlos und undeutlich gemalt, als wollte es in den Schatten der Bildgrundierung treten. Neben dem Triptychon standen zwei große geschnitzte Holzfiguren, sie erinnerten an Hirtenjungen von Weihnachtskrippen, aber noch mehr an Priesterseminarzöglinge in Nachthemden.

Mateusz war im Nachthemd dagestanden, barfuß auf kaltem Steinboden, »Sammlung« hatte dies geheißen, wenn ein Zögling nach dem Abendgebet noch abkommandiert wurde, im Arkadengang neben der Statue des ihm zugewiesenen Heiligen strammzustehen, mit Blick hinunter in den Innenhof, Blick hinauf in den Sternenhimmel, um über »die drei Fragen« nachzudenken, bis er vom Pater Prior gerufen wurde, um die Antworten zu geben, manchmal nach zwei oder drei Stunden, manchmal erst am nächsten Tag vor dem Morgengebet. Wie groß ist der Zweifel an der Stärke deines Glaubens? Wie sicher bist du, den Zweifel zu besiegen? Durch welche Taten willst du die Stärke deines Glaubens beweisen?

Mateusz war von einer eigentümlichen Erregung erfasst worden, nicht bloß einer allgemeinen Aufgeregtheit oder Angst, sondern buchstäblich Erregung, einer sexuellen oder erotischen Energie, als er die Glätte und Kälte des Steins unter sei-

nen Fußsohlen spürte, die Kälte, die über die Füße in ihm
aufstieg und seine Muskeln, sein Gewebe hart und straff machte, während er zugleich die glatte Oberfläche des Steins wie
die Haut eines Körpers empfand, Marmorhaut, Heiligenhaut,
Mutter-Gottes-Haut, die er berührte, an die er sich schmiegte, mit der er verschmolz. Er hatte sich neben der Figur des
heiligen Sebastian hinstellen müssen und nicht gewusst, ob
es Zufall oder eine mit Bedacht gewählte Entscheidung des
Priors war, als er ihn angewiesen hatte, hier seine Sammlung
durchzuführen.

Mateusz hatte das Gespräch mit dem Pater gesucht, nicht
weil er Zweifel an seinem Glauben hatte, sondern Zweifel
daran, wie er seinen Glauben leben wollte. Er war bereit für
den Kampf, aber er wollte einen Sohn in die Welt setzen, so
wie sein Vater und sein Großvater es getan hatten, bevor sie
in den Kampf gingen.

– Du willst, dass dein Name weiterlebt? Dein Blut? Etwas
von dir? Du wirst ewig leben, wenn du stirbst, aber du willst
hier auf Erden weiterleben?

Mateusz war nun wieder Ryszard gewesen und hatte keine
Antwort geben können.

Sammlung. Vor dem Morgengebet war er gefunden worden,
lang hingestreckt auf den Steinplatten des Gangs liegend, als
hätte er versucht, möglichst viel Haut mit dem Stein in Berührung zu bringen. Er war stark unterkühlt gewesen, dann
hatte er tagelang gefiebert. Danach beantwortete er die drei
Fragen. Durchaus überzeugend und zur Zufriedenheit des
Priors. Aber im Seminar konnte er nicht bleiben.

Der glühende Schmerz. Mateusz wandte den Blick von den
Krippenfiguren ab, sah um sich. Er hatte beten wollen. Hier
konnte er es nicht. Er drückte eine Hand gegen sein Zwerchfell, stöhnte, wischte sich den Schweiß von der Stirn. Er hatte
nicht mehr viel Zeit.

Er atmete tief ein und aus, verließ die Flughafenkapelle und ging zum Gate.

Ursprünglich hätte er nach Erledigung seines Auftrags nach Warschau zurückfliegen sollen. In der Nacht war aber ein Umschlag für ihn im Hotel abgegeben worden, der ihm am Morgen an der Rezeption ausgehändigt wurde. Darin fand er ein Flugticket nach Istanbul sowie die Reservierungsbestätigung eines Istanbuler Hotels. Mateusz wusste, das war kein neuer Auftrag, konnte keiner sein. Jeder neue Auftrag begann mit einem Dossier über die Zielperson und wurde bis ins Detail geplant und vorbereitet. Und noch nie hatte ein Soldat nach Erledigung eines Auftrags schon am nächsten Tag einen neuen bekommen. Der Rückzug in die Etappe danach hatte für die Sicherheit jeder Aktion eine ebenso große Bedeutung wie die exakte Planung davor. Er konnte sich das nur so erklären: Die Zielperson war nach Istanbul ausgewichen, aber das hieß auch, dass er den falschen Mann erschossen hatte. Oder aber, dies war eine Falle. Wenn man sich seiner entledigen wollte, dann war das die einfachste Methode: Er hatte bedingungslosen Gehorsam geschworen. Ein Tier musste man in die Falle locken. Einem Soldaten musste man bloß den Marschbefehl geben, in die Falle zu gehen.

Irgendetwas war da faul. Für Operationen außerhalb des Schengen-Raums hatten sie eigene Spezialisten. Mateusz hatte zwar Vertrauen in seinen Pass, der sicherlich perfekt gemacht war, aber die Kontrollen an der Schengen-Grenze waren doch genauere, und er wollte sich nicht darauf verlassen müssen, dass sein Pass auch diesen standhielt.

Er war zum Flughafen gefahren und hatte versucht, mit seinem ursprünglichen Ticket nach Warschau einzuchecken. Die Frau am Schalter sagte, dass er diesen Flug doch storniert hätte.

Nein.

Doch. Sie sind nicht mehr auf der Passagierliste, Monsieur. Sie haben gestern Abend storniert.

Missverständnis! Ich will diesen Flug.

Es tut mir leid, ich kann Ihnen keine Bordkarte ausstellen. Sie haben kein Ticket mehr für diesen Flug.

Aber bezahlt!

Die Frau tippte in den Computer, schaute, tippte, schaute und sagte: Der Ticketpreis abzüglich Stornogebühr ist Ihrer Kreditkarte wieder gutgeschrieben worden.

Meine Kreditkarte? Ich habe nicht – gut! Dann ich will neues Ticket. Ich kaufe neues Ticket.

Es tut mir sehr leid, Monsieur, aber der Flug ist ausgebucht. Es gibt keinen Platz mehr.

Aber ich muss nach Polen. Heute.

Sind Sie Pole, Monsieur? Ja? Wir können auch polnisch sprechen, drogi Panie. Mein Vater ist Pole. Er kam als Hydraulik nach Brüssel, plombier. Hat hier meine Mutter kennengelernt. Wir werden eine Lösung finden. Gdy zaleje woda, trzeba wymienić rurę.

Es gab noch einen freien Platz für den Flug nach Krakau in zwei Stunden. Oder eine Stunde später nach Frankfurt, mit Anschluss nach Warschau. Er nahm den Flug nach Krakau. Er wollte so schnell wie möglich zurück nach Polen.

So kam es, dass er schließlich im selben Flieger saß wie Martin Susman. Aber welche Bedeutung haben schon Zusammenhänge, Verflechtungen und Vernetzungen, wenn die Betreffenden nichts davon wissen?

Martin Susman ärgerte sich über seine Schnapsidee, die warme Unterwäsche gleich auf der Reise anzuziehen. Damit er nicht fror, wenn er in Krakau ankam. Schon im Taxi zum

Flughafen fing er an zu schwitzen wie ein Schwein. Das Taxi war natürlich geheizt, wahrscheinlich überheizt, und in seinem Kaninchenfell fühlte er sich, als hätte er hohes Fieber. Warum sagte man im Deutschen »schwitzen wie ein Schwein«? Als Sohn eines Schweinebauern wusste er natürlich, dass Schweine nicht schwitzen, nicht durch die Haut transpirieren können. Als Kind hatte er diese Redewendung einmal verwendet – warum? Weil man so sagt. Sein Vater hatte ihn zurechtgewiesen. Schweine schwitzen nicht. Und man muss nicht alles machen, was andere machen, wenn andere Unsinn reden, dann musst du ja nicht auch Unsinn reden!

Aber warum sagt man so?

Weil viele Menschen ein Problem mit Blut haben. Wenn sie früher, bei den Hausschlachtungen, gesehen haben, wie stark die Schweine bluten, dann haben sie das Blut Schweiß genannt. Eine Umschreibung, verstehst du? Das klingt nicht so schlimm. Die Jäger sagen heute noch Schweiß zum Blut der Tiere, und der Hund, der ein angeschossenes und blutendes Tier sucht und stellt, heißt Schweißhund.

Aber wir sagen Blutwurst und nicht Schweißwurst.

Genug, hatte Vater gesagt, geh rein und hilf der Mutter!

Er hatte diese Floskel seither nicht mehr verwendet, aber jetzt, im Taxi zum Flughafen, war sie plötzlich wieder da, in seinem Kopf, und die Erinnerung daran, dass eigentlich Blut gemeint war, Blutvergießen, Ströme von Blut, ein Blutbad.

Martin Susman hatte, als er am Flughafen ankam, eine ganze Packung Papiertaschentücher zum Schweiß-Abwischen verbraucht, er hielt einen Klumpen nassen Papiers in der Hand, als er aus dem Taxi stieg, nun hatte er auch keine Taschentücher mehr, er wischte sich mit dem Ärmel übers Gesicht, es war aussichtslos, er schwitzte und schwitzte. Blut. Er wollte neue Taschentücher kaufen, lief hin und her, wodurch er nur noch mehr schwitzte. Schließlich beschloss er, direkt zum Gate zu gehen, möglichst langsam, sich dort hinzusetzen, vielleicht hörte er dann auf zu schwitzen, wenn er sich nicht bewegte. Er war wütend auf sich selbst, das hätte ihm doch klar sein müssen, dass es völlig absurd war, diese Unterwäsche in Situationen anzuziehen, in denen er ohnehin nicht frieren würde. In Krakau würde man ihn am Flughafen abholen, in einem geheizten Taxi zu einem geheizten Hotel bringen, dort würde er Gelegenheit haben sich umzuziehen, er hätte die Unterwäsche dann dort, vor der Weiterfahrt ins Lager, anziehen können – aber jetzt war es sehr fraglich, ob die völlig schweißnasse Unterwäsche im Hotel rechtzeitig trocknen würde, wahrscheinlich wird sie im Hotelzimmer zum Trocknen hängen, während er dann im Lager ohne Unterwäsche der mörderischen Kälte ausgesetzt war.

Er hatte Wallungen. Selbsthass. Er war jetzt 38 Jahre alt und noch immer nicht imstande, sich alleine, einer Situation und ihren Anforderungen entsprechend, anzuziehen. Der Begriff »lebenstüchtig« fiel ihm ein, wie oft hatte er das gehört: Dieses Kind ist nicht lebenstüchtig! Nicht lebenstüchtig! Aber zum Glück haben wir ja den Florian!

Von »Lebenstüchtigkeit« war es nicht weit zu »Lebenswille«. Er wusste oder glaubte zu wissen, wie das zusammenhing. Untrennbar. Das schaukelt sich hoch oder zieht sich wechselseitig hinunter. Bei Individuen, Familien, gesellschaftlichen Gruppen, ganzen Gesellschaften. Er hatte Glück: Seine Lebensuntüchtigkeit führte nicht zu einem schnellen Ende des Lebens, sein Lebenswille konnte brechen, doch er konnte noch lange gebrochen durchs Leben gehen. Aber er bekam Angst, wenn in den Medien immer wieder diese Lebensratgeber auftauchten und ihre ideologischen Phrasen zu blinken begannen: »Man muss loslassen können«, »Man muss lernen, sich fallenzulassen« … Sie wussten nicht, was sie da redeten. Man konnte das an den vier archäologischen Schichten bei Ausgrabungen studieren, da war immer sehr genau datierbar, wann es begonnen hatte: das Loslassen, das Sichfallenlassen, der Tod, den die Lebensratgeber predigten. Die dritte Schicht.

Knapp vor dem Durchgang zum Security-Check bot sich ihm ein seltsames, verwirrendes Bild. Er hatte den Eindruck, als würden sich da inmitten der Passagierströme zwei Teams gegenüberstehen, das eine in gelben Dressen, das andere in blauen. Gab es da ein Spiel, einen Wettkampf? Ein Spiel nicht, aber einen Wettkampf schon, in gewissem Sinne. Eine junge Frau im gelben Dress sprach ihn an: Entschuldigen Sie, mein Herr, fliegen Sie nach Polen?

Ja, sagte er. Sie sah ihn an, es war ihm peinlich, was musste sie sich denken, als sie sein nasses Gesicht, seine geröteten Augen sah? Sie lächelte, sprach schnell weiter. Sie sei Aktivistin der Menschenrechtsorganisation »Stop Deportation« und –

Wie bitte?

Stop Deportation, sagte sie und zeigte auf den Slogan auf ihrem T-Shirt:

NO BORDER
NO NATION
STOP DEPORTATION

Es geht darum, dass ein Mann abgeschoben werden soll, der –

Nun kam ein Mann vom blauen Team, ein Polizist, er sagte: Werden Sie belästigt, mein Herr? Zu Ihrer Information: Es handelt sich hier um eine angemeldete und bewilligte Kundgebung, aber wir können diese Kundgebung auflösen, wenn sich Passagiere belästigt fühlen.

Nein, nein, sagte Martin Susman, es ist okay, es ist okay. Ich werde nicht belästigt.

Er strich sich mehrmals den Schweiß von der Stirn ins Haar.

Der Polizist nickte, entfernte sich, sprach einen anderen Passagier an, der von einem Aktivisten in ein Gespräch verwickelt wurde.

Susman erfuhr, dass ein Tschetschene abgeschoben werden solle, der in seiner Heimat politisch verfolgt und gefoltert worden sei. Über Polen sei er in die EU gekommen. Nun solle er nach Polen abgeschoben werden, von dort werde er an Russland ausgeliefert. Russland werde von den Behörden für Tschetschenen als sicher eingestuft. Das sei blanker Zynismus. Es sei mehrfach nachgewiesen worden, dass nach Russland abgeschobene Tschetschenen in Folterkellern verschwinden.

Die Frau gab ihm ein Flugblatt. Das ist der Mann, sagte sie, Aslan Achmatow. Er ist traumatisiert, und ihm drohen erneute Folter und der Tod. Das ist ein Menschenrechtsskandal, Monsieur. Stimmen Sie mir zu? Hier steht, was Sie als Passagier tun können, um die Abschiebung zu verhindern, wenn Sie diesen Mann im Flugzeug sehen. Verlangen Sie mit dem Piloten zu sprechen und fordern Sie ihn auf, die Abschiebung aus humanitären Gründen und aus Gründen der Flugsicherheit abzubrechen. Er hat die Bordgewalt, er kann den Transport von Passagieren, die nicht freiwillig mitfliegen, ablehnen.

Sie sprach immer schneller, während er das Flugblatt las.

Steht alles hier! Weigern Sie sich, Platz zu nehmen und sich anzuschnallen, machen Sie die anderen Passagiere darauf aufmerksam, dass es sich hier nicht um einen normalen Transport, sondern um einen gewaltsamen Akt handelt und –

Entschuldigen Sie, sagte Martin, aber hier steht, es handelt sich um den Flug LO 236 nach Warschau. Aber ich fliege nach Krakau!

Oh! Pardon! Ich hätte – natürlich. Danke. Ich danke Ihnen für Ihre Geduld, Ihr Verständnis. Behalten Sie bitte das Flugblatt! Wegen der allgemeinen Informationen. Es gibt ja immer mehr Deportationen und – danke! Und einen guten Tag!

Sie drehte sich um, er sah ihr kurz nach, sie sprach einen anderen Passagier an, auf dem Rücken ihres T-Shirts stand »Resistance is possible«.

Als alle Passagiere Platz genommen hatten und das Boarding abgeschlossen war, stand eine Frau auf und ging, rechts und links in die Sitzreihen blickend, nach vorne. Vor dem Übergang in die Business Class stellte sich ihr eine Stewardess in den Weg –

Suchen Sie die Toilette, Madame? Die befindet sich am Ende der Maschine. Aber Sie können die Toilette jetzt nicht benutzen, Madame. Sie müssen sich bitte hinsetzen und sich anschnallen.

Ich will nicht auf die Toilette, sagte sie, und dann laut: Ich möchte den Flugkapitän sprechen! In diesem Flugzeug soll sich ein Passagier befinden, der nicht freiwillig mitfliegt. Und ich will wissen –

Bitte! Sie müssen –

Wir müssen wissen, ob er sich tatsächlich gegen seinen Willen in dieser Maschine befindet. Bitte rufen Sie den Kapitän!

Sie drehte sich um, ging den Mittelgang zurück. Mesdames, Messieurs, in dieser Maschine befindet sich ein Mann, der abgeschoben werden soll. Bitte helfen Sie mit, dass dieser Mann –

Bitte Madame! Sie müssen sich hinsetzen und –

Die Frau ging unbeirrt weiter, kam an der Reihe vorbei, in der Susman saß.

– wir müssen ihm ermöglichen, die Maschine zu verlassen.

Der Sitznachbar von Martin Susman starrte in seine Zeitung,

die Frau auf dem Gangsitz nebenan schloss die Augen, der Mann neben ihr auf dem Fensterplatz wischte unausgesetzt über sein Smartphone.

Martin Susman stand auf, um besser sehen zu können, was nun passierte. Sofort war eine Flugbegleiterin bei ihm, die ihn aufforderte, unverzüglich Platz zu nehmen und sich anzuschnallen.

Ja, sagte er, Moment! Ich wollte nur – Er öffnete die Gepäckablage, um aus seiner Tasche die Packung Nikotin-Kaugummi herauszuholen, nun blieb die Frau stehen, wandte sich an einen Passagier und fragte: Sind Sie Herr Achmatow?

Der Mann reagierte nicht. Er hatte eine Kapuze über den Kopf gezogen, das Kinn an der Brust.

Sprechen Sie Englisch, Sir? Sind Sie Mr Achmatow?

Mateusz Oswiecki sah auf und schüttelte den Kopf. Die Frau zögerte, sie war im ersten Moment nicht sicher, ob er verneinte, Englisch zu sprechen, oder ob er verneinte, die gesuchte Person zu sein. Sie sahen einander an. Mateusz hatte nicht genau verstanden, worum es ging, aber er begriff, dass diese Frau den Start verzögerte, und er hasste sie dafür. Er sah ihr ins Gesicht, ihre Blicke trafen sich und –

In diesem Moment geschah etwas mit ihm. Im Zwerchfell, da wo sein Schmerz saß. Es war, als wäre eine Ader geplatzt, und nun breitete sich warm und süß Blut in seinem Bauch aus. Er hatte keinen Gedanken, kein Satz bildete sich in seinem Kopf. Er hatte plötzlich ganz schwere Lider, er kämpfte damit, die Augen offen zu halten, um zu sehen, wie diese Frau ihn ansah, er wollte in diesem Blick verweilen, eine Sehnsucht auskosten, die er nicht gekannt hatte, und das Gefühl einer Geborgenheit, das er gekannt, aber vergessen hatte, aber nun war es als Erinnerungsbild da: wie er als Kind, stark fiebernd, wie durch einen Nebel das Gesicht der Mutter gesehen hatte, die sich über das Krankenbett gebeugt hatte und lächelte. Dieses Bild seiner Mutter wie eine Erscheinung im Nebel, es hatte ihm alle Angst genommen, auch die Angst davor, zu sterben, wenn er doch nachgab und die Augen schloss. Das war Kitsch. Er war kein Kind mehr, er hatte hart werden müssen und verachtete Rührseligkeit. Was er jetzt empfand, war unklar, so verschwommen wie das Erinnerungsbild. Die Sehnsucht nach einer geborgenen Kindheit, weil man sie gehabt oder weil man sie nicht gehabt hatte, teilen alle, Terroristen genauso wie Pazifisten. Er wollte nur … ihr Blick … da ging die Frau schon weiter. Sie bat um Verständnis für die Verzögerung des Starts, bat um Mithilfe, die Abschiebung zu verhindern. Martin Susman sah ihr nach, die Passagiere waren still, saßen reglos da, bei einigen meinte er an ihren Blicken zu erkennen, dass sie mit der Frau sympathisierten, andere schlossen die Augen, senkten den Kopf, da stand plötzlich ein Stewart neben ihm: Sie müssen sofort Platz nehmen, bitte setzen Sie sich und schnallen Sie sich an! Der Stewart legte mit sanftem Druck eine Hand auf Martins Schulter, verstärkte den Druck. Als Martin sich auf den Sitz fallen ließ, hörte er eine Männerstimme: Halt endlich die Klappe und setz dich hin!

Eine andere Stimme: Hören Sie doch auf, den Start zu verhindern! Sie sind im falschen Flieger! Der Mann befindet sich in der Maschine nach Warschau! Das stand doch in dem Flugblatt!

Die Frau: Er wurde umgebucht auf diesen Flug. Wegen der Proteste gegen seine Abschiebung. Ich habe eine SMS bekommen, dass er sich jetzt in dieser Maschine befindet. Um ihn so ohne Aufsehen nach Polen abzuschieben.

Nun stand ein junger Mann unmittelbar vor Martin Susman auf und rief: No Deportation! Von weiter vorn eine Frauenstimme: Solidarité!

Martin Susman lehnte sich aus seinem Sitz heraus und schaute nach hinten in den Mittelgang, die Frau stand nun in der letzten Reihe, er sah, wie sie sich zu einem Passagier hinunterbeugte. Wegen seiner verdrehten Haltung spürte er einen heftigen Spannungsschmerz im Rücken, von den Lendenwirbeln bis in den Nacken, er sollte aufstehen, dachte er, aber er wollte kein Risiko eingehen, welches Risiko? Er stand auf, streckte sich, drückte seine Hände in den Rücken, der junge Mann vor ihm setzte sich wieder, die Stewardess und der Stewart waren verschwunden, und er hörte, wie die Frau zu einem Passagier in der letzten Reihe sagte: Mr Achmatow? Sind Sie Mr Achmatow?

Yes!

Der Mann stand auf. Das war er wirklich? Er war nicht gefesselt und ohne Polizeibegleitung. Aber er wirkte benommen, irgendwie ruhiggestellt.

Die Frau zeigte ihm das Flugblatt mit seinem Foto, um sicherzugehen, er sagte Yes!

Es ist vorbei, sagte die Frau. Keine Angst, bleiben Sie stehen, bleiben Sie einfach stehen, und wir werden die Maschine verlassen.

Der Mann begann zu weinen. Er führte seine Hände ans Gesicht, die Handgelenke aneinandergedrückt, als wäre er gefesselt.

Polizisten kamen an Bord, führten die beiden ab. Passagiere applaudierten. Warum? Wegen der Zivilcourage der Frau? Oder weil die Staatsgewalt einschritt? Oder weil das Flugzeug nun endlich starten konnte? Jeder hatte seinen Grund. In Summe ergab das: Applaus!

Frigges Flug ging in vier Stunden. Dubra packte den Koffer. Und er hatte noch einen Termin mit seinem Kollegen George Morland von der DG AGRI. Zwischen der AGRI und der TRADE hatte es immer schon Konflikte und Kompetenzstreitigkeiten gegeben, das war geradezu Tradition, um nicht zu sagen: ein altes Spiel. Aber nun war der Konflikt eskaliert, und damit konnte man nicht mehr lächelnd umgehen, Kompromisse von Fall zu Fall schließen und dann miteinander auf ein Bier gehen oder, wenn die Chemie mit den Bio-Bauern nicht stimmte, höflich bedauernd keine Zeit haben, um auf ein Bier zu gehen. Jetzt herrschte Krieg, da musste man aufrüsten und die Entscheidung suchen. Der Streitpunkt, der zur Eskalation geführt hatte, waren ausgerechnet die Schweine. Das war es, was Frigge »die Schweinerei« nannte, andere in der Kommission sprachen in Hinblick auf den Konflikt zwischen TRADE und AGRI gar vom »Krieg der Schweine«. AGRI wollte durch Kürzung von Subventionen einen Rückgang der Schweineproduktion erreichen, um den Preisverfall von Schweinefleisch auf dem europäischen Markt zu stoppen, TRADE aber wollte die Schweineproduktion verstärkt fördern, weil sie im Außenhandel, vor allem mit China, große Wachstumschancen sah. Deshalb wollte TRADE ein Mandat, um den Export von Schweinefleischprodukten in Drittländer für ganz Europa zu verhandeln, und durchsetzen, die Schweineproduktion in Europa entsprechend der Nachfrage auf den Weltmärkten auszurichten, AGRI aber wollte bloß den Binnenmarkt regulieren, gemeinsame Standards durchsetzen, wobei die Veterinär-Standards wiederum in die Verantwortung der DG SANCO fielen. Und beide wollten sie die Außenhandelsverträge in der Souveränität der einzelnen Staaten belassen.

Das Ergebnis dieser Kompetenzstreitigkeiten war jedenfalls, dass jedes europäische Land allein und nur für sich mit China verhandelte, Europa wurde auseinanderdividiert, durch die Konkurrenz der europäischen Staaten kam es zu einem noch größeren Preisverfall, sowohl auf dem Binnenmarkt wie auch im Außenhandel, während kein Staat mehr allein die internationale Nachfrage bedienen konnte, weil ja gleichzeitig die Schweinebauern zum Aufgeben gedrängt wurden. Frigge fand das völlig verrückt. Und dieser Morland machte ihn rasend. Frigge fragte sich – warum eigentlich? Warum regte er sich auf? Die Kommission hatte nun einmal im Moment kein Mandat, für alle Mitgliedstaaten zu verhandeln, die Mitgliedstaaten waren froh, inzwischen die Lage für sich nutzen zu können und das Maximum jeweils für sich alleine herauszuholen. Es war natürlich ein Trugschluss, irgendwann würden sie es merken, aber im Moment konnte er das nicht ändern, er könnte die Dinge einfach über seinen Schreibtisch wandern lassen, emotionslos zuschauen, niemandem auf den Nerv gehen und irgendwann wieder weiter nach oben rutschen – aber nein! Er fand diese Situation so irrational, dass er nicht emotionslos bleiben konnte. Also blockierte er das Business as usual, wo er nur konnte, um eine Entscheidung zu erzwingen.

Der Kompetenzstreit beruhte darauf, dass das Schwein eine Querschnittmaterie war: das lebende Schwein im Stall »gehörte« der DG AGRI, nach der Schlachtung, als Schinken, Eisbein, Schnitzel, Wurst oder was auch immer, jedenfalls als »processed agricultural good« war die DG GROW zuständig, und erst wenn es Europa verließ, sozusagen als Schwein im Frachtschiff oder im LKW, gehörte es der DG TRADE. Das Problem war, dass man über das Schwein im Container nicht verhandeln konnte, wenn man über das Schwein im Heimatstall nicht bestimmen durfte. Die GROW war in dieser Frage inoffensiv. Dort beschäftigte man sich mit Regeln für die Auflistung von Inhaltsstoffen, Definitionen von Höchstgrenzen beim Einsatz von Pharmazeutika und Chemikalien, Qualitätskriterien. Ihnen war das Schwein buchstäblich Wurst, es sollte nur richtig etikettiert sein. Das

Match musste zwischen AGRI und TRADE entschieden werden.

George Morland war einem Gespräch mit Frigge seit Wochen ausgewichen. E-Mails hatte er mit Vertröstungen beantwortet: Lass uns demnächst darüber reden, alle Fakten auf den Tisch legen. Terminvorschläge von Frigge aber beantwortete er stereotyp mit dem Hinweis auf seinen aktuell besonders dichten Terminkalender. Die Kommissare hielten sich zurück. Sie waren neu und wollten sich erst einarbeiten. Aber die Zeit drängte. Die niederländische, die deutsche und die österreichische Regierung waren in ihren Verhandlungen mit China am weitesten. Die deutsche Kanzlerin ist im Lauf des vergangenen Kalenderjahrs acht Mal in China gewesen. Nächste Woche sollte der österreichische Präsident mit einer Flugzeugladung von Ministern, Interessenvertretern von Industrie, Handel und Landwirtschaft nach Peking fliegen, zualleroberst auf der Agenda: der Schweinehandel. Gleich danach hatten sich noch einmal die Holländer in Peking angesagt. Wenn es einem dieser Länder gelang, einen substantiellen bilateralen Vertrag mit China abzuschließen, dann war es politisch gesehen eher unwahrscheinlich, dass die EU ein Verhandlungsmandat bekam. Und dann wird das große Stechen beginnen, ganz brutal, das Unterbieten, der Versuch, die Nachbarn auszubooten. Statt gemeinsam vorzugehen, werden sie sich gegenseitig umbringen und mit ihrer Gier nach nationalem Wachstum eine europäische Krise produzieren. Das war so klar wie Kloßbrühe, um es mit Kai-Uwes Worten zu sagen. Morland wusste natürlich, dass Kai-Uwe Frigge an diesem Tag dienstlich verreisen musste. Und es war perfide, dass er ihm schließlich just diesen Terminvorschlag machte: drei Stunden vor Frigges Boarding.

Frigge war cool geblieben und hatte den Termin angenommen. Und nun saß er diesem Schwein gegenüber. Das war eine billige Assoziation, aber Frigge konnte nicht anders. Er ertrug diesen Morland nicht, hielt ihn für hinterhältig, zynisch und verantwortungslos. Das konnte schon einen starken Ausdruck rechtfertigen. Aber dazu kam Morlands Erscheinung: sein rundes rosafarbenes Gesicht, seine kleine breite Nase mittendrin, wie eine Steckdose. Er war Mitte dreißig, sah aber viel jünger aus, dieses britische Oberschichtkind, als würde er sich erst seit kurzem rasieren, weshalb seine Wangen immer so rötlich gereizt glühten. Er hatte dickes rotes Haar, das er zu einem Bürstenhaarschnitt trimmte, Frigge dachte: Borsten.

Frigge kam aus einer Hamburger Lehrerfamilie. Hanseatischer Internationalismus, Einsicht in die historische deutsche Schuld, ein großer abstrakter Anspruch auf Friede und Gerechtigkeit in der Welt, persönlicher Fleiß und Anstand, Misstrauen gegen Moden und Mainstream – das waren die Pflöcke, die seine Eltern eingeschlagen hatten, um das Feld abzustecken, in dem er aufwuchs. Er wusste, dass er, was Morland betraf, ungerecht war. Aber er wusste auch: Er hatte verdammt gute Gründe dafür.

Morland betrachtete seine Fingernägel, während er seine Sicht der Dinge erklärte. Frigge schloss die Augen, er wollte das nicht sehen, diese blasierte Art. Morland hatte in jedem Punkt recht. Ja, so war es. Das war die Situation. Aber der Unterschied bestand ja nicht darin, dass Frigge die Lage anders sah, sondern darin, dass Morland die Situation vernünftig fand und verteidigte, während Frigge aus dieser Situation herauskommen wollte.

Okay, George, sagte Frigge, stelle dir einmal Folgendes vor: Du wärst ein leibeigener Bauer!

– Warum sollte ich das tun?

– Nur ein Gedankenspiel! Also –

– Mit einem solchen Gedanken möchte ich nicht spielen!

– Also gut. Es gab einmal Leibeigenschaft. Right? Das ist dir bekannt. Und nun stelle dir vor: Ein leibeigener Bauer kommt zu seinem Herrn und sagt, er müsse mit ihm reden.

– Durften Sklaven so ohne weiteres mit ihren Herren reden?

– Weiß ich nicht, egal, es geht ja jetzt nur darum, was er sagt, der Leibeigene, nicht der Sklave, aber meinetwegen auch der Sklave, egal, er sagt: Herr, ich finde die Leibeigenschaft überhaupt nicht gut, sie ist menschenunwürdig, sie widerspricht der Bibel –

– Diese Geschichte steht in der Bibel? Kannte ich nicht.

– In der Bibel steht, dass vor Gott alle Menschen gleich sind, und das war ein Argument des Leibeigenen, also –

– Konnte er überhaupt lesen? Und Latein? Meines Wissens gab es im Mittelalter die Bibel nur auf Latein, und die meisten Menschen waren Analphabeten.

– Okay. Ohne Bibel. Jedenfalls der Leibeigene ist mit der Leibeigenschaft nicht einverstanden. Und er schlägt mit einigen vernünftigen Gründen seinem Herrn vor, ihm die Freiheit zu geben. Was wird ihm der Herr antworten?

– Du wirst es mir sagen.

– Er wird dem Bauern erklären, dass er Leibeigener sei, weil schon sein Vater Leibeigener war und sein Großvater Leibeigener beim Großvater des Herrn war, die Welt so sei, wie sie sei, und zwar seit Generationen, seit jeher, und das müsse doch einen Sinn haben.

– Das würde ich ein vernünftiges Argument nennen. Oder nicht?

– Okay, George, jetzt sage mir: Gibt es noch Leibeigenschaft?

– Das weiß ich nicht. Irgendwo auf der Welt?

– George! Noch einmal! Ein leibeigener Bauer irgendwo in Europa, er beklagt sich und –

– Er wird im Mittelalter wohl eher geviertteilt worden sein, als seine Freiheit zu erlangen, nehme ich an.

– Genau. Und der Herr sagt, das war immer so. Aber jetzt frage ich dich noch einmal: Gibt es noch Leibeigenschaft? Siehst du! Worauf ich hinauswollte: Alles, was du gesagt hast, ist richtig, stimmt vollkommen – aber nur inside the box. Objektiv aber ist es absurd, und perspektivisch auf jeden Fall unhaltbar. Immer wieder ist verschwunden, was für die Ewigkeit gemacht schien und –

– Du meinst die EU?

– Nein, ich meine die nationalen Interessen. Es ist doch absurd, wenn die europäischen Staaten einen gemeinsamen Markt bilden, aber im Außenhandel keine Gemeinsamkeit herstellen. Dass jedes Schwein, das Europa verlässt, nur mit einem Visum seines Nationalstaats auf den Weltmarkt kommen kann. Okay, es ist so, aber es wird irgendwann anders sein, weil die Dinge sich ändern. Also könnten wir es gleich vernünftiger gestalten.

– Ich werde über deine Geschichte mit der Leibeigenschaft nachdenken. Obwohl ich nicht sicher bin, ob es exakt das ist, was wir ein sinnvolles Beispiel nennen.

Kai-Uwe Frigge wusste natürlich, warum sich Morland gegen die Weiterentwicklung der Gemeinschaftspolitik stemmte: Er war kein Europäer, sondern in erster Linie Brite, und in der Kommission war er nicht europäischer Beamter, sondern eben ein Brite in der europäischen Beamtenschaft. Und es war eiserne Politik Großbritanniens, jeden weiteren noch so kleinen Transfer von nationaler Souveränität nach Brüssel zu unterbinden. Sie haben mit EU-Geldern ihr völlig verrottetes Manchester renoviert, aber sie sind nicht dankbar, sondern halten die heute herausgeputzten Fassaden von Manchester für den Beweis dafür, dass der Manchester-Kapitalismus immer wieder alle Konkurrenten besiegen wird. Dieses schwammige, parfümierte Schwein begann den Tag wahrscheinlich mit dem Absingen von »Rule Britannia!« beim Early-Morning-Tea, und – Frigge atmete tief durch. Dann stand er auf, sagte:

Well, ich muss zum Flughafen. Reden wir nächste Woche weiter!

Jederzeit, sagte Morland.

Frigge hatte einen starken Abgang vorbereitet. Während er seinen Mantel anzog, sagte er: Übrigens, ich nehme an, dass du darüber informiert bist. Die deutsche Regierung wird in den nächsten Wochen einen bilateralen Handelsvertrag mit China abschließen. Okay, nur Schweinehandel. Das ist für United Kingdom nicht von so großem Interesse.

Das ist sicher?

Ja. Das ist fix.

Frigge knöpfte den Mantel zu, schob Unterlagen in seine Aktentasche.

Es ist exklusiv, praktisch das Einfallstor der deutschen Wirtschaft auf den chinesischen Markt. Und da geht es nicht nur um Exportstatistiken.

Er gab Morland die Hand.

Die großen Investoren werden das zu interpretieren wissen, die Finanzmärkte werden Reaktionen zeigen. Der Finanzplatz London City wird an Bedeutung verlieren, die Börse in Frankfurt wird dramatisch gewinnen.

Frigge schlug Morland auf die Schulter.

Ist es nicht komisch? Englische Misere, nur wegen deutscher Schweine? Okay, ich muss los. Ruf mich nächste Woche an, wir müssen das Gespräch unbedingt fortsetzen. Ich bin sicher, wir finden einen Weg, um das vernünftiger zu gestalten, gerechter. Aber da muss sich die Kommission einig sein.

Frigge öffnete die Tür, sah sich nochmals nach Morland um,

sagte kopfschüttelnd: Schweine! – und lachte. Er grinste
noch im Taxi zum Flughafen.

Einundvierzig zweiundvierzig dreiundvierzig vier fünf sechs
sieben acht neun undvierzig fünfzig! Durchatmen! Einund-
fünfzig zweiundfünfzig drei vier
er ging in der Mitte der Straße, jeder Schritt ein Aufstampfen,
ein Keuchen der Schrittzahl, sieben acht und neunundfünf-
zig sech-zig! Durchatmen! Einundsechzig zwei dreiund –
warum zählte er die Schritte, er wollte wissen, wie viel Schritte es waren vom Eingangstor bis zum Ende, vom Eingang ins
Ende bis zum Ausgang vom Ende, er wollte die Dimension
dieses Ortes erfassen, dieser unendlich lang erscheinenden Lagerstraße, der Straße in die Unendlichkeit. Unschuldig schnee-
weiß lag die Straße vor ihm, unschuldig weiß das ganze riesige Areal, warum assoziiert man Weiß mit Unschuld, selbst
hier, an diesem Ort, die Farbe mörderischer Kälte unter dem
Totenlicht der Wintersonne. Der Rauch des Atems vor dem
Mund, bei jeder Zahl, sechs sieben achtund neunundsechzig
sieb- -zig! Eisiger Wind blies in sein Gesicht.
Da spürte Martin Susman einen leichten Druck auf seiner
Schulter, einundsiebzig zweiundsiebzig dreiund – eine Hand
auf seiner Schulter: Sie müssen sich bitte anschnallen!
Er schreckte auf, öffnete die Augen. Ja, sagte er, natürlich!
Der Rückflug von Krakau nach Brüssel. Keuchte er? Er atmete schwer. Er schloss den Sicherheitsgurt, griff hinauf zu
der Luftdüse und drehte sie zu. Dann fielen ihm wieder
die Augen zu, er spürte den kalten Schweiß auf seiner Stirn,
er fröstelte. Er hatte sich natürlich erkältet. Er hatte Angst
vor dieser Reise gehabt, sich nur widerwillig, mit großer Ab-
wehrhaltung, auf den Besuch der Gedenkstätte und des Museums vorbereitet, aus Angst vor dem Schock, zu sehen, was
unbeschreiblich war. Aber die Musealisierung tötet den Tod,

und das Wiedererkennen verhindert den Schock des Erkennens. Die Getränkeautomaten, wo die Touristen im Lager für zehn Zloty warme Getränke oder Schokoriegel kaufen konnten, hatten ihn mehr schockiert als die schon so oft auf Fotos oder in Dokus gesehenen Haufen von Haaren, Schuhen oder Brillen. Die Kälte war das Entsetzlichste. Sie drang überall hinein, in seine Haut, in seine Knochen, der Eishauch im langen Korridor der Geschichte. Im Festzelt von Auschwitz war es noch einigermaßen erträglich gewesen, aber Birkenau war gnadenlos, noch nie in seinem Leben hatte er so gefroren. Seine Großmutter hatte stets mehrere Röcke und Westen übereinander getragen und immer wieder gesagt: »Wer sich warm hält, kommt davon!« So mehrschichtig bekleidet stand sie sogar im Stall, in der Stallwärme. Und bei klirrender Kälte pflegte sie zu sagen: »Da holt man sich den Tod!« Diese Erinnerung, auf der Heimreise, zurück in seine geheizte Brüsseler Wohnung, war ihm peinlich, als hätte er laut zu seiner Sitznachbarin gesagt: In Birkenau – da habe ich mir den Tod geholt. Eine Kälte, ich sage Ihnen! Was soll ich viel erzählen? Da habe ich mir den Tod geholt!

Er schnaufte. Die Nase war verstopft. Er gähnte, im Grunde ein gieriges Luftholen, dann begann er wieder zu dösen. Er hatte den Gangsitz in einer Dreierreihe. Er hörte die Stimmen seiner beiden Sitznachbarinnen, wie aus der Ferne, wie aus der Erinnerung. Sie sprachen Deutsch, heiter und angeregt.

Er sah sich wieder über die Lagerstraße gehen, keuchend, wie besessen die Schritte zählend, er stemmte sich gegen den Wind, ging weit nach vorn gebeugt, Wolken schlossen wie schwere Augenlider den Himmel, die weite weiße Fläche wurde aschgrau. Er spürte, wie alles in ihm nachgab, er widerstand diesem Gefühl nicht, sein Kopf sank auf die Brust. Da spürte er Aufwind, er fühlte sich hochgetragen, verlor den Boden unter den Füßen, er flog. Er wunderte sich darüber, dass er fliegen konnte, zugleich hatte er ein wunderliches Vertrauen, es war irgendwie logisch, ganz selbstverständlich, so leicht und körperlos aufzusteigen in die Luft. Sah jemand her? Er hatte den Wunsch, dass alle Welt herschaute und dies sah: wie er hochflog, wie er kreiselnd und schaukelnd in den Luftströmungen zu den Wolken aufstieg. Er hörte die deutschen Stimmen, so nah, so fern, sie redeten über etwas ganz anderes, über Kunst und Literatur, über Bücher, und er sah aufgeschlagene Bücher wie Vögel hochfliegen, ihr Gesang erfüllte die Luft, während er hinunterschaute auf das weite Feld. Von oben – das war erstes Semester Archäologie – konnte man unter die Oberfläche der Erde sehen, man sah in eine Tiefe, die man, wenn man über die Erde ging, nicht wahrnahm. Man sieht, wenn man geht und um sich blickt, eine schneebedeckte Fläche. Überfliegt man sie, sieht man Strukturen, Flächen, die sich voneinander abgrenzen, das Feld löst sich auf in ein Raster von Feldern. Je nachdem, was sich unter der Oberfläche befindet, unschuldige Erde oder vergrabener Zivilisationsschutt, Leichen, Steine von versunkenen Gebäuden, Wasseradern oder alte Keller und Kanalsysteme oder zugeschüttete Klärgruben und Latrinen, reagiert die Oberfläche anders, wächst die Vegetation stärker oder schlechter, je mehr Geschichte, desto differenzierter das Feld aus der Vogelperspektive. Auf der dünnen Erdschicht über den Steinen versunkener Zivilisation wächst die Vegetation weniger üppig als über einem Massengrab, wo das Gras sprießt, wie man es vom Gras erwartet: Rasch wächst es drüber! Aber auch bei einer geschlossenen Schneefläche werden Unterschiede sichtbar: Die Bodentemperatur ist anders auf unschuldiger Erde als auf einer bloß dünnen Erdschicht, die über Steinen liegt oder über verrottendem Holz oder über einem Massengrab, noch nach Jahrzehnten wärmt der Verwesungsprozess von Leichen den Boden, und da ist also der Schnee eisig, dort ist er harschig, und hier ist er glasig und taut bereits. Wer darüberfliegt, sieht diese Raster und erkennt, wo man graben muss.

Er sah Professor Krinzinger vor sich, seinen alten Lehrer, der sagte: Die moderne Archäologie beginnt nicht mit Graben, sie beginnt mit Fliegen!

Plötzlich flog der Professor an seiner Seite, rief ihm etwas zu – Was? Es war so ein starkes Dröhnen in der Luft, dass Martin ihn nicht sofort verstand, er sah, wie der Professor immer wieder mit dem Daumen nach unten deutete und dabei etwas rief.

Was?

Runter! Runter!

Jetzt verstand er ihn: Komm runter! Wir haben eine andere Aufgabe. Wir Archäologen müssen Zivilisation ausgraben und nicht Verbrechen!

Aber –

Wir gehen auf unsicherem Grund, aber wir treten fest auf, mit unseren Stiefeln, wir stampfen den Boden fest, auch leichten Schritts ist jeder Schritt ein Tritt, Hauptsache, die Füße sind warm, Martin sah Stiefel, überall warme Stiefel – und hörte jetzt deutlicher diese Frauenstimmen, die er schon die ganze Zeit im Ohr hatte.

– Ich fand den Roman ganz gut. Aber die Träume haben mich genervt.

– Der Roman ist ein Klassiker.

– Ja, darum wollte ich das Buch endlich mal lesen. Aber ich mag Träume in Romanen nicht. Immer wieder träumt sie etwas, das wird dann minutiös beschrieben, ganz surreal, soll wohl poetisch sein. Ich sag mal so: Was eine Figur sieht und erlebt, kann ich nachvollziehen, aber Träume –

– Aber der Roman spielt im Faschismus. Da kann man schon Albträume haben.

– Nee, ich sag mal so: Wenn in einem Buch ein Traum vorkommt, schlafe ich lieber selbst.

Martin sah diese vielen Stiefel, warm und bequem, eine deutsche Schulklasse auf Exkursion in Auschwitz. Eine Lehrerin: Thorsten! Was ist mit dir? Träumst du? Schließ dich hier an!

Zwei Jugendliche sprechen Türkisch. Ein Lehrer fordert sie auf, hier nicht Türkisch zu sprechen, einer antwortet: Genau hier sprechen wir nicht Deutsch!

Martin schwindelte. Es war, als drehte er sich, immer schneller, alles um ihn herum verschwamm, nur manchmal blitzte ein Bild auf, hörte er einen Satz, irgendwer sagte etwas über Kohle, ein Schüler fragte: Was bitte ist Kohle?

Eine Durchsage. Hier spricht der Kapitän. Anschnallen. Turbulenzen.

Martin Susman steht vor dem Krematorium Auschwitz Stammlager. Er hat die Gaskammer gesehen, die Verbrennungsöfen, es sieht genauso aus wie auf den Fotos, die er kannte, Schwarz-Weiß-Fotos, und was er jetzt wirklich gesehen hatte, war tatsächlich schwarz-weiß. Er fühlte sich – wie? Er konnte es nicht sagen, er hatte kein Wort dafür, weil »betroffen« kein deutsches Wort mehr war, sondern eine Art von deutschem Hansaplast für die Seele. Das war ein Gedanke, aber im Traum stand er ihm vor Augen. Er stand vor dem Gebäude und zündete sich eine Zigarette an. Da tauchten plötzlich zwei Männer in Uniform auf, liefen auf ihn zu, der eine schlug ihm gegen die Hand, in der er die Zigarette hielt, der andere sagte etwas auf Polnisch, dann auf Englisch: No smoking here!

Auf Martins Brust baumelte ein Badge: »GUEST OF HONOUR / GOSC HONOROWY / EHRENGAST in Auschwitz«. Er hielt den Uniformierten den Badge entgegen, da kam Herr Zeromski gelaufen, rief: Herr Doktor, Herr Doktor, wir müssen ins Zelt! Die Feier beginnt.

Er wachte auf, weil das Flugzeug rüttelte, schwankte und bebte. Ein Kind schrie.

Am nächsten Tag meldete er sich krank. Er blieb fünf Tage zu Hause. Drei Tage fieberte er. Am fünften Tag notierte er seine Idee und entwarf ein erstes Konzept für das Jubilee Project.

Fünftes Kapitel

Erinnerungen sind nicht
unzuverlässiger als alles andere,
was wir uns ausmalen.

Liebe ist eine Fiktion. Fenia Xenopoulou hatte das Getue, das um die Liebe gemacht wird, nie verstanden. Sie hielt dieses Gefühl für ein unbewiesenes Vorkommen in einer anderen Welt, wie Wasser auf dem Mars. Die Menschen lasen davon in diesen bunten Illustrierten wie »Chrisi Kardia« oder »Loipón«, die von den Liebesaffären der Hollywood-Schauspieler und Popstars und den Traumhochzeiten der Prinzessinnen berichteten. Manche hielten Liebe für möglich, weil sie die Sehnsucht danach verspürten, aber alle, die Fenia kannte, hatten sich irgendwann ergeben. Ihre Mutter hatte einmal beim Friseur über die unglücklich liebende Lady Diana gesagt: »Das, was sie nie bekommen hat, habe ich viel billiger nie bekommen!«

In Fenias Familie hatte ihres Wissens nie ein Mensch geliebt. In dem emphatischen Sinn, dass ein Überschwang von Gefühlen der Anlass für eine Hochzeit oder die Enttäuschung von Gefühlen der Grund für eine Tragödie gewesen wäre. Ausgenommen ihr Onkel Kostas, der ältere Bruder ihres Vaters, den sie nie kennengelernt hatte, der aber in den Erzählungen der Familie lebte, als der Verrückte, der in den Tod gegangen ist, weil er unsterblich verliebt gewesen war. Dieser Widerspruch hatte Fenia als Kind sehr beunruhigt: unsterblich in den Tod. Wahrscheinlich war gar nicht so oft von ihm die Rede gewesen, wie es ihr rückblickend erschien, und es war nur so, dass das, was sie hörte, ihre Fantasie besonders angeregt und sie in Angst versetzt hatte. Onkel Kostas hatte geliebt, fanatisch, wie es hieß, und weil er die Angebetete nicht bekommen konnte, sei er weggegangen und habe sich dem Widerstand angeschlossen. Bei dem Wort »Angebetete« hatte die kleine Fenia an die

Jungfrau Maria denken müssen, an religiöse Verzückung, und das war vielleicht gar nicht so falsch. Aber noch mehr hatte sie damals der Begriff »Widerstand« beschäftigt. Sie wusste nicht, welcher Krieg oder Bürgerkrieg da geherrscht hatte, das war vor ihrer Geburt, und auch wenn es sehr kurz vor ihrer Geburt gewesen war, war es für sie doch so fern wie der Peloponnesische Krieg, von dem sie damals oder wenig später in der Schule hörte. Der Onkel Kostas, hieß es, sei »nicht mehr zurückgekommen«. In ihrer Phantasie befand sich der »Onkel im Widerstand« in einer Unterwelt, wo die Toten, aber unsterblich Verliebten, gegen dieses Verhängnis kämpften, das Liebe hieß und Anbetung. Diese Unterwelt hatte sie sich dunkel, sehr schwül und feucht vorgestellt, auf unklare Weise gefährlich und jedenfalls nicht als Ort, wo man unbedingt hin möchte – auch wenn sie nichts wie fort wollte aus ihrem von der Sonne verbrannten zypriotischen Dorf, dem steinigen, ausgedörrten Land mit den armseligen Olivenbäumen, deren silbriges Schimmern auch nur ein Betrug war, nämlich Schönheit für andere, für entzückte Touristen, deren Geld das Dorf überleben ließ, das von den Oliven schon lange nicht mehr leben konnte. Die Touristen kamen, um zum »Bad der Aphrodite« geführt zu werden. Das Wasser dieser Quelle soll dem darin Badenden ewige Jugend schenken. Hier hatte sich die Liebesgöttin mit Adonis vergnügt. Allerdings war diese Sehenswürdigkeit bloß ein unscheinbares Naturbecken in den Felsen oberhalb des Dorfes, fast immer ausgetrocknet, daneben ein großes Holzschild, auf dem stand:

NON POTABLE WATER

PLEASE DO NOT SWIM

Die Touristen fotografierten das trockene Becken und das Schild und lachten. Das also waren die Jünger der Göttin der Liebe. Fenia verkaufte ihnen nach der Schule Mineralwasser, das sie in zwei Kühltaschen auf den Berg schleppte. Sie sparte. Sie wollte weg.

Es dauerte Jahre, bis sie begriff, dass der Onkel seit langer Zeit wirklich tot war, als Partisan gefallen, irgendwo verscharrt. Partisanen, dachte sie nun, waren Menschen, die die Realität nicht anerkannten, insofern hatten sie tatsächlich eine große Gemeinsamkeit mit Verliebten. Sie fand es verrückt, völlig verrückt, als Grieche gegen griechische Generäle zu kämpfen, statt sich gegen die Türken zu wehren, die die halbe Insel besetzt hatten.

Fenia hatte eine andere Vorstellung vom Glück und vom Kampf, durch den sie ihr Glück erringen wollte. Sie wollte hinaus. Hoch hinaus. Als zypriotische Griechin mit entsprechenden Zeugnissen war ihr die Möglichkeit auf einen Studienplatz in Griechenland gegeben. Sie wollte nach Athen. Die Mutter unterstützte Fenias Plan mit ihren bescheidenen Ersparnissen. Liebte Fenia ihre Mutter? Sie wusste, dass es letztlich um Zins und Zinseszins ging: um das Geld, das sie, nach einem erfolgreichen Studium, würde nach Hause schicken können. Die ganze Familie spannte die Muskeln an. Das war die Definition von Liebe, die Fenia verstand. Der Vater mobilisierte mit kleinen Geschenken und großem Starrsinn Menschen, die er kannte, die wiederum andere kannten, bis er für Fenia einen Platz auf einem Schiff von Limassol nach Lavrio organisiert hatte. Es war ein Frachtschiff, das keine Passagiere mitnahm. Der Kapitän erklärte sich bereit, Fenia mitzunehmen, gleichsam als geduldeten blinden Passagier. Die Fähre wäre zu teuer und ein Flug unerschwinglich gewesen. Von Lavrio nach Athen musste sie sich alleine durchschlagen. Das war nicht schwierig, auf dieser Strecke fuhr ein Lastwagen nach dem anderen. Eine Freundin hatte ihr prophezeit: Du wirst mit Sex bezahlen müssen. Fenia zahlte nicht. Die Fahrer ließen ein hübsches junges Mädchen einsteigen und hatten dann eine respektgebietende, eisige Frau neben sich auf dem Beifahrersitz. In Athen kam sie bei entfernten Verwandten unter. Mit der Entfernung steigt der Preis für familiäre Solidarität. Die Verwandten forderten zu viel »Kostbeitrag«, viel mehr als zuvor brieflich vereinbart. Ihr Budget, ihre und ihrer Mutter Ersparnisse, schmolz zu schnell dahin. Sie durfte sich nichts aus dem Kühlschrank nehmen, was sie nicht selbst gekauft hatte – obwohl sie doch Kostbeitrag zahlte. Wenn die Familie abends Fleisch aß, bekam sie nur das Gemüse und die Kartoffeln, und am Ende den Knochen der Lammkeule, soweit noch etwas dran war. Sie fühlte sich gedemütigt, war aber zu stolz, um das nach Hause zu berichten. Sie hielt ihren Rucksack gepackt und schaute sich um. Eine Studienkollegin nahm sie mit ins »Spilia tou Platona«, das angesagte Lokal der Chrysi Neolaia, der »goldenen Jugend« Athens.

– Ist das nicht teuer?

– Es ist teuer. Wir investieren nur einen Drink. Und dann werden wir sicher von Männern eingeladen! Die interessantesten Männer verkehren in der Spilia!

Dort lernte sie den Doktor kennen, den Anwalt Jorgos Chatzopoulos, von ihr bald Chatz oder Schatz genannt, wobei nicht klar war, ob das bloß ihre Koseform von Chatzopoulos war oder eine Anspielung auf die Naziliebchen, die seinerzeit als »germaniki Schatz« gebrandmarkt worden waren: Jorgos Chatzopoulos war der Erbe einer Kanzlei, die sein Großvater während der deutschen Besatzung übernommen hatte, nachdem der jüdische Anwalt, dem sie gehört hatte, deportiert worden war. Aber Fenia wusste das gar nicht. Und sie überschätzte Jorgos. Sie holte ihren Rucksack und zog bei ihm ein. Für sie war er der erste Mann von Welt. Fünfzehn Jahre älter, großzügig, ein Mann, der in teuren Restaurants mit Kellnern über französische Weine diskutieren konnte. Fast hätte sie gedacht, dass es das doch gibt: dieses Prinzessinengefühl der Liebe. Sie heirateten. Bei der Hochzeit musste Fenia lachen, als Schatz in einer Rede zu den Festgästen von »ewiger Liebe« sprach. Das klang wie eine schmalzige Geschichte aus »Xrisi Kardia«, dem »Goldenen Herz«-Blatt. Und tatsächlich hatte er die Fotos der Hochzeit an das Blatt verkauft – es erschien aber nur ein kleiner Artikel, halbe Seite mit zwei Fotos, und später stellte sich heraus, dass »verkauft« auch nicht ganz korrekt war: Er hatte dafür bezahlt!

Wie stolz die Eltern waren. Und sie machten sich Sorgen, als sie bald darauf mitbekamen, dass Fenia unglücklich war. Sie machten sich nicht etwa Sorgen um Fenia, sondern um deren Ehe. Es ging zu schnell, dass diese Ehe sich entzauberte. Wenn sie sich Schatz hingab im Whirlpool seiner Wohnung, dann spürte sie unerträglich deutlich, wie schal das alles war: Er war so stolz auf seinen Whirlpool, er genoss nicht den Luxus, zu dem er es gebracht hatte, sondern das Gefühl, damit zu beeindrucken, er genoss Symbole eines privilegierten Lebens, aber nicht das Leben selbst, er war begeistert davon, dass er, er, diese schöne junge Frau besitzen konnte, er war verliebt in sich selbst, sie aber hatte bald das Gefühl, austauschbar zu sein, er glaubte »Liebe zu machen« – eine Formulierung, die sie blöder fand als jeden ordinären Ausdruck – und machte doch nur Selbstliebe.

Sie kam durch ihn in andere Kreise, und dort sah sie, dass er nicht die große Nummer war, als die er in der »Spilia« aufgetreten war, sondern ein nervöser Biedermann, der sich schleimig an die wirklich Reichen anbiederte, im Grunde ein Winkeladvokat, der mit den fauligen Fischen, die er an Land zog, gut genug verdiente, um zu glauben, dass er schon im Vorzimmer von Geld und Macht saß.

Als Fenia sich zurückzog und immer konsequenter eigene Wege ging, glaubte Schatz plötzlich, sie doch zu lieben. Er zeige es durch emotional vorgebrachte Vorhaltungen, durch eine neurotische Verlustangst, die er für einen Liebesbeweis hielt, durch einen Gefühlssturm, der so heftig war, dass man ihn mit Mordlust verwechseln konnte. Besonders skandalös fand Fenia, dass er Dankbarkeit einforderte. Das war doch verrückt: Dankbarkeit von anderen einzufordern, nachdem man sich selbst befriedigt hatte!

Er hatte ihr das Studentenleben ökonomisch erleichtert, okay, aber sie hätte es ohne ihn genauso geschafft, während er ohne sie weniger Spaß und, so wie er sie ausstaffiert und vorgeführt hatte, in seinen Kreisen weniger Renommee gehabt hätte. Sie studierte Ökonomie, und diese Bilanzrechnung war unter ihrem Niveau. Und das Stipendium für England hatte sie ohne seine Hilfe errungen, und damit kam sie weg, sie wollte hinaus, hoch hinaus.

Es wurde eine Wochenend-Ehe, in immer größeren Abständen, zunächst in London, dann in Brüssel. Das letzte Mal, als sie ihn in ihrem Bett sah, als sie aufwachte und seine verschwitzten grauen Locken, sein vom Alkohol verquollenes Gesicht betrachtete, dachte sie: Er ist mir heute fremder als beim ersten Mal.

Sie fand, das war eine gute Definition für das Ende.

Dieser Gedanke machte sie fröhlich. Sie war beim Frühstück so vergnügt und entspannt wie schon lange nicht mehr. Weil ihr alles klar war. Das war der Moment, in dem Schatz wirklich Größe zeigte. Er verstand die Situation nicht falsch, wirkte selbst auch befreit, war launig und sagte, als er mit seinem Trolley aus ihrem Apartment hinausging: Liebe ist eine Fiktion.

Ja.

Mach's gut!

Ja. Du auch.

Und wie verrückt war es, völlig verrückt, dass Fenia jetzt an ihrem Schreibtisch saß, unfähig zu arbeiten, weil sie sehnsüchtig wartete, so sehnsüchtig wie eine Liebende – auf den Anruf von Fridsch. Er war gestern von seiner Dienstreise nach Doha zurückgekommen, hatte heute Vormittag ein Gespräch mit Queneau gehabt, bei dem er auch beiläufig Fenias Anliegen erwähnen wollte, um auszuloten, welche Möglichkeiten es gab, dass sie von der Kultur wegkam. Er hatte versprochen, sie gleich danach anzurufen. Sie saß da, starrte das Telefon an. Nahm den Hörer ab, legte ihn wieder auf. Nein, sie rief ihn nicht an, er sollte sie anrufen. Sie nahm ihr Smartphone, sah nach, ob sie seinen Anruf versäumt oder er eine Nachricht geschickt hatte – nein, sie legte es neben die Tastatur ihres Computers, checkte die E-Mails, siebenundvierzig ungelesene Nachrichten, aber keine von ihm, sie nahm erneut das Smartphone, ja, sie hatte natürlich guten Empfang, sie legte es wieder auf den Tisch. Was sie verwirrte: Ihr war vollkommen egal, was Fridsch von dem Gespräch berichten würde, ob Queneau eine Andeutung gemacht hatte, die man dahingehend interpretieren könnte, dass er bereit wäre, ihren Wunsch nach einem Wechsel im Geiste der Mobilité zu unterstützen – sie wollte die Stimme von Fridsch hören. Egal, was er zu berichten hatte. Einfach nur seine Stimme hören. Sie fühlte sich wie – ja, wie? Das war doch verrückt: Sie hatte Sehnsucht nach seiner Stimme.

Martin Susman kam um acht Uhr in die Arche. Von der Kantine wehte der Geruch frisch aufgebackener Croissants ins Foyer. Der Duft, dem er normalerweise nicht widerstehen konnte, erinnerte ihn heute an eine Chemiefabrik, und er nahm dies als Zeichen dafür, dass er noch nicht ganz gesund war. Vor dem Lift traf er zwei junge Männer von der Task Force Ukraine, die in der 6. Etage arbeiteten. Bohumil Szmekal hatte sie »die Salamander« genannt, ein Ausdruck, der mittlerweile in der Arche allgemein verwendet wurde, wenn von den Mitarbeitern dieser »Task Force« die Rede war. So konnte man über sie, »die Salamander«, verächtlich oder ironisch reden, auch wenn sie in der Kantine am Nebentisch saßen. Das ist die neue Generation bei uns, hatte Bohumil erklärt, keine Europäer, sondern einfach Karrieristen in den europäischen Institutionen, sie sind wie Salamander, man kann sie ins Feuer werfen, aber sie verbrennen nicht, ihr Hauptmerkmal ist ihre Unzerstörbarkeit.

Es waren junge Männer in korrekten engen Anzügen, mit großen Krawattenknoten und pomadisiertem Haar, schon optisch der schärfste Gegensatz zu den Mitarbeitern in der Kultur, sie waren glatt und wendig und auf eine Weise förmlich höflich, die Kassándra »niederschmetternd« nannte, fünf Minuten Smalltalk mit den Salamandern, und ich bin depressiv!

Was ist eure Aufgabe?, hatte Bohumil einen Salamander gefragt, als die Task Force Ukraine hier über ihren Köpfen einquartiert wurde. Er erfuhr, dass sie Hilfsprogramme für die Ukraine entwickeln sollten, um die Demokratiebewegung nach der Maidan-Revolution zu unterstützen. Die Herausforderung bestand darin, Geld zu verteilen, das sie nicht hatten. Es wurde ihnen kein neues, eigenes Budget zur Verfügung gestellt. Sie machten daher klassisches Repackaging – wenn man Neues nicht hat, wird Altes neu verpackt. Sie verpackten also alte, längst bestehende Hilfsprogramme mit neuen Titeln und neuen Bedingungen in neuen Kombinationen zu neuen Hilfspaketen, wodurch mit alten Budgets neue Verteilungskämpfe entstanden, die zu neuen Statistiken führten, in denen neue Prozentangaben und graphische Kurven neue Dynamik zeigten. Diese Aufgabe war die ideale Feuertaufe für diese jungen Karrieristen: Es gab am Ende nichts zu gewinnen als das eigene Überleben in den gegebenen Bedingungen beziehungsweise das Fortbestehen von alten Bedingungen bei verbesserten eigenen Zukunftschancen.

Dass er nun mit den zwei Salamandern auf den Lift warten musste, besserte Martin Susmans Laune nicht.

Wie es ihm gehe? Natürlich wäre »Ausgezeichnet!« die richtige Antwort gewesen, aber Martin war vom Teufel geritten, er sagte »Scheiße!«, weidete sich am Gesichtsausdruck der Salamander und fügte hinzu: Ich habe mich schwer erkältet! –

Das tut mir sehr leid!

Sehr leid!, sagte auch der zweite Salamander.

Und nun ging Martin aufs Ganze: Es war arschkalt in der Ukraine!

Oh! Sie waren in der Ukraine?

Yes, Sir! Und es ist kein Wunder, dass mein Immunsystem zusammengebrochen ist! Die Menschen dort sind so frustriert, so enttäuscht von uns, von der EU. Sie fühlen sich im Stich gelassen und –

Die Salamander glänzten: O ja, wir kennen das Problem, Sie haben völlig recht! Wir –

Völlig recht!

Wir wissen, wir müssen jetzt –

Da kam der Lift, die Tür öffnete sich.

Dritter, richtig?

Ja, sagte Martin.

Der Salamander drückte auf Drei und Sechs und sagte: Wir müssen unsere Kommunikation verbessern. Sie haben völlig recht! Deshalb bündeln wir jetzt unsere Kräfte in der Kommunikation!

Die Kommission muss sich besser verkaufen, und wir –

Der Lift hielt, die Tür öffnete sich. Sich verkaufen! Wenn die wüssten, dachte Martin, was sie da sagten! Auf Wiedersehen!

Haben Sie einen schönen Tag!

Einen schönen Tag! Und gute Besserung!

Die Lifttür glitt hinter Martin zu, er holte tief Luft, mit offenem Mund, seine Nase war verstopft. Er war zu früh wieder zur Arbeit gegangen, andererseits: Er musste schnellstens sein Papier zum Jubilee Project fertig machen, um es endlich Xeno zu mailen. Das hätte er auch von zu Hause machen können, aber wie er sie kannte, würde sie ihn dann gleich ins Besprechungszimmer rufen, um mit ihm und einigen anderen Kollegen aus der Abteilung über das Papier zu reden. Also musste er da sein und sich bereithalten.

Er ging an ihrem Arbeitszimmer vorbei, die Tür war zu. Er ging an Bohumils Zimmer vorbei, die Tür war offen, Bohumil stand mitten im Raum auf einer Stehleiter. Als er Martin sah, rief er Ahoj!

Ahoj!

Martin war so langsam im Kopf, dass ihm erst in seinem Zimmer einfiel, dass er eigentlich stehen bleiben und Bohumil hätte fragen sollen, was er da auf der Leiter tat. Egal. Er polierte eine Stunde lang, die ihm wie eine Ewigkeit erschien, seine Bullet Points, mailte sie an Xeno. Dann trug er langsam seinen E-Mail-Rückstau ab. Das meiste beantwortete sich von selbst oder hatte sich während seines Krankenstands bereits erledigt. Da war eine Mail von Florian. »Lieber Bruder, du Kuckucksei! Nächste Woche fliege ich nach Peking, Wirtschaftsdelegation mit UHBP und dem Präs. der Wirtschaftskammer. So wie es aussieht – habe Infos des österr. Handelsdelegierten in Peking – werden die anstehenden Verhandlungen zum Erfolg – der sich als Katastrophe erweisen wird. Der Präs. ist ahnungslos, der Vertrag, der unterschrieben wird, macht uns erpressbar. Ich frage mich, wer hier die Schweine sind … Du musst unbedingt –« Martin Susman stand auf und streckte sich. Er wollte rauchen, er brauchte unbedingt eine Zigaret-

te. So krank konnte er also nicht mehr sein. Noch keine
Reaktion von Xeno. Er schaute hinüber zu Bohumil, aber
der war nicht mehr da, auch die Leiter war weg. Martin ging
hinaus auf die Feuerleiter, rauchte frierend zwei Zigaretten,
dann ging er wieder in sein Zimmer. Er schrieb den Dienst-
reise-Bericht, machte die Dienstreise-Spesenabrechnung, er-
ledigte noch einigen administrativen Kram, das heißt: Er
füllte Tabellen aus. Dann bearbeitete er die Studentenanfra-
gen – da waren wieder zwei, die ein Praktikum machen wollten, diese Anfragen leitete er weiter. Ein Student schrieb eine
Doktorarbeit in European Studies an der Universität Passau,
sein Thema war Europäische Kulturpolitik, abgeleitet vom
Zitat von Jean Monnet: »Wenn ich noch einmal anfangen könnte, dann würde ich mit der Kultur beginnen.« Martin Susman
wusste nicht, warum, aber solche Mails kamen im Schnitt
zwei Mal pro Woche. Der Student erbat zu diesem Zitat eine
Stellungnahme der Generaldirektion für Kultur der Europäischen Kommission. Die Antwort schrieb sich von selbst. Es
gibt keinen Nachweis, dass Monnet diesen Satz tatsächlich
gesagt oder gar irgendwo veröffentlicht hat. Und selbst wenn
er ihn gesagt hätte, dann wäre ohne eine weitere Ausführung
völlig unklar, was damit konkret gemeint war: »Mit Kultur
beginnen«. Die Ode an die Freude singen und dann erst die
Montanunion gründen? Kultur sei a priori universal, habe also immer schon eine Gemeinsamkeit und Verbundenheit
zwischen Menschen hergestellt, die endlich auch politisch
verwirklicht werden musste. Und der Austausch von Regio-
nalkulturen, der sich tatsächlich für das Zusammenwachsen
Europas als eminent wichtig erwiesen hat, sei nur durch die
politischen Errungenschaften des europäischen Projekts immer intensiver möglich geworden: durch den Wegfall der
Grenzen, der Reise- und Niederlassungsfreiheit, den freien
Handel auf einem gemeinsamen Markt.

Er hielt inne. Waren das Phrasen? Andererseits: Gibt es eine Wahrheit, die man hundert Mal wiederholen kann, ohne dass sie zur Phrase wird? Seine verstopfte Nase machte ihm zu schaffen, er fürchtete, dass der Schnupfen sich zu einer Sinusitis auswachsen könnte, er spürte ein beängstigendes Pochen in der Stirn. Warum hielt er sich so lange mit dieser Mail an den Studenten auf? Sein Papier für das Jubilee Project – das waren doch keine Phrasen, die er da geschrieben hatte. Noch immer keine Antwort von Xeno. Das wunderte ihn. Er sah auf die Uhr. Es war ein Uhr. Und Xeno reagierte nicht. Warum reagierte sie nicht?

Er stand auf, ging aus dem Zimmer, raus aus seiner Arbeitszelle. Im Gang traf er Bohumil.

– Bist du krank?

– Ja.

– Liebeskrank?

– Wie kommst du drauf?

– Du schaust so aus. Völlig konfus.

David de Vriend stand mitten in seinem Zimmer und fragte sich, warum er da stand. Er hatte eben noch etwas vorgehabt, etwas tun wollen – aber was? Nein, jetzt fragte er sich das nicht, er sah sich einfach um, als suchte er erst eine Beschäftigung oder – sein Blick fiel auf das Telefon – als wartete er auf etwas, ja, als erwartete er einen Anruf. Er setzte sich in seinen Sessel, mit Blick auf das Telefon. Vergessen! Er hatte das Gefühl, vergessen worden zu sein, völlig vergessen von allen Menschen und sogar vom Tod. Aber wen gab es denn noch, der sich seiner erinnern sollte?

Das Januarlicht, eine silbrig graue Fläche im Rahmen des Fensters, wie die Tür eines Schließfachs oder eines Safes. Der Schlüssel verloren, die Kombination vergessen. Oder die eiserne Kellertür eines Bunkers, dahinter der dunkle Stollen zum Tod.

Er stand wieder auf, trat an das Fenster. Da unten lag der Friedhof. Wer sollte sich denn an ihn erinnern? Lagen doch schon alle dort, unter den Steinen unter dem grauen Dunst. Nein, nicht alle.

Er war eigenbrötlerisch geworden, als die ihm nahestehenden Menschen nach und nach starben. Deren Kinder gingen längst schon eigene Wege, die sie weit weg führten, in eine Welt mit mehr Glück oder ganz anderem Unglück. In seiner letzten Zeit in Sainte-Catherine war er noch ab und zu auf der Straße gegrüßt worden – wer war das? Ein ehemaliger Schüler, wird auch schon grauhaarig! Und er hatte erstaunt zurückgegrüßt. Das war alles. Und jetzt saß er alleine in der Seniorenresidenz Huis Hanssens, sollte Gemeinschaftsräume mit Menschen teilen, die aus seiner Generation waren, aber nie seine Zeitgenossen gewesen sind, weil sie seine Erfahrungen nicht teilen mussten, ihr Unglück war das Alter, sein Unglück war das Leben. Nein, da gab es nichts zu teilen, außer Ausdünstungen, von den Mottenkugeln der Anzüge und Kleider, von Urin, Schweiß, vermodernden Körperzellen, nur Tränen haben keinen Geruch. Er hatte vergessen wollen, aber das hatte nur dazu geführt, dass er vergessen wurde.

Er setzte sich an den Tisch. Da lag ein Kugelschreiber. Er stand wieder auf, sah sich um, da musste doch irgendwo sein Notizblock liegen. Wo war der Notizblock? Vor ein paar Tagen war eine Frau Doktor da gewesen, eine Psychologin von einem städtischen Amt, das für die Altersheime zuständig war, um ein so genanntes Akkommodationsgespräch mit ihm zu führen, ein – was? Ein Betreuungsgespräch. Sie hatte den großen Notizblock mitgebracht. Sie sei gekommen, um ihm, wie sie sagte, den Eintritt in den Lebensabend zu erleichtern und Hilfestellung zu geben bei der Gestaltung seines Lebensabends, vor allem um ihm allfällige Angst zu nehmen vor dem Lebensabend – sie sagte unausgesetzt Lebensabend, bis David de

Vriend sie unterbrach: Es wäre zwar genauso verlogen, aber doch irgendwie netter, wenn sie statt »Lebensabend« einfach »Lebensabschnitt« sagen würde. Dass es der letzte sei, wisse er ohnehin, aber selbst da könne es noch sonnige Tage geben und nicht nur einen ewigen Abend. Die Frau Doktor war so bemüht einfühlsam. Was de Vriend besonders unerträglich fand, war, dass diese dünne Frau ihren Kopf kahlgeschoren hatte – warum? War das jetzt Mode? Er hatte in letzter Zeit immer wieder Glatzköpfe auf den Straßen gesehen, junge Menschen mit Glatzen und Tätowierungen. Wussten sie, was sie da taten, was sie damit aussagten, welche Assoziationen sie weckten? Er hatte die geschorenen Köpfe und die Skelette vergessen wollen, und nun schickten sie ihm diese Frau. Es machte ihn aggressiv. Gehen Sie! Sie beleidigen mich – und er wurde pathetisch: Sie beleidigen das Gedächtnis der Welt!

Die Frau Doktor war einfühlsam. Sie fragte nach, schließlich erklärte sie sich: sie habe eine Chemotherapie hinter sich. Brustkrebs. Aber sie legte Wert darauf, weiter zu arbeiten, weil –

De Vriend schämte sich. Und schwieg. Schwieg und ließ sie reden, kein falsches Wort mehr, ab und zu nickte er, und er nickte, als sie aus der Tasche diesen Notizblock zog, ihn auf den Tisch legte und sagte: Das habe ich Ihnen mitgebracht. Ein kleiner Tipp: Notieren Sie Ihre Gedanken und Absichten. Ich kenne das, glauben Sie mir: Man hat einen Gedanken, und dann vergisst man ihn wieder. Aber wenn Sie ihn gleich aufschreiben, dann können Sie immer überprüfen, habe ich das getan, was ich vorgehabt habe, habe ich mich darum gekümmert, was ich mir überlegt habe. Es ist ein gutes Training gegen das Vergessen, wenn man sich angewöhnt, immer alles aufzuschreiben.

Wo war der Notizblock? Da. Neben dem Bett.

Er setzte sich an den Tisch, nahm den Kugelschreiber. Der Block war großformatig, oben hatte er eine Leiste aus Karton, unter der man die Blätter abtrennen konnte. Auf dieser Leiste stand neben dem Wappen der Region Brüssel: »Bruxelles ne vous oublie pas! / Brussel zal u niet vergeten!«

Er wollte eine Liste anlegen, die Namen all derer aufschreiben, die mit ihm überlebt hatten und noch lebten oder vielleicht noch lebten, weil er keine Nachricht von ihrem Tod bekommen hatte. Warum? Er hatte doch Erinnerungen. Sie drängten sich vor. In seinem Gedächtnis leuchteten Namen auf, er sah Gesichter, hörte Tonfälle, er sah in dunkle Augen, sah Gesten und Bewegungen, und er spürte den Hunger, diese Häckselmaschine des Lebens, die das Körperfett frisst, dann die Muskeln zermalmt und dann die Seele, die man, wenn überhaupt, erst entdeckt, wenn der Hunger zur Metapher wird: Lebenshunger. Er spürte diesen Hunger jetzt, nicht mehr so stark, aber er spürte ihn, und er wollte diese Liste machen, aufschreiben, mit wem er diesen Hunger geteilt hatte und – er sah auf. Hunger war der falsche Begriff, mit Hunger bezeichnet man das Gefühl der Satten, die eine Mahlzeit ausließen. Das hatte mit dem Hunger, den er überlebt hatte, nichts zu tun. Die Lebenden und die Überlebenden sprachen nur zufällig dieselbe Sprache, produzierten ein ewiges Missverständnis, indem sie dieselben Begriffe verwendeten.

Er setzte an zu schreiben: »Überlebende«. So wollte er seine Liste nennen, das war seine Idee: Wer war noch da, der seine Sprache sprach. Da läutete das Telefon. Er hielt inne. Begann das Wort »Überlebende« zu schreiben, das Telefon nervte, er legte den Kugelschreiber auf den Tisch und hob ab.

Es war Frau Joséphine. Warum er denn nicht zum Essen komme? Er wird doch nicht das Mittagessen vergessen haben? Wir müssen doch etwas essen, nicht wahr, Herr de Vriend? Sie brüllte ins Telefon. Wir werden doch nicht hungern wollen, nicht wahr?

Er sei der einzige von den Mobilen, der nicht in den Speisesaal gekommen sei und –

Der einzige – was?

Es gibt Fisch, mit Reis und Gemüse, das ist bekömmlich und gesund. Und –

Ja. Ja. Ich habe die Zeit übersehen. Ich komme schon.

David de Vriend band eine Krawatte um, zog ein Sakko an und fuhr mit dem Lift hinunter in den Speisesaal. Er schaute, ob es einen Tisch gab, an dem er alleine sitzen konnte. Nein. Frau Joséphine stürzte auf ihn zu, brachte ihn an einen Tisch. Sagte, sie sei froh, dass er gekommen sei, sie habe sich schon Sorgen gemacht. Wir wollen doch keinen Schwächeanfall haben, nicht wahr, Herr de Vriend.

An dem Tisch saßen zwei Männer und eine Frau, die Frau Joséphine ihm vorstellte: Ein pensionierter Richter, ein emeritierter Universitätsprofessor für Geschichte und eine ehemalige Standesbeamtin, alle drei verwitwet. Sie waren sehr freundlich und de Vriend fand sie auf Anhieb widerlich. Sie waren so – de Vriend suchte nach einem Wort – so, wie sagt man in diesem Leben? Sie waren schon längere Zeit hier, kannten das System, die Strukturen, die Gebräuche, hatten ihre Kontakte zur Direktion und zum Personal, sie kannten sich aus und hatten sich eingerichtet, mehr noch: Sie konnten einem Neuankömmling helfen, aber ihm auch das Leben schwer machen. Das war nach wenigen Minuten klar. Und dann kam die Frage: Und was haben Sie gemacht im Leben?

De Vriend verstand natürlich, dass sie bloß wissen wollten, welchen Beruf er ausgeübt hatte, aber er verschluckte sich an der Suppe, hustete, da kam schon sein Fisch-Teller, während seine Tischgenossen bereits die Nachspeise aßen, Crème de lait. De Vriend schob den Suppenteller weg, begann den Fisch zu essen, er aß schnell, nicht weil er den Vorsprung der ande-

ren aufholen, sondern weil er dieses Mittagessen schnellstmöglich hinter sich bringen und gehen wollte, er schlang den Fisch hinunter und spürte plötzlich eine Gräte, die in seine Luftröhre schlüpfte und stecken blieb, er stieß ein paar Mal kräftig Luft aus, um die Gräte zu lösen, aber er hatte das Gefühl, dass sie sich nur noch mehr verhakte, sich quer legte, er bekam Panik, er hechelte, immer wieder sich kräftig räuspernd und Luft holend, die Luft heftig ausstoßend. Er sprang auf, beugte sich vor, versuchte die Gräte abwechselnd zu schlucken oder hervorzudrücken, aber sie steckte in der Luftröhre fest, nahm ihm den Atem. Er schlug sich gegen die Brust, stieß mit aller Kraft Luft aus, ihm wurde rot vor Augen, und er schrie. Zunächst ein krächzendes, anschwellendes Aaaaa, dann ein Fluch, der Professor und die Standesbeamtin sprangen auf, von anderen Tischen schaute man erschrocken her, Frau Joséphine kam herbeigeeilt. Der Professor schlug ihm auf den Rücken, sagte Atmen! Er sagte immer wieder Atmen! Atmen! Die Standesbeamtin versuchte ihm ein Glas Wasser zu reichen, Frau Joséphine stellte sich hinter ihn, schlang ihre Arme um seine Brust, drückte und schüttelte ihn, er stieß sie mit dem Ellenbogen weg, keuchte.
Die Standesbeamtin versuchte ihre Finger in seinen Mund zu stecken, de Vriend schlug sie weg, sie taumelte und fiel auf einen Stuhl.
Er schrie hysterisch, dass das nicht wahr sein dürfe, er habe ein KZ überlebt und jetzt sterbe er an einer Gräte, bis er plötzlich innehielt, weil er merkte, dass er die Gräte nur noch als leichte Irritation spürte, und nicht einmal mehr sagen könnte, ob die Gräte wirklich noch in seinem Schlund steckte. Etwas Speichel rann aus seinem Mund, er setzte sich, keuchte und sagte schließlich: Es ist gut. Es ist gut.
Alles in Ordnung?
Ja.

Ganz sicher?

Ja.

Brauchen Sie einen Arzt?

Nein.

De Vriend atmete ein paar Mal tief durch, entschuldigte sich und ging in sein Zimmer.

In seinem Zimmer legte er sich hin, aber er empfand eine so starke Unruhe, dass er nicht liegen bleiben konnte, er stand wieder auf, setzte sich an den Tisch. Da lag der Notizblock. Darauf stand ein Wort, in seiner Handschrift: »Überleben«. Er hatte vorhin, vor dem Mittagessen, »Überlebende« schreiben und eine Liste anlegen wollen, war aber durch das Telefon gestört worden. Jetzt stand nur »Überleben« da, das hatte er geschrieben. Warum? Er zündete sich eine Zigarette an und schloss die Augen.

Es war ausgerechnet ein Totengräber, der den Weg zur Ewigen Liebe kannte. Professor Erhart hatte schließlich ihn angesprochen und nach dem Mausoleum der bedingungslosen Liebe gefragt, und dieser Mann wusste Bescheid. Es heißt zur Ewigen Liebe, nicht zur bedingungslosen Liebe, sagte er, auf seine Schaufel gestützt, ich weiß gar nicht, ob es das gibt, bedingungslose Liebe. Ewige Liebe, ja. Sie meinen das Mausoleum mit dem Lichtherzen auf dem Sarkophag, ja? Na eben. Da sind Sie hier auf dem falschen Friedhof. Das Mausoleum der Ewigen Liebe befindet sich auf dem Friedhof von Laeken.

Wo?

Laeken. Im Norden Brüssels.

Er nahm ein Taxi, döste ein während der Fahrt, die länger dauerte, als er erwartet hatte, und befand sich in einer eigentümlichen Trance, als er in Laeken ankam. Der Arm mit dem Bluterguss schmerzte ihn, aber jetzt, in seinem fast schlafwandlerischen Zustand, empfand er diesen Schmerz nur als leichten, angenehmen Druck, als hätte sich seine verstorbene Frau bei ihm eingehängt, er spürte sie an seinem Arm, als ginge sie neben ihm, und bei jedem Schritt schien er sich mehr anzupassen an den Rhythmus ihrer Schritte und an ihr Tempo. Natürlich war das verrückt. Er schüttelte den Kopf, buchstäblich, rief sich zur Räson. Jetzt spürte er den Schmerz im Arm stärker, und auch das unangenehm taube Gefühl in seinen geschwollenen Füßen, die er behutsam einen vor den anderen setzte, als wären sie ungewohnte Prothesen.

Gleich nach dem Eingangstor befand sich ein Büro der Friedhofsverwaltung. Dort bekam er auf Nachfrage den Plan der Friedhofsanlage, auf dem die Gräber von Berühmtheiten und die geschichtlich bedeutsamen Denkmäler und Gedenkstätten eingezeichnet waren. Der Beamte markierte auf diesem Plan noch eigens mit einem X, wo sich das Mausoleum der Ewigen Liebe befand. Der Professor wunderte sich darüber, dass der Beamte ihm die Auskunft mit todtraurigem Gesicht gab, ihm den Plan geradezu mit dem Ausdruck der Bestürzung überreichte. Was hatte es mit diesem Mausoleum auf sich, dass die Frage danach zu einer solchen Reaktion führte? Dann dachte er, dass es sich wohl um eine Déformation professionnelle handelte. Der Mann arbeitete auf einem Friedhof und irgendwann war sein Gesicht eben zur Maske des Beileids geworden. Und so war selbst die ewige Liebe – in Gestalt eines Mausoleums – für ihn nichts anderes als ein Trauerfall.

Professor Erhart hatte den Tod seiner Frau noch nicht verwunden. Er fragte sich, ob ihm die Zeit, die angeblich alle Wunden heilt, überhaupt noch gegeben war. Und wenn ja, ob das überhaupt wünschenswert wäre. Der Schmerz, den er seit dem grauenvollen Sterben und schließlich dem Tod seiner Frau spürte, erinnerte ihn so – ja: so lebendig an das große späte Glück, das er mit ihr gehabt hatte, und er war sicher, dass diese Erinnerung zu einer bloßen Phrase werden würde, wenn diese Wunde tatsächlich vernarbte.

Er ging mit dem Plan in der Hand über den Kiesweg und wunderte sich, dass er kein Knirschen hörte. In allen Filmen und Romanen knirschen die Kieswege. Er blieb stehen. Es war so still. Stumm wiegten sich die Äste der Bäume im Wind, lautlos das Flügelschlagen der Krähen. Weit vorn kreuzten einige Menschen die Allee, wie Schatten, die still vorbeiglitten, so wie am Himmel die grauen Wolken. Er ging weiter und – ja, doch: als läge eine Watteschicht auf dem Kies, hörte er nun ganz leise seine Schritte.

Dann stand er vor dem Grabmal. Er vergewisserte sich mehrmals, dass es tatsächlich das gesuchte Mausoleum der Ewigen Liebe war, aber es gab keinen Zweifel. Es war traurig. Was hatte er erwartet? Natürlich nicht den Tadsch Mahal, aber doch etwas Stolzes, etwas, das, im schönsten Menschenmaß, der Idee und der Erfahrung einer unendlichen Liebe einen baulichen Ausdruck gab, Ewigkeit im Material der Ewigkeit, dem Stein. Aber das hier war eine Ruine. Das Dach, in dem sich die berühmte, genau vermessene Öffnung befunden hatte, durch die ein Lichtherz auf den Sarkophag fallen sollte, war eingeknickt, die linke Seite des Mausoleums war eingesunken, wodurch sich Risse und Verschiebungen zwischen den Steinquadern gebildet hatten, aus denen Unkraut wuchs, die mit zwei flammenden Herzen verzierte Eisentür war verrostet und mit einer Kette versperrt, ein Türflügel hing schief in den Angeln, wodurch sich ein Spalt ergab, durch den man ins Innere blicken konnte, aber man sah nicht den Sarkophag, sondern nur Dreck, sogar Plastikmüll, wie war er da hineingekommen?

Links daneben steckte ein primitives, bereits vermorschtes

und vermoostes Holzschild schief im Boden, das darauf hinwies, dass die Pacht für diesen Grabplatz per August 1990 abgelaufen war und allfällige Nachkommen sich bei der Friedhofsverwaltung melden mögen. Daneben stand ein Schild aus Emaille in schmiedeeisernem Rahmen, das dieses Mausoleum als Kulturdenkmal auswies.

Die Idee einer ewigen Liebe, die Ewigkeit so wörtlich nimmt, dass sie sich noch ihres Nachlebens versichert, hatte Alois Erhart fasziniert. Aber solange die Ewigkeit auch nur etwas Menschengemachtes war, nichts Absolutes, sondern ein Verhältnis zwischen Menschen, im Grunde eine Vereinbarung, geht sie wie alles Menschengemachte irgendwann zu Ende, schnell und gnadenlos.

Das hätte er wissen müssen. Es hatte eine kleine Ewigkeit gedauert, nämlich bis zu seinem sechzigsten Lebensjahr, also vierzig Ehejahre, dass er selbst dieses Gefühl zum ersten Mal zutiefst spürte: ewige Liebe. Und da hatte er gesagt: Ich werde dich ewig lieben!

So pathetisch! Und er war tatsächlich erstaunt über sich selbst gewesen, als er diesen Satz ausgesprochen hatte. Er hatte damals das Gefühl gehabt, angekommen zu sein. Und später wunderte er sich darüber, dass ihm nicht gleich klar gewesen war, dass es keine Ewigkeit geben konnte: Sie ist nichts anderes als eine kurze Rast auf der Reise der Geschichte. Ich weiß, ich werde dich ewig lieben, hatte er gesagt – und schon zwei Jahre danach ist seine Frau gestorben. Und ob es nun ein Leben nach dem Tod gibt oder nicht, also das ewige Leben – der Satz von der ewigen Liebe ist, genauso wie das Gefühl, das diesen Satz hervorbrachte, nur noch Erinnerung, eben Geschichte.

Pathos! Eigentlich ist es so gewesen: Alois Erhart hatte sechzig Jahre alt werden müssen, um zu erfahren, dass es das wirklich gab: guten Sex.

Sein Lebtag lang hatte er das anwachsende Geraune und Gerede über »guten Sex« nicht verstanden. Hatte er wirklich gedacht: »sein Lebtag«? Das hätte von seinem Vater sein können, der hat solche Formulierungen verwendet. Jedenfalls: »Guter Sex«, das hielt er für Gequatsche, für die dubiose Ideologisierung eines menschlichen Triebs, die sich nicht annähernd so einsichtig begründen und erklären ließ wie die Frage, was »gute Küche« in Hinblick auf den menschlichen Nahrungstrieb sei. Alois Erhart war von der Fraktion »Man isst, was zu Hause auf den Tisch kommt«. Man ist dankbar und schlägt sein Kreuzzeichen drüber. Er war ein Nachkriegskind, ein Kind des Wiederaufbaus, er wusste, was Bedürfnisse sind, und er verstand bald, dass bei zunehmendem Wohlstand die Ansprüche wuchsen, aber er verstand nicht, warum guter und freier Sex ein Anspruch sein sollte, etwas, das politisch diskutiert und erkämpft werden musste, als wäre es eine Sozialleistung, die jedem Menschen zustehe, wie freier Hochschulzugang oder das Pensionsrecht. Das war in den sechziger und siebziger Jahren des vorigen Jahrhunderts gewesen, es war seine Generation, die die »sexuelle Revolution« ausgerufen hatte, aber er hatte nicht dazugehört.

Sein Vater besaß ein Sportartikel-Geschäft auf der Mariahilfer Straße, einer der großen Einkaufsstraßen von Wien, also gute Lage, aber was nützt die beste Geschäftslage in einer Zeit ohne Kaufkraft? Der Vater hatte das Geschäft als junger Mann, begeistert von der damals »neuen Zeit«, euphorisch und risikofreudig im Jahr 1937 eröffnet, gerade noch Zwischenkriegszeit. Warum Sportartikel? Der Vater war fanatischer Turner, er nannte sich »Turnbruder« als Mitglied der Turnvater-Jahn-Gesellschaft Wien, außerdem war er Fußballer, er spielte bei Wacker Wien, wo er, nach dem Verkauf von Josef Mahal an die Wiener Austria, als dessen Ersatz früh einen Platz in der Ersten bekam. »Der Jud Mahal hat mir mit seiner Gier Glück gebracht«, hatte der Vater erzählt, »er ist für zehn Schilling pro Spiel zur Austria gewechselt, so bin ich in die Kampfmannschaft gekommen und war mit fünf Schilling mehr als zufrieden!«

Geschäftseröffnung. Aber das Geschäft ging schlecht. Wer kaufte in Zeiten der Massenarbeitslosigkeit und Hyperinflation Fußballschuhe, wenn schon das Geld für normale Schuhe fehlte? Viele Kinder gingen damals barfuß in die Schule. Der Vater polierte Fahrräder im Geschäft, verkaufte ab und zu ein »Jahn-Leibchen«, im Volksmund – warum auch immer – »Ruder-Leiberl« genannt, und schrammte dem Konkurs entgegen. Im Jahr 1939 schöpfte er Hoffnung, als er es durch seine Kontakte schaffte, einen größeren Posten Zelte und »Feldgeschirr« an das »Jungvolk« und die »Hitlerjugend Wien« zu verkaufen, im Jahr darauf sperrte er zu. 1944 wurde das Haus in der Zollergasse, wo die Eltern wohnten, ausgebombt, sie überlebten im Luftschutzkeller und zogen in das noch bestehende Lager des Geschäfts in der Mariahilfer Straße. Hier kam Alois Erhart zur Welt. »Du bist ein Lager-Kind«, sagte seine Mutter gern, und er fand diesen Satz so normal wie »Die Zeiten waren damals schlecht«. Erst als Student begriff er, wie unfassbar zynisch das war, und er verbot ihr schreiend, dies noch einmal zu sagen. Es brauchte wieder Jahre, bis er verstand, dass seine Mutter viel zu naiv war, um schuldig zu sein, beziehungsweise dass ihre Schuld in ihrer Naivität lag und sie deshalb jeder Anschuldigung enthoben war. Wenn sie ihren »Loisl«, der im Lagerraum ihres Geschäfts zur Welt gekommen war, ein »Lagerkind« nannte, dann war das für sie bloß ein Spiel mit Worten, die ihr geläufig waren, weil sie irgendwie herumschwirrten, ein hilfloser Spaß im hilflosen Elend, das sie erlebt hatte. Sie war eine »deutsche Mutter«, deren großes Herz und Empathiefähigkeit zu den Menschen, die ihr nahestanden, missbraucht worden war, ohne dass sie es je verstanden hätte. Die Nazis hatten ihre Vorstellung von Frau und Mutter zum Ideal erklärt, und dieses Ideal, ohne dass sie ein anderes gehabt hätte, konnte doch nicht durch eine Niederlage in einem Krieg außer Kraft gesetzt werden. Es war zeitlos in Zeiten, die schlecht waren, und umso mehr galt es in Zeiten, die besser wurden. »Opferbereit«, das war auch so ein Wort, und sie war es, jetzt erst recht, als ihr Sohn studierte, und sie weinte, wenn der Herr Student heimkam und sie als alte Nazihexe beschimpfte. Jetzt sagte sie gerne Sätze, die mit den Worten begannen: »Wenn ich einmal nicht mehr bin …« – dann werde sie ihm fehlen. Dann werde er begreifen, was sie für ihn getan habe. Dann werde es ihm leidtun, wie ungerecht er zu ihr gewesen sei. Dann werde er schon sehen, dass. Er werde schon sehen, was. Er werde schon sehen, wie. Wenn sie einmal nicht mehr ist. Sie, die in den Augen ihres Sohnes in einer vergangenen Zeit feststeckte, erwartete Gerechtigkeit in ihrem Nachleben, da prallten in ihrer Seele Ewigkeiten aufeinander, das ewig Gestrige und das ewige Leben nach dem Tod. Immer öfter wich Alois seiner Mutter aus, ihrem Anblick, wenn er am Küchentisch lernte, den Gesprächen mit ihr, dem Streit, den Tränen, und er lief in die Mariahilfer Straße, zum Geschäft, setzte sich mit seinen Skripten ins Lager. Aber das war keine Regression, keine Rückkehr des »Lagerkinds«. Es war eine Flucht nach vorn. In die Zukunft, die sich hier abzeichnete. Der Wirtschaftsaufschwung wurde nun deutlich spürbar, die Geschäfte seines Vaters gingen immer besser. Seit der Weltmeisterschaft 1954 waren die Fußballschuhe mit den neuartigen Stollen der größte Wunsch aller kickenden Buben, und jetzt, Anfang der Sechziger, konnten es sich die meisten Väter leisten, ihren Söhnen diesen Wunsch zu erfüllen. Und echte Lederbälle. Und echte Dressen. Alles musste »echt« sein, kein Ersatz und kein Als-ob mehr, kein Sich-Begnügen mit dem, was »da war«, weil man es im Mangel noch irgendwie gehabt hatte. Was jetzt da war, war in den Auslagen der Geschäfte und in den Regalen der Supermärkte, und man konnte es kaufen und man konnte es sich leisten. So wie die Mutter nun Fru Fru kaufte, statt wie früher selbstgemachte Marmelade in ein Glas saure Milch einzurühren. Das Selbstgemachte war Ersatz, das Gekaufte war echt. Das Geschäft des Vaters ging jetzt gut, und er stellte einen Verkäufer an, den Herrn Schramek, einen alten Bekannten aus seiner Turnerbund-Zeit, und schließlich auch ein Lehrmädchen, die Trude.

Die Trudi. Sie war sechzehn, hatte einen sehnigen Körper, mit dem sie sich geschmeidig zwischen den Regalen bewegte. Wie ein edles Tier, dachte Alois – unsicher, ob diese Assoziation nicht ziemlich dumm war. Sie hatte einen »Bubikopf«, einen Kurzhaarschnitt, wie er damals bei jungen Frauen modern war und den Alois äußerst kess fand. Der fadenscheinige Stoff ihres blauen Arbeitsmantels schien fast durchsichtig, wenn sie die Lichtbahnen kreuzte, die durch die Fenster in den Raum fielen, da sah er die Konturen ihres Körpers, als hätte er einen Röntgenblick. Sie war ein sehr ernstes Mädchen, aber manchmal, wenn er etwas sagte, lachte sie so unschuldig fröhlich, dass Alois hingerissen war und, statt zu lernen, darüber nachdachte, wie er sie das nächste Mal zum Lachen bringen könnte. Ihm fiel auf, dass sie immer öfter unter irgendeinem Vorwand vom Geschäft nach hinten ins Lager schaute. Aber über seine vorbereiteten Witze lachte sie nicht.

Ein Jahr später heirateten sie. Alois brauchte eine Einverständniserklärung seines Vaters, Trudi war als Kriegswaise bereits volljährig geschrieben.

Die Flucht nach vorn: Auszug von zu Hause. Alois Erharts Vater kannte von früher einen Parteigenossen, der jetzt bei der Vergabe von Sozialwohnungen der Gemeinde Wien Einfluss hatte. So kam das junge Paar zu einer billigen Wohnung im Friedrich-Engels-Hof im 11. Bezirk, just in dem Jahr, als die roten Buchstaben auf der Front dieser kommunalen Wohnanlage erneuert und ersetzt wurden. »Friedrich« und das »s« von Engels war von Nazis abgeschlagen worden, der Wohnblock hatte in der NS-Zeit »Engel-Hof« heißen müssen.

Im nun renovierten Engels-Hof, in ihrer kleinen Gemeindewohnung, war Alois Erhart nichts ferner als die Wohngemeinschaften und Kommunen, in denen damals die sexuelle Revolution diskutiert wurde.

Vierzig Jahre später begriff er, was »guter Sex« ist. Dass es diese Sensation wirklich gab.

Sie waren zusammengeblieben, nachdem sich längst Liebe und Begehren getrennt hatten. Sie waren zusammengeblieben, nachdem beide, Liebe und Begehren, ausgezogen waren. Respekt und Solidarität waren in ihre Wohngemeinschaft eingezogen. In seinem Freundes- und Bekanntenkreis war Alois Erhart der Einzige, der nicht geschieden war. Er sagte: Es ist eine gute Ehe.

Es war ein Sonntag, sie hatten lange geschlafen, aber aus irgendeinem Grund standen sie nicht wie üblich gleich auf. Ein sonniger Tag, durch die beiden Fenster des Schlafzimmers fielen Lichtbahnen auf ihr Bett. Er sah sie an. Sein Rücken tat ihm weh. Sie legte ihre Hand auf seinen Rücken. Er blinzelte in das Licht, und dann – warum tat er das plötzlich? Er setzte sich auf und schlug die Decke zurück. Er schob ihr Nachthemd hoch, spürte dabei einen kurzen stechenden Schmerz in seinen Lendenwirbeln wie einen Stromschlag. Er stöhnte, sie zog das Hemd aus. Sie lächelte. Erstaunt? Fragend? Er betrachtete ihren Körper, studierte ihn, las jede Falte und jedes blaue oder rote Äderchen und jedes Fettpölsterchen wie eine Landkarte, auf der ein langer gemeinsamer Weg eingezeichnet war, ein Lebensweg mit Höhen und Tiefen, und er drückte sich erregt an sie, weinte, drückte, das Licht, der Röntgenblick, und plötzlich, in größter Erregung, spürte er es: ein Verschmelzen, in dem ihre Seelen sich berührten.

Und sie lachte. Trudi. Ihre Seelen berührten sich. Das war das Geheimnis, dachte Alois Erhart, das also war der »gute Sex«, der ihm eine bis dahin ungeahnte Befriedigung gab und der zugleich Begehren und Gier immer wieder aufs Neue entfachte: einen Körper so zu berühren, dass die Seelen sich berührten.

Zwei Jahre später war Trudi tot. Die ewige Liebe. So kurz die Ewigkeit.

Rauchpause?

Okay!

Nein, warte! Nicht Feuerleiter, sagte Bohumil. Viel zu kalt, du bist ohnehin schon krank. Komm in mein Zimmer!

Aber der – Martin deutete mit dem Zeigefinger nach oben, er wusste nicht, was Rauchmelder auf Englisch heißt. Bohumil verstand ihn:

Ich habe vorhin die Batterie rausgeholt. Der ist tot.

Bohumil setzte sich an seinen Schreibtisch, steckte sich eine Zigarette in den Mund und grinste wie ein kleiner frecher Junge. Martin Susman setzte sich auf den Besucherstuhl ihm gegenüber, schaute zur Decke.

Und zur Sicherheit habe ich den Sensor noch mit einem Pflaster zugeklebt. Feuer?

Martin zündete sich eine Zigarette an.

Ich bin Beamter, sagte Bohumil, ich bin es gewohnt, Fleißaufgaben zu machen. Einen toten Alarm noch zukleben – wenn das keine Metapher für unsere Arbeit ist! Jedenfalls frieren wir nicht. Aber sag mir: Was hast du in der Ukraine gemacht?

Ich? In der Ukraine? Wie kommst du drauf?

Habe ich gehört. Ein Salamander hat erzählt, dass du in der Ukraine warst, und er fand sehr wertvoll, was du berichtet hast –

Unsinn! Wie kommen die drauf? Ich war in Polen. Auschwitz. Weißt du doch!

Darum hat es mich ja gewundert. Was sagt uns das über unsere Task Force hier im Haus? Glauben die Salamander, dass Auschwitz in der Ukraine ist?

Und wenn sie recht haben? Auschwitz ist überall.

Du hast Fieber.

Ja.

Warum gehst du nicht nach Haus und legst dich ins Bett?

Ich warte auf Xeno. Ich muss mit ihr reden.

Martin nahm sein Smartphone heraus, dabei verhedderten sich seine Finger im Band des Auschwitz-Badge, den er immer noch in seiner Sakkotasche hatte, er schaute nach, ob er eine Nachricht von Xeno hatte, im selben Moment schaute Fenia Xenopoulou zwei Zimmer weiter auf ihren Blackberry, ob nicht endlich eine Nachricht von Fridsch gekommen sei. Diese Gleichzeitigkeit ist nicht konstruiert und war auch kein Zufall, sondern bloß größte Wahrscheinlichkeit: denn mittlerweile kontrollierte Fenia jede Minute ihr Telefon.

Martin zog den Badge aus der Tasche und steckte sein Smartphone ein.

Wie war es in Auschwitz?

So!, sagte Martin und reichte Bohumil den Badge.

Guest of Honour in Auschwitz, sagte Bohumil. Das ist krass.

Dreh ihn um! Und lies, was da steht.

Verlieren Sie diese Card nicht. Im Verlustfall haben Sie keine Aufenthaltsberechtigung im Lager. – Ist das … das ist – Bohumill drehte die Karte hin und her – echt? Diesen Badge hast du tatsächlich in Auschwitz bekommen? Und vom Hals baumeln lassen? Im Ernst?

Natürlich, das ist sehr ernst. Am Jahrestag der Befreiung von Auschwitz ist das Lager für Touristen gesperrt, da kommen ja Staatschefs, hohe Repräsentanten und Diplomaten aus allen möglichen Ländern, da gibt es natürlich gewisse Sicherheitsvorkehrungen, ich meine, ich verstehe das, aber –

Aber dieser Badge ist wie ein schlechter Witz, wie eine Parodie –

Ja. Alles. Als ich mir auf der Lagerstraße eine Zigarette anzündete, im Freien, auf der Lagerstraße, vor den Ruinen des Krematoriums, stand plötzlich ein Mann in Uniform vor mir und sagte: No smoking in Auschwitz.

Bohumil schüttelte den Kopf, blies Rauch aus und sagte: Hitler war Nichtraucher –

Es war grotesk. Wie auch die Automaten im Lager, wo man heiße Getränke bekommt. Die Automatenfirma heißt »Enjoy!« Es war so entsetzlich kalt in Auschwitz, und ich war froh, dass ich da einen heißen Kaffee bekam. Aber vielleicht schockiert oder verwundert uns bloß die Normalität, dort, wo wir sie nicht erwarten. Ich meine, dieser Badge ist keine zynische Parodie, er ist perfekt normal. Dass er grotesk wirkt, dass er anders formuliert, anders gestaltet sein müsste, denken wir nur an diesem Ort. Wie alles irgendwie anders sein müsste – das denken wir nur an diesem Ort. Aber wenn wir das jetzt umkehren, wenn wir überall das Normale, das Gewohnte in diesem Licht sehen würden … Verstehst du, was ich meine? Darum habe ich vorhin gesagt: Auschwitz ist überall. Wir sehen es nur nicht. Wenn wir es sehen könnten, dann würden wir das Bizarre, das Zynische einer Normalität begreifen, die hier in Europa doch eine Antwort auf Auschwitz sein sollte, eine Lehre, die aus dieser Geschichte gezogen wurde. Versteh mich nicht falsch, es geht nicht um einen sensibler gestalteten Badge oder um pietätvollere Kaffeeautomaten, ich meine grundsätzlich –

Ja, okay. Bohumil drückte seine Zigarette aus. Das Gespräch wurde ihm zu philosophisch. Er hatte ein heiteres Wesen, er fand, dass ein bisschen Ironie völlig ausreichte, um ein kritischer Zeitgenosse zu sein. Er hatte keine Karriereplanung, aber er hatte auch keine Lust, das, was er hatte oder was er vielleicht erreichen konnte, aufs Spiel zu setzen. Er mochte Martin, aber manchmal fand er dessen Schwermut mühsam. Nachdenklich betrachtete er seinen Aschenbecher. Er war aus schwarzem Gusseisen und stellte die Karikatur eines Afrikaners dar, mit wulstigen Lippen, krausem Haar und Baströckchen, der seine Handflächen zur Schale formte, um die Zigarettenasche aufzunehmen. Er saß auf einem Sockel, auf dem stand: »Le Congo reçoit la civilisation belge.« Er hatte diesen Aschenbecher vor Jahren auf dem Brüsseler Flohmarkt auf der Place du Jeu de Balle gekauft.

Weißt du – hob Martin an.

Ja? Sagte Bohumil.

In diesem Moment kam Kassándra herein, sie stutzte, als sie die Rauschwaden sah, Martin drückte seine Zigarette im Aschenbecher aus, der ihm jetzt erst auffiel, Bohumil schrie: Es brennt! Hilfe! Die Akten! Die Akten! Ruf die Feuerwehr! Er lachte, stand auf, öffnete das Fenster. Keine Sorge, sagte er, ich habe den Rauchmelder gekillt.

Ihr seid Kinder, sagte Kassándra. Martin! Du wirst gesucht! Xeno will dich sprechen!

Das Schwein wurde in kürzester Zeit zum Medienstar. Zunächst war in der Gratiszeitung Metro nur ein kurzer Bericht darüber erschienen, dass einige Passanten in Sainte-Catherine ein frei herumlaufendes Schwein gesehen haben wollten. Der Artikel war in ironischem Ton verfasst, so als ginge es um die angebliche Sichtung eines UFOs, illustriert war der Artikel mit dem Archivfoto irgendeines herzigen Ferkels, untertitelt war es mit dem Satz: »Wer kennt dieses Schwein?« Daraufhin riefen immer mehr Menschen bei der Redaktion an oder schrieben E-Mails, dass sie dem Schwein ebenfalls begegnet waren, und beschwerten sich, dass sie dies auch der Polizei gemeldet hätten, ihre Wahrnehmung von der Polizei aber nicht ernst genommen worden sei, und dass der Ton des Artikels und die Illustration eine Verharmlosung und eine Täuschung der Öffentlichkeit darstellten, da es sich um ein viel größeres und aggressives Tier gehandelt habe, vielleicht ein Wildschwein, jedenfalls eine öffentliche Gefahr.

Metro erkannte nun das Potential dieser Geschichte und setzte mit einer Titelgeschichte nach. Sie hatten Bewohner von Sainte-Catherine befragt, »besorgte Bürger«, die sich im Stich gelassen fühlten und nicht wussten, ob sie ihre Kinder noch unbegleitet zur Schule gehen lassen oder ob Frauen noch alleine ausgehen konnten, solange eine womöglich tollwütige Wildsau auf den Straßen ihr Unwesen trieb. Eine Madame Eloise Fourier fragte an der Metro-Redaktion an, ob ein Pfefferspray zur Verteidigung gegen Wildschweine empfehlenswert wäre, was Professor Kurt van der Koot, Professor an der Vrije Universiteit Brussel, auf Nachfrage von Metro verneinte. Ein Pfefferspray könnte die Unberechenbarkeit einer Sus scrofa, so der Fachterminus, nur vergrößern. Pfeffer, wie übrigens auch Salz und Kümmel, sei daher nur für Schweinebraten zu empfehlen. Dieser schlechte Witz des Professors, der bis dahin einer größeren Öffentlichkeit unbekannt gewesen war und der, wie man dann erfuhr, als Verhaltensforscher Spezialist für Wölfe war, löste einen Shitstorm in den sozialen Medien aus, der dazu führte, dass der Funke nun auf andere Zeitungen übersprang. Die Zeitung Le Soir brachte ein Interview mit dem Polizeichef des Kommissariats Centre Ville, einem

Flamen, der schon die längste Zeit auf der Abschussliste der Zeitung stand. Dabei verband sich der Wunsch der Zeitung, diesen Mann hinzurichten, mit dessen Naivität, mit der er Harakiri beging (»Welche Vorkehrungen haben Sie getroffen?« »Ich habe den städtischen Hundefängern Anweisung gegeben, dieses Schwein, wenn sie ansichtig werden, es dingfest zu nehmen.« »Wieso den Hundefängern?« »Wir haben viele streunende Hunde. Deshalb hat die Stadt Hundefänger. Aber wir haben kein Schweinefänger.« Dazu merkte die Zeitung an: »Der Plan ist so perfekt wie sein Französisch.«) Immer mehr Augenzeugen meldeten sich, De Morgen brachte nun jeden Tag einen Stadtplan von Brüssel-Region, auf dem mit Fähnchen graphisch markiert wurde, wo und wann das Schwein wieder gesehen worden war. Dabei fiel schließlich auf, dass das Schwein mittlerweile omnipräsent war. So wurde es zum Beispiel an einem Tag in Anderlecht, kurz darauf in Uccla und dann schon wieder in Molenbeek gesichtet.

Professor Kurt van der Koot, bemüht, seinen Ruf wiederherzustellen, veröffentlichte in De Morgen einen betont sachlichen Kommentar, in dem er die Höchstgeschwindigkeit, die ein Schwein im vollen Lauf erreichen könne, mit den Distanzen, die es zurückgelegt haben musste, in Beziehung setzte und somit nachwies, dass es rein empirisch nur zwei Möglichkeiten gebe: entweder, These eins, es handle sich nicht um bloß ein Schwein, sondern es müsse mehrere geben. Denn gemäß Weg-Zeit-Diagramm sei es gänzlich unmöglich, dass ein einzelnes Schwein überall dort gewesen sein könne, wo es Augenzeugen gesehen haben wollen. Oder aber, These zwei, es gebe überhaupt kein Schwein, sondern nur die Fiktion eines Schweins in den Köpfen einer verantwortungslos verunsicherten Bevölkerung, also eine hysterische kollektive Projektion. Es habe zwar in der Geschichte einige verbürgte Fälle von solcher kollektiver Hysterie gegeben, etwa die in der Stadtchronik von Nürnberg erwähnte Beobachtung eines Einhorns im Jahr 1221, er sei aber skeptisch, dass es sich beim Brüsseler Schwein tatsächlich um einen vergleichbaren Fall handle: denn bei allen historischen Beispielen habe es sich um Fabelwesen und nicht um eigentlich domestizierte Tiere gehandelt, darüber hinaus sei seit dem Ausgang des Mittelalters nie wieder ein Fabeltier mit übernatürlichen Eigenschaften, wie etwa Omnipräsenz, gesichtet und beschrieben worden. Davon leitete er ab, dass es sich in diesem Fall also weder um ein fiktionales Schwein noch um ein einzelnes Schwein handeln konnte, sondern um eine Horde von Schweinen, die jeweils an verschiedenen Plätzen Brüssels beobachtet wurden.

Eine Horde! Und was machte der Polizeipräsident?

Sechstes Kapitel

Kann man ein Comeback
der Zukunft planen?

The past forms the future, without regard to life.

Schwer zu sagen, warum dieser Satz Fenia Xenopoulou glücklich machte oder, wenn glücklich vielleicht ein zu großes Wort war, sie jedenfalls heiter stimmte. Fridsch hatte angerufen, endlich hatte er angerufen und ihr gesagt, dass kurzfristig ein Wechsel in eine andere Generaldirektion kaum möglich sei. Die Kommission sei ja erst vor kurzem neu aufgestellt worden, und der Präsident erwarte gerade jetzt von den Beamten vor allem der Führungsebenen, dass sich jeder an seinem Platz erst einmal bewährte. Für Wechsel und Rochaden sei es viel zu früh. *But* – Fridsch sagte, um der nun folgenden tröstlichen Seite dieser Information gehörig Nachdruck zu verleihen, besonders betont *but*, machte eine kurze Pause – und Xeno dachte an butter, letzter Tango in Paris, dann an butterflies, sie spürte butterflies in the stomach, zumindest hatte sie diese Assoziation, und Fridsch sagte nochmals *but*, und: sie sei auf dem Radar von Queneau und auch anderen sehr einflussreichen Spitzenbeamten, ihre bisherige Arbeit sei durchaus anerkannt, ihre bisherigen Leistungen, wirklich sehr anerkannt, und jetzt ginge es nicht darum, was sie sich wünsche, sondern darum, dass sie sichtbar bleibe und immer wieder auffalle – Xeno hörte zu, sie war nicht enttäuscht, es war okay, ja ja, es war okay, und dann – sie wusste nicht mehr, was er dann gesagt hatte, wie der Übergang war, jedenfalls sagte er plötzlich den Satz: »The past forms the future, without regard to life.« Dieser Satz blieb in ihrem Kopf hängen, sie dachte noch eine Weile nach dem Telefonat darüber nach, übersetzte ihn für sich in ihre Muttersprache und stellte fest, dass es nicht nur bei internationalen Verträgen und

Gesetzen auf die kleinsten Feinheiten jedes einzelnen Worts in den jeweiligen Übersetzungen ankam, sondern auch bei einem so höchstpersönlichen – ja, was? Satz. Einfach Satz. Über das Leben. Ihr Leben. Ein Lebenssatz, der so klar war wie ein juristischer Paragraph, der aber auf Griechisch, wie sie mit Verwunderung feststellte, Interpretationen erforderte, die den Satz heillos verwirrten … Mit welchem Begriff müsste man *the past* übersetzen? Die Vergangenheit, *parelthón*, und die Geschichte, *istória*, sind im Griechischen nicht so weitgehend deckungsgleich wie in *the past*, das ja doch auch irgendwie *history* miteinschließt. Alles Geschehene? Wem geschehen? Individuelle Geschichte? Also das Erlebte, die Biographie? Oder allgemein, sozusagen Weltgeschichte? Im Englischen lässt man das alles offen, dennoch hat man das Gefühl von größter Präzision. Im Griechischen muss man in der Übersetzung diese Fragen klären – und alles wird dadurch weniger klar und irgendwie beschränkter, Auslegungssache. Hat das Vergangene einen definierten Beginn und ein definiertes Ende oder ist unbestimmt, wann es begann und ob es endete? Wiederholt es sich oder war es – beziehungsweise ist es – einmalig? Davon hing dann die Konstruktion des griechischen Zeitworts ab, im Englischen stand es im Präsens, aber in der Übersetzung musste vielleicht der Aorist gewählt werden oder das Imperfekt oder das Perfekt, je nachdem, wie man definierte, was das Vergangene tat oder getan hatte. Und es erheiterte sie, dass dieser englische Satz letztlich also genau dies aussagte: dass sich ihre Herkunft in Widerspruch zu ihrem Leben befand – vielleicht war diese Erkenntnis schon die Übersetzung oder zumindest eine gültige Interpretation von »The past forms the future, without regard to life«.

Sie ließ Martin Susman rufen. Schließlich kam er in ihr Zimmer, blieb unschlüssig stehen. Fenia lächelte. Er war verwundert, so kannte er sie nicht. Dass sie ihn mit einem Lächeln empfing. Dass sie ein freundliches Gesicht machte. Er konnte das nur falsch verstehen. War sie so angetan von seinem Papier? Das hätte er nicht erwartet, er hatte schon bereut, dass er dieses Dokument fiebernd, also unkontrolliert, geschrieben und abgeschickt hatte, andererseits –

Es war der Anzug. Martins verbeulter, billiger, grauer Anzug. Ein Mann mit einem Minimum von Gefühl für Eleganz, dachte Fenia, würde nie einen solchen Anzug kaufen. Aber ein Mann, dem die Idee oder der Anspruch von Eleganz völlig egal war, auch nicht. Der würde mit lässiger Indifferenz irgendetwas Funktionales und doch Bequemes tragen, aber nie und nimmer solch ein Maus-Kostüm. Fenia sah Martin an und stellte sich vor, wie er in einem Bekleidungshaus, in der Abteilung, die für ihn völlig unangemessen »Herren« hieß, mehrere Anzüge an einer Stange durchwinkte, plötzlich auf diesen grauen Anzug zeigte und sagte: Den will ich probieren.

Nimm bitte Platz, Martin.

Sie fand das so komisch. Die Vorstellung, wie er in der Umkleidekabine in diesen Anzug schlüpfte, sich im Spiegel betrachtete und dachte: Ja! Passt! Und wie er sich vor dem Spiegel kurz hin und her bewegte und zum Verkäufer sagte: Ich lasse ihn gleich an!

Sie musste ein Lachen unterdrücken.

Martin war verunsichert beglückt. Ein verwirrendes Gefühl.

Du hast mein Papier gelesen?, fragte er.

Ja, natürlich, sagte sie. Sie konnte nicht ablassen von seiner Erscheinung, lächelnd stach sie Blicke in seinen Anzug wie Nadeln in eine Voodoo-Puppe. Er hatte immer so einen grauen Anzug an, sie hatte ihn nie anders gesehen. Sie stellte sich vor, dass er einen neuen Anzug brauchte. Der einzige neue, in dem er sich im Spiegel wiedererkannte, war wieder genau der gleich graue Anzug. In jedem anderen würde er denken: Das bin ich nicht. Gewohnheit gibt nicht Sicherheit, sondern macht unsicher. Gegenüber allem anderen. Nadelstreifen: zu förmlich. Blau, das war vielleicht etwas für die Nacht, aber nicht für den Tag. Ein hellerer Stoff, zu dandyhaft. Jedes Muster, jeder modische Schnitt, das war doch nichts für die Arbeit, das Büro ist ja kein Catwalk. Fenia stellte sich vor, wie der Verkäufer sich bemühte, ihm Alternativen zu zeigen, nein, nein, Martin würde zu schwitzen beginnen, geradezu in Panik geraten, der graue Anzug ist okay, würde er sagen, ich bleibe beim Grauen, das bin ich. Der mit dem Grauen.

Fenia Xenopoulou senkte den Kopf, sie hatte Martins Konzept ausgedruckt vor sich auf dem Schreibtisch liegen, sie strich mit der Kuppe ihres Mittelfingers ganz leicht über das Papier, hin und her und hin und her, dann sah sie auf, sah Martin an und sagte: Auschwitz! Was hast du dir dabei gedacht? Ich muss gestehen, ich bin erschrocken, als ich das las. Ich dachte, du bist – warte! Hier: Auschwitz als Geburtsort der Europäischen Kommission. Steht da! Ich dachte, das ist verrückt. Was hast du, Martin? Bist du krank?

Er schwitzte, wischte mit der Hand den Schweiß von der Stirn ins Haar, sagte: Ich war einige Tage krank, ja. Ich habe mich verkühlt in – ich habe mich verkühlt auf der Reise. Aber. Es geht schon wieder.

Gut. Aber kannst du mir das erklären? Wir suchen eine Idee, die wir ins Zentrum unserer Jubiläumsfeier stellen können, ja müssen. Da waren wir uns doch einig: Ein Jubiläum ist ein Anlass, aber noch keine Idee. Also, wie können wir erreichen, dass die Menschen merken, die Kommission ist notwendig, mehr noch, wie soll ich sagen? Dass wir sexy sind, dass wir etwas haben – sie räusperte sich –, ja, dass man froh ist, dass es uns gibt. Dass man Erwartungen an uns hat. Dass es etwas gibt, das uns verbindet. Verstehst du? Das wäre die Idee. Und du kommst mit Auschwitz.

Noch vor einer halben Stunde, als er bei Bohumil im Zimmer geraucht hatte, wäre Martin Susman froh gewesen, wenn Xeno ihm mitgeteilt hätte, dass sein Vorschlag ein völliger Unsinn sei, wir werfen das weg und vergessen es. Er hatte sich davor gefürchtet – aber es doch erhofft. Lieber jetzt die kurze Demütigung, hatte er gedacht, als dann die ganze Arbeit, die zweifellos zu einer Reihe von Verwerfungen und Komplikationen im Haus führen würde. Aber so, wie ihm Xeno jetzt kam, diese gepanzerte Frau, mit einem Lächeln, das ihn zunächst überrascht hatte, aber das eigentlich aussah wie mit Photoshop in ihr Gesicht gepinselt, diese geistlose Künstlichkeit, der er schwitzend gegenübersaß, das konnte er nicht akzeptieren. Er hatte –

Ich habe doch in dem Papier erklärt, warum wir von Auschwitz ausgehen müssen. Okay, es waren nur ein paar Stichworte, ich dachte –

Dann erkläre es mir noch einmal, Martin.

Sie stand auf, sie hatte einen schwarzen Rock an, mit einem diagonal verlaufenden, rot eingefassten Reißverschluss. Martin dachte: als wäre ihr Schoß durchgestrichen! Und doch mit einem Mechanismus versehen, um ihn blitzschnell öffnen zu können!

Kaffee? Sie hatte auf einem kleinen Seitentisch eine eigene Nespresso-Maschine stehen. Milch? Zucker? Martin schüttelte den Kopf. Sie setzte sich wieder hinter den Schreibtisch, hielt ihre Kaffeetasse mit beiden Händen. Martin musste daran denken, dass er genau so auch den Kaffeebecher in Auschwitz gehalten hatte, um seine klammen Finger zu wärmen.

Martin hustete. Sorry, sagte er und: Das ist doch die Idee der Kommission, so steht es in den Gründungsdokumenten, den damaligen Absichtserklärungen und Sideletters! Okay, es klingt ziemlich abstrakt, aber es ist doch auch völlig klar: Die Kommission ist keine internationale, sondern eine supranationale Institution, sie vermittelt also nicht zwischen Nationen, sondern steht über den Nationen und vertritt die gemeinsamen Interessen der Union und ihrer Bürger. Sie sucht nicht Kompromisse zwischen Nationen, sie will die klassischen nationalen Konflikte und Widersprüche in einer nachnationalen Entwicklung überwinden, also im Gemeinsamen. Es geht um das, was die Bürger dieses Kontinents verbindet, und nicht um das, was sie trennt. Monnet hat geschrieben – Wer?

Jean Monnet. Er hat geschrieben: Nationale Interessen sind abstrakt, das Gemeinsame der Europäer ist konkret.

Fenia sah, dass eine Mail hereingekommen war. Ja, und?, sagte sie. National, supranational – das war für sie Haarspalterei, sie war Zypriotin, aber der nationalen Identität nach war sie Griechin. Die Mail war, wie sie sah, von Fridsch. Sie öffnete die Mail und sagte: Was hat das mit Auschwitz zu tun?

Das, was die Kommission ist oder sein soll, sagte Martin, konnte man doch erst nach Auschwitz denken. Eine Institution, die die Staaten dazu bringt, nach und nach nationale Souveränitätsrechte aufzugeben und –

Wann? Wo?, tippte Fenia. (Fridsch hatte gefragt, ob sie Lust und Zeit hätte, mit ihm zu Abend zu essen.)

Auschwitz! Sagte Martin. Die Opfer kamen aus allen Ländern Europas, sie trugen alle dieselbe gestreifte Kleidung, sie lebten alle im Schatten desselben Todes, und sie alle hatten, so sie überlebten, denselben Wunsch, nämlich die für alle Zukunft geltende Garantie der Anerkennung der Menschenrechte. Nichts in der Geschichte hat die verschiedenen Identitäten, Mentalitäten und Kulturen Europas, die Religionen, die verschiedenen so genannten Rassen und ehemals verfeindete Weltanschauungen so verbunden, nichts hat eine so fundamentale Gemeinsamkeit aller Menschen geschaffen wie die Erfahrung von Auschwitz. Die Nationen, die nationalen Identitäten, das war alles hinfällig, ob Spanier oder Pole, Italiener oder Tscheche, Österreicher, Deutscher oder Ungar, das war alles hinfällig, die Religion, die Herkunft, das alles war aufgehoben in einer gemeinsamen Sehnsucht, dem Wunsch zu überleben, dem Wunsch nach einem Leben in Würde und Freiheit.

Italiener? (Fridsch)

O. K.! (Fenia)

Diese Erfahrung und die Einigkeit, dass sich dieses Verbrechen nie mehr wiederholen darf, haben erst das Projekt der Einigung Europas möglich gemacht. Also, dass es uns gibt! Und deshalb ist Auschwitz –

Fenia sah Martin an, sagte: *But* –

Das ist die Idee! Die Überwindung des Nationalgefühls. Wir sind die Hüter dieser Idee! Und unsere Zeugen sind die Überlebenden von Auschwitz! Die Überlebenden sind nicht nur Zeugen der Verbrechen, die in den Lagern begangen wurden, sie sind auch die Zeugen der Idee, die daraus entstanden ist, der Idee, dass es erwiesenermaßen etwas Gemeinsames gibt, und –

Pasta Divina, 16, Rue de la Montagne. 8 pm? (Fridsch)

O. K.! (Fenia)

Martin hatte das Gefühl, dass Xeno nachdenklich wurde, und er setzte nach: Die Sicherheit eines Lebens in Würde, Glück, Menschenrechte, das ist doch seit Auschwitz ein ewiger Anspruch, oder? Das versteht doch jeder. Das müssen wir klarmachen: dass wir die Institution dieses Anspruchs sind. Die Hüter dieses ewig gültigen Vertrags. Nie wieder – das ist Europa! Wir sind die Moral der Geschichte!

Fenia sah ihn erstaunt an. Wie lebendig dieser schwitzende graue Mann plötzlich war.

Dafür sind Menschen in den Tod gegangen, ihr Tod war ein Verbrechen und für jeden Einzelnen absolut sinnlos, aber doch bleibt diese Konsequenz: Dafür sind sie letztlich in den Tod gegangen, und das bleibt ewig!

Auch wenn das Xeno jetzt nicht wirklich bewusst war, es klang wie ein Echo aus der tiefen dunklen Höhle ihrer Vorgeschichte, es klang wie: unsterblich in den Tod.

Sie sah Martin an. Sie wirkte nun sehr ernst, sehr nachdenklich. Martin fragte sich, ob er sie jetzt womöglich überzeugt hatte, obwohl er noch gar nicht fertig war mit seiner Argumentation.

Fenia hatte nie viel über sich selbst nachgedacht, und wenn, dann über Möglichkeiten, über Ziele, aber nicht über Befindlichkeiten und Gefühle. Wohlbefinden, das war für sie der Idealzustand von Gefühllosigkeit, in einem sehr umfassenden Sinn, und das hieß: nicht behelligt zu werden von Stimmungen. Gefühle, das waren für sie Stimmungen.

Hast du Zigaretten?

Ja, natürlich, sagte Martin erstaunt.

Fenia stand auf, öffnete das Fenster und sagte: Würdest du mir eine geben?

Ich wusste nicht, dass du rauchst.

Manchmal. Sehr selten. Eine.

Sie standen dicht nebeneinander im engen Winkel des geöffneten Fensterflügels und rauchten, Martin erwartete, dass sie etwas sagte, er hatte den Eindruck, dass sie etwas sagen wollte, aber sie paffte, mit dem verkniffenen Gesicht des Amateurrauchers, es war eisig kalt, schließlich sagte Martin: Es ist die letzte Chance!

Sie sah ihn erstaunt an. Es war so furchtbar kalt am offenen Fenster, Martin dachte, man müsste enger zusammenrücken, um sich gegenseitig zu wärmen, er erschrak, versuchte etwas Abstand zu gewinnen, und sie sagte: Wie bitte?

Es werden immer weniger, sagte Martin. Sehr bald wird es niemand mehr geben, der ein Vernichtungslager überlebt hat. Verstehst du? Wir müssen sie ins Zentrum der Jubiläumsfeier stellen – Das ist die Idee: Sie bezeugen, zu welch grauenhaften Verbrechen der Nationalismus im alten Europa geführt hat, und zugleich bezeugen sie all das Gemeinsame, das durch die Lager so radikal klar wurde, nämlich dass …

Es war so verdammt kalt am offenen Fenster.

… und für all das Gemeinsame in Sachen Würde und Rechtszustand steht die Kommission, und deswegen …

Martin warf die Zigarette aus dem Fenster, trat einen Schritt zurück, Fenia schnippte ihre Zigarette ebenfalls hinaus und schloss das Fenster.

Weiß man, wie viele noch leben?

Ich weiß es nicht. Ich weiß nur, dass zum Jahrestag der Befreiung von Auschwitz kaum ein Dutzend da waren, und alle waren sie zwischen fünfundachtzig und fünfundneunzig, schätze ich. Vor wenigen Jahren sind angeblich noch mehr als zweihundert gekommen.

Gut. Dann finde das heraus: Wie viele sind noch am Leben? Und dann müssen wir diskutieren, wie wir das konkret machen, wie wir sie ins Zentrum der Feierlichkeit stellen. Alle, oder – weißt du, was ich jetzt vor mir sehe? Tausende –

So viele leben sicher nicht mehr!

Nein, warte! Wenn wir sie alle einladen mit ihren Familien und Nachkommen, die Kinder, Enkelkinder, Urenkel, das sind dann vielleicht Tausende, und dann, wie soll ich sagen – sie machte eine weit ausholende Handbewegung –, dann erklären wir uns alle symbolisch zu ihren Kindern, und unsere Kinder erklären wir zu ihren Enkeln und –

Ich weiß es nicht genau, aber ich glaube, dass die meisten

Nachkommen der Auschwitzüberlebenden nicht in Europa leben.

Ja. Aber. Ändert das etwas? Ja, vielleicht. Also –

Sie überlegte, dann sagte sie: Die anderen Punkte deines Papiers sind okay, das lassen wir einmal so. Das sind die üblichen Dinge, die bei so einer Feier bedacht werden müssen. Aber was wir jetzt schnell brauchen, sind Fakten und Zahlen. Wie viele leben noch, vor allem in Europa?

Wieder dachte sie nach. Martin fragte sich, ob er sich wieder hinsetzen sollte. Aber sie selbst machte keine Anstalten, sich wieder zu setzen, sie stand vor dem Fenster, sah hinaus, sagte schließlich: Vielleicht genügt einer. Im Grunde brauchen wir nur eine Symbolfigur, für das geeinte Europa, für das Gemeinsame, für den Anspruch unserer Arbeit hier.

Zuerst will sie Tausende, dann nur einen – in welche Richtung sollte er jetzt weiterarbeiten? Er sah sie an. Sie sah an sich hinunter, wischte Asche von ihrer Bluse.

Als Professor Erhart zum ersten Meeting der Reflection Group »New Pact for Europe« kam, war er der Einzige mit einer Aktentasche. Das war wirklich komisch: Es fiel ihm selbst sofort auf, und er hatte das Gefühl, dass dies auch von den anderen registriert wurde, ob mit Belustigung oder bloßem Erstaunen, jedenfalls wurde es bemerkt.

Er war der Letzte, der eintraf, weil er sich auf dem Weg zunächst verirrt hatte. Das Treffen fand im Résidence Palace hinter dem Ratsgebäude in der Rue de la Loi statt, eine Adresse, die im Grunde nicht zu verfehlen war, man kam aus der Metro-Station Schuman heraus und stand praktisch davor. Allerdings gab es neben dem Ratsgebäude eine Baustelle, davor einen gesperrten Gehsteig, Absperrgitter, Betonklötze. Alois Erhart hatte gedacht, dass er um die ganze Baustelle herumgehen müsste, um hinter das Ratsgebäude zu kommen, also ging er die Rue de la Loi weiter, aber er fand keine Gelegenheit, links abzubiegen und zu einer Parallelstraße zu kommen, die zurück zur Hinterseite des Ratsgebäudes führte. Da sah er den Eingang zur Metro-Station Maelbeek, das bedeutete, er war von Schuman bereits eine ganze Metro-Station zurückgegangen. Eine so lange Umleitung, das konnte doch nicht sein! Andererseits: Er sah keine andere Möglichkeit, ging unschlüssig noch ein Stück weiter die Straße hinunter. Da kam endlich eine Seitengasse nach links. Er bog ab, Rue de Trèves, dann wieder links, die Rue Jacques de Lalaing, er las die Straßennamen, als könnte es ihn beruhigen, dass die Straßen, in denen er sich verirrte, Namen haben. Er blieb stehen und nahm den Stadtplan von Brüssel aus seiner Aktentasche, suchte, stellte fest, dass er, wenn er die Jacques de Lalaing weiterginge, auf die Chaussée d'Etterbeek käme – die unter der Rue de la Loi durchführte, ohne eine Möglichkeit, zumindest war keine eingezeichnet, wieder hinauf zur Rückseite des Ratsgebäudes zu gelangen. Also machte er kehrt und ging den ganzen Weg zurück. Wieder bei der Baustelle angelangt, entdeckte er, dass es einen kleinen unscheinbaren Durchschlupf zwischen Gittern und gelben Sperrholzplatten zum Résidence-Palace-Gebäude gab.

Als er das Gebäude betrat, wusste er natürlich nicht, wohin er sich nun wenden sollte. In der Mitte des Foyers gab es einen Info-Point, wo zwei Mädchen saßen, die Professor Erhart mit größter Freundlichkeit Auskunft gaben. Nein, sie wüssten nicht, wo das European Policy Center hier im Haus sei. Der Think-Tank »New Pact for Europe« sei ihnen völlig unbekannt. Ob er einen Namen habe. Professor Erhart nannte seinen Namen, ein Mädchen tippte in den Computer, sagte mit freundlichem Lächeln, es tue ihr leid, es tue ihr sehr leid, aber es befinde sich niemand mit diesem Namen im Haus. Aber das ist doch mein Name, sagte der Professor, ich dachte,

Sie wollten meinen ... okay, ich möchte zu – warten Sie! Er
öffnete seine Tasche, er hatte die Mail, mit der er über alle
organisatorischen Details des ersten Meetings informiert worden war, ausgedruckt. Er zog das Blatt aus der Tasche. Hier,
sagte er, Mister Pinto, European Policy Center, erstes Treffen
der Reflection Group New Pact for Europe, sehen Sie! Max
Kohnstamm Room, 4th floor –
Oh, sagte das Mädchen, alles klar! 4. Stock! Der Lift ist da
hinten rechts.
Er war also als Letzter eingetroffen. Aber viel zu spät kam er
nicht. Hätte er sich nicht verlaufen, wäre er viel zu früh da
gewesen. Er war sonst immer der Erste, aus Angst, zu spät
zu kommen.
Er hatte seine Tasche die ganze Zeit in der linken Hand gehalten, wegen der Schmerzen, die er immer noch im rechten
Arm hatte. Nun spürte er auch einen ziehenden Schmerz im
linken. Er hob die Tasche und drückte sie mit gekreuzten Ar-
men an seine Brust. Er wollte seine Arme entlasten, aber es
sah aus, als verwendete er seine Tasche als Schild, als wollte
er sich ängstlich wappnen. Das war das Bild, das er abgab, als
er den Raum betrat.
Ein Mann kam mit breitem Lächeln auf ihn zu.
Mister Erhart?
Yes.
Der Professor aus Österreich!
From Vienna, yes.
Ich bin António Oliveira Pinto, der Leiter unserer Reflection
Group. Schön, dass Sie da sind, sagte der Mann. Er sprach
perfekt Deutsch.
Bedaure die Verspätung, die Baustelle –
Ja, sagte der Mann fröhlich lachend, Europa ist eine verwir-
rende Baustelle. Und darum sind wir hier, unser Job ist, zu
diskutieren, was bauen wir da eigentlich?

Ich bin kein Architekt, und –

Haha, Wiener Schmäh, nicht wahr? Sehr gut. Also, ich schlage vor, Sie stärken sich erst mal, und in zwanzig Minuten beginnen wir im Meeting-Room mit der Vorstellungsrunde. Kein Architekt, haha, sehr gut!

Alois Erhart stand da, mit seiner Tasche vor der Brust, schaute sich um. Auf einem Tisch war ein Buffet aufgebaut, an einer Reihe von Stehtischen standen Männer und Frauen, die Mitglieder des Think-Tanks, sie aßen mit Plastikgabeln von Papptellern und unterhielten sich und sahen her, oder sie redeten nicht, lächelten und sahen her.

Alois Erhart nahm jetzt die Tasche wieder in die linke Hand, um die rechte frei zu haben, damit er einen Teller halten konnte – aber wie sollte er jetzt den Nudelsalat oder das Roastbeef auf den Teller geben? Er klemmte die Tasche unter die linke Achsel, nahm den Teller in die linke Hand, versuchte mit der rechten etwas Nudelsalat aus der Schüssel … – da fiel die Tasche zu Boden. Er bückte sich, um sie aufzuheben, dabei rutschte der Nudelsalat, den er bereits auf seinen Teller geschaufelt hatte, auf den Boden. Er stellte die Tasche wieder ab, sie fiel um. Das machte ihn seltsamerweise nervös: dass die Tasche nicht stand, sondern lag. Er nahm sie und lehnte sie an die Wand. Irgendwie beunruhigte ihn das: dass dort die Tasche lehnte und er, wenn er sich am Buffet bediente, so weit weg von ihr war. Also stellte er seinen Teller ab, holte die Tasche wieder, stellte sie zwischen die Füße, während er sich am Buffet bediente. Nun musste er zu einem der Stehtische gelangen. Er versuchte, den Teller in der Rechten, einen Becher mit Apfelsaft in der Linken, mit kleinen engen Schritten die Tasche zwischen seinen Füßen irgendwie mitzunehmen, dabei wäre er fast gestolpert, nun gab er der Tasche einen leichten Tritt, machte einen Schritt und gab der Tasche wieder einen Schubs mit dem Fuß, um sie so bis zum Tisch vor sich herzuschieben, und spätestens jetzt stand er beziehungsweise seine Tasche im Zentrum der Aufmerksamkeit. Und Professor Erhart sah, dass niemand sonst hier eine Tasche hatte – einige trugen Rucksäcke, standen selbstgewiss mit ihren Höckern und freien Händen da, die anderen hatten Trolleys an ihrer Seite, auf die sie sich lässig mit einer Hand stützten. Und er, der alte Mann mit der Schultasche.

Es war tatsächlich seine Schultasche. Er hatte sie sehr spät bekommen, erst in der Oberstufe des Gymnasiums. Vorher ist kein Geld dagewesen. Oder sein Vater war der Meinung, dass der Kauf einer Schultasche eine unnötige Ausgabe sei, wo er doch in seinem Geschäft Sporttaschen auf Lager hatte. Sie waren aus Stoff, eine Art Seesack, der mit einer Kordel verschlossen wurde, die dann zugleich eine Schlaufe bildete, die als Henkel diente. Im Grunde war es ein etwas größerer Turnbeutel, und der junge Alois schämte sich, dass sein Vater, immerhin Ladenbesitzer, also Unternehmer, ihn zwang, mit diesem seltsamen Beutel, wie ihn kein anderer Schüler hatte, in das bürgerliche Gymnasium in der Amerlingstraße zu gehen. Als er endlich eine echte Schultasche bekam, war er überglücklich. Sie war aus Leder, handgenäht. Der Vater hatte sie beim Weinberger gekauft, einem »Ledergalanteriewarenerzeuger« ein kleines Stück weiter unten auf der Mariahilfer Straße, mit einem schönen Preisnachlass, nachdem er dem Taschner beim Kauf einer Schi-Ausrüstung für dessen Sohn sehr entgegengekommen war.

Alois war so stolz auf seine Ledertasche, dass er sie, wenn er schlafen ging, neben das Bett stellte, um sie sofort im Blick zu haben, wenn er aufwachte. Er liebte das Geräusch, wenn die Steckschlösser aus glänzendem Nickel beim Packen der Tasche für den Schultag mit einem hellen Klicken einrasteten. Von Zeit zu Zeit pflegte er die Tasche mit einer Fettpaste, damit das Leder nicht brach. Die Tasche hatte einen Riemen, den man an der Rückseite in Schlaufen einfädelte, wenn man sie auf dem Rücken tragen wollte, aber diesen Riemen verwendete Alois nie, er trug die Tasche lieber wie ein Erwachsener in der Hand, und der Riemen kam ihm irgendwann abhanden.

Später kamen dann die modernen Schultaschen auf, bunt, grell gemustert, aus irgendeinem künstlichen Material, im Grunde plastifizierte Pappe, und Alois empfand eine Mischung aus Abscheu und Mitleid, wenn er die Kinder sah, die diese lächerlichen Snoopy- und Batman-Koffer auf dem Rücken in die Schule schleppten. Seine Ledertasche begleitete ihn bis heute. Das Leder war inzwischen etwas weicher geworden und hatte eine schöne, matt glänzende Patina. Und er brachte in dieser Tasche alles unter, was er für einen Anlass wie diesen brauchte. Eine Klarsichthülle mit zwei Blättern mit Stichworten für das fünfminütige Eingangsstatement, das er, wie die anderen auch, bei der Eröffnungsrunde geben sollte, eine Klarsichthülle mit den ausgedruckten E-Mails, die er von Herrn Pinto in Vorbereitung zu diesem Treffen erhalten hatte, eine Mappe mit seinem Papier zur Reform der Union, das er, sobald sich Gelegenheit dazu ergab, präsentieren wollte, ein Notizblock und ein Federpennal. Er fragte sich, was die anderen in ihren prall gefüllten Rucksäcken und Trolleys mitbrachten.

An einem Stehtisch erste freundliche Wortwechsel. Oh, Sie sind Professor Erhart? Freut mich sehr. Freut mich. Sehr erfreut. Ich bin, ich bin, ja und ich bin. Der. Die. Der. Freut mich, Sie kennenzulernen. Freut mich, Sie kennenzulernen. Ein Franzose begann etwas zu erzählen, Professor Erharts Schulfranzösisch reichte nicht aus, dessen französischen Dialekt zu verstehen – bis er erkannte, dass der Franzose Englisch sprach, und er widmete sich seinem Nudelsalat. Da klatschte António Oliveira Pinto ein paar Mal in die Hände, rief: Meine Damen und Herren, ich darf Sie bitten, bitte, wir möchten beginnen.

Das ging ja schnell: Professor Erhart spürte schon jetzt, dass er hier fehl am Platz war beziehungsweise mit seinen Anliegen in dieser Runde keine Chance hatte. Alle waren sich so ähnlich. Nur er war anders. Er war darüber informiert, dass sich dieser neue Think-Tank sechs Mal in diesem Jahr für jeweils zwei Tage treffen sollte, um am Ende dem Kommissionspräsidenten ein Papier mit den Ergebnissen ihrer Analysen und Vorschläge für Auswege aus der Krise und für eine Festigung der Union zu überreichen. Alois Erhart hatte sich gewundert, dass man nur zwölf Tage und diese verteilt auf ein ganzes Jahr Zeit habe, um ein Konzept zur Lösung der europäischen Krise zu entwickeln. Aber er hatte diese Einladung auch als Chance gesehen: seine Ideen in dieses System einzuspeisen.

Nun saßen sie alle im Kreis im Max Kohnstamm Room, Alois Erhart zog seine Blätter mit den Stichworten für sein erstes Statement aus der Tasche, alle anderen holten aus ihren Rucksäcken oder Trolleys Laptops heraus oder Tablets, António Oliveira Pinto sagte mit dem breiten strahlenden Lachen eines Mannes, der soeben den größten Glücksmoment seines Lebens hatte, Once again welcome, da machte es einen Knall, die Frau neben Erhart zog den Kopf ein, ein Mann sprang auf, einem anderen rutschte der Laptop von den Knien – was war das? Ein Vogel war gegen die Fensterscheibe geflogen, ja, das musste es gewesen sein, ein Vogel – einer, der behauptete, es gesehen zu haben, sagte: ein großer schwarzer Vogel … man sprang auf, drängte sich vor dem Fenster, es war tatsächlich ein kleiner Blutfleck zu sehen und eine Feder, die da klebte.

Seltsam, dass Alois Erhart, dieser im Grunde seines Herzens so glücklich konservative Mensch, in dieser Runde zum traurigen Revolutionär werden sollte.

Wäre Kommissar Émile Brunfaut nicht beurlaubt worden, er hätte sich nicht die Zeit genommen, zum Arzt zu gehen. Und dann hätte er vielleicht auch nie versucht, das Rätsel des Falls »Atlas-Mord« zu lösen.

Nun lag er mit freiem Oberkörper und offener Hose auf der Pritsche des Arztes und merkte beklommen, dass ihn Angst überkam, eine stille, lähmende Angst. Tief einatmen! Ausatmen! Eine Angst, die ihm den Atem nahm. Seltsam, dass Brunfaut bisher nie an die eigene Sterblichkeit gedacht hatte, obwohl er doch ständig mit Leichen konfrontiert war. Aber es war eben er, der lebte und der die Aufgabe hatte, die am Tod Schuldigen der gerechten Strafe zuzuführen. Und die hieß in der Regel »lebenslang«, was selbst bei vorzeitiger Entlassung eines Täters nach der unabsehbaren Ewigkeit eines Lebens klingt, dessen Ende niemand kennt.

Gefährliche Verfolgungsjagden, Schusswechsel und dergleichen, das gab es im Fernsehen, aber nicht bei seiner Arbeit, und wenn, dann gab es dafür Spezialisten, er selbst aber hatte dies in all seinen Dienstjahren kein einziges Mal erlebt, er war noch nie in eine Situation gekommen, in der er Todesangst kennenlernen musste. Aber jetzt, bei diesem Arzt, der kein Gerichtsmediziner und kein Forensiker war, sondern ein ganz normaler praktischer Arzt, der ihn eben untersucht hatte, hier ein bisschen drückend, dort ein bisschen klopfend, da –

Brunfaut knöpfte sein Hemd zu, während der Doktor die Überweisung in die Klinik schrieb, zur genauen Abklärung der Symptome, da –

Da musste er an den Tod denken. Den eigenen. Ohne Koketterie. Der Doktor hatte einen Verdacht. Er wusste etwas. Und im Spital werden sie bestätigen, was der Doktor wusste oder ahnte. Die Krankheit zum Tod. Brunfaut hatte plötzlich keinen Zweifel daran, dass er zuschaute, wie sein Todesurteil verfertigt wurde. Er erlebte diesen Moment als unwirklich und zugleich sich selbst als auf eine bisher nicht gekannte radikale Weise wirklich. Niemand ist so sehr aus der Welt gefallen und zugleich bei sich wie einer, der plötzlich in undurchdringlichem Nebel verloren ist. Panik und Überlebenswille zerreißen den Körper, der Kopf wird heiß, die Brust kalt und klamm. Der Doktor schlug in die Tastatur, sehr unrhythmisch, immer wieder mit hochgezogenen Brauen auf den Computerbildschirm starrend, tip tip tip Pause klick Pause tip tip Pause, dann wie ein Trommelwirbel und dann ein Aussetzen, wie die Töne eines verzweifelten Herzens, angeschlossen an einen Verstärker. Und Brunfaut, als würde er Übungssätze in eine Fremdsprache übersetzen, die er erst lernte, formulierte in seinem Kopf nach und nach Fragen, langsam und unsicher: Wie reagieren, wie werde, ich? reagieren, wenn der Befund, wenn ich den Befund habe, schwarz auf weiß? Aufbäumen und kämpfen? Kämpfen wollen? Werde ich mich fallenlassen, mich aufgeben? Selbst belügen, belügen lassen, verrückt hoffen? Werde ich Selbstmitleid – oder Lust, werde ich noch Lust empfinden können, Lust empfinden lernen, an letzten Genüssen? Werde ich wütend sein, oder, oder zärtlich sein können? Zärtlich zu wem?

Der Doktor räusperte sich, und Brunfaut musste plötzlich lächeln. Das waren noch Zeiten, als Kranksein idyllisch und paradiesisch war – ganz schnell, höchstens eine Sekunde lang, hatte er jetzt dieses Bild im Kopf: Er, hineingekuschelt in ein weiches Federbett, von der Schule befreit, die Mutter so zärtlich, ihre Hand auf seiner heißen Stirn, so fürsorglich, sie macht Tee, und zu seiner Stärkung kocht sie dann sein Lieblingsessen. Dösen, Träumen, Lesen. Die süße Erfahrung von Liebe in Gestalt von Mitleid und Sorge. Und die Gewissheit: Alles wird gut. Alles war gut …

Der Doktor telefonierte: … Gleich in der Früh ist nicht

möglich? … Verstehe … also 13 Uhr? … D'accord! Besten Dank, Herr Kollege!

Morgen um 13 Uhr bitte im Europa-Hospital St. Michel, sagte der Doktor, wenn möglich nüchtern. Mit diesem Überweisungsschein, hier bitte! Die Abklärung, also die erforderlichen Untersuchungen werden vielleicht drei Tage in Anspruch nehmen. Sollte es länger dauern, können Sie auf jeden Fall über das Wochenende nach Hause gehen. Das wird der Primar, Doktor Drumont, entscheiden. Ich habe gerade mit ihm gesprochen. Bei ihm sind Sie in besten Händen.

Und da geschah etwas Seltsames mit Émile Brunfaut: Die Angst erlöste ihn. Das war tatsächlich sein Gefühl und schließlich sein Gedanke: Erlösung.

Das Todesurteil, oder sagen wir: das Begreifen der Sterblichkeit empfand er plötzlich als Befreiung zur Tat. Er musste tun, was getan werden musste. Es war beurlaubten Polizisten verboten, auf eigene Faust weiter zu ermitteln. Aber welche Strafe hatte er jetzt noch zu fürchten? Zu sterben, im Wissen, nicht gehandelt zu haben, das wäre die einzige Strafe, die er fürchten müsste, das wäre der qualvollste Tod. Pathetisch? Geschichte ist nichts anderes als eine Pendelbewegung zwischen Pathos und Banalität. Und der Sterbliche wird einmal dahin, dann dorthin gestoßen.

Kommissar Brunfaut stand auf, sah auf den Doktor hinab, mit dem Blick, den sein Großvater gehabt hatte. Der berühmte Widerstandskämpfer, nach dem eine Straße in Brüssel benannt worden war. Der Blick des Großvaters, vor dem er sich als Kind gefürchtet hatte. Als er, der kleine Émile, mit leichtem Fieber, mit Schnupfen und Halsschmerzen mit dem von der Mutter gekochten Salbeitee im Bett gelegen hatte, Kranksein war Idylle und Paradies, da stand der Großvater vor ihm, schaute auf ihn hinunter und sagte: Kranksein gibt es nicht. Man ist erst krank, wenn man umfällt. Und dann ist man tot.

Und die Mutter, die gerade mit dem Tee ins Zimmer kam, schrie: Was redest du da? Lass das Kind in Ruhe! Warum machst du ihm Angst?

Brunfaut nahm den Einweisungsschein für die Klinik, bedankte sich beim Doktor und ging. Er blickte in Gedanken hinab auf das Kind, das er gewesen war, das Kind war erschrocken, das Kind hatte Angst. Er nicht.

Er war jetzt im Widerstand. Solange er nicht umfiel. La Loi, la Liberté!

Langsam ging er in Richtung Zentrum, er hatte Zeit, die er überbrücken musste, er war erst in einer Stunde mit seinem Freund Philippe Gaultier verabredet, im Restaurant l'Ogenblik in den Galerien bei der Grand Place.

Er kaufte bei Neuhaus an der Grand Place Pralinen –

Von diesen hier, bitte, in so einer kleinen Schachtel für neun Stück!

Neunmal »Le désir«! D'accord. Soll ich sie als Geschenk verpacken?

Ja bitte.

Die Dame wird eine Freude haben. Ich finde, »Le désir« ist unsere beste Praline!

Welche Dame? Das schenke ich mir selbst.

Oh.

Brunfaut sah die Verkäuferin an und hatte plötzlich Mitleid. Und Selbstmitleid. Er hatte eine Idylle zerstört, auch wenn sie nur die Fiktion einer Verkaufssituation war. Warum war er so achtlos? Er konnte sich das doch nicht mehr erlauben: Achtlosigkeit. Er zahlte, nahm die kunstvoll verpackte kleine Schachtel in Empfang und sagte: Ich habe es mir anders überlegt. Ich will diese Pralinen doch einer Dame schenken – einer Dame, deren Lächeln mich heute verzaubert hat.

Und er überreichte der Verkäuferin das Päckchen.

Er lief hinaus.

Es ist alles in Ordnung, dachte er, mit Ausrufezeichen und mit Fragezeichen, solange die Scham stärker brennt als die Todesangst.

Er war dann nur eine Viertelstunde zu früh im l'Ogenblik. Er trank ein Glas Champagner, während er auf Philippe wartete.

Philippe war Leiter des EDV-Zentrums der Brüsseler Polizei, fünfzehn Jahre jünger als Brunfaut und trotz dieses Altersunterschieds sein bester Freund. Nicht zuletzt verband sie, dass sie beide »Träger des nassen Schals« waren, so nannten sie sich als Anhänger des Fußballclubs RSC Anderlecht, die kaum ein Heimspiel versäumten – sie hatten so viele Tränen in ihren Fan-Schal geweint, dass er nie wieder trocken werden konnte. Sie waren, wie sie bei einem Bier nach der Arbeit einmal feststellten, beide der Meinung, dass nach dem unfassbaren Bestechungsskandal, damals, als bekannt wurde, dass der Club vor dem Halbfinalrückspiel im UEFA-Cup gegen Nottingham Forest den Schiedsrichter mit 27 000 britischen Pfund bestochen hatte, ein Zeichen hätte gesetzt werden müssen, ein Zeichen für einen Neubeginn. Und wenn es auch nur ein ganz simpel symbolisches gewesen wäre, eine kleine Änderung im Vereinsnamen, um klarzumachen, dass ab jetzt dieser Verein neu startete und nichts mehr mit Korruption und Bestechungen zu tun hatte. RSC Anderlecht – wie hätte die Änderung aussehen können? Das R streichen, hatte Émile Brunfaut gesagt, nur um ein Zeichen zu setzen.

Aber warum das R.?

Le Roi, la Loi, la Liberté! Worauf können wir verzichten? Le Roi!

Sie lachten. So fanden sie sich auch schnell politisch in Übereinstimmung, in Hinblick auf das belgische System, auf diesen zerrissenen Staat, der nicht hilflos durch einen König zusammengehalten werden sollte, sondern durch den gemeinsamen Rechtszustand einer Republik. Obwohl: Die Entscheidung des Königs, in der Zeit, in der Belgien den EU-Ratsvorsitz innehatte, keine Regierung zu ernennen, um die notwendigen europapolitischen Entscheidungen nicht durch innenpolitische Koalitionsstreitereien zu blockieren, fanden sie beide gut. Nie, sagte Philippe, hatte Belgien besser funktioniert als in dieser Zeit ohne Regierung.

Sie pilgerten ins Constant-Vanden-Stock-Stadion in Anderlecht, weinten in ihre Schals und neckten einander. Philippe schwärmte davon, dass er noch Franky Vercauteren hatte spielen sehen, so einen bräuchten sie heute wieder, einen genialen Torjäger. Ach, du hast ja keine Ahnung, hatte Émile gesagt, er, der Ältere, hatte noch Paul van Himst gesehen, gegen den war Vercauteren schon eine lahme Ente.

War früher alles besser? Nichts war besser, es war einfach alles ganz anders.

Ja, sicher! Anders! Aber war es nicht doch besser? Früher war Anderlecht ein jüdischer Bezirk von Brüssel. Es war das geheime Zentrum von Brüssel, wegen des Clubs und wegen der Cafés und Läden. Jetzt ist es ein muslimischer Bezirk, die Juden sind fort, und keiner, den ich kenne, käme auf die Idee, hierherzukommen und in ein Café zu gehen, schon gar nicht mit einer Frau, die dürfte ein Café bei den Moslems gar nicht erst betreten.

Du kennst doch Gerrit Beers, von der Spurensicherung? Er ist jetzt nach Anderlecht gezogen, er sagt, die Wohnungen sind dort billiger, es ist alles viel mehr easy-going, und er ist Raucher. Hier schert sich keiner um das Rauchverbot. Er bekommt einen erstklassigen Kaffee, und die Männer mit ihren Wasserpfeifen kümmern sich nicht darum, wenn er sich dazu eine Zigarette anzündet.

Wie in Molenbeek.

Ja. Die Zeiten ändern sich. Bald gibt der Club das Stadion hier auf und zieht in das neue König-Baudouin-Stadion. Dann wird der Club noch Anderlecht heißen, aber nicht mehr in Anderlecht spielen. Und du wirst sagen, früher war alles besser. Und heute beschwerst du dich, weil Anderlecht nicht mehr so ist wie vor zwanzig Jahren.

Ja, so schlecht waren sie heute nicht. 2:1 gegen Leuven, das war schon okay.

Vor drei Jahren hatte Philippe Émile gebeten, sein Trauzeuge zu sein. Ein Jahr später wurde Philippe Vater, und Émile wurde Pate der kleinen Joëlle. Er war nun mehr als ein Freund, er war Familie.

Émile Brunfaut trank sein Glas Champagner aus und bestellte noch eines. Philippe war genau der Mensch, den er jetzt brauchte: ein genialer Informatiker, zugleich völlig vertrauenswürdig und solidarisch. Hoffte er. Nein, er war sich dessen sicher.

Er bekam sein zweites Glas, nippte daran, da stand Philippe vor ihm: Der Rest des Lebens beginnt mit Champagner und endet mit Kräutertee! Und? Wie war es beim Arzt?

Sie umarmten sich, Philippe nahm Platz, sagte: Und was ich auch wissen möchte: Hast du es schon überführt und verhaftet?

Es? Was? Wen?

Na, das Schwein. Hast du heute keine Zeitung gelesen?

Ach so, das Schwein. Ich habe eine Spur. Wir haben Gen-Material sichergestellt. Du musst morgen die DNA abgleichen mit der von allen Schweinen, die in der Europol-Datenbank registriert sind.

Philippe lachte. Du weißt, ich stehe dir immer zur Verfügung.

Genau darüber wollte ich mit dir reden.

Sie redeten und aßen und tranken. Früher war das Essen besser. Findest du? Ja. Aber hier hat sich doch überhaupt nichts geändert. Ja, außer das Essen. Wieso? Den Lammbraten haben wir hier schon vor zehn Jahren gegessen. Ja, schon, aber er war früher besser. Na ja, vielleicht, aber sonst – immerhin hat sich hier sonst nichts geändert. Vielleicht hätte ich besser den gegrillten Wolfsbarsch genommen, mit dem Spargelrisotto. Spargel, jetzt im Winter? Der kommt aus Thailand, stand auf der Karte. Spargel aus Thailand, komm, hör auf! Wir haben doch hier immer das Lamm gegessen, es ist doch okay. Ich weiß nicht, es schmeckt nach Leiche, ich habe doch früher nie den Gedanken gehabt, dass ein Lammbraten eine Leiche ist. Ach, hör auf, was ist denn los mit dir? Es ist okay. Ja, es ist okay.

Brunfaut erzählte, dass der Arzt ihn ins Europa-Hospital überwiesen habe, dort werde er morgen durchgecheckt.

Hat er irgendeinen Verdacht geäußert?

Nein. Er hat nur gesagt, das gehöre genauer untersucht.

Er geht auf Nummer sicher. Ist doch gut. Und dann hast du Klarheit. Also ich würde mir da jetzt keine Sorgen machen.

Ja, vielleicht. Vielleicht hast du recht. Auf jeden Fall: Ich bin nicht außer Gefecht.

Das heißt?

Du weißt, dass mir der Atlas-Fall entzogen und ich beurlaubt wurde?

Ja.

Weißt du, warum?

Ich dachte, du würdest es mir erzählen.

Ich weiß es aber nicht.

Du weißt es nicht? Sie haben es nicht begründet?

Nein.

Ich brauche noch ein Glas Wein.

Hör zu, Philippe, alle Daten, die den Fall Atlas betreffen, sind gelöscht worden. Ich war am Tatort, die Spurensicherung war am Tatort, ich habe erste Vernehmungen durchgeführt – das alles existiert nicht mehr. Alle Akten, Protokolle und Dokumente sind spurlos verschwunden, der Mord ist verschwunden, als hätte es die Leiche, die ich gesehen habe, nicht gegeben. Als ich zu meinem Computer zurückkam, war alles weg, wie abgesaugt. Da hat jemand gehackt. Wahrscheinlich nicht nur in meinen Computer, sondern ins ganze System. Und der Staatsanwalt spielt mit. Ich möchte wissen, warum?

Das verstehe ich.

Du musst mir helfen.

Der Kellner servierte ab, und Philippe schnippte mit den Fingern, deutete dorthin, wo eben noch Émiles Teller gewesen war, und sagte: Die Leiche ist verschwunden!

Mach keine Witze! Es tut mir leid, was ich vorhin gesagt habe. Ganz im Ernst: Der Fall ist verschwunden, und wenn es jemanden gibt, der vielleicht zurückverfolgen kann, wie das geschehen ist und wer das gemacht hat, dann bist das du. Du bist der Chef-Informatiker, du kontrollierst das ganze EDV-System der Brüsseler Polizei. Du musst die Lücke finden.

Wie soll ich das begründen? Ich kann in der Abteilung eine solche Recherche nicht beginnen, ohne einen Grund dafür anzugeben. Noch dazu gegen eine Weisung des Staatsanwalts.

Weißt du von der Weisung des Staatsanwalts? Nein. Na eben. Du musst das nicht begründen. Du musst es einfach tun.

Es ist zu kompliziert, dir jetzt zu erklären, wie das mit dem Zugang zum Zentralspeicher funktioniert, wie viele Sicherungen da eingebaut sind und wie viel Bürokratie notwendig ist, um nur zwei von vielleicht zwanzig Schritten weiterzukommen.

Du musst es ja nicht offiziell machen, meine Frage ist ja nicht, ob du glaubst, dass du eine Bewilligung bekommst, sondern ob du das kannst.

Es wäre gegen das Gesetz.

Hör zu, Philippe, ein Mord ist ein Offizialdelikt, eine Straftat, die die Staatsanwaltschaft von Amts wegen verfolgen muss. Wenn aber die Staatsanwaltschaft dies nicht tut, sondern im Gegenteil den Mord vertuscht, dann ist das Gesetz durch den Staat selbst gebrochen worden, und diejenigen, die dann illegale Mittel einsetzen, um das aufzuklären, sind die Verteidiger des Gesetzes. Wenn du mir hilfst und wir Erfolg haben, dann werden es wir sein, die dem Gesetz entsprochen haben.

Also gut. Ich versuche das zunächst einmal von deinem Zugang aus. Gib mir dein Passwort. Wenn da gleich etwas auffliegt, dann hast du im Urlaub mit deinem Computer gespielt, okay?

Okay.

Eine Mousse au Chocolat?

Sicher. Warum sollten wir ausgerechnet heute unsere Gewohnheiten ändern? Wie geht es Joëlle?

Matek wusste, dass er keine Chance hatte, spurlos unterzutauchen. Sie wussten mittlerweile, dass er nicht in die Maschine nach Istanbul eingestiegen war. Sie würden sicherlich auch in Betracht ziehen, dass er doch nach Polen geflogen ist, obwohl sie sein Ticket nach Warschau storniert hatten. Es war für sie keine Schwierigkeit, in kürzester Zeit herauszufinden, dass er auf der Passagierliste eines Flugs nach Krakau stand. Als er in Krakau ankam, konnte er also davon ausgehen, dass sie nur einen Schritt hinter ihm zurück waren.

Das hatte er als Żołnierz Chrystusa schon in der Grundausbildung gelernt: Versuche erst gar nicht, keine Spuren zu hinterlassen – es ist unmöglich. Versuche nicht, deine Spuren zu verwischen – nichts macht Verfolger so sicher, auf der richtigen Fährte zu sein, als wenn sie auf Spuren stoßen, die du zu verwischen versucht hast. Wenn du also schon nicht vermeiden kannst, Spuren zu hinterlassen, dann produziere noch mehr Spuren! Viele Spuren, widersprüchliche Spuren! Während sie sie auswerten, gewinnst du einen Vorsprung. Wenn sie zurückkommen vom Verfolgen falscher Spuren, hast du deinen Vorsprung vergrößert.

Natürlich wusste er, dass sie wussten, dass er das wusste – aber das änderte nichts daran, dass sie den Spuren nachgehen mussten, die er produzierte, und ob sie das misstrauisch oder naiv taten, war egal.

Er kalkulierte, dass er drei Tage brauchen würde, um herauszufinden, was in Brüssel schiefgelaufen war und warum sie ihn dann, gegen den ursprünglichen Plan, nach Istanbul schicken wollten. Drei Tage Vorsprung, das war machbar, das war Routine, und dann würde er weitersehen.

Nach seiner Ankunft am Flughafen Krakau ging er zum Info-Desk und ließ sich selbst ausrufen: Herr Mateusz Oswiecki möge sich bitte zum Schalter der Firma Krakow Express Shuttle Pastuszak begeben. Herr Oswiecki bitte! Ihr Fahrer wartet auf Sie beim Schalter Express Shuttle Pastuszak!

Er wusste, dass die Personen, die ausgerufen wurden, achtundvierzig Stunden gespeichert blieben. Dann ging er zum Schalter des Shuttle-Service. Er hatte den Transfer in die Stadt noch am Flughafen Brüssel per Mail gebucht. Wenn sie seine Mailbox hackten, hatten sie nun zwei Hinweise. Er zahlte mit Kreditkarte. Dritter Hinweis. Er ließ sich zum Hotel Europejski, ulica Lubicz, bringen.

Morgen Mittag würden sie wissen, was er ohnehin nicht hätte verheimlichen können: dass er in Krakau angekommen war. Einen Tag später würden sie wissen, wo er abgestiegen ist. Indem er ihnen die Adresse selbst auf dem Silbertablett servierte, konnte er sie auf eine falsche Fährte setzen und sie die drei Tage, die er brauchte, ins Leere laufen lassen: Er checkte im Hotel ein und bat die Rezeptionistin, nachzuschauen, wann am nächsten Tag der erste Zug nach Warschau ging. Sie tipp-

te in den Computer, schaute, schüttelte den Kopf und sag-
te: Sie wollen wirklich den ersten Zug? Der geht um 4.52
und –
Das ist zu früh!
Der nächste geht um 5.41, kommt an um –
Der nächste bitte!
Dann gibt es Züge um 6.31, dann 7.47 und –
Der um 6.31! Wann kommt er an?
Um 8.54, und der Zug um 7.47 kommt um 10.00 an.
Das ist zu spät. 8.54 Ankunft ist perfekt. Sagen Sie nochmal,
sechs Uhr …?
Sechs Uhr einunddreißig. Von Krakow Główny.
Sehr gut. Können Sie bitte das Bahnticket gleich hier online
für mich kaufen und ausdrucken? Hier ist meine Kreditkar-
te. Und ich zahle auch das Zimmer gleich. Dann spare ich
morgen früh Zeit.
Bardzo zadowolony, panie Oswiecki.

Matek brachte seinen Rucksack aufs Zimmer, schrieb auf
dem Briefpapier des Hotels einen Brief, den er zusammen
mit einer seiner Kreditkarten in ein Kuvert steckte, das er ad-
ressierte und zuklebte. Dann verließ er das Hotel. Morgen
Nachmittag hatten sie sechs logisch zusammenpassende Spuren, dass er in Krakau angekommen und gleich am nächsten
Morgen nach Warschau weitergereist war. Aber er würde in
Krakau bleiben. Bis sie das begriffen, hatte er Zeit.
Er spazierte zur Starowiślna, dort kannte er einen dieser du-
biosen Läden mit gebrauchten Handys. Tatsächlich, den Laden gab es noch. Er kaufte ein altes, primitives Nokia und
eine 100-Zloty Prepaid Card. Matek sah den Jungen an, der
das Telefon mit einer aufgebogenen Heftklammer aufbrach
und die Karte einlegte, er betrachtete ihn wie ein abstoßen-
des und zugleich auch Mitleid erregendes Tier in einem Ter-

rarium. Alles an diesem Jungen war Hilferuf oder Schrei nach Aufmerksamkeit und zugleich Demonstration von Trotz und Verachtung. Seine groteske Frisur, seitlich ausrasiert, das Deckhaar lang und kunstvoll verstrubbelt, die dicken blauschwarzen Strähnen mit Gel fixiert. Er trug ein rotes T-Shirt mit einem großen Stinkefinger auf der Brust. Auf seinem rechten Oberarm war eine Wolfsangel tätowiert, darunter eine kniende nackte Frau, umrankt von Ketten. Interessanter als diese kindische Kraftmeierei aber war der linke Unterarm: Kein Zweifel, der Junge fügte sich regelmäßig Selbstverletzungen zu. Eine ganze Reihe roter Linien, mehr oder weniger frisch verkrustete Ritzungen, wahrscheinlich durch eine Rasierklinge. Matek kannte das aus dem Priesterseminar. Er kannte das Gefühl, wenn die Glückshormone ausgeschüttet werden, die den Schmerz lindern, die man aber so explosiv nur bekommt, wenn man sich Schmerz zufügt, wenn man den Schmerz von der Seele mit einer Rasierklinge auf die Außenhaut umleitet. Endorphine und Adrenalin, darum ging es. Er hatte gehört, dass Frauen diese Sensation im Stress und Schmerz einer Geburt erleben. Das hat Gott so eingerichtet. Ritzungen und Schnitte auf Armen und Bauch, das ist im Seminar verbreitet gewesen, gelegentlich auch, wechselseitig zugefügt, am Rücken, selten an den Genitalien.

Der Junge presste die Teile des Handys zusammen, bis sie mit einem lauten Klack einrasteten, drückte einige Tasten, schaute auf das Display und sagte: Dopasować!

Dziękuję, sagte Matek, zahlte die achtzig Zloty für das Handy und hundert Zloty für die Karte, dann zögerte er, tat so, als fiele ihm plötzlich noch etwas ein, blickte nachdenklich in seine Geldbörse, sagte: Ich habe noch eine Frage, vielleicht kannst du mir helfen! Er nahm einen Hundert-Euro-Schein heraus, legte ihn auf den Tresen, die Hand darauf.

Kennst du zufällig jemanden, der nach Warschau fährt?

Der Junge schaute auf Mateks Hand, die auf dem Geldschein lag.

Müsste mich umhören. Worum geht es? Mitfahrgelegenheit?

Nein. Ein Brief. Den könnte er mitnehmen.

Matek legte noch einen Hundert-Euro-Schein auf den Tresen.

Warum gehen Sie nicht zur Post?

Die Postämter sind seit einer halben Stunde geschlossen. Und der Brief ist eilig.

Ich glaube, mein Bruder hatte vor, morgen nach Warschau zu fahren. Hat ein Mädchen dort. Müsste ihn fragen.

Matek legte noch einen Fünfziger hin.

Der Brief müsste um spätestens zehn Uhr dort sein.

Es wird ihm egal sein, wenn er etwas früher als geplant fährt.

Er wird sehr früh losfahren müssen. Spätestens um halb sieben.

Er wird noch Geld fürs Benzin haben wollen.

Wollte er nicht ohnehin fahren, zu seinem Mädchen?

Matek zog die Hand von den Geldscheinen zurück, holte den Brief aus der Brusttasche seiner Jacke, legte ihn auf die Banknoten.

Ich bin morgen um zehn Uhr wieder hier. Wenn ich bis dahin per SMS eine Bestätigung bekommen habe – er hielt das Nokia in die Höhe –, dass der Brief angekommen ist, gibt es diese Summe noch einmal. Da hat er genug Benzingeld, da kann er sein Mädchen noch zwanzig Mal besuchen und ausführen. Wenn die Liebe so lange hält.

Sie ist treu.

Das ist gut. Treu sein ist immer gut. Die Adresse steht hier auf dem Umschlag.

Matek ging.

Er schlenderte die Starowiślna hinunter in Richtung Zentrum, zum Rynek Główny, dem Hauptmarkt. Die Schönheit und Erhabenheit dieses weitläufigen mittelalterlichen Platzes berührte ihn jedes Mal aufs Neue, wenn er in diese Stadt kam. Der riesige quadratische Platz war mit Palästen umrahmt, nur die Marienkirche brach die strenge Symmetrie. Sie trat mit ihren beiden Türmen aus der Fassadenfront dieser Platzseite gleichsam einen Schritt hervor, stellte sich quer, frech, stolz, alles überragend, die beiden Türme verschieden hoch, der Grund dafür wurde in alten Legenden erzählt, Matek kannte sie natürlich, aber er hielt diese Legenden für eine geradezu heidnische Anmaßung. Für ihn war völlig klar, dass es nur einen Grund für diesen Bruch von Symmetrie und Harmonie geben konnte: Nicht einmal beim Bau eines Gotteshauses darf es den Menschen gegeben sein, etwas Vollkommenes zu erschaffen, denn vollkommen ist nur Gott und sein Schöpfungsplan selbst. Aus Menschenhand kann es keine Vollkommenheit geben, die sich mit Gottes Vollkommenheit messen kann, auch nicht in dem Glauben, ihm durch diesen Anspruch die höchste Ehre zu erweisen. Die Marienkirche, die sich zum Markt quer stellte, dadurch den Menschen, die da ihren Geschäften nachgehen, symbolisch auf die Zehen stieg, sich dabei hoch aufrichtete, um nach den Sternen zu greifen, mit dem einen Turm zu kurz, mit dem anderen doch schon näher am Himmel, Ausdruck des menschlichen Strebens, das wächst, an der Vollendung aber scheitert – diese Kirche war für Matek der sinnigste Ausdruck des Verhältnisses der Menschen zu Gott. Ganz anders als Notre-Dame – ein Jahr zuvor hatte Matek einen Auftrag in Paris gehabt. Natürlich hatte er die Kathedrale von Notre-Dame sehen wollen, und natürlich war er zunächst beeindruckt, als er vor ihr stand. Aber – was? Da hatte er es begriffen. Dieser selbstherrliche, im Grunde aufgeblähte Kleingeist, mit dem darauf vertraut wurde, dass geometrische Regeln, umgelegt auf bombastische Größe, die göttliche Harmonie des Universums widerspiegeln können, hatte ihn irritiert, er hatte es als Lästerung empfunden. Und das war wohl der Grund, warum Gott mit kalter Indifferenz zugeschaut hatte, als der häretische Philosoph Abélard mit der Mesner-Tochter Héloïse auf dem Altar dieser Kathedrale Unzucht beging. Matek hatte zugehört, als eine Reiseführerin in der Kirche, vor dem Altar, einer Gruppe haltlos kichernder englischer Touristen diese Geschichte erzählte: Und hier, auf diesem Altar, Ladies and Gentlemen, ist es passiert, hier hat der junge Doktorand der Philosophie Pierre Abélard seine große Liebe Héloïse, die Tochter des Mesners dieser Kathedrale, entjungfert. Immer wieder erzählt, immer wieder besungen, Abélard und Héloïse, dies hier war der Altar ihrer Liebe! Matek fand die Entscheidung des Papstes, diesen Abélard kastrieren zu lassen, völlig richtig und gerecht, ja geradezu milde, aber selbst diese Strafe, die tatsächlich vollzogen wurde, wie die Führerin erzählte, konnte, so dachte Matek, nicht rückgängig machen, dass dieses eitle Gotteshaus entweiht war und es auch blieb. Das hatte er gespürt. Wie anders die Marienkirche hier in Krakau. Er blickte an ihr hinauf, jetzt war es 19 Uhr, und wie zu jeder vollen Stunde begann der Krakauer Turmbläser das Przerwany Hejnał zu spielen: ein Trompetensignal zur Warnung vor heranrückenden Feinden, das plötzlich abbricht. Zur Erinnerung an jenen Trompeter, der beim Tatarenangriff 1241 von einem Pfeil in die Kehle getroffen wurde, spielte man es nur bis zu jenem Ton, den er als letzten noch hatte blasen können, bevor er fiel.

Matek schaute suchend den Ostturm hinauf, wo an einem Fenster der Trompeter stehen musste, konnte ihn aber nicht sehen, da brach das Hejnał schon ab.

Er ging nicht hinein in die Kirche. Er konnte nicht beten im

Gewitter zahlloser fotografierender Touristen. Er wandte sich um, überquerte den Platz, vorbei an den Tuchhallen, er konnte sich nicht sattsehen, aber er wusste auch, er durfte nicht zu genau schauen. Die Läden mit den schönen alten Portalen verkauften Ansichtskarten, die die schönen alten Läden zeigten, als sie noch nicht Ansichtskarten und billige Souvenirs verkauft hatten. Die Gasthäuser warben mit Tafeln, die »Traditionelle polnische Küche« versprachen, und pflegten keine andere Tradition als die der raschen Abfertigung von Touristen. Neben der Kirche, wo früher die große, staatliche Buchhandlung gewesen war, befand sich jetzt der Flagshipstore der Modekette Zara. In den ehemaligen Tuchläden konnten Touristen Andenken an das alte jüdische Krakau kaufen, Postkarten mit alten Fotografien und CDs mit Klezmer-Musik, aber auch geschmacklose Karikaturen von Juden im Stürmer-Stil, zum Beispiel holzgeschnitzte Figuren des gierigen Juden mit Geldbeutel oder Goldmünze in der Hand.

Er verließ den Platz und bog in die Grodzka ein, da am Eck hatte er früher so gerne das süße polnische Reisbrot gekauft, jetzt hieß der Laden »Quality Burger«. Er ging die Grodzka weiter bis zum Ende, immer weiter, er ging und ging, die Stradomska entlang, immer weiter, die rhythmischen Schritte und das gleichmäßige Atmen waren jetzt sein Gebet, immer weiter, bis er zur Paulińska kam, da kannte er ein kleines Gasthaus, die Kuchnia Adama, wo er etwas essen wollte. Hier gab es den besten Bigos der Stadt, und auch wenn es für diesen Eintopf hundert verschiedene, mehr oder weniger offizielle Rezepte gab, für Matek war er nur hier, nur zwei Mal ums Eck von den Touristentrampelpfaden entfernt, authentisch. Auf keinen Fall durfte er frisch gekocht serviert werden, er war erst so richtig gut, wenn er über Tage hindurch immer wieder aufgewärmt wurde. Bei Adam stand der Bigos-Kessel zumindest eine Woche lang auf dem Herd. So konnte der

Bauchspeck sein Fett ganz an das Kraut abgeben, der scharfe rote Paprika sein Aroma voll entfalten, die Fleischwürfel wurden wunderbar mürbe, dennoch: Diese Worte sind nur ein Summen und die Reime der Lieder, die auf den Bigos Adama gesungen wurden, sind Zufall, nur der Magen wird den Bigos verstehen.

Matek aß schweigend, natürlich, er war ja alleine, aber er aß, auch wenn er alleine war, immer so, als müsste er das Sprechverbot während der Mahlzeiten einhalten. Ein kurzes, fast lautlos gemurmeltes Tischgebet, mit gesenktem Kopf, dann schweigend essen. Doch an diesem Abend hatte er so viele Gedanken, wie ein Stimmengewirr, im Kopf. Er hörte seine Mutter, die sein Vertrauen, behütet und beschützt zu sein, eben dadurch zerstörte, dass sie ihn, um ihn zu schützen, weggegeben hatte, in die Verliese eines Untergrunds, wo es das alles nicht mehr gab, diesen glückseligen Dampf der Küche einer liebenden und lächelnden Mutter. Vor ihm dampfte der Bigos, und er konnte sich selbst hören, wie es aus ihm herausgesprudelt war, wenn er mit seiner Mutter beim Essen saß, beim Bigos oder den Gołąbki, Heldenphantasien, wo hatte er sie aufgeschnappt, diese Legenden, die er aufgeregt erzählte, während sie ihm lächelnd zuhörte und sagte: Vergiss nicht zu essen! Und er hatte damals noch gar nicht gewusst, dass sie eine Waffe unter dem Rock trug, die Pistole des toten Vaters. Wo war Vater? Das war noch gar nicht begriffen, solange sie ihn in die Arme nahm, und dann hatten sich ihre Arme geöffnet und sie hat ihn abgeliefert, in die Hände heiliger Männer, die Vater genannt wurden, und er hatte plötzlich Brüder, in einem Verlies, aus dem er nach Jahren der Askese herausstieg als Żołnierz Chrystusa, um eine Heimat zu verteidigen, in der er nie gewesen ist. Wer ist jemals dort gewesen? Der Großvater nicht, der Vater nicht – und er selbst ist vertrieben worden, gerade als er in sie eintreten wollte, durch einen Hintereingang, durch die Tür, die seine Mutter plötzlich zugeworfen hatte. Und er hörte die Stimme des Pater Prior, der ihm verständnisvoll und mit einem Lächeln, das triefte vor Fett wie dieser Bigos, erklärte, dass er, Mateusz, der liebe Matek, nicht berufen sei zum Priesteramt, sondern zum Soldaten Christi. Er war gehorsam, er ist immer gehorsam gewesen, zuerst weil er Weltvertrauen gehabt hatte und dann weil er in Sinn und Vernunft des Gehorsams eingeschult wurde, und jetzt saß er vor einer Falle, und er wusste nicht, warum, aber er zweifelte nicht daran: Sie hatten ihm eine Falle gestellt. Er hörte seine Mutter, er hörte den Pater Prior, er hörte Stimmen, unklar, unverständlich, von Menschen, die er nicht kannte, die aber über ihn sprachen wie über eine Figur auf einem Schachbrett. Silentium!, rief er und noch einmal: Silentium! Er rief es lautlos, nur in seinem Kopf. Er wollte schweigend essen. Er atmete seufzend tief ein, den Oberkörper aufrichtend, und blickte hinüber zur Kellnerin, die neben dem Schild »Rauchen verboten« stand und rauchte.

Er ging zu Fuß zurück zum Hotel, machte im Zimmer seine Kraftübungen, dann legte er sich schlafen.

Als er um sechs Uhr morgens das Hotel verließ, standen vor dem Hotel bereits die Sightseeing-Busse, »Auschwitz. Best price!«

Er ging zum Kazimierz-Viertel, nahm im Rubinstein ein ausgiebiges Frühstück zu sich, dann rief er Wojciech an, seinen alten Freund aus Seminar-Tagen, der damals bei den Schulbrüdern in Poznań den apostolischen Schutznamen Szymon, der Maurer, erhalten hatte. Er war nun Pater des Augustinerklosters, das zur Kirche St. Katharina in Krakau gehörte. Matek kannte seinen Tagesablauf, die Konventmesse musste vorüber sein, jetzt war er bis zur Terz erreichbar.

Mateusz, mein Bruder! Bist du in Krakau? Wie geht es dir?

Ja, ich bin in Krakau. Es geht mir gut. Ich erinnere mich so gerne zurück, wie wir durch die Klostergärten gingen und redeten. Wir müssen reden.

Ach, die Gärten. Wir haben sie verpachtet, als Parkplätze. Traurig, aber ein gutes Geschäft. Die Renovierung der Kirche verschlingt Unsummen. Ja, lass uns reden, nach der Non?

Ich habe einen Rucksack mit.

Du bist willkommen.

Matek sah sich um. Niemand schaute her. Er schob den Hemdärmel ein wenig zurück, wischte das Messer mit der Serviette ab und ritzte mit sanftem Druck seinen linken Unterarm. Das verdammte Messer war stumpf, ein typisches Gastronomie-Messer, er kippte es leicht und zog die Klinge über die Haut und nochmals mit stärkerem Druck, da endlich öffnete sich die Haut einen kleinen Spalt und Blut quoll hervor, er schloss die Augen und legte das Messer weg.

Um halb zehn kam die SMS: »Werde deine Grüße gerne ausrichten!«

Bruder Tomasz in Warschau hatte also den Brief erhalten. Tomasz wird mittagessen gehen und mit Mateks Kreditkarte bezahlen. Dann wird er in die Potockich gehen, zu dem großen Taschen- und Koffergeschäft, mit der Kreditkarte einen Koffer kaufen und später am Bahnhof mit der Kreditkarte ein Zugticket nach Budapest lösen. Das werden sie herausfinden. Tomasz wird dann die Kreditkarte zerschneiden und wegwerfen. Matek schätzte, dass er 72 Stunden Vorsprung hatte, bis sie die Spuren überprüft hatten.

Er ging zur Toilette, ließ kaltes Wasser über seinen Unterarm laufen, sehr lange, bis er das Gefühl hatte, dass der Arm taub war, dann ging er. Er ging zu dem Handy-Laden in der Starowiślna, der Junge trug dasselbe T-Shirt wie am Vortag, Matek legte das Geld auf den Tresen.

Es war ein für diese Jahreszeit ungewöhnlich warmer und sonniger Tag.

Er schlenderte durch die Stadt, die ulica Józefa hinunter, auf der Reisegruppen hinter hochgehaltenen Täfelchen oder Wimpeln hergingen, in der ulica Bożego Ciała bog er links ab, da war die Kirche Corpus Christi, die erste katholische Kirche nach dem Judenviertel, er trat ein, hier war offenbar gerade die Morgenmesse zu Ende gegangen, die Menschen erhoben sich aus den Bänken, strebten zum Ausgang, Matek stand da wie ein Fels in der Brandung, rechts und links von ihm strömten die Menschen vorbei und hinaus, bis er sich umdrehte und mit ihnen die Kirche verließ, als wäre er Teil einer Gruppe, zurück zur Józefa, ein Haustor stand offen und gab den Blick frei in einen schönen versteckten Innenhof, hinter einem baufälligen Durchgang voller Müllsäcke, ein Tourist stand dort und fotografierte mit seinem Smartphone, Rufe einer Fremdenführerin: »This way, please!«, eine Frau sagte »… would be a perfect hideaway!«, ein Mann lachte, »You cannot escape«, die Gruppe bewegte sich weiter zur St.-Katharina-Kirche, Gärten hinter Gittertoren, Parkplätze in den Gärten, ein junger Mann begann zu laufen, lief auf eine Frau zu, sie umarmten sich, schlenderten Hand in Hand weiter, an der blinden, schweigenden Fassade des Klosters entlang, vorbei am Platz mit dem Millennium-Altar, der aus einer Gruppe von sieben großen Bronzefiguren bestand, überlebensgroße Heilige, Kirchenmänner, eine deutsche Frau stand davor und sagte: »Da, schau einmal, dieser da, das ist doch wohl der polnische Papst!«, ein Mann sagte: »Ja, das ist Wojtyla!«, ein anderer: »Nein, da steht Św. Stanisław (1030-1079)«. Priester liefen vorbei, bogen ab in die Augustiánska, dann kamen zwei Frauen mit schweren Taschen, als würden sie den Priestern nachlaufen, schon waren sie um die Ecke verschwunden, die Reisegruppe war inzwischen weitergezogen, und die Millenniumsstatuen blickten mit toten Augen auf einen leeren Platz.

Die Union drohte zu zerbrechen. Sie befand sich in der größten Krise seit ihrer Gründung. Florian Susman hatte sich seit vielen Jahren aus tiefer Überzeugung für dieses Projekt engagiert, und er war selbstverständlich auch bereit gewesen, Verantwortung zu übernehmen. Man mault nicht, man übernimmt Verantwortung – das war schon das Credo seines Vaters gewesen. Wer einen Betrieb aufbaut, geht Risiken ein. Wie kann man sie verantwortungsbewusst einschätzen und kalkulieren? Florian konnte sich gut an die Zeit erinnern, als seine Eltern nach dem Abendessen noch lange am Tisch saßen und mit ernsten Gesichtern die Chancen und Gefahren abwogen, die eine kreditfinanzierte Investition in eine konzessionierte betriebliche Schlachtanlage mit sich brachte. Die Schulden könnten ihr Untergang sein, aber die Feigheit vor diesem Schritt konnte erst recht den Untergang des Hofs bedeuten. Es gab eine riskante Chance, aber es gab nicht die Chance, »auf Nummer sicher zu gehen«. Die Eltern saßen da und rechneten, sie formulierten Einwände und hatten gleich auch Argumente, um die Einwände zu zerstreuen, sie warfen Bedenken auf die eine Waagschale, Hoffnungen auf die andere, nein, Bedenken gegenüber den Bedenken. Florian hatte zugehört, es war seltsam, dass die Eltern ihn nicht ins Bett geschickt hatten, vielleicht ist der Vater der Meinung gewesen, dass der Thronfolger das ruhig alles hören sollte, während Martin, der Jüngere, auf dem Sofa lag und las, bis er einschlief und schließlich von der Mutter ins Bett getragen – nein, so zärtlich ist es nicht gewesen –, ins Bett gestoßen wurde.

»Götter, Gräber und Gelehrte«. Florian war erstaunt, ja gerührt, dass ihm jetzt sogar der Titel des Buchs einfiel, das sein Bruder damals immer wieder gelesen hatte, während er, Florian, nur dasaß und zuhörte, wie die Eltern darüber redeten, was sie verantworten konnten und mussten. Damals. An langen Abenden.

Florian fuhr langsam. Er hatte Zeit. Er musste erst am Abend in Budapest sein, es war früher Nachmittag, und er befand sich bereits zwanzig Kilometer vor Nickelsdorf, der österreichisch-ungarischen Grenze. Er fuhr wie in Trance, mit Tempomat, leiser Musik aus dem Autoradio, Regionalprogramm, volkstümliche Schlager, die immer wieder von Werbung unterbrochen wurden: »Ich möchte so gern ein Trüffelschwein sein«, quäkte eine Stimme, worauf eine sonore Stimme antwortete: »Aber geh, Schweinderl, meinst net, dass unsere Kartofferl viel besser schmecken? Ja, schon, Bauer, grunz. Bist halt mein Kartoffelschweinderl. Bin ich dann auch was Besonderes? Ja, natürlich.«
Da schaltete Florian das Radio ab.

In jener Zeit, als der Vater, der kleine Schweinebauer, den kaum rentablen Hof zum Schweinemast- und Schlachtbetrieb ausbaute, hatte er auch beschlossen, sich in Interessenvertretungen zu engagieren. Bald schon übernahm er Ämter in Fachverbänden und im österreichischen Bauernbund. Man darf nicht abwarten, was die für uns machen, man muss selbst etwas tun, hatte er gesagt. Er konnte mitreden, aber er konnte die Bedingungen der Branche nicht verbessern, schon gar nicht konnte er den Preisverfall aufhalten. So setzte er auf Masse, um bei der immer kleineren Gewinnspanne auf seine Rechnung zu kommen. Die weiteren Investitionen erhöhten die Schuldenlast, aber sie erhöhten auch den Umsatz. Und dies erhöhte Vaters Gewicht in den Gremien. Florian fragte sich, ob Vater, dieser zunehmend genervte und gereizte Mann, irgendwann in einer stillen Stunde sich gefragt hatte, ob es einen Weg zurück gab, zu dem Punkt, wo sich Notwendigkeit und Freiheit in Balance befanden, wo Mühe und Fleiß mit Zufriedenheit und Sicherheit belohnt wurden. Wahrscheinlich nicht. Es gibt Wege, die sind nur Hinwege, ohne Möglichkeit zu wenden. Wie diese Autobahn, auf der er dahinglitt, und wenn ihm auf dieser Fahrbahn etwas entgegenkam, dann konnten es nur Geister sein, eine Gefahr.

Und plötzlich hatte Florian in die Schuhe des Vaters steigen müssen. Verantwortung übernehmen. Und er stellte fest, dass die Schuhe zu klein waren. Das ist ungewöhnlich bei Söhnen starker Väter. Aber es wurde ihm sehr bald klar: Um zu retten, was der Vater aufgebaut hatte, brauchte er größere Schuhe, und zwar gleich um einige Nummern größere. Österreich war der EU beigetreten, und die nationalen Interessenvertretungen begriffen lange Zeit nicht, dass sie in der Falle saßen. Sie verteidigten den nationalen Markt, der nur noch in den Köpfen alter Funktionäre existierte, machten es sich in einem System von Förderungen bequem, das nicht zu gerechten Preisen führte, sondern, bei wachsendem Bürokratieaufwand, zur Abhängigkeit von Almosen, für die es mittelfristig nicht einmal eine Garantie gab, und es existierte kein Plan für die Zeit danach, wenn die Übergangsbestimmungen ausliefen, die bei den Beitrittsverhandlungen vereinbart worden waren. Er erinnerte sich an eine Sitzung in der Bundeswirtschaftskammer in Wien, in der es um Strategien für die Schweineproduzenten gehen sollte. Er war damals jung, noch sehr unsicher. Die Schuhe des Vaters drückten ihn. Er war verblüfft, wie feindselig die alten Funktionäre reagierten, wenn er Fragen stellte – als würde er nicht Fragen stellen, sondern alles in Frage stellen, vor allem sie, die Herren einer untergegangenen Welt, die Fürsten von Atlantis.

Er ist naiv gewesen, aber das Wichtigste hatte er begriffen: Er brauchte größere Schuhe, mit nationalen Interessenverbänden kam er unter den neuen Bedingungen in Europa nicht weiter. Damals hatte er begonnen, sich bei der Union der Europäischen Schweineproduzenten, der EPP, zu engagieren. Und nun war er seit einem Jahr ihr Präsident.

Er wurde von einem Polizeiauto mit Blaulicht und Martinshorn überholt, gleich darauf von einem zweiten. Schließlich von einem Rettungsfahrzeug.

Einmal im Jahr trafen sich die Vertreter der EPP in einer europäischen Stadt zu einer dreitägigen Generalversammlung. Dabei wurde der Präsident gewählt beziehungsweise der amtierende Präsident bestätigt. Es gab Erfahrungsaustausch, Diskussionen über die Widersprüche zwischen europäischen Richtlinien und nationalen Sonderregelungen, Erstellung von Forderungskatalogen an die europäischen Regierungen und an die Kommission, Besichtigung lokaler Betriebe und jedes Jahr ein Hauptthema – diesmal war es »Europäischer Schweine-Außenhandel«.

Für dieses Jahr hatte die ungarische Sektion die Einladung zum jährlichen Treffen ausgesprochen. Darauf war es in der Union der Schweineproduzenten zu Tumulten und noch in der Phase der organisatorischen Vorbereitung der Konferenz zu organisiertem Widerstand gekommen. Das hatte statuarische und politische Gründe. Nach den Statuten der EPP kam ein Vertreter des einladenden Landes in den Vorstand der EPP. Nun war aber Ungarn politisch verfemt, weil die ungarische Regierung europäische Schweinezüchter, die nach der Wende in Ungarn investiert und sich an ungarischen Betrieben beteiligt hatten, kalt enteignete und bislang die Mahnschreiben der Europäischen Kommission, zum Bruch des europäischen Rechts Stellung zu nehmen, und schließlich die Aufforderung, diese Verstöße innerhalb einer bestimmten Frist zurückzunehmen, einfach ignorierte. Es bildete sich eine Fraktion, die den Boykott Ungarns forderte. Es waren vor allem die Holländer und die Deutschen, die verlangten, die Jahreskonferenz in einer anderen Stadt auszurichten, vorgeschlagen wurde Madrid, denn Serano- und Iberico-Säue waren stark im Kommen. Dagegen vertraten vor allem die Österreicher, die Italiener und die Rumänen die Position, dass die Konferenz erst recht in Ungarn abgehalten werden müsse, um ein deutliches Zeichen zu setzen, dass die EPP gewillt war, die Interessen ihrer Mitglieder in Ungarn selbst zu verteidigen.

Es begann zu regnen. Florian Susman schaute auf das Display seines Navis: nur noch zehn Kilometer bis zur Grenze. Und wieder Sirenengeheul, ein weiteres Rettungsfahrzeug brauste vorbei.

Florian hatte als Präsident alle Hände voll zu tun gehabt, ein Zerbrechen der EPP zu verhindern und einen Kompromiss zwischen den Lagern herzustellen. Der Kompromiss war brüchig, er bestand im Grunde aus Absichtserklärungen, die dann auf der Konferenz erst diskutiert werden sollten. Aber immerhin, es war ein Kompromiss, und die Konferenz konnte wie geplant in Budapest stattfinden. Die ungarische Sektion, als Gastgeber, hatte sich bereit erklärt, eine Protestnote an die ungarische Regierung mit zu unterschreiben – mal sehen, ob sie das wirklich tun werden. Denn die großen ungarischen Schweineproduzenten hatten von der Renationalisierung der Betriebe profitiert, andererseits: Jetzt waren sie unterkapitalisiert, und der Export ungarischer Mangalica-Schweine war um fast 25 Prozent zurückgegangen. Aber das war ja das Hauptthema der diesjährigen Konferenz.

Florian Susman hatte nicht die Befürchtung, dass er als Präsident abgewählt werden könnte. Immerhin war ihm dieser vorläufige Kompromiss gelungen, was allgemein anerkannt wurde, und es hatte sich auch bis jetzt kein Gegenkandidat in Stellung gebracht.

Wieder Sirenen und Blaulicht. Es flackerte im Rückspiegel, zuckte auf der nun etwas angelaufenen Windschutzscheibe. Er schaltete das Gebläse ein, zwei Polizeiautos rasten an ihm vorbei.

Er war sicher, dass er als Präsident bestätigt werden würde, aber er fragte sich, ob er das überhaupt noch wollte. Er war nicht mehr naiv. Im Gegenteil, er drohte zu dem Typus Pragmatiker zu werden, wie er ihn früher immer verachtet hatte: einer, der immer nur das gerade Mögliche machte, das Notwendige aber nicht durchsetzen konnte. Er steuerte auf einen Abgrund zu, er konnte versuchen zu bremsen, aber er konnte das Steuer nicht herumreißen.

Es gab für die Spaltung der EPP in Wahrheit keine Lösung, er sah jedenfalls keine: Es ging bei dieser Konferenz in Budapest gemeinsam mit den Ungarn gegen die Europäische Kommission, weil sie nicht imstande oder willens war, eine höhere Exportquote für Schweine mit China zu verhandeln, und zugleich ging es mit der Europäischen Kommission gegen die Ungarn, weil sie EU-Recht brachen.

Wenn es die Union der europäischen Schweineproduzenten zerreißen sollte, welchen Sinn hatte es da, Verantwortung zu übernehmen, wie absurd war es, das alles nicht zu wollen, aber zu sagen: Ich übernehme Verantwortung. Wofür? Als Hampelmann der Erfahrung, dass Menschen sich organisierten, die gemeinsame Interessen hatten, um dann, in dieser Gemeinschaft, so unerbittlich Interessenkonflikte auszutragen, bis es keine Gemeinsamkeit mehr gab.

Da sah er Menschen vor sich auf der Autobahn. Fußgänger! Auf der Autobahn! Sie marschierten ihm entgegen! Geistergänger! Männer, Frauen, Kinder. Gebeugt unter Kapuzen von Regenjacken oder mit Plastiktüten auf dem Kopf, manche mit Decken über den Schultern oder über den Köpfen, manche trugen Taschen, andere zogen Koffer, die Scheibenwischer schlugen rhythmisch hin und her, wie Hände, die dieses Bild verwischen wollten, wegwischen, da hörte er das Navi: »Bitte nach Möglichkeit wenden! Bitte nach Möglichkeit wenden!« Das war verrückt! Er war auf einer Autobahn, das Navi sagte Wenden, und Fußgänger kamen ihm entgegen. Er schaltete den Warnblinker ein, rollte im Schritttempo, da sah er wieder Blaulicht, Polizeiwagen auf dem Pannenstreifen, Polizisten, die Leuchtstäbe schwenkten. Er hielt an. Immer mehr Menschen traten aus dem grauen Regenvorhang in das Scheinwerferlicht. Es waren viele. Dutzende. Hunderte.

David de Vriend hatte in seinem Leben, besser gesagt seinem Überleben, nie die Erfahrung gemacht, dass etwas besser wurde oder ihm weiterhalf oder ihn gar rettete, wenn er bemüht freundlich war. Und er erwartete auch keine Freundlichkeit. Höflichkeit, ja. Höflichkeit war Zivilisation. Korrektheit. Daran musste und wollte er festhalten. Aber warum sollte er, wenn er »Sehr erfreut« sagte, so tun, als wäre er wirklich sehr erfreut?

Er hatte Gefühle zeigen können, wenn er sie wirklich hatte. Liebe, diese Selbstlosigkeit, die das Schönste von einem selbst zum Vorschein bringt, und Dankbarkeit, eine so innige und existentielle Dankbarkeit, dass sie sogar verlorenes Gottvertrauen ersetzt. Und er hatte gelernt, Gefühle zu verstecken, Angst oder das Gefühl von Leere, Gefühle, die er nicht mehr loswerden, aber immerhin wegpacken konnte. Und er hatte gelernt, auf eine so sensible Weise misstrauisch zu sein, dass diese Eigenschaft unauffällig und erhellend wie ein Nachtsichtgerät funktionierte. Aber Freundlichkeit, vor allem die überfallartige Freundlichkeit gegenüber Fremden, war für ihn bloßes Schmierentheater von Charakterdarstellern, so grotesk wie ein bemüht freundlich blickendes Glasauge.

Goedemiddag, sagte er und nickte höflich, als er beim Verlassen seines Apartments den Mann sah, der gerade die Tür zum Nachbarapartment aufschloss. Bonjour, sagte der Mann, der sofort zwei Schritte auf ihn zuging, wobei der Strahl der Deckenleuchte in sein schlohweißes Haar fiel, dass es aufleuchtete wie ein Heiligenschein. Bonjour, Monsieur.

David de Vriend nickte noch einmal und wollte rasch weitergehen, schaute aber, nur eine Sekunde, aber doch zu lang, verwundert diesen Mann an, der im Licht des Deckenspots leuchtete. Er trug einen Regenmantel mit Moiré-Effekt, der bei der kleinsten Bewegung zwischen Hellgrün und Beige changierte, sein Gesicht glänzte wie soeben eingecremt.

Bonjour, Monsieur, permettez-moi de me présenter, sagte der Mann, nannte seinen Namen, Romain Boulanger, streckte de Vriend seine Hand hin und strahlte, als wäre das der glücklichste Moment seines Lebens.

De Vriend schüttelte ihm förmlich die Hand, sagte seinen Namen, und Aangenaam, verbesserte sich: Enchanté! Das war alles noch sehr höflich, aber es drohte ein bedrängend freundliches Gespräch zu werden.

Oh, er spreche Französisch.

Er hätte sagen sollen, leider nicht gut, sich entschuldigen und weitergehen, aber er sagte Oui, Monsieur. Viele Flamen sprachen ein akzeptables Französisch, und David de Vriend sprach es perfekt. Er war seinerzeit, nach seiner Flucht aus dem Deportationszug, zwei Jahre lang von einer wallonischen Familie versteckt worden, in Villers-la-Ville, von seinem vierzehnten bis zum sechzehnten Lebensjahr, bis er knapp vor Kriegsende denunziert wurde. Französisch war damals seine zweite Muttersprache geworden, seine Ersatzelternsprache, in einem existentiellen Sinn für ihn die Sprache der Liebe. Er verabscheute es augenblicklich, wie outriert dieser Fremde, wie hieß er noch gleich, »Quel bonheur« sagte und noch einmal

»Quel bonheur«, welch ein Glück, und lossprudelte: er sei der neue Nachbar, heute hier eingezogen, wie schön, dass er gleich seinen Nachbarn kennenlerne, er hoffe auf gute Nachbarschaft, aber es beginne ja schon bestens, ein Glück, dass Monsieur de Vriend Französisch spreche, er habe heute ja schon die Erfahrung machen müssen, dass einige im Haus nur Flämisch sprächen, sogar vom Personal, also das habe ihn zunächst doch etwas verunsichert, dass es in der Maison Hanssens Personal gebe, das nicht frankophon sei, nicht sattelfest, gleich eine Betreuerin, die ihn in die Hausregeln einweisen sollte, eine Madame Godelieve, unaussprechlicher Name – Godelieve.

Ja, Monsieur, ob er sie kenne? Jedenfalls, er habe sie nicht verstanden, aber zum Glück sei es möglich gewesen, das zu regeln, er werde nun von Madame Joséphine betreut –

Ein Glück!

Der Mantel von Monsieur Boulanger wechselte unausgesetzt die Farbe.

Ja, Monsieur, sehr nett, sehr hilfsbereit, aber – er machte ein verschmitztes Gesicht und hob seinen Zeigefinger – man dürfe nie Schwester zu ihr sagen, aber es sei ja wirklich wahr, das hier sei ja kein Hospital, auch wenn sie so ein Häubchen trage, ob er sie kenne?

David de Vriend nickte.

Jedenfalls, es freue ihn ungemein, einen so netten Nachbarn zu haben. Ob er schon länger hier sei, er müsse ihm unbedingt, unbedingt, von seinen Erfahrungen erzählen und Tipps geben, vielleicht beim Essen oder später bei einem Glas Wein.

David de Vriend brachte es nicht über sich, freudig auf diesen Vorschlag einzugehen, ja, selbstverständlich, sehr gerne zu sagen, er suchte nach einer höflichen Antwort, die ihn zu nichts verpflichtete, zugleich war er davon abgelenkt, dass ihn das Gesicht dieses Mannes an jemanden erinnerte, aber er wusste nicht, an wen. Monsieur Boulanger machte einen kleinen Schritt, wodurch er den direkten Lichtkegel des Spots verließ, sein Haar und sein Gesicht hörten plötzlich zu strahlen auf, wurden grau, und er sagte: Ich halte Sie auf! Hatte er tatsächlich »arrêter« gesagt? Entschuldigen Sie bitte! Ich halte Sie nicht länger auf! Wir sehen uns!

Als de Vriend den Speisesaal betrat, stellte er fest, dass es keinen Tisch mehr gab, an dem er alleine sitzen konnte. Er wollte kehrtmachen und ins Le Rustique gehen, mittlerweile hatte er Ermäßigungsmarken für dieses Lokal bekommen, aber da wurde er von Frau Joséphine bereits entmündigt: Da sind wir ja, sagte sie so laut, dass er zusammenzuckte, und schob ihn energisch zu einem Tisch, an dem der Professor saß, den »wir«, wie Frau Joséphine rief, schon kennengelernt haben, nicht wahr, Herr de Vriend, damals bei dem kleinen Missgeschick mit der Fischgräte, nicht wahr, aber heute besteht keine Gefahr, es gibt eine leckere Waterzooi. Professor, darf ich Ihren Bekannten de heer de Vriend zu Ihnen setzen?
Wie es ihm gehe, ob er sich im Haus wohlfühle, ob er Verwandte habe, die zu Besuch kämen – David de Vriend beantwortete höflich, aber sehr knapp die Fragen, mit denen der Professor – wie hieß er gleich? – Konversation machen wollte. Dann kam ein Moment des Schweigens, während sie die Vorspeise aßen, Fenchel-Orangen-Salat, und de Vriend überlegte, ob es unhöflich wäre, den Professor noch einmal nach dessen Namen zu fragen, also zuzugeben, dass er ihn schon wieder vergessen hatte, während er selbst vom Professor mit Namen angesprochen worden war, und er dachte, dass es korrekter wäre, es doch zu tun, statt seine kleine Unachtsamkeit mühsam und letztlich peinlich zu überspielen.
Der Professor zeigte sich gar nicht indigniert, gab freudig

Auskunft. Er heiße Gerrit Rensenbrink, sagte er, holte seine Brieftasche hervor, nestelte eine Visitenkarte heraus, schob den Teller weg und legte die Karte vor sich hin. Professor an der Universität Leuven, sagte er, plötzlich hatte er einen Kugelschreiber in der Hand und strich »Katholieke Universiteit Leuven« auf der Karte durch. Er sei ja emeritiert. Leiter der Forschungsstelle für Politische Geschichte, sagte er und strich die entsprechende Zeile auf der Karte durch. Sein Forschungsschwerpunkt sei Geschichte des Nationalismus gewesen und da insbesondere die Geschichte der Kollaboration in Belgien und den Niederlanden während des 2. Weltkriegs. Was strich er jetzt durch? Die Mailadresse und die Telefonnummer. Die gebe es ja nicht mehr, sagte er.

Dann sagte er: Bitte, und schob David de Vriend die Karte hin. In diesem Augenblick gab es einen Knall, das war Monsieur Boulanger, der beim Betreten des Speisesaals die Tür hinter sich allzu schwungvoll ins Schloss geworfen hatte. David de Vriend sah auf, Émile Boulanger hob entschuldigend beide Hände, sagte Pardon, Messieursdames, sah sich um, erblickte de Vriend und eilte freudig zu seinem Tisch.

Puis-je me joindre à vous? Sagte er, und: Wunderbar, dass wir unser Gespräch so schnell fortsetzen können.

Er setzte sich, nickte Professor Rensenbrink zu, es war mehr als ein Nicken, es war geradezu eine Verbeugung im Sitzen, und sagte: Ich bin sozusagen der Neue. Darf ich mich vorstellen, ich heiße –

Er begann zu sprudeln und de Vriend fühlte sich plötzlich unsagbar müde. Die Vorspeisenteller wurden abserviert, es klapperte, da kamen schon die Teller mit dem Waterzooi, es klapperte und klapperte, plötzlich Schweigen – Professor Rensenbrink hatte gesagt, er spreche leider nicht Französisch.

Oh! Und Monsieur Boulanger sprach nicht Niederländisch.

De Vriend hatte immer gerne Waterzooi gegessen, jedenfalls nie ein Problem damit gehabt, manchmal gab es eben Waterzooi, in der Schulkantine hatte es ab und zu Waterzooi gegeben, und er hatte immer gegessen, was es gab. Natürlich zog er Coq au Vin vor, wenn er in einem Restaurant Huhn bestellen wollte, aber er wäre nie auf den Gedanken gekommen, daraus ein Problem zu machen, wenn es Waterzooi gab, gab es Waterzooi, und er war dankbar. Er sah auf die Fleischteile, blickte auf, Professor Rensenbrink und Monsieur Boulanger schauten ihn an, verzweifelt? Irgendwie hilflos? Aber das hatte nichts mit dem Waterzooi zu tun, das, wie de Vriend meinte, seltsam roch. War das ein Gewürz, das er nicht kannte, oder war das bereits der Geruch von Verwesung?

Vous devez m'aider! Sie müssen mir helfen, Monsieur de Vriend! Der Monsieur spricht nicht Französisch, wären Sie so freundlich zu übersetzen?

De Vriend nickte.

Boulanger sagte, während er Rensenbrink nochmals zunickte: Mon nom est Romain Boulanger –

Son nom est Romain Boulanger –

Ik begrijp dat –

J'étais journaliste jusqu'à récemment chez Le Soir … Seit zehn Jahren sei er in Ruhestand, als freier Autor schreibe er allerdings noch ab und zu Kommentare, man könne es eben nicht lassen, die Herren wüssten doch gewiss, wie es sei, man könne sich ja nicht aus seinem Leben von einem Tag auf den anderen verabschieden, es sei natürlich nichts Wichtiges, das er noch schreiben dürfe, aber er sei dankbar, dass sie ihn noch schreiben lassen, und es mache Spaß, zum Beispiel die Geschichte mit dem Phantomschwein, Sie haben das vielleicht mitbekommen, dieses Schwein, das … aber egal – er hielt inne und machte eine Kopfbewegung, die bedeutete, dass de Vriend das bitte für Professor Rensenbrink übersetzen möge.

Allors, sagte de Vriend, il a dit qu'il était un journaliste. Retraité.

Aber er schreibe noch immer. Über ein Schwein.

Boulanger sah ihn verwundert an, zögerte, de Vriend sagte, c'est tout, und Boulanger setzte fort: Ja, wenn er ein Weingut hätte, würde er sich mit Leidenschaft darum kümmern, oder wenigstens ein Haus mit Garten, vielleicht würde er nur Rosen schneiden und lesen. Aber er habe eben bloß ein Apartment gehabt, ein schönes großes Apartment in Ixelles, aber was gäbe es da schon zu tun, und dann sei seine Frau gestorben, danach habe ihn das alles beengt, das Apartment, es sei ein großes Apartment gewesen, aber es habe ihn beengt, nach dem Tod seiner Frau sei da kein Alltag mehr möglich gewesen, also eine Fortsetzung seines Alltags, nur noch ein Hin- und Herschlurfen zwischen den Wänden, und er habe das nicht mehr verwalten können –

Wie bitte?

Verwalten, das sei ihm alles zu viel geworden, und zugleich zu wenig, ob die Herren das verstünden, es sei jedenfalls nicht mehr sein Leben gewesen –

Wat heeft hij gezegd?

David de Vriend atmete tief durch und gab wieder, was Boulanger gesagt hatte, und als er das Erstaunen von Professor Rensenbrink sah, fügte er hinzu, dass das doch verständlich sei. Dass Monsieur Boulanger nach dem Tod seiner Frau –

Oui, Monsieur, sagte Boulanger, aber, Sie haben, ich dachte –

In diesem Moment spürte de Vriend eine Beklemmung in der Brust, die ihm den Atem nahm, zugleich wurde ihm heiß, es war brennende Scham, er begriff, dass er –

Er hatte, was Monsieur Boulanger auf Französisch gesagt hatte, nicht übersetzt, sondern immer nur auf Französisch wiederholt.

Er senkte den Kopf, sah auf die Fleischteile auf seinem Teller, stand auf und lief weg, hinaus aus dem Speisesaal, dessen Tür mit einem Knall ins Schloss fiel.

Siebentes Kapitel

Wie kann man nicht an die Zukunft glauben,
wenn man von der Sterblichkeit weiß?

Die Tage wurden immer wärmer, für die Jahreszeit untypisch warm. Bei Begegnungen in den Korridoren, in der Kantine oder vor dem Lift machte man nun launige Bemerkungen über die Erderwärmung.

Wir in Brüssel sind eindeutig Gewinner dieser Entwicklung!

Das wird man uns auch wieder vorwerfen: noch ein Privileg für die Brüsseler Beamten!

Das warme Wetter habt ihr mir zu verdanken, ich habe immer nur Deos mit Treibgas benutzt!

Mit der Klima-Richtlinie schneiden wir uns aber ins eigene Fleisch!

Hält sich ohnehin keiner dran – ihr werdet sehen, bald haben wir Palmen hier in Brüssel!

Aber das war eben die Arche und nicht die Generaldirektion Klimapolitik, und in Wahrheit lachte niemand über die banalen Smalltalk-Witzchen, sondern einfach deshalb, weil in dieser verregneten Stadt in einer eigentlich kühlen Jahreszeit seit Tagen die Sonne schien. Die Sonne wurde reflektiert von den strahlenden Gesichtern der Menschen, sie strahlte aus ihren Augen, sie glitzerte in den Fensterscheiben, und sie glänzte auf dem Blech des Straßenverkehrs.

Martin Susman hatte nach der Besprechung mit Xeno das Papier für das Jubilee Project ausgearbeitet, sie hatte dazu schriftliche Kommentare gemacht, nun musste er das Papier entsprechend um- und weiter ausarbeiten, damit es zur Grundlage einer Inter-Service Consultation werden konnte. Das wäre der nächste Schritt. Er hatte versprochen, das Papier Ende der Woche abzugeben, aber es gab noch einige offene Fragen, zumindest eine große unbeantwortete Frage. Die musste er schnellstens mit Bohumil klären, der damit betraut war. Er besuchte ihn in seinem Zimmer, fragte, ob er Lust auf einen Mittagsimbiss habe.

Bei dem Wetter könnten wir zur Place Jourdan schlendern. Zum Beispiel zur Brasserie L'Esprit. Ich glaube, man kann sogar im Freien sitzen.

Gute Idee! Soll ich anrufen und einen Tisch reservieren?

Ja bitte, ich hole inzwischen meine Jacke!

In der Rue Joseph II fuhren Traktoren.

Ist das eine Bauerndemo?

Was?

Martin schrie: Bauerndemo?

Bohumil zuckte mit den Achseln.

Eine lange Kolonne von Traktoren. Manche hatten Anhänger, auf denen Menschen standen, die etwas riefen, was im Lärm der Motoren, der Hupen und Trillerpfeifen aber unterging.

Seitenstraßen waren durch quer gestellte Polizeiautos abgesperrt.

Martin und Bohumil gingen Richtung Rond-Point Schuman, es war unmöglich, sich zu unterhalten. Sie sahen, dass von der Rue Archimède und der Avenue de Cortenbergh ebenfalls Traktoren herantuckerten, Traktoren mit Mistfuhren, dazwischen gingen Gruppen von Menschen mit Heugabeln und Sensen. Es sah bedrohlich aus, zugleich wie aus der Zeit gefallen, Wut in folkloristischem Kostüm. Auf dem Schuman-Kreisverkehr, zwischen dem Kommissions- und dem Ratsgebäude und weit in die Rue de la Loi hinein standen Traktoren, es wurde Mist abgeladen, Transparente wurden aufgerollt, es stank nach Diesel, schwarze Abgaswölkchen schwebten im Sonnenlicht, auf einem Ladewagen stand eine junge Frau, barbusig, die eine Tricolore schwenkte, Martin blieb stehen und schaute, Polizisten winkten ihn weiter, continuer s'il vous plaît, doorlopen alstublieft, lotsten die Passanten zwischen Absperrgittern durch, sie kamen auf die Rue Froissart, hier wurde es ruhiger, aber sie gingen schweigend weiter zur Place Jourdan.

In der Brasserie, genauer: vor der Brasserie, denn man konnte tatsächlich draußen sitzen, zündeten sich Martin und Bohumil Zigaretten an, warfen einen Blick auf die Speisekarte, bestellten die Empfehlung des Tages, Waterzooi de la mer, dazu Weißwein und Wasser, Bohumil blies Rauchkringel in die Luft und sagte: Es ist wie Urlaub, nicht wahr? Ich fürchte mich schon vor dem Heimkommen.

Heimkommen? Was meinst du?

Ich muss am Freitag heim nach Prag. Am Samstag heiratet meine Schwester.

Die Kellnerin brachte den Wein, Bohumil nippte an seinem Glas, sagte: Und das wird furchtbar. Sie heiratet Květoslav Hanka – der Name sagt dir nichts, aber in Prag ist er ziemlich bekannt, mehr noch, berüchtigt. Er ist ein, wie sagt man auf Englisch, wir sagen křikloun. Ja, ein Rowdy. Ein ziemlich radikaler Abgeordneter der Úsvit, das ist bei uns die Nationalisten-Partei, natürlich radikale EU-Gegner. Das ist doch völlig wahnsinnig, oder? Ich arbeite in der Europäischen Kommission, und mein Schwager arbeitet an der Zerstörung der EU.

Im Ernst? Und jetzt sag nicht, dass du Trauzeuge bist.

Nein, natürlich nicht. So viel Feeling hat meine Schwester. Noch. Das war klar, dass sie nicht einmal daran dachte, mich zu fragen. Ich habe sie ziemlich beschimpft, als sie mir von ihrer Liebe erzählt hat. Erfahren habe ich es zuerst aus dem Fernsehen. Ich schaue ja ab und zu im Internet tschechische Nachrichten. Und da sah ich ihn, in einem Bericht über eine

Charity-Veranstaltung, Charity! Diese Mörder organisieren Charity-Veranstaltungen für arme Täter! Und da sah ich ihn, den Herrn Abgeordneten, und eine Stimme sagte: in Begleitung seiner charmanten neuen Freundin – und was sehe ich? Meine Schwester! Ich habe sie sofort angerufen und zur Rede gestellt. Sie sagte nur: Männer!

Männer?

Ja, sie meint, politische Differenzen sind ein Spleen von Männern. Frauen sind für die Liebe zuständig und Männer für idiotische Kämpfe.

Das ist deine Schwester?

Da wurde das Essen serviert, Bohumil steckte seinen Löffel in den Teller und schaufelte herum, als wollte er das Unterste zuoberst kehren, schüttelte den Kopf, sagte: Kannst du dir die Hochzeit vorstellen? Das Hochzeitsfest? Die ganze Faschistenszene von Prag wird dort sein, und Květoslav hat die Fotorechte an Blesk verkauft –

An wen?

Blesk. Eine Zeitung. Übersetzt: Lightning. Ein Boulevard-Blatt.

Lightning? Offenbar das Gegenteil von Enlightenment.

Bohumil machte ein gequältes Gesicht

Ich würde nicht hinfahren, sagte Martin.

Es ist meine Schwester. Und unsere Mutter hat gesagt, wenn ich nicht komme, dann bringt sie sich um.

Ich würde nicht hinfahren, wiederholte Martin. Er war verwundert. Er mochte Bohumil, und er glaubte ihn zu kennen. Er hätte nicht gedacht, dass sein leichtlebiger Kollege, der eben noch so heiter in die Sonne geblinzelt hatte, solch ein existentielles Problem haben könnte. Er dachte, dass er –

Bohumil sagte etwas, Martin verstand nur: Vorkriegszeit, hatte er tatsächlich Vorkriegszeit gesagt? Da läutete Martins Mobiltelefon, er hob ab, sagte: Ich rufe zurück, ich bin in einer

Besprechung, und fragte Bohumil: Entschuldige, was hast du gesagt?

Bohumil löffelte sein Waterzooi, schob plötzlich den Teller weg, sagte: Eigentlich mag ich das nicht!

Was?

Ich bin kein Historiker, sagte er, aber für mich war das immer Geschichte, irgendwie früher, verstehst du, Steinzeit, und dieses Kapitel der Steinzeit hieß Vorkriegszeit: dass radikale politische Gegensätze quer durch Familien gehen, der eine geht zu den Faschisten, der andere zu den Kommunisten, und so weiter. Habe ich in der Schule zu wenig aufgepasst? Aber das habe ich in Erinnerung, so wurde es erzählt: Früher, in finsteren Zeiten, ging politischer Hass quer durch Familien. Was ist das für ein Albtraum? Wieso habe ich heute, heute, diese finsteren Zeiten in meiner Familie? Mein Vater kommt übrigens nicht zur Hochzeit.

Und das ist für deine Mutter kein Grund, sich umzubringen?

Nein, im Gegenteil. Ihr wäre es recht, wenn er sich umbringt. Sie haben sich getrennt, und sie prozessieren.

Martin hatte etwas Wichtiges mit Bohumil besprechen wollen, wegen des Jubilee Project, er verschob es auf später, wenn sie wieder im Büro waren, jetzt hatte er das Gefühl, dass er, ausgerechnet er, ihn, ausgerechnet ihn, Bohumil, irgendwie aufheitern musste. Er hob sein Glas, sagte: Ich kann dich trösten. Denk an Herman Van Rompuy!

Bohumil sah ihn fragend an.

Das muss man sich vorstellen: Van Rompuy war Präsident des Europäischen Rats, also ein Präsident der Europäischen Union, seine Schwester ist Vorsitzende der belgischen Maoisten, und sein Bruder ist Mandatar der belgischen Nationalisten, ein beinharter flämischer Separatist. In der Zeitung habe ich gelesen: Die Familie trifft sich nur einmal im Jahr – zu Weihnachten!

Bohumil, der gerade einen Schluck Wein trank, prustete los: Zu Weihnachten! Der Europapräsident, der Nationalist und die Maoistin!

Und da singen sie »Stille Nacht«!

Stille Nacht! Bruhaha! Ist das wahr?

Ja. Angeblich. Habe ich gelesen. War eine Story in De Morgen.

Bohumil sagte lachend: Ein Glas trinken wir noch!

Als sie zurück ins Büro gingen, hatte sich die Demo bereits aufgelöst, sie gingen über den Schuman zwischen Absperrgittern an Misthaufen vorbei, die auf städtische Reinigungswagen geschaufelt wurden. Es stank. Es lachte die Sonne.

Auf dem Rückweg ins Büro war Bohumil schweigsam und nachdenklich. Im Lift sagte er: Ich storniere den Flug am Freitag. Ich gehe nicht zu der Hochzeit. Ich will nicht zusammen mit Květoslav Hanka auf einem Foto sein, das dann in Blesk erscheint.

Und deine Mutter?

Ich werde ihr sagen: Ich komme zu Weihnachten.

Dann boxte er Martin auf den Oberarm, sagte grinsend: Stille Nacht!

Eine halbe Stunde später saßen Martin, Bohumil und Kassándra im Besprechungszimmer, zu einem Update der Vorarbeiten für das Jubilee Project. Xeno hatte im Kommentar zu Martins Papier angemerkt, dass eruiert werden müsse, wie viele Verfolgte und Opfer des Holocaust heute noch am Leben seien. Gibt es ein zentrales Register der Überlebenden von Konzentrations- und Vernichtungslagern? Wie viele leben heute in Europa, wie viele in Israel, den USA oder anderswo? Gibt es eine Institution, die als repräsentative Vertretung der Überlebenden ein Kooperationspartner bei der Organisation des Events sein kann?

Dies müsse man wissen, um zu entscheiden, ob man tatsächlich alle Holocaust-Überlebenden nach Brüssel einladen könne oder wenigstens eine Gruppe, die wirklich repräsentativ wäre.

Das hat uns sehr überrascht, sagte Bohumil. Wir hatten natürlich erwartet, dass es ein zentrales Register der Holocaust-Überlebenden gibt. Aber wir haben keines gefunden.

Kassándra: Alle Institutionen, von denen wir Auskunft erbeten haben, haben nicht geantwortet. Yad Vashem zum Beispiel. Keine Antwort. Auf Nachfrage kam schließlich doch eine, aber die ist auch keine, hier, bitte: die Mail sei an einen dafür zuständigen Mitarbeiter weitergeleitet worden. Danach passierte wieder tagelang nichts. Ich schrieb wieder hin, mit der Bitte, mir den Namen und die Mail-Adresse dieses Mitarbeiters mitzuteilen, damit ich direkt mit ihm in Kontakt treten könne. Keine Antwort. Bis heute nicht. Dann das Wiesenthal Center in Los Angeles: keine Antwort. Auf Nachfrage bekamen wir dann die Auskunft, dass die Dokumentation der Opfer der Shoa nicht Aufgabe des Wiesenthal Centers sei. Sie hätten nur eine Liste der noch lebenden NS-Kriegsverbrecher, sie sei auf ihrer Homepage veröffentlicht, aber sie verfügten über kein Register der noch lebenden Opfer der Shoa. Wir mögen uns an Yad Vashem wenden. Wir haben diese Mail an Yad Vashem weitergeleitet, mit nochmaliger Bitte um Auskunft – keine Reaktion. Wir haben alle Gedenkstätten angeschrieben, Auschwitz, Bergen-Belsen, Buchenwald, Mauthausen und so weiter, aber nur von Mauthausen kam eine Antwort.

Und was schrieb Mauthausen?

Hier: dass sie nur eine Liste der Überlebenden von Mauthausen selbst hätten, aber nicht einmal diese sei vollständig, was auf das Chaos nach der Befreiung im Mai 45 zurückzuführen sei. Die Überlebenden, so sie das Lager gleich verlassen konnten, hätten sich an verschiedene Behörden und Institutionen gewandt, um Hilfe und Papiere zu bekommen, das sei nicht zentral gesammelt worden. Und von der unvollständigen Personendatei, über die der Gedenkdienst Mauthausen verfüge, sei es wiederum nur ein kleiner Teil, von dem sie aktuelle Daten hätten – und nicht einmal die seien gesichert. Die Menschen, von denen man Adressen habe, würden jedes Jahr zur Befreiungsfeier eingeladen. Wer nun jahrelang auf diese Einladung nicht reagiert, kann gestorben sein oder aber auch bloß verzogen. Der Direktor der Mauthausen-Gedenkstätte verwies uns – Überraschung! – an Yad Vashem, aber auch an die Shoa Foundation von Steven Spielberg. Ein interessanter Hinweis! Und im Anhang schickten sie uns den Text des Mauthausen-Schwurs, um uns, also die Kommission, daran zu erinnern, dass die Römischen Verträge sich darauf beriefen. Der Direktor schrieb – Moment, ja, hier habe ich es: die Losung »Nie wieder Auschwitz« sei problematisch, weil sie ein Lager an die Spitze stelle, also letztlich ein Ranking der Lager mache, aber der Schwur von Mauthausen sei universal und stehe ebendeshalb auch am Beginn des europäischen Einigungsprojekts, auch wenn man heute nichts mehr davon höre.

Martin nickte. Das ist ja der Grund, warum wir – er brach ab, sagte: Wir verwenden Auschwitz als Chiffre, aber im Grunde hat er unsere Idee verstanden. Und, hast du an Spielberg geschrieben?

Ja.

Keine Antwort?

Doch. Kurz und bündig. Es gäbe nur eine Liste der Überlebenden, die bereit waren, als Testimonials ihre Lebensgeschichte vor einer Kamera zu erzählen. Aber weder wüssten sie, wie viele Shoa-Opfer insgesamt noch lebten, sie wüssten nicht einmal, wie viele ihrer Zeitzeugen mittlerweile noch am Leben seien. Die Aufnahmen wurden mit Menschen gemacht, die sich von sich aus gemeldet hatten. Das Archiv sei frei zugänglich. Näheres sollen wir anfragen bei –

Yad Vashem.

Genau. Das heißt, wir wissen gar nichts.

Das ist wirklich seltsam, sagte Martin. Völlig verrückt. Die Nazis haben jeden Menschen, der in ein KZ deportiert wurde, in Listen eigetragen, mit Namen, persönlichen Daten, Geburtsdatum, Beruf, letzte Adresse, sie haben sie durchnummeriert, ununterbrochen wurden sie gezählt, fein säuberlich wurden die Ermordeten aus Listen gestrichen – und nach der Befreiung löst sich alles in Luft auf –

Die Nazi-Bürokratie!

Aber alle Bürokratie? Man hätte sie doch erfassen müssen, um sie –

Nein, sagte Bohumil. Viele wollten oder konnten nicht in die Länder zurück, aus denen sie vertrieben oder deportiert worden waren. Niemand hatte Interesse an noch einer Liste von »displaced persons«. Man hat sie erstversorgt und dann gehen lassen, die gehen konnten.

Ich kann das nicht glauben, sagte Martin. Yad Vashem rekonstruiert alle Namen der Menschen, die in den Lagern ermordet wurden, aber sie haben kein Interesse an denen, die überlebt haben? Ich kann das nicht glauben. Diese Liste muss existieren, aber es scheint ein Interesse daran zu geben, sie geheim zu halten.

Come on, Martin, sagte Kassándra, es gibt keine Verschwörung. Welchen Sinn sollte sie haben? Es gibt sehr viele Gründe dafür, warum wir die Zahl der Überlebenden nicht kennen. Sie konnten, als sie sich nach der Befreiung irgendwohin durchschlugen, keine Adresse zurücklassen. Sie hatten ja noch keine Adresse. Und als sie dann an irgendeinem Ort begonnen haben, ihr Leben wiederaufzubauen, haben sie nicht an ihr ehemaliges Konzentrationslager geschrieben, um mitzuteilen, wo sie jetzt erreichbar sind – bitte Martin, versteh doch, KZ-Überlebende sind keine Alumni! Okay, manche meldeten sich bei den Gedenkstätten, stellten sich als Zeitzeugen zur Verfügung, um von ihren Erlebnissen zu berichten, manche kamen zu den Befreiungsfeiern, manche kamen Jahrzehnte später, mit ihren Enkelkindern, das war ihr Triumph über Hitler, manche aber wollten nie mehr etwas damit zu tun haben, manche sind sehr bald nach der Befreiung gestorben, sie waren zwar Überlebende, und dann plötzlich ganz normale Todesfälle der Nachkriegszeit, manche empfanden Scham und wollten nicht wieder in einer Kartei erfasst werden, manche schwiegen, weil sie merkten, dass keiner ihre Geschichte hören wollte, nicht einmal in Israel wollte man ihnen zuhören, den peinlichen Juden von der Schlachtbank, wie hätte das alles erfasst und systematisiert werden sollen?

Wir haben ein Problem, sagte Bohumil. Die Liste, die Xeno wollte, gibt es nicht. Es ist sinnlos, den Grund dafür zu erforschen. Und es gibt eine einfache Lösung des Problems. Worum geht es denn wirklich? Um das Narrativ der Europäischen Kommission. Du sagst, sie ist entstanden als Antwort auf den Holocaust, das soll sich nie mehr wiederholen können, wir garantieren Frieden und Rechtzustand. Okay, aber um das zu bezeugen, brauchen wir keine vollständige Liste der Opfer, die noch leben. Willst du sie in der Rue de la Loi Appell stehen lassen? Und durchzählen?

Hör auf! Sei doch still!

Es gibt Shoa-Überlebende, die kennt man, sagte Kassándra, die könnten wir einmal auflisten und schauen, wer von ihnen eine Botschaft bei unserer Feier –

Habt ihr bei Eurostat nachgefragt?

Warum hätten wir das tun sollen?

Bitte, Bohumil, sagte Martin. Wir haben eine europäische Statistik-Behörde. Die haben Statistiken für alles. Die wissen alles. Die wissen, wie viele Hühnereier heute in Europa gelegt wurden. Die werden auch wissen, wie viele Holocaust-Opfer heute noch in Europa leben. Kassándra, mach bitte die Anfrage, und wir reden weiter, wenn wir die Antwort haben.

Kassándra schrieb »Eurostat« auf ihren Notizblock, sah Martin an: Ich will ja nichts sagen, aber warum willst du über Menschen, die zu Nummern gemacht worden sind, jetzt ausgerechnet eine statistische Auskunft, eine Zahl?

Sie öffnete den Knopf an der Manschette ihrer Bluse, schob den Ärmel hoch, schrieb mit ihrem Tintenroller 171185 auf ihren Unterarm und streckte ihn Martin entgegen.

Was –? Was ist das?

Mein Geburtsdatum, sagte Kassándra.

Martin Susman arbeitete oft bis sieben, halb acht. Er hatte kein schlechtes Gewissen, als er an diesem Tag das Büro um halb fünf verließ. Dringendes stand nicht mehr an, und was an Routinearbeiten in der nächsten Stunde vielleicht noch anfiel, konnte er am nächsten Morgen erledigen. Er hatte nichts zu essen zu Hause, aber er hatte keinen Hunger. Er beschloss, auf dem Weg zur Metro ein Bier zu trinken, im James Joyce Pub in der Rue Archimède. Dort fuhren Panzerfahrzeuge. Er ging ein Stück weiter, zur Charlemagne, auch dort und auf der Rue de la Loi fuhren Militärfahrzeuge, deren grün-braun lackierter Stahl das Licht der Abendsonne zu verschlucken schien. Soldaten patrouillierten, Polizisten lenkten Autos um und wiesen Passanten zwischen Absperrgittern in enge Korridore, die zur Metro-Station führten, wobei der direkte Abgang vor dem Ratsgebäude gesperrt war.

Die Situation erinnerte Martin an Filme, die er irgendwann

gesehen hatte, »Z« oder »Missing«, oder an Dokus im Fernsehen. Er sah selten fern. Aber wenn er in schlaflosen Nächten doch durch die Programme zappte, dann blieb er immer bei historischen Dokus hängen, Geschichte interessierte ihn mehr als Geschichten, vor allem historische Filmdokumente faszinierten ihn, alte Wochenschaufilme genauso wie Amateuraufnahmen, die ausgegraben und in Dokumentarfilmen verwendet wurden, während eine sonore Stimme bedeutungsschwer von einer untergegangenen Zeit erzählte. Jetzt hatte er solche Bilder im Kopf, von den Panzern auf dem Wenzelsplatz nach der Niederschlagung des Prager Frühlings, von den Panzerfahrzeugen, die durch die Straßen Santiago de Chiles fuhren, nach dem Pinochet-Putsch, von der Militärpräsenz in den Straßen Athens nach dem Putsch der Obristen, zittrige Amateur-Super-8-Filme und Schwarz-Weiß-Szenen aus alten Fernsehnachrichten, Martin hatte den Eindruck, dass dieses historische Material jetzt auf die Straße projiziert wurde, durch die er ging, und eine virtuelle Realität schuf, für die ihm die Spielkonsole fehlte. Wie große Käfer bewegten sich die Panzer durch die autofreie Straße, die wenigen Passanten drückten sich an Häusern und Gittern vorbei und wurden vom Abgang zur Metro verschluckt.

Martin hatte keine Angst, er erinnerte sich, dass es einen Rats-Gipfel der europäischen Staats- und Regierungschefs gab. Das waren hier die begleitenden Schutzmaßnahmen. Er ging ins James Joyce Pub, schnatternd standen Menschen in Anzügen und mit gelockerten Krawatten an der Theke. Es war Happy Hour.

Auf dem Heimweg kaufte er noch ein Sixpack Jupiler im Shop Ecke Rue Sainte-Catherine.

Goedenavond.

Bonsoir, Monsieur.

Au revoir!

Tot ziens.

Zu Hause zog er die Hose aus, sie zwickte ihn, er ging aus dem Leim, er verachtete sich dafür, aber ohne Vorsätze zu fassen, in Brüssel zählte man die Zeit nicht in Jahren, sondern in Kilos. Er rauchte in Hemd und Unterhose eine Zigarette am offenen Fenster, dann setzte er sich in den Fauteuil am Kamin, in dem die alten Bücher standen, zündete die Kerze an, warum? Weil sie da war. Er trank Bier, sah zu, wie Insekten durch das offene Fenster ins Zimmer flogen und das Licht der Kerze suchten, in die Flamme hineinflogen und verbrannten.

Für ihn der Beweis, dass es keinen Gott gab, keinen Sinn in der Schöpfung, also keine Schöpfung. Denn was soll der Sinn darin sein, eine Gattung zu erschaffen, die erst in der Nacht aktiv wird, dann aber, in der Dunkelheit, das Licht sucht – nur um darin zu verbrennen? Wofür sind diese Tiere nützlich, welchen Beitrag zu der behaupteten oder erhofften Harmonie in der Natur leisten sie? Wahrscheinlich haben sie sich vorher noch irgendwie vermehrt, Nachkommen in die Welt gesetzt, die sich, so wie sie, den ganzen hellen Tag irgendwo in einem Dämmerzustand befinden, um dann bei Einbruch der Dunkelheit auszuschlüpfen und das Licht zu suchen, das sie verschlafen haben, nur um ihr Leben aus einem grotesken Todestrieb sofort zu beenden. In der Dämmerung beginnt der Flug in den Tod. Sie kleben an Fenstern, hinter denen Licht ist, als böte das Glas Nahrung, sie umschwirren Lampen und Laternen, als gäbe es so nahe am Licht etwas anderes als Blendung, und wenn sie eine Kerze oder anderes offenes Feuer entdecken, dann finden sie ihre Bestimmung, den sofortigen Tod, in den sie sich stürzen, also in die Finsternis, aus der sie kamen.

Kurzentschlossen stieg Kommissar Brunfaut schon bei der Station Schuman aus, statt bis Merode zu fahren. Zwischen diesen beiden Metro-Stationen lag der Parc du Cinquantenaire, allgemein der »Jubel-Park« genannt, durch den er nun an diesem strahlend schönen Tag einen wohltuenden Spaziergang machen wollte. Er verordnete sich diesen Fußmarsch, bedrückt von der kalten Angst, die ihn in der U-Bahn erfasst hatte, vor der Röhre, in die man ihn im Spital hineinschieben würde. Er hatte Zeit genug, er war in seiner Nervosität viel zu früh von zu Hause aufgebrochen.

Der Aufgang Justus Lipsius war gesperrt, er wurde von der Menge weitergeschoben zum Aufgang Berlaymont, wo es zu einem Gedränge kam, weil die Rolltreppe, die hinaufführte, nicht funktionierte. Die Leute wichen auf die Treppe aus, auf der sie aber immer wieder stehen blieben und sich zur Seite drückten, um den Passanten, die herunterkamen, Platz zu machen. Gleichzeitig wurden sie aber von den Nachrückenden angeschoben, von Trolleys und Rucksäcken gestoßen. Brunfaut drückte seine kleine Reisetasche an den Körper, er hörte Geschrei, das von oben vom Ausgang herunterhallte, schrilles Pfeifen, einige Passanten, die die Treppe hochgingen, machten kehrt, immer mehr Menschen kamen nun von oben herunter, Brunfaut hatte keine Ahnung, was da vorging, aber er ließ sich zurückdrängen und schwamm nun in der Menge zurück zum Bahnsteig. Da kam schon ein Zug, Brunfaut stieg ein und fuhr die eine Station weiter bis Merode.

Gleich neben dem Metro-Ausgang auf der Avenue des Celtes befand sich die Brasserie La Terrasse. Hier wollte er nun bei einem Bier die Zeit bis zu seinem Termin überbrücken. Die Terrasse war gut besucht, aber es gab einen freien Tisch, und obwohl das Lokal direkt an einer großen und lauten Straße lag, hatte Émile Brunfaut das Gefühl, sich hinter der Wand von Grünpflanzen in einer Oase der Ruhe zu befinden. Ruhe. In Ruhe nachdenken. Was? Worüber? Er sollte eine Lebensentscheidung treffen. Er dachte es so pathetisch: Lebensentscheidung. Und war augenblicklich überfordert. Obwohl er jetzt schon einige Zeit damit gelebt hatte, dass man ihn entlassen hatte, nicht formal, aber doch: Aus seinem Leben entlassen, fühlte es sich für ihn immer noch so »plötzlich« an, seltsam, wie lange ein »Plötzlich!« dauern kann.

Zugleich fragte er sich, welchen Sinn es haben sollte, eine Lebensentscheidung zu treffen, nur weil er dieses Wort im Kopf hatte, während er nicht einmal wusste –

Der Kellner. Brunfaut bestellte ein Bier.

Ob er auch zu speisen wünsche?

Er verneinte. Er wollte nur ein Bier.

– während er nicht einmal wusste, ob er überhaupt noch Lebenszeit hatte.

Der Kellner brachte das Bier, legte gleich auch den Rechnungsbon auf den Tisch, und einen Zettel, auf dem stand: »Reserviert 12.30«. Er bat, gleich kassieren zu dürfen. 12.30 – das war in zehn Minuten. Es war offensichtlich, dass der Kellner den Tisch schnell wieder frei haben wollte, falls noch jemand kam, der auch essen wollte.

Brunfaut war immer eine respektgebietende Person gewesen, allein schon durch seine physische Präsenz, mit dem großen, raumgreifenden Körper. Nun war er wie betäubt, wie klein und schwammig er sich fühlte, als er zum Kellner aufblickte.

Er stand auf. Er atmete tief ein und blähte sich auf. Sie hätten mir gleich sagen müssen, dass dieser Tisch reserviert ist! Ich habe keine Lust, das Bier so schnell runterzustürzen! Sie knallen mir da diesen »Reserviert«-Zettel vor die Nase, nachdem ich bestellt habe, ich finde das zynisch und demütigend. Auf Wiedersehen!

Aber – Monsieur! Sie können, warten Sie! Sie können nicht einfach gehen! Sie müssen das Bier bezahlen.

Warum? Ich trinke es ja nicht.

Dann muss ich die Polizei rufen.

Hier, mein Dienstausweis! Ich komme wie gerufen!

Oh! Entschuldigen Sie, Herr Kommissar! Selbstverständlich können Sie hier an diesem Tisch bleiben, solange Sie wollen, ich werde selbstverständlich die Reservierung umdisponieren, Herr Kommissar!

Ich habe keine Lust mehr!

Das war nur eine kurze Phantasie, die ihn, so kindisch sie war, nur noch mehr demütigte. Tatsächlich zahlte er, sagte: Kein Problem, ich muss in zehn Minuten ohnehin gehen. Ich habe einen Termin und –

Was und? Er gab noch viel zu viel Trinkgeld.

Er schaute ein paar Minuten vor sich hin, sah das Bier an – wie hatte er vergessen können, dass …? Er stand auf und ging, ohne vom Bier auch nur einen Schluck getrunken zu haben.

Émile Brunfaut überquerte die Avenue des Celtes und ging die Rue de Linthout hinauf. Die Nummer hatte er vergessen, aber er ging immer weiter, dachte, dass er das Spital, auch wenn er die Hausnummer nicht wusste, wohl erkennen würde.

Er erkannte es nicht. Er lief viel zu weit. Irgendwann wurde ihm das klar und er machte kehrt. Er schaffte es, statt zu früh fast zu spät zu kommen. Er schwitzte. Er würde schon bei der Aufnahme und dem ersten Arztgespräch den denkbar schlechtesten Eindruck machen.

Da! Jetzt sah er es! Das Europa-Hospital. Es sah von außen aus wie eine neugotische Kathedrale. Darum war er vorbeigelaufen. Wer erwartet schon, dass ein Spital aussieht wie ein historisches Gotteshaus?

Er ging hinein – und befand sich plötzlich in einer Raumstation. Weiße Kunststoffflächen, Alusilber, blaues Licht, bunte Lichtbänder auf dem Boden, als Leitsystem zu den verschiedenen Abteilungen, Brunfaut wunderte sich, dass die Menschen, die da gingen oder saßen, nicht schwerelos durch den Raum schwebten. Andererseits: Es war, ganz banal, bloß das Foyer eines Spitals. Alles abwaschbar, klinisch glänzend. Wie die Kulisse eines Science-Fiction-Films wirkte es nur deshalb, weil man durch die Fassade einer gotischen Kathedrale in diesen Raum eintrat.

Brunfaut stand vor der Wegweiser-Tafel. Das Erste, was er bewusst wahrnahm, war: »Psychiatrie«. Dann erst sah er »Innere Medizin«. Er folgte dem blauen Lichtband des Leitsystems.

Anmeldung, Aufnahme, Zuweisung des Zimmers, erstes Arztgespräch mit Anamnese. Dann erklärte Doktor Drumont, welche Untersuchungen er für erforderlich hielt und dass es möglich sei, sie alle im Lauf von zwei Tagen durchzuführen. Er werde das entsprechend einteilen. Danach, sei er sicher, werde man eine Diagnose für Brunfauts Beschwerden haben. Ob der Herr Kommissar nüchtern sei? Brunfaut bejahte. Er habe heute nichts gegessen und nichts getrunken. Sehr gut, sagte der Primar, dann können wir ja die Blutabnahme gleich erledigen. Das wird Schwester Anne machen. Sie kommt zu Ihnen ins Zimmer. Und ich werde veranlassen, dass Sie gleich danach eine kleine Stärkung bekommen.

Die Schwester, die nach der Blutabnahme den Tee mit Waffeln und einigen Erdbeeren brachte, fragte Brunfaut auch gleich nach seinem Wunsch für das Abendessen.

Ich sehe auf Ihrem Krankenblatt, Sie sind nicht – sie sah ihn an: noch nicht auf Diät gesetzt. Also Normalkost. Da können Sie wählen zwischen Fleisch oder Vegetarisch.

Brunfaut blickte auf den Teller mit den zwei Waffeln und den drei Erdbeeren und sagte: Bitte beides, Madame.

Wie, beides?

Ich nehme an, dass es bei der Fleischspeise eine Beilage gibt?

Es gibt Boulettes Sauce Lapin.

Und dazu?

Kartoffelpüree und Karotten.

Na eben, das ist ja vegetarisch. Ich nehme also die Bouletten, da habe ich beides.

Brunfaut hatte Angst. Er hatte eine solche Angst nie zuvor gehabt. Irgendetwas in ihm bäumte sich aber dagegen auf, zwang ihn geradezu, so zu tun, als würde er das alles nicht ernst nehmen. Auf seinem Bett lag sein Pyjama, wie eine körperlose Leiche. Auf einem Haken neben dem Bett hing schlaff sein Morgenmantel: Das war er, nach seinem Verschwinden. Er zog sich nicht aus, legte sich noch nicht ins Bett. Die Schwester ging. Er aß eine Waffel, nahm einen Schluck Tee, er lächelte, als er sich dabei ertappte, wie er mit angehaltenem Atem horchte und dann, die Zimmertür öffnend und nach rechts und links blickend, schaute, ob die Luft rein war. Er verließ das Zimmer, fuhr mit dem Lift hinunter ins Foyer, um in der Kantine ein Bier zu trinken.

Kein Alkohol in der Spitalskantine. Also trat er aus der Weltraumwelt hinaus, durch die neugotische Fassade ins Freie, ging ein paar Schritte im Strom der Menschen, die nicht an den Tod dachten, fand ein Straßencafé, bestellte ein Bier.

Ein kleines Bier, Monsieur?

Ein Großes, bitte.

Er saß so, dass er eine Apotheke vor Augen hatte.

Er schwitzte, wischte mit seinem Taschentuch den Schweiß

von der Stirn. Hatte er Fieber? Nein, es war einfach ein heißer Tag. Die Sonne brannte durch den Spalt zwischen zwei
Sonnenschirmen auf seinen Hinterkopf und Rücken. Er schob
seinen Stuhl ein Stück zur Seite, zog sein Sakko aus.

Da läutete sein Handy. Es war Philippe.

Hör zu, sagte er, ich habe einiges zu erzählen. Nicht am Telefon. Das Bild ist noch nicht klar, aber es gibt einige sehr
interessante – wie soll ich sagen? Symptome. Ich weiß nicht,
ob ich weitermachen kann, es ist sehr riskant. Wir müssen das
besprechen. Können wir uns morgen treffen?

Ich bin im Spital, sagte Brunfaut. Du weißt doch, ich werde
durchgecheckt. Morgen habe ich eine Reihe von Untersuchungen, aber –

Wie geht es dir? Was sagt der Arzt?

Wie du sagst: Interessante Symptome, aber das Bild ist noch
nicht klar. Kannst du morgen Abend?

Am frühen Abend. Halb sieben, sieben.

Gut. Dann besuche mich im Europa-Spital, Rue de Linthout. Wenn du mit der Metro kommst, dann ist das Station
Merode.

D'accord. Bis morgen.

Émile Brunfaut war in einem Zweibettzimmer untergebracht,
aber das zweite Bett war zum Glück nicht belegt. So konnte
er am Abend einige Anrufe erledigen, ohne einen anderen zu
nerven oder sich gezwungen zu fühlen hinauszugehen, er
konnte den Fernsehapparat, der gegenüber den Betten über
dem Esstisch an der Wand montiert war, einschalten und wieder ausschalten, ohne sich darüber mit jemandem einigen zu
müssen, er sah sich die Abendnachrichten an, es gab ein Interview mit dem Polizeipräsidenten, der den Vorwurf der
Untätigkeit zurückwies, es sei nun einmal schwer möglich,
eines Schweins habhaft zu werden, wenn man nicht wisse,

wann und wo es das nächste Mal zuschlagen werde. – Hat er jetzt wirklich »zuschlagen« gesagt, fragte sich Brunfaut. Da kam schon die Frage der Journalistin: Was er mit »zuschlagen« meine? Er meinte plötzlich auftauchen und Passanten verunsichern, wobei – entnervt schaltete Brunfaut den Fernseher ab, was er ebendeshalb konnte, weil er alleine im Zimmer war. So konnte er dann auch in einer sehr unruhigen Nacht hemmungslos unruhig sein, sich im Bett hin- und herwerfen, immer wieder aufstehen, im Bad Wasser trinken, auf die Toilette gehen, die Spülung betätigen, die so laut rauschte, dass er alleine schon erschrak, er konnte fluchen, wenn er sich auf dem Rückweg zum Bett an der Bettkante stieß, er konnte schnarchen und furzen, ohne angespannt darauf achten zu müssen, dezent zu sein.

Aber dieses Glück im Unglück war am nächsten Tag vorbei. Frühmorgens wurde er zu einem EKG abgeholt, und als er zurück ins Zimmer kam, befand sich ein Mann im zweiten Bett. Er lehnte am hochgeklappten Kopfteil des Bettes, er war sehr zart, sehr blass, fast durchsichtig, sein dünnes blondes Haar war streng gescheitelt. Er trug einen Nadelstreifenpyjama! Dunkelblaue Seide, die zarten Streifen in Orange. Er hatte die Beine angezogen, auf dem Schoß ein Laptop.

In Brunfauts Kopf pochte noch der Begriff »ventrikuläre Extrasystolen«, wie in Watte eingebettet in die beruhigenden Worte des Kardiologen. Und da war jetzt dieser Mann in seinem Zimmer – der so freudig grüßte, als wäre er begeistert, nun nicht mehr alleine zu sein. Brunfaut grüßte zurück, stand nun zwischen den beiden Betten, nickte dem Mann noch einmal zu und sah, dass auf der Brust seines Pyjamas ein Wappen aufgenäht war, eine hellblaue Schlange – was ...? Der Mann streckte Brunfaut die Hand entgegen, sagte: Ich bin Maurice Géronnez.

Sehr erfreut. Brunfaut sagte seinen Namen und verbeugte

sich, eigentlich beugte er sich nur etwas vor, um das Wappen besser sehen zu können, die Schlange war ein stilisiertes S, daneben stand Solvay, darunter Brussels School of Economics. Brunfaut war verblüfft. Er selbst besaß einen Schal und ein T-Shirt von RSC Anderlecht, seinem Patenkind Joëlle hatte er für die Taufe zum Spaß im Fan-Shop eine Strampelhose in den Anderlecht-Farben gekauft, aber er hatte noch nie erlebt oder gehört, dass jemand den Fan-Pyjama einer Universität trug.

Monsieur Géronnez wollte natürlich sofort Krankengeschichten austauschen, Brunfaut sagte kurz, dass er bloß für eine Durchuntersuchung hier sei, reine Vorsichtsmaßnahme.

Na ja, sagte Géronnez, sie werden schon etwas finden, sie finden immer etwas, ab fünfzig kann man Gift drauf nehmen, dass sie etwas finden, und wenn die Ärzte bei einem 50-plus-Mann nichts finden, dann frage ich mich, was haben die studiert? Dann muss man das Spital wechseln. Aber keine Angst, hier sind Sie in guten Händen, das Europa ist das beste Krankenhaus, hier finden sie immer etwas. Bei mir ist es die Milz. Ist es nicht seltsam? Ausgerechnet die Milz. Sie werden jetzt fragen, warum ist das seltsam? Sagen Sie mir, was macht die Milz, was ist ihre Aufgabe? Sehen Sie! Sie wissen es nicht. Niemand weiß das, fragen Sie Ihre Freunde, Ihre Bekannten, fragen Sie Menschen auf der Straße. Die Leber, ja! Das Herz, sowieso! Die Lunge, die Nieren, man muss nicht Medizin studiert haben, um zu wissen, was diese Organe tun, was ihre Funktion ist. Aber die Milz – na sagen Sie schon: Was ist die Aufgabe der Milz? Sehen Sie, das ist doch eigenartig! Die Milz führt ein Schattendasein. Dabei könnten all die anderen Organe, über die wir glauben Bescheid zu wissen und die wir für so wichtig halten, auf Dauer gar nicht arbeiten, wenn die Milz nicht wäre. Die Milz kontrolliert alle anderen Organe, weiß alles, überprüft sie ununterbrochen. Sie wehrt

Krankheiten der anderen Organe ab, entfernt schädliche Partikel aus dem Blut, speichert weiße Blutkörperchen, die sie bei Bedarf ausschüttet, man kann sagen: aussendet wie eine Eingreiftruppe. Das Herz merkt nicht, wenn die Leber ein Problem hat, oder umgekehrt, die Nieren versuchen ihren Job zu machen, egal ob die Lungenfunktion eingeschränkt ist oder nicht, aber die Milz, die merkt alles von allen und reagiert auf alle. Und alles, was die Milz tut, nehmen die anderen Organe wahr. Sie ist der große Kommunikator, zugleich der Geheimdienst, den keiner beachtet. Und warum beachtet keiner die Milz? Warum weiß keiner, was die Milz tut? Genau deshalb: weil sie in der Regel nicht auffällig wird. Die Milz ist das Organ, das nur ganz selten Probleme bereitet. Sie löst die Probleme anderer Organe, sie wehrt nach Möglichkeit deren Krankheiten ab, aber selbst wird sie so gut wie nie krank. Wissen Sie, was ich glaube? Ich glaube, dass wirklich etwas dran ist an dieser Theorie von der Psychosomatik. Das ist mein Verdacht. Sie können sich noch so gesund ernähren, Sie werden magenkrank, wenn Sie im übertragenen Sinn immer etwas runterschlucken müssen, verstehen Sie, was ich meine?

Ja, das ist bekannt.

Sehen Sie. Und bei mir ist es die Milz. Kein Zufall. Ich bin sozusagen beruflich eine Milz, und vor einiger Zeit habe ich bemerkt, ich schaffe es nicht mehr, ich konnte nicht mehr akzeptieren, was meine Aufgabe war, und –

Sie sind beruflich … was? Ich meine, Milz ist kein Beruf.

Brunfaut stöhnte.

Ich arbeite in der Europäischen Kommission, sagte Géronnez, in der ECFIN, das ist die Generaldirektion Wirtschaft und Finanzen. Ich bin verantwortlich für die Kommunikation. Ich bin sozusagen zwischen den verschiedenen Organen der Kommunikator, der im Schatten steht. Ich muss zusammenhalten und koordinieren, was da jeder vor sich hin arbeitet, alles aufbereiten und nicht zuletzt die Reden schreiben, mit denen der Kommissar das nach außen vertritt. So, und jetzt stellen Sie sich einen Organismus vor, die Lunge schwer belastet vom Kettenrauchen, die Leber von Alkoholexzessen, der Magen von Lebensmittelchemie, und Sie sollen das alles entgiften – und die Reden schreiben, mit denen der Mund verkündet, dass alles insofern in bester Ordnung ist, als die größten Anstrengungen unternommen werden, ein besseres Funktionieren des Organismus zu gewährleisten, zum Beispiel dadurch, dass zur Einsparung des Nägelschneidens nun alle Finger amputiert werden. Ich konnte das nicht mehr, Monsieur Brunfaut. Es hat vor drei Jahren begonnen, dass ich Schwierigkeiten bekam, weil ich nicht mehr funktionieren konnte. Damals bekam ich die Studie auf den Tisch, die die Webster und Portsmouth University gemeinsam mit der Wirtschaftsuniversität Wien durchgeführt hat – warten Sie!

Er klopfte auf die Tastatur seines Laptops! Hier! Ich habe das abgespeichert. The Impact of Fiscal Austerity on Suicide Mortality. Das ist fürchterlich, eine Langzeitstudie über den Zusammenhang zwischen den Sparprogrammen für Griechenland, Irland, Portugal und Spanien und der Entwicklung der Selbstmordraten in diesen Ländern. Ich will Sie da jetzt nicht mit Statistiken und Zahlen langweilen, aber nur so viel, hier: Mit Beginn des Sparprogramms in Griechenland stieg die Selbstmordrate im ersten Jahr um 1,4 Prozent, klingt wenig, eine kleine Zahl, aber bitte, das sind Menschen, und jetzt kommt es: Im dritten Jahr schnellt die Kurve dramatisch nach oben, und da haben wir eine Zahl, bei der wir von einer Epidemie sprechen müssen, und 91,2 Prozent der Suizid-Fälle betreffen Menschen über sechzig, deren Pensionen und Gesundheitsversicherungen gekürzt oder gar gestrichen wurden, im vierten Jahr wächst der Anteil der über Vierzigjährigen in der Suizidstatistik, überwiegend alleinstehende Langzeitarbeitslose. Im fünften Jahr entspricht der Rückgang der Arbeitslosenzahl mit einer marginalen Differenz von 0,8 Prozent der Anzahl der Suizidfälle des Jahres. Und jetzt umgekehrt, warten Sie – er tippte – hier: Irland. Das Lieblingsbeispiel meines Kommissars. Hier ist das Wirtschaftswachstum wieder angesprungen! Die Vorzugsschüler! Aber was zeigt diese Studie: Die zuvor dramatisch gestiegene Selbstmordrate ist nicht zurückgegangen. Die Studie zeigt, dass der Konjunkturaufschwung nicht dort ankam, wo zuvor das soziale Netz zerstört worden ist. Verstehen Sie?

Die zarten Nasenflügel des Mannes vibrierten.

Ich muss gestehen, ich war entrüstet, als ich das las. Ich schrieb ein Papier für den Kommissar, für die Mittwoch-Konferenz der Kommission, ich weiß noch, der erste Satz lautete: »Wir sind Mörder«, und machte einige Points, was er, also der Kommissar, vorschlagen müsse, damit die Kommission ihrer Aufgabe, dem Schutz der europäischen Bürger, gerecht werde. Ich schickte eine Kopie an den Generaldirektor, er ist immerhin zuständig für die Ökonomie der Mitgliedstaaten, jedenfalls, seit damals habe ich Beschwerden. Es ist die Milz, sie schafft die Entgiftung nicht mehr und –

In diesem Augenblick kam die Schwester herein. Monsieur Brunfaut? Ich bringe Sie zur Sonographie.

Brunfaut entschuldigte sich und folgte der Schwester. Ein Redenschreiber, der ununterbrochen redete, das war ihm zu viel. Auch wenn er sich eingestehen musste: Im Grunde war dieser Mann ein Waffenbruder.

Der Bluterguss auf Professor Erharts Unterarm, den er sich beim Sturz gegen den Heizkörper im Hotel zugezogen hatte, war zu einem dunkelblau verfärbten Fleck beträchtlichen

Ausmaßes geworden, der aussah wie ein schlechtgemachtes Tattoo der geographischen Fläche Europas.

Professor Erhart hatte sich nach der Sitzung der »Reflection Group« geweigert, zu einem gemeinsamen Abendessen mitzukommen, und war sofort mit der Metro nach Sainte-Catherine zurückgefahren. Nun saß er im Schanigarten der Brasserie Van Gogh, direkt neben der Kirche, er hatte im Vorbeigehen, auf dem Weg von der Metro-Station zum Hotel, die hier auf einem Eisbett drapierten Austern, Hummer und Krabben gesehen und sich kurzentschlossen an einen Tisch gesetzt, um es sich gutgehen zu lassen. Das war wörtlich sein Gedanke: Er wollte es sich gutgehen lassen. Als Trost. Zum Trotz. Nach dem demütigenden Eklat, den es vorhin bei der Sitzung gegeben hatte.

Es war Abend, aber immer noch so heiß, dass Professor Erhart sein Sakko auszog und über die Sessellehne hängte. Da sah er sein unfreiwilliges Tattoo. Er erschrak. Er tastete es sanft mit den Fingerkuppen ab, stöhnte leise, aber es war nicht der Schmerz, jedenfalls nicht der lokale, es war seine Verzweiflung, sein Seelenbrennen.

Er hatte sich aufgeführt wie einer dieser antiautoritären Studenten, mit denen er vor vielen Jahren als Professor zu tun bekommen hatte. Auch wenn er mit ihnen besser hatte umgehen können als die meisten seiner Kollegen, weil er imstande war, Talente zu erkennen und die Ideen ernst zu nehmen, für die sie glühten, war ihm doch völlig klar, dass ihm selbst ein solches Auftreten nicht anstand. Er war Professor und hatte sich nicht professoral verhalten. Konnte man sagen, dass er eben ein unkonventioneller Professor war? Nicht in diesen Zeiten, wo alles Unkonventionelle nur anerkannt wurde, wenn es gleich als Mainstream auftrat. Sein Verhalten war nur dumm und skandalös. Es wäre besser gewesen, er hätte bei der Sitzung des Think-Tanks möglichst lange geschwiegen, sich dann mit ein paar kurzen Statements zu Wort gemeldet und sich langsam diplomatisch vorgetastet. Aber es war so unfassbar dumm, was er sich hatte anhören müssen. Na und? Dummheit kann man auch ganz ruhig und sachlich beantworten. Wenn zum Beispiel ein Experte die These aufstellt, dass – bildlich gesprochen – unser Problem Übergewicht heißt und es die beste Methode zur Bekämpfung des Übergewichts wäre, noch mehr zu essen, um den Körper dazu zu zwingen, mehr auszuscheiden, und diese vermehrte Ausscheidung würde zu einer Gewichtsreduktion führen, dann musste man doch nicht brüllen und den Experten einen Idioten nennen. Es wäre ein Leichtes gewesen, es anders zu machen. Wirklich? Eben nicht. Das war ja das Gespenstische, dass in dieser Runde von Anfang an der Konsens geherrscht hatte, dass die Krise Europas nur mit eben den Methoden gelöst werden könne, die zu der Krise geführt hatten. More of the same. Diese oder jene Strategie hat nicht funktioniert? Dann wurde sie eben nicht konsequent genug umgesetzt! Konsequent weitermachen! More of the same! Mit dieser oder jener Entscheidung wurden die Probleme nur vergrößert? Nur vorübergehend! Nicht nachlassen mit diesen Anstrengungen! More of the same! Es hatte ihn wahnsinnig gemacht.

Er bestellte ein Dutzend Austern, und dann einen halben Hummer. Dazu einen Chablis.

Chablis haben wir nur in der Bouteille, Monsieur. Glasweise gibt es den Hauswein, einen Sauvignon.

Dann bringen Sie mir vom Chablis eine Flasche.

Er strich mit den Fingerkuppen immer wieder ganz sanft über seinen blauen Fleck.

Die Austern. Er schlürfte eine nach der anderen und fragte sich, warum er geglaubt hatte, dass er das genießen könne. Austern essen. Der Geschmack von Austern erinnerte ihn an keinen früheren Glücksmoment. Darum konnten sie ihn nicht glücklich machen. Das Beste am Lobster war, dass nicht viel dran war. Für die Zangen hatte er keine Geduld. Er hatte ja keinen Hunger. Er hatte es sich nur gutgehen lassen wollen. Eine halbe Flasche Wein hatte er schon getrunken. Auf dem Platz spielte ein Mann mit Ziehharmonika deutsche Schlager aus den dreißiger Jahren. Erhart kannte sie, seine Eltern hatten diese Platten gehabt. Jetzt genoss er doch etwas: das Ablecken der Finger, bevor er sie in die Tasse mit warmem Wasser und Zitronenscheiben tauchte.

Das Beste war, dass dieser eine deutsche Ökonom, mitten in der hitzigen Debatte, die auf Englisch geführt wurde, auf Deutsch zu Erhart sagte: »Mäßigen Sie sich!« Mäßigen! Ausgerechnet er sollte sich mäßigen in dieser maßlos dummen Diskussion. Ein griechischer Finanzexperte beschrieb minutiös, wie die griechische Haushaltsschuld zustande gekommen sei, und erklärte mit der Autorität eines Mannes, der sich nach Oxford in Sicherheit gebracht hatte, dass es ohne weitere tiefe Einschnitte in das griechische Sozialsystem nicht gehen werde. Ausgerechnet ein italienischer Politologe stimmte sofort zu und mahnte die Notwendigkeit an, die Stabilitätskriterien einzuhalten. Dabei gestikulierte er, beide Hände mit ausgestreckten Zeigefingern in Achter-Schleifen bewegend, als würde er einen Kinderchor dirigieren. Der französische Philosoph – Erhart hatte es zunächst spannend gefunden, dass auch ein Philosoph in diesen Think-Tank eingeladen worden war – insistierte darauf, die deutsch-französische Achse wieder zu stärken, eine Forderung, der selbst die Kollegin aus Rumänien zustimmte. Einen kleinen Meinungsunterschied gab es nur zwischen den beiden Deutschen, die sich nicht darauf einigen konnten, ob Deutschland seinen Führungsanspruch in Europa »mit mehr Selbstbewusstsein« oder aber »mit mehr Demut« ausüben sollte. So war es dahingegangen, und Erhart hatte sich gefragt, was mit diesen Menschen passiert war, dass sie, nach Jahren des Studiums und des Kampfes um Lehrstühle und verantwortungsvolle Positionen, nun nichts anderes wussten als dies: die seit Jahren und Jahren geübte Praxis jetzt als Desiderat für die künftige Politik zu formulieren. Dafür brauche ich keinen Think-Tank, hatte Erhart dazwischengerufen, dafür brauche ich nur eine Boulevard-Zeitung!

Dann ging es los, bis der eine Deutsche, der weit über die Grenzen der Fachschaft Wirtschaftswissenschaften der Universität Aachen hinaus unbekannt war, Erhart auf Deutsch zurief: »Mäßigen Sie sich!«

Ein britischer Professor für Kulturwissenschaften, Universität Cambridge, sagte, das Fundament des gemeinsamen Europas sei das Christentum und wir erlebten heute, dass uns diese einzige Gemeinsamkeit sowohl allgemein gesellschaftspolitisch als auch in unserem individuellen Verhalten abhandenkomme.

Da war Professor Erhart aufgesprungen und –

Nein, sagte er, er wolle kein Dessert. Er trank seine Flasche Wein aus, zahlte und ging. Er hatte alles erwartet, aber nicht die Karikatur von allem. Er kannte Kollegen in verschiedenen Ländern – er war mit ihnen in Kontakt –, mit denen man produktiv diskutieren konnte, es gab viele Initiativen, Stiftungen, NGOs, bei denen man voraussetzen konnte, dass sie wussten, worum es in Europa ging. Er korrespondierte mit ihnen, verfolgte ihre Blogs. Aber viel zu wenig sickerte in die breitere Öffentlichkeit durch. So hatte er eben große Hoffnungen in diesen »New Pact«-Think-Tank gesetzt, der direkt mit dem Präsidenten der Europäischen Kommission verbunden war. So nah an der Macht. Aber offenbar existierte so nah an der Macht nur noch eine Blase, so geistlos wie eine Seifenblase, aber doch unzerstörbar: Wenn man mit einer Nadelspitze hineinstach, platzte sie nicht, sondern trudelte elastisch nur noch höher. Er stolperte. Fast. Er fing sich. Das Brüsseler Pflaster. Die Menschen saßen in den Straßencafés und blinzelten in die untergehende Sonne. Ein Jongleur hielt vier, sechs, acht, acht! Bälle in der Luft. Der Ziehharmonikaspieler. Erhart warf ihm eine Münze in den Hut, er spielte Junge komm bald wieder! Touristen machten mit Selfie-Sticks Fotos vor der Kirche. Erhart überquerte den Platz, ging aber nicht weiter zum Hotel, sondern bog in die Rue Sainte-Catherine ab. Er ging ziellos, schaute ab und zu in Auslagen, erblickte aber immer nur sein bleiches Gesicht mit der großen schwarzen Brille und dem weißen Haar, das wie elektrisiert vom Kopf abstand. Er kam in die Rue des Poissoniers, sah dort an der Ecke ein Kaffeehaus, Café Kafka, fand das sinnig und kehrte auf ein Glas Wein ein. Nun war er schon gehörig beschwipst. Er hatte immer gerne getrunken, aber in der Regel in feierlichen Momenten, nicht aus Frust. Die Flasche Chablis hatte er vorhin nur deshalb bestellt, weil er gelernt hatte, zu Austern trinkt man Chablis. Seine Frau hatte solche Sachen gewusst. Trudi. Wenn sie noch lebte, würde er sie anrufen, und sie würde sagen: Du musst es morgen besser machen. Du hast eine Vision. Beschimpfe nicht die anderen! Versuche nur, ihnen deine Vision zu erklären.

Er zahlte und ging weiter. Er überquerte den Boulevard Anspach, sah linker Hand eine schöne alte Geschäftsfassade, sie wirkte wie ein elegantes Juweliergeschäft, er ging darauf zu, warum? Er brauchte keinen Schmuck. Trudi war tot. Und sie hatte sich auch nie etwas aus Geschmeide gemacht. Es war die Fassade. Auf dem Schild über dem Geschäft stand »Mystical Bodies«. Er sah in die Auslage. Nadeln und Stifte, mit Steinchen am einen Ende, Zeichnungen – was war das? Schließlich begriff er: Hier wurden Piercings und Tattoos angeboten.

Er trat ein. Ein junger Mann, der an einem großen leeren

Schreibtisch saß, wie man sich ihn im Büro eines Staatspräsidenten vorstellen würde, sah auf.

Erhart sagte, dass er gerne eine Tätowierung hätte. Er empfand die Situation als so unwirklich und zugleich plastisch wie eine intensive Traumfrequenz. Er hatte gedacht, dass Tätowierer selbst immer von oben bis unten tätowiert waren, aber dieser Junge hatte kein Tattoo, jedenfalls nicht sichtbar.

Sie wollen –

Ja, sagte Erhart und zog sein Sakko aus, streckte dem Jungen seinen Arm entgegen: Ich will 12 fünfzackige Sterne hier drauf, um dieses – auf diesen blauen Fleck.

Das ist ein Hämatom.

Ja.

Und ich soll Ihnen Sterne da drauf tätowieren?

Ja, bitte.

Aber warum?

Sieht es nicht aus wie Europa?

Wie bitte?

Sehen Sie! Das hier ist die Iberische Halbinsel, und dieser kleine Vorsprung ist doch eindeutig der Stiefel, oder?

Italien?

Ja. Und da, wo es ausfranst, ist Griechenland. Sieht man doch.

Okay, mit sehr viel Phantasie. Aber die Proportionen stimmen nicht, es ist, nein, das ist nicht Europa, das ist ein Zerrbild. Wie auch immer, es wird abheilen – hoffe ich zumindest für Sie.

Ich sehe in diesem Fleck Europa. Und ich will jetzt die Sterne dazu. Was würde das kosten?

Nein. Ich mache das nicht. Da sind Blutgefäße verletzt, Kapillaren geplatzt, da steche ich nicht rein, das kann ich nicht kontrollieren. Ich würde das nicht anrühren. Und in ein paar

Wochen ist das sowieso verschwunden. Dann hätten Sie da
Sterne, aber der Grund ist verschwunden, warum –
Also keine Sterne für ein verschwindendes Europa?
Sorry, Mann, ich mache das nicht.

Niemand in der Arche hatte sich vorstellen können, welch
gewaltigen Sturm das Jubilee Project in der Kommission
auslösen würde. Dabei hatte sich der Sturm genauso angekündigt, wie sich große Stürme eben ankündigen: durch eine
geradezu gespenstische Ruhe.
Zunächst hatte die Eurostat brav geliefert. Die Antwort war
ausführlich, gespickt mit Zahlen, aber nicht hilfreich.
Statisten! Hatte Bohumil achselzuckend auf Deutsch zu Martin gesagt.
Du meinst: Statistiker!
Ja.
Bereinigt von Zahlentabellen, Formeln und Graphiken teilte
die Eurostat etwas mit, das Martin so verblüffte, dass er das
Papier drei Mal las und dann noch eine Stunde ungläubig an-
starrte. Was der Referent der Eurostat schrieb, bedeutete im
Grunde, dass das Individuum bei allen statistikbasierten Hoch-
rechnungen ein Störfaktor sei, dachte Martin. Man könnte
die Auskunft auch so lesen: Gott mit seinem unerforschba-
ren Willen macht alle verfügbaren statistischen Daten über
Menschen letztlich zu Makulatur.
Man wisse, wie viele neunzigjährige Frauen und Männer heute
in Europa leben. Und man wisse, dass sich die Schere in der
Lebenserwartung zwischen Frauen und Männern mit zunehmendem Alter schließt. Neunzigjährige Frauen hätten heute
im statistischen Durchschnitt noch vier Jahre, Männer noch
dreidreiviertel Jahre Lebenserwartung. Die Zahl der Shoa-
Überlebenden im Jahr 1945 könne nur geschätzt werden. Über
das Verhältnis von Männern und Frauen gäbe es gar keine

Angaben. Aber wenn man nun davon ausgehe, dass sich die unterschiedliche Lebenserwartung von Männern und Frauen mit zunehmendem Alter ohnehin angleicht, und eine Hochrechnung der Lebenserwartung der Shoa-Überlebenden ohne Differenzierung nach Geschlecht vornehme, um herauszufinden, wie viele aller Wahrscheinlichkeit nach heute noch leben, so scheitere dieser Versuch daran, dass die Lebenserwartung in verschiedenen Ländern unterschiedlich hoch ist und man die Verteilung der Überlebenden auf diese Länder nicht kennt. Es mache einen Unterschied, ob es sich um einen Shoa-Überlebenden in Deutschland, in Polen, in Russland, in Israel oder in den USA handelt. Und dann müsste noch berücksichtigt werden, ob jemand begütert ist oder unterhalb der Armutsgrenze lebt. Es gebe die Schätzung eines israelischen Demographen aus dem Jahr 2005, siehe Anmerkung, dass 40 Prozent der Shoa-Überlebenden an oder unterhalb der Armutsgrenze leben. Diese Menschen hätten zweifellos die schlechtesten Karten, und man sei verführt anzunehmen, dass von diesen mittlerweile niemand mehr am Leben ist, was aber nicht belegt werden könne, weil eine andere Statistik dagegen spricht: Menschen, die in ihrer Jugend längere Hungerperioden erlebt haben, hätten eine höhere Lebenserwartung und könnten sich auch im Alter auf Mangel physisch besser einstellen als jene, die nie diesen physiologischen Anpassungsdruck erlebt haben. Nun sei aber bekannt, dass nicht nur Shoa-Überlebende, sondern auch große Teile der Zivilbevölkerung in den vom Krieg betroffenen oder in den besetzten Gebieten unter epidemischem Hunger gelitten hätten, weshalb es keine Formel gebe, mit der man die Lebenserwartung und die wahrscheinliche Zahl der heute noch lebenden Shoa-Überlebenden exklusiv herausrechnen könnte.

Und nun kam der Referent der Eurostat auf die eingangs erwähnte Lebenserwartung der heute Neunzigjährigen zurück.

Er schrieb: »Wenn wir davon ausgehen, dass die jüngsten der gegenwärtig noch lebenden Shoa-Überlebenden im Jahr 1929 geboren wurden – denn sie mussten bei Einlieferung in ein KZ zumindest 16 Jahre alt sein, alle Jüngeren gingen sofort ins Gas –, dann wissen wir auf Grund der Lebenserwartungsstatistiken nur, dass es eine gewisse Anzahl von Überlebenden geben muss. Aber selbst wenn wir ihre genaue Zahl wüssten, könnten wir nicht sagen, ob die Statistik auf sie noch zutrifft, das heißt, ob sie dem statistischen Mittelwert entsprechen. Sie alle müssen über neunzig Jahre alt sein, haben also theoretisch noch eine durchschnittliche Lebenserwartung von dreidreiviertel bis vier Jahren. Es ist aber möglich, dass schon in einem Jahr hundert Prozent der uns unbekannten Zahl verstorben oder aber hundert Prozent noch am Leben sind. Beides liegt innerhalb der Schwankungsbreite.« Und dann kam der Satz, der Martin nun vor den Augen tanzte, als stünde er in Großbuchstaben da: »DAS IST NICHT MEHR STATISTIK, DAS IST SCHICKSAL!«

Martin leitete diese Auskunft der Eurostat mit einem Kommentar an Xeno weiter. Er schlug vor, die Frage vorläufig offen zu lassen, ob man möglichst viele Shoa-Überlebende (soweit man sie erfassen könne) oder eine kleine, repräsentative Gruppe (Vertreter aus verschiedenen Ländern) oder nur einen exemplarischen Repräsentanten in den Mittelpunkt der Jubiläumsfeier stellen sollte. Entscheidend sei zunächst, ganz allgemein Zustimmung zu der Idee zu bekommen: Das Jubiläum sollte als Gelegenheit wahrgenommen werden, einer breiten europäischen Öffentlichkeit zu zeigen, dass die Kommission nicht bloß »die Hüterin der Verträge der Union« sei (so wie es auf der Homepage der Kommission stand), sondern vor allem auch die Hüterin des größeren und umfassenderen Schwurs, dass sich ein europäischer Zivilisationsbruch wie Auschwitz nie wieder ereignen würde. Diese »Ewigkeitsklausel«, schrieb Martin, müsse als das eigentliche Herz der Kommission vermittelt werden, denn sie mache die Kommission nicht bloß zu einer abstrakten »Bürokratie«, sondern »zu einer moralischen Instanz«, wobei durch die Präsentation letzter Testimonials der Shoa der notwendige emotionale Bezug der Öffentlichkeit zur Arbeit der Kommission hergestellt werden könne. Das schlechte Image der Kommission beruhe letztlich darauf, dass sie als Apparat einer bloßen Wirtschaftsgemeinschaft gesehen werde, die für eine Wirtschaftspolitik stehe, die von immer mehr Menschen abgelehnt wird. Nun müsse konsequent an die Grundidee erinnert werden, mit den Worten von Jean Monnet: »Alle unsere Anstrengungen sind die Lehre unserer historischen Erfahrung: Nationalismus führt zu Rassismus und Krieg, in radikaler Konsequenz zu Auschwitz.«

Aus diesem Grund hat der erste Kommissionspräsident, der Deutsche Walter Hallstein, seine Antrittsrede in Auschwitz gehalten. Später ist diese Idee von den Kommissionspräsidenten Jacques Delors und Romano Prodi aufgegriffen worden. Und auch der neue Präsident habe am 27. Januar bei der Befreiungsfeier in Auschwitz gesprochen und dort festgehalten, dass »die wirtschaftliche Verflechtung der Nationen nicht Selbstzweck zur bloßen Generierung von Wirtschaftswachstum« sei, sondern »notwendige Voraussetzung für den tieferen Sinn des Europäischen Projekts: in Zukunft nationalen Eigensinn und somit letztlich den Nationalismus zu verhindern, der zu Ressentiments und Aggressionen gegen andere, zur Spaltung Europas, zu Rassismus und letztlich zu Auschwitz« führe.

Abschließend schrieb Martin in seiner Mail an Xeno, dass er dringend empfehle, das Projekt nicht aus dem EU-Haushalt, sondern ausschließlich aus dem Budget der Kommission zu finanzieren. Auf diese Weise wären keine Abstimmungen mit

dem Rat und dem Parlament nötig (mit den absehbar lang-
wierigen Verhandlungen und letztlich unproduktiven Kom-
promissen), und der Image-Gewinn käme am Ende zur Gän-
ze der Kommission zugute.

Xeno setzte Mrs Atkinson in Kenntnis und bat um Zustimmung, das Projekt ausschließlich mit Mitteln aus dem Kommissionsbudget zu finanzieren. Mrs Atkinson hatte allerdings inzwischen andere Sorgen. Vor einigen Tagen war in
sozialen Netzwerken das Gerücht aufgetaucht, dass die Kommission, bestochen von Lobbyisten der großen Pharmakon-
zerne, ein Verbot der Homöopathie plane. Eineinhalb Millionen Protestmails aus ganz Europa waren innerhalb eines
Tages eingegangen und hatten den Server der Kommission
fast zum Absturz gebracht. Die deutsche BILD-Zeitung brachte die Falschmeldung in Riesenlettern als Aufmacher, wenn
auch mit Fragezeichen, »Brüsseler Beamte durchgeknallt?«.
Auch die Sun, die Kronenzeitung, die Blesk, A Hola und sogar El País, France Soir und, wenn auch nicht auf Seite eins,
Libération berichteten. Und alle diese brüllenden Meldun-
gen mündeten in den Aufruf, gegen die Konzerne und ihre
Lobbyisten bei der Kommission zu protestieren. Mrs Atkinson saß händeringend an ihrem Schreibtisch. Ihre langen zarten Finger waren kalt und bläulich. Sie knetete, drückte und
massierte sie, während sie darüber nachdachte, auf welche
Weise sie diesem Unsinn wirkungsvoll entgegentreten konnte. Eine Presseaussendung mit klarem Dementi hatte nur die
Neue Zürcher Zeitung aufgegriffen, was aber zu einem neu-
erlichen Shitstorm in den Sozialen Medien führte: man kenne
doch die Konzerne, die in der Schweiz ihren Sitz hatten. Atkinson fragte sich, warum Medien, die man wohl kaum als
antikapitalistische Kampfblätter bezeichnen konnte, mit solcher Wollust zu einem Kampf gegen Konzerne aufriefen –

und dabei vor allem die Europäische Kommission prügelten, die doch selbst einen Kampf gegen die unkontrollierte Macht von Konzernen führte. Hatte die Kommission nicht erst unlängst Strafen in Milliardenhöhe gegen Microsoft und Amazon durchgesetzt?

Mrs Atkinson war ausgebildete Ökonomin und keine Kommunikationsexpertin, auch wenn dies nun ihr Arbeitsgebiet war. Sie war angetreten, um das Image der Kommission zu verbessern, sie hatte eine Offensive geplant und war seither nur in der Defensive. Der Kommissionspräsident hatte sie wegen dieser Homöopathie-Geschichte zu sich bestellt: Ob sie einen Plan habe, wie diese Rufschädigungen gestoppt und die Leistungen der Kommission besser kommuniziert werden könnten.

Ja. Selbstverständlich.

Und wann werde man die Wirkung dieses Plans sehen können?

Das könne sie jetzt nicht sagen.

Er würde – vorsichtig formuliert – einen Plan nur dann einen Plan nennen, wenn eine wünschenswerte Wirkung realistisch und auch bald überprüfbar wäre.

Yes, Sir.

Sie knetete ihre Hände. Fenia Xenopoulous Idee brachte sie jetzt nicht weiter. Aber sie war dankbar für deren Einsatz. Mittel- oder langfristig konnte sie helfen. Sie schrieb zurück: »Ich sage Finanzierung aus Kommissionsbudget zu – erbitte aber genauen Kostenplan, Auflistung der benötigten Ressourcen, auch personell. Go ahead!«

Xeno gab nun Martin ihr Okay. Bitte bis morgen eine »note« für die Inter-Service Consultation. Mit: Voraussichtliche Höhe der nötigen Finanzmittel, Zeitplan, erforderliche

Ressourcen, auch personell, gewünschte Beiträge der anderen DGs.

Danach suchte sie pflichtbewusst unter all den Papieren auf ihrem Schreibtisch, auf dem Beistelltisch und im Regal den Roman, den sie nun schon seit gut drei Wochen nicht mehr weitergelesen hatte, den Lieblingsroman des Präsidenten. Sie hatte endlich von seinem Büro einen Termin bekommen. Das traf sich gut. Nun hatte sie etwas, das sie herzeigen konnte: das Projekt, mit dem sie die Kultur, dieses Mauerblümchen in der Kommission, in den Mittelpunkt der öffentlichen Aufmerksamkeit stellen würde. Wer das schaffte, und das musste der Präsident doch einsehen, sollte eine wichtigere Position in der Kommission bekommen. Am besten in der DG TRADE, wo sie mit Fridsch zusammenarbeiten könnte. Andererseits: War es gut, so eng mit dem Mann zusammenzuarbeiten, den sie – was? Sie hatte eine Scheu, das Wort »lieben« auch nur zu denken. Und sie hatte das Gefühl, dass auch er erst lernen musste, eine gewisse professionelle Distanz zu überwinden. Während des Abendessens neulich beim Italiener war er auf eine Weise höflich und freundlich gewesen, wie man es gegenüber guten Bekannten oder geschätzten Mitarbeitern war, aber dann, als sie miteinander ins Bett gingen, da hat er am Ende geweint. Das ist nur Schweiß, sagte er, als sie ihm die Tränen aus dem Gesicht wischte, aber sie war sich ganz sicher, es waren Tränen des Glücks und der Rührung.

Da fand sie den Roman. Sie wusste ja, was sie mit dem Präsidenten besprechen wollte, aber sie dachte, es würde bestimmt nicht schaden, wenn sie, in seinem Lieblingsbuch lesend, sich noch ein bisschen mehr auf ihn einstimmen würde.

Sie blätterte hin und her, schließlich begann sie an irgendeiner Stelle zu lesen – und hielt schockiert inne, als sie diesen Satz las: »Einmal ließ sie eine Kosmetikerin kommen, um Schminkvarianten auszuprobieren für die Zeit, da sie im Sarg liegen würde, betrauert von ihrem weinenden Geliebten.« Was sie schockierte, war, dass sie sich augenblicklich selbst in dieser Situation sah: im Sarg liegend, perfekt geschminkt, mit einem Lächeln, wie es nur der Gedanke an den Geliebten beim Eintritt in die Ewigkeit ins Gesicht zaubern kann. Und Fridsch –

Achtes Kapitel

»Get into trouble, good trouble.«

Um die Pietà herum rotierte Blaulicht, über der Pietà kreise
der Rettungshubschrauber. Immer mehr Menschen, Männer
und Frauen, Alte, Junge und Kinder, strömten in diese Szene, manche blieben erschrocken stehen, schauten, aber die
meisten begannen zu laufen, liefen auf die Polizisten zu, die
in einer Reihe quer über der Fahrbahn standen, mit ausgestreckten Armen. Halt! Stehenbleiben! Die Polizisten versuchten, die Menschen aufzuhalten, die Autobahn zu sper-
ren, damit der Rettungshubschrauber landen konnte, aber
die anwachsende Menschenmasse stürmte auf sie zu und
an ihnen und den quer stehenden Polizeiautos vorbei. Diese
Menschen verstanden die Situation nicht, sie sahen nicht die
Verletzten, maßen den Autowracks keine Bedeutung bei, sie
dachten nur, dass sie hier aufgehalten und wieder zurückge-
schickt werden sollten, vielleicht hielten sie den Rettungshubschrauber für einen Polizei- oder Militärhubschrauber,
eine hilflose Drohgebärde des österreichischen Grenzschut-
zes, das konnte sie nicht aufhalten, sie hatten die ungarisch-
österreichische Grenze passiert, so weit waren sie schon gekommen, sie wollten weiter nach Deutschland, sie ließen sich
nicht mehr aufhalten.

Es waren auch bereits Journalisten da, die filmten und fotografierten und im Weg standen. Und das Bild der Pietà inmitten dieses Chaos sollte um die Welt gehen: die schwarz
gekleidete Frau mit Kopftuch, die auf einem Koffer saß,
quer über ihrem Schoß lag ein Mann im Business-Anzug.
In ihrem Gesicht der Regen wie Tränen. Mit ihrer Rechten
stützte sie seinen Kopf, die Linke hatte sie in die Höhe ge-
streckt, den Kopf zurückgeworfen, blickte sie nach oben, auf

dem Foto wirkte es, als klagte die Frau mit dem Kopftuch verzweifelt den Himmel an. Sie schaute hinauf zum Hubschrauber.

Dieser Frau war am schnellsten klar gewesen, dass der Mann irgendwie stabilisiert werden musste.

Sie hatte, ihren Koffer hinter sich herziehend, das Krachen, den Knall gehört, etwas, das sich anhörte wie eine Explosion, sie hatte, noch ohne etwas zu verstehen, gesehen, wie die Menschen vor ihr auseinanderliefen, zur Seite sprangen, schrien, und plötzlich war sie vor dem Autowrack gestanden, aus dem ein stöhnender Mann heraushing.

Das war Florian Susman.

Menschen waren ihm zu Fuß auf der Autobahn entgegengekommen, Polizeiwagen waren mit Blaulicht und Sirenen an ihm vorbeigefahren und ein Stück weiter vorn stehen geblieben. Er war nur noch Schritttempo gefahren, hatte schließlich ganz abgebremst und den Wagen angehalten. Er hatte die Warnblinkanlage eingeschaltet. Er hatte einen Polizisten gesehen, der, einen Leuchtstab schwenkend, auf ihn zukam. Der Polizist war vielleicht noch zwanzig Meter entfernt gewesen, als er plötzlich schrie, auf eine Weise schrie, dass Florian für den Bruchteil einer Sekunde, die zugleich ein Moment der Ewigkeit war, nur dieses Schreien sah, er sah den offenen Mund des Polizisten durch die regennasse Windschutzscheibe wie herbeigezoomt und dabei grotesk verzerrt. Da hechtete der Polizist zur Seite.

An das Krachen, den gewaltigen Stoß, das aggressive Geräusch des brechenden Blechs, das Knallen der explodierenden Reifen konnte sich Florian später nicht erinnern, nur an diesen ganz kurzen Moment, in dem er sich mit einem Staunen, das größer war als Schock und Schmerz, als Gefangener in einer engen Kapsel fühlte, die von einer unfassbaren Macht hin und her geschleudert wurde. Er sah, eingeklemmt, verwischte Bilder, an denen er entlangschlitterte, ein wirrer Film, seltsamerweise ohne Ton.

Er kam erst im Unfallkrankenhaus wieder ganz kurz zu Bewusstsein, als ihm mit einer großen Schere die Kleidung vom Leib geschnitten wurde. Er schlug die Augen auf, die Schere fuhr über seinen Oberkörper, teilte sein Polohemd, er wurde gleichsam aufgeklappt, er sah ein Gesicht vor sich, hörte: Verstehen Sie mich? Können Sie mich verstehen?

Er sagte etwas von Schweinen, die Schweine, es war nicht verständlich, dann verlor er wieder das Bewusstsein.

Ein burgenländischer Taxifahrer, der schon mehrmals an diesem Tag zum Grenzübergang Nickelsdorf gerast war, um Flüchtlinge nach Wien zum Westbahnhof zu bringen, von wo sie mit Zügen nach München weiterfahren konnten, hatte eilig die nächste Fuhre holen wollen, es war ein schnelles gutes Geschäft, jeder dieser armen Teufel zahlte anstandslos den dreifachen Fuhrlohn. Er hatte in seiner Eile, seiner Gier, seiner Hektik, nicht gesehen, dass der Verkehr vor ihm zum Stillstand gekommen war. So ist er ungebremst in Florian Susmans Wagen hineingedonnert.

Die Frau, die Florian mit Hilfe ihres Sohns vorsichtig aus dem Wrack gehoben, ihn dann auf ihren Schoß gelegt und seinen Kopf gehalten hatte, war seine Rettung. Florian hatte einen gebrochenen Rückenwirbel, aber seine vorsichtige Bergung und Stabilisierung hatte verhindert, dass das Rückenmark verletzt wurde, sonst wäre er gelähmt gewesen. Das verstand Florian erst, als Martin ihm die Zeitungen mit dem Foto der Pietà ins Krankenhaus mitbrachte. »Du bist auf dem Cover!«

Auf Grund dieses Fotos war das christliche Abendland, das sich vor dem Ansturm der Muslime fürchtete, eine historische Sekunde lang sentimental berührt. Die Muslima, die Florian rettete, war eine Madonna.

Was wäre alles anders gekommen, wenn Florian diesen Unfall nicht gehabt hätte? Vielleicht hätte Martin Susman die Turbulenzen, die sein Jubilee-Papier auslöste, verhindern oder zumindest eindämmen können, wenn er in Brüssel geblieben wäre, statt sofort nach Wien zu fliegen, um seinem Bruder beizustehen. So aber kam es, während Martin sich in Wien um seinen Bruder kümmerte, in der Europäischen Kommission in Brüssel zu Konflikten und Auseinandersetzungen, die sich sehr schnell auf eine Weise hochschaukelten, dass es keine rationale Lösung mehr geben konnte und nicht einmal einen Kompromiss. Und wer war an dieser Aufregung schuld, wer hatte diese verrückte Idee gehabt? Mrs Atkinson? Xeno? Martin.

Allerdings: Kann es Schuldige geben, wenn jeder nur seine Pflicht tut? Was ist Pflicht? Die Einhaltung der bürokratischen Regeln, der festgelegten Verfahren? Oder die Verteidigung von Interessen, denen man verpflichtet ist oder sich verpflichtet fühlt? Alles wird zwischen den großen Rädern oben und den kleinen Rädchen unten zermahlen, und am Ende ist nichts geschehen, auch wenn das Krachen und Knirschen des Mahlvorgangs zunächst Nervosität und Aufregung verursacht hat. Dabei waren Xeno und er, vor seiner Abreise nach Wien, noch völlig sicher gewesen, dass das Jubilee Project nun reibungslos seinen Lauf nehmen würde. Sie hatten die Ruhe vor dem Sturm bereits für das Fehlen von Einwänden, für stillschweigende Zustimmung gehalten. Und sie fühlten sich bestätigt und geschützt durch die Aufmunterung und den Schutz von »ganz oben«.

Xeno hatte nämlich endlich den Termin beim Kommissionspräsidenten bekommen, zwei Tage vor dem Inter-Service-Meeting, das sie wegen des Jubilee Project einberufen hatte. Also in Wahrheit nicht beim Präsidenten höchstselbst, sondern bei seinem Kabinettschef. Schon dies war aber eine Auszeichnung, eine Anerkennung ihrer Arbeit und ein deutliches Interesse an ihrer Person, denn in der Regel bekamen Beamte in der Position Xenos einen Termin höchstens bei einem Mitarbeiter des Kabinetts. War dieses Privileg vielleicht die Folge der Interventionen von Fridsch, der sie nachdrücklich für höhere Weihen empfohlen hatte? Andererseits: Hatte sie nicht noch mehr erwartet, nämlich einen Termin beim Präsidenten selbst? Hatte sie sich aus diesem Grund nicht minutiös auf ihn vorbereitet, seine Biographie, seine Vorlieben, seine Schrullen studiert, sogar sein Lieblingsbuch gelesen? Aber das ist ihr dann doch klar geworden, als ihr dieser Termin in Aussicht gestellt (»Worum geht es?«, »Wir werden uns bemühen!«), sie aber immer wieder vertröstet wurde, bis Fridsch ihr schließlich sagte: Ein Termin beim Präsidenten ist bloß ein Termin mit einem Mitarbeiter seines Kabinetts! Erst recht, wenn man von der Kultur kommt.

Er lächelte.

Stell dir vor, sagte er, dass der Präsident gar nicht wirklich existiert. Nach Jacques Delors gab es keinen Präsidenten mehr! Danach gab es nur noch Marionetten. Das Kabinett zieht die Fäden. Jedes Wort, das der Präsident sagt, sagen seine Bauchredner. Alles, was er entscheidet, ist längst entschieden, und wenn er etwas unterschreibt, wird seine Hand geführt. Hast du im Fernsehen gesehen, wie der Präsident bei einem Treffen mit Staatschefs den einen plötzlich an der Krawatte zieht und dem anderen einen kleinen Schubs gibt? Das ist das einzig Unvorbereitete und Eigenständige, was er sich erlauben kann, sozusagen seine persönliche Note in dieser Mechanik der Macht, das ist sein ironisches Spiel: Er, der an so vielen Fäden hängt, macht sich pantomimisch darüber lustig, indem er zieht und schubst, als wäre er selbst der Strippenzieher. Also, hatte Fridsch gesagt, du wirst deinen Termin beim

Präsidenten bekommen, aber erwarte nicht einen Termin mit der Marionette.

Und dann saß Xeno dem Kabinettschef des Kommissionspräsidenten gegenüber, Romolo Strozzi, der, wie sie seinem Wikipedia-Eintrag entnommen hatte, mit vollem Namen Romolo Augusto Massimo Strozzi hieß, letzter und kinderloser Spross einer alten italienischen Adelsfamilie. Es kursierten in den europäischen Institutionen einige Anekdoten über ihn und seine sehr unkonventionelle Art, er galt als »bunter Hund«, und Xeno stellte erstaunt fest, dass das womöglich auch ganz wörtlich zu verstehen war: Strozzi trug einen blauen Anzug, ein gelbes Einstecktuch, eine rote Anzugweste, die seinen Bauch hervorhob und zugleich zusammenhielt. Er war nicht dick, nur gerade so mollig, dass er, nicht zuletzt auch mit dem Signalrot seiner Weste, demonstrierte, wahrlich kein Asket zu sein. Das war ungewöhnlich auf dieser Ebene der Macht, die beherrscht war von den »Enarchen«, den Absolventen von Kaderschmieden wie der École Nationale d'Administration, sehr schlanke Männer mit unauffälligen, nicht zu teuren Anzügen, asketisch in jeder Hinsicht: fähig, stunden- und nächtelang zu verhandeln. Sie schienen kaum Essen zu brauchen und so gut wie keinen Schlaf, sie kamen mit wenigen Worten aus, mit wenigen Gesten, sie vermieden die Überzuckerung ihrer Seele durch die Süße der Empathie, sie brauchten keine Öffentlichkeit, ihnen genügte der Stoffwechsel im Inneren der Macht, sie entsagten dem äußeren Glanz. Es gab in ihrem Leben und in ihrer Arbeit kein Ornament, alles war so klar wie unsichtbar. Diesen Typus Mann konnte Xeno professionell einschätzen, das hatte sie gelernt und darauf war sie in ihren Eliteschulen vorbereitet worden, damit hatte sie in ihrer bisherigen Karriere Erfahrungen gemacht – und nun saß sie diesem barocken italienischen Grafen gegenüber, der ihr sein rotes Bäuchlein entgegenstreckte und wie ein Operetten-dirigent mit großer Gestik sprach, wobei sein Siegelring vor ihren Augen tanzte. Es war nicht lächerlich, es war durchaus ehrfucht- und respektgebietend, anders wäre es bei einem Mann in seiner Position auch nicht vorstellbar gewesen. Es war nur so, dass Xeno von seiner Art verwirrt war und nicht damit zurechtkam. Er war nicht nur perfekt in Italienisch, Deutsch, Englisch und Französisch, er eröffnete das Gespräch lippenleckend vor Vergnügen auf Altgriechisch. Als Xeno ihn nur fassungslos anschaute, entschuldigte er sich: sein Neu-griechisch sei leider so rudimentär, dass es ihr Schmerzen bereiten würde. Und er vergesse immer wieder, dass Alt-griechisch für Griechen eine so fremde Sprache sei wie Kisua-heli.

Ἐν ἀρχῇ ἦν ὁ λόγος, sagte er und fügte hinzu: Ἀλλ' ὁ λόγος ἦν ἁμαρτοεπής. Am Anfang war das Wort. Aber das Wort ist falsch gewesen. Je suis désolé, sagte er lachend.

Xeno war eingeschüchtert vom Überfall seiner Heiterkeit. Sie hatte sich unmittelbar vor diesem Termin über den Conte Strozzi schlaugemacht, um ihn einschätzen zu können, um nicht überrascht zu werden und in der Verhandlung mit ihm möglichst schnell richtig reagieren zu können. Aber sie be-griff erst jetzt, zu spät, was all das wirklich bedeutete, was sie über ihn gehört und gelesen hatte: Die Strozzis waren bereits vom römisch-deutschen Kaiser Friedrich II. in den Adels-stand erhoben worden, sie waren verwandt und verschwägert mit österreichischem, deutschem und tschechischem Hoch-adel. Romolo Strozzis Großvater war ein Kriegsverbrecher als Kommandant einer Einheit der 9. Italienischen Armee, die 1941 und 1942 in Montenegro Massenerschießungen durch-führte, aber sein Vater wurde 1964 als Absolvent der diplo-matischen Akademie jüngstes Mitglied des Verhandlungs-teams, das für die italienische Regierung den Fusionsvertrag der Europäischen Gemeinschaft vorbereitete, der zur Einsetzung des gemeinsamen Rats und der Kommission führte. Sein österreichischer Großonkel Nikolaus Graf Khevenhüller war ein fanatischer Nationalsozialist, der noch im Januar 1945 stellvertretender Gauleiter von Kärnten wurde, aber gleich Anfang Mai nach Spanien abtauchte, wo er bis zu seinem Tod 1967 als »Berater« der spanischen Geheimpolizei DGS mit einem Ehrensold von Generalísimo Franco unbehelligt lebte. Seine Großtante Marion, eine von Tirpitz, wiederum heiratete den deutschen Widerstandskämpfer Ulrich Hesse, war eine sozialdemokratische Kommunalpolitikerin in Hannover und Sekretärin des Verbands der Opfer des Nationalsozialismus.

Diese Familiengeschichte war wohl der Grund für das berühmteste Zitat, das Romolo Strozzi zugeschrieben wurde: »L'Europe, c'est moi!«

Eine solche Familiengeschichte war natürlich faszinierend, aber für Xeno letztlich auch rätselhaft: Es war ihr völlig wesensfremd, dass all dies fortwirken und die Biographie eines Menschen prägen konnte. Sie hatte ein Familienbild, dem zufolge Vorfahren etwas waren, woüber man erst etwas wusste, seit es Fotografien gab, und auch dann wusste man nicht viel mehr als die Namen, im Grunde waren es Menschen, die wahrscheinlich nicht viel anders gelebt hatten als die Eltern, Menschen, die zusammenhielten und sich halfen, gefangen in ihren Verhältnissen, das musste so gewesen sein, denn es gab keine Geschichten über sie, sie haben keine Geschichten gemacht, nur ab und zu gab es einen Sonderfall wie ihren Onkel Kostas, das war der mit der unsterblichen Liebe, und dann, am Ende, gab es den radikalen Bruch: Das war sie selbst, die alles zurückgelassen hatte. Als Xeno den ausführlichen Wikipedia-Eintrag über Romolo Strozzi gelesen hatte, war sie von all den Herkunfts- und Familiengeschichten dieses Mannes nicht

sonderlich beeindruckt gewesen: Das war für sie Geklimper –
Strozzi war Kabinettschef des Kommissionspräsidenten, aber
der Eintrag tat so, als wäre er hauptberuflich Nachfahre, und
das fand Xeno verrückt. Wirklich erstaunt und beeindruckt
hatte sie eine andere Information: Romolo Strozzi hatte bei
den Olympischen Sommerspielen 1980 eine Medaille im
Fechten gewonnen: Bronze in Säbel Einzel.

Hast du das gewusst?, hatte sie Fridsch gefragt.

Ja, hatte er gesagt, das habe ich gehört. Das waren die Spiele
in Moskau. Man sagt, dass Strozzi davon profitiert habe, dass
sehr viele Länder, ich weiß nicht wie viele, damals die Spiele
boykottiert haben, wegen des Einmarsches sowjetischer Trup-
pen in Afghanistan. Dadurch waren einige Weltklasse-Fech-
ter gar nicht dabei.

Aber er hat sich qualifiziert, er hat gekämpft, und er hat eine
Medaille gemacht.

Ja, das hat er. Und weißt du, was interessant ist? Das hat mir
Queneau erzählt, als wir einmal über Strozzi sprachen: Die
Italiener haben die Spiele zwar nicht boykottiert, aber sie
sind auch nicht unter ihrer Nationalflagge angetreten. Sondern unter der olympischen Fahne: die fünf Ringe auf weißem
Grund. Und bei den Siegerehrungen italienischer Sportler
wurde nicht ihre Nationalhymne gespielt, sondern die Ode
an die Freude. Die Familie Strozzi soll damals großen Einfluss auf diese Entscheidung des italienischen Olympischen
Komitees gehabt haben.

Xeno sah Strozzi an, der Siegelring tanzte vor ihren Augen,
und was sie über diesen Mann mit dem roten Bäuchlein im
Kopf hatte, war: Olympia-Medaille im Fechten! Sie kannte
sich bei diesem Sport nicht aus. Warum sollte sie? Strozzi hatte seine Medaille mit dem Säbel gewonnen. Das war nicht
Florett. Hätte Xeno den Unterschied gekannt, sie hätte jetzt
auch den Gesprächsverlauf besser einschätzen können.

Sie hatte erwartet, dass er ohne Umschweife zur Sache kommen würde. Solche Männer haben wenig Zeit. Er würde sie geradeheraus fragen, was er für sie tun könne, dann Interesse zeigen oder Interesse heucheln, und sie müsste sehr schnell und sehr präzis ihr Anliegen so vorbringen, dass seine Reaktion in Richtung »Interesse haben« ausschlägt. Aber zu ihrer Verblüffung sagte er: Wissen Sie, was mich interessiert? Da hätte ich jetzt gerne Ihre Meinung. Was sagen Sie zum Burkini-Verbot? Sie als Frau. Würde mich wirklich interessieren. Sind Sie der Meinung, dass Männer wie der Bürgermeister von Nizza bestimmen dürfen, was Frauen anzuziehen haben, besser gesagt, in diesem Fall: dass sie sich ausziehen müssen? Eine Frau muss sich ausziehen, das ist unsere christliche Kultur? Ja? Was sagen Sie? Wenn Sie wüssten, wie viele Anfragen wir da haben. Dass die Kommission hier Stellung nehmen müsse.

Xeno war sprachlos.

Strozzi lächelte. Bisschen viel verlangt, sagte er. Also ich bin ja privat der Meinung, dass der Burkini die Frauen vor Hautkrebs schützt.

Xeno wusste nicht, ob Strozzi im Ernst erwartete, dass sie –

Aber der Ruf nach einem Verbot wird immer lauter, sagte er. Auf welcher Grundlage könnten wir das tun? Kampf gegen Fanatismus und Orthodoxie? Es gibt keine Richtlinie, die uns dazu verpflichtet. Zum Glück. Wir könnten in Europa das Licht ausmachen und den Laden schließen. Denn wir müssten dann auch den Kaftan und den Streimel verbieten, und –

Den was?

Den Streimel. Das ist dieser riesige runde Pelzhut der orthodoxen Juden.

Aber da gibt es schon einen Unterschied, sagte Xeno fast ohne Stimme.

Natürlich gibt es einen Unterschied. Bei allem, was sich gleicht, gibt es Unterschiede. Und alles, was sich von anderem unterscheidet, gleicht sich! Ich sage Ihnen etwas: Wir müssten dann sogar die Businessanzüge verbieten. Ich bin hier im Haus umzingelt von Männern in Businessanzügen. Das ist wie eine Uniform. Schauen alle gleich aus. Es ist furchterregend. Und glauben Sie mir, alle diese Männer sind auf ihre Weise Orthodoxe und Fanatiker. Würden Sie jetzt sagen, die sollen ihre Anzüge ausziehen?

Xeno sah Strozzi fassungslos an, der lachte, sich zurücklehnte und die Arme weit ausbreitete. Dann beugte er sich vor, immer noch lächelnd, aber nun wohlig auf ernste Neugier umschaltend, und sagte: Aber ich will Ihre kostbare Zeit nicht stehlen. Sagen Sie mir geradeheraus, was ich für Sie tun kann.

Dass Strozzi sagte, er wolle ihre Zeit nicht stehlen, war nicht nur die ironische Umkehrung der Situation, es war eine klassische Kreisfinte, wie ein Fechter sagen würde. Xeno konnte ihm nicht in die Parade fahren, weil sie nicht einmal wusste, was eine Parade ist. Sie hatte keine Vorstellung davon, wie das Fechten einen Mann prägen kann. Darum war sie, die sich immer so genau auf jede Situation vorbereitete, auf Strozzi in Wahrheit überhaupt nicht vorbereitet. Das Umgehen der klaren Absicht des anderen, das Ausweichen und Antäuschen, der Aufbau der Finten, Kreisfinte, Stoßfinte, Hiebfinte, und dann der Treffer, nach einem plötzlichen, unerwarteten Ausfall. Und ehe der andere es sich versieht, ist alles vorbei, man schüttelt sich die Hand, mit dem Ausdruck des Respekts und größter Ehrerbietung. Und schon wurde Xeno von einem Stagiaire zum Lift gebracht, hinunterbegleitet ins Foyer des Berlaymont, sie trat hinaus in das Licht einer geradezu explodierenden Sonne, ging wie betäubt zurück in die Rue Joseph II, in ihr Büro. Was war das jetzt?

Mit der unerwarteten Ouvertüre auf Altgriechisch hatte er sie verwirrt und sie dann dadurch überrumpelt, dass er zum Französischen wechselte. Sie stieg darauf ein, obwohl sie sich im Französischen unsicher fühlte, sie hätte lieber Englisch geredet, das sie, wie ja auch er, perfekt beherrschte. Strozzi musste das gewusst haben, er war hundertprozentig gebrieft. Auf Französisch konnte Strozzi sich im Verlauf dieses Gesprächs freier und eleganter bewegen als sie und die Mensur nach Belieben beherrschen. Und die Burkini-Geschichte – hatte er das wirklich ernst gemeint? Das konnte er nicht ernst gemeint haben – das war die perfekte Täuschung. Sie war so verblüfft, dass sie dann nicht mehr alert war, sie hatte die Konzentration verloren. Und jetzt, auf dem Weg zurück in ihr Büro, war ihr noch nicht klar, welche Konsequenzen das Gespräch haben sollte. Im Gegenteil: Sie sagte sich immer wieder, dass sie sich letztlich gut geschlagen hatte, sie interpretierte die wesentlichen Momente des Gesprächs in ihrem Kopf immer wieder neu, als würde sie einen Filmclip abspielen, zurücklaufen lassen, wieder abspielen, bis sie davon überzeugt war: Ja, es war ein Triumph. Sie hatte Schwächen gezeigt, aber schlussendlich war es ein Sieg!

Sie hatte gewusst, dass er gewusst hatte, dass es ihr eigentlich um den Wechsel in eine andere Generaldirektion ging. Denn aus diesem Grund hatte sie ursprünglich um einen Termin angesucht. Das war auch der Grund dafür, warum sie ihn so lange nicht bekommen hatte. Denn so machte man das nicht. Und ohne Intervention hätte sie diesen Termin auch nie bekommen. Und nun hatte sie dieses Thema gar nicht angeschnitten. Sie hatte das Jubilee Project präsentiert. Sie fand, das war perfektes Bandenspiel. Sie würde Bedeutung und Meriten der Kommission in die Auslage stellen und das Image der Kommission in der europäischen Öffentlichkeit verbessern. Sie war es, die die Idee dazu hatte, das Konzept hatte und die das konnte. Danach würde klar sein, dass sie eine wichtigere Position in dieser Institution verdiente. Das musste jetzt gar nicht mehr explizit ausgesprochen werden. Was sie jetzt brauchte, war bloß die Zustimmung und förmliche Unterstützung des Präsidenten. Würde er erklären, dass dieses Jubiläumsfest sein Wunsch war, dann wäre eine Situation hergestellt, hinter die es kein Zurück mehr gibt, dann müssten alle an einem Strang ziehen. Xeno hatte Strozzi Martins Papier überreicht, ihm in Grundzügen die Idee erklärt, besonderes Augenmerk darauf gelegt, dass dies klar war: es gehe um die Kommission, nicht um »die EU«, es gehe darum, der Kommission das Image einer Institution von weltfremden Bürokraten zu nehmen und sie als Hüterin der Lehren aus der Geschichte und der Menschenrechte zu positionieren. Es sei darum auch wichtig, das Projekt ausschließlich aus dem Budget der Kommission zu finanzieren, und es bedürfe natürlich vor allem der vollen Unterstützung durch den Präsidenten. Dieses Projekt müsse doch im Interesse des Präsidenten sein, gerade in Zeiten wie diesen, da die Kommission ein veritables Image-Problem habe. Sie stelle sich vor, dass das Jubiläumsfest mit einer Grundsatzrede des Präsidenten eröffnet werden müsse und –

D'accord, hatte Strozzi gesagt, d'accord. Ich glaube, dass ich die Elastizität meiner Kompetenzen nicht überdehne, wenn ich –

Pardon?

Ich glaube, sagte er lächelnd, dass ich das Pouvoir habe, ohne Rückfrage Ihnen gleich diese Zusage zu geben: Der Präsident unterstützt diese Idee und wird bei der Eröffnung eine Rede halten. Ein Protokoll unseres Gesprächs mit dieser Zusage werde ich gleich anschließend schreiben lassen. Das geht Ihnen heute noch zu.

Das war Xenos Triumph. Sie hatte, was sie wollte. Das sagte sie sich vor, als sie in 70, Rue Joseph II angekommen war und sich erst einmal einen Kaffee in der Kantine holte. Sie steuerte mit ihrem Kaffee auf einen Tisch im Hof zu, an dem zwei Salamander saßen, sie setzte sich dazu, empfand plötzlich ein warmes Gefühl der Sympathie für Conte Strozzi, ja, die Businessanzüge sollten verboten werden, sie fragte, ob jemand eine Zigarette habe, das war jetzt der Moment für eine Ausnahme-Zigarette, die Salamander prallten zurück, als hätte sie nach Arsen oder Opium gefragt. Da kamen Martin und Bohumil mit Kaffeebechern in den Hof, Xeno winkte sie herbei, sagte: Good news! Das Jubilee Project ist ab jetzt Wunsch des Präsidenten. Hat jemand eine Zigarette für mich?

Sie hatte ein mulmiges Gefühl. Sie verdrängte es. Was sie verdrängte, war, dass Strozzi am Ende noch zwei oder drei Sätze über die weitere Planung gesagt hatte: Ach ja, darum werde ich mich kümmern, wie wir die Mitgliedstaaten in das Projekt einbinden.

Die Mitgliedstaaten? Also den Rat?, hatte Xeno gesagt. Wozu? Wir waren uns doch einig, das Projekt ist Sache der Kommission.

Ja, das ist klar. Aber die Mitgliedstaaten haben die Kommission gegründet.

Bien sûr.

Da ist Xeno eben nicht alert gewesen. Dieses »Bien sûr« öffnete definitiv ihre Deckung. Sie merkte den Säbelhieb nicht. Und schon war sie verabschiedet. Mit ihrem »Bien sûr« hatte sie die Institutionen am Hals, die, wie Martin mit gutem Grund vorgeschlagen hatte, nicht involviert werden sollten, Rat und Parlament. Statt an einem Strang wurde nun an einem Knäuel von Fäden gezogen, maßgeblich wurden viele Interessen, statt das gemeinsame Interesse. Und schon wenige Tage später hatte sie, die so bestrebt war, Visibilité zu zeigen, nur noch den Wunsch, unsichtbar zu sein, alles bei Martin abzuladen – der da schon im Lorenz Böhler Unfallkrankenhaus in Wien am Krankenbett seines Bruders saß.

Aber zuvor gab es noch das Inter-Service-Meeting. Auch da lief noch alles bestens. Die meisten Generaldirektionen ignorierten die Sitzung. Für jeden in der Kommission, der ein Projekt voranbringen wollte, war allgemeines Desinteresse daran eine große Erleichterung. So konnte man, ohne sich mit zahllosen Meinungen und Gegenmeinungen, unproduktiven Vorschlägen und kleinlicher Kritik herumschlagen zu müssen, sofort größere Schritte machen und Fakten schaffen, hinter die es dann kein Zurück mehr gab. Informiert hatte man alle.

Natürlich kam jemand von der DG COMM (Kommunikation), schließlich war das Projekt ja ursprünglich von Mrs Atkinson ausgegangen, mit der Xeno auch in regelmäßigem Kontakt stand. Eine Vertreterin kam von der DG HOME (Migration und Inneres), was sich als sehr produktiv herausstellen sollte, weil das Holocaust-Gedenken zu den Arbeitsbereichen dieser Generaldirektion gehörte und sie diesbezüglich einiges an Kompetenz und Kontakten einbringen konnte. Ein junger Mann kam von der DG TRADE (Handel), das hatte Fridsch veranlasst, der offenbar über Xenos Projekt informiert sein wollte, der junge Mann selbst machte nur ein paar Notizen und nickte ab und zu. Überraschend war, dass jemand von der DG JUST (Justiz und Verbraucher) kam. Das hatte, wie sich herausstellte, damit zu tun, dass der in der JUST für die Zusammenarbeit mit der EAC (Kultur) zuständige Beamte der Enkel französischer Holocaust-Überlebender war. Das hatte Martin sofort interessiert: ob dessen Großeltern noch lebten? Leider nein. Seit über dreißig Jahren nicht mehr.

Keiner von der AGRI da?, fragte Martin ironisch zu Beginn der Sitzung.

Die DG AGRI (Landwirtschaft) war das Ressort mit dem größten Budget, gleichsam ein Staat im Staat, mit beinharter Interessenpolitik, aber bekanntermaßen wenig Engagement für die Interessen anderer Generaldirektionen. Der Vertreter der COMM sagte: Die Bauern sind erst zuständig, wenn Gras über die Sache gewachsen ist.

In dieser Runde gab es selbstverständlich nicht nur keinen Einwand gegen eine große Image-Kampagne der Kommission, es stellte auch niemand die Idee in Frage, Auschwitz-Überlebende in den Mittelpunkt des Jubiläums der Kommission zu stellen. Die Information, dass dieses Projekt der Wunsch des Präsidenten sei, was er mittlerweile bestätigt hatte, tat ein Übriges, dass Martins Papier in toto akzeptiert wurde und nur noch einige pragmatische und organisatorische Punkte diskutiert wurden: Zeitplan, Finanzmittel, Ressourcen, auch personell. Nach knapp eineinhalb Stunden war das Meeting beendet, und nun schien definitiv alles auf Schienen zu stehen.

Freitagnachmittag. Auf dem Heimweg hatte Martin Susman im Käseladen am Vieux Marché ein Baguette, eine Flasche Sancerre Blanc und eine kleine Käseauswahl gekauft. Der Verkäufer, ein junger Mann, dem bei allem, was er genießerisch schnitt und liebevoll verpackte, selbst schon das Wasser im Mund zusammenlief, hatte ihm dazu einen Feigensenf aufgeschwatzt, aus dem Tessin, neu im Sortiment. Sie werden es nicht glauben, sagte er, aber der ist besser als die Moutarde aux Figues aus dem Burgund, und er küsste vor Begeisterung schmatzend seine Fingerkuppen. Und zum Ziegen-käse, sagte er, gehört unbedingt Feigensenf, aber was sage ich da, das wissen Sie doch, aber diesmal, sagte er, müssen Sie unbedingt den Tessiner nehmen.

Ja, dann nehme ich diesmal den Tessiner, sagte Martin, der noch nie hier Feigensenf gekauft hatte.

Zu Hause legte Martin den Käse auf einen Teller, stellte ihn mit dem Senf auf den Tisch. Käse mit Senf? Er brach ein Stück vom Baguette ab, es schmeckte wie Watte. Es war stickig heiß, Martin zog die Schuhe und die Hose aus, öffnete ein Fenster. Der Wein war nicht gekühlt. Er legte die Flasche in das Tiefkühlfach, nahm ein Jupiler aus dem Kühlschrank, stellte sich an das offene Fenster und sah hinunter auf den Platz. Er trank das Bier aus der Flasche, rauchte dazu eine Zigarette, schaute aus dem Fenster, auf das Gewimmel da unten, die Asche fiel von seiner Zigarette, auf dem Teller schmolz und zerfloss der Käse.

Das Bild, das sich Martin beim Blick aus dem Fenster darbot, erinnerte ihn an ein Kinderbuch, das er geliebt und, noch bevor er lesen konnte, immer wieder lange studiert hatte. Es hieß »Die Stadt« und war ein Suchbilderbuch, großformatig, mit dicken kartonierten Seiten, die bunte Wimmelbilder zeigten. Seine Mutter hatte nie Zeit gehabt, das Buch mit ihm anzuschauen, er wusste auch nicht mehr, von wem er es geschenkt bekommen hatte, aber es musste ein Geschenk gewesen sein, denn seine Eltern hätten ihm das nie gekauft. Aber Florian, sein älterer Bruder, hatte sich manchmal am Abend zu ihm aufs Bett gesetzt und sie hatten gemeinsam in das Buch geschaut, so wie er jetzt auf den Platz – Wo ist die Blumenverkäuferin?

Da!

Wo ist der Polizist?

Da!

Wo ist der Briefträger?
Da!
Wo ist das Feuerwehrauto?
Da!
Wo ist der Springbrunnen?
Da!
Wo ist der Gemüsestand?
Da!
Wo ist der Mann mit der kurzen Hose und dem Fotoapparat?
Da!
Wo ist die Frau mit der Einkaufstasche?
Da!
Wo sind die Soldaten mit den Maschinengewehren?
Da, da, da, da und da!

Da läutete sein Smartphone. Martin schaute auf das Display, er kannte die Nummer nicht, hob ab.
So, in der Unterhose mit einer Bierflasche in der Hand entgeistert auf »die Stadt« schauend, erfuhr er, dass sein Bruder im Unfallkrankenhaus lag.

Als Alois Erhart zwölf Jahre alt war, wurde er Mitglied beim MAC, dem Mariahilfer Athletik Club, einem kleinen, rührigen Sportverein des Bezirks. In Erharts Erinnerung war das der Wunsch seines Vaters und nicht sein eigener gewesen. Da hatte es keine Diskussion gegeben: Alois hatte selbstverständlich Mitglied des »Clubs« zu werden. Was würden sonst die Leute reden? Ist der Sohn des Sportartikelhändlers gar unsportlich? Die Welt war kleiner damals, man dachte in Bezirksidentitäten. Wenn man im 6. Wiener Bezirk lebte, dann wusste man tunlichst alles, wer was wie und warum, von der Laimgrube rüber zum Magdalenengrund runter über Gumpendorf bis zur Linken Wienzeile. Alois Erhart konnte sich erinnern, dass sein Vater von einer Hochzeit, die in der Pfarr-kirche St. Ägyd am Gumpendorfer Platz stattgefunden hatte, schwärmte: »Das war die schönste Hochzeit, die Mariahilf je gesehen hatte!« Mariahilf! Nicht Wien! Man war »Mariahil-fer«, und wenn man die Mariahilfer Straße runterging, über die Babenbergerstraße in den Ersten, dann ging man »in die Stadt«. Im Café Kafka in der Capistrangasse wurde ge-tratscht, dass man den »Bua«, den Sohn vom »Sport-Erhart«, immer nur mit Büchern, aber nie mit einem Ball gesehen hat-te. Und schon war Alois Mitglied im »Club«. Er musste eine »Sektion« wählen. Gymnastik kam nicht in Frage, das war für Frauen. Geräteturnen war ihm völlig wesensfremd, davor fürchtete er sich schon in der Schule, in der Turnstunde schaff-te er am Reck nicht einmal einen Felgaufschwung. Allerdings fand er den Turnlehrer im MAC witzig und sympathisch: Já-nos Görgey, ein 56er-Flüchtling aus Ungarn, der sich selbst »Turnvater János« nannte, empfing ihn mit betörend ungari-schem Akzent: »Wo man turnt, da kannst du ruhig verharren, denn böse Menschen haben keinen Barren!« Aber nein, kein Barren, kein Pferd, kein Reck! Berühmt war der MAC für sei-ne Boxsektion. Sie stellte in drei Gewichtsklassen die öster-reichischen Meister. Der Boxtrainer, Toni Marchardt, zwick-te Alois in den Oberarm, sagte mit heiserer Stimme etwas Unverständliches und schaute so verächtlich, dass Alois in seiner Meinung bestärkt wurde, dass Boxen kein Sport, son-dern eine Verhaltensauffälligkeit von Verrückten ist. Er war bereit, sich in der Fußball-Sektion einzuschreiben, da kannte er die Regeln, über Fußball wurde auch in der Schule disku-tiert, also würde er dann mit mehr Kompetenz mitreden kön-nen, und er dachte, da müsse er bloß ein bisschen mitlaufen und nicht weiter auffallen, es gab immer andere, die unbe-dingt den Ball wollten.

Der Ball.

Eines Tages gab der Trainer, Herr Horak, nach dem Training, das eine Schlammschlacht bei strömendem Regen auf der Denzel-Wiese gewesen war, Alois den Vereinsball mit nach Hause. Damals spielte man noch mit handgenähten Lederbällen, so genannten »echten«, das war ein Wertgegenstand, mit dem sich die Mitglieder des Clubs auch abhoben von den Gassenjungen, die im Park mit »Fetzenlaberln« oder billigen Plastikbällen, besseren Luftballons, spielten.

Alois hatte die Aufgabe, diesmal die Ballpflege durchzuführen, das hieß, den von Schlamm, Kot und Regennässe arg malträtierten Ball zu reinigen, die kleinen Risse und Brüche im Leder mit Lederfett »einzulassen« und dann, wenn das Leder wieder »seine Fettn hat«, den Ball mit einem weichen Tuch abzureiben und zu polieren, »als wär's das Paar Schuh, das man anzieht bei einer Audienz beim Kaiser«.

Alois Erhart lächelt still in sich hinein. Eigentlich, dachte er, hatte er damals schon etwas gelernt, was er noch gar nicht begreifen konnte: wie beharrlich selbst im Banalen die Geschichte fortwirkt.

Vielleicht hatte Herr Horak eine pädagogische Anwandlung und glaubte, er könne Alois zu mehr Engagement und Identifikation mit dem Club bewegen, wenn er ihm diese Aufgabe übertrug. Vielleicht hatte Herr Horak bemerkt, dass Alois schon keine Lust mehr zeigte, in den Club zu kommen, beim Training geschunden zu werden, beim Spiel selbst auf der Reservebank zu sitzen, aber Werbeträger seines Vaters zu sein, als Einziger mit den neuesten Fußballschuhen mit Wechselstollen, erhältlich bei »Sport-Erhart«.

Alois nahm den Ball also mit nach Hause, am Sonntag sollte er ihn zum Spiel gegen die Ottakringer wieder mitbringen. Eines der wichtigsten Spiele der Saison, denn gegenüber Ottakring herrschte eine besondere Rivalität: Die Mariahilfer nannten damals die Ottakringer verächtlich »die Bayern« oder gar »die Germanen«, das hatte historische Gründe, die niemand mehr genau kannte. Angeblich soll Ottakring als Wiener Vorstadt von bayrischen Einwanderern gegründet worden sein. Diese Legende verschmolz damals irgendwie mit dem weit verbreiteten Hass auf die »Piefkes«, die Deutschen, die natürlich an allem Unglück in Krieg, Nachkrieg und Besatzungszeit schuld waren. Das war grotesk, aber es heizte die Emotionen noch weiter auf, die es ohnehin schon wegen der traditionellen Rivalität der Innenstadtbezirke mit den äußeren, den Bezirken auf der anderen Seite des Gürtels, gab.

Dann also kamen die Ottakringer. Und die Mariahilfer hatten keinen Ball.

Der lag in Alois' Zimmer, in der dunklen Ecke neben dem Schrank. Alois war nicht zu dem Spiel erschienen. Als er beschlossen hatte, nicht mehr in den Club zu gehen, hatte er den Ball vergessen und daher auch nicht zurückgebracht.

Man kann sich vorstellen, was am Montag im Café Kafka in der Capistrangasse getratscht wurde. Vater Erhart konnte den Skandal nur bereinigen, indem er dem Club einen funkelnagelneuen »Echten« spendete sowie eine Garnitur Dressen. Und er nahm sich seinen Sohn zur Brust.

Alois Erhart saß auf einer Bank im Brüsseler Friedhof, hatte den Kopf zurückgeworfen, die Augen geschlossen und lächelte. Warum fiel ihm das alles jetzt wieder ein?

Verlässlichkeit, hatte sein Vater gesagt, ist im Leben das A und O. Mach, was du willst, aber das muss in deinem Leben ein ehernes Gesetz sein: Gegenüber zwei Gruppen von Menschen musst du absolut verlässlich sein, gegenüber den Menschen, die du liebst, und gegenüber den Menschen, die du brauchst.

Ich liebe Herrn Horak nicht, sagte Alois.

Der Vater sah ihn schweigend an.

Und ich brauche ihn auch nicht.

Bist du sicher? Bist du sicher, dass du ihn nie brauchen wirst? Und keinen von all deinen Mannschaftskameraden?

Alois sah seinen Vater schweigend an.

Also? Hast du begriffen? Wiederhole, was ich dir gesagt habe.

Ich muss verlässlich sein.

Wem gegenüber?

Denen, die ich liebe, und denen, die ich brauche.

Nein, mein Sohn, wir waren schon weiter. Also: wem gegenüber?

Alois sah seinen Vater schweigend an.

Du musst immer verlässlich sein. Grundsätzlich. Gegenüber denen, die du liebst, das versteht sich von selbst. Aber auch allen anderen gegenüber, weil du nie weißt, wen du brauchen kannst und wer dir schaden kann. Also?

Ich muss immer verlässlich sein.

Wenn du etwas versprichst, was musst du tun?

Es einhalten.

Wenn du eine Aufgabe übernimmst, was musst du tun?

Die Aufgabe, die Aufgabe –

Erfüllen, ja.

Wenn man von dir etwas erwartet, und du hast nicht sofort klargemacht, dass du das nicht kannst, und du hast auch keine guten Gründe, warum du das nicht machen willst, was musst du tun?

Alois sah seinen Vater an.

Richtig: es tun! Ich will nie wieder im Kafka beschuldigt werden, dass ich meinen Sohn nicht erziehen kann, alles klar?

Ja, Vater.

Warum fiel Alois Erhart das alles jetzt ein, halb gerührt, halb belustigt, während er auf einer Bank des Brüsseler Friedhofs saß, auf ein Grab schaute und wartete?

Er hatte sich geärgert, weil er wieder nach Brüssel geflogen ist, zum zweiten Meeting des »New Pact for Europe«-Think-Tanks. Er hatte sich geärgert, als er den Flug buchte, er hatte sich geärgert, als er den Koffer packte, geärgert im Taxi zum Flughafen, im Flugzeug gekocht vor Wut über sich selbst, er war aggressiv zu der flötenden jungen Frau an der Rezeption beim Einchecken ins Hotel Atlas, weil ihm das alles so furchtbar auf die Nerven ging, dieses wichtigtuerische Trolley-Rollen in Brüssel, dieses bedeutsame Eilen zu Meetings, dieses Beantworten von Floskeln mit Floskeln, die raunende Transformation von keinen Ideen in ein babylonisches Kauderwelsch, es erschien ihm sinnlos, völlig aussichtslos, es war verbrannte Zeit. Er wollte den Ball in die Ecke rollen und vergessen.

Aber er hatte zugesagt. Er war in diesem Team. Mehr noch, er hatte sich bereit erklärt, die Keynote zur Eröffnung dieser zweiten Beratungsrunde zu halten. Diese Aufgabe hatte er übernommen. Der Ball lag bei ihm. Deshalb war er gekommen. Er war verlässlich.

Er lächelte.

Er musste es sein. Es steckte in ihm drinnen, und diese Verlässlichkeit hatte ihn weit getragen. Von Mariahilf rund um die Welt zu sich selbst. Was war dagegen die Enttäuschung, die er beim ersten Treffen des Think-Tanks empfunden hatte? Was war das gegen die belanglose Verachtung – er, der Menschenfreund, musste es sich eingestehen: ja, die Verachtung, die er gegenüber den Mitgliedern der Gruppe empfand?

Konnte er das so pauschal sagen? Dass sie alle verächtlich waren? Es gab schon Unterschiede. Zumindest Abstufungen der Verächtlichkeit und Abstufungen ihrer Wirksamkeit. Professor Erhart teilte die Mitglieder des Think-Tanks in drei Klassen ein: Da waren einmal die Eitlen. Na gut, eitel waren im

Grunde alle, in gewissem Sinne auch er. Man müsste präzisieren: die Nichts-als-Eitlen. Für sie war der Think-Tank von größter Bedeutung – weil sie dabei waren. Darin erschöpfte sich auch schon dessen Bedeutung, weil es nur darum ging, die eigene Bedeutung in sich zu spüren und sie abstrahlen zu lassen. Erhart kannte diese Typen, er wusste, wie sie zu Hause, an ihren Universitätsinstituten oder anderen Institutionen, an denen sie arbeiteten, bedeutsam raunten: »Morgen muss ich übrigens nach Brüssel, Herr Kollege, Sie wissen ja, ich bin in der Advisory Group des Kommissionspräsidenten!« Das war ihr Lebenselixier: die Wirkung auf ihr unmittelbares berufliches Umfeld, der Stolz, es so weit gebracht zu haben, dass sie nicht mehr zuhören mussten, sondern ihr Ohr leihen konnten. Sie waren leicht zu begeistern, nämlich von sich selbst, wenn sie redeten, rhetorische Demonstrationen des reinen Glücks, dass sie mitreden konnten. Sie hatten nie einen originellen Gedanken und konnten auch keinen Gedanken verstehen und anerkennen, der nicht schon von ihresgleichen hundertfach wechselseitig zitiert und mit Fußnoten abgesichert war. Im Grunde waren sie harmlos. Waren sie das wirklich? Sie waren diejenigen, mit denen in solchen Gruppen, wenn es um Entscheidungen und Beschlüsse ging, die Mehrheit hergestellt werden konnte.

Und dann gab es die Idealisten. Allerdings: Waren nicht gewissermaßen alle Idealisten? Auch er. Nur ihre Ideale waren verschieden. Was dem einen ideal erschien, zum Beispiel ein vielfach größeres Einkommen als andere zu haben, weil er sich in einer Leistungsgesellschaft mit seiner Leistung durchgesetzt hatte, widersprach dem Ideal von Verteilungsgerechtigkeit eines anderen. Das waren Banalitäten, die Erhart schon im ersten Semester Volkswirtschaft diskutiert hatte. Im Grunde nannte man Idealisten nur diejenigen, die nichts davon hatten, welche zu sein. Die Nichts-als-Idealisten. Sie waren zunächst Bündnispartner gegen die Eitlen, aber sehr schnell scheiterte das Bündnis daran, dass es immer irgendeinen Aspekt, irgendein Detail gab, das ihren selbstlosen Idealen widersprach. Und da konnten sie nicht mit. Sie waren so selbstlos, dass sie, »um in den Spiegel schauen zu können« und sich selbst zu sehen, irgendetwas haben mussten, das sie ganz alleine hatten. Das waren dann sie. Wenn es zu Abstimmungen und Entscheidungen kam, waren sie ganz plötzlich nicht mehr kompromisslos: Da war es ihre Sorge, ein größeres Übel durch die Zustimmung zu einem kleineren Übel zu verhindern. Allerdings waren die Nichts-als-Idealisten für die Herstellung einer Mehrheit meistens nicht maßgeblich. Sie waren zu wenige. In der Regel genügten für die Mehrheit die Nichts-als-Eitlen. Allerdings war auffällig, dass die Idealisten in der Regel mit den Eitlen stimmten. Offenbar erschien ihnen das Vertraute, das sich von selbst versteht, als ungefährlicher, als kleineres Übel im Vergleich zum Ungewissen, das sie mit ihrem Gewissen nicht vereinbaren konnten. Blödes Wortspiel, dachte Erhart, Ungewissen – Gewissen, und entschuldigte sich bei sich selbst. Andererseits auch nicht so schlecht. Er lächelte. Jedenfalls funktionierte dieser Betrug verblüffend gut: Das Gewisse, das Realistische, das immer auftrat mit Tabellen und Statistiken, mit Kästchen und Pfeilen, und was konnte man da realistisch machen, wieder Kästchen und Pfeile, Blatt um Blatt wurde auf dem Flipchart mit Kästchen und Pfeilen gefüllt, mit Flipchart-Markern in verschiedenen Farben, allein die Bewegung, die dann notwendig war, um so ein Flipchart-Blatt über den Flipchart-Rahmen hinweg nach hinten zu schlagen, das hatte etwas Großes, etwas Dynamisches, und wusch! Und auf einem neuen Blatt neue Kästchen, die mit Pfeilen verbunden wurden … – nur: So funktionierte weder die Welt noch irgendeine Gegenwelt, sicherlich auch nicht die Nachwelt. Aber man musste nur ein Kästchen für die Idealisten machen, in ein Kästchen eines ihrer Ideale hineinschreiben, ein paar Pfeile von diesem Kästchen hinauf zum Präsidenten machen, ein paar Pfeile von unten hin zu diesem Kästchen, dabei ausrufen: Demand-driven, bottom-up, nicht top-down, und schon hatte man im Gewirr der Pfeile und Verbindungslinien ein Netz, in dem die Idealisten gefangen waren.

Da lächelten die von der dritten Gruppe: Sie lächelten wissend, wie die Eitlen, aber besser wissend und zuletzt lachend, also am besten lachend, wenn die Idealisten nur das Schlimmste verhindert hatten. Das waren die Lobbyisten. Allerdings musste man da auch differenzieren: War er, Professor Alois Erhart, selbst nicht auch ein Lobbyist? Lobbyist einer Idee? Lobbyist bestimmter Interessen, auch wenn gerade sie, seiner Meinung nach, zum Nutzen der Allgemeinheit waren? Solch eine Idee hatten diese Lobbyisten nicht, sie konnten sich nicht einmal vorstellen, dass es sie geben könnte. Allgemeinheit, allgemeines Interesse, das war für sie etwas, dem sie verkaufen mussten, was sie zu verkaufen hatten. Verkaufen und kaufen, das war ihre Welt, und vielleicht glaubten sie sogar, dass darin das einzige allgemeine Interesse lag. Sie waren in solchen Advisory Groups nicht Vertreter von Konzernen, sie waren Vertreter der Stiftungen von Konzernen. Man durfte nicht geringschätzen, was sie alles förderten, finanzierten, unterstützten, man sollte nicht einmal daran herummäkeln, was sie in bloße kulturelle Alibis investierten, das alles hatte tatsächlich da und dort großen gesellschaftlichen Nutzen, und Professor Erhart wollte das auch nicht abstreiten, er war ein alter Hase nicht nur als Ökonom, sondern auch in Hinblick auf Drittmittel-Akquise an seiner Universität. Aber was ihn wahnsinnig machte und auch an diesem Think-Tank so verzweifeln ließ, war, dass sie jede Diskussion irgendwann kaperten und in immer demselben Mantra aufhoben: Wir brauchen mehr Wachstum! Was auch immer diskutiert wurde, es führte zur Frage: Wie schaffen wir mehr Wachstum? Eingewachsene Zehennägel waren ein Problem von Wachstum, warf Erhart einmal ein und erntete nur Unverständnis, aber der allgemeine Vertrauensverlust in die europäischen Institutionen war Folge von mangelndem Wachstum, der bedrohliche Erfolg des Rechtspopulismus – ganz klar: Gäbe es mehr Wachstum, gäbe es kein Wachstum des Rechtspopulismus. Und wie konnte man mehr Wachstum generieren? Klar, durch mehr Liberalisierung. Statt der Union gemeinsame Regeln zu geben, sollte jeder Mitgliedstaat für sich möglichst viele Regeln abbauen. So würde es zwar nie zu einer wirklichen Union kommen, aber zu Wachstum, und das wäre das Beste für die Union. Am Ende, das war schon jetzt völlig klar, würde die »New Pact for Europe«-Gruppe dem Kommissionspräsidenten ein Papier überreichen, in dem vorgeschlagen wird: Wir müssen für mehr Wachstum sorgen. Der Präsident wird sich höflich bedanken, die wichtige Arbeit der Gruppe loben – und dann das Papier ablegen, ohne es zu lesen, denn lesen musste er dieses Papier nicht, um bei der nächsten Grundsatzrede oder auch schon im nächsten Interview sagen zu können: Wir müssen für mehr Wachstum sorgen!

Erhart wusste, dass diese Lobbyisten nicht unbedingt Zyniker waren, nicht alle. Sie glaubten wirklich, was sie sagten, erstens weil sie es nicht anders gelernt hatten, und zweitens weil sie gelernt hatten, damit ihr Geld zu verdienen. Ihr Mantra wurde gut bezahlt, alles andere weniger oder gar nicht. Das ist immerhin eine Erfahrung. Man konnte einem Menschen das Streben nach Wohlstand nicht vorwerfen, auch nicht das Streben nach Reichtum, aber doch dies: käuflich zu sein. Und sie sind es. Objektiv. Mit ihrer Ignoranz gegenüber Ideen, die nicht in das Schema passten, für dessen

Verteidigung sie bezahlt wurden. Wenn sie von der Zukunft redeten, dann redeten sie von einer möglichst reibungslosen Verlängerung der Gegenwart und nicht von der Zukunft. Das verstanden sie nicht, weil sie glaubten, die Zukunft bestehe aus den Trends, die sich unaufhaltsam durchsetzen. Bei der letzten Sitzung sagte ein Lobbyist: Der Trend geht jetzt eindeutig in Richtung xy – wir müssen dafür sorgen, dass wir für diese Entwicklung fit sind! Da hatte Erhart gesagt: Ende der zwanziger Jahre ging der Trend eindeutig in Richtung Faschismus in ganz Europa. War es richtig, sich für diese Entwicklung fit zu machen, oder wäre es nicht richtig gewesen, Widerstand zu leisten?

Die Eitlen waren fassungslos, die Lobbyisten grinsten, und blöderweise nickten nur die Idealisten, die dann aber ohnehin absprangen, weil es in den weiteren Ausführungen von Erhart Details gab, denen sie nicht folgen konnten.

Ja, Erhart war naiv gewesen. Seine Publikationen der letzten Jahre hatten dazu geführt, dass er in diesen Kreis eingeladen wurde. Aber er hatte das überschätzt. Er hatte tatsächlich geglaubt, er könne nun durch kontinuierliche Mitarbeit in dieser Advisory Group, gleichsam im Vorzimmer des Kommissionspräsidenten, nach und nach Einfluss auf die politischen Eliten bekommen und etwas bewegen. An Konzepten mitarbeiten, die geeignet wären, die Europäische Union zu retten. Und dann würde der Ball bei der politischen Führung Europas liegen.

Aber so spielte es nicht. Das war ihm allzu schnell klar geworden.

Aber seine Keynote würde er halten. Das hatte er noch zugesagt. Auch wenn es ihn wahnsinnig machte, wie aussichtslos alles war. Er hatte sich verpflichtet, er war verlässlich. Und er war es auch seinem Lehrer Armand Moens schuldig, auf dessen Grab er nun schaute. Er war gegen Mittag in Brüssel angekommen, das Meeting mit seiner Keynote begann erst um 18 Uhr. Zur Überbrückung der Zeit hatte er beschlossen, noch einmal zum Brüsseler Friedhof zu fahren und das Grab seines Lehrers zu besuchen – den er als Einstieg in seine Rede zitierte: »Das 20. Jahrhundert hätte die Transformation der Nationalökonomie des 19. Jahrhunderts in die Menschheitsökonomie des 21. Jahrhunderts sein sollen. Das ist auf so grauenhafte und verbrecherische Weise verhindert worden, dass danach die Sehnsucht neu und noch dringlicher wiedererstand. Allerdings nur im Bewusstsein einer kleinen politischen Elite, deren Nachfolger bald beides nicht mehr verstanden: die kriminelle Energie des Nationalismus und die Konsequenzen, die aus dieser Erfahrung bereits gezogen worden waren.«

Er hatte sein Referat komplett umgeschrieben, nachdem er beschlossen hatte, nicht mehr in den Club zu gehen. Er sah keine Veranlassung mehr, ein Jahr lang mit großer Geduld zu versuchen, von der Reservebank ins Spiel zu kommen. Er würde nie ins Spiel kommen. Das war sein Fehler gewesen: zu glauben, mitspielen zu können und gleichzeitig die Regeln zu ändern. Das ging nicht. Nie und nimmer würde er einen aus diesem Kreis überzeugen können, so wenig, wie man ein Fließband stoppen konnte, wenn man jeden Tag, geduldig seine Handgriffe machend, den Kollegen sagte, dass man andere Vorstellungen von sinnvoller Arbeit hätte. Also würde er seine Pflicht erfüllen und seine Keynote halten – aber so, dass klar war, dass er damit den Club verließ. Er hatte einen radikalen, für diese Runde völlig verrückten Text geschrieben. Er hatte jetzt einmal den Ball. Und er hatte verlässlich dafür gesorgt, dass der Ball sein Fett abbekam.

Reden Sie auch schon mit den Toten?

Professor Erhart sah auf, vor ihm stand ein alter Mann, dessen hellblaue Augen zu den buschigen schwarzen Augenbrauen einen seltsamen Kontrast bildeten: Dadurch hatte der Mann etwas Strahlendes und Finsteres zugleich. Er hatte sehr schütteres Haar, das aber immer noch schwarz war, es sah aus, als wären die Haare mit Tusche auf seinen gebeugten Schädel gezeichnet worden. Er trug einen sehr guten Anzug, der etwas zu groß war und zu warm für diesen heißen Tag. Der Mann hatte gesagt: Praat U ook al met de doden? Professor Erhart verstand nicht. Er konnte nicht Flämisch und er wusste, dass man bei dieser Sprache fast immer falschlag, wenn man als Deutschsprachiger glaubte, etwas zu verstehen. Sollte er auf Englisch sagen, dass er nicht verstehe? Da fiel ihm »Kannitverstaan« ein, aber bevor er es sagen konnte, wiederholte der alte Mann den Satz auf Französisch. Erharts Französisch war schlecht, er ist ein Jahr lang Gastdozent an der Panthéon-Sorbonne Paris 1 gewesen, er hatte auf Englisch vorgetragen, sich in dieser Zeit bemüht Französisch zu lernen, aber rasch gelernt, dass es besser war zu sagen, dass man die Sprache nicht beherrschte.

Diesen Satz allerdings konnte er bilden: »Die Toten antworten nicht.«

Das Problem mit Fremdsprachen, wusste Erhart, wenn man sie nicht zumindest stiefmuttersprachlich beherrschte, war, dass man immer nur sagt, was man sagen kann, und nicht, was man sagen will. Die Differenz ist das Niemandsland zwischen den Grenzen der Welt. Eigentlich hatte er sagen wollen: »Die Toten haben ihre Antworten schon gegeben, bevor die Lebenden die Fragen hatten.« Aber so weit reichte sein Französisch nicht.

Der alte Mann lächelte. Ob er sich setzen dürfe?

Natürlich. Bitte sehr.

David de Vriend nahm Platz, sagte: Es gibt zu wenig Bänke hier! Diese ist die einzige bis – er warf die Hand weit nach vorn – bis zu den Kriegshelden.

Er keuchte, machte ein paar tiefe Atemzüge. Das Gehen strengte ihn schon sehr an. Eigentlich hatte de Vriend den Nachmittag in seinem Zimmer verbringen wollen, bei geschlossenen Jalousien, bis die ärgste Hitze vorbei war. Nach kurzer Zeit hatte er in dem dunklen Raum das Zeitgefühl verloren.

Er wusste nicht mehr, wie lange er einfach dagesessen und gegrübelt hatte. Er bekam Durst.

Er öffnete den Kühlschrank, nahm den Notizblock heraus.

Das war der Block, auf dem er die Namen der Überlebenden aufgeschrieben hatte, die ihm nach und nach eingefallen waren, weil es mit ihnen im Lauf der Jahre sporadischen Kontakt gegeben oder weil er ab und zu etwas über sie gehört oder gelesen hatte. Da standen neun Namen. Fünf davon waren durchgestrichen. Er sah die Liste verwundert an. Da fiel ihm ein, dass er noch einen Namen durchstreichen musste: Gustave Jakubowicz. Nach der Befreiung von Auschwitz hatte er in Brüssel und Paris Jura studiert und war ein bedeutender Menschenrechtsanwalt geworden, in den letzten Jahren – längst in Rente – vertrat er Flüchtlinge, die abgeschoben werden sollten. De Vriend hatte die Nachricht von dessen Tod in der Zeitung gesehen. Er suchte den Kugelschreiber. Er zog die Jalousie hoch, sah verwundert, in welch grellem Licht der Friedhof lag, das Grün der Baumkronen, das Weiß des Kieswegs, das Silbergrau der Steine, alles schien zu leuchten.

Da hatte er beschlossen, hinauszugehen.

Alois Erhart dachte, dass der alte Mann, der sich zu ihm auf die Bank gesetzt hatte, Ansprache brauchte, reden wollte, und es war ihm jetzt unangenehm, neben diesem schnaufenden Mann zu sitzen und nichts zu sagen. Kriegshelden? Was meinte er? Wahrscheinlich gab es weiter vorn auf diesem Friedhof eine Sektion für Tote des Weltkriegs. Was sollte er darauf sagen? Er suchte nach Worten. Ja, mein Herr, sagte er schließlich, sehr wenig Bänke. Und dann: Besuchen Sie Verwandte, die im Krieg – nun wusste er das französische Wort für »gefallen« nicht, was heißt »gefallen«? Na klar, er konnte ja »gestorben« sagen, »sterben« wusste er – da sagte der Mann bereits: Nein, ich gehe spazieren. Für uns ist dieser Friedhof der Auslauf.

Für uns?

Ich wohne da im Altersheim. Maison Hanssens. Das ist alles.

Nun ging ein Mann vorbei, den Erhart in einem ersten Impuls grüßen wollte, weil er ihn zu kennen glaubte, er kam ihm bekannt vor, woher? Wer war er? Ja, da fiel es ihm ein, das war der Kommissar mit dem riesigen Blähbauch, der ihn damals im Hotel befragt hatte, bei seinem ersten Brüssel-Besuch. Er ging zügigen Schritts vorbei, ohne herzuschauen, sein Bauch, dachte Erhart, war kleiner geworden.

Professor Erhart sah auf die Uhr. Es war Zeit aufzubrechen, sich im Hotel frisch zu machen und zum Meeting zu fahren.

Kommissar Brunfaut verlangsamte seinen Schritt, er bekam Atemnot. Sein Hemd klebte schweißnass auf Bauch und Rücken, er zog das Sakko aus. Er hatte unterschätzt, wie lang diese Allee war, die zu den Soldatengräbern führte. Bei den Opfern des 2. Weltkriegs gab es ein Denkmal, »Le Mur des Fussilés«, nicht zu verfehlen, gegenüber befand sich eine Parkbank. Dorthin hatte ihn Philippe bestellt. Brunfaut war spät dran, und Philippe hatte ihm am Telefon eingeschärft, pünktlich zu sein. Es werde nämlich noch jemand dazukommen, der nur sehr wenig Zeit habe.

Wer?

Wirst du sehen. Ich kann das am Telefon nicht sagen.

Es betrifft –?

Ja, genau!

Warum dort?

Das wollte – mein Freund. Und dort können wir in aller Ruhe reden. Zu den Denkmälern kommen kaum Friedhofbesucher, nur Politiker am Tag der Feier des Kriegsendes. Und der war schon. Dort gibt es dann nur uns und ein paar verdorrte Kränze vom Feiertag.

Brunfaut sah auf die Uhr. Er war schon fast 15 Minuten zu spät. Er begann zu laufen. Da sah er sich von außen, fand, dass er einen unerträglich peinlichen Eindruck machte, mit seinem hektischen Zuckeln, das kein Gehen mehr war, aber auch noch kein Laufen. Er ging wieder langsamer, verwischte mit seinem nassen Taschentuch den Schweiß in seinem Gesicht. Warum war es so heiß? Das war Brüssel, nicht der Kongo!

Da sah er endlich vor sich die Carrés mit den weißen Kreuzen. Und dort! Das musste das Denkmal sein, das Philippe gemeint hatte.

Er sah es deutlich vor sich, ging und ging und hatte doch das Gefühl, nicht näher zu kommen. Es war ein Albtraum.

Es war Wochen her, seit Philippe ihn im Spital besucht hatte, um ihm zu berichten, was er mit seinen Möglichkeiten über den Atlas-Fall herausfinden konnte. Besser gesagt: über das Verschwinden des Atlas-Falls.

Unser Informatik-Department, hatte Philippe erklärt, ist nicht schlecht, wir können schon einiges, und ich habe die Grenze der Legalität sehr frei interpretiert. Aber du darfst nicht vergessen: Wir sind die Brüsseler Polizei – also technisch nie auf dem letzten Stand. Erschwert wird das Ganze durch ein Netz von Geheimhaltungsstufen – wie soll ich dir das erklären? Es ist ungefähr so: Wenn es zum Beispiel eine Information gibt, besser gesagt den Hinweis auf eine Information, bei der, sagen wir, der französische Geheimdienst Interesse an besonderer Geheimhaltung hat, dann bekommt vielleicht unsere Sureté de l'État einen Zugang, aber nicht unsere Polizei. Versucht man das zu hacken, dann gibt es bei denen natürlich Alarm. Jetzt stell dir vor, wenn die merken, dass der Hackerangriff von der Polizei kam. Und dann gibt es noch die Europol. Hier sollten die Polizeidienste der europäischen Mitgliedstaaten zusammenarbeiten und sich austauschen. Das Problem ist aber, dass der Austausch nicht funktioniert. Jeder Staat will natürlich alles von den anderen wissen, aber keiner will etwas herausrücken. Da kommen sie mit ihren Verfassungen – was ihnen alles die nationale Verfassung leider, leider nicht erlaubt. Das heißt, da bewegt sich nichts, jede Information wird zu einer Nadel im Heuhaufen. Es gibt immer einen, der weiß, wo die Nadel steckt, aber wer weiß, wo dieser eine steckt, der das weiß? Das heißt, wir haben zwei Heuhaufen. Nein, wir haben Hunderte Heuhaufen, und in zweien steckt je eine Nadel, die wir suchen. Aber wenn es gelingt, sie zu finden, dann heißt das, dass wir den Safe gefunden haben, in dem das verwahrt ist, was uns interessiert. Nun müssen wir den Safe knacken. Und wenn das gelingt, dann ist das Erste, was wir beim Öffnen des Safes sehen, ein neuer Tresor mit einer noch komplizierteren Kombination. Du verstehst, ja? Ich gebe dir jetzt ein konkretes Beispiel aus der Praxis: Wenn ein Terroranschlag passiert ist, dann gab es in allen Sicherheitsstufen und auf allen Ebenen hinter vielen verschlossenen Tresortüren alle Informationen, die geeignet gewesen wären, diesen Anschlag zu verhindern. Aber sie wurden nicht zusammengeführt. Das erfahren wir dann manchmal aus den Zeitungen. Und dann muss irgendwo in Europa ein Innenminister zurücktreten. Aber das ändert nichts am System. Umgekehrt, wenn einmal auf der Basis geheimdienstlicher Erkenntnisse ein Anschlag verhindert werden soll, dabei aber eine Panne passiert, dann haben die Geheimdienste kein Interesse daran, dass das in den Zeitungen steht, und dann verschwindet der Fall. Ein Toter in einem Hotelzimmer, das ist ja nicht wie dreißig Tote nach einer Bombe am Flughafen. Das kann man vertuschen. Das muss man vertuschen. Die Geheimdienste haben ja kein Interesse daran, dass Ermittlungen und Untersuchungen eingeleitet werden und öffentlich diskutiert wird, warum ein Polizist einen Touristen in einem Hotelzimmer abknallt. Und damit sind wir beim Fall Atlas. Ich kann es nicht beweisen, aber ich bin hundertprozentig davon überzeugt, dass das eine Geheimdienstgeschichte ist. Die Sureté? Nein. Und auch nicht der SGRS. Die Geschichte ist größer. Viel größer. Wir haben mit der Rekonstruktion deiner Festplatte begonnen. Alles, was auf einem Computer abgespeichert war und gelöscht wurde, kann man rekonstruieren. Es sei denn, die Dokumente wurden nicht am Computer gelöscht, sondern im Zentralrechner. Na gut, das ist basic. Jedenfalls, so sind wir vorgegangen. Du musst nicht nur Schwachstellen finden, durch die du in andere Systeme eindringen kannst, du musst es auch so machen, dass der Angriff nicht rückverfolgt werden kann. Solange wir uns im belgischen System bewegten, war es relativ einfach. Es ist mir ja doch einigermaßen vertraut, ich weiß, wie unsere Leute ticken, und ich weiß auch, wo sie sparen müssen, unter welchen Einschränkungen und Behinderungen sie arbeiten. Und das ist jetzt typisch belgisch: Die Sicherheitspolizei hat wirklich viel investiert in die Verschlüsselung ihrer Dokumente, in Sicherheits- und Abwehrmaßnahmen gegen Zugriffe von außen. Aber was sie vergessen hat, ist der Schutz ihres Papierkorbs. Was zentral gelöscht wird, kommt in einen zentralen Papierkorb, ist ja logisch. Vielleicht haben sie auch noch eine Sicherheitskopie irgendwo, an die komme ich natürlich nicht ran. Aber es liegt auch im Papierkorb, vereinfacht gesagt. Und den kann ich durchwühlen. Ist das nicht komisch? Sie haben gedacht, dass ein Angreifer von außen sich für ihre geheimen Dokumente interessiert, aber sie haben sich nicht vorstellen können, dass jemand in ihrem Papierkorb sucht. Jedenfalls, so haben wir uns vorgetastet. Irgendwo muss es eine Schwachstelle geben, wo wir an mehr Informationen rankommen, nicht nur, was wurde gelöscht und vertuscht, sondern auch, wer wollte das und warum? Schau nicht so. Ich sage es dir ja gleich – was ich glaube, denn beweisen kann ich gar nichts. Wir haben tatsächlich eine Schwachstelle gefunden. Es ist für uns unmöglich, die Rechner der Geheimdienste zu hacken, das ist für uns so, als würde man versuchen, mit einem Zahnstocher einen Safe zu öffnen. Aber man kann das Netz erkennen, das sie bilden, und wenn ich alle Indizien richtig interpretiere, dann sitzt da mitten drinnen die Nato. Ja. Die Nato – aber warte! Jetzt kommt es: Das System hat aber doch einen Schwachpunkt. Und das ist der Rechner des Erzbistums Posen. Ja, Posen. Was heißt, was ist das? Das ist die älteste römisch-katholische Diözese Polens. Dort laufen einige Informationen von Geheimdiensten zusammen, aber in viel größerem Ausmaß gehen von dort Informationen an die Nato und kooperierende Geheimdienste. Da schaust du! Du weißt ja, dass Armin de Boor mir hilft – als Armin und ich da gelandet waren, sahen wir uns fassungslos an, und dann musste Armin lachen. Das ist irre, sagte er, schnell, gib den Zugangscode ein! Es ist ein Wort, nur ein Wort. Ja, sagte ich, aber welches? Wir müssen versuchen den Schlüsselbund zu knacken. Er lachte und sagte, siehst du nicht? Die ticken ganz simpel, gib »Judas«

ein. Es muss ein Wort sein, das ein katholischer Pater sinnig findet. Aber »Judas« war es nicht. Armin sagte, Moment, vielleicht schreibt man Judas auf Polnisch anders. Er öffnete ein Übersetzerprogramm, wir erfuhren, dass man Judas auf Polnisch Judasz schreibt. Aber das war es auch nicht. Armin holte Bier aus dem Kühlschrank, wir tranken, plötzlich sagte er: Klar! Natürlich nicht Judas. Sie wollen ja nichts verraten, sie wollen alles wissen. Er tippte etwas in den Übersetzer, dann setzte er das als Passwort ein – und das Tor öffnete sich. Das Passwort war »Bozeoko« – Auge Gottes.

Das Auge Gottes?

Ja.

Die katholische Kirche?

Erzbistum Posen. Ja.

Émile Brunfaut stöhnte.

Was ist? fragte Philippe.

Meine Milz, sagte Brunfaut.

Dass das Vertuschen des Mords im Hotel Atlas nicht bloß auf einen belgischen Staatsanwalt zurückging, sondern dass die Nato da irgendwie die Finger im Spiel hatte, war für Émile Brunfaut tatsächlich »zu groß«. Wir vergessen das, hatte er zu Philippe gesagt. Vergessen kann ich das nicht, hatte Philippe geantwortet, aber tun werde ich nichts mehr.

Wir rühren das nicht mehr an, sagte Émile.

Nein, wir rühren das nicht mehr an! Wann kommst du aus dem Spital? Nächsten Sonntag um 15 Uhr spielt der Club gegen Brügge.

Wir müssen dabei sein.

Wir werden dabei sein!

In den Wochen danach hatte sich Émile Brunfaut vor allem um seine Gesundheit gekümmert. Das hieß, dass er, wenn er rauchte, es mit schlechtem Gewissen tat, sein Duvel und dann seinen geliebten Rosé Glas für Glas nur ausnahmsweise trank, das Mort Subite allerdings strich, und bei allem, was er aß, das sichtbare Fett wegschnitt und an den Tellerrand schob. Seine Frites sah er lange misstrauisch an, bevor er davon »nur kostete«, indem er bloß zwei Drittel der Portion aß, das war seine Diät, denn die Moules waren praktisch nur Eiweiß. Immerhin machte er öfter als früher Wege zu Fuß. Nach drei Wochen kehrte er allerdings ganz zu seinen alten Gewohnheiten zurück und hielt das Befreiungsgefühl und den Genuss, den er dabei empfand, für klare Symptome seiner Genesung. Er meldete sich zurück zum Dienst, bekam seine Marke wieder, seinen Dienstcomputer und eine Menge bürokratischer Arbeit. Es gab mehr Berichte als Tote, und Kommissar Brunfaut fand das mit heiterer Gelassenheit ganz in Ordnung. Maigret schaute bei ihm im Zimmer vorbei, um in einem verworrenen Smalltalk zu testen, ob Brunfaut den Mord im Atlas wirklich vergessen hatte. Aber wie kann man überprüfen, ob jemand etwas vergessen hat, ohne ihn daran zu erinnern? Brunfaut war so belustigt von Maigrets Naivität, dass er sich definitiv darin bestätigt fühlte, wieder ganz der Alte zu sein. Nein, er rührte den Fall nicht mehr an.

Er konnte es bloß nicht ganz lassen.

Die Nato – das war ihm allerdings zu heftig. Er hätte auch nicht gewusst, wie er etwas in dieser Richtung, wie vorsichtig auch immer, ermitteln hätte können. Aber was er hatte, war der Name des Opfers, besser gesagt dessen drei Namen, denn es sind drei verschiedene Pässe im Hotelzimmer gefunden worden. Diese Namen hatte Brunfaut gleich, als er zu diesem Fall gerufen worden war, auf seinem Spiralblock notiert, und den hatte er noch, ein Spiralblock konnte nicht gelöscht werden. Und was ihn auch beschäftigte, war die Frage, was die katholische Kirche beziehungsweise eine Diözese damit zu tun haben konnte. Mit den Namen kam er nicht weiter, keiner der drei Namen war polizeilich erfasst, ja nicht einmal irgendwo in Europa standesamtlich oder meldeamtlich registriert. Letzteres konnte nur bedeuten, dass alle drei Pässe gefälscht waren. Das war für ihn und seine Möglichkeiten eine Sackgasse. Und die Beteiligung des Bistums Posen? In den Notizen, die er machte, schrieb er immer VAT, als Kürzel für Vatikan, weil er sich nicht vorstellen konnte, dass ein katholisches Bistum mit Geheimdiensten zusammenarbeitete, ohne dass der Vatikan davon Kenntnis hatte. Er konnte nur spekulieren. Also hatte er nicht gelogen, als er Philippe und nicht zuletzt auch Maigret deutlich machte, dass er seine Finger von diesem Fall ließ. Er starrte ja bloß leere Kästchen an, wie ein kompliziertes Sudoku, das er nicht auflösen konnte.

Umso überraschter war er, als Philippe ihn plötzlich in dieser Angelegenheit auf den Friedhof bestellte. Offenbar war er auch stillschweigend an dem Fall drangeblieben und hatte nun einen Fisch an der Angel.

Als Brunfaut endlich schwitzend und keuchend beim Mur des Fussilés ankam, schaute er sich suchend nach der Bank um, auf der Philippe und »sein Freund« auf ihn warten sollten. Aber da war keine Bank. Nicht vor diesem riesigen Monument »AUX VICTIMES INNOCENTES DE LA FURIE TEUTONNE«. Vielleicht dahinter, auf der anderen Seite? Oder seitlich? Oder hatte Philippe ein anderes Denkmal gemeint? Er sah das Feld mit den zahllosen weißen Kreuzen. Es war nicht so, dass er noch nie einen Soldatenfriedhof gesehen hatte, aber zum ersten Mal war er schockiert darüber, dass er – das schön fand. Er stand da, atmete tief durch und fand dieses große, heckenumsäumte Quadrat mit den immergleichen weißen Kreuzen schön. Nach all den Grabhügeln, Grabplatten, Grabsteinen, Gruften, Mausoleen, Kapellen, mit denen die Toten oder deren Nachkommen die anderen übertrumpfen wollten, nach all den Skulpturen weinender Putten, weinender Engel, weinender Mütter, in Granit, in Marmor, in Bronze und in Edelstahl, nach all dem Wuchern von kriechenden und sich aufbäumenden Pflanzen, nach all der Unruhe im endlosen Feld der letzten Ruhe war es hier endlich still. Die absolute optische Ruhe. Er fand das schön in einem radikal ästhetischen Sinn, als wäre dieser Teil des Friedhofs eine Installation, das Projekt eines Künstlers, der sich mit der Formensprache der Ruhe beschäftigte, befreit von jeglichem Sinn. Wenn er einen Schritt nach links machte oder einen Schritt nach rechts, dann ergaben sich in diesem Feld mit den streng in gleichen Abständen und gleichen Reihen aufgestellten Kreuzen immer andere Perspektiven, Linien, Diagonalen, Fluchtlinien, und er fand dies sinnig: Fluchtlinien. Wechselnde Fluchtlinien, die aber perspektivisch immer in dieselbe Richtung zeigten, in die Ewigkeit. Die Ewigkeit war überall, so wie am Ende die Befreiung von Sinn und Bedeutung. Zu Ehren der Schicksale war jedes konkrete Schicksal ausgelöscht, dem Gedenken an die Opfer wurde der Gedanke geopfert, dass jedes einzelne Leben einzigartig und unwiederbringlich war. Es gab nur Form, Symmetrie, Harmonie. Eingliederung in ein ästhetisches Bild. Schon gar nicht im Tod gab es Widerstand. Brunfaut war entsetzt, weil er, das schwitzende, keuchende, stinkende Lebewesen, das schön fand. Nicht gut. Schön.

Aber wo war Philippe? Brunfaut stand vor dem Memorial und sah sich um. Da sah er, dass plötzlich ein Schwein durch eine Hecke brach und zwischen den weißen Kreuzen zu wühlen begann. Das Schwein! Es stieß den Rüssel in die Erde, immer wieder, bohrte ihn hinein, scharrte mit den Klauen, stieß mit seinem Rücken gegen ein Kreuz, das daraufhin schief da-stand, das Schwein grub und wühlte weiter, das Kreuz begann langsam zu kippen. Kommissar Brunfaut, der im Laufe seines Berufslebens noch nie bewaffneten Männern gegenübergestanden war, diese Situation aber in Simulationsübungen hatte trainieren müssen, empfand gegenüber diesem Tier eine Angst und Hilflosigkeit, die er nicht kannte. Er wusste nicht, was tun. Sein Gedanke war, auf das Schwein zuzugehen, als könnte er es verhaften. Wie lächerlich war das. Sein Impuls war davonzulaufen. Er, flüchten, vor einem Schwein? Was immer Brunfaut in diesem Moment getan hatte – er selbst konnte es später nicht mehr sagen –, machte er ein oder zwei Schritte vorwärts, oder wich er ein paar Schritte zurück oder beides, ein unentschiedenes Vor-und-Zurück, das Schwein hob den Schädel, stieß einen schrecklichen Laut aus und rannte davon, eine animalische Gewalt, in einer schnurgeraden Diagonale quer durch das Feld der harmonischen Symmetrie – und Brunfaut stellte stöhnend fest, dass er saß. Er saß auf dem Kiesweg, in der einen Hand sein nasses Taschentuch, die andere verkrallt in die Steine auf dem Weg. Mit Abschürfungen an den Handballen und mit einem stechenden Schmerz vom Steißbein hinauf in den Rücken. Und über den Gräbern wehte der Wind.

Zurück im Hotel, ging Professor Erhart unter die Dusche, zog ein frisches Hemd an, dann den leichten blauen Leinenanzug – er sah sich im Spiegel: Europablau. Er lächelte innerlich. Zufall! Auf eine Krawatte verzichtete er.
Dann nahm er die Mappe mit der Keynote aus seiner Schultasche. Die Laschen an den Schnappschlössern wurden brüchig. Er dachte, dass er sie zu Hause mit etwas Lederfett einreiben müsste. Neben dem Bett stand ein Sessel, im Grunde eine Sitzschale, ungepolstert, mit rotem Nappaleder überzogen. Erhart setzte sich hinein und legte die Füße auf das Bett.

Es war unbequem und beengend. Er hievte sich mühsam wieder aus diesem halben Ei und setzte sich auf das Bett. Er wollte seine Rede noch einmal durchgehen, bevor er zu dem Meeting ging. Er hatte sie auf Englisch geschrieben, sein Englisch war ausgezeichnet, seit seinen Gastdozenturen vor vielen Jahren an der London School of Economics und der University of Chicago, dennoch hatte er sie von einem befreundeten Englisch-Professor gegenlesen lassen.

Diese Rede willst du wirklich halten?

Ja.

Da wäre ich gerne dabei.

Erhart memorierte halblaut seine Rede, in dem Tempo, in dem er sie dann halten würde. Er hatte die Stoppuhr seines Smartphones mitlaufen lassen. Siebzehn Minuten. Zwei Minuten zu lang. Das war egal. Es ging nicht um zwei Minuten, es ging um sein Leben. Das war zu pathetisch. Er fragte sich, was mit ihm los war. Er fühlte sich wie aus der Zeit gefallen. Er saß auf dem Bett, mit den Blättern seines Vortrags auf dem Schoß, und blickte auf die düstere braune Tapete des Hotelzimmers. Warum fiel ihm das jetzt ein: Fremdwörter, Wörter, die ihm fremd gewesen sind, mit Rührung fielen ihm Wörter ein, die er sich als Kind von der Mutter erklären ließ, wenn er sie in einem Buch gelesen und nicht verstanden hatte: frönen, hartleibig, Labsal, Behuf, dünken, dauern –

Mutti, da steht: Die ausgemergelten Kutschpferde dauerten ihn. Das verstehe ich nicht.

Du weißt doch, was Kutschpferde sind! Pferde, die Kutschen ziehen.

Ja, das weiß ich. Aber: Sie dauerten ihn. Heißt das, dass die Pferde so langsam waren, und zu lange brauchten, um die Kutsche wohin zu ziehen?

Nein, das heißt: Sie taten ihm leid.

Er war dann lange dagesessen, mit beklommenem Erstaunen, dass Dauer etwas mit Leid zu tun hatte oder Mitleid. Professor Erhart gab sich einen Ruck und machte sich auf den Weg.

Neuntes Kapitel

La fin, un prolongement du présent –
nous-mêmes une condition préalable du passé.

Das Schwein wurde von einer Überwachungskamera des Hotel Sheraton an der Place Charles Rogier gefilmt, eine ganz kurze Sequenz, man sieht das Schwein ins Bild kommen, langsam, mit erhobenem Schädel, als würde es genüsslich flanierend die frühsommerliche Luft schnuppern, ein Passant springt zur Seite, andere bleiben erstaunt stehen, einige holen ihre Mobiltelefone heraus, um das Schwein zu fotografieren, und da ist es schon aus dem Bild verschwunden. Dieses Video wurde auf YouTube hochgeladen, unter dem Titel »Aankomst van een afgevaardigde op de conferentie van de dieren«, von einem User, der sich Zinneke nannte. Im Sheraton wurde eine Untersuchung gestartet, wer vom Sicherheitspersonal, der Zugriff auf die gespeicherten Daten der Überwachungskameras hatte, dieser Zinneke war – der Hotelmanager befürchtete einen Image-Schaden, wenn ein Video öffentlich kursierte, das ein freilaufendes Schwein vor dem Eingang des Sheraton zeigte. Aber es gab keinen Image-Schaden, im Gegenteil. Der Film wurde auf Facebook geteilt und in kürzester Zeit mehr als dreißigtausend Mal gelikt. Die Metro-Zeitung konnte nun ein Bild des Schweins veröffentlichen, worauf der Zeitung weitere Bilder zugespielt wurden, die von den Überwachungskameras des Carrefour in der Chaussée de Louvain, des Postamts in der Avenue de la Brabançonne und der österreichischen Botschaft in der Rue Kortenberg stammten. Alle diese Bilder waren so unscharf oder verwackelt, dass Professor Kurt van der Koot, der nun eine fixe Kolumne in Metro bekam, nicht mit letzter Sicherheit sagen konnte, ob es sich immer um ein und dasselbe Schwein oder um verschiedene Schweine handelte. Eine Horde würde die Menschen beunruhigen, dachte er nun, aber ein einzelnes Schwein, das durch Brüssel spazierte, würde sie rühren, in ihnen eine geradezu kindliche Tierliebe wecken, das hätte das Zeug zur Legendenbildung. Kurt van der Koot war kein Feind seiner Beliebtheit und wollte sich daher nicht gegen kollektive Bedürfnisse stellen. So startete er bereits fünf Tage nach der Veröffentlichung des ersten Videos auf YouTube in der Metro-Zeitung die Aktion: »Brüssel hat Schwein! Wie soll es heißen?« Namensvorschläge an die Redaktion. Drei Wochen bis Einsendeschluss. Die Zeit bis dahin überbrückte Professor van der Koot mit der Serie »Das Schwein als universelle Metapher«: In täglich neuen Folgen zeigte er die Bandbreite von Gut und Böse, von Glück und Verhängnis, von sentimentaler Liebe, Verachtung und tiefem Hass, für Erotik und Gemeinheit, für die das Schwein als Sinnbild herhalten musste, es war das einzige Tier, das als Metapher die ganze Breite menschlicher Empfindungen und ideologischer Weltbilder abdeckte, vom Glücksschwein bis zur Drecksau, von »Schwein haben« bis »ein Schwein sein«, er wagte sich sogar in politische Gefilde vor und räsonierte über die Begriffe »Judensau« und »Nazischwein«, dann wieder über das verbotene Schwein in den Religionen und die geliebten Schweinchen Babe, Piggy und Schweinchen Schlau. Die Serie wurde ein großer Publikumserfolg, nicht zuletzt durch die Illustrationen: Fotos von herzigen Schweinchen, Faksimiles alter Karikaturen, die Kaiser, Generäle und Präsidenten als Schweine darstellten, Reproduktionen von Gemälden, die das Schwein in der Kunst zeigten (besonders viele Likes bekam eine Zeichnung von Tomi Ungerer, die eine Muttersau zeigte, die ihren Ferkeln ein Märchen vorlas: »Es war einmal ein Metzger …«), Figurinen und Nippes, vom Sparschwein bis zum Schwein als Koch, vom Gejagten bis zum Jäger, und Fotos von Alltagsgegenständen, es gab, wie van der Koot selbst mit größtem Erstaunen feststellte, kaum einen Gegenstand des täglichen Gebrauchs, der nicht irgendwann die Form eines Schweins angenommen hatte: Bierkrüge, Salzstreuer, Hausschuhe, Kappen, sogar Toaster …

Die Redaktion berief eine Jury von Prominenten ein, die aus den eingesandten Vorschlägen zunächst eine Longlist, später eine Shortlist ermitteln sollte, um dann erst den Siegernamen zu küren. Der Jury gehörten an: der Volksmusik-Sänger Barthold Gabalier, die Schauspielerin Sandra Vallée, der Fußballprofi und Torschützenkönig der Jupiler Pro League Jaap Mulder, die Witwe des früheren Brüsseler Bürgermeisters Daniela Collier, der seit seinen Mohammed-Karikaturen unter Polizeischutz stehende Cartoonist Roger Lafarge, der Schriftsteller und Brüssel-Chronist Geert van Istendael, der Zwei-Sterne-Koch Kim King, Maître de Cuisine im »Le Cochon d'Or«, und der Künstler Wim Delvoye, bekannt dafür, dass er seine Bilder auf Schweine tätowierte. Der Jury-Vorsitzende und Sprecher der Jury war natürlich Universitätsprofessor Kurt van der Koot.

Romolo Strozzi war ein Mann, der kaum aus der Fassung zu bringen war. Was andere überraschen mochte, löste bei ihm höchstens eine ironische Gestimmtheit aus. Nichts war ihm fremd – was also konnte ihn erstaunen? Er hatte viel erlebt, und was er nicht erlebt hatte, war ihm als Erfahrungsschatz seiner Familie und seiner Vorfahren weitergegeben worden. Zudem war er sehr belesen. Und in dem Feld, das er beruflich beackerte, kannte er jeden Krümel, jeden Stein, jedes Unkraut. So hatte er auch unmerklich schmunzeln müssen, als diese Fenia Xenopoulou plötzlich das Lieblingsbuch des Präsidenten zitierte, bemüht beiläufig, aber eindeutig taktisch geplant. Es zeigte, dass sie sich mit einiger neurotischer Energie vorbereitet hatte. Aber ihn hatte dies nicht verblüffen können. Er wusste, Menschen machen alles Mögliche. Ihre Finte ging ins Leere. Hatte sie wirklich gedacht, dass er dem Präsidenten berichten würde: Übrigens, diese Frau Xenopoulou hat denselben Lieblingsroman wie Sie, Monsieur le Président? Hatte sie wirklich gedacht, das gäbe dann einen Pluspunkt?

Er setzte sich an einen Tisch vor dem Café Franklin, Ecke Rue Franklin und Rue Archimède, auf die Archimède-, also Schattenseite. Es war ein sehr heißer Tag, und er wollte eine kleine Zigarre rauchen, während er auf Attila Hidegkuti wartete, den Protokollchef des Präsidenten des Europäischen Rates. Er musste informell mit ihm über Frau Xenopoulou und ihr so genanntes Jubilee Project reden.

Da stand plötzlich ein großes Schwein vor ihm. Ein Mensch in einem grotesken Schweinekostüm, einem Ganzkörperkostüm aus rosa Plüsch. In der Hand hielt er eine Stange, auf der eine Tafel montiert war. Er lehnte die Tafel an die Hauswand, setzte sich an den Nebentisch, nahm den Kopf ab, also seinen Schweinekopf, zum Vorschein kam ein gerötetes, schweißüberströmtes Männergesicht, schweißnasses blondes Haar. Der Mann, er war etwa so alt wie Strozzi, fuhr sich mit seinem rosa Plüschärmel mehrmals übers Gesicht und sagte zu der Kellnerin, die gerade Strozzis Kaffee servierte: Bitte ein Bier!

Sie wundern sich? Kann ich verstehen, sagte er, sich Strozzi zuwendend. Bitte verachten Sie mich nicht. Ich bin seit Monaten arbeitslos. In meinem Alter ist es schwierig. Schließlich habe ich mich mit einem Schild auf den Boulevard Anspach gestellt, vor die Börse: »Nehme jede Arbeit an!« Daraufhin habe ich diesen Job bekommen. Ein Schild herumtragen. Im Schweinekostüm durchs Europa-Viertel. Werbung, sagte er und wischte sich wieder den Schweiß ab.

Strozzi wandte sich um, las das Schild:

Slagerij
Van Kampen
Fijnste vlees, beste worst!
Voor bestellingen:
Let op! Nieuw telefoonnummer!

Viele Leute lachen. Manche fragen mich, wie ich so etwas tun kann. Kann sich keiner mehr vorstellen, wozu Menschen in der Not imstande sind? Glauben Sie, bei dieser Hitze in diesem Kostüm, das ist ein Spaß?

Strozzi holte sein Portemonnaie heraus, die Kellnerin brachte dem Mann das Bier, lächelte und fragte: Etwas dazu? Vielleicht einen Maiskolben?

Strozzi warf einen Fünfer auf den Tisch und ging. Auf der anderen Straßenseite tippte er eine SMS an Attila: Treffen nicht im Franklin! Bin im Kitty O'Shea's, blvd Charlemagne.

Er stand in Unterhose und Socken auf dem kleinen Balkon und bürstete sorgfältig seinen Anzug aus. Die Kieswege des Friedhofs waren an diesen warmen, trockenen Tagen sehr staubig, jeder Schritt zwischen den Reihen der Toten wirbelte Staub auf, der die Hosenbeine hochkroch und sich auch im Gewebe des Sakkos verfing. David de Vriend ging sehr sorgfältig mit seiner Kleidung um. Seit der Rückkehr ins Leben, nach der Befreiung, legte er größten Wert auf gute Anzüge aus erstklassigem Tuch. Als Lehrer hatte er zwar kein großes Einkommen gehabt, aber doch genug verdient, um sich schließlich Anzüge nach Maß anfertigen zu lassen und keinen mehr von der Stange zu tragen. Er bürstete und dachte an Brot. Warum dachte er an Brot? Er bürstete sorgfältig und geduldig, er war glücklich mit seiner Kleiderbürste, die er vor vierzig Jahren bei »Walter Witte« gekauft hatte, dem

Geschäft für »Waren für den täglichen Bedarf« auf dem Boulevard Anspach. Herr Witte persönlich hatte ihm diese Bürste empfohlen, beste Qualität, Herr de Vriend, diese Bürste wird Sie überleben, die beste Kleiderbürste, deutsches Rosshaar, händisch eingezogen in den Korpus aus Eichenholz! De Vriend hatte kurz gestutzt, »Deutsches – was? Rosshaar?«, und plötzlich bemerkt, dass er ohne innere Widerstände die Qualität des täglichen Bedarfs wichtiger nehmen konnte als den Spuk der Geister von gestern. Er kaufte diese deutsche Bürste, die ihn überleben würde, die unschuldig war, und vielleicht waren es auch die Hände, die sie gefertigt hatten. Er bürstete seinen Anzug aus, im Zimmer läutete das Telefon, er hörte es, aber bezog es nicht auf sich. Der Klingelton war ihm nicht vertraut, auch erwartete er keinen Anruf. Es wird immer gesagt, wer ein Konzentrations- oder Vernichtungslager überlebt hat, könne für den Rest seines Lebens kein Stück Brot mehr wegwerfen. Das ist jetzt wieder in der Zeitung gestanden. Die Tochter von Gustave Jakubowicz hat es in einem Interview in De Morgen gesagt, nach dem Tod ihres Vaters, des berühmten Menschenrechtsanwalts: Wir Kinder mussten oft hartes Brot essen, wir bekamen erst frisches, wenn das alte aufgegessen war, Vater konnte kein Brot wegwerfen, das konnte er einfach nicht. De Vriend bürstete. Gustave, ach Gustave! Das Telefon läutete wieder. Gustave hat erstklassige Anzüge geliebt und das frische Baguette in den Körbchen der Restaurants. Keine fadenscheinige Kleidung mehr, gute dicke Stoffe! Nichts von der Stange, schon gar nichts Gestreiftes, und keine Mütze, keine Kopfbedeckung! Wer im Lager gewesen war, wusste, was es hieß: keine Mütze. Das war der Tod. Darum hieß es danach: Leben. Freiheit. Bester Stoff und ein freier Kopf. De Vriend bürstete routiniert, er stand in der Unterhose auf dem Balkon, ein Hosenbein des Anzugs über den linken Arm gezogen, und strich rhythmisch über den Stoff, in diese Bewegung versunken wie ein Geigenspieler. Irgendwo läutete schon wieder ein Telefon. Er hatte vier Maßanzüge. Für den Winter zwei aus dickem Tweed, einen Harris in Fischgrat und einen etwas weicheren Donegal in Salt & Pepper. Für die Übergangszeit einen nachtblauen in Schurwolle und einen leichteren, aber trotzdem angenehm wärmenden aus Mohair in Anthrazit. Er hatte keinen Sommeranzug. Er hatte schon zu viel gefroren in seinem Leben, für ihn war der Sommer auch nur eine Übergangszeit. Ein heißer Tag machte ihm nichts aus, und der graue Mohair, den er gerade ausbürstete, war so wunderbar leicht. Wie lange hatte er ihn schon? Viele Jahre, es waren sicher schon – viele Jahre.

Da spürte er eine hart zupackende Hand auf seinem Oberarm, diese Hand zog ihn zurück, beinahe wäre ihm die Bürste hinuntergefallen. Ja was machen wir denn da, schrie Frau Joséphine. Wir können doch nicht nackt auf dem Balkon stehen, nicht wahr, Herr de Vriend.

Er sah sie an, und sie drückte noch immer seinen Oberarm und sagte viel zu laut: Jetzt gehen wir hinein und ziehen uns was an, nicht wahr.

Er war doch nicht schwerhörig. Er verstand sie nur deshalb nicht gleich, weil sie so schrie.

Haben Sie das Telefon nicht gehört, schrie sie. Also wir gehen jetzt schön hinein, na kommen Sie, ja, und da, sehen Sie, da liegt ja Ihr Hemd, das ziehen wir jetzt an und – aber das ist ja ganz feucht, da haben Sie aber sehr geschwitzt, nicht wahr, da müssen wir ein frisches, nicht wahr, da nehmen wir ein frisches.

Sie öffnete energisch seinen Schrank, schaute, griff hinein, und de Vriend sagte: Nein! Er wollte das nicht, er wollte das nicht zulassen, dass jemand einfach seinen Spind öffnete und in seinen Sachen – aber da sagte sie schon: Das ist ein schönes Hemd, ein so schönes weißes Hemd, das ziehen wir jetzt an!

Frau Joséphine nahm ihm die Bürste ab, die er immer noch in der Hand hielt, legte sie auf das kleine Tischchen, die Anzughose war de Vriend vom Arm gerutscht und lag auf dem Boden. Sie half ihm ins Hemd, dabei sah sie wieder die tätowierte Nummer auf seinem Arm, rasch fädelte sie den Arm in den Hemdärmel, wollte Brav! sagen, aber sagte nichts.

Sie hob die Hose vom Boden auf, hielt sie ihm hin. Schweigend. Er zog sie an. Schweigend. Er knöpfte das Hemd zu, schloss den Hosengürtel. Sie schaute sich um, sah, dass die Schuhe neben dem Bett standen, er sah, wohin sie schaute, ging zum Bett, setzte sich und schlüpfte in die Schuhe. Er sah sie an, sie sah ihn an, dann beugte er sich vor und schnürte die Schuhe zu. Er richtete sich auf, sah sie an. Sie nickte.

Frau Joséphine war eine routinierte Altenbetreuerin. Sie hatte in ihren fast schon zwanzig Dienstjahren sehr viel gesehen. Und sie hatte im Zug ihrer Ausbildung auch einen Psychologiekurs und erst vor zwei Jahren ihren letzten Fortbildungskurs gemacht. Sie selbst war am meisten davon überrascht, dass sie plötzlich sagte: Auschwitz?

Er nickte.

Er wollte aufstehen. Aber konnte nicht. Er blieb auf dem Bett sitzen.

Sie dachte, dass sie jetzt zu weit gegangen war. Also ging sie einen Schritt weiter: Wie war das? Wollen Sie erzählen?

Sie spürte ein atemabschnürendes Grauen. Weil sie diese Frage gestellt hatte.

De Vriend saß auf dem Bett, sah sie an, dann sagte er: Wir sind Appell gestanden. Wir sind Appell gestanden. Das war alles.

Nachdem Joséphine das Zimmer verlassen hatte, blieb de Vriend noch eine Weile auf dem Bett sitzen, dann stand er auf, ging durch das Zimmer, sah sich um – da sah er seine Bürste.

Langsam zog er sich aus, nahm die Bürste, schob ein Hosenbein über seinen linken Arm, stellte sich nackt auf den Balkon und begann zu bürsten.

Kabinettschef Strozzi wusste natürlich, dass der Präsident der Kommission sich unmöglich gegen eine Initiative aussprechen konnte, die das Image der Kommission aufpolieren und ihr Ansehen heben wollte. Deshalb hatte er Fenia Xenopoulou sofort die Unterstützung des Präsidenten zugesichert. Eine Carte blanche. Zugleich wusste Strozzi aber auch, dass dieses seltsame Projekt mehr Probleme produzieren würde, als dadurch zu gewinnen wäre. Die Idee des Jubilee Project war verrückt, und auch wenn man sie natürlich sehr gut begründen konnte, wie Frau Xenopoulou durchaus bewiesen hatte, so war sie doch politisch alles andere als opportun. Deshalb war die Carte blanche eine Finte gewesen, ein beliebter Trick des alten Bürokratie-Haudegens Strozzi: Wenn man eine Idee abstechen möchte, dann muss man ihr zunächst zustimmen und volle Unterstützung versprechen. Daraufhin hat noch jeder freudig die Deckung geöffnet. Das Schöne daran ist, dass man dann den entscheidenden Hieb oft gar nicht mehr selbst führen muss. Das war ein alter Fechter-Witz: Wenn es dir gelingt, deinen Gegner dazu zu bringen, Harakiri zu begehen, dann musst du nicht mehr angreifen, sondern nur noch aufpassen, dass er nicht dir röchelnd in die Arme fällt. Und bei Fenia Xenopoulou hatte das wieder einmal funktioniert: Begeistert von seiner Zustimmung hatte sie dann natürlich achtlos seinem Vorschlag zugestimmt, die Vertreter der Nationen, die die Kommission gegründet hatten, von diesem

Kommissionsprojekt in Kenntnis zu setzen. Was hätte sie dagegen vorbringen sollen? Zugleich war er ja auch schon aufgestanden und hatte ihr damit das Ende des Gesprächs signalisiert. Sie wird später nie sagen können, er sei ihr in den Rücken gefallen. Im Gegenteil: Das war offenes Visier. Nun musste er nur noch dafür sorgen, dass sie nicht in seine Arme sinkt und mit ihrem Blut seine Weste befleckt. Und da genügte ein Gespräch: mit seinem Freund Attila, dem Protokollchef des Ratspräsidenten.

Es war eine verrückte Gesprächssituation: diese beiden ranghohen Beamten im Kitty O'Shea's, dem Irish Pub hinter dem Berlaymont-Gebäude, mit Eistee an einem von verschüttetem Bier klebrigen Tisch sitzend, umgeben von schnatternden und schreienden Guinness-Trinkern und Dart-Spielern.

Abgehört können wir hier jedenfalls nicht werden, bei diesem Lärm, sagte Attila Hidegkuti in seinem charmanten Hunglish, was ist Änglisch mit ún-ga-rísche Ák-zänt.

Strozzi lächelte. Er hatte seit einigen Jahren eine ausgezeichnete Gesprächsbasis mit Attila, sie hatten schon viele Probleme in feiner Abstimmung miteinander gelöst. Wenn es zu Konflikten zwischen Kommission und Rat kam, also sehr oft, oder wenn der Kommissionspräsident etwas vom Ratspräsidenten wollte, also nicht unbedingt selten, dann sprach Strozzi lieber mit Hidegkuti als mit dem Kabinettschef des Ratspräsidenten, Lars Ekelöf, diesem Hardcore-Lutheraner aus Schweden, dem der barocke italienische Graf naturgemäß unheimlich war. Umgekehrt hatte Strozzi einmal voll Verachtung über Ekelöf gesagt: Man kann sich in strittigen Punkten nicht mit einem Mann einigen, der sich in jedem Punkt moralisch überlegen fühlt und daher jeden Kompromiss als Verrat an seiner Moral empfindet! Und er hatte ironisch lächelnd hinzugefügt: Ekelöf kann nur deshalb nie aus der Deckung gelockt werden, weil er nur aus Deckung besteht, er ist die Deckung an sich. Könnte man sie umgehen, wäre dahinter nichts, nur ein verwehender Geruch, das Verduften von Selbstgerechtigkeit.

Der Widerspruch zwischen Nord und Süd, er verlief genau zwischen diesen beiden Männern, die nördlich und südlich der Rue de la Loi in Brüssel arbeiteten.

Und wir Ungarn wér-den dá-zwischen zérr-rieben! (Hidegkuti).

Besorgt sah Hidegkuti jetzt auf die Dartspieler, die unangenehm knapp neben ihm standen. Die Pfeile fliegen hier tief, sagte er.

Ein Dartspieler grüßte ihn, Hidegkuti grüßte nickend zurück, rückte mit seinem Stuhl ein wenig zur Seite, da hob ein anderer der Spieler grüßend sein Bierglas und prostete Hidegkuti und Strozzi zu.

Come on, wir stellen uns dort rüber, sagte Strozzi und dann: Das sind die Briten. Britische ENDs. Seit Beginn der Austrittsverhandlungen bereiten sich einige hier mit Bier und Dart nur noch auf ihre Heimkehr vor. Sie sind mir lieber als die Engländer, die weiterarbeiten, solange der Austritt nicht besiegelt ist, aber nichts anderes tun, als fleißig unsere Arbeit zu obstruieren.

Hast du mich deshalb hierher gebeten? Hast du Probleme mit Beamten in meinem Haus?

Nein, sagte Strozzi und erzählte ihm vom Jubilee Project.

Hidegkuti verstand augenblicklich, dass dieses Projekt zu Verwerfungen führen musste. Es war nicht so sehr die Tatsache, dass die Kommission einen Alleingang plante, gegen die anderen europäischen Institutionen oder zumindest ohne sie einzubeziehen, auch wenn schon dies natürlich höchst problematisch war, nein, es war grundsätzlich die Idee: Testimonials aufmarschieren zu lassen, die mit ihren Biographien und Schicksalen bezeugen sollten, dass der Nationalismus zu den größten Verbrechen der Menschheitsgeschichte, letztlich zu Auschwitz geführt hatte, weshalb es die moralische Verpflichtung der Kommission sein musste, an der Überwindung der Nationen zu arbeiten. Von der Floskel »Nie wieder Auschwitz« den Anspruch »Überwindung des Nationalismus, letztlich Überwindung der Nationen« abzuleiten und dies der europäischen Öffentlichkeit als moralischen Anspruch und als politische Aufgabe der Europäischen Union zu verkaufen, das würden die nationalen Staats- und Regierungschefs nie akzeptieren.

Wir haben Experten für alles, sagte Hidegkuti. Wir können Regen machen, und wir können das so machen, dass die Kommission im Regen steht.

Ich weiß, sagte Strozzi. Darum erzähle ich dir das ja.

»Nie wieder Auschwitz« ist gut und richtig.

Ja.

Das könnt ihr jeden Sonntag in einer Rede sagen.

Ja. Damit man es nicht vergisst. Niemals vergessen, das muss man immer wieder sagen.

Genau. Aber das ist kein politisches Programm.

Moral war noch nie ein politisches Programm.

Vor allem, wenn die Moral Konflikte produziert.

Genau. Der Rat könnte das nie akzeptieren: Überwindung der Nationen. Das hieße Krieg. Gegen die Kommission. Und Aufruhr der Menschen in allen Ländern gegen Europa.

Genau.

Also?

Ich habe dich verstanden. Wir werden dieses Pró-ject nie-der-métzeln, bevor Licht der Öffentlichkeit es erblickt.

Strozzi wusste, dass er sich auf seinen Freund Attila verlassen konnte.

Und Attila Hidegkuti leistete ganze Arbeit. Viel Arbeit war es nicht. Eine Unterschrift, ein Anruf, im Grunde ein Fingerschnippen. Damit wurde eine Kugel angestoßen, die die nächste anstieß und so fort. So entstand eine Eigendynamik, von der bald niemand mehr wusste, wer sie wirklich ausgelöst hatte, die aber ununterbrochen Energie weitergab, bis die letzte Kugel ins Nichts rollte, ins Out, in ein schwarzes Loch. Darum ging es. Das war Hidegkutis Job. Am Ende ist selbst der, der alles ausgelöst hat, auch nur eine dieser Kugeln gewesen, die eine andere anstieß, im Grunde eine Murmel oder nur ein Körnchen, letztlich etwas Unsichtbares, ein Atom – der spaltbare Kern unfassbarer politischer Energie. Schon am nächsten Tag rief der ungarische Außenminister seinen »geschätzten Kollegen und lieben Freund«, den österreichischen Außenminister, an und informierte ihn darüber, dass die Kommission unter dem Vorwand von Jubiläumsfeierlichkeiten einen Prozess einleiten wollte, der zur Abschaffung der europäischen Nationen führen sollte.

Du weißt, was es bedeutet, lieber Freund, wenn die EU dekretiert, dass Österreich keine Nation ist, fragte er. Man konnte gar nicht sagen: scheinheilig – denn die Nation war wirklich sein Heiligtum. Allerdings die eigene, die ungarische. Ob Österreich eine Nation war oder ein Betriebsunfall der Geschichte, in seinem Größenwahn zu Recht zurückgestutzt zu einem Kleinstaat von Mischlingen, war ihm letztlich egal, auch wenn er »privat«, wie er gerne sagte, eher zu Letzterem neigte. Aber er wusste, dass er einen Bündnispartner hatte, wenn er den Nationalismus des Nachbarn, wie er es gegenüber seinem Regierungschef formuliert hatte, »ein bisschen an den Eiern kratzte«.

Rund 86 Milliarden Neurone kommunizierten, in Millisekunden fanden an Tausenden Zellen komplexe elektrische

Prozesse statt, chemische Botenstoffe taten ihre Schuldigkeit und die Synapsen funktionierten, kurz: Der österreichische Außenminister dachte nach. Und nur wenige Wimpernschläge später hatte er die Alternativen ausgelotet und eine Entscheidung getroffen. Variante eins war, vorläufig nichts zu tun, zu warten, bis die Kommission mit diesem Projekt an die Öffentlichkeit ging, und dann als Verteidiger der österreichischen Nation in den Ring gegen »die EU« zu steigen. Da glühten die Synapsen zunächst vor Wollust, aber was war das? Sie begannen rot zu blinken. Die Anti-EU-Klientel hatte er mit seinen Stellungnahmen zur europäischen Flüchtlingspolitik bereits gut bedient, ein Schritt weiter, ins Feld grundsätzlicher Ablehnung der europäischen Idee (und es war gut, dass sie letztlich ohnehin so unklar war), würde nicht nur »die Wirtschaft« verstören, sondern ihn in die Nähe der Partei der rechten Rabauken rücken, die mit ihrem »Österreich-zuerst«-Nationalismus immer mehr Zustimmung erhielten. Er wollte nicht der Schmiedl neben dem Schmied sein, er wollte populär werden ohne Anruch des Populismus, also war klar: Wenn Nation und Nationalismus grundsätzlich zu einem großen öffentlichen Thema wurden, hatte er schlechte Karten. Daher Variante zwei: Er musste dieses Projekt verhindern. Wenn er eine Grundsatzdiskussion über die Nation und ihre Verteidigung verhindern konnte, dann konnte er bei jeder einzelnen Sachfrage als Vertreter der österreichischen Interessen, der Interessen der nationalen Wähler auftreten, und zugleich auch als Europäer – da wäre er der Schmied.

Er bedankte sich bei seinem lieben Freund, dem ungarischen Kollegen, versprach »selbstverständlich« akkordierte Zusammenarbeit, trommelte sein Büro zusammen und verteilte die Aufgaben. Alle verließen eilfertig sein Zimmer, nur der Pressesprecher blieb und räusperte sich. Er erinnerte den Minister daran, dass sie noch den Fragebogen ausfüllen mussten.

Welchen Fragebogen?

Für Madonna, diese Frauenzeitschrift. Wo wir letzte Woche das Fotoshooting hatten.

Ach ja. Dann füll es doch aus.

Ich würde es doch gerne mit dir durchgehen, Herr Minister. Die privaten Fragen. Zum Beispiel: Lieblingsbuch.

Was schlägst du vor?

Es ist in Österreich Tradition, dass Politiker bekennen: »Der Mann ohne Eigenschaften«. Drunter geht es eigentlich nicht. Und Tabu ist auf jeden Fall ein lebender Autor. Die Leut wollen keinen Lebenden.

Na gut, dann sind wir gut österreichisch. Der Mann ohne Eigenschaften. Den hat ja schon, so viel ich weiß, der Kreisky geliebt.

Und der Sinowatz, der Klima und der Gusenbauer.

Nur die Roten?

Nein, auch der Mock, der Khol und sogar der Molterer.

Na drunter kann ich nicht gehen.

Und jetzt: die Lieblingsfigur in der Literatur?

Was ist denn los mit dieser Frauenzeitschrift? Arbeiten da lauter Germanistinnen?

Nein, Herr Minister. Sind nur diese zwei Fragen. Dann kommt schon Musik und Essen.

Na gut. Also Lieblingsfigur. Wie heißt denn der aus dem »Mann ohne Eigenschaften«?

Ulrich. Würde ich aber nicht empfehlen. Wie gesagt: ohne Eigenschaften. Habe außerdem gegoogelt: Er hat dann ein Problem mit Inzest. Schlage vor: Arnheim.

Wer ist das?

Passt für dich, Herr Minister. Wird als »großer Mann« bezeichnet, Politiker und Intellektueller. Und hat eine innige platonische Liebesbeziehung.

Im Ernst?

Im »Mann ohne Eigenschaften«.
Geil!

Am nächsten Tag wies die polnische Regierung die polnischen Beamten in den Kabinetten an, diese »Kampagne« der europäischen Kommission, die gegen den Stolz der polnischen Nation gerichtet sei, abzudrehen. Vor allem sei die DG COMM darauf hinzuweisen, dass das Vernichtungslager Auschwitz ein deutsches Verbrechen und daher ein ausschließlich deutsches Problem sei. Die Bundesrepublik Deutschland sei herzlich eingeladen, das deutsche Vernichtungslager auf polnischem Boden abzumontieren und in Deutschland als Museum auszustellen. Jedenfalls würde sich eine Erinnerungskultur von Verbrechen, die von Besatzungsmächten auf polnischem Boden begangen wurden, nicht als moralischer Baldachin über einer Wirtschaftsgemeinschaft eignen.

Vom österreichischen Außenminister traf eine Note beim Präsidenten des Europäischen Rats ein, die unmissverständlich klarmachte, dass die Republik Österreich dafür und dagegen sei: Sie unterstütze die Initiative der Europäischen Kommission, könne allerdings in der geplanten Form keine Zustimmung geben. Das Außenamt, im Namen der österreichischen Bundesregierung, befürworte vorbehaltlos die Initiative der Europäischen Kommission, »Europa den Bürgern besser zu kommunizieren«, allerdings sei in Österreich nicht kommunizierbar, dass ein polnisches Lager, in dem es abertausend österreichische Opfer gegeben hatte, nun eine Begründung dafür sein solle, die österreichische Nation in Frage zu stellen.
Der Botschafter der Ständigen Vertretung der Tschechischen Republik bei der Europäischen Union übermittelte eine diplomatische Protestnote, die schärfer formuliert war: Die tsche-

chische Regierung werde es nicht zulassen, dass die Europäische Union eine Kampagne der so genannten Geschichtsbewältigung plane, mit der Tschechien einmal mehr von der Landkarte gestrichen werde. Dafür gebe es kein Mandat und könne es keines geben.

Wenige Stunden später kam ein ähnlich lautendes Schreiben von der Ständigen Vertretung der Slowakei.

Attila Hidegkuti lächelte. Die kleinen Länder waren erwartungsgemäß am schnellsten im Widerstand, wenn ihre nationale – was? Identität? Ehre? oder gar Daseinsberechtigung? in Frage gestellt wurde. Darauf konnte man sich verlassen. Damit konnte man arbeiten. Die große und entscheidende Frage war nun, wie würde Deutschland reagieren? Und Frankreich? England war aus dem Spiel, auch wenn sie noch im Spielfeld herumstanden. Hidegkuti hielt es für möglich, dass das Vereinigte Königreich seine Beamten im Haus anwies, das Projekt zu unterstützen und darauf zu drängen, es öffentlich anzukündigen, um es dann innenpolitisch ausschlachten zu können, als weiteren Beweis für die Notwendigkeit des Brexit. England, dachte Hidegkuti, könne man als weiteres Druckmittel gegen die Arche und die DG COMM einsetzen, um das Projekt tunlichst zu stoppen, bevor es öffentlich wurde.

Lars Ekelöf war betont beherrscht, als er in Hidegkutis Zimmer kam. Den Anspruch, jederzeit und überall absolut korrekt zu sein, hatte er so verinnerlicht, dass er nur einen Moment lang den Impuls gehabt hatte, zu Hidegkuti ins Zimmer zu stürzen und ihn anzubrüllen: »Was soll der Scheiß?« Aber unkontrollierte Emotionen und schmutzige Sprache, die einen anderen beleidigen oder kränken konnten, erlaubte er sich nicht. Nie. Natürlich hatte er den Verdacht, dass bei diesen eigenartigen Protesten, die von den Außenministerien und Botschaftern einiger Mitgliedstaaten im Kabinett des Präsidenten eingingen, Hidegkuti irgendwie seine Finger im Spiel hatte. Dieser ungarische Husar mit seinen stets schalkhaft blitzenden Augen und diesem wabbeligen Grinsen über dem Doppelkinn hatte doch immer seine Finger im Spiel. Er konnte es nicht beweisen, aber er hatte den Verdacht, dass Hidegkuti immer wieder Probleme erfand, mit deren Lösung er sich dann beim Präsidenten wichtigmachte. Und das lief jedes Mal an ihm, Ekelöf, dem Kabinettschef, vorbei. Er atmete tief durch, trat ein und sagte: Ich habe da ein kleines Problem, ich bin sicher, du kannst mir helfen.

Hidegkuti konnte.

Da macht sich eine besonders engagierte Person in der Kommission wichtig, erklärte er. Aber ich habe schon mit dem Präsidenten gesprochen. Wir warten jetzt einmal ab. Die Sache stranguliert sich von selbst.

Lars Ekelöf war nicht der Typ, der wartete und zusah, wie etwas »sich strangulierte«. Was war das wieder für eine unerträgliche Wortwahl des Protokollchefs? Er ging der Sache nach – und das führte dazu, dass zunächst einmal Mrs Atkinson Probleme bekam.

Hidegkuti lächelte. Es lief alles so, wie er es vorhergesehen hatte.

Wer die Freiheit liebt und wer die Wahrheit liebt, der verlernt zu lieben. Das hatte sein Großvater einmal gesagt, und Émile Brunfaut, damals noch Schüler, war schockiert gewesen, ohne genau verstanden zu haben, warum. Er hatte lange über diesen Satz nachgedacht, wie über ein Rätsel, das ihn höchst beunruhigte, und er hatte sich diesen Satz wohl deshalb gemerkt. Brunfaut sah den Großvater noch vor sich, wie er erzählte und schließlich diesen Satz sagte, sein zerfurchtes, missmutiges Gesicht, das der kleine Émile damals so falsch verstanden hatte, nämlich als Ausdruck von einschüchternder Selbstgerechtigkeit und Empathielosigkeit – wenn er damals schon diese Wörter gekannt hätte. Wahrscheinlich hatte der Großvater von der Zeit im Widerstand erzählt, was sonst, und davon, dass Misstrauen, radikales Misstrauen eine Lebensversicherung war, keine gute, aber die einzige. Man konnte sich selbst und die, die einem am nächsten standen, nur dann einigermaßen schützen, wenn man möglichst wenig mit ihnen teilte und selbst denen, die man liebte, nicht vertraute. Tapfere, wunderbare Frauen und Männer sind verraten worden von Freunden, Brüdern, Vätern und sogar von ihren eigenen Kindern, von Menschen, die sie geliebt haben. Die Liebe war kein Raum der Freiheit und sie bot keinen Schutz.

Erst später, da war sein Großvater schon lange tot, hatte Brunfaut den Satz langsam zu verstehen begonnen: als er Polizist wurde. Als er lernte, grundsätzlich misstrauisch zu sein, nichts von dem zu glauben, was ihm erzählt wurde, allen Anschein als versuchte Verschleierung zu betrachten und jede schnelle und offene Erklärung zunächst für einen Versuch von Vertuschung zu halten. Aber er hatte sich geschworen, diese Déformation professionnelle nicht zu akzeptieren, auf keinen Fall zuzulassen, dass sie in sein Privatleben, in sein Verhältnis zu den Menschen, die er liebte, hineinwirkte.

Natürlich denkt man nicht jeden Tag seines Lebens an einen solchen Vorsatz. Aber nun hatte Brunfaut Anlass, daran zu denken, und er hielt sich zugute, dass er es eigentlich ganz gut gemacht hatte: Er liebte zärtlich und ohne Misstrauen die Menschen, die ihm nahestanden, er liebte ohne Furcht die Freiheit, und er liebte mit unerschütterlichem Grundvertrauen die Wahrheit, sei es in Form von Offenheit gegenüber seinen Lieben, sei es als Ergebnis von Nachforschungen und

Ermittlungen und, sei's drum, sogar als Anspruch der liberalen Presse.

Zugleich aber musste er sich eingestehen – und dieser Gedanke schockierte und verwirrte ihn jetzt –, dass das alles vielleicht nicht mehr stimmte. Er liebte? Wirklich? Musste er sich nicht eingestehen, dass er nun sagen müsste: Er hatte geliebt?

Er konnte nicht mehr vorbehaltlos lieben. Er hatte es mit einem Schlag verlernt. Konnte das wahr sein?

Das Erlebnis auf dem Friedhof. Es hatte ihn erschüttert. Und es war nicht das Schwein, das ihn zunächst in so große Verwirrung und Schrecken versetzt hatte, nein, es war vielmehr die Tatsache, dass er danach mit zerrissener Hose, Rückenschmerzen und Abschürfungen an der Hand noch eine gute halbe Stunde herumgeirrt ist, ohne Philippe zu finden, geschweige denn dessen »Freund«, der doch Anlass ihrer Verabredung an diesem Ort gewesen war. Er hatte dann eine Bank gefunden, sich hingesetzt und Philippe mehrmals angerufen, aber immer nur das Tonband gehört. Und dann war auch noch ein alter Mann vorbeigekommen, hatte sich neben ihn auf die Bank gesetzt und gesagt: Reden Sie auch schon mit den Toten?

Das alles war entsetzlich, Brunfaut ist geflüchtet, nun wirklich im Laufschritt, die ganze lange Allee hinauf, vorbei auch am Grab seines Großvaters, laufend und keuchend bis zum Ausgang und zu seinem Auto. Mit höllischem Seitenstechen, als würde sich ein großes Fragezeichen wie eine Sichel in sein Seelengeflecht schlagen, ein Schmerz, der tiefer saß als die Abschürfungen, ein Schmerz, den er schließlich benennen konnte, als er wieder zu Hause war und in der Badewanne lag. Was ihm wehtat, war das plötzliche, tiefe Misstrauen, besser gesagt: der Verlust von Vertrauen.

Selbst sein professionelles Misstrauen als Polizist hatte auf einem Grundvertrauen basiert: dem Vertrauen in den Rechts-staat. Gut, es hatte immer wieder politische Interventio-nen gegeben, wenn einflussreiche Männer in Affären ver-strickt waren, aber im Grunde war das kindisch, es konnte die Mühlen der Justiz behindern, aber das Recht auf Dauer nicht aushebeln, schon gar nicht bei Offizialdelikten wie Mord. Der vertuschte Atlas-Mord aber hatte sein Vertrauen bereits mehr erschüttert, als er sich eingestehen wollte. Die Frage war nun, wie man damit umging: wie Großvater? Oder wie Philippe? Und das war es, was ihm jetzt so wehtat: dass er Philippe plötzlich nicht mehr traute. Seinem besten Freund, dem Vater seines Patenkinds Joëlle. Auf einmal sah er ihn in einem schiefen Licht, alles, was er ihm erzählt hatte, war diffus, über die Nato und den Vatikan, Gruselge-schichten, dazu angetan, sofort die Finger von diesem Fall zu lassen, und plötzlich kommt er mit neuen Informationen, unklar welche, das würde ein Informant erklären, auf dem Friedhof – und dann war weder er noch der geheimnisvolle Informant da, und plötzlich ist er auch telefonisch nicht er-reichbar.

Brunfaut stubbste die Plastikente an, die zwischen seinen Knien auf dem Wasser schaukelte, und fragte sich, ob Philip-pe nicht vielleicht den Auftrag hatte, ihn zunächst davon zu überzeugen, dass weitere Nachforschungen sinnlos waren und ihn höchstens in Gefahr brachten, und dann mit der In-formanten-Legende zu überprüfen, ob er wirklich die Finger von dem Fall gelassen hatte oder sich immer noch neugierig damit beschäftigte.

Das Bad tat ihm gut. Es linderte seinen Schmerz nicht, aber es entspannte ihn. Er hatte das Gefühl, nun klar zu denken, aber just dies, was er dachte, beunruhigte ihn. Er machte Wellen, die Ente tanzte stoisch auf dem Wasser, stieß an sei-nen Bauch, drehte sich und schaukelte zwischen seinen Knien, er gab ihr einen Tritt, sie hüpfte, um sich dann wieder im Wasser zu wiegen.

Brunfaut hatte den Staatsanwalt nie gemocht. Respektiert, ja. Aber zugleich verachtet. Ein Mann, der sich so blind mit dem Staat identifizierte, dass er die Mächtigsten und Einflussreichsten des Staats mit dem Staat verwechselte und daher, natürlich nur in Ausnahmefällen, im Staatsinteresse sogar bereit war, das Recht zu beugen, das der Staat garantieren sollte. Aber hatte Brunfaut ihn lieben müssen, um ihn zu verstehen? Nein. Wann immer er auftauchte, war klar, da ging es um bestimmte Interessen. Und diese Interessen waren klar. Im Grunde war das immer wahrhaftig, und diese Wahrheit bedurfte keines Vertrauensverhältnisses und keiner Liebe. Ach Philippe! Brunfaut schlug mit der flachen Hand ins Wasser. Ich habe dir vertraut. Hast du mich betrogen?

Das Wasser wurde kalt, und Brunfaut fragte sich, ob er nicht wegen eines unglücklichen Zufalls einer großen Täuschung unterlag. Vielleicht stimmte sein Verdacht gar nicht und Philippe war immer noch der treue Freund, den er lieben und dem er vertrauen konnte.

Aber das Misstrauen war in sein Herz gesetzt, es war da und konnte nicht mehr durch Beschluss verbannt werden.

Die Ente war der Behälter eines Shampoos gewesen, eines Kindershampoos, »garantiert keine Tränen«, er hatte diese Shampoo-Ente als Kind geliebt und sie, nachdem sie leer war, immer aufgehoben, später sogar über alle Umzüge und Änderungen der Lebensverhältnisse hinweg. Am Bürzel hatte die Ente einen Schraubverschluss, hier konnte man das Shampoo herausrinnen lassen.

Brunfaut drückte die Ente mit beiden Füßen unter Wasser. Wenn er die Füße zurückzog, hüpfte die Ente wieder herauf, schaukelte und schwamm.

Sie konnte nicht untergehen. Sie würde immer obenauf sein.

Darauf konnte man sich verlassen. Brunfaut schraubte den Drehverschluss auf, drückte die Ente hinunter, nun begann Wasser in sie einzudringen, er legte die Arme auf den Badewannenrand, spreizte die Beine und sah zu, wie die Ente langsam unterging.

Wieder wäre Professor Erhart fast zu spät gekommen. Er nahm wie immer die Metro, stieg Schuman aus, aber der Aufgang Justus Lipsius war gesperrt. Also nahm er den Aufgang Berlaymont. Da befand er sich dann nicht nur auf der falschen Seite der Rue de la Loi, sondern auch unterhalb der Straße, in dieser seltsamen Mulde, in der das Berlaymont-Gebäude stand. Als er um die Einfriedungsmauer der Mulde herumgegangen und zur Straße hinaufgestiegen war, stellte er fest, dass es nicht möglich war, die Rue de la Loi zu überqueren. Entlang des Gehsteigs waren Absperrgitter aufgestellt, dahinter standen Militärfahrzeuge. Militärpolizisten winkten die Menschen, die von der Metro heraufkamen, ungeduldig weiter. Weitergehen! Nicht stehenbleiben!
Ich muss da hinüber, sagte Erhart, ich muss zum –
Gehen Sie weiter! Weitergehen!
Er wäre besser hinauf zum Schuman-Rondo gegangen, um von dort auf die Justus-Lipsius-Seite zu kommen, aber Erhart verstand die winkenden Bewegungen des Polizisten so, dass er in die andere Richtung gehen sollte, just dort hinunter, wo er sich das letzte Mal schon verlaufen hatte. Er schritt schnell aus, mit schwingenden Armen, in der Rechten trug er seine alte Schultasche, die bei diesem hektischen Gang immer wieder gegen sein Knie oder in seine Kniekehle schlug. Er musste bis Maalbeek gehen, dort konnte er endlich die Straßenseite wechseln. Das nächste Mal, dachte er, werde er mit der Metro nicht bis Schuman fahren, sondern gleich bei der Station Maalbeek aussteigen. Falls es überhaupt ein nächs-

tes Mal geben wird. Nach der Keynote, die er in zehn Minuten halten sollte. Er lief das ganze Stück zurück, bis zur Baustelle neben dem Justus-Lipsius-Gebäude, wo er den Durchschlupf zwischen den Baugittern und Sperrholzplatten suchte, den Korridor zum Résidence Palace, wo das Meeting stattfand. Natürlich hatte sich seit dem letzten Mal hier alles verändert, es sah nur unverändert chaotisch aus. Er wandte sich nach links, machte dann ein paar Schritte nach rechts, er sah nur Gitter, hinter seinem Rücken die Militärfahrzeuge, vor ihm die Absperrgitter, er fühlte sich wie ein gefangenes oder in die Enge getriebenes Tier. Er keuchte, drückte nun seine Tasche an die Brust, die Tasche mit dem Vortrag, der im Grunde eine Rede über die Freiheit war. Über Befreiung. Zumindest eine Rede der Selbstbefreiung.

Erhart war natürlich der Letzte. Nicht wirklich zu spät, aber doch der Letzte. Jetzt sind wir komplett, jubelte Mr Pinto. Wollen Sie noch einen Kaffee, bevor wir beginnen? Wasser?
Ja bitte, sagte Erhart. Er sah sich um, grüßte dahin, dorthin, wurde zurückgegrüßt. Wie perfekt sie alle waren. Nicht das winzigste Partikelchen Straßenstaub an ihren Schuhen – kannten sie einen anderen Weg? Hatten sie nicht auch die Baustelle überqueren müssen? Keine zerknitterten Hosen und Jacken, auf keinem Hemd auch nur der kleinste Schweißfleck. Wie waren sie hierher gekommen? Es war so schwül draußen, man musste gar nicht so wie er um die Absperrungen laufen, man schwitzte schon, wenn man nur langsam ging.
Mister Pinto fragte: Wären Sie jetzt bereit, Professor?

Professor Erhart war bereit. Immer. Sein Leben war ein ewiger Bereitschaftsdienst. Die Zeiten ändern sich, aber im Grunde blättert nur das Lose ab vom Zeitlosen. Er trank seinen Kaffee aus, nickte.

Als er zum ersten Mal zu einem Kongress eingeladen worden war, als blutjunger Universitätsassistent, hatte er sich extra für diesen Anlass einen neuen Anzug gekauft. Er durfte damals ein Referat beim Wissenschaftsforum in Alpbach halten, dem Bergdorf in den Tiroler Alpen, wo sich jährlich Eliten aus der Wirtschaft, berühmte Wissenschaftler verschiedener Disziplinen und arrivierte Künstler zum Gedankenaustausch trafen. Sein Professor, Doktor Schneider, hatte Erhart diese Einladung verschafft, um ihn zu fördern oder ihn zumindest bei Laune zu halten, immerhin hatte Erhart schon einige Aufsätze geschrieben, die dann Professor Schneider unter seinem Namen veröffentlichte. Erhart hatte sich geehrt und geschmeichelt gefühlt, und ihm wurde erst später bewusst, zu welch lächerlicher Willfährigkeit ihn diese Aussicht auf Ehre verführen konnte: Er sollte nicht einen öffentlichen Vortrag halten, sondern nur ein kurzes Referat in einem Arbeitskreis – aber dennoch: Er würde in Alpbach dabei sein und, wenn er sich bereit hielt, in Kontakt kommen mit berühmten und einflussreichen Menschen. Er wollte also den bestmöglichen Eindruck machen. Daher: ein neuer Anzug, sein erster Dreiteiler, und neue Schuhe. Er schmierte noch Lederfett auf die Schuhe, die er noch nie getragen hatte, und polierte sie. Und dann stand er in einem Raum herum, wo es Kaffee und Topfengolatschen gab, die neuen Schuhe drückten ihn, und in seinem neuen Anzug fühlte er sich verkleidet, das war nicht er selbst, der diesen Anzug buchstäblich trug.

Er sah zu, wie Sir Karl Popper auf die gebeugten Rücken österreichischer Politiker und Beamter hinabblickte – die plötzlich hochstoben und zum gerade eintretenden amerikanischen Außenminister schwärmten, um, noch tiefer gebeugt, in der hohlen Hand die Asche seiner Zigarre aufzufangen.

Und dann sah Erhart ihn: Armand Moens.

Erharts erster Kongress. Und Armand Moens' letzter öffentlicher Auftritt vor seinem Tod, wenige Wochen später. Das einzige Aufeinandertreffen von Lehrer und Schüler, Erhart hätte damals vielleicht sogar gesagt: zwischen Gott und Apostel – und sie sprachen ausgerechnet über Kleidung.

Erhart war überrascht, mit welcher Indifferenz dieser berühmte Mann gekleidet war. Er trug eine verbeulte Cordhose, einen grauen Pullover, auf dessen Brust Flecken (von Kaffee?) waren, darüber eine billige blaue Nylon-Jacke.

Erhart näherte sich, um sich vorzustellen und dem verehrten Wissenschaftler seine Reverenz zu erweisen.

Moens war alt und krank. Er war am Ende. Erhart bereute augenblicklich, ihn angesprochen zu haben. Er hätte gerne mit ihm über sein Buch diskutiert, »Das Ende der Nationalökonomie und das Wirtschaftssystem einer nachnationalen Republik«, aber als Erhart ihm gegenüberstand, war ihm augenblicklich klar, dass das nicht mehr möglich war. Die gelbe Gesichtshaut mit den braunen Flecken, die wässrigen Augen, die vom Speichel feuchten Lippen – da kam ein Student mit einem Buch von Moens und bat ihn um eine Signatur. Es war für Erhart unerträglich, zuzuschauen, wie lange Moens brauchte, um zittrig seinen Namen zu schreiben. Erhart wusste nicht mehr, was er dann gesagt hatte, er wusste nur noch, dass Moens nicht darauf einging, sondern sagte: Es schauen alle hier so verkleidet aus.

Erhart: Wie bitte?

Sehen Sie nicht? All diese Menschen mit ihren Anzügen, die sie in Wien, Paris und Oxford tragen – er tat sich schwer beim Sprechen – diese, diese Kostüme, hier, vor dem Zirbenholz und der ganzen Alpenästhetik – verkleidet! Wirken verkleidet! Und die anderen, die gekommen sind mit Loden und Trachten, weil Tirol, sie dachten, Trachtenjanker, weil Tirol – sie schauen erst recht verkleidet aus. Schauen Sie! Lauter verkleidete Menschen. Ein Wissenschaftskarneval!

Erhart wusste nicht, was er darauf antworten sollte, schließlich sagte er: Wir sollten uns nie verkleiden!

Und Armand Moens sagte verblüffend laut und schroff: Nein!

Zurück in Wien, am Institut, schrieb Alois Erhart auf einen Zettel:

»NEIN!«
Armand Moens

… und pinnte ihn an die Wand vor seinem Schreibtisch. Er wusste, dass das kindisch war, aber zugleich auch wieder nicht. Es war ein kleiner Stromstoß. »Nein!« war nie falsch. Nie? Nein!

Er knöpfte sein zerknittertes Sakko zu, um die Schweißflecken auf seinem Hemd zu verdecken, und folgte Mr Pinto in den Raum, wo er seine Keynote halten sollte.

Als Kassándra Mercouri an diesem Tag mit dem Rad ins Büro fuhr, traf sie, wie meistens, auf der Rue d'Arenberg mit Bohumil zusammen. Kassándra war aufgeregt, ungeduldig, wollte gleich lossprudeln, erzählen von ihrem Wochenende, sie war so stolz auf das, was sie herausgefunden hatte, es war verblüffend, es war so wichtig – aber stattdessen sagte sie: Was hast du? Was ist los?

Der immer so heitere, ausgelassene, kindisch tollkühne Radfahrer Bohumil trat schweigend in die Pedale, mit verkniffenem Gesicht, holte keinen seiner »Sie stehen im Weg!«-Sticker aus der Tasche, wenn ein Auto auf dem Radweg stand. Sie hatte sich immer Sorgen gemacht, wenn er diese riskanten Manöver machte, aber jetzt war sie besorgt, weil er sie nicht machte.

Jetzt erzähl schon! Was ist los?

Ich war am Wochenende zu Hause. In Prag.

Kassándra musste sich hinter Bohumil zurückfallen lassen, als sie um ein Auto, das in zweiter Spur stand, herumfuhren, während ein Bus links von ihnen vorbeidonnerte. Dann schloss sie wieder zu ihm auf, Bohumil schwieg.

Also du warst in Prag. Familie besucht? Allons! Was ist passiert?

La famille est la mort de la raison!

Bohumil!

Eigentlich nichts Besonderes. Es hat mich nicht überrascht. Oder sagen wir so: Ich wundere mich jetzt, dass es mich überrascht hat. Ich war bei den Eltern. Eh bien! Eltern sind Eltern. Dann wollte ich meine Schwester treffen, zum Essen im U Zavêsenyho, Ente mit Rotkraut, wie immer. Sie wollte nicht!

Deine Schwester wollte dich nicht treffen?

Nicht im Restaurant, nur wir zwei. Sie wollte, dass ich zu ihr nach Hause komme.

Das ist doch nett.

Nein. Sie weiß, wie gern ich die Ente im U Zavêsenyho habe. Und es ist doch immer so gewesen! Dort haben wir uns getroffen, gegessen und uns alles erzählt, alle Neuigkeiten, alle Geheimnisse, alle Gerüchte! Nein, ich wollte nicht zu ihr nach Hause. Sie hat unlängst geheiratet und –

Du kennst ihren Mann? Dann warst du also bei ihnen beiden eingeladen?

Sie hat gesagt, du warst nicht bei unserer Hochzeit! Sie hat gesagt: Ich weiß natürlich, warum. Jetzt kommst du zu uns und gibst meinem Mann die Hand. Ich mache eine Ente. Aber du gibst meinem Mann die Hand. In unserem Haus.

Und was ist das Problem?

An einem vor ihnen parkenden Auto schwang die Tür auf.

Bohumil bremste so abrupt ab, dass er fast kopfüber vom Rad fiel. Kassándra verriss ihr Rad nach links und gleich wieder nach rechts, fast wäre sie von einem Lieferwagen erfasst worden. Sie blieb stehen und stieg ab. Ihr Herz klopfte, es schlug gegen den Brustkorb und gegen ihre Schläfen. Bohumil stieg ab, schrie den Autofahrer an, der die Tür ohne zu schauen geöffnet hatte. Der Mann entschuldigte sich ein ums andere Mal, Bohumil schob sein Rad an dem Auto vorbei, an Kassándras Seite, ließ es fallen, setzte sich auf die Kühlerhaube eines parkenden Autos und weinte.

Kassándra setzte sich neben ihn, legte den Arm um seine Schulter, sagte: Es ist nichts passiert. Es ist nichts passiert. Es ist noch einmal gut gegangen!

Nichts ist gut gegangen!

Der Autofahrer stand kreidebleich da, Kassándra wedelte mit der Hand, bedeutete ihm, er solle abhauen.

Nichts ist gut gegangen, sagte Bohumil noch einmal und wischte den Handrücken über seine Augen. Ich bin also hin, ins Haus meiner Schwester. Sie wollte, dass ich ihrem Mann die Hand gebe. Und dann hat er mir den Handschlag verweigert. Er, bitte, er hat meine ausgestreckte Hand ausgeschlagen. Ignoriert. Mich angeschaut, mit seinem feisten, selbstzufriedenen Gesicht, die Hände in den Hosentaschen, und hat zu mir gesagt: Y smrade zasranej!

Wie bitte?

Tu es un crétin d'idiot!

Non! Ce n'est pas vrai!

Doch! Ich sei gekauft von den Konzernen, verrate für ein üppiges Gehalt in Brüssel die nationalen Interessen der Tschechischen Republik, ich sei ein Volksschädling und so weiter. Das alles in der Diele von ihrem Haus. Neben den Garderobenhaken.

Und was hast du gesagt, was hast du gemacht?

Bohumil lachte auf, schniefte und sagte: Was ich gemacht habe? Meine Hand wieder zurückgezogen. Und dann habe ich zu meiner Schwester gesagt: Wenn wir noch lange da in der Diele diskutieren, verbrennt inzwischen die Ente. Und sie: Es gibt keine Ente. Es gab nur die Klarstellung.

Kassándra drückte ihn, drückte seinen Kopf auf ihren Busen, streichelte seinen Kopf. Es war lächerlich: Sie streichelte seinen Fahrradhelm.

Da stand plötzlich ein Mann vor ihnen, der sie anbrüllte. Der Besitzer des Autos, auf dessen Kühlerhaube sie saßen. Bohumil sah auf, nahm aus seiner Umhängetasche einen Sticker heraus, löste bedächtig die Folie ab, stand auf und klatschte dem Mann den Aufkleber auf die Stirn. Der Mann taumelte zurück, Bohumil nahm sein Rad und sagte zu Kassándra: Los! Wir müssen zur Arbeit!

Kassándra war verblüfft, wie schnell sie auf dem Rad saß, sie traten kräftig in die Pedale, schweigend, erst in der Avenue des Arts sagte Bohumil: Meine Schwester ist fünf Jahre jünger als ich. Als sie in der Schule war, habe ich für sie die Hausaufgaben gemacht. Niemand hat gesagt, sie ist dumm oder faul. Sie war die Prinzessin. Jetzt bekommt sie ein Kind von einem Faschisten. Und niemand in der Familie regt sich auf. Er ist nett zu den Verwandten, singt mit schöner Stimme alte Volkslieder, er sieht einigermaßen gut aus, er verdient gut, und er ist kein Kommunist. Das ist es, was heute bei uns zählt.

Kassándra wusste nicht, was sie sagen sollte. Erst als sie angekommen waren, ihre Räder abgeschlossen hatten und zum Lift gingen, sagte sie: Ich habe auch einiges von meinem Wochenende zu berichten.

Vor dem Lift standen zwei Salamander. Sie grüßten mit überschwänglicher Höflichkeit, die Lifttür ging auf, ein Salamander fragte: Vierter, nicht wahr?

Kassándra bejahte, der Salamander drückte Drei und Vier, fragte freundlich: Hatten Sie ein schönes Wochenende?

Das Wochenende war scheiße, sagte Bohumil.

Und Kassándra spürte einen Kick, eine freche, verrückte Lust, und sagte zu ihrer eigenen Überraschung: Ja, und bis jetzt war auch der Montag scheiße!

Oh!

Der Lift schwebte hoch, sehr langsam, in dieser Situation bedrückend langsam, und Bohumil sagte: Und der Lift ist auch scheiße.

Kassándra kicherte. Innerlich.

In der Dritten sprangen die beiden Salamander aus dem Lift, Bonne journée!

Bonne journée!

und Bohumil lachte. Kassándra sagte: Ich bin froh, dass du wieder lachen kannst. Und jetzt will ich von meinem Wochenende erzählen. Dir und Xeno. Es ist wichtig. Und es wird dich überraschen.

Fenia Xenopoulou saß bereits an ihrem Schreibtisch, mit einem Becher Kaffee aus der Kantine. Es sollte wieder drückend heiß werden, das Fenster stand offen, schon jetzt, um acht Uhr morgens, war die Luft warm, aber Fenia Xenopoulou schien zu frösteln. Sie hielt den Becher mit beiden Händen umfasst, als wollte sie sich daran wärmen. Aber das war vielleicht nur Gewohnheit. Ihr war nicht kalt. Höchstens seelisch. Sie hatte einen Kater. Nicht physisch, aber moralisch. Sie hatte die Nacht bei Fridsch verbracht und hatte es zunächst nicht geschafft, ihm zu sagen, dass – sie hatte dann doch, viel zu spät, als der Moment wahrlich nicht mehr günstig war, den Vorschlag gemacht, dass – und er – schläft ein – und sie – hielt den Kaffeebecher mit beiden Händen und schämte sich, dass sie dann – sie hatte das Kissen auf sein Gesicht gedrückt und – sie wollte nur sehen, ob er noch zu einer Regung fähig ist, oder sind Männer, wenn das Eiweiß weg ist, zu keiner Regung mehr fähig? Er hat sich freigestrampelt, sie weggeschlagen, geschrien, und sie ist in Tränen ausgebrochen – na gut, da hat er sie in den Arm genommen und –

Kassándra kam ins Zimmer, warum war sie so aufgedreht? Wir müssen reden, hast du Zeit, es ist wichtig, für das Jubilee Project, ach, du hast Kaffee, gute Idee, ich hole mir auch einen und sage Bohumil Bescheid, ist dir das recht, in zehn Minuten hier bei dir?

Hast du eine Zigarette?

Nein, ich rauche nicht. Aber wenn du rauchen willst, dann reden wir besser in Bohumils Zimmer, er hat das Ding da oben, wie soll ich sagen – also, bei ihm kann man rauchen ohne Alarm.

Eine Viertelstunde später saßen sie in Bohumils Zimmer, Kassándra hatte Kaffee für alle geholt, Xeno rauchte zum ersten Mal vor Zeugen drei Zigaretten hintereinander, und Kassándra erzählte von der Dossin-Kaserne in Mechelen.

Kassándra liebte es, am Wochenende Ausflüge mit der Bahn zu machen. Sie genoss es, dass »von Brüssel aus alles so nahe war«, wie sie gerne sagte, ihr Europa, man war in weniger als eineinhalb Stunden in Paris, in zweieinhalb Stunden in London, in Amsterdam oder Köln in weniger als zwei Stunden. Manchmal fuhr sie Sonntag Früh los und am Abend wieder zurück, manchmal fuhr sie schon samstags und übernachtete einmal. Sie besuchte dann Museen und Galerien, traf Freunde in Bistros und gönnte sich ab und zu ein nettes kleines Teil in einer Boutique. An diesem Wochenende aber hatte sie nicht den Thalys genommen, sondern einen Regionalzug: Nach Mechelen, nur etwa dreißig Kilometer, weniger als eine halbe Stunde, von Brüssel entfernt.

Sie hatte in Le Soir den Nachruf auf Gustave Jakubowicz gelesen, den berühmten Brüsseler Anwalt, der, wie sie wusste, auch eine wichtige Rolle in der Geschichte des Europäischen Gerichtshofs für Menschenrechte gespielt hatte, der Mann war eine Legende, hochaktiv bis zuletzt, bis er jetzt eben mit knapp neunzig Jahren gestorben war. Aber was die besondere Aufmerksamkeit von Kassándra erregt hatte, war die Zeile über den Autor des Nachrufs: »Jean Nebenzahl, wissenschaftlicher Mitarbeiter des Dokumentationszentrums für Holocaust und Menschenrechte der Kaserne Dossin in Mechelen«. Die Dossin-Kaserne war während der Besatzungszeit das belgische Sammellager der SS gewesen, von wo aus Juden, Roma und Widerstandskämpfer nach Auschwitz deportiert wurden. Kassándra hatte vielleicht einmal davon gehört, dass diese Kaserne nun ein Museum war, aber sie wusste nicht, dass es dort eine Forschungsstelle gab, eine wissenschaftliche Institution, die die Geschichte der Deportationen nach Auschwitz systematisch aufarbeitete. Sie schrieb eine Mail an Jean Nebenzahl, der prompt antwortete: Er sei gerne bereit, sie am Sonntag zu treffen, mit ihr durch die Ausstellung zu gehen und alle ihre Fragen, so gut er könne, zu beantworten.

Kassándra war eine engagierte Beamtin. Sie fuhr nach Mechelen und traf Jean Nebenzahl, weil sie dachte, dass dies für das Jubilee Project interessant sein könnte. Aber sie wäre nie auf den Gedanken gekommen, dafür Überstunden zu verrechnen oder erst dann nach Mechelen zu fahren, wenn dies »als Dienstreise bewilligt« wurde und danach »abgerechnet« werden konnte. Es interessierte sie, es war ein Sonntagsausflug, bei dem sie etwas Neues sehen, etwas lernen konnte, und wenn es sich tatsächlich als hilfreich für das Projekt erweisen sollte, umso besser.

Und Jean Nebenzahl war ein engagierter Wissenschaftler,

der sich selbstverständlich auch an einem Sonntag, »außerhalb seiner Dienstzeiten« zur Verfügung stellte, wenn jemand von der Europäischen Kommission auf seine Arbeit aufmerksam wurde und deshalb nach Mechelen kam. Es wurde immer schwieriger, Menschen für die Arbeit dieser Forschungsstelle zu interessieren und die Mittel dafür aufzutreiben. So war er geradezu gerührt vom Interesse dieser europäischen Beamtin – die er auch sofort gegoogelt hatte: Tätigkeitsfeld, Fotos.

Sie müssen sich nicht bedanken, sagte er, ich bin ja kein seelenloser Bürokrat, auch wenn ich in diesem Haus am Schreibtisch von Eggert Reeder sitze. Wer das war? Er war der deutsche Militärverwaltungschef in Belgien, hat die Deportation von mehr als dreißigtausend Juden nach Auschwitz organisiert, er wurde nach dem Krieg zu zwölf Jahren Zuchthaus verurteilt – und dann von Konrad Adenauer begnadigt. Er ist ja nur an einem Schreibtisch gesessen. Er war doch nicht für die Ermordung der Juden in Auschwitz verantwortlich. Er hat sie in seinen Bürostunden nur auf Listen geschrieben, damit sie geordnet auf die Schlachtbank geliefert werden konnten. Er war eindeutig kein Fanatiker, er hat nie Überstunden gemacht. Er bekam nach der Begnadigung eine Beamtenpension der Bundesrepublik Deutschland. Er hatte genug Dienstjahre. Und ich sitze heute an seinem Schreibtisch und arbeite mit diesen Listen.

Jean Nebenzahl war ein gutaussehender Mann, etwa so alt wie Kassándra, und vom Typ her sehr ähnlich: nicht dünn – Kassándra war misstrauisch gegenüber hageren Männern, sie fand, dass sie zu Askese, also zu Rigidität und Freudlosigkeit neigten, aber Jean war auch nicht dick –, die Dicken fand Kassándra formlos, nicht attraktiv und ohne Selbstkontrolle, aber man sollte nicht verallgemeinern, also die meisten, jedenfalls viele Dicke standen bei Kassándra im Verdacht, sich gehenzulassen. Jean war einfach ein Mann, groß, stark – und doch weich, so sah sie, was er in seiner Selbsteinschätzung als »ein bisschen zu mollig« bezeichnet hätte. Und sie war hingerissen von seinen braunen Augen und seinem gelockten schwarzen Haar.

Und warum, glaubst du, soll uns interessieren, dass du dich verliebt hast, fragte Xeno.

Es gab in Bohumils Arbeitszimmer nur zwei Stühle, den Schreibtischstuhl und einen Besucherstuhl. Bohumil hatte Xeno seinen Schreibtischstuhl angeboten, Xeno wollte aber lieber stehen. Sie sah mit genervtem Gesichtsausdruck auf Kassándra hinab, die auf dem Besucherstuhl saß. Kassándra sprang auf: Versteht ihr nicht? Ich habe es doch deutlich gesagt! Sie ha-ben die Lis-ten! In Mechelen! Hier ist das Archiv des SS-Sicherheitsdienstes, der für die Deportationen zuständig war, vollständig erhalten. Wir haben mit der ganzen Welt korrespondiert und hatten alles hier vor unserer Nase: Mit dem Bummelzug dreißig Minuten von uns entfernt! Ich weiß jetzt auch, wie viele Auschwitz-Überlebende noch leben, und habe ihre Namen.

Wie viele sind es?

Sechzehn, sagte Kassándra.

Sechzig?

Sechzehn!

Sechzehn? Weltweit?

Soweit sie auf Deportationslisten standen und dann als Überlebende registriert wurden, kurz: soweit sie in irgendeiner Form erfasst wurden und bekannt sind – ja.

Und von ihnen gibt es Kontaktadressen?

Jean sagte: Nicht hundertprozentig auf dem letzten Stand. Kann sein, dass sie bei einigen nicht mehr stimmen, weil es ja nicht mit jedem regelmäßigen Kontakt gibt. Aber grundsätzlich ja.

Und in welchem – wie soll ich sagen? Zustand? Ich meine, wie sind sie gesundheitlich – ich meine, könnten sie anreisen und auftreten?

Von fünf ist bekannt, dass sie regelmäßig auftreten, in Schulen oder anderen Zeitzeugenprogrammen.

Fünf?

Ja. Und einer ist ein besonderer Fall. Ein gewisser David de Vriend. Und er lebt hier in Brüssel. Jean meinte, wenn er unser Projekt richtig versteht, dann wäre dieser de Vriend unser idealer Zeitzeuge.

Warum?

Er ist nicht nur einer der letzten Auschwitz-Überlebenden, er ist auch der letzte noch lebende Jude aus dem legendären 20. Deportationszug nach Auschwitz. Das war der einzige Deportationszug, der von Widerstandskämpfern überfallen, auf offener Strecke angehalten wurde. Mit Zangen zerschnitten sie den Draht, mit dem die Verriegelungen der Viehwaggontüren gesichert waren, schoben die Türen auf und riefen den Juden zu, sie sollen rausspringen und fliehen. Wer sprang, bekam fünfzig Franc und eine sichere Adresse zugesteckt. Die meisten hatten Angst, sie fürchteten, von den Deutschen erschossen zu werden, wenn sie zu flüchten versuchten. Sie blieben im Zug, der nach einem kurzen Schusswechsel der SS-Wachmannschaft mit den Widerstandskämpfern die Fahrt fortsetzte. Alle, die nicht gesprungen sind, gingen sofort nach der Ankunft in Auschwitz ins Gas. Aber de Vriend war einer von denen, die aus dem Zug sprangen.

Aber du sagtest doch, dass er in Auschwitz war.

Diese Flucht aus dem 20. Deportationszug war im April 43. Er kam zu einer Familie in einem Dorf, weiß jetzt den Namen nicht mehr, die hat ihn als Neffen aus Brüssel ausgegeben. Er war blutjung damals und schwer traumatisiert: Die Eltern sind im Zug geblieben. Er hätte bei der Familie, die ihn aufgenommen hatte, das Kriegsende abwarten können, aber er wollte kämpfen, vielleicht die Eltern befreien? Europa befreien? Er schloss sich im Juni 44 als Jüngster der Widerstandsgruppe »Europe libre« an, das war die Gruppe um Jean-Richard Brunfaut, von dem ihr vielleicht gehört habt, also zumindest kennt ihr die Rue Brunfaut. Diese Gruppe wurde legendär, wegen ihrer tollkühnen Aktionen, aber auch deswegen, weil sie sich politisch von allen anderen Widerstandsgruppen unterschied: Sie war die einzige, die mit ihrem Namen nicht für ein freies Belgien, sondern für ein freies Europa eintrat. Sie wollten nach dem Krieg, nach dem Sieg über die Nazis, auch gleich die Abschaffung der belgischen Monarchie und die Gründung einer Europäischen Republik. Brunfaut und seine Genossen engagierten sich auch bis an ihr Lebensende gegen die faschistischen Regime in Spanien und Portugal, gegen Franco und Salazar, die die Siegermächte bei der Befreiung Europas seltsamerweise vergessen hatten. Jedenfalls: David de Vriend wurde im August 44 verraten, verhaftet und nach Auschwitz deportiert. Er wurde nicht ins Gas geschickt. Er war jung und stark. Er überlebte die Monate bis zur Befreiung. Nach dem Krieg wurde er Lehrer. Er ist nicht wie viele andere Überlebende als Zeitzeuge ab und zu in Schulen aufgetreten, er wollte Lehrer werden, um sich jeden Tag um die nächsten Generationen kümmern zu können. Er wollte nicht Zeuge, er wollte Erzieher sein. Also, was sagt ihr? Wenn wir Martins Idee weiterverfolgen, und wir haben ja dafür den Sanktus des Präsidenten, dann müssen wir doch diesen Mann in den Mittelpunkt der Feier stellen. Da haben wir alles: ein Opfer des Rassismus, einen Widerstandskämpfer, ein Opfer von Kollaboration und Verrat, einen Zeugen des Vernichtungslagers, einen Visionär des nachnationalen Europas auf der Basis der Menschenrechte, die Geschichte und die Lehre aus der Geschichte in einer Person, in der Person dieses Lehrers.

Sehr schön, sagte Xeno. Welch mitreißende Emphase. Es gibt da nur ein kleines Problem.

Schwester Joséphine machte sich Sorgen um de Vriend. Sie war eine gerechte Frau, die alle ihre »Schützlinge«, wie sie sie nannte, möglichst gleich zu behandeln versuchte, ob sie ihr sympathisch, unangenehm oder gar widerlich waren, ob sie sich kommunikativ oder abweisend gaben, freundlich oder aggressiv. Joséphine fand, dass sie alle gute Gründe dafür hatten, so zu sein, wie sie sich hier zeigten, biographische Gründe, die in diesem Haus deutlich zutage traten, wenn sie begriffen, dass sie in der Maison Hanssens nichts anderes mehr zu tun hatten, als ihrem Lebensende entgegenzudämmern, während sie noch so taten, als wären sie Gäste in einem Kurhotel.

Alle, die sie betreute, waren am Ende ihres Lebens, aber mit ihrem Leben noch nicht fertig. Das war Joséphines Erfahrung, ihre Einsicht. Sie stellte sich jeden Tag vor, was das bedeutete. Für jeden Einzelnen. Und da waren sie alle gleich, und in dieser Gleichheit unterschied sie nicht mehr zwischen pflegeleichten und lästigen Schützlingen, sympathischen und unsympathischen. David de Vriend hatte nie das Bedürfnis gezeigt, mehr als nötig mit ihr zu kommunizieren. Und wenn er sich für etwas bedankte, dann klang das mehr nach einer Verabschiedung als nach einer Bezeugung von Dankbarkeit. Man konnte also nicht sagen, dass de Vriend ein Schützling war, den man lieben musste und dem man daher besonders liebevoll seine Aufmerksamkeit schenken wollte. Und doch fand Joséphine, dass sie eine besondere Verantwortung für Herrn de Vriend hatte. War es wegen der Nummer auf seinem Arm? Sie fragte sich das und verbot sich zugleich diesen Gedanken. Sie war gerecht, zu jedem gleich aufmerksam. Jedem hatte das Leben mitgespielt.

So stürmte sie mit den besten Absichten in de Vriends Zimmer, mit zwei Zeitungen, und schrie: Sie kommen nie –
De Vriend saß in seinem Fauteuil, nur mit einer Unterhose bekleidet.

Joséphine schrie: Ich habe Sie schon seit Tagen nicht mehr im Gemeinschaftsraum gesehen, wo die Zeitungen liegen. Aber wir müssen doch Zeitungen lesen, nicht wahr, Herr de Vriend? Oder wollen wir nicht mehr wissen, was in der Welt los ist? Nein, nein, wir wollen doch Bescheid wissen, wir wollen doch neu-gier-ig bleiben, nicht wahr, Herr de Vriend. Was lesen Sie denn am liebsten, Herr de Vriend? Le Soir oder De Morgen? Ich glaube, Sie sind ein De-Morgen-Leser, nicht wahr? Jetzt wollen wir ein bisschen unsere kleinen grauen Zellen trainieren und lesen, und – natürlich ging Joséphine die Apathie von diesem de Vriend auf die Nerven, aber sie versuchte doch, ihn zu animieren, alert zu bleiben, neugierig, kommunikativ, bevor er ganz wegdämmerte.

David de Vriend nahm die Zeitung, starrte sie an, dann begann er langsam zu blättern, bis er plötzlich gebeugt in die Zeitung starrte.

Wollen wir einen Artikel gemeinsam lesen? Interessiert Sie –

De Vriend stand auf, ging durch das Zimmer, ging hin und her, schaute, suchte, Schwester Joséphine sah ihn verwundert an: Was suchen Sie?

Meinen Notizblock. Haben Sie nicht gelesen? Todesfälle. Ich muss einen Namen, schon wieder einen Namen aus meiner Liste streichen.

Zehntes Kapitel

Gdy wszystko było na próżno,
nawet najpiękniejsze wspomnienie nas nie pocieszy.
I jak tu szukać usprawiedliwienia?

Émile Brunfaut stand nackt mit dem Rücken zum Spiegel im Badezimmer und versuchte sich über die Schulter zu schauen, um festzustellen, ob ein Bluterguss oder eine Abschürfung auf der Höhe von Steiß- oder Kreuzbein zu sehen war. Zunächst hatte das Bad ihn entspannt, aber je länger er in der Badewanne saß, desto stärker wurde der Schmerz über dem Gesäß, zweifellos Folge seines Sturzes.

Seine Halswirbel knackten und knirschten, aber er schaffte es nicht, seinen Kopf so weit zurückzudrehen, dass er im Spiegel sein Rückenende sehen konnte. Nun kamen zu den Schmerzen im Steiß noch Verspannungsschmerzen im Nacken dazu. Natürlich wusste Brunfaut, dass sein Körper nicht so biegsam, beweglich und elastisch sein konnte wie der einer russischen Turnerin, aber es deprimierte ihn doch, dass er gar so steif war. Sein Kollege Jules Meunier hatte, »um nicht einzurosten«, sogar im Kommissariat in Arbeitspausen immer wieder Yoga-Übungen gemacht, bei längeren Besprechungen zwischendurch sogar einen Kopfstand. Wie lächerlich Brunfaut das gefunden hatte! Andererseits aber auch so schrullig, dass es fast schon wieder sympathisch war. Aber das hätte Brunfaut nie zugegeben. Wahrscheinlich hatte Jules recht gehabt. Brunfaut war davon überzeugt, dass Jules völlig problemlos seinen Kopf zurückdrehen und in aller Ruhe Rücken und Steiß im Spiegel betrachten konnte, ohne Verspannung und ohne Schmerzen. Ach Jules! Wie elastisch und beweglich du tatsächlich für dein Alter noch warst, als mir der Fall Atlas entzogen wurde und ich gehen musste. Hast dich aus dem Stand von mir abwenden können, ohne Verspannung und ohne Schmerzen!

Brunfaut versuchte nun, seinen Nacken zu massieren, da hinten war alles bretthart – da läutete das Telefon. Er lief vom Bad ins Schlafzimmer, wo er sich ausgezogen hatte, aber da war sein Telefon nicht, er lief ins Wohnzimmer, da lag es, auf dem Schreibtisch. Er hob ab und erstarrte. Es war Philippe.

Hör zu, sagte Brunfaut, wir reden nicht am Telefon darüber. Ja, ich will, dass du mir das erklärst. Natürlich. Treffen wir uns – wo? Café Kafka? Wo ist das? Rue des Poissonniers? Ecke Rue Antoine Dansaert. Verstanden. In eineinhalb Stunden? D'accord.

Als Brunfaut im Café ankam, war Philippe noch nicht da. Er war gut fünfzehn Minuten zu früh, das musste also gar nichts bedeuten, dennoch hatte er sofort das mulmige Gefühl, dass Philippe irgendein Spiel mit ihm spielte und ihn wieder sitzenließ.

Sitzenlassen – aber wie denn? Émile Brunfaut konnte ja kaum sitzen. Das Steißbein tat unerträglich weh. Nur wenn er sein Gewicht auf eine Beckenhälfte verlagerte, war das Sitzen einigermaßen erträglich. Aber wie lange konnte er das durchhalten? Er stand auf und stellte sich an die Theke. Gequält verlagerte er immer wieder das Gewicht von einem Bein auf das andere, trank in einem Zug sein Bier aus, bestellte noch eines, dazu einen Genever. Er sah auf die Uhr. Er würde sicher keine halbe oder drei viertel Stunde auf einen Philippe warten, der dann ohnehin nicht kam. Sicher nicht. Höchstens zehn Minuten. Er kippte den Schnaps hinunter, nahm sein Bierglas und ging hinaus vor das Café. Wie heiß es war. Er konnte sich an keinen Frühling oder Frühsommer in Brüssel erinnern, der so heiß, so drückend, so brutal gewesen ist. Der Asphalt, die Pflastersteine, die Hausmauern speicherten die Hitze, strahlten sie ab, und selbst ein Lufthauch war keine Erlösung, sondern schlug einem die Hitze ins Gesicht wie ein Keulenschlag. Dazu kam jetzt, in diesem Moment, ein ganz seltsames, unnatürlich erscheinendes Licht, es war knapp vor Sonnenuntergang, aber man sah hier in der Straßenschlucht natürlich nicht die Sonne, man sah nur gelblich rosa Lichtbahnen, die – Brunfaut sah hinauf – den Himmel wie mit einem giftigen Lack überzogen.

Émile Brunfaut war ein poetischer Mensch. Er wusste es nur nicht, weil er wenig las. Und Poesie überhaupt nicht. Von allen Gedichten, die er seinerzeit in der Schule gelernt hatte, viele waren es nicht, war ihm nur ein einziges in Erinnerung geblieben: »À une Passante«, weil ihn die Zeile »Un éclair ... puis la nuit! – Fugitive beauté« damals eigentümlich berührt hatte. Später, als er schon Kommissar war, hatte er seine Mannschaft, wenn sie im Dunkeln tappte, mit der Paraphrase aufgemuntert: La nuit ... puis l'éclair! – Le fugitif est visible. Das war, seiner Meinung nach, die einzige poetische Leistung seines Lebens gewesen. Aber da unterschätzte er sich. Jetzt war er von diesem Licht schmerzhaft berührt und er empfand es als Metapher – und das war zweifellos ein poetischer Akt. Das schiefe Licht. Plötzlich war alles in schiefes Licht getaucht. Das Vertraute bekam einen giftigen Anstrich, und – er sah auf dem Eckhaus gegenüber das Straßenschild: »Poissonniers« – es schillerte fischig.

Er wäre gerne länger in diesem Licht verharrt, in dieser Stimmung – nicht dass sie ihm angenehm war, aber ja, doch: Er fand sie stimmig. Stimmung, stimmig, ja, es stimmte. Das war es, das war das Licht seiner seelischen Schmerzen, aber er ertrug die körperlichen nicht. Er trank sein Bier aus, wollte ins Café hineingehen und zahlen, nach Hause fahren, da stand plötzlich Philippe vor ihm, umarmte ihn, warum so fröhlich, und warum drückte er ihn gar so fest?

Brunfaut stöhnte kurz auf und löste sich aus der Umarmung. Philippe machte ein besorgtes Gesicht, fragte: Was ist? Hast du Schmerzen?

Warum empfand Brunfaut den besorgten Gesichtsausdruck seines Freundes als gar so übertrieben? Wie konnte Philippe glauben, dass er auf dieses Schmierentheater hereinfiel? Wenn es aber keines war, wie konnte er selbst glauben, dass sein bester Freund dazu fähig wäre?

So wütend, als würde er mit dem Fuß aufstampfen, um sich zu vergewissern, dass der Boden nicht schwankte und ihm nicht unter den Füßen weggezogen wurde, sagte er: Ja, er habe Schmerzen, er sei auf dem Friedhof gestürzt. Auf dem Friedhof. War da nicht etwas?

Er atmete tief durch: Wir waren dort verabredet, nicht wahr? Du warst nicht da. Du kannst mir das sicher erklären.

Mein Gott, warum bist du gestürzt? Hast du dich verletzt?

Und wenn ich jetzt sage: Weil ich nicht dich gesehen habe, aber ein Phantom?

Philippe wollte offensichtlich etwas sagen, sagte es aber nicht, schüttelte den Kopf, dann deutete er auf Brunfauts leeres Bierglas: Gehen wir rein, wir brauchen etwas zu trinken.

Es war die Zeit, in der sich das Café rasch füllte. Nun war kein Tisch mehr frei, aber Émile Brunfaut sagte, dass er ohnehin nicht sitzen könne.

Es hat mich auf den Arsch gesetzt. Bei unserem Treffpunkt auf dem Friedhof. Es ist das Steißbein. Es tut höllisch weh.

Er gab dem Mann hinter der Theke ein Zeichen: zwei Bier!

Ich werde auch nicht lange stehen können. Also reden wir nicht lange um den heißen Brei herum. Was ist passiert? Warum warst du nicht da? Was hat es mit diesem geheimnisvollen Freund auf sich, den wir dort treffen sollten? Ist dein Freund der alte Mann, der mich fragte, ob ich mit den Toten rede? Willst du mir erklären, dass das eine Losung war, an der ich ihn erkennen sollte? Und warum warst du dann telefonisch nicht erreichbar? Bitte Philippe, erkläre mir das. Und ich bitte dich herzlichst: Erkläre es mir so, dass ich es verstehen kann.

Du wirst es nicht glauben, sagte Philippe, aber –

Da bekamen sie ihr Bier.

Émile Brunfaut hob sein Glas, sagte: Santé! Ich werde es also nicht glauben. Und weiter?

Hör zu, sagte Philippe. Man kann das alles sehr einfach erklären. Das Problem ist nur, dass es zwar sehr logisch ist, zugleich aber höchst unglaubwürdig klingt.

Du wirst es schaffen, dass ich dir glaube.

Das glaube ich nicht. Ich habe dich noch nie so misstrauisch erlebt, du wirst zu deinem eigenen Großvater, du musst aufpassen, es ist dieses Misstrauen, das Vertrauen zerstört. Egal, ich erzähle dir jetzt die Geschichte, ganz kurz, damit du bald wieder ins Bett gehen kannst. Übrigens, Joëlle schickt dir Grüße, und sie fragt, wann du endlich wieder einmal bei uns vorbeikommst. Ich werde ihr sagen, dass sie Geduld haben muss, weil du krank bist. Also: Es begann damit, dass ich einen Brief bekam. Wir hatten die Geschichte, du weißt, was ich meine, bereits abgehakt. Und da kam der Brief. Ich betone: Brief. Keine Mail, keine elektronische Nachricht. Ich hätte ihn fast übersehen, weil ich mein Postfach im Haus nur noch ausräume, um alles sofort in die Mülltonne zu werfen. Ist doch immer nur Werbung. Jedenfalls, in diesem Brief schrieb mir eine Person, die sich selbst tatsächlich »Personne« nannte, dass sie mich zurückverfolgt habe.

Zurückverfolgt?

Ja. Ich bin offenbar damals bei meinen Versuchen, in unserer Angelegenheit weiterzukommen und herauszufinden, wie der Fall Atlas auf deinem Computer gelöscht werden konnte, irgendwie zumindest in den Vorhof eines Systems gelangt, das daran – sagen wir vorsichtig – beteiligt war. Genau weiß ich es ja nicht. Jedenfalls hat dort jemand bemerkt, dass ich

versucht habe, hineinzuhacken. Und wenn das jetzt ein großes Ding ist, dann weiß dieser Personne in kürzester Zeit,
dass ich das war. Wie ich heiße, wo ich wohne, alles. Die haben diese Möglichkeiten. Personne schrieb mir also einen
Brief – und begründete auch diese Form der Kontaktaufnah-
me: der gute, alte, mit Snail-Post verschickte Brief sei die einzige Form von Kommunikation, die nirgendwo abgespeichert,
mitgelesen, ausgewertet und gegen dich verwendet werden
kann. Was früher »Toter Briefkasten« hieß, das Versteck für
geheime Nachrichten, ist heute der ganz normale Hausbrief-
kasten. Also gut. Du kennst ja Léo Aubry vom Labor. Ein guter
Junge. Immer hilfsbereit. Und absolut vertrauenswürdig, nicht
wahr? Eben. Ich habe ihm den Brief gegeben. Das Papier: Al-
lerweltspapier, das meistverkaufte, in jedem Diskounter bekommst du davon 500 Blatt für vier Euro. Der Drucker, soweit man von der Tinte einen Rückschluss ziehen kann, ein
einfacher Canon, der meistverkaufte Drucker in Belgien. Auf
dem Papier nicht die winzigste DNA-Spur oder sonst etwas,
das einen Hinweis auf den Absender geben könnte.
Bien. Aber was stand in dem Brief?
Dass ich mich weit vorgewagt hätte. Dass das unmöglich in
meiner Dienststelle mit meinen Vorgesetzten abgesprochen
sein könne. Ich sei offenbar, außerhalb meines Jobs, ein Ein-
zelkämpfer. Er sei das auch.
Er? Woran hast du erkannt, dass es sich bei Personne um
einen Mann handelt?
Gute Frage. Ich bin davon ausgegangen.
Ach ja? Und weiter?
Er – ich bin sicher, es ist ein Mann. Er schrieb weiter, er sei
nicht der Typ Whistleblower, der bereit sei, sein Leben zu
zerstören, aber er sympathisiere mit allen, die nach Ritzen suchen, durch die die Wahrheit sickern kann.
Das war seine Formulierung?

Ja. Und er bot mir Hilfe an. Wenn ich an einer Fortsetzung der Kommunikation mit ihm interessiert sei, soll ich weitere Versuche, ins System einzudringen, unterlassen, denn er könne nicht länger gewährleisten, dass der Alert, den ich auslöste, unterdrückt wird. Er wird mich dann mit den Informationen, die ich brauche, versorgen. Wenn ich einverstanden sei, soll ich am nächsten Tag zu einer bestimmten Uhrzeit auf Google folgende Suchanfrage eingeben: Regentanz der Hopi-Indianer.

Hopi was? Was erzählst du mir da? Das ist doch verrückt!

Nein, das ist nicht verrückt. Offenbar hat dieser Personne die Möglichkeit, zu sehen, was ich an meinem Computer mache. Und wenn ich das eingebe, was er verlangt, und eine der Seiten, die dann angeboten werden, anklicke, dann weiß er, dass ich seinen Vorschlag annehme – ohne dass das in irgendeiner Form im System auffällig wird.

Und das hast du dann so gemacht?

Ja.

Ich brauche noch ein Bier.

Ich auch. Und weißt du, was dann kam? Ich gab also ein: »Regentanz Hopi-Indianer«, und Google empfahl mir sofort: »Systemtheorie und neue soziale Bewegungen. Identitätsprobleme in der Risikogesellschaft«.

Verstehe ich nicht.

Da gibt es nichts zu verstehen. Das ist ein Buchtitel, und in diesem Buch gibt es offenbar ein Kapitel über Hopi-Indianer und Regentänze. Warum auch immer. Das habe ich angeklickt.

Und?

Zwei Tage später hatte ich den nächsten Brief.

Und wie hast du geantwortet?

Indem ich zu bestimmten Zeiten, die er vorgab, in meinem Computer Suchanfragen auf Google machte. Die Stichwörter waren meine Antwort beziehungsweise meine Fragen. Er saß offenbar irgendwo, wo er kontrollieren konnte, wer was auf Google sucht.

Wie oft habt ihr – ich meine: Wie lang ging das so?

Drei Wochen? Vielleicht vier.

Und du hast mir nichts davon erzählt? Wir waren bei Anderlecht gegen Mechelen, wir haben in unsere Schals geweint, wie bitte kann Mechelen 2:0 gegen uns gewinnen? Wir haben dann noch fünf Bier getrunken, mindestens, alles Mögliche geredet, aber du hast nichts erzählt, nicht von diesem Personne. Das muss doch damals – das muss doch in dieser Zeit gewesen sein.

Ja, aber ich wollte erst wissen, ob das seriös ist. Es hätte ja auch ein Spinner sein können.

Aber es war kein Spinner?

Nein. Besser gesagt: Ich weiß es nicht. Er gab interessante und glaubwürdige Hinweise. Von ihm kam das Dossier über die Zusammenarbeit des Vatikans mit den westlichen Geheimdiensten. Ich habe das gelesen, es war verblüffend, geradezu phantastisch, aber zugleich auch völlig logisch und nachvollziehbar, es waren Puzzleteile, die perfekt passten. Schau, kein Geheimdienst der Welt hat die Ressourcen, die finanziellen und personellen Mittel, ein Agentennetz aufzubauen, das sich auf eine Weise über den Globus spannt, die dem Stand der Globalisierung auch nur annähernd entspricht. Jetzt haben sie also ihre Agenten in den Brennpunkten. Aber wer vertraut ihnen, wer gibt ihnen Informationen? Nur die, die ohnehin mit den Regierungen dieser Geheimdienste zusammenarbeiten, das heißt: Was diese Agenten berichten, unterscheidet sich nicht wesentlich von dem, was auch der Botschafter nach Hause berichtet. Und weiter: Wo ist der nächste Brennpunkt? Was wird morgen zu brennen beginnen, während Millionen investiert werden in die Arbeit von vielleicht dreißig Agenten, die in Krisengebieten in ein paar noch funktionierenden Hotels mit Wellness-Bereich sitzen? Und zwanzig der dreißig sind vom CIA, die steigen sich an einem Ort gegenseitig auf die Füße, aber woanders haben sie niemanden. Und das ist bitte der mächtigste Geheimdienst. Also gut, jetzt eine einfache Frage: Wer aber hat in jedem Kaff einen Agenten sitzen? Der Vatikan. Warum? In jedem Kaff gibt es einen Priester. Wer erfährt in jedem Winkel die geheimsten Geheimnisse? Der Pfaffe, nicht zuletzt über die Beichte. Auch wenn das vielleicht nicht alles abdeckt, ist es doch um ein Vielfaches mehr, als selbst die bestausgestatteten Geheimdienste an Informationen zu organisieren vermögen. Und deshalb, mein Freund, wetteifern die Geheimdienste mit allen Mitteln um die Gunst des Vatikans, um Zusammenarbeit und Austausch mit der Kirche. Das war im Kalten Krieg so, und das ist mittlerweile nicht einmal mehr ein Geheimnis. Jetzt gibt es einen anderen Feind. Es ist nicht mehr der gottlose Kommunismus, der Feind heute heißt Islam.

Aber ... Warte! Ein Moslem wird doch nicht zu einem Pfarrer gehen und beichten, dass er einen Anschlag verübt hat oder einen plant. Das ist doch verrückt.

Nein, natürlich nicht. Aber brave Christenmenschen erzählen dem Pfarrer, was ihnen Verdächtiges aufgefallen ist, zum Beispiel bei den neuen Mietern in der Nebenwohnung oder im Nebenhaus oder im Haus gegenüber, sie sitzen mit Ferngläsern an ihren Fenstern und schauen in die Fenster der Häuser auf der anderen Straßenseite. Ist Neugier eine Sünde? Unsere Neugier sicher nicht. Aber genauso wie wir in der Regel berichten, was wir ermittelt haben, so beichtet der Christ. Und deshalb existiert die im Kalten Krieg aufgebaute Achse zwischen den Geheimdiensten und dem Vatikan noch immer.

Glaubst du das?, fragte Brunfaut.

Philippe stutzte, dann lachte er. Ich bin nicht religiös. Ich glaube nicht. Und du kannst jetzt glauben, was du willst. Ich gebe dir die Fakten. Was macht übrigens dein Steiß?

Noch ein Bier und ein Genever, und es geht besser.

Gut. Da halte ich mit. Nun gibt es von Personne einen Hinweis darauf, dass die Kirche eine Art von Todesschwadron unterhält, die mit Billigung der Geheimdienste mutmaßliche Terroristen oder so genannte Hassprediger einfach abknallt. Also Menschen, von denen Terrorakte erwartet werden, gegen die der Rechtsstaat aber nicht genug Handhabe hat, um sie legal aus dem Verkehr zu ziehen. Und damit sind wir beim Fall Atlas. Gotteskrieger machen den Job, und die Geheimdienste unterstützen sie dadurch, dass sie den jeweiligen Fall anschließend in Luft auflösen. Personne schickte mir eine Liste mit vierzehn Mordfällen, die es im vergangenen Jahr in Europa gab, über keinen von ihnen stand etwas in den Zeitungen.

Hast du das überprüft?

Ja. Ich fand auf keinen der aufgelisteten Mordfälle auch nur den geringsten Hinweis. Das heißt: Es hat sie nicht gegeben, oder die Vertuschung war so perfekt, dass es eben keinen Hinweis geben kann.

Aber jetzt kommen wir ins Gefilde von Verschwörungstheorien.

Nein, kommen wir nicht. Denn wenn du heute Hinweise auf den Atlas-Mord suchst, wirst du auch nichts finden. Nichts. Absolut nichts. Aber wir wissen, es hat ihn gegeben. Und was wir brauchen, ist nicht ein Beweis für die vierzehn Mordfälle auf der Liste, sondern eine Erklärung für den Mord im Hotel Atlas. Und die Erklärung von Personne klingt verdammt logisch! Santé!

Irgendetwas störte Brunfaut. Und seine Erfahrung als Polizist sagte ihm: Wenn dich an einer Legende etwas stört, dann ist mit großer Wahrscheinlichkeit wirklich etwas daran faul.

Ich verstehe nicht, warum du mich nicht eingeweiht und auf dem Laufenden gehalten hast, sagte er.

Habe ich doch, sagte Philippe. Das heißt, ich kenne dich doch. Ich wusste, ich muss dir mehr bieten als solch eine Geschichte. Fakten. Also wollte ich Personne treffen. Daher habe ich zu der vereinbarten Zeit in meinem Computer nur noch Suchanfragen mit Variationen des Stichworts »Treffen« gemacht. Drei Tage später ein Brief, mit dem Vorschlag: Treffen auf dem Friedhof, so wie ich es dir dann auch gesagt habe.

Und da hast du endlich dein Rendezvous mit diesem Phantom – und gehst nicht hin?

Was sagst du da? Ich war doch dort. Natürlich. Ich habe keine Ahnung, wo du warst. Vielleicht am falschen Denkmal, vielleicht zur falschen Stunde, was weiß ich. Ich jedenfalls war dort. Und ich saß auf der Bank. Und ich wartete auf Personne und auf dich. Da läutete mein Handy. Ich hob ab, und eine Stimme sagte: Mister Philippe Gaultier? Ich sagte Ja. Er fragte: Sitzen Sie auf der Bank, die wir als Treffpunkt vereinbart haben? Ich begriff, wer das war, und sagte Ja. Er: Stehen Sie bitte auf. Ich: Wie bitte? Warum? Er: Stehen Sie bitte auf. Ich stand auf, er: Drehen Sie sich bitte um und sagen Sie mir, was Sie sehen. Ich fand das grotesk, ich sagte: Hören Sie, ich will keine Spielchen, und er: Keine Spielchen. Was sehen Sie? Ich sagte: Einen Baum! Und dachte: Wie lächerlich ist das, was soll das? Er sagte: Dahinter? Ich: Gräber. Soldatengräber. Weiße Kreuze! Er: Sehr gut. Und dahinter? Ich: Nichts. Nur ein riesiges Feld von weißen Kreuzen. Er: Dann heben Sie den Blick. Was sehen Sie jetzt? Ich: Nichts. Ich weiß nicht, was Sie hören wollen. Er: Ich will hören, was Sie sehen. Ich: Nichts, Bäume, Himmel. Er: Und zwischen Bäumen und Himmel? Hinter dem Friedhof? Ich: Ja, zwei große

Gebäude, wie zwei riesige Blöcke Emmentaler. Er: Genau. Wissen Sie, was das ist? Ich: Die Nato? Er: Richtig. Und jetzt haben Sie die Informationen, die ich Ihnen geben kann. Arbeiten Sie damit, oder geben Sie auf! Ciao, Herr Polizist!

Du warst auf dem Friedhof und bekamst diesen Anruf?

Ja. Dann habe ich noch eine Dreiviertelstunde auf dich gewartet, dann bin ich gegangen.

Und warum hattest du dein Telefon ausgeschaltet? Ich habe dich mehrmals angerufen, weil ich dich nicht gefunden habe und –

Mein Telefon war gestört. Ich konnte plötzlich weder anrufen noch angerufen werden. Und als es wieder funktionierte, habe ich dich sofort angerufen. Darum sind wir ja jetzt da.

Brunfaut fand diese Geschichte toll. Wirklich spannend. Hätte er Philippe gar nicht zugetraut. Aber er glaubte ihm kein Wort. Wie weh ihm das tat.

Ich habe starke Schmerzen, sagte er. Sei mir nicht böse, ich muss nach Hause. Er sah, dass Philippe seinen Schnaps nicht angerührt hatte. Émile nahm das Glas, kippte es hinunter, sagte À bientôt, mon ami! Dann humpelte er hinaus. Er merkte, dass er hinkte, das wollte er nicht, er versuchte, aufrecht und ohne sichtbare Beschädigung zu gehen, aber das gelang ihm nicht, er humpelte hinaus aus dem Kafka und hätte schreien wollen.

Dass Matek nicht nach Istanbul, sondern nach Krakau geflogen war, hatten sie noch am selben Tag gewusst. Und dass die Hinweise, er wäre gleich am nächsten Tag nach Warschau weitergereist, eine von ihm gelegte falsche Fährte waren, wussten sie drei Tage später. Matek hatte keine Bestätigung dafür, aber er ging davon aus. Und er wusste auch, dass er Pater Szymon, seinen engen Freund aus Seminar-Tagen, in einen Gewissenskonflikt bringen würde, wenn er nach drei

Tagen nicht abreiste. Szymon hatte ihm Unterschlupf im Augustinerkloster gegeben, in dem Glauben, dass Matek wieder eine Zeit der Einkehr und Kontemplation brauchte. Szymon war absolut loyal, Matek wusste, dass er sich auf ihn verlassen konnte, aber er wusste auch, dass Szymon es nie würde verstehen können, dass er, Matek, sich in Wahrheit hier im Kloster vor Kirchenoberen versteckte. Sie kannten seine Kontakte, also war klar, dass sich Szymon ab dem vierten Tag in ihrem Fadenkreuz befand. Und ebenso klar war, wie sich Szymon im Konflikt zwischen treuer Freundschaft und dem Gehorsamsgelübde, das er als Priester abgelegt hatte, entscheiden würde. Matek hatte die drei Tage zur Meditation genutzt, seine Lage überdacht, Kraft getankt. Aber nun musste er das Kloster verlassen. Er hatte zwei Möglichkeiten: weiterzureisen, in billigen Hotels abzusteigen, wo man es mit Meldezettel und Ausweis nicht so genau nahm, keine Bankkarte und keine Kreditkarte zu verwenden, tunlichst auch Überwachungskameras an öffentlichen Orten zu meiden, den Laptop nie einzuschalten. Er wäre ein U-Boot, unsichtbar, unauffindbar. Allerdings: Er hätte keine Möglichkeit, herauszufinden, was da in Brüssel, im Hotel Atlas, schiefgelaufen war und was sie jetzt mit ihm vorhatten. Und sein Bargeld würde noch für maximal eine Woche reichen. Diese Woche als U-Boot würde seine Situation nicht verbessern, und keine Erkenntnisse bringen. Zweite Möglichkeit: Er begab sich in die Höhle des Löwen! Er musste herausfinden, was geschehen ist und wie es um ihn bestellt war. Und es gab nur einen Ort, wo er dies in Erfahrung bringen konnte: Poznań. Sie würden nicht erwarten, dass er, nachdem er untergetaucht war, nun direkt in die Zentrale kommen würde. Es war gefährlich. Andererseits: Wenn es schiefging, könnte er Demut zeigen und geltend machen, dass er doch freiwillig heimgekommen sei.

Er umarmte Szymon zum Abschied, sagte: Danke Bruder, drückte seine beiden Hände, Gott schütze dich!

Szymon lächelte: Gott schütze dich! Und – gute Reise nach Poznań!

Matek war schwer aus der Fassung zu bringen. Er war unausgesetzt auf der Hut, kalkulierte alle Möglichkeiten, war, wie er dachte, in jeder Situation auf jede Eventualität vorbereitet. Er hatte das kalte Blut eines Mannes, der in vierter Generation Soldat war. Aber damit hatte er nicht gerechnet. »Gute Reise nach Poznań!« – das traf ihn wie ein Schlag, der ihn kurz betäubte. Er atmete einmal tief durch, stellte seinen Rucksack ab und sagte: Du weißt –

Szymon nickte.

– dass ich nach Poznań fahre? Aber ich habe dir das nicht gesagt.

Du wirst dort erwartet. Und du hast nichts zu befürchten.

Was weißt du, Bruder Szymon? Und warum hast du mir nichts gesagt?

Du hast mich nicht gefragt. Du bist zu den Exerzitien erschienen, zum gemeinsamen Gebet und der Pflege des Schweigens, und du bist zu den Mahlzeiten gekommen, ausgenommen am Abend, und hast geschwiegen, nicht nur bei der Suppenruhe. Sonst hast du stundenlang in der Kapelle vor der »Gottesmutter vom Trost« gekniet. Wenn mich ein Bruder fragt, gebe ich Auskunft, aber du hast nicht gefragt.

Aber du hast Auskunft gegeben?

Ja.

Du wurdest nach mir gefragt?

Szymon nickte.

Matek schaute zu Boden, hob langsam den Kopf. Er sah den schwarzen Habit Szymons, den schwarzen Ledergürtel, die schwarze Mozetta, aus deren Kragen ein grauer Hals hervorkam, auf dem unter der schwarzen Kapuze das graue Gesicht

Szymons saß, Matek senkte seinen Blick wieder, betrachtete seine eigenen Hände, auch sie waren grau, er ließ sie fallen, sie verschwanden im Grauschwarz über dem schwarzen Stein des Fußbodens in diesem düsteren Vorraum. Matek sah nun Szymon direkt ins Gesicht. Szymons Lippen waren rot. Als hätte er sie sich blutig gebissen. Jetzt frage ich dich, sagte Matek. Was weißt du? Was kannst du mir sagen?

Du hattest eine Aufgabe. Ich weiß nicht welche. Es ging etwas schief. Ich weiß nicht, was. Es war nicht deine Schuld. Du wirst erwartet. Du hast nichts zu befürchten. Das soll ich dir sagen, solltest du mich fragen.

Matek sah Szymon an, nickte, nahm dessen Kopf zwischen seine Hände, zog ihn zu sich und drückte seinen Mund auf Szymons blutrote Lippen. Das Blutrot, das einzige Leuchten in diesem Raum, der in diesem Moment ein Weltraum war und zugleich nur eine Schleuse hinaus in die Welt.

Dann trat er aus dem Kloster ins Freie, in das bedrohliche, in das bedrohte Freie.

Nach den Tagen in der stillen Düsternis hinter den dicken Mauern traf ihn das grelle Licht des Tages wie ein Blitz.

Die DG AGRI hatte auf die Inter-Service Consultation in Sachen Jubilee Project nicht reagiert und niemand zum Meeting geschickt. Die Organisation von Jubiläen und Feierstunden, das interessierte keinen in dieser Generaldirektion, und schon gar nicht, wenn im Mittelpunkt der Feier nicht eine Leistungsschau der europäischen Agrarpolitik stehen sollte. Und es interessierte die AGRI noch weniger, wenn die DG COMM die Vorbereitung der Feierlichkeiten ausgerechnet der Kultur übertrug, dieser »Arche im Trockendock«, wie sie George Morland einmal genannt hatte. Der Elefant wusste, dass man aus einer Mücke nicht wirklich einen Elefanten machen kann.

Und jetzt war es ausgerechnet dieser George Morland von der AGRI, der, nach den ersten Querschüssen vom Rat, auch in der Kommission Fäden zu knüpfen begann, die zu Fallstricken für das Projekt werden sollten.

George Morland war, wie die meisten englischen Beamten, im Haus nicht sehr beliebt. Die Briten, das hatte sogar der Präsident selbst einmal gesagt, akzeptieren hier nur eine einzige verbindliche Regel: dass sie grundsätzlich eine Ausnahme sind. Tatsächlich standen die Engländer immer im Verdacht, die Interessen der Gemeinschaft gegenüber den Interessen Londons hintanzustellen. In vielen Fällen war der Verdacht begründet. In anderen Fällen aber war es komplizierter: Das Vereinigte Königreich war ja tatsächlich, ob man wollte oder nicht, prinzipiell ein Sonderfall. Die englische Krone hatte Besitztümer, die allerdings rechtlich kein Teil des Vereinten Königreichs waren, wie die Isle of Man oder die Kanalinseln, was in Hinblick auf die Entwicklung einer europäischen Steuerpolitik ein unlösbares Problem darstellte: die Steueroasen eines Mitglieds, auf die es rechtlich keinen Zugriff gab. Die Queen war formal Staatsoberhaupt der Commonwealth-Staaten, was zu juristischen Spitzfindigkeiten etwa in allen Handelsverträgen führen musste, die die EU mit Nicht-EU-Staaten abschloss. Hätte man diese besondere Situation nicht jedes Mal in Ausnahme-Regelungen berücksichtigt, wäre zum Beispiel Australien plötzlich ein Teil des europäischen Binnenmarkts gewesen. Es war von Anfang an nicht einfach mit England gewesen, aber es gab durchaus Engländer, die in Brüssel zu Europäern wurden. Und man musste auch George Morland zugutehalten, dass er in seinen Jahren in Brüssel nicht nur ein paar Brocken Französisch gelernt, sondern auch wichtige europapolitische Arbeit geleistet hatte. In seiner Funktion in der AGRI war er stets ein glühender Verteidiger und Förderer der kleinteiligen Landwirtschaft gewesen, und auch wenn er es deshalb tat, weil er die englische Landschaft im traditionellen Sinn gepflegt und nicht von riesigen Agrarindustriekomplexen und Monokulturen zerstört sehen wollte, so war ebendies auch von allgemeinem europäischen Interesse. Und da ließ sich Morland, dieser Upper-Class-Sprössling, auch nicht von Agrar-Industrie, Saatgut-Konzernen und ihren Lobbyisten bestechen. Er beziehungsweise seine Familie hatte beträchtlichen Grundbesitz im östlichen Yorkshire, der an mehrere kleine Farmer verpachtet war. Morland kannte ihre Leistungen und ihre Nöte. Ihre Interessen gegen die radikale Intensivierung der Landwirtschaft zu verteidigen, war ein klassischer Fall von Eigennutz, der dem Gemeinnutz diente. Die einzige Monokultur, die er akzeptierte, war der Golfplatz.

Morland war also ein sehr ambivalenter Fall. Er wusste, dass er nicht beliebt war, aber das hatte mit seiner Arbeit in der Kommission zunächst wenig zu tun. Er hatte schon in seiner Jugend darunter gelitten, erst als Schüler und dann als Student in Oxford. Er war eine unglückliche, auf den ersten Blick komische Erscheinung und hatte bei allem Bemühen kein gewinnendes Wesen. Sein rundes, rosafarbenes Gesicht, seine platte Nase, das starke rote Haar, das er nur in Form eines Bürstenhaarschnitts bändigen konnte, der kleine stämmige Körper – er hatte als Kind viele Nächte in sein Kissen geweint, wegen der Spottnamen, die ihm nachgerufen wurden. Vor Schlimmerem als Spott hatte ihn seine Herkunft geschützt, die ihn – in einer Art seelischer Notwehr – schließlich überheblich machte, zugleich aber auch besonders ehrgeizig. Er lernte, sich durch Ämter und Karriere Respekt zu verschaffen, wobei er, mit ironischem Lächeln, ganz alte Schule war: Im Zweifelsfall sollte ihn fürchten, wer ihn partout nicht schätzen wollte.

Now is the winter of our discontent / Made glorious summer by this sun of Brussels.

Aber die Sonne verdunkelte sich. Er war ein END, Expert National Détaché, seine Zeit in Brüssel lief ab. Und ihm war in all dem Chaos der Verhandlungen wegen des Austritts Großbritanniens aus der Union ein schwerer Fehler unterlaufen, der ihn zu Hause gehörig Reputation gekostet hatte. Die Deutschen hatten tatsächlich einen bilateralen Handelsvertrag mit China abgeschlossen, der ihnen den chinesischen Markt für ihre Schweineproduktion öffnete. Schweine! Er hatte das nicht ernst genommen, er war maßgeblich daran beteiligt gewesen, alle Versuche zu boykottieren, einen Gemeinschaftsvertrag der Union mit China zustande zu bringen, er hatte Privilegien für das Vereinigte Königreich verteidigen wollen und die Konsequenzen nicht absehen können. Dieser Kai-Uwe Frigge hatte doch tatsächlich recht gehabt! Die Turbulenzen am Finanzmarkt London City waren beträchtlich und hatten den Wechsel wichtiger Fonds nach Frankfurt beschleunigt. Auf Grund von Schweinen! Morland war fassungslos gewesen. Welche enorme ökonomische Bedeutung es hatte, dass China auch den Schlachtabfall von Schweinen importieren wollte, war ihm völlig unverständlich gewesen. Die Iren hatten in den Zeiten der Hungersnot um ein paar Pence Schweinefüße gekauft und stundenlang ausgekocht, das war elendes Essen in der größten Misere, und Schweineohren hatte in London der Butcher den Stammkunden für ihre Hunde geschenkt. Und der Schweineschädel – nun ja. In das Maul eines toten Schweins hatte er seinen Penis gesteckt, als Initialritus für die Mitgliedschaft im Oxforder Bullingdon Club, der exklusiven Studentenverbindung für Zöglinge aus den besseren Familien. Das tun zu müssen, um dabei sein zu dürfen, war seine letzte Demütigung gewesen, gemildert durch Rausch und Gejohle. Danach nur noch Anerkennung. Schwein kann Spuren von Tories enthalten. Ja. Haha! Wie sie jetzt lachten, die Deutschen. Sie verkaufen Abfall zum

Filetpreis, aber England hat keinen Anteil, und demnächst ist UK ganz draußen.

Es ist verrückt, völlig irrational, aber diese Schweinegeschichte war ein wesentlicher Grund dafür, dass George Morland nun zur radikalen Obstruktion überging. Wenn England schon den Schaden hatte, dann sollte es wenigstens die Schädiger verspotten können. Und alles, was der Kommission nun misslang, stärkte die britische Position bei den kommenden Verhandlungen. Und wenn die Kommission, angeblich unter Schirmherrschaft des Präsidenten, eine Image-Kampagne vorbereitete, dann soll sie scheitern. Ein schlechtes Image der Kommission war gut. Für England.

Morland kippte in seinem Schreibtischstuhl nach hinten und feilte seine Fingernägel. Was war der Grund dafür, dass seine Nägel plötzlich einrissen, splitterten und brachen? Er feilte und dachte nach. Von Zeit zu Zeit blies er den Abrieb von seiner Brust.

Und die gute Mrs Atkinson! Morland lächelte. Es war zwar nicht von nationaler und schon gar nicht von europapolitischer Bedeutung, aber es wäre doch eine hübsche Fußnote in der Geschichte seiner politischen Bemühungen, wenn mit dem Scheitern des Jubilee Project auch diese frigide Person mit ihrem Muff beschädigt wäre. Sie hatte nur wegen dieser Frauenquote den Job bekommen, den er angestrebt hatte und für den er zunächst auch als Favorit gehandelt worden war. George Morland würde es nie zugeben, es wäre nicht exakt das, was er als »objektive Notwendigkeit« bezeichnen würde, aber der bloße Gedanke, Mrs Atkinson zu Fall bringen zu können, gefiel ihm sehr.

Er hatte, wenn er alles recht bedachte, eine klare Vorstellung davon, was nun zu tun war. Ein paar Verabredungen zum Mittagessen mit maßgeblichen Kollegen von anderen Generaldirektionen, am besten im Martin's, das hatte einen schönen Garten, da waren die Raucher unter den Kollegen glücklich und viel entspannter, offener, dort müsste er ihnen maßgeschneiderte Argumente servieren, die sie beunruhigten und gegen das Projekt einnahmen.

Morland wechselte die Feile. Nach grob kam nun fein.

Das würde zunächst eine gewisse Eigendynamik bewirken, Gerede, Rumoren, und diese Unruhe müsste man dann vorsichtig in die Richtung lenken, dass das Bedürfnis nach einer Ratsarbeitsgruppe entstünde, um das Problem auszudiskutieren und zu lösen.

»Das Problem lösen.« Auch in Hinblick auf diese Formulierung war George Morland konservativ. In den letzten Jahren hatte sich eine erstaunliche Sprachverschiebung im Haus durchgesetzt, und niemandem ist es aufgefallen, zumindest hat es niemand kommentiert oder gar in Frage gestellt. Wenn früher gesagt wurde: »ein Problem lösen«, so hieß das jetzt: »das Problem einer Lösung zuführen«. Wenn gesagt worden war: »eine Entscheidung treffen«, so wird jetzt gesagt: »eine Entscheidung herbeiführen«. Statt »etwas zu analysieren«, musste es jetzt »einer Analyse unterzogen werden«. Wenn es geheißen hatte, dass »Vorkehrungen getroffen werden«, so wurden jetzt »Vorkehrungen auf den Weg gebracht«. Man könnte ein ganzes Lexikon der neuen »Comitology-Language« anlegen, und es war erstaunlich, wie in diesem Babylon gewisse sprachliche Tendenzen sofort Allgemeingut in allen Sprachen wurden. George Morland war sensibel genug, dies zu bemerken. Er war kein Semiotiker, kein Hermeneutiker, kein Sprachwissenschaftler, aber er hatte doch das deutliche Gefühl, dass diese Entwicklung ein Zeichen war, eine Bedeutung hatte, die symptomatisch für den Zustand der Kommission war, für ihre Hilflosigkeit, ihre Erstarrung. »Etwas auf den Weg bringen« war doch eindeutig etwas anderes, etwas Defensiveres als »etwas tun«. Diese Formulierungen verrieten, dass es nicht mehr um ein Ziel ging, sondern nur noch um den Weg. So ungefähr sah er das. Aber er akzeptierte es nicht. Er beharrte auf dem guten alten »ein Problem lösen«, und in diesem Fall hieß das ohne Umschweife: Kill the project, kill Mrs Atkinson.

Nun nahm er die weiche Nagelbürste, um allfällige winzige Feilstaub-Rückstände zu entfernen, dann holte er aus der Schreibtischlade den farblosen Nagellack. Vergnügt lackierte er seine Fingernägel und dachte mit einem dezenten Anflug von Hohn an Mrs Atkinson, die ihre kalten Finger mit den abgekauten Nägeln in einem Muff versteckte.

Und bereits zwei Wochen später konnte er sich ganz unverdächtig dem allgemeinen Wunsch nach der Bildung einer Ratsarbeitsgruppe anschließen, in der Zuständigkeit des CAC (»Cultural Affairs Committee«).

Mrs Atkinson wusste sofort: Das war das Ende des Projekts – das sie selbst doch gar nicht wirklich gewollt hatte. Es war ja bloß eine Initiative der Kultur gewesen. Nach außen war das Projekt völlig mit dieser Xenopoulou verbunden, die sich da enorm wichtiggemacht hatte. Xeno wiederum war sich nicht so sicher, sie fand, wenn es noch Diskussionsbedarf gab, dann sollte sich Martin darum kümmern. Das Projekt war doch Martin Susmans Idee gewesen. Und sie hatte ihm alle organisatorische Arbeit übertragen.

Und Martin war nicht da.

Auf dem Grundstück des Altersheims Maison Hanssens hatte sich ursprünglich eine Grabsteinmanufaktur befunden. Piet Hanssens, Steinmetz in vierter Generation, war ohne Nachkommen gewesen und hatte auch niemand gefunden, der die Manufaktur übernehmen und weiterführen wollte. Als er mit dreiundsiebzig Jahren wegen seiner Quarzstaublungenkrankheit eine demütigende Odyssee durch Spitäler und Pflegeanstalten erleben musste und nicht mehr arbeiten konnte, vermachte er testamentarisch sein Haus, die Werkhalle und den Grund der Ville de Bruxelles, unter der Bedingung, dass die Stadt beziehungsweise die Region Brüssel an dieser Stelle ein würdiges Alters- und Pflegeheim errichtete. Dann schloss er die Augen. Die finanziell klamme Stadt nahm das Erbe an, aber es dauerte Jahre, bis schließlich mit Hilfe von EU-Geldern, aus dem Europäischen Fonds für regionale Entwicklung und dem Europäischen Sozial-Fonds, die ehemalige Grabstein-Manufaktur zu einem modernen »Kompetenz-Zentrum für Senioren-Pflege« um- und ausgebaut werden konnte. In der ehemaligen Werkhalle befand sich nun der Speisesaal, im ehemaligen Schauraum die Bibliothek und der Gemeinschaftsraum des Altersheims, sonst war nichts von der ursprünglichen Bausubstanz übrig geblieben, nichts erinnerte mehr an die Geschichte dieses Ortes.

Fast nichts. Hinter dem Seitenausgang neben der Bibliothek, der eigentlich eine Fluchttür war, standen auf einem Grünstreifen ein knappes Dutzend blanke Grabsteine ohne Gravuren, übrig gebliebene Schaustücke der alten Manufaktur. Es war unklar, ob diese Steine einfach vergessen oder als Reminiszenz an die Geschichte des Ortes bewusst dort belassen worden waren. Niemand, außer dem Hauswart, Monsieur Hugo, der auch die Grünflächen um das Haus herum mähte, bekam sie normalerweise zu Gesicht.

Und dann entdeckte sie David de Vriend. Er hatte das Haus verlassen wollen, er wusste nicht mehr warum, er war einen Augenblick verwirrt, als er im Erdgeschoss den Lift verließ, was wollte er, wohin wollte er, hinaus, er ging nach links, statt nach rechts zum Ausgang, stand plötzlich vor der Fluchttür, drückte den großen roten Querbalken, mit dem man sie öffnen konnte, und befand sich vor den Grabsteinen, die er verwundert ansah – er war doch nicht zum Friedhof gegangen, er hatte doch nur etwas essen gehen wollen. Er nahm wahr, dass auf diesen Grabsteinen keine Namen standen – ein Friedhof der Namenlosen? Aber warum so wenig Steine? Warum so ein kleiner Friedhof? Tausende, Hunderttausende Menschen hatten keinen Namen mehr gehabt, als sie sterben mussten, die Namen von Millionen Menschen sind ausgelöscht worden, bevor sie in den Tod geschickt wurden, sie waren zu Nummern gemacht worden, aber zahllos, und hier – er schaute und begann zu zählen – waren nur: zwei, drei, vier, fünf – da nahm ihn ein Pfleger am Arm, de Vriend hatte durch das Öffnen der Fluchttür einen Alarm ausgelöst.

Was machen Sie denn da? Wollten Sie hinausgehen? Ja? Das ist die falsche Tür. Kommen Sie, ich bringe Sie – wohin wollen Sie denn?

David de Vriend sagte nun bestimmt, dass er essen gehen wollte.

In den Speisesaal?

Nein! Hinaus, in das Gasthaus, in das – er deutete mit dem Zeigefinger: In das, dort! Nebenan.

Wenig später saß er im Le Rustique, die Kellnerin brachte ein Glas Rotwein, und er schämte sich. Das war wieder ein Moment der Klarheit. Und Klarheit hieß Scham. Er fragte sich, warum er –

Natürlich wusste er, warum er –

Und er wurde wütend. So wollte er nicht –

Es war unerträglich heiß. De Vriend zog sein Sakko aus, krempelte die Hemdärmel auf, wischte sich mit seinem Taschentuch den Schweiß von der Stirn. Er konnte nicht denken. Es war zu laut. Am Nebentisch die schnatternde Großfamilie, die kreischenden Kinder. Genervt sah er hinüber –

und lächelte. Das war ein Reflex. Er hatte immer gelächelt, wenn er Kinder sah. Beglückt, oder verständnisvoll, oder einfach aus Höflichkeit.

Da sah er, dass ein Mädchen neugierig zu ihm hersah. Wie alt mochte sie sein? Vielleicht acht. Ihre Blicke trafen sich. Da kam sie zu ihm an den Tisch.

Bitte, nein! Dachte er.

Cool!, sagte sie und zeigte auf die tätowierte Nummer auf de Vriends Arm.

Ist das echt?

Ja, sagte er und zog sein Sakko an.

Cool!, sagte sie und zeigte ihm ein Klebetattoo auf ihrem Unterarm.

Vier chinesische Schriftzeichen.

Ist aber nicht echt, sagte sie. Ich darf noch nicht echt.

Weißt du, was das heißt, fragte de Vriend. Nein? Aber es gefällt dir? Ja?

Er tippte auf die Zeichen.

Auf das erste: Alle

Das zweite: Menschen

Das dritte: sind

Das vierte: Schweine

…

Hab mich verlesen, sagte er und tippte

auf das erste: alte

und das vierte: schweigsam.

Prof. Alois Erhart folgte António Oliveira Pinto in den Meeting Room. Er sah die Mitglieder der Reflection Group im Halbkreis um den Stuhl herum sitzen, auf dem er Platz nehmen sollte: Ein Halbkreis von Laptops und Tablets, dahinter gesenkte Blicke, auf die Bildschirme gerichtet, er hörte das leise schnelle Klicken von Tastaturen.

Erhart stand da, schließlich setzte er sich. Nach und nach richteten sich die Blicke auf ihn.

Hier sollte nur eine Diskussion stattfinden? Das täuschte. Es ging um seine Hinrichtung, um das Ende seines Lebens in der Expertenwelt. Aber hatte Erhart es nicht darauf angelegt? Was sagt man in Erwartung einer Hinrichtung? Letzte Worte. Jetzt ist es so weit, dachte er, genau darauf wollte er seit langem hinaus: Letzte Worte.

Wie fröhlich Herr Pinto alle Anwesenden begrüßte! Nur der griechische Professor, der in Oxford lehrte, tippte noch schnell etwas in seinen Laptop, es musste ganz wichtig und dringend sein, zumindest war es eine Demonstration von Wichtigkeit und Dringlichkeit. Erhart lächelte, sagte: Sind Sie fertig, Herr Kollege? Können wir beginnen?

Letzte Worte. Das war eine Geschichte, die auf Erharts erste wissenschaftliche Publikation zurückging, die in der Vierteljahreszeitschrift zur Wirtschaftsforschung der Universität Wien erschienen war. Damals war er noch Wissenschaftliche Hilfskraft. In dieser Publikation referierte er die Theorie der nachnationalen Volkswirtschaftslehre von Armand Moens und unterkellerte sie mit einigem neuen statistischen Material über die Entwicklung des Welthandels. Voll Stolz hatte Erhart damals ein Exemplar seines Aufsatzes an Armand Moens geschickt – der, zu Erharts Verblüffung, umgehend antwortete. Den Antwortbrief hatte Alois Erhart an diesem Tag mit, und ein Auszug daraus war Teil des kleinen Referats, das er nun hielt.

Zunächst begann Erhart mit dem Zitat von Armand Moens: »Das 20. Jahrhundert hätte die Transformation der Nationalökonomie des 19. Jahrhunderts in die Menschheitsökonomie des 21. Jahrhunderts sein sollen. Das ist auf so grauenhafte und verbrecherische Weise verhindert worden, dass danach die Sehnsucht neu und noch dringlicher wiedererstand. Allerdings nur im Bewusstsein einer kleinen politischen Elite, deren Nachfolger bald beides nicht mehr verstanden: die kriminelle Energie des Nationalismus und die Konsequenzen, die aus den Erfahrungen mit dem Nationalismus bereits gezogen worden waren.«

Einige tippten in ihre Laptops. Erhart wusste nicht, ob sie mitschrieben oder Mails beantworteten. Es war ihm egal. Er hatte noch dreizehn bis fünfzehn Minuten, er hatte Zeit, sein Moment kam noch.

Erhart erläuterte ganz kurz die globale Wirtschaftsentwicklung bis zum Ersten Weltkrieg und mit einigem Zahlenmaterial den radikalen Rückschlag durch Nationalismus und Faschismus – und er sah, dass bereits jetzt, in Minute 5 seines Referats, einige sich langweilten. Nichts langweilte sie so sehr wie die Erinnerung an Faschismus und Nationalsozialismus. Das war ein finsteres Kapitel, das Buch mit diesem Kapitel ist zugeschlagen, ein neues Buch ist längst aufgeschlagen, diese Buchhaltung ist jetzt super, außer in einigen faulen Staaten, dort muss man durchgreifen, das ist unsere Aufgabe, wir halten nichts von Kapiteln in alten Büchern, wir sind die neuen Buchhalter.

Nur ein Beispiel, sagte Erhart, für die Zäsur durch die Jahre 1914 bis 45: Wenn sich der Welthandel in den nächsten Jahren linear so weiterentwickelt wie in den vergangenen zwanzig Jahren – wobei wir nicht einmal sicher davon ausgehen können –, dann wird im Jahr 2020 das Volumen des Welthandels von 1913 erreicht sein. Das heißt, wir nähern uns erst langsam wieder dem Stand der Globalisierung der Vorkriegszeit.

Das ist Unsinn! Das kann doch nicht sein!

Sie wachten auf! Ach, wenn sie wüssten, dass sie noch lange nicht aufgewacht waren!

Warum sagen Sie »Unsinn«, Herr Kollege? Das ist gesichertes statistisches Material, sagte Erhart. Ich wollte Sie nur daran erinnern, ich hätte nicht gedacht, dass Sie es gar nicht kennen.

Dann brachte Erhart noch drei Moens-Zitate, mit denen er aus der Entwicklung der transnationalen Ökonomie die Notwendigkeit neuer demokratischer Institutionen ableitete, die die nationalen Parlamente ablösen mussten. Gut, der Bogen war da jetzt sehr verkürzt, aber Erhart hatte nicht mehr viel Zeit, und er wollte zum Schock kommen.

Er atmete tief durch, dann sagte er: Und nun möchte ich Ihnen etwas erzählen. Ich habe jetzt ein paar Mal Armand Moens zitiert. Das haben Sie geschluckt. Sie haben sich vielleicht gedacht, okay, Moens ist nicht Mainstream, aber es sind doch Zitate eines bekannten Ökonomen, und Sie, meine Damen und Herren, zitieren in Ihren Arbeiten und Ihren Wortmeldungen eben andere, Sie zitieren die Namen, die jetzt Mainstream sind. Sie suchen nicht nach der Wahrheit, weil Sie den Mainstream für den letzten Stand der Wahrheit halten. Warten Sie! Warten Sie! Ich sage nicht, dass ich weiß, was die Wahrheit ist. Ich sage nur, dass wir uns das fragen müssen. Und ich sage, dass wir ihr nicht unbedingt näher kommen, wenn wir uns am Zeitgeist orientieren, also an den gegenwärtig machtvollen Interessen von Wenigen, für die die Mehrheit der Menschen nur ein Abschreibposten in ihrer Buchhaltung ist. Egal. Was ich erzählen will: In meiner allerersten wissenschaftlichen Publikation habe ich mich mit der Theorie von Armand Moens auseinandergesetzt. Voll Stolz schickte ich ihm diesen Aufsatz. Ich hatte es nicht erwartet, aber er antwortete. Ich möchte Ihnen eine Stelle aus seinem Brief vorlesen: Lieber Herr Erhart und so weiter und so weiter, ja, hier: Was Sie getan haben, ist für mich schmeichelhaft und stellt Ihnen ein gutes Zeugnis aus. Sie haben mich zustimmend zitiert und dabei alle Zitierregeln eingehalten. Was Sie geliefert haben, ist eine perfekte erste Publikation, nach den Spielregeln unseres Betriebs. Aber stellen Sie sich vor, Sie müssten jetzt sterben, und diese Publikation wäre das, was von Ihnen bleibt. Wären Sie dann noch immer damit zufrieden? Haben Sie keine Gedanken, keine Visionen, die weit über das hinausgehen, was Sie zitiert haben? Ist dieser Aufsatz wirklich das, was Sie der Welt mitteilen wollten, das, was nur Sie sagen können, das, was weiterwirken soll, falls Sie keine Gelegenheit mehr haben, noch etwas zu sagen? Ich sage: NEIN!

NEIN in Großbuchstaben geschrieben, sagte Erhart.

Und jetzt sage ich Ihnen noch etwas: Wenn Sie sich wirklich, wie Sie in Ihrem Begleitbrief schreiben, als mein Schüler verstehen, dann müssen Sie zuallererst dies lernen: Bei allem, was Sie öffentlich sagen, bei allem, was Sie publizieren, müssen Sie von der Vorstellung ausgehen, dies könnten Ihre letzten Worte sein. Bei Ihrem nächsten Vortrag – stellen Sie sich vor, Sie wüssten, dass Sie unmittelbar danach sterben müssen – was würden Sie in diesem Fall sagen? Einmal noch können Sie etwas sagen, einmal noch, auf Leben und Tod. Was wäre das? Ich bin sicher, Sie würden etwas anderes sagen als das, was Sie in diesem Aufsatz geschrieben haben. Und wenn nicht, dann hätten Sie auch diesen Aufsatz nicht schreiben müssen. Verstehen Sie mich? Es gibt zahllose Sätze, mit denen man sein Leben behaupten, einen Dienstposten erobern und ihn verteidigen kann, Sätze, die am Ende in Gesammelte Werke und in Festschriften eingehen, und ich sage nicht, dass sie alle falsch sind oder unnötig, aber was wir dringend brauchen, sind Sätze mit dem existentiellen Anspruch letzter Worte, die dann nicht in einem Archiv schlummern, sondern Menschen aufwecken, vielleicht sogar Menschen, die heute noch gar nicht geboren sind. Also, lieber Herr Erhart, schicken Sie mir noch einen Text. Ich möchte gerne wissen, was Sie schreiben unter der Voraussetzung: Das ist meine letzte Chance, noch etwas zu sagen. Und dann sage ich Ihnen, ob es sinnvoll ist, dass Sie weiter publizieren.

Erhart blickte auf. Er erzählte nicht, dass er nach diesem Brief wochenlang unfähig gewesen war zu schreiben, bis er erfuhr, dass Armand Moens gestorben war. Er sah, dass eine eigentümliche Stimmung im Raum herrschte, die er nicht einschätzen konnte. António Pinto rief: Vielen Dank für diese interessante – äh, Anregung, Professor Erhart, will jemand –

Moment, bitte, sagte Erhart, ich bin noch nicht fertig.

Pardon, sagte Pinto, es kommen also noch last words, sozusagen. Bitte, Professor!

Ich habe, sagte Erhart, zu zeigen versucht, dass wir etwas völlig Neues brauchen, eine nachnationale Demokratie, um eine Welt gestalten zu können, in der es keine Nationalökonomie mehr gibt. Bei dieser These, die ich bis zu meinem Tod vertreten werde, gibt es zwei Probleme. Erstens: Nicht einmal Sie, die Eliten der internationalen Wirtschaftswissenschaften, Mitglieder unzähliger Think-Tanks und Beratergremien von EU-Staaten, können sich das vorstellen, können diesen Gedanken akzeptieren. Sie alle denken immer noch in den Kriterien nationaler Haushalte und nationaler Demokratien. Als gäbe es keinen gemeinsamen Markt und keine gemeinsame Währung, als gäbe es keine Freizügigkeit für die Finanzströme und die Wertschöpfungsketten. Sie glauben im Ernst, dass irgendetwas in Europa besser wird, wenn man den griechischen Staatshaushalt, also einen nationalen Staatshaushalt, auf eine Weise saniert, dass das Gesundheitssystem und das Bildungssystem und das Pensionssystem in Griechenland zusammenbrechen. Dann ist für Sie alles in Ordnung. Wissen Sie, was Ihr Problem ist? Sie sind Katzen in einer Box, und es ist nicht einmal sicher, dass Sie existieren. Sie und Ihre Theorien werden als Realität bloß vorausgesetzt. Diese Voraussetzung ermöglicht, dass man Rechnungen anstellen kann, und weil diese Rechnungen möglich sind, gilt das gleich als Beweis, dass diese Rechnungen die Realität widerspiegeln und es gar nicht anders sein kann. Warten Sie, warten Sie! Sie können sich gleich aufregen, ich möchte nur noch ein paar Sätze sagen. Okay, ich anerkenne: Sie sind Experten des Status quo. Niemand kennt ihn besser als Sie, niemand hat mehr Insider-Wissen als sie! Aber Sie haben keine Ahnung von der Geschichte, und Sie haben kein Bild von der Zukunft. Oder? Warten Sie, Professor Stephanides, eine Frage: Wenn Sie zur Zeit der griechischen Sklavenhaltergesellschaft gelebt hätten und man hätte Sie gefragt, ob Sie sich eine Welt ohne Sklaven vorstellen können – Sie hätten gesagt: Nein. Nie und nimmer. Sie hätten gesagt, die Sklavenhaltergesellschaft ist die Voraussetzung der Demokratie! Oder? Nein, nein, Professor Matthews, warten Sie. Bitte. Sie stelle ich mir vor in Manchester, zur Zeit des Manchester-Kapitalismus. Wenn man Sie damals gefragt hätte, was man tun müsse, um den Standort Manchester zu sichern, Sie hätten gesagt: Auf keinen Fall darf man diesen Gewerkschaften nachgeben, die statt eines 14-Stunden-Tags einen 8-Stunden-Arbeitstag fordern, ein Verbot der Kinderarbeit und die sogar eine Alters- und Invalidenrente wollen, denn das würde die Attraktivität des Standorts total gefährden – und, Professor Matthews, was ist jetzt? Gibt es Manchester noch? Und ersparen Sie sich dieses überhebliche Grinsen, Herr Mosebach. Mit der Radikalität, mit der Sie heute deutsche Interessen verteidigen, wären Sie mit früherer Geburt als Angeklagter bei den Nürnberger Prozessen gelandet. Und das ist Ihnen nicht einmal klar. Aber zittern Sie nicht, lieber Mosebach, Menschen wie Sie werden immer begnadigt, denn das sieht doch jeder Gutachter: Sie meinen es nicht böse, Sie sind nur verblendet. Sie sind ein Mitläufer. Und das ist das Problem von Ihnen allen. Sie alle sind Mitläufer. Sie sind entrüstet, wenn Ihnen das heute einer sagt, aber Sie sind genau die, die morgen, wenn es eine Katastrophe und dann gar einen Prozess gibt, zu Ihrer Entschuldigung sagen werden, dass Sie doch nur Mitläufer gewesen sind, kleine Rädchen. Und jetzt frage ich Sie: Wissen Sie überhaupt, worüber wir diskutieren? Wir diskutieren über die Weiterentwicklung der Europäischen Union – einer nachnationalen Gemeinschaft, geboren aus der Einsicht in den historischen Fehler, den Sie wieder für »normal« halten: So ist die Welt, so sind die Menschen, sie wollen sich über die Zugehörigkeit zu einer Nation definieren, sie wollen definieren, wer dazugehört und wer die anderen sind, und sie wollen sich besser fühlen als andere und sie wollen, wenn sie sich vor anderen fürchten, diesen den Schädel einschlagen, das ist ganz normal, so sind die Menschen, Hauptsache das nationale Budget ist im Rahmen der vereinbarten Kriterien.

Danke, vielen Dank, Professor Erhart, sagte António Pinto, gibt es Fragen von Seiten –

Bitte, Mr Pinto, ich bin noch nicht fertig. Bitte noch zwei Minuten.

Die Schultasche war Erhart vom Schoß gerutscht und zu Boden gefallen, ebenso die Blätter mit seinem Vortrag, er sprach schon die längste Zeit frei, sein Referat war ihm aus dem Ruder gelaufen, aber das, worauf er hinauswollte, die Pointe seiner radikalen Intervention, die wollte er unbedingt noch anbringen. Bitte noch zwei Minuten, für mein Resümee. Nein, für meine Vision. Wirklich Last words. Okay? Okay! Also, ich fasse zunächst zusammen: Konkurrierende Nationalstaaten sind keine Union, auch wenn sie einen gemeinsamen Markt haben. Konkurrierende Nationalstaaten in einer

Union blockieren beides: Europapolitik und Staatspolitik. Was wäre jetzt notwendig? Die Weiterentwicklung zu einer Sozialunion, zu einer Fiskalunion – also die Herstellung von Rahmenbedingungen, die aus dem Europa konkurrierender Kollektive ein Europa souveräner, gleichberechtigter Bürger machen würde. Das war ja die Idee, das war es, wovon die Gründer des europäischen Einigungsprojekts geträumt haben – denn sie hatten ihre Erfahrungen. Aber das alles ist nicht durchsetzbar, solange das Nationalbewusstsein gegen alle historischen Erfahrungen weiter geschürt wird und solange der Nationalismus weitgehend konkurrenzlos ist als Identifikationsangebot an die Bürger. Wie kann man also das Bewusstsein fördern, dass die Menschen auf diesem Kontinent europäische Bürger sind? Da gäbe es viele kleine Maßnahmen. Zum Beispiel könnte man alle nationalen Pässe durch einen Europäischen Pass ersetzen. Ein Pass der Europäischen Union, in dem der Geburtsort vermerkt ist, aber nicht die Nationalität. Ich glaube, dass allein dies etwas im Bewusstsein der Generation bewirken würde, die mit einem solchen Pass aufwächst. Und das würde nicht einmal etwas kosten.

Erhart sah, dass die Idealisten in der Runde zwar die Köpfe wiegten, aber bereit waren, über diese Idee zumindest nachzudenken.

Aber das ist nicht genug, setzte er fort. Wir brauchen auch und vor allem ein starkes Symbol für den Zusammenhalt, es muss ein konkretes gemeinsames Projekt sein, das als gemeinsame Anstrengung das Gemeinsame in die Welt setzt, wir brauchen etwas, das allen gehört und sie als Bürger der Europäischen Union verbindet, weil es die Bürger des gemeinsamen Europas waren, die es wollten und produzierten und nicht bloß geerbt haben. Eine erste, kühne, große, bewusste Kulturleistung der nachnationalen Geschichte, und sie muss zugleich von politischer Bedeutung und psychologischer Symbolkraft sein. Worauf will ich hinaus?

Erhart sah, dass einige nun doch den Eindruck erweckten, als wären sie gespannt, was nun kommen werde. Er holte tief Luft und sagte: Die Europäische Union muss eine Hauptstadt bauen, muss sich eine neue, eine geplante, eine ideale Hauptstadt schenken.

Professor Stephanides lächelte: Die Diskussion, welche Stadt in Europa den Status einer Hauptstadt der Union erhalten soll, ist tot. Das ist Schnee von gestern. Es war eine vernünftige Entscheidung, keiner Stadt, auch Brüssel nicht, diesen Titel zu geben, sondern die europäischen Institutionen auf verschiedene Städte in verschiedenen Ländern zu verteilen.

Sie haben mich nicht verstanden, Kollege Stephanides. Ich sagte nicht, eine Stadt sollte den Titel Hauptstadt bekommen. Mir ist schon klar, dass das nur weiter den Nationalismus anheizt, in den Ländern, deren Bürger sich dann von der Hauptstadt, die zugleich Hauptstadt einer anderen Nation ist, fremdbestimmt fühlen. Das ist ja auch das Problem von Brüssel. Obwohl ich ja Brüssel als EU-Hauptstadt zunächst für sinnig hielt: die Hauptstadt eines gescheiterten Nationalstaats, die Hauptstadt eines Landes mit drei Amtssprachen. Aber nein, ich meinte: Europa muss eine neue Hauptstadt bauen. Eine neue Stadt, deren Errichtung die Leistung der Union ist, und nicht eine alte Reichs- oder Nations-Hauptstadt, in der die Union nur Untermieterin ist.

Und wo wollen Sie diese Stadt bauen? In welchem Niemandsland? In der geographischen Mitte des Kontinents? Die reichste und mächtigste Nation Europas schafft es nicht einmal, einen Flughafen für eine Hauptstadt zu bauen, und Sie träumen gleich vom Bau einer ganzen Stadt? Mosebach schüttelte milde lächelnd den Kopf.

Also eine Art europäisches Brasilia? Ich finde das als Gedankenexperiment interessant, sagte Dana Dinescu, die rumänische Politikwissenschaftlerin, die in Bologna lehrte.

Natürlich, sagte Erhart, kann man diese Stadt nicht in ein Niemandsland bauen. Es gibt in Europa kein Niemandsland mehr, keinen Quadratmeter Boden, der nicht eine Geschichte hat. Und deshalb muss die europäische Hauptstadt natürlich an einem Ort gebaut werden, dessen Geschichte maßgeblich für die Einigungsidee Europas war, eine Geschichte, die unser Europa überwinden will, zugleich aber niemals vergessen werden darf. Es muss ein Ort sein, wo die Geschichte spürbar und erlebbar bleibt, auch wenn der letzte gestorben ist, der sie erlebt oder überlebt hat. Ein Ort als ewiges Fanal für die künftige Politik in Europa.

Erhart sah in die Runde. Gab es jemanden, der schon ahnte, was nun kommen würde? Dana lächelte und blickte ihn neugierig an. Stephanides schaute betont gelangweilt zum Fenster. Mosebach tippte etwas in seinen Laptop. Pinto sah auf die Uhr. Aber zehn Sekunden später starrten sie alle Erhart mit offenen Mündern an. Fassungslos. Dreizehn Sekunden später war Erhart, der renommierte Professor Emeritus, als Mitglied des Think-Tanks »New Pact for Europe« Geschichte.

Er sagte: Und deshalb muss die Union ihre Hauptstadt in Auschwitz bauen. In Auschwitz muss die neue europäische Hauptstadt entstehen, geplant und errichtet als Stadt der Zukunft, zugleich die Stadt, die nie vergessen kann. »Nie wieder Auschwitz« ist das Fundament, auf dem das Europäische Einigungswerk errichtet wurde. Zugleich ist es ein Versprechen für alle Zukunft. Diese Zukunft müssen wir errichten, als erlebbares und funktionierendes Zentrum. Haben Sie den Mut, über diese Idee nachzudenken? Das wäre doch ein Ergebnis unserer Reflection Group: eine Empfehlung an den Präsidenten der Kommission, einen Architekturwettbewerb auszuschreiben, für die Planung und Errichtung einer europäischen Hauptstadt in Auschwitz.

Alois Erhart legte den Koffer auf sein Bett im Hotel Atlas, um zu packen. Er hatte ein heißes Gesicht, dachte, dass er fieberte. Das eben Erlebte brannte in ihm. Er zog die Vorhänge zur Seite und schaute aus dem Fenster, hinunter auf den Platz. Zeitlupe, dachte er. Es war da unten ein Gewimmel in Zeitlupe. Bei drückender Hitze bewegte sich alles ganz langsam, als wären die Bewegungen aller eine gemeinsame Bewegung mit einem gemeinsamen Ziel – das möglichst lange nicht erreicht werden soll.

Erhart hatte gelernt, dass das europäische Einigungsprojekt auf diesem Konsens beruhte: Nationalismus und Rassismus hatten zu Auschwitz geführt und durften sich nie mehr wiederholen. Dieses »Nie wieder!« begründete alles Weitere, die Souveränitätsabgabe der Mitgliedstaaten an supranationale Institutionen und die bewusste Gestaltung einer transnationalen, verflochtenen Ökonomie. Das begründete auch das Hauptwerk von Armand Moens, der als Ökonom darüber nachzudenken begann, wie nachnationale Ökonomie politisch organisiert werden müsse. Dieser Frage hatte auch Professor Erhart sein Leben als Wissenschaftler gewidmet. Sein Leben, das Leben seines Lehrers, die erlebte Zeitgeschichte, die Wahrung von sozialem Frieden, die Zukunft des Kontinents, das alles beruhte auf zwei Worten: »Nie wieder!« So sah das Erhart. »Nie wieder!« ist ein Versprechen auf Ewigkeit, ist ein Anspruch, der ewige Gültigkeit behauptet. Jetzt starben die letzten, die überlebt hatten, was nie wieder geschehen sollte. Und dann? Hatte selbst die Ewigkeit ein Ablaufdatum? Jetzt hatte eine Generation die Verantwortung übernommen, die sich wenigstens in Sonntagsreden noch verpflichtet fühlte, raunend und mahnend dieses »Nie wieder«

auszusprechen. Aber dann? Wenn der Letzte gestorben sein wird, der bezeugen kann, aus welchem Schock heraus Europa sich neu erfinden wollte – dann war Auschwitz für die Lebenden so weit abgesunken wie die Punischen Kriege.

Wenn Alois Erhart einen mächtigen, objektiven Grund brauchte, um sich seine Schmerzen zu erklären und sich ihnen wehrlos auszuliefern, dann dachte er in solch großen politischen und geschichtsphilosophischen Kategorien. Das war dann eben der Weltschmerz, gegen den es kein Mittel gab.

Pragmatiker kannten Mittel. So wie sein Vater. Erharts Vater hatte 1942 eine Einberufung zur OrPo bekommen, Ordnungspolizei, Bataillon 316, die nach Posen verlegt wurde, um dort unter dem Titel »Partisanenbekämpfung« Erschießungen von Juden durchzuführen. Diesen Stellungsbefehl hatte Alois Erhart nach dem Tod seines Vaters in einer Mappe mit Papieren in dessen Schreibtisch gefunden. Der Vater war bereits vor der Annexion Österreichs NSDAP-Mitglied geworden, wurde dann Ausstatter für Sport- und Feldausrüstung des BDM Wien, der Hitlerjugend und des Turnerbunds. So konnte er lange als »kriegswichtig« einer Einberufung entgehen. Als er das Geschäft schließen musste, wurde seine Einberufung unvermeidlich. Wegen seiner guten Kontakte und seiner Verdienste wurde er allerdings nicht an die Front geschickt, sondern mit einem Polizeibataillon hinter die Linien.

Sein Vater ist im Krieg in Posen/Poznań gewesen? Er, Alois Erhart, ist im Lager des Geschäfts zur Welt gekommen, während sein Vater in Polen als »Polizist« Juden exekutierte? Und hat später nie darüber geredet? Erhart hatte diese Dokumente lange ungläubig studiert und schließlich seine Mutter darüber befragt. Sie war, als Vater starb, bereits dement, ging wenige Monate später dem Vater nach. Aber noch lebte sie und Erhart versuchte, sie zu einer Erinnerung zu bewegen, aber sie schaute nur, lachte plötzlich, sagte: Polen? Und begann zu singen. *Sto lat, sto lat,* sie sang, emphatisch und mit glücklichem Gesichtsausdruck. Alois verstand kein Wort, er schüttelte sie an den Schultern und rief Mutter! Mutter! Was singst du da? Erhart versuchte, sich Worte einzuprägen, auch wenn er sie nicht verstand, *sto lat* und *Jeszcze raz* konnte er sich merken, weil Mutter diese Worte immer wieder singend wiederholte, er lief auf die Toilette und schrieb sie auf, phonetisch, ungefähr so, wie sie klangen. Dann zurück zur Mutter, sie saß da, still, verträumt, sagte nichts mehr.

Erhart fragte am nächsten Tag eine Kollegin von der Slawistik, sie sagte, dass die Worte, die er aufgeschrieben habe, »Hundert Jahre« und »Noch einmal« bedeuten. Und sie glaube, dass Erharts Mutter ein altes polnisches Volkslied gesungen habe, allerdings sei »Sto lat« auch ein Trinkspruch. Ob ihm das weiterhelfe?

Nein.

Woher kannte seine Mutter ein polnisches Volkslied? Was hatte sein Vater in Poznań gemacht? Und wieso singt die Mutter, die keine Erinnerung mehr hat, auf Polnisch »Noch einmal! Noch einmal! Noch einmal!«?

Alois Erhart packte seinen Koffer, in Gedanken und Erinnerungen versunken. Er hielt inne. Warum packte er? Sein Rückflug ging erst übermorgen, das Zimmer im Hotel Atlas war bis übermorgen gebucht und bezahlt. Weil morgen noch eine Sitzung des »New Pact«-Think-Tanks stattfinden sollte. Und nur, weil er nicht mehr teilnehmen, sich dort nicht mehr blicken lassen wollte, musste er doch nicht sofort abreisen. Er hatte auch kein Flugticket, das umgebucht werden konnte. Also – noch ein Tag in Brüssel.

Er setzte sich an den Schreibtisch, öffnete seinen Laptop, wollte ein Gedächtnisprotokoll der Sitzung schreiben, die Reaktionen der Mitglieder dieser Gruppe zusammenfassen. Der

Reihe nach, gemäß den Kategorien, nach denen er sie einge-
teilt hatte. Er begann mit »Die Eitlen« – aber bevor er weiter-
schreiben konnte, sah er, dass das automatische Korrektur-
programm dies zu »Die Eliten« verbessert hatte.

Ist gut, dachte er und klappte den Laptop zu.

Matek nahm den IC um 11.04 von Krakow Główny nach
Poznań Gł. Die Fahrt sollte knapp 5 Stunden 20 dauern.
Sie war für ihn nach weniger als drei Stunden zu Ende. Denn
kurz nach Łódź löste der Lokführer eine Notbremsung aus,
wodurch Matek, der just in diesem Moment aufgestanden
war, um auf die Toilette zu gehen, durch den Mittelgang des
Waggons geschleudert wurde, gegen eine Sitzlehne und dann
gegen die Tür prallte und liegenblieb. Er versuchte aufzuste-
hen, aber er konnte sich nicht aufstützen, sein rechter Arm
stand unnatürlich weg, seine Beine gehorchten ihm nicht,
er konnte sie nicht anziehen und auf die Knie kommen, irgendetwas war mit seinem Bauch, als wäre hinter seinem Na-
bel etwas geplatzt, als hätte sich eine gewaltige Energie befreit, die nun glühend durch seine Eingeweide strömte, er
hörte Menschen wimmern, es musste auch andere Verletzte
geben, er versuchte nochmals, sich aufzurichten, aber er konnte nur den Kopf etwas heben, den er stöhnend wieder sinken
ließ. Jemand beugte sich über ihn, sagte etwas, es war eine
Frauenstimme, die Matek Vertrauen einflößte, geradezu ein
Gefühl von Geborgenheit gab, er schloss die Augen. Er sah
einen kleinen Jungen über ein Feld laufen, der einen Drachen steigen ließ. Andere Kinder liefen dem Jungen nach,
sie wollten ihm den Drachen abjagen, aber der Junge war
schneller, und je schneller er lief, desto höher stieg der Drachen, die Leine wickelte sich so schnell von der Kordel ab,
dass sie ihm regelrecht die Handflächen ritzte und zersägte,
nun tauchten Männer mit Pistolen und Gewehren auf, die

auf den Drachen schossen, aber das große, mit rot-weißem Tuch bespannte Kreuz flog schon so hoch, dass die Kugeln es nicht mehr erreichten, seine Hände bluteten, das Blut tropfte auf das Feld, der Drachen stieg immer höher hinauf in den Himmel, da sah er seitlich die Mutter stehen, sie applaudierte lachend, und der Junge ließ los, der Drachen stieg hinein in die Sonne, dorthin wo sie nicht mehr blendete, sondern tiefrot und schließlich schwarz wurde.

Am nächsten Tag berichteten die Zeitungen europaweit von dem Zugunglück. Ein Selbstmörder hatte sich auf der Bahnstrecke zwischen Łódź und Zgierz vor den IC nach Poznań geworfen, was den Zugverkehr auf dieser Strecke für mehr als drei Stunden blockierte.

Diese Meldung war ungewöhnlich. Es handelte sich um ein verhältnismäßig kleines, lokales Unglück, und es gab einen Konsens zwischen den Medien, über solche Vorkommnisse nicht zu berichten, um Nachahmungstaten zu verhindern. Dass dieser Fall doch den Weg in die Medien, sogar in die europäischen Medien fand, hatte einen einfachen Grund: Der Tote war, zumindest als Toter, von allgemeinem Interesse. Bei dem Mann, der sich vor den Zug geworfen hatte, handelte es sich um den achtzigjährigen Adam Goldfarb.

Ab 1942 hatte es neben dem Ghetto Łódź auch ein Jugendkonzentrationslager gegeben, in dem jüdische Kinder schon ab einem Alter von zwei Jahren eingesperrt wurden. Und Adam Goldfarb war der letzte Überlebende dieses Jugendkonzentrationslagers von Łódź. War der letzte Überlebende gewesen. Das Motiv dieses »Mahners«, so stand es in der Zeitung, sei nicht bekannt.

Elftes Kapitel

Wenn etwas zerfällt,
muss es Zusammenhänge gegeben haben.

Die erste Sitzung der Ratsarbeitsgruppe, Betreff: Jubilee Project der Europäischen Kommission, fand ausgerechnet am Nachmittag des Tages statt, an dem die belgischen Zeitungen und auch einige deutsche und französische den Skandal kommentierten, den die neue Ausstellung in den Musées royaux des Beaux-Arts in Brüssel ausgelöst hatte. Wie so mancher große Skandal hat auch dieser klein angefangen. Zunächst waren nach der Vernissage der Ausstellung »Kunst auf dem Abstellgleis – vergessene Moderne« einige kurze, eher betuliche, wenig inspirierte Berichte in lokalen Medien erschienen. Wenn eine Sammelausstellung Werke vergessener Künstler zeigt, dann fällt es selbst den gewöhnlich besonders ambitionierten Kunstkritikern schwer, die gezeigte Auswahl zu kritisieren und etwa einzuklagen, dass der eine oder andere Künstler, der in dieser Ausstellung hätte gezeigt werden müssen, vergessen wurde. Die Ausstellung präsentierte ja nur vergessene Künstler, und jeder Kritiker, der unter diesen Vergessenen einen vermisst hätte, der vom Kurator der Ausstellung vergessen wurde, wäre in eine Falle getappt: Er würde an einen Vergessenen erinnern, nur um ihn anzufügen an die Liste der Vergessenen. Da stellte sich eine Frage von unendlicher kunsttheoretischer Komplexität: Gibt es Kunst, die in einer bestimmten Epoche bedeutsam ist, dann aber zu Recht vergessen wird? Offenbar. Aber warum? Wir vergessen ja nicht die Epoche, warum aber vergessen wir Exempel ihrer Kunst? Gibt es vorbildlich vergessene Kunst, gibt es den paradigmatischen vergessenen Künstler? Und wie sehr verdient ein vergessener Künstler das Verdikt »Vergessen«, wenn ein Kritiker an ihn erinnert, und wie sehr ist er dann doch nicht oder erst recht vergessen, wenn der Kritiker bloß einmahnt, dass er in der Liste der Vergessenen nicht vergessen werden dürfe?

Aus diesem Grund war die Ausstellung kein großer Erfolg bei der Kritik – es herrschte der Tenor: Im Grunde handelte es sich um Kunst, die sich letztlich auf dem Markt nicht durchsetzen konnte. Aber sie war auch kein Misserfolg – denn alle gezeigten Kunstwerke sind irgendwann nach 1945 immerhin von den königlichen Museen angekauft worden, wurden also zu einer bestimmten Zeit doch anders eingeschätzt, als hervorragend im Kontext ihrer Zeitgenossenschaft, zumindest als Arbeiten vielversprechender junger Künstler. Und einige Kritiker setzten sich daher mehr oder weniger originell mit ebendieser Frage auseinander: Wie kommt es, dass etwas wichtig genommen und gleich darauf vergessen wird?

Thomas Hebbelinck, der Kurator der Ausstellung, verriet in einem Interview in De Standaard den verblüffend banalen Grund für die Konzeption dieser Ausstellung: Die königlichen Museen bereiteten eine große Francis-Bacon-Ausstellung vor, allein die Versicherungsprämien der Leihgaben, die von anderen Häusern angefordert wurden, verschlinge einen so großen Teil des Budgets, dass die Notwendigkeit entstand, zur Überbrückung eine Ausstellung zu machen, die nichts kostete. Also mit Werken aus dem Bestand des Hauses, aus dem Depot. So sei die Idee entstanden, Ankäufe von Künstlern zu zeigen, die vergessen wurden, eine Idee, die er tatsächlich spannend und einer Diskussion würdig fände. Denn die Frage, was wir vergessen und warum wir vergessen und ob sich in ausgestellten Werken vielleicht gar ein kollektiver Wunsch nach Verdrängung zeigt, sei doch von grundsätzlicher Bedeutung.

Damit schien diese Ausstellung medial abgehakt.

Doch dann kam in De Morgen der große geschliffene Essay von Geert van Istendael, dem berühmten Brüsseler Intellektuellen, der zuletzt auch als Mitglied der Jury »Brüssel sucht

einen Namen für sein Schwein« medial auffällig wurde. Er
eröffnete eine völlig neue Front in einer Auseinandersetzung,
die einen Tag lang halbherzig und dann schon gar nicht mehr
geführt worden war: Er setzte sich nicht mit der vergessenen
Kunst auseinander, sondern nur mit der Form, wie Kurator
Hebbelinck sie in Szene gesetzt hatte. Die Ausstellung hatte
den Titel »Kunst auf dem Abstellgleis«. Durch den großen
Ausstellungsraum waren Eisenbahnschienen gelegt worden,
am Ende befand sich ein Prellbock, was, wie van Istendael
schrieb, wohl ausdrücken sollte: Hier ist Endstation. Die Be-
sucher der Ausstellung wurden an die linke Seite der Gleise
geführt, während sich die Kunstwerke, Plastiken, Gemälde
und Zeichnungen, sehr dicht gehängt und aufgestellt, auf
der rechten Seite befanden.
Geert van Istendael eröffnete seinen Essay mit dem Satz:
»Bei dieser Ausstellung, die einem sehr zu denken gibt, fehlt
nur ein kleines, aber wichtiges Detail: Über dem Tor in die
Ausstellung der Satz ›Kunst macht frei‹.«
Und er stellte die Frage, ob das Museum beziehungsweise der
Kurator dieser Ausstellung der Meinung sei, man könne das
Verhältnis von gescheiterter und erfolgreicher Kunst mit der
Selektion an der Rampe von Auschwitz vergleichen. Links das
Leben, rechts der Tod. Die Präsentation von Kunst, die sich
auf dem Kunstmarkt nicht durchgesetzt hat, als eine Masse
von Werken zu präsentieren, die am Ende einer Bahnstrecke
in den Tod geschickt wird – denn wie sonst seien die Bahn-
gleise und der Prellbock zu interpretieren? –, während auf
der linken Seite den Besuchern gesagt wird, dass sie zu den
Überlebenden zählen, sei nicht nur eine Verharmlosung
von Auschwitz, sondern zeige auch die Dummheit und Un-
angemessenheit der Idee, ständig auf Auschwitz verweisen zu
müssen. Und es stelle sich die Frage, so van Istendael, »was
der größere Skandal ist: schlechte Kunst mit Juden gleichzu-

setzen oder den Kunstmarkt als eine Art Doktor Mengele zu sehen. So oder so, diese Ausstellung ist ein Skandal, zugleich aber hoffentlich der letzte seiner Art: Denn ab jetzt ist die Faschismuskeule ein Requisit aus Papiermaché, gefertigt aus dem ins Wasser gefallenen Katalog einer schlecht gemachten Ausstellung von Pappkameraden, die sich Künstler nennen.«

Das saß. Und plötzlich war die vom Feuilleton nur sehr müde kommentierte Ausstellung ein Skandal, der in politischen Kommentaren und Leitartikeln breitgetreten wurde.

Sogar der große alte Mann der bürgerlichen belgischen Presse, der seit mehr als zehn Jahren pensionierte Chefredakteur von De Financieel-Economische Tijd, Tom Koorman, meldete sich in De Tijd mit einem Kommentar zurück: Diese Ausstellung sei ein Verbrechen, weil sie kein Verbrechen mit dem größten Verbrechen gleichsetze. Die freie Welt habe auch die Freiheit, zu vergessen, und der freie Markt, auch der Kunstmarkt, definiere sich eben nicht über die Anbetung von Asche.

Diese geistlose, zumindest unglückliche Formulierung »Anbetung von Asche« im Zusammenhang mit Auschwitz führte zu weiteren aufgeregten Reaktionen, auch wenn Koorman es gewiss nicht so gemeint hatte, wie es interpretiert wurde. Aber auch Kurator Hebbelinck hatte nichts von alldem beabsichtigt, was ihm in den Reaktionen und Kommentaren unterstellt worden war. Jedenfalls gab es an diesem Tag, an dem die Ratsarbeitsgruppe zusammentrat, keine Zeitung, in der »der Missbrauch von Auschwitz« nicht Thema war.

Und George Morland sagte gleich zu Beginn des Meetings – aber bitte außer Protokoll –: Wenn diese Ausstellung, die doch zweifellos eine gewisse Verwandtschaft zur Idee der COMM hat, bereits Teil des geplanten Jubilee gewesen wäre – well, das wäre nicht exakt das gewesen, was ich als großen Image-Gewinn für die Kommission bezeichnen würde.

Als Mrs Atkinson das Protokoll der Sitzung las, wusste sie, dass sie das Projekt in dieser Form – ja: vergessen konnte. Es gab nun zwei Möglichkeiten: das Projekt definitiv der Arche zuzuschieben – und sie damit scheitern zu lassen. Das würde kaum noch Rumoren im Haus zur Folge haben, denn niemand erwartete von der Arche etwas wirklich Erhellendes. Was hatte ihr Kollege Jean-Philippe Dupont unlängst über die Arche gesagt? »J'adore les lucioles, vraiment, elles sont magnifiques. Mais quand je veux travailler, elles ne me donnent simplement pas assez de lumière!«

Oder aber sie insistierte auf der Grundidee, Jubilee Project zur Verbesserung des Images der Kommission, trennte sich allerdings von der inhaltlichen Idee, die von der Arche gekommen war. Das war ja ein Vorschlag der Arbeitsgruppe: »Warum die Juden? Warum nicht Sport?«

Ja, dachte sie. Warum nicht? Die völkerverbindende Idee des Sports, damit könnte man arbeiten, im Sinne von Artikel 165 Absatz 1, AEU-Vertrag, wie hier im Protokoll vermerkt wurde. Das Sport-Ressort war auch der Generaldirektion für Bildung und Kultur zugeordnet, so könnte sie also weiter mit Frau Xenopoulou zusammenarbeiten, und sie könnten sich weiterhin darauf berufen, dass der Präsident seine grundsätzliche Unterstützung für das Jubilee Project gegeben hatte. Auch das war im Protokoll festgehalten. Allerdings wurde ein Alleingang der Kommission dezidiert abgelehnt, wodurch der Sinn des Projekts, einen Image-Gewinn der Kommission zu erreichen, hinfällig würde. Akzeptiert wurde lediglich, dass das Projekt ausschließlich aus dem Budget der Kommission finanziert werden sollte, was aber schwerlich zu akzeptieren wäre, wenn Rat und Parlament sich anhängten und bei der Planung mit all ihren dauernden Einwänden mitredeten. Und konnte man der Kultur überhaupt zumuten, ihre Idee abzulehnen und sie gleichzeitig zu verpflichten, eine ganz andere Idee umzusetzen, allerdings ohne Aussicht auf einen exklusiven Imagegewinn?

Grace Atkinson knetete ihre Finger. Die Brüsseler Küche tat ihr gut. Sie hatte schon acht Pfund zugenommen, und sie war erstaunt darüber, dass auch die Durchblutung ihrer Hände und Füße nun besser zu funktionieren schien. Und keine Spur mehr von Blässe, von bleicher Gesichtshaut wie Papier. Sie hatte jetzt rote Wangen, wie auf den Porträts von Sir Thomas Lawrence, dem Lieblingsmaler der Queen. Das war vielleicht auch Folge des Gläschens Champagner oder, sie wollte ja nicht übertreiben, Prosecco, das sie ab und zu trank. Sie hatte die Erfahrung gemacht, dass ein Gläschen, nur ein kleines Gläschen, maximal zwei, ihre Phantasie anregte, ihr Verstand wurde offener, zugleich war sie entschlossener, nur ihre Finger knetete sie noch aus Gewohnheit.

Sie knetete und dachte nach. Zunächst müsste sie herausfinden, wie Fenia Xenopoulou auf das Protokoll der Ratssitzung reagierte.

Sollte sie ihr eine Mail schreiben und ein Treffen vorschlagen, um zu besprechen, wie man die vorliegenden Einwände adaptieren könnte?

Unsinn. Da gab es nichts zu adaptieren. Und eine solche Mail käme daher schon einer definitiven Distanzierung von der Idee gleich, die von der Arche geliefert worden war.

Grace Atkinson fühlte sich schlecht. Sie war ein loyaler Mensch. Sie hatte das Engagement von Fenia Xenopoulou ehrlich geschätzt. Loyalität und Fairness, das waren für sie keine Phrasen, sondern tief in ihrer Seele verankerte Prinzipien, das menschliche Rüstzeug, um in Würde und durchaus mit dem Anspruch auf Erfolg seinen Weg zu gehen. Sie war in etwas hineingeraten, wo berufliches und menschliches Überleben vielleicht von ganz anderen Parametern abhing, und sie wusste nicht, ob das damit zu tun hatte, dass hier

Menschen mit ganz verschiedenen kulturellen Prägungen zusammenarbeiten mussten oder, weil große bürokratische Systeme grundsätzlich zu solchen Widersprüchen führten. Sie hatte zuvor in Gremien der University of London gearbeitet, dann im Kabinett des englischen Außenministers. In beiden Fällen hatte es sich um schlanke Strukturen gehandelt, wenngleich sie nicht transparent waren. Im Grunde hatte sich alles hinter verschlossenen Türen abgespielt; die berühmten Polstertüren, sie waren Metapher und Realität gleichzeitig. Aber hier, hier war sie unausgesetzt unter Beobachtung, und alle Mails wurden abgespeichert und einer Akte zugeordnet, die dann nach einer gewissen Zeit nach Florenz kam, ins Archiv der Europäischen Union, wo Historiker saßen und darin herumstocherten. Wenn eine Entscheidung im Kabinett des Ministers in London zu treffen war, dauerte die Debatte maximal dreißig Minuten, inklusive der Rituale und Floskeln am Beginn und am Ende. Da saßen Menschen zusammen, die denselben Background hatten, eine vergleichbare Herkunft, daher auch dieselben Schulen besucht hatten, dieselbe Sprache mit demselben Akzent sprachen, an dem sie einander erkannten, sie alle hatten Ehepartner aus derselben gesellschaftlichen Schicht, sie hatten zu achtzig oder neunzig Prozent deckungsgleiche Biographien und weitgehend identische Erfahrungen. Es gab ein Problem? In zwanzig Minuten waren sich diese weißen, protestantischen Eliteschulen-Abgänger einig. Was ein anderer in diesem Kreis sagte, klang, als führte man ein Selbstgespräch. Aber hier in Brüssel? Da saßen ständig Menschen zusammen, mit verschiedenen Sprachen und verschiedenen kulturellen Prägungen, vor allem aus den Staaten im Osten kamen viele auch aus Arbeiter- oder Handwerkerfamilien, sie hatten ganz unterschiedliche Erfahrungen, und alles, was Grace Atkinson in zwanzig Minuten zu klären gewohnt war, dauerte hier Stunden, Tage, Wochen.

Sie fand das faszinierend. Sie musste sich eingestehen, dass die Entscheidungen, die im Zirkel der Eliten in England so schnell getroffen werden konnten, in der Regel nicht den Interessen der Mehrheit der britischen Bevölkerung entsprachen, egal wer regierte. Hier war es umgekehrt. Es gab so viele, so unendlich mühsame Kompromisse, dass deswegen niemand mehr, egal wo, verstand, dass seine Interessen in diesem Kompromiss irgendwie aufgehoben waren. Es war komplizierter, aber es war auch spannender, doch manchmal dachte sie: Man müsste autoritär durchgreifen können, mit Weisungs- und Durchgriffsrecht und –

Mrs Atkinson schluckte. Der Gedanke schockierte sie. Jedenfalls keine Mail. Sie hätte es nicht fair gefunden, sich aktenkundig von Frau Xenopoulou zu distanzieren. Absolut nicht fair. Sie schenkte sich noch ein Glas Prosecco ein und beschloss, Fenia Xenopoulou anzurufen.

Als Fridsch anrief und fragte, ob sie in der Mittagspause Zeit habe, dachte Xeno, dass es um die Verwerfungen ginge, die das Jubilee Project ausgelöst hatte. Es sei für sie sehr wichtig, hatte er gesagt, eine Information, die er ihr dringend mitteilen müsse, und er hatte ein Lunch in der Rosticceria Fiorentina, Rue Archimède, vorgeschlagen. Okay, hatte sie gesagt, in einer Stunde in der Rosti.

Xeno war nicht naiv. Aber jetzt, bei der Lektüre des Protokolls der Ratsarbeitsgruppe, fragte sie sich doch, wie sie so überrascht werden konnte von Dynamiken, die sie, mit all ihren Erfahrungen, doch hätte voraussehen und erwarten müssen. Und warum sie die Spielchen, die da gespielt wurden, plötzlich widerlich fand, obwohl sie Routine waren. Sie kannte das doch seit Jahren. Allgemeine Zustimmung zu der Idee, und dann so viele einzelne Einwände und Änderungsvorschläge, dass von der Idee nichts mehr übrig blieb.

In dem Roman, den Xeno gelesen hatte, dem Lieblingsroman des Präsidenten, gab es eine Stelle, in der der Kaiser seiner Geliebten verspricht, dass er mit all seiner Macht, die doch von den Göttern gegeben sei, den alten Menschheitstraum vom Fliegen verwirklichen möchte. Dieses Wunder, wenn er es denn in die Welt setzen könne, würde nicht nur seine Herrschaft befestigen, sondern zugleich auch den Glauben der Menschen in ihre Möglichkeiten entfesseln und daher Glück und Wohlstand seines Reichs befördern. Er rief die bedeutendsten Philosophen, Priester und Wissenschaftler seiner Zeit zusammen, um an der Lösung dieser Aufgabe zu arbeiten – die sehr schnell daran scheiterte, dass all diese weisen Männer sich nicht einmal darauf einigen konnten, welcher Vogel der richtige sei, um ihm das Geheimnis des Fliegens zu entreißen. Sie sahen nicht das Fliegen, sie sahen nur die Unterschiede der Vögel.

Was Xeno besonders verblüffte, war die Reaktion der Deutschen. Das Protokoll begann ganz routiniert mit »Allgemeine Zustimmung zu dem Vorschlag von COMM und EAC, eine Jubiläumsfeier zum runden Jahrestag der Gründung der Europäischen Kommission auszurichten, mit dem Ziel, das Image der Kommission zu verbessern (PT, IT, DE, FR, HU, BG, SI, AT, FR, UK, NL, HR, LV, SE, DK, EE, CR, EL, ES, LU). BG unterstrich besonderes Interesse an dieser Initiative, die in die Zeit seiner Ratspräsidentschaft fallen würde.«

Und so ging es zunächst weiter, höfliche Zustimmungen, bis die ersten Einwände kamen: »Zustimmung zum Budgetvorschlag, aber MS (IT, DE, FI, EE, CR, HU, SI, HR, FR) forderten verbindliche Zusage, dass auch im Falle einer Kostenüberschreitung die Finanzierung des Projekts ausschließlich aus dem Verwaltungsbudget der Kommission erfolgen dürfe, ohne das allgemeine Budget zu belasten. Rat und Parlament würden dem nicht zustimmen. Dessen ungeachtet insistierten MS (DE, IT, FR, HU, PL) auf Einbindung des Rats und Parlaments bei der inhaltlichen Ausrichtung des Projekts.«

Das war schon ein starkes Stück. Aber fassungslos war Xeno, als sie die inhaltlichen Einwände las, vor allem von Seiten Deutschlands: »DE stellte die Idee, Auschwitz als Fundament der europäischen Einigung, in Frage und betonte, dass die Muslime in Europa nicht aus dem europäischen Einigungswerk ausgeschlossen werden dürfen. (Zustimmung: UK, HUN, PL, AT, HR, CR)«

Xeno hielt sich für abgebrüht. Sie hatte im Lauf ihrer Karriere genug Erfahrungen mit Widerständen, Blockaden und bürokratischen Hürden gemacht. Und auch wenn sie in letzter Zeit unsicherer geworden war, was ihre weitere Karriere betraf, so hatte sie sich doch immer darauf verlassen können, dass sie Widerstände antizipieren konnte und dann entsprechend darauf vorbereitet war. Aber dieser Einwand der Deutschen und die Liste der zustimmenden Staaten, ausgerechnet dieser, machte sie wirklich sprachlos. Damit hatte sie nicht gerechnet: dass sich die Deutschen Sorgen um die Muslime machten und dass ausgerechnet die Länder, die innenpolitisch am radikalsten das »christliche Abendland« verteidigten, hier den Deutschen zustimmten. Und dass just die Ungarn ihrer Besorgnis Ausdruck verliehen, dass die Zustimmung einer breiteren europäischen Öffentlichkeit nicht gegeben sei, wenn das Verbrechen an den Juden in den Mittelpunkt der angeblich identitätsstiftenden Feierlichkeiten gestellt werde, ohne auch daran zu erinnern, dass die Juden nun mit den Palästinensern genau das machten, was ihnen selbst zuvor widerfahren war. Für diesen Einwand bekamen sie den Beifall der linken Abgeordneten (aus DE, GR, ES, PT, IT). Und sie, die Ungarn, erinnerten auch daran, dass sie im kommenden Jahr den Vorsitz der Internationalen Allianz für Holocaust-Gedenken (IHRA) innehaben werden und daher ohnehin schon eine Reihe von Gedenkveranstaltungen vorbereiteten. Und dann die Italiener: »Vorschlag IT, die Jubilee-Feierlichkeiten in Rom abzuhalten, zur Erinnerung an die Römischen Verträge. Festveranstaltung im Palazzo Montecitorio, mit den Präsidenten des Parlaments, des Rats und der Kommission, des Wirtschafts- und Sozialausschusses, der Zentralbank und des Ausschusses der Regionen –«, und den folgenden Zusatz fand Xeno besonders perfid: »… so sich diese auf eine gemeinsame feierliche Erklärung einigen können (Zustimmung: UK, DE, HUN, CR, LV, AT)«. Xeno fragte sich zum ersten Mal, warum immer wieder Menschen bei Entscheidungen mitredeten, die nicht einmal die Basics kannten. »Zur Erinnerung an die Römischen Verträge« – die Kommission hatte ihren Ursprung nicht in den Römischen Verträgen, sondern im Pariser Vertrag und in ihrer heutigen Form im Gipfel von Den Haag. Und keiner in der Ratsarbeitsgruppe sagte etwas gegen den Vorschlag der Italiener, das Jubiläum der Kommission in Rom zu feiern? Nicht einmal die Franzosen, die es doch besser wissen müssten? Niemand wusste mehr irgendetwas. Wie man so viel vergessen und trotzdem so viel reden konnte! So gesehen war der ergänzende Vorschlag der Italiener schon wieder rührend: »Im Anschluss Volksfest im Zentrum Roms.«

Den Vorschlag, eingebracht von den Polen mit den Worten »Warum die Juden? Warum nicht der Sport?«, fand Xeno so skandalös, dass sie nicht nur innerlich, sondern buchstäblich den Kopf schüttelte. Es bliebe, wenn man der massiven Zustimmung zu dieser Idee folgte, dann zwar in ihrem Ressort, da die Arche auch für europäischen Sport zuständig war, aber sie hatte da noch weniger Kompetenzen und Möglichkeiten als bei der Kultur. Die nationalen populistischen Parteien waren ein Klacks im Vergleich zum Nationalismus der Sportverbände der Mitgliedstaaten.

In diesem Moment kam Kassándra ins Zimmer, um zu berichten, dass sie die letzte Adresse von David de Vriend beim Meldeamt herausgefunden habe: an der Place du Vieux Marché-aux-Grains in Sainte-Catherine. Aber das Haus sei vor kurzem abgerissen worden.

Wer ist David – wie?

Das haben wir doch besprochen. Er wäre ideal für unser Projekt. Und es gibt keine Bestätigung für sein Ableben. Wahrscheinlich ist er jetzt in einem Altersheim. Das finden wir noch heraus.

Ableben?, sagte Xeno. Sie war nun sehr müde. Keine Bestätigung? Ich danke dir!

Sie sah auf die Uhr. Ich muss weg, sagte sie. Mittagspause, eine Besprechung!

Fridsch war schon da, als Xeno zur Rosti kam. Er saß an einem Tisch vor dem Lokal, in der prallen Sonne, als wäre die Straße eine Bühne und die Sonne ein Scheinwerfer, der nur auf ihn gerichtet war. Sie hatte diesen Gedanken, als sie ihn schon von Weitem sah und auf ihn zuging, und zugleich wunderte sie sich zum ersten Mal über das Wort Scheinwerfer: Schein-Werfer!

Sie konnte nicht erkennen, ob auch er sie schon gesehen hatte. Fridsch trug eine verspiegelte Sonnenbrille. Das fand Xeno entsetzlich. Sie hasste verspiegelte Sonnenbrillen. Man sah die Augen des Menschen nicht. Das war für Xeno die ärgste Vermummung, schlimmer noch als Nikab und Burka, wo man wenigstens noch die Augen sah, das Fenster in die Seele des Menschen, wie man sagt. Außerdem erinnerten sie diese Brillen an Männer, vor denen sie in ihrer Kindheit Angst gehabt hatte. Vor denen sie von ihrem Vater gewarnt worden war: Wer solche Brillen trägt, wer seine Augen nicht zeigt, hat ein dunkles Geheimnis. Und wer hat ein Geheimnis? Natürlich die Geheimpolizei. Darum heißt sie ja so. Die verrät Menschen, die dann ins Gefängnis kommen, oder ermordet sie gleich, hatte Vater gesagt, dann schützend seinen Arm um sie gelegt und sie an sich gedrückt.

Wie sie Fridsch kannte, hatte er diese Brille auf dem Flohmarkt gekauft, aber wenn er sie jetzt trug, dann musste man womöglich damit rechnen, dass Spiegelbrillen wieder in Mode kamen.

Er sprang auf, um sie zu begrüßen. Weil sie seine Augen nicht sah, sah sie zum ersten Mal überdeutlich, dass er Haare in der Nase hatte. Sie standen aus den Nasenlöchern hervor wie Spinnenbeinchen. Zugleich sah sie ihren eigenen Blick in seinen Gläsern. Sie hasste Haare in der Nase. Sie rasierte ihre Achseln, ihre Beine, trimmte ihr Schamhaar, und der Mann war nicht einmal imstande, diese blöden Härchen aus den Nasenlöchern wegzuknipsen.

Was war mit ihr los? Das fragte jetzt auch Fridsch: Was hast du?

Ärger –

Blendet dich –

– mit dem Projekt.

– die Sonne? Wir –

– Ja.

– können auch hineingehen. Ich habe –

– Ja?

– alternativ drinnen und draußen einen Tisch reserviert.

Er war so fürsorglich. Und drinnen würde er auch seine Brille abnehmen, dachte Xeno.

Das Projekt, vergiss es! Wir reden gleich darüber, sagte Fridsch, während er die Tür des Restaurants aufhielt, ihr den Vortritt ließ, ihr nachblickte und sie dabei optisch abtastete – mit dem Stolz des Mannes, der diese Frau erobert hatte und der zugleich von sich selbst gerührt war, weil dieser Stolz ihn

mit Gefühlen von Zärtlichkeit erfüllte. Zarter Zärtlichkeit.
War das eine Tautologie? Es gab da doch sicher Abstufungen.
Zarteste Zärtlichkeit! So als würde man die Hand auf den
Bauch einer schwangeren Frau legen – was dachte er da?
Er dachte gar nichts, nicht in Worten, aber könnte man seine
Gefühle in ein Programm einspeisen, das sie in Sprache über-
setzt, dann kämen ungefähr diese Sätze heraus.
Fridsch hatte sein Haar streng gescheitelt. Dieses Signal von
Pedanterie und Korrektheit irritierte Xeno. Was irritierte sie
jetzt gerade nicht? Als sie Platz genommen hatten, Fridsch
seine Brille abnahm und sich über den Tisch Xeno entgegen-
beugte, fuhr sie ihm ins Haar, bis der Scheitel zerstört war,
lachte, vielleicht eine Spur zu künstlich, und sagte: Besser!
So siehst du fünf Jahre jünger aus.
Will ich das? Vor fünf Jahren war ich nicht so glücklich wie
jetzt!
Diese Reaktion machte sie sprachlos. Da kam die Wirtin,
brachte die Speisekarten, nahm die Bestellung für Getränke
auf. Fridsch bestellte Wasser, Xeno Wein.
Da habt ihr alles, was man braucht, zum Predigen und zum
Trinken, sagte die Wirtin, Xeno nickte höflich, sie hatte das
nicht verstanden, die Wirtin sprach Bayrisch. Sie war Italie-
nerin, aus Mailand, hatte aber, bevor sie nach Brüssel kam,
jahrelang ein Restaurant in München geführt und dort Deutsch
gelernt. Und sie kannte Fridsch, wusste, dass er Deutscher
war.
Sie ist wegen eines Manns nach Brüssel gekommen, sie sagt
»Mannsbild«, wenn sie erzählt, er habe sehr gut ausgesehen,
ein »Feschak« sei er gewesen, aber, wie sich dann herausgestellt
habe, »nicht gut beinander«, kurz: »eine Mogelpackung«.
Fridsch liebte dieses Lokal, kannte all die Geschichten.
Unlängst hat sie zur Sperrstunde da mit ihrer Musikanlage
die Internationale abgespielt, erzählte Fridsch. Da waren ein

paar Gäste sehr verwundert. Weißt du warum? Aus Heimweh nach Mailand, hat sie gesagt.

Xeno sah ihn verständnislos an.

Fridsch lachte. Ihr Vater, erzählte er, war ein glühender Anhänger von Internazionale Milano, das ist der berühmte Fußballclub von Mailand. Und als der Club ins Finale des Europa-Cups kam, gegen Real Madrid, ist er nach Wien gereist. Warum nach Wien?

Weil dort das Finale stattfand. Also Inter Mailand gegen Real Madrid. Vor dem Spiel sollte die österreichische Militärkapelle die beiden Club-Hymnen spielen.

Warum die Militärkapelle?

Weiß ich nicht. Das war eben so. Glaubst du, die Wiener Philharmoniker spielen auf dem Fußballplatz? Jedenfalls: Die Kapelle spielte zuerst die Hymne von Real Madrid. Dann sollte die von Mailand kommen. Aber man hatte der Kapelle irrtümlich die Noten der Internationale gegeben statt der Clubhymne von Internazionale Mailand. Also ertönte plötzlich die kommunistische Internationale. Und einige italienische Spieler haben tatsächlich auch mitgesungen: Wacht auf, Verdammte dieser Erde!, keine Ahnung, wie die italienische Übersetzung ist. Bei Real spielte Ferenc Puskás, damals wahrscheinlich der beste Fußballer der Welt. Ein Ungar, der 1956 vor den sowjetischen Panzern aus Budapest geflohen war. Er war so verstört, als er vor dem Spiel die kommunistische Hymne hörte, dass er danach nur noch geschockt über das Feld irrte, weshalb Inter Mailand 3:1 gegen den Favoriten Real Madrid gewann. Und deswegen, zur Erinnerung an diesen Triumph, spielte ihr Vater zu Hause immer wieder die Internationale und deswegen hat sie –

Fridsch sah, dass es Xeno überhaupt nicht interessierte, was er da erzählte. Aber er war so fröhlich, so glücklich, sein Herz war voll, sein Mund ging über. Da kam die Wirtin, brachte die Getränke. Sie hatten noch keinen Blick in die Speisekarten geworfen, bestellten einfach das Tagesmenü.

Anyway, sagte Fridsch, was ich dir sagen wollte, es ist sehr wichtig. Hör zu, dein Jubilee Project, also –

Hast du das Protokoll der Arbeitsgruppe gelesen?

Natürlich.

Und was ist da jetzt noch wichtig?

Nichts –

Sie fiel ihm ins Wort, ein bisschen zu laut, so dass man von den Nebentischen herschaute: Was redest du da? Nichts ist wichtig, und das ist so wichtig, dass du mich herbestellst, um mir das zu sagen?

Nein, hör doch zu! Was ich sagen wollte: Es gibt nichts, was du für das Projekt noch tun kannst, es ist tot. Es wird noch eine Zeitlang als typischer Kommissions-Zombie durch ein paar Abteilungen und Instanzen geistern und dann endgültig begraben werden. Was du jetzt tun musst, ist: dich freizuspielen. Lass es von den Sherpas zu den Totengräbern tragen. Du kannst die Idee nicht verteidigen. Du kommst damit nicht durch. Du bist aus dem Spiel. Die COMM wollte ein Jubiläumsfest, der Präsident sagt, dass er eine gute Idee unterstützen würde, die Ratsarbeitsgruppe sagt, dass es keine gute Idee gibt, beziehungsweise macht andere schlechte Vorschläge, die alle keine Chance haben, weil das alles nur Alibi-Vorschläge sind, verstehst du? Wenn irgendwer immer noch glaubt, er könne damit Lorbeeren ernten, dann lass ihn. Aber wenn jemand peinlich damit scheitert, dann bist es nicht du. Okay? Du bist aus dem Spiel, weil du – und jetzt kommt es – …

Fridsch wollte jetzt Fanfarentöne imitieren, um die Pointe einzuleiten, da brachte die Wirtin die Blattsalate und wünschte einen guten Appetit, sie sagte es auf Bayrisch, schwer zu transkribieren, es klang wie: »Angurten!«

Weil du, setzte Fridsch fort, dann schon ganz woanders bist.

Mit einem schönen Karriereschritt zum Beispiel in der TRADE oder in der HOME.

Was redest du da?

War es nicht das, was du wolltest? Und ich habe den Catch entdeckt, wie es geht. Hör zu! Du bist doch Zypriotin, oder?

Ja. Das weißt du doch.

Aber war Zypern schon EU-Mitglied, als du nach Brüssel kamst?

Nein. Ich bin damals –

Du bist damals mit einem griechischen Ticket gekommen.

Ja. Ich bin ja Griechin.

Also was jetzt? Griechin oder Zypriotin?

Warum lachst du so? Machst du dich über mich lustig? Was ist so komisch daran: Ich bin griechische Zypriotin.

Also ganz langsam, sagte Fridsch: Griechenland ist Mitglied der Europäischen Union. Mittlerweile ist auch die Republik Zypern Mitglied der Union. Aber damals, als Zypern noch nicht Mitglied war, bist du, eine Zypriotin, als Griechin hierhergekommen.

Ja, das war damals meine Chance. Ich konnte als griechische Zypriotin einen griechischen Pass bekommen und –

Und jetzt hast du eine ganz andere Chance. Weil seit einiger Zeit auch die Republik Zypern Mitglied der Union ist. Eine kleine Insel. Noch dazu eine halbe kleine Insel. Mit weniger als einer Million Einwohner, ein Staat mit ungefähr so viel Einwohnern wie Frankfurt. Das ist doch bizarr, oder? Und was machen die Menschen dort? Sind sie Fremdenführer, Tauchlehrer, Olivenbauern? Ich weiß es nicht. Ich weiß nur eines –

Xeno schaute ihn an, seine fröhlichen Augen, er steuerte auf eine Pointe zu, sie begriff noch nicht, welche, irgendetwas war ihr unangenehm, wie eine sehr subtile Beleidigung, die sie aber noch nicht verstand, jetzt hätte sie nichts dagegen gehabt, wenn er seine Spiegelbrille wieder aufgesetzt hätte.

Diese winzige Republik Zypern schafft es nicht, die Quote der Beamten, die ihr hier auf allen Ebenen der Hierarchie zustehen, zu erfüllen, alle Posten, die Zyprioten beanspruchen können, zu besetzen. Sie haben zu wenig qualifizierte Menschen. Verstehst du jetzt, worauf ich hinauswill?

Das war das Wichtige, was du mir sagen wolltest?

Ja. Ist das nicht wunderbar? So logisch. So einfach. Du besorgst dir einen Pass der Republik Zypern und bekommst mit deinem CV sofort eine Direktion.

Aber dann müsste wer gehen.

Die Briten gehen. Andere gehen in Pension. In einem Monat muss eine Direktion bei uns in der TRADE neu besetzt werden. Und dann eine in HOME. Und wenn die Zyprioten, die erst fünfzig Prozent der Posten, die ihnen zustehen, besetzt haben, wen vorschlagen können –

Aber ich habe den Concours bestanden, ich sitze schon lange nicht mehr auf einem nationalen Ticket.

Umso besser! Die Republik Zypern wird es sehr zu schätzen wissen, eine so erfahrene und unkündbare Landsfrau in verantwortungsvolle Position in der Kommission zu bringen.

Und ich muss nur – ein neuer Pass?

Ja. Den du selbstverständlich sofort bekommen kannst.

Fridsch strahlte. Er wunderte sich, dass Fenia keine Anzeichen von Begeisterung zeigte.

Angurten!

Sie aßen jetzt ihre Ravioli, sprachen nur noch wenig. Fridsch dachte, dass sie diese Information erst verdauen musste. Das andere Wichtige, was er ihr auch noch sagen wollte, das Private, schob er auf. Gefühle waren so schwer zu verstehen, und kaum hatte man sie in Worte gefasst, waren sie schon wieder so unsicher. Er dachte, es wäre besser, wenn sie ihm erst einmal dankbar war.

Nach dem Lunch saß Fenia Xenopoulou wieder an ihrem Schreibtisch, begann Mails zu beantworten, tippte so routiniert wie geistlos Floskeln vor sich hin – und kam bald ins Stocken. Wie sollte sie mit dem Vorschlag umgehen, den Fridsch gemacht hatte? Bald sah sie nicht mehr den Bildschirm, sondern Erinnerungsbilder, und ihre Finger lagen reglos auf der Tastatur. Sie lehnte sich zurück. Diese Sache mit dem Pass, das war doch – sie sprang auf, öffnete das Fenster. Die dicke, sonnenwarme Luft, die nun in das klimatisierte Zimmer strömte, erinnerte sie an Kindersommer in Zypern. Ist der Himmel damals auch wolkenlos gewesen, so war es für sie doch keine wolkenlose Zeit, wie sie Kinder aus begüterten Familien zwischen Liebkosungen und Spielen auf sonnigen Wiesen erlebten. Sie sah, dass sie sich im geöffneten Fensterflügel spiegelte, aber nur sehr schemenhaft, als wäre dieses Bild die Projektion aus einer fernen Zeit, nein, doch nicht, sie sah, wie hart ihr Mund geworden war, die Falten rechts und links vom Mund, im Spiegelbild schienen sie wie mit dem Luftpinsel hingetupft. Das war sie und doch eine andere, das war – sie lief zurück zum Schreibtisch, nahm das Telefon und rief Bohumil an: Kannst du kurz zu mir kommen?

Er kam sofort, und Xeno bat ihn um eine Zigarette.

Die Zigaretten hab ich in meinem Zimmer, ich hol sie gleich, sagte er, dann blickte er hinauf zum Rauchmelder: Soll ich auch die Leiter mitbringen und das Ding da oben zukleben?

Ist nicht nötig, sagte sie, ich rauche am Fenster.

Er kam zurück, gab ihr das Päckchen, sagte: Du kannst es behalten. Sind nur noch fünf drinnen. Ich habe noch ein Päckchen im Zimmer.

Danke. Das ist sehr nett. Hast du Feuer?

Sie stand rauchend am Fenster, sah Bohumil an, auf eine Weise, die ihm unangenehm war. Als stünde sie neben sich. Und als schaute sie durch ihn hindurch. War es wegen des Jubilee Project? Er wusste natürlich, dass es da Probleme gab, er hatte eigentlich erwartet, dass sie ihn deshalb sprechen wollte. Aber sie sprach das Thema nicht an. Es war gespenstisch. Sie war doch eine beinharte Pragmatikerin, er hatte sie noch nie so verstört erlebt. Okay, sagte er, machte einen Schritt zurück und wollte schon hinausgehen, da sagte Xeno: Hast du einen Pass?

Bohumil sah sie erstaunt an.

Ich meine, sagte sie, was für einen Pass hast du?

Sie erwartete, dass er sagen würde: natürlich einen tschechischen Pass. Und sie hätte genickt und ihn um dieses »natürlich« beneidet. Aber dann war sie einen Moment lang sprachlos. Denn er sagte: Ich habe einen österreichischen Pass. Warum fragst du?

Sie sah ihn an, hielt die Zigarette vor ihren Mund, ohne daran zu ziehen, kniff die Augen zusammen, streckte dann die Hand mit der Zigarette aus dem Fenster, schüttelte den Kopf und sagte: Hast du jetzt gesagt, einen österreichischen Pass?

Ja. Ich habe einen österreichischen Pass. Warum?

Das möchte ich von dir wissen. Warum? Du bist doch Tscheche.

Ja, aber ich bin in Wien geboren. Meine Großeltern sind 1968, als die russischen Panzer den Prager Frühling niederschlugen – du weißt: Prager Frühling?

Xeno nickte.

Da sind meine Großeltern nach Österreich geflüchtet. Mit meinem Vater. Der damals sechzehn Jahre alt war. Zehn Jahre später hat mein Vater meine Mutter geheiratet, sie war ebenfalls Kind geflüchteter Tschechen in Wien. Aber da waren beide schon österreichische Staatsbürger. Ich kam zur Welt und war natürlich auch österreichischer Staatsbürger. Im Dezember 1989, also gleich nach der Revolution, sind wir zurück nach Prag. Das war der Triumph meiner Eltern, die Wende. Da war ich zehn. 2002 machte ich den Concours in Brüssel. Ich habe Politikwissenschaften studiert, in Prag, aber ich wollte hinaus, und da war es gut, dass ich meinen österreichischen Pass noch hatte, weil Österreich war bereits EU-Mitglied, aber Tschechien noch nicht. Deshalb bin ich hier, und – er lächelte – deshalb bin ich Raucher und habe immer ein paar Päckchen Vorrat.

Xeno sah ihn fragend an.

Well, ich bin als kleines Kind jeden Abend mit den Eltern in der verrauchtesten Kneipe von Wien gesessen, im Azyl, das war der Treffpunkt der geflüchteten und exilierten tschechischen Dissidenten. Meine Eltern gingen jeden Abend hin, für Babysitter hatten sie kein Geld, also nahmen sie mich einfach mit. Dort diskutierten sie stundenlang mit Václav Havel, wenn er in Wien war, Pavel Kohout, Karel Schwarzenberg, Jaroslav Hutka und wie sie alle hießen. Dabei rauchten sie Kette, alle. Ich saß daneben oder schlief daneben, ich war schon nikotinabhängig, bevor ich selbst meine erste Zigarette rauchte.

Er lachte. Brach das Lachen ab, als er Xenos Gesicht sah.

Und?, fragte sie.

Das war nicht das Ende, sagte er – er hatte nicht »and?«, sondern »end?« verstanden –, oder vielleicht doch: für meinen Vater. Havel wurde Präsident, Schwarzenberg Außenminister, Kohout bekam fast den Literaturnobelpreis, zumindest erzählte er das, und Hutka, der ein Star auf Radio Free Europe geworden war, tourte mit seinen Protestliedern durch das Land, bis eine Generation herangewachsen war, die diese Lieder nicht mehr verstand. Da ging er mit dem Titel »Le-

bende Legende« in Pension. Mein Vater wurde Unterrichts-
minister – und hatte am Tag der Vereidigung einen Herzinfarkt. Er ging in die tschechische Geschichte ein als »der Zehn-
Minuten-Minister«.

Das tut mir leid.

Danke. Mir auch.

Jedenfalls, dann kannst du also Deutsch, sagte Xeno.

Lausig, sagte Bohumil auf Deutsch.

Lousy?

Yes.

Aber warum? Wenn du –

Weil ich es seit meiner Rückkehr nach Prag nie wieder gesprochen habe, also seit ich zehn war. Und in der Wiener
Zeit habe ich in der Volksschule zwar Deutsch gelernt, aber
zu Hause immer Tschechisch gesprochen. Es ist eigentlich
nur eines geblieben: Ich muss immer lachen über deutsche
Lehnwörter im Tschechischen. Zum Beispiel »pinktlich«. Das
ist ein tschechisches Wort, das aus dem Deutschen kommt.
Es bedeutet alles, was unsympathisch und abstoßend und typisch deutsch ist: Es bedeutet pedantisch, unflexibel, unsen-
sibel, auf gnadenlose Weise gründlich, selbstgerecht, mit preu-
ßischer Disziplin – da sagt man auf Tschechisch, wenn jemand
so ist, er ist pinktlich.

Er lachte. Und brach sofort ab. Xenos maskenhaftes Gesicht.

I see, sagte sie. Und – der Pass? Du hattest nie ein Problem
damit?

Nein, warum? Was für ein Problem? Es ist doch egal, welchen Pass ich habe, es ist ein europäischer Pass.

Xeno hatte die Zigarette aus dem Fenster geworfen, jetzt zog
sie eine neue aus dem Päckchen, steckte sie zwischen die Lippen und hielt Bohumil ihren Mund entgegen, es sah aus wie
ein Kussmund, wenn man sich die Zigarette wegdachte.

Er gab ihr Feuer, sie bedankte sich und sah aus dem Fenster, was Bohumil als dezenten Hinweis verstand, dass er sich nun zurückziehen könne.

Er sagte okay, well, sie sagte nichts, sah aus dem Fenster. Also ging er. Er hatte das Gefühl, eine Prosektur zu verlassen. Ob er die Tote identifizieren könne? Sie sei ihm bekannt, aber er sei sich nicht sicher.

Was war Xenos Problem? Sie war von Bohumils Geschichte so überrascht, dass sie wie versteinert war. Dieser heitere Bohumil. Aber so einfach war es nicht. Sie war gespalten. Sie war zwei. Sie verstand nicht, warum sie das sein sollte. Seine Geschichte war in gewisser Weise ihre. Und doch war ihre ganz anders. Das verwirrte sie. Zunächst.

Sie besaß einen Pass, der immer ihr europäischer Pass gewesen war, und nicht ein Ausweis ihrer nationalen oder ethnischen Identität. Er war für sie die Eintrittskarte in das Reich der Freiheit, der Freizügigkeit und Niederlassungsfreiheit Europas, er war ihr Freibrief, in Europa ihren Weg gehen zu können. Χαῖρε, ὦ χαῖρε, Ἐλευθερία, hatte sie als Schülerin in Zypern mit Inbrunst mitgesungen, wenn bei Anlässen die Nationalhymne gespielt wurde: Holde Freiheit, sei gegrüßt! Aber dass man als griechische Zypriotin zu einer zypriotischen Nationalistin werden muss, auf diesen Gedanken wäre sie nie gekommen, das war ihr vollkommen fremd. Warum sollte der Geburtsort mehr Bedeutung haben als die Ansprüche, die man als Mensch haben konnte, ja musste? Freiheit, das verstand sie, aber Zypern über alles, das wäre ihr nie in den Sinn gekommen. Deshalb hatte es sie auch nicht im Geringsten erstaunt, als sie nach Griechenland zum Studium kam und merkte, dass man hier dieselbe Hymne sang. Χαῖρε, ὦ χαῖρε, Ἐλευθερία. Das war also für sie kein nationales Bekenntnis, und es war für sie auch nicht im Geringsten rätselhaft, warum zwei Länder dieselbe Hymne hatten, diese Hymne war für sie einfach ein Freiheitslied – und wie gut es für sie passte: Die du aus der heiligen Griechen Knochen / wutentbrannt entsprossen bist!

Ihre Wut sollte sie weit tragen. Wut war Energie, eine Produktivkraft. Das Versprechen der Freiheit konnte doch nicht bedeuten: Verkümmere in deiner Enge, aber deine Gedanken sind frei! Sieh doch die Olivenbäume im dürren Hain vor deinem Haus! Wie wenig sie brauchen, und doch schimmern ihre Blätter in der Sonne wie Silber!

Sind deine Gedanken frei, dann müssen es deine Möglichkeiten auch sein, deine Taten, deine Handlungen. Das ist ihr schon mit zwölf klar gewesen, als sie für Touristen aus aller Herren Länder Mineralwasserflaschen zum ausgetrockneten Bad der Aphrodite schleppte. Aus aller Herren Länder, das hatte sie in der Schule gelernt, sind sie immer schon nach Zypern gekommen, die Herren, weil Zypern so nah ist zur Türkei, zu Griechenland, zu Syrien und Ägypten, also immer schon eine Schnittstelle war zwischen Europa, Asien und Afrika. Zypern war keine Nation, diese Insel war ein kleines Schiff, es schaukelte auf den Wogen der Geschichte und den Gezeiten der Nationen und Reiche, die auftauchten und wieder untergingen.

Als sie ihren griechischen Pass erhalten hatte, hätte sie nie gedacht, dass sie damit nun das Land ihrer Herkunft verlassen und verraten habe. Der griechische Pass war für sie ein Reisedokument, von der Insel, die eine Taube im Wappen hatte, auf den Kontinent, der sich als Friedensprojekt bezeichnete und ihr Karrierechancen bot. Und jetzt fand sie es völlig verrückt, dass sie diesen Pass aufgeben und ihn gegen einen anderen eintauschen sollte, der nichts anderes konnte und nichts anderes versprach als der alte – ihr aber abverlangte, sich als griechische Zypriotin zu entscheiden, ob sie Griechin oder Zypriotin sei. Sie sollte ihren Pass, den sie als europäisches Dokument betrachtet hatte, gegen einen eintauschen, der nun ein nationales Bekenntnis war – um in Europa Karriere machen zu können. Ja, das war verrückt. Sie hatte lange genug in der Kommission gearbeitet, um diese Erfahrung zu haben: dass die Nationalisten immer brutaler auf dieses Europa einprügelten, in dem sie frei ihren Weg gehen wollte, mit all ihrer Wut, die sie mitbrachte aus der Enge, und die, wie sie jetzt plötzlich dachte, vielleicht unbewusst eine Wut auf die Beschränkungen war, die einem abverlangten zu sagen: Ich bin ... Zypriotin. Oder Griechin. Oder sonst was. Wer sagt: Du bist – der meint: Bleib, wo du bist!

Der Vorschlag von Fridsch stellte ihr ganzes Leben auf den Kopf. Identität war doch nur ein Papier. Würde sie eine andere werden, wenn sie das Papier wechselte? Würde sie eine andere sein, wenn sie statt »Freiheit, sei gegrüßt!« nun »Freiheit, sei gegrüßt!« singen sollte, die Hymne des neues Passes, die identisch war mit der Hymne des alten Passes? Ja – weil sie eine Freiheitshymne ausgetauscht hätte gegen eine Nationalhymne, und derselbe Text und dieselbe Melodie hätten daher eine ganz andere Bedeutung. Sie war in Zypern geboren, als Griechin, und sie war in Griechenland Griechin, geboren in Zypern. Es war verrückt, dass ihr nun abverlangt wurde, diese Identität als eine doppelte zu sehen, die ihr eine Entscheidung abverlangte: Du bist schizophren, entscheide dich, wer du bist!

Das Furchtbare war, dass sie insgeheim wusste, dass sie sich mit ihrem Grübeln selbst belog. Natürlich würde sie die Chance ergreifen und den Pass wechseln. Sie brauchte zwei Stunden, um es sich einzugestehen. Sie war Pragmatikerin. Und das war nichts anderes als eine pragmatische Entscheidung. Warum sie solche Skrupel hatte? Weil sie irgendwie spürte, dass dabei etwas in ihr starb. Und wer stirbt schon gern? Die Aussicht auf ein besseres Leben danach, ob es nun Gott oder Karriere heißt, ist dann nur ein verzweifelter Trost.

Sie schrieb eine Mail an Mrs Atkinson, hielt inne und schloss das Dokument. Es erschien das Fenster »Als Entwurf sichern?«.

Sie hätte gern, dass im Leben möglich wäre, was der Computer anbietet: Entwürfe zu sichern. Sie klickte auf »Nicht sichern«, lehnte sich zurück und dachte: Okay.

Es war fast 17 Uhr. Sie schrieb noch eine Rund-Mail an ihre Mitarbeiter: »Besprechung wg. Begräbnis Jubilee Project morgen 11 Uhr.«

Dann wird auch Martin Susman zurück sein.

Sie löschte »Begräbnis« und klickte auf Senden.

Sie schaltete den Computer aus und ging. Sie hatte keine Lust, »nach Hause« zu gehen, in ihr kleines, funktionales Apartment, das im Grunde ein Schlafplatz mit begehbarer Garderobe war. Aber sie wollte auch nicht mehr hierbleiben, an einem Arbeitsplatz, den sie mit ihrer heutigen Entscheidung eigentlich schon verlassen hatte. Irgendwo noch etwas trinken? Sie war unschlüssig. Wenn, dann im Het Lachende Varken, dem Café in der Straße, in der sie wohnte.

Sie ging die Rue Joseph II hinauf zur Metro-Station Maelbeek. Auf dem Bahnsteig sah sie auf zur Info-Tafel: nächster Zug in sechs Minuten.

Das gab es also wirklich. Dass ein Mann in einen Käfer verwandelt werden konnte.

Dieser Gedanke war nur ein kleines, aber typisches Symptom dafür, dass der starke und robuste Florian Susman plötzlich ein anderer war: geschockt, hilflos, verzweifelt. Er war kein belesener Mann. Der mit den Büchern ist immer sein kleiner Bruder Martin gewesen.

Was liest du da schon wieder? Indianergeschichten?

Nein. Da wird ein Mann in ein Ungeziefer verwandelt, in einen Käfer.
Von einem Zauberer?
Nein. Einfach so. Ganz plötzlich. Er wacht auf und ist ein Käfer.

Wie verrückt er damals seinen kleinen Bruder gefunden hatte. Wie konnte man so etwas lesen, seine Zeit mit solch seltsamen Büchern verschwenden? Er war das Vater-Kind gewesen, der designierte Thronfolger, vom Vater abgöttisch geliebt, wenn auch ohne Zärtlichkeit behandelt. Er, der einmal den Hof übernehmen sollte, durfte kein Weichei sein, niemals schwach und verträumt. Gefühle sprach der Vater nicht aus. Wenn er sie zeigte, dann durch einen anerkennenden Blick, ein Nicken oder indem er Florian unbeholfen den Arm um die Schulter legte, mit kurzem Druck, der ausdrückte: Mein Sohn!

Martin ist der Mutter-Sohn gewesen, ein verträumtes Kind, das viel weinte, viel las und sich oft fürchtete. Dann lief er zur »Mutti«, die ihn schützte, aber sich zugleich auch schwertat, zärtlich zu sein: Sie war hart geworden im Lebenskampf, hatte schlaflose Nächte wegen der Schulden, die sie auf sich genommen hatten für den Ausbau des Hofs zum Schweinemast- und Schlachtbetrieb. Alle Muskeln waren angespannt. Wer ein Gewicht zu stemmen hat, kann nicht streicheln. Das bedeutete nicht, dass sie ihn ablehnte, auch wenn sie sich manchmal irritiert fragte, warum er so war, wie er war, und so dachte sie, dass er sich abhärten musste, einen Panzer brauchte, und nicht zuletzt, dass er, auch wenn er noch so ungeschickt war, Bereitschaft zeigen sollte, seinen Anteil zu übernehmen bei der Arbeit, die anfiel. Dann schickte sie ihn, wenn sie ihn beim Lesen erwischte, in den Stall. Es war sinnlos, weil die Masttiere damals bereits maschinell gefüttert und die Ställe von zwei Angestellten maschinell ausgemistet wurden, Martin also nur im Weg stand. Schließlich lief er wieder in die Küche. Dann durfte er beim Kochen helfen – oder am Küchentisch lesen. Bis er aufdecken musste, wenn die Männer zum Essen kamen, der Vater, der große Bruder, die zwei Angestellten mit dem strengen Geruch, Männer. In einen Käfer verwandelt? Einfach so? Ohne Zauberer? So ein Blödsinn!

Kannst du dich erinnern, fragte Florian, wie alt wir damals waren? Vierzehn und sechzehn? Und jetzt lag er da wie ein auf den Rücken gefallener Käfer. Jetzt war er verwandelt in einen hilflosen Käfer. Plötzlich. Einfach so. Und wartete darauf, versorgt zu werden. Wartete auf Infusionen gegen die Schmerzen, wartete auf das Essen, wartete auf Zuwendung. Wenn er konnte, las er, zunächst nur Zeitungen, dann auch Bücher, die Martin ihm brachte. Wenn das Lesen ihn anstrengte, seine Augen müde und seine Arme schwer wurden, dann döste er, grübelte vor sich hin, träumte. Inzwischen kümmerte sich der kleine Bruder um eine Reihe von Dingen, die anfielen und erledigt werden mussten, während Florian hilflos auf dem Rücken lag. Gespräche mit dem Stationsarzt und Telefonate mit der Versicherungsanstalt, bei der Florian eine private Zusatzversicherung hatte. Er holte Erkundigungen ein, welcher Chirurg den besten Ruf hatte, um diesen dafür zu gewinnen, die komplizierte und gefährliche Operation an Florians Rücken durchzuführen, es musste ein Meister seines Fachs sein –
Ein Zauberer?
Nein, ganz pragmatisch ein Meister, sagte Martin.
Martin verständigte die Innung, den Wirtschaftsbund, Geschäftspartner Florians, den Vorstand der European Pig Producers, forderte auf Florians Bitte von der EPP einen Bericht

von der Konferenz in Budapest an, stand in ständigem Kontakt mit Marlene, Florians Frau, die die Stellung im Betrieb halten musste, er organisierte einen Rechtsanwalt, spezialisiert auf Verkehrsdelikte und Unfallschaden, beauftragte ihn mit der Vertretung seines Bruders gegenüber der Versicherung des Taxifahrers, der an dem verheerenden Unfall schuld gewesen war, was auf einen Zivilprozess hinauslief, zur Durchsetzung der Ansprüche auf Schadensersatz und Schmerzensgeld.

Inzwischen las Florian oder starrte zur Decke. Ein verblüffender Rollentausch, einfach so, plötzlich, ganz ohne Zauberer.

Florian hatte nun eine Titanplatte und zwölf Schrauben im Rücken, das Rückgrat war stabilisiert, Rückenmark nicht verletzt, die Gefahr einer Lähmung war gebannt. Man gratulierte Florian zu seinem Glück im Unglück.

Er lag auf dem Rücken, träumte, manchmal seufzte oder stöhnte er, und er lächelte, wenn sein Bruder etwas flüsterte, Schweiß von seiner Stirn tupfte, seine Hand nahm.

Als der Vater starb, war er so alt wie ich jetzt, sagte Florian. Ich war jung damals, aber ich konnte ... – meine Kinder, wenn ich jetzt gestorben wäre – Elisabeth ist sieben, Paul ist fünf – es wäre ...

Ist es nicht seltsam, dass mir das jetzt passiert ist, in dem Alter, das der Vater hatte, als er – weißt du, was seltsam ist? Ich habe nie über den Tod nachgedacht. Nicht einmal am offenen Grab vom Vater. Eine Schaufel Erde hinuntergeworfen und – ja, ich war unter Schock. Aber ich dachte nicht über den Tod nach, sondern über mich. Der Tod ist für einen Lebenden immer der Tod von anderen.

Er grübelte.

Wenn ich jetzt gestorben wäre, ich hätte mich nicht verabschieden können, sagte er. So wie unser Vater sich nicht verabschieden konnte.

Er schwieg. Dann sagte er: Ist es besser, wenn man sich verabschieden kann? Oder ist es dann nur noch leidvoller?

Er dachte nach.

Wenn ich jetzt gelähmt wäre, hättest du mir geholfen, Schluss zu machen? Ich hätte dann nicht mehr leben wollen. Hätte ich mich auf dich verlassen können? Ich glaube jetzt, ich kann mich auf dich verlassen.

Nein, sagte Martin.

Martin reizte unverbrauchte Urlaubstage, Anspruch auf Pflegeurlaub und schließlich noch die Möglichkeit unbezahlter Freistellung so weit aus wie nur möglich. Der Frühling kam, laue Luft strömte durch offene Fenster herein, die ersten Pollen, das Spitalzimmer war überheizt, denn dem Kalender nach müsste es noch kühler sein, und es wurde nach dem Kalender geheizt und nicht nach der Realität, Florian schob die Decke weg, schrie Au!, wenn er niesen musste, die Erschütterung tat immer noch am Rücken weh, er schwitzte, dann fröstelte er im Luftzug der offenen Fenster, Martin musste ihn wieder zudecken, bis Florian die Decke wieder wegschob, wütend, das Einzige, was er energisch tun konnte, der auf dem Rücken liegende Käfer.

Martin hatte ein kleines Apartment in Wien behalten, im zweiten Bezirk, damit er eine Absteige hatte, wenn er ab und zu auf ein paar Tage nach Hause kam, aber es war nie ein Zuhause gewesen, es war eine Absteige, eine Kochnische, in der er noch nie mehr gekocht hatte als Kaffee, nie eine andere Schublade geöffnet hatte als die, in der sich der Flaschenöffner befand, in dem von Mal zu Mal Marmelade verschimmelte und die Haltbarkeit von Butter ablief. Ein Zimmer mit Bett und Tisch. Und Kisten. Acht große Umzugskisten. Sie hatte er hier abgestellt, als er seine frühere Wohnung aufgab, weil er nach Brüssel umzog. Mittlerweile wusste er gar nicht mehr, was in diesen Kisten war. Sein Zuhause. Er hatte auch noch immer ein Zimmer im Betrieb, im Elternhaus, bei den Schweinen, drei Stunden von Wien entfernt, das war auch kein Zuhause, was sollte er dort?

Manchmal ging er abends, wenn er vom Spital kam, um die Ecke ins Gasthaus Zum Sieg. Dort bekam er ein anständiges Gulasch, am Freitag einen sehr guten Fisch. Einmal wurde er Zeuge, wie ein Deutscher, der von einem Wiener in dieses Gasthaus mitgenommen wurde, mit geradezu panischer Irritation fragte: Zum Sieg? Das ist doch hoffentlich kein Nazi-Lokal!

Der Kellner, der gerade vorbeiging und dies hörte, stützte seine Arme auf den Tisch, beugte sich vor und sagte: Oida! Sieg der Arbeiterklasse! Verstehst mi?

Martin musste lächeln. Das war wie ein Winken von Geistern der Geschichte, wie ein Scherben, zutage gebracht in einer archäologischen Grabungsstätte. Später kam der Kellner bei ihm vorbei und sagte: War nur ein Schmäh! Weißt eh! Wir heißen Zum Sieg, weil es das Gasthaus gibt seit dem Sieg von Aspern, dazumal der Sieg der Österreicher über Napoleon!

Eine Schicht tiefer, noch ein Scherben.

An einem Samstag frühstückte er am Karmelitermarkt, dort traf er Felix, einen ehemaligen Kollegen aus der Studentenzeit. Er hätte ihn nicht erkannt. Er wurde erkannt. Er log: Wie schön, dass wir uns wiedersehen! Sie tranken Kaffee, redeten, und Martin hielt sich für Sentimentalitäten bereit. Es funktionierte. Früher, ja früher! Und weißt du noch: damals?

Ja, damals. Sie blinzelten in die Sonne, tranken Kaffee, gingen zu Wein über. Und plötzlich wurde die Sentimentalität zu Weinerlichkeit. Martin erzählte – warum ausgerechnet ihm? Warum diesem Fremden, mit dem biographischen Vorwand, ein alter Freund zu sein? Vielleicht ebendeshalb! – Martin erzählte ihm, dass er gefährdet sei, depressiv, er leide unter Depressionen und –

Depressionen? Geh bitte, sagte Felix mit morbider Heiterkeit. Sag mir eines: Putzt du dir vor dem Schlafengehen die Zähne?

Martin sah ihn fassungslos an. Ja, natürlich, sagte er.

Felix lachte. Dann hast du keine Depression. Solange man Zähne putzt, ist man nicht depressiv. Höchstens deprimiert, sagte er. Ich weiß, wovon ich rede! Und er schob seine Ärmel zurück und zeigte ihm die Narben an seinen Pulsadern.

Wann war das?

Ist doch egal, sagte Felix. Jedenfalls: Zähne geputzt habe ich damals nicht mehr!

Inzwischen erholte sich Florian, langsam, aber doch. Er wollte nicht mehr lesen. Er kehrte ins Leben zurück. Und – das war seltsam: Er begann zugleich, auf gewisse Weise mit seinem Leben abzuschließen.

Er erfuhr, dass bei der Jahresversammlung der Union der Europäischen Schweineproduzenten in Budapest ein neuer Präsident gewählt worden war. Das war zu erwarten gewesen. Durch seinen Unfall während der Hinfahrt hatte er ja nicht erscheinen und den Vorstand der EPP vom Grund seines Fernbleibens auch nicht verständigen können. Es war klar, dass dies damals nur missinterpretiert werden konnte. Als hätte er kein Interesse mehr an seinem Amt, ja nicht einmal mehr an einer regulären Amtsübergabe. Dass also ein neuer Präsident gewählt worden war, konnte er nachvollziehen, das kränkte ihn nicht, aber was ihm größte Sorgen bereitete, mehr noch: geradezu wütend machte, war, dass ein Ungar zum neuen Präsidenten gewählt wurde, der unsägliche Balázs Gyöngyösi, ein radikaler Nationalist, der seine Mitarbeit und sein Engagement in dieser europäischen Organisation bislang nur dazu genutzt hatte, sich Vorteile für seinen eigenen großen Mangalica-Zuchtbetrieb zu verschaffen. Er versuchte, die European Pig Producers als Lobbyisten zu missbrauchen, um das »Ungarische Mangalica-Schwein« als geschützte Herkunftsbezeichnung markenrechtlich registrieren zu lassen und dadurch österreichische und deutsche Mangalica-Züchter auszubooten. Nebenbei war Gyöngyösi immer wieder durch antisemitische Äußerungen auffällig geworden. Für ihn war die EU eine Verschwörung des Weltjudentums zur Zerstörung der europäischen Nationen, der von ihm so genannten »Wirtsvölker«. All diese Widersprüche, von der EU Rechtsschutz für seine ungarischen Rasseschweine zu fordern, zugleich die EU abzulehnen, eine Schweinezucht zu betreiben, aber seine Todfeinde, die Juden, als Schweine zu bezeichnen, waren nicht nur grotesk, sie waren in Florians Augen ehrenrührig und gefährlich für die Union. Er hatte daher vorgehabt, einen Antrag auf Ausschluss von Balász Gyöngyösi aus der EPP zu stellen. Und nun war ausgerechnet dieser Mann der neue Präsident der EPP. Wie war das möglich?

Ungarische Schweinemäster und Schlachter waren bei dieser Konferenz in Budapest natürlich besonders zahlreich vertreten. Angeblich hatte Gyöngyösi Dutzende von ihnen mit Bussen zur Versammlung gekarrt. Sein Gegenkandidat war ein Spanier, ein gewisser Juan Ramón Jiménez, den Florian nicht kannte. Das Problem war offenbar, dass sich die Deutschen und die Holländer der Stimmen enthalten haben, während sich die Delegierten der kleinen Länder hinter dem Ungarn versammelten, was reichte, um die Franzosen, Italiener und Spanier zu überstimmen.

Später erfuhr Florian den Grund: Die Deutschen hatten tatsächlich inzwischen einen bilateralen Handelsvertrag mit China unterschriftsreif ausgehandelt, ebenso die Niederländer. Die Union der Europäischen Schweineproduzenten und die Frage, wer nun deren Präsident sein sollte, war ihnen nun –

– scheißegal!, rief Florian. Das ist ihnen jetzt, mit Verlaub, scheißegal!

Er starrte zur Decke, lag reglos da, aber Martin hatte das Gefühl, dass tief in ihm ein Tier brüllend gegen Gitterstäbe sprang.

Tage später. Mail von Gabor Szabó, dem einzigen ungarischen Kollegen, der mit Florian noch Kontakt hielt. Martin las vor. Ungarische Schweineproduzenten verhandeln bilateral mit China. Delegation unter Führung von Balázs Gyöngyösi war in Peking. »Stell dir vor: Es gab einen ersten Empfang, mit Essen und vor allem mit Trinksprüchen, und Balázs hob das Glas und sagte, wie sehr er sich freue und geehrt sei und auf freundschaftliche Beziehungen anstoße und so weiter. Und dann: Die chinesische Regierung sei ein Vorbild für uns Ungarn, wegen der Klarheit und Entschlossenheit, mit der sie die Interessen des Volkes vertrete, zum Wohle des Volkes, und besondere Bewunderung verdiene zum Beispiel die Konsequenz, mit der damals gegen die Staatsfeinde am Tian'anmen-Platz durchgegriffen wurde. – Die Chinesen waren hochgradig irritiert. Sie waren weder darauf vorbereitet noch daran interessiert, dass das Massaker am Tian'anmen angesprochen wurde. Bei den folgenden Verhandlungen hätte man sich genauso gut wechselseitig die Telefonbücher von Budapest und Peking vorlesen können. Bereits auf dem Rückflug war Balázs als Delegationsleiter und als Präsident der Interessengemeinschaft Ungarischer Schweineproduzenten abgesetzt.«

Florian lächelte. Dann starrte er wieder an die Decke. Er grübelte. Martin drückte seine Hand. Florian zog sie zurück.

Irgendwann fühlte sich Martin von seinem Bruder ausgesaugt wie von einem Vampir. War das ein Zeichen dafür, dass nun alles wieder so war wie zuvor, oder fast so? Florian konnte bereits zeitweise auf der Seite liegen, kurz aufstehen und einige wenige Schritte gehen.

Ich muss zurück nach Brüssel.

Ich werde dir nie vergessen, was du für mich getan hast.

Ich fliege nächsten Montag. Ich helfe dir noch am Wochenende bei der Überstellung in die Reha-Klinik.

Danke.

Was wirst du dann machen? Wenn du rauskommst?

Siehst du doch.

Was?

Na was mache ich denn? Still liegen.

Ich meinte, wenn du da raus bist.

Sag ich doch. Die EU zahlt Stilllegungsprämien für Schweinezüchter. Man bekommt Geld für jedes Schwein, das man nicht mehr mästet. Ich werde alle Mitarbeiter kündigen. Ich werde von meiner Stube aus zuschauen, wie der Betrieb verfällt. Irgendwann können ihn deine Nachfolger ausgraben und ihre Schlüsse ziehen. Inzwischen kassiere ich die Stilllegungsprämie.

Das meinst du nicht ernst!

Doch. Ich werde mein Kapital in Deutschland investieren, mich an einem großen Mastbetrieb beteiligen, wahrscheinlich bei Tönnies Fleisch, da habe ich durch die EPP gute Kontakte, und mich mit meinen Erfahrungen und meiner

Expertise einbringen. Oder auch nicht. Jedenfalls: Ich liege still. Kannst du in die Zukunft schauen?

Nein.

Du siehst nichts?

Nein.

Ich auch nicht. Ich sehe nichts mehr.

Der so genannte »Pyjama-Flieger« nach Brüssel (Montag um 7 Uhr morgens) war natürlich ausgebucht. Da flogen all die Beamten und MEPs, die das Wochenende in Wien verbracht hatten und nun zur Arbeit zurückkehrten, österreichische Lobbyisten und Vertreter von Interessenverbänden, die schon am Vormittag Termine hatten und am Abend oder am nächsten Tag zurückflogen. Und wahrscheinlich war, wie so oft, auch ein engagierter Lehrer mit einer Schulklasse an Bord, im Rahmen der geförderten Aktion »Junge Europäer besuchen das Europäische Parlament«. Martin hatte erst für den Nachmittagsflug einen Platz bekommen, was ein Glück war, weil er den Morgenflug und wahrscheinlich sogar den Mittagsflug verschlafen hätte. Er hatte bis fast vier Uhr nachts nicht einschlafen, den Kopf nicht abschalten können. Er hatte seinen Bruder am späten Nachmittag nach Klosterneuburg in die Rehabilitationsklinik gebracht, dann bei dem Griechen auf der Taborstraße drei Flaschen Mythos-Bier gekauft, etwas Käse und eine Flasche »Drama«-Weißwein, nebenan beim Türken ein Fladenbrot.

Er aß und trank und schaute auf die Umzugskisten, versuchte sich vorzustellen, wie es sein würde, wenn er das nächste Mal das Elternhaus, seinen Bruder und die Familie besuchte und buchstäblich kein Schwein da wäre, die Ställe, die große Masthalle, die Schlachtanlage, alles leer, stillgelegt, die weißen Kacheln nicht blutig und dann auch nicht glänzend weiß, wenn der Herr Hofer sie mit dem Schlauch abgespritzt und gewaschen hätte, sondern staubgrau, staubtrocken, Herr Hofer in Frühpension, alle Mitarbeiter gekündigt, die Natur würde in die stillgelegten Hallen eindringen, Efeu, Farne, Schlingpflanzen, Unkraut zu wachsen beginnen auf dem Mist, der von den Schweinen zurückgeblieben war, von der letzten Generation der Schweine vor der Stilllegung ... Die Fenster brachen, bei Frost platzten in den kalten Ställen die Wasserrohre, in den Wänden entstanden Risse, Flugsamen nistete sich ein, trieb aus und verwurzelte, allerlei Pflanzen fraßen den Verputz und sprengten die Wände, schufen ein Biotop für Mäuse, Ratten, Igel, Ameisen, Spinnen, Mauersegler, Hornissen, verwilderte Katzen, und Martin trank das dritte Mythos und sah schon das Dach der Masthalle einstürzen, die vor dem Wohnhaus der Familie stand, dem ursprünglichen Wohntrakt des alten Bauernhofs, der inzwischen zwei Mal aufgestockt und erweitert worden war, und Martin machte die Weinflasche auf und fragte sich, ob sie dann wirklich an den Fenstern stehen oder auf der Bank vor dem Haus sitzen werden und zuschauen, wie die Wurzeln von Unkraut und Wildwuchs und die Klauen von allerlei Getier hineinschlugen in die untergehende Familiengeschichte. Und wenn der Betrieb zu Staub zerfällt und versinkt – wie lange wird sein Bruder die Stilllegungsprämie kassieren können?

Er sollte schlafen gehen. Er putzte die Zähne. Er lächelte in sich hinein: Das war ein gutes Zeichen. Ein weniger gutes Zeichen war, dass er sich danach wieder an den Tisch setzte, doch noch eine Zigarette rauchen und noch ein Glas Wein trinken wollte. Er dachte darüber nach, was ihn nun in Brüssel erwartete. Natürlich hatte er auf Grund von Rund-Mails mitbekommen, dass es Probleme mit dem Jubilee Project gab. Er hatte natürlich auch das Protokoll der Ratsarbeitsgruppe erhalten. Er hatte es überflogen – und nicht besonders ernst genommen. Für ihn war maßgeblich, dass Xeno das Projekt offenbar weitertreiben wollte, zumindest war kein Stop! von ihr gekommen. An manchen Abenden war er am Computer gesessen, um Ergänzungen und weiterführende Gedanken zum Projekt zu notieren. Auch wenn er beurlaubt war, er wollte, wenn er zurückkam, etwas vorlegen können. Zumindest hat er an manchen Abenden, nach den Nachmittagen beim Bruder im Spital, nicht gewusst, was er sonst tun sollte.

Vor allem einer Idee war er nachgegangen: Wenn man Auschwitz-Überlebende als Zeitzeugen für die Idee des Europäischen Friedensprojekts und für die historische Aufgabe der Europäischen Kommission präsentiert, dann wäre es doch logisch und sinnvoll, auch Beamte aus der Gründungszeit der Kommission einzubinden, sie erzählen zu lassen, mit welchen Ideen, Absichten und Hoffnungen sie damals ihre Arbeit aufgenommen hatten. Martin war überzeugt davon, dass die Beamten der ersten Generation viel genauer wussten, worum es ging, als die gegenwärtigen Eliten der Bürokratie. Das wäre, dachte Martin Susman, gleichsam die zweite Zangenbacke. Auf der einen Seite die Überlebenden der Vernichtungslager, die an den Schwur erinnerten: nie wieder Nationalismus und Rassismus. Auf der anderen Seite die Vertreter der Gründergeneration der Europäischen Kommission, die daran erinnerten, dass es genau darum ging: um die Entwicklung einer supranationalen Institution zur Überwindung des Nationalismus, letztlich der Nationen.

Er hatte Kassándra eine Mail geschrieben: Was hältst du davon?

Kassándra: Ich kümmere mich darum.

Eine Woche später. Kassándra: Erste Generation Kommission: a) tot. b) dement. c) nicht dement, nicht reisefähig. Willst du weiterarbeiten an dieser Idee? Ev. Videobotschaften von c)?

Martin hatte den »Drama«-Wein ausgetrunken, fühlte sich aber noch immer nicht in der Lage, ins Bett zu gehen und zu schlafen. Er fand in der Küche eine Flasche Grappa. Tu es nicht, dachte er und öffnete die Flasche. Er taumelte leicht, als er von der Kochnische die drei Schritte zum Tisch zurückging.

Vielleicht, dachte er, sollte man das Jubilee Project ganz anders organisieren. Aufs Ganze gehen. Kompromisslos. Wenn Demenz und Tod verhinderten, dass noch jemand Auskunft geben und sich darin erinnern konnte, worum es eigentlich gegangen war und worum es immer noch ging – dann müssten eben Demente und Tote auftreten und dafür einstehen. Würden sie nicht Schrecken und Mitleid erregen und vielleicht Reinigung bewirken? Sogar Verstehen. Plötzlich versteht eine demente Gesellschaft, was sie hatte sein wollen, plötzlich erinnert sich ein todkranker Kontinent an die Medizin, die ihm Heilung versprochen, die er aber abgesetzt und vergessen hatte. Wie? Wie könnte man das durchspielen? Schauspieler? Man müsste Schauspieler engagieren, die als die Beamten der Gründerzeit der Kommission auftreten, keine berühmten Schauspieler, die bereits für die Darstellung aller möglichen Rollen gefeiert wurden, sie wären wieder nur sie, nur eben in einer anderen Rolle, Stars des Pluralismus, dem alles gleich gültig ist, nein, man bräuchte alte Schauspieler, die große Idealisten waren, nie Stars wurden, sich nie ganz durchsetzen konnten, obwohl sie ihr Handwerk beherrschten, und die Erfahrungen gemacht hatten, die sie und ihre Arbeit prägten, aber den nächsten Generationen nichts mehr bedeuteten, als es mehr um Ruhm als um Wahrheit ging und um die Phrasen der Wahrheit als Grundlage für Ruhm, um Ruhm als Geschäftsgrundlage statt als Leuchtfeuer von Sinn und Bedeutung. Gescheiterte Schauspieler müssten das nicht spielen, sie wären das, was die toten Gründerväter zeigen würden, wenn man sie morgen auf eine Bühne holen könnte: den unveräußerlichen Respekt gegenüber den Idealen ihrer Jugend, die Verzweiflung über ihr Scheitern und das Vergessen-Werden, die Sehnsucht nach Wiederentdeckung und Erinnert-Werden und die Würde einer Idee, die schöner ist als all das Geröll, unter dem sie begraben wurde. Gab es nicht achtzig- oder neunzigjährige gescheiterte Schauspieler, die nicht gaga waren und sich noch Texte merken konnten? Sie wären die authentischen Repräsentanten der europäischen Gründerzeit.

Martin trank Schnaps aus dem Zahnputzbecher.

Er sah es vor sich wie einen Film: Der Aufmarsch der Toten, auf großer Leinwand, sie marschierten in einem Sternmarsch durch alle Gassen und Straßen zum Berlaymont-Gebäude, eine Demonstration der verdrängten Geschichte, ein Fanal der Gründer des Europäischen Einigungsprojekts, und dann kam der Sarg. Was für ein Sarg? Wer lag darin? Der letzte Jude, na klar, der letzte Jude, der ein Vernichtungslager überlebt hatte. Gestorben in schicksalhafter Koinzidenz just am runden Geburtstag der Kommission! Da fand im Rahmen des Jubiläums ein pompöser Umzug statt, ein feierliches Begräbnis, mehr als ein Staatsbegräbnis, das erste übernationale, europäische Unionsbegräbnis, der Kommissionspräsident erneuert vor dem Sarg den Schwur: Nie wieder Nationalismus, Rassismus, Auschwitz! Und die Ewigkeit wäre, nach dem Tod des letzten Zeitzeugen, verlängert, der Schlussstrich überschritten und die Geschichte wieder mehr als ein Pendel, dessen Schwingungen die Menschen in geistlose Trance versetzt. In Martins Film zogen nun schwarze Wolken auf, in einem dramatischen Spektakel des Himmels, so radikal wie eine Sonnenfinsternis, die Wolken schoben sich vor die Sonne, vor alles Licht, atemberaubend schnell, im Zeitraffer – das Kino stockte jetzt kurz, weil Martin am Wort »Zeitraffer« hängen-blieb, er rauchte und starrte vor sich hin und dachte: Zeitraffer. Dann schossen die Wolken weiter, es wurde immer dunkler, ein Sturm kam auf, der den Menschen die Hüte von den Köpfen riss, er sah Hüte, die durch die Luft wirbelten, immer dunkler und …

Ohnmacht. Es war nicht Schlaf. Martin fiel irgendwann gegen vier Uhr morgens in Ohnmacht.

Er nahm ein Taxi zum Flughafen, schlief während der Fahrt fast ein. Er döste während des Flugs. Er aß Aspirin wie Smarties. Am Flughafen Brüssel nahm er auf Level o den Bus zum Europa-Viertel. Von dort ging er die paar Schritte zur Metro-Station Maelbeek, da der Zugang Berlaymont wieder einmal gesperrt war. Er wollte nur noch nach Hause. Nie zuvor hatte er seine Brüsseler Wohnung so innig als sein Zuhause empfunden. Am Bahnsteig schaute er zur Anzeigentafel: noch vier Minuten.

Professor Erhart musste um 11 Uhr aus dem Atlas auschecken, das war zu früh, um gleich zum Flughafen zu fahren. Er ging langsam über den Vieux Marché aux Grains, zog seinen Koffer hinter sich her, der am Kopfsteinpflaster hüpfte und sprang, als wollte Brüssel ihn abschütteln. Was sollte er tun, um die Zeit zu überbrücken? Essen gehen? Ja. Aber er hatte sehr spät gefrühstückt, war ohne Hunger. Er ging Richtung Metro-Station Sainte-Catherine. Was tun? Es war unerträglich heiß, er begann zu schwitzen. Er hatte in der Zeitung von der Ausstellung »Vergessene Moderne« gelesen, und welch heftige Auseinandersetzungen sie ausgelöst hatte. Vielleicht sollte er sich diese Ausstellung ansehen? Er war unschlüssig. Als er zur Kirche Sainte-Cathrine kam, ging er kurzentschlossen hinein. Er hatte Zeit. In der Kirche würde es kühler sein. Er war so oft an dieser Kirche vorbei, aber nur ein einziges Mal hineingegangen, an seinem ersten Abend in Brüssel, damals war er vor einem Platzregen geflüchtet. Die Kirche sah eigentlich aus wie ein Dom. Vielleicht war sie kunst- oder kulturhistorisch interessant.

Kaum war er eingetreten, fragte er sich, was er hier suchte. Vereinzelt saßen Betende in den Sitzreihen, Touristen hielten Smartphones oder Tablets in die Höhe und machten Fotos, immer wieder flackerten die Blitzlichter auf, während an den Seitenaltären die Flammen der Votivkerzen zitterten. Er ging auch in Wien nie in eine Kirche. Warum sollte er also in Brüssel eine Kirche besichtigen? Als er zwölf Jahre alt war, war er mit seiner Schulklasse in den Stephansdom geführt worden. Nicht einmal aus religiösen Gründen, sondern: Heimatkunde. Und mit fünfzehn hatte er seine Großmutter, die, als sie den Tod anklopfen hörte, zur Last-Minute-Gläubigen wurde, einmal in die Weihnachtsmette begleitet. Aber erst, nachdem sie ihm zwanzig Schilling zugesteckt hatte. Seither war er in keiner Kirche mehr gewesen. Er war froh, dass er nicht religiös erzogen worden war, einverstanden mit dem grundsätzlichen Atheismus seiner Eltern, auch wenn er erst viel später, viel zu spät, begriffen hatte, dass sie stramme Nationalsozialisten gewesen waren und deshalb antiklerikal.

Er ging im linken Seitenschiff nach vorn, da sprach ihn ein Mann an, der einen schwarzen Anzug und Kollar trug:

Est-ce que vous l'aimez aussi?

Pardon?

Die schwarze Madonna!

Erhart folgte dem Blick des Mannes, sah die Madonnenstatue.

Ein Wunder! Sie sehen es natürlich?

Was meinen Sie? Ihr Gesicht? Weil es schwarz ist?

Nein. Schauen Sie sich einmal ihre Hand an. Sehen Sie? Der

Daumen ist abgeschlagen. Die Protestanten haben damals, in der Reformationszeit, die Kirche verwüstet und diese Statue da vorne in den Kanal geworfen, dabei ist der Daumen abgebrochen. Sehen Sie die Bruchstelle? Und jetzt zählen Sie die Finger! Na! Sehen Sie? Fünf Finger! Die Katholiken haben die Madonna geborgen, in die Kirche zurückgebracht und wieder aufgestellt. Und obwohl ihr ein Finger abgeschlagen wurde, hatte sie dann wieder fünf Finger! Ein Wunder! Sehen Sie es?

Mit strahlendem Lächeln bekreuzigte er sich.

Kann es sein, sagte Erhart, dass sie davor sechs Finger hatte?

Der Mann im schwarzen Anzug sah ihn an, drehte sich um und ging weg.

Professor Erhart verließ die Kirche, ging weiter zur Metro-Station. Er hatte vor bis zur Gare Centrale zu fahren und dort einen Zug zum Flughafen zu nehmen. Aber er wäre viel zu früh am Flughafen gewesen, würde, um die Zeit totzuschlagen, apathisch durch Taxfree-Shops wandern, schließlich ein schlechtes Sandwich essen, ein Bier trinken, aus Langeweile noch ein Bier, dann wieder herumgehen, einen Kaffee trinken, dann irgendwo sitzen und warten. Schließlich würde er, weil die Zeit nicht und nicht verging, belgische Schokolade kaufen, weil man Schokolade aus Belgien mitbrachte, aber er hatte niemanden, dem er etwas mitbringen könnte oder wollte, Trudi hatte gerne Schokolade gegessen, er hatte ihr ab und zu eine dieser Milka-Rollen mit der blauen Quaste mitgebracht, am Anfang zum Rendezvous, später einfach so, als kleine Aufmerksamkeit, wenn er von der Uni heimkam, und als es um die Ecke vom Institut, in der Grillparzerstraße, noch dieses alte Süßwaren-Geschäft gab, den »Bonbon Kaiser«, geführt vom alten Herrn Kaiser, der Sätze sagte wie »Empfehlungen an die Frau Gemahlin, Herr Professor«, als er noch Assistent war, und er hatte sich gefreut, wenn Trudi sich freute, aber er selbst machte sich nicht so viel aus Schokolade, warum jetzt welche kaufen? Das letzte Mal hatte er am Brüsseler Flughafen, nur damit die Zeit verging, eine Bonbonniere von Neuhaus gekauft, sie lag dann wochenlang zu Hause in der Küche herum. Irgendwo lag sie noch immer. Er stieg bei Gare Centrale nicht aus, sondern fuhr weiter, bis Maelbeek, dort, ganz in der Nähe der Station, kannte er ein italienisches Lokal, wo er einmal nach einem »New Pact«-Meeting gegessen hatte. Es war sympathisch und unkompliziert, und das Essen war so gut, dass man es auch genießen konnte, wenn man keinen Hunger hatte. Er fand die Osteria Agricola Toscana tatsächlich wieder. Beim Warten auf das Essen und dann beim Essen und Weintrinken dachte er über seine Zukunft nach. Zumindest nahm er sich das vor und versuchte es. Es war nicht so einfach. Das Einzige, was er mit großer Sicherheit über die nächste Zukunft wissen konnte, war, dass er all das, was er jetzt aß und trank, verstoffwechseln und, zurück in Wien, ausscheiden würde. Er ermahnte sich zu weniger banalen Gedanken. Es war nicht so einfach. Das Essen schmeckte ihm. Aber es kam ihm wie eine Verschwendung vor: so gutes Essen nur für ihn, der es mit niemandem zelebrieren konnte. Der Wein war sehr gut. Er dachte über seine Zukunft nach. Er dachte, dass er genauso gut darüber nachdenken konnte, ob es ein Leben nach dem Tod gab. Ja doch, dachte er, es hieß Nachleben. Konnte er etwas hinterlassen, das fortwirkte? Hatte er einen Nachlass, der weiterwirken konnte? Ein Testament? Er dachte, dass er vielleicht noch Zeit hatte, ein Buch zu schreiben. Konnte man ein Buch so planen und schreiben, dass es ein Testament war und ein Erbe definierte, das Künftige tatsächlich antraten? Vielleicht eine Autobiographie? Vielleicht sollte er eine Autobiographie schreiben, seine Erfahrungen und Überlegungen, damit irgendwann einmal zumindest die Erinnerung daran möglich war, was hätte sein können und unerlöst weiterschwelte. In der Autobiographie von Armand Moens hatte er gelesen: »Geschichte ist nicht nur die Erzählung davon, was war, sondern auch die stetige Verarbeitung der Gründe, warum Vernünftigeres nicht sein konnte.« Das müsste das Motto seiner Autobiographie sein, dachte er und bestellte einen Espresso und die Rechnung. Er wollte eine Autobiographie schreiben, die nicht sein bescheidenes Leben erzählte, sondern das Nicht-Gelebte. Das Nicht-Gelebte seiner Zeit. Nun wurde die Zeit knapp. Er musste zum Flughafen. Er zahlte die ganze Flasche Wein.

Er wurde nervös, er hatte die Zeit übersehen.

Sollte er zum Schuman-Rondo gehen und den Bus zum Flughafen nehmen? Oder zurück zur Metro-Station, drei Stationen zur Gare Centrale und mit dem Zug zum Flughafen? Er dachte, dass der Zug schneller war als der Bus. Er rannte mit seinem hüpfenden Koffer zur Station Maelbeek, stolperte die Rolltreppe hinunter, merkte zu spät, dass sie außer Betrieb war, schaute am Bahnsteig nervös zur Anzeigetafel: Noch zwei Minuten.

David de Vriend hörte den Schrei »Bleib da!«, er hielt sich die Ohren zu, aber da hörte er es noch dröhnender in seinem Kopf, dieses »Bleib da!«, als würde es zwischen seinen Schläfen immer wieder hin und her und zurückgeworfen, Nachhall um Nachhall, »Bleib da!«, und er wusste, jetzt musste er gehen. Sofort. Kein Nachdenken mehr, nur ein Entschluss. Sofort raus von hier und weg.

Er schloss nicht einmal die Tür hinter sich. Er begegnete niemandem. Im Treppenhaus, unten im Foyer, drüben im Speisesaal, vorn in der Bibliothek, überall war es ruhig, kein Mensch zu sehen. Nach dem Mittagessen schliefen die meisten Heimbewohner, oder sie machten Spaziergänge, entweder die Rue de l'Arbre Unique hinunter bis zum Bach mit den Trauerweiden, Vögel füttern, oder auf dem Friedhof, bis zur Bank, Ausruhen, dann zurück zum Tee. Die Betreuerinnen hatten jetzt im Personalzimmer ihr Kaffeestündchen und tauschten sich über ihre Problemfälle aus.

De Vriend verließ die Maison Hanssens wie eine Welt ohne Menschen. Oder wie einen Zugwaggon von Toten. »Du stürzt uns ins Unglück!« – das waren die letzten Worte gewesen. Er musste weg, so schnell wie möglich weg. Wohin?

Es war ein Entschluss gewesen, der ihm keine Zeit gelassen hatte, Für und Wider abzuwägen. Hinaus! Sich losreißen und hinaus!

Er ging zum Friedhofstor, aber er ging nicht in den Friedhof hinein, er hatte eine Adresse, zu der er hinmusste.

Als er aus dem Zug gesprungen war, hatte ihm ein junger Mann ein Kuvert zugesteckt, darin befanden sich ein Zettel mit einer sicheren Adresse und zwanzig Francs. Es ging alles so schnell. Nach einem Schusswechsel setzte sich der Zug wieder in Bewegung, aber das sah er so langsam, das Anrollen des Zugs, die offene Schiebetür des Viehwaggons wie ein schwarzes Loch, dahinter seine Eltern und sein kleiner Bruder, es war, als rückte dieses Bild Zentimeter um Zentimeter weiter, Schüsse und ein Stampfen und Schnaufen, das schneller werdende Rattern der Schläge von Eisen auf Eisen, ein Stoß, der Mann stieß ihn noch einmal und schrie: Lauf! Such die Adresse, die du da – und er deutete auf das Kuvert, das er ihm soeben in die Hand gedrückt hatte –, da drinnen! Und der Zug gewann an Fahrt, das schwarze Loch, hinter dem seine Familie kauerte, war vorbei, da rollte noch ein schwarzes Loch vorbei und noch eines, und er drehte sich um und sah Menschen über die Felder laufen, wie viele waren das, hundert? Er sah, wie da und dort einzelne stürzten oder niederbrachen, von Kugeln im Rücken getroffen, und er warf sich zu Boden, rollte die Böschung des Gleiskörpers hinunter und blieb flach liegen, bis der Zug vorbei war, aus dem die SS-Wachmannschaft den Flüchtenden nachschoss. Erst dann lief er los.

Er sah vor sich auf dem Feld Menschen, die sich hingeworfen hatten und nun aufstanden. Er lief an Menschen vorbei, die dalagen und nicht mehr aufstanden. Er lief hinein in die Nacht. Er hatte eine Adresse.

Er wusste den Weg nicht. Da kam ein Bus, hielt vor dem Friedhofstor.

Bus Nr. 4 – de Vriend sagte das nichts. Er stieg ein. Der Bus fuhr an. Brachte ihn weg. Er ließ alles zurück. Seine Eltern und sein kleiner Bruder kamen nach der Ankunft in Auschwitz sofort ins Gas. Er hätte sie nicht retten können, wenn er nicht aus dem Zug gesprungen, wenn er bei ihnen geblieben wäre. Es war auch keine Zeit, um zu diskutieren: Sollen wir springen oder nicht springen? Was haben wir in dem einen, was in dem anderen Fall zu erwarten? Er war gesprungen. Er hatte überlebt. Sein Vater, dieser kleine Buchhalter, dieser schwache, zärtliche Mann mit den traurigen dunklen Augen, der nichts anderes zum Funktionieren der Welt beitragen konnte als seine gnadenlose Korrektheit, sein Vertrauen in die Kontrolle von Soll und Haben, mit bemühtem Stolz, der eigentlich Trotz war gegen die Zeiten und gegen das ironische, herablassende Lächeln der Größeren und Wendigeren. Selbst zu Hause, ganz privat in den eigenen vier Wänden, wenn niemand zusah, führte er das Schauspiel absoluter Korrektheit auf, als würden König und Regierung zuschauen und anerkennend nicken. Und seine Mutter, auch sie sah er, wenn er sich an sie erinnerte, immer mit diesem traurig ergebenen Blick, beide hatten sie diese traurigen Augen nicht deshalb, weil sie kommen sahen, was dann kommen sollte, sondern, weil sie glaubten, dass alles immer so bleiben würde, wie es war. Sie hatten sich keine Sorgen gemacht, sie hatten sich nur in den Sorgen eingerichtet, die sie für ihr Leben hielten – und nicht für Pflastersteine auf dem Weg in ihren Tod. De Vriend hatte sie nur ein einziges Mal schreien, ja brüllen hören: Bleib da! Wäre er geblieben, er wäre ins Gas gegangen wie sie. Er hatte und hätte sie nicht retten können. Ist das Schuld?

Er hatte eine Adresse.

Fremde Menschen hatten ihn Stolz und Widerstandskraft gelehrt. Sie hatten ihn geliebt wie ein eigenes Kind. Als er schließlich verraten wurde, reichte die Zeit nicht mehr, um einen starken jungen Mann durch Arbeit zu ermorden. Er hatte Glück gehabt. Unglück, Glück im Unglück, Unglück, wieder Glück im Unglück.

Er fand die Adresse nicht. Er saß im Bus und merkte, dass er leere Taschen hatte. Er musste sich erinnern. Er musste den Weg finden, ihn wiedererkennen. Er stöhnte. Er musste sich erinnern. Aber da war nur ein schwarzes Loch. Er sah aus dem Fenster. Was da vorbeizog, war keine Erinnerung. Kein Wegweiser, nichts, das sich mit Erfahrung verband. Fassaden.

Nun war nichts. Die Bustüren öffneten sich und schlossen sich. Dann schaukelte der Bus wieder an Fassaden vorbei. Die Türen öffneten sich und schlossen sich. Das war alles.

Die Tür des Waggons wurde aufgerissen. Eine Stimme schrie: Raus! Springt raus!

Die Bustüren öffneten sich. Bleib! Du stürzt uns ins Unglück!

De Vriend sprang aus dem Bus. Fast wäre er gefallen. Ein Mann an der Busstation fing ihn auf.

Lauf! Zu dieser Adresse da –

De Vriend sah sich um, sah Menschen die Straße hinunter-eilen, er lief ihnen nach. Wo war er? Vor einem schwarzen Loch. Da war ein kurzer Moment des Wiedererkennens: Metro-Station Maelbeek. Das sagte ihm etwas. Was? Er ging hinein, die Treppe hinunter. Er musste den Weg wiedererkennen. Er ging auf den Bahnsteig und dachte, das ist der Weg.

Noch eine Minute.

Ein Mann mit einer Tasche. Eine Frau, die etwas in ihr Smartphone tippte. Ein Mann mit einem Koffer. Der Zug fuhr ein, hielt. Die Türen öffneten sich. Er sah in der offenen Tür vor sich ein Kind an der Hand seiner Mutter. Das Kind riss sich los, als es aus dem Zug sprang.

Da detonierte die Bombe.

Als Schwester Joséphine zusammen mit Monsieur Hugo, dem Hauswart der Maison Hanssens, das Zimmer von David de Vriend ausräumte, fand sie ein Blatt Papier, auf dem Namen aufgelistet waren.

Monsieur Hugo warf drei Hemden in einen Umzugskarton, sagte: Viel hat er nicht gehabt.

Schwester Joséphine nickte. Alle Namen auf dieser Liste waren durchgestrichen.

Die wenigsten haben viel, sagte Hugo. Ich arbeite seit acht Jahren hier im Haus, sagte er, und noch immer wundere ich mich, wie wenig am Ende von einem Menschen bleibt.

Ja, sagte Joséphine. Sie setzte sich, schaute verwundert auf das Blatt. Am Ende der Liste der durchgestrichenen Namen hatte David de Vriend seinen eigenen Namen gesetzt.

Er hatte schöne Taschentücher, mit Monogramm, sagte Hugo und warf die Taschentücher in den Karton.

Nur David de Vriends eigener Name war nicht durchgestrichen.

Tolle Anzüge hat er gehabt! Wirklich erstklassig. Da werden sie sich freuen bei der Obdachlosen-Hilfe. Aber, wenn einer in so einem Anzug bettelt, bekommt er keinen Cent. Einem Mann in diesem Anzug – er hielt de Vriends Tweed in die Höhe – dem hilft kein Mensch.

Joséphine hätte gern gehabt, dass er schwieg. Sie sagte nichts. Da, vor ihr auf dem Beistelltischchen lag ein Kugelschreiber. Sie nahm ihn, hielt ihn wie ein Messer.

Was hat er eigentlich gemacht im Leben?, fragte Monsieur Hugo. War er irgendwie prominent? Ein Politiker oder hoher Beamter? Ich meine – weil die Kommission sein Begräbnis organisiert.

Das stille Begräbnis einer Epoche, dachte Joséphine.

Was ich vermisse, sind die Klassiker, sagte Monsieur Hugo, Fotoalben, Taschenkalender, Tagebücher. Sehr ungewöhnlich. Er hatte nichts, nicht einmal ein Fotoalbum, das hat doch normal jeder, sagte er und warf die Schuhspanner in den Karton.

Joséphine fragte sich, was sie mit dieser Namensliste machen sollte. In den Karton werfen? Oder in den Papierkorb? Sollte sie den Namen David de Vriend auch durchstreichen? Hatte er das wollen? Hat er das Blatt deswegen hier auf das Tischchen gelegt, zusammen mit dem Kugelschreiber? Damit sie dann –

Monsieur Hugo warf Zahnbürste, Zahnpasta, Nagelschere, Deo und Rasierapparat in einen Plastikbeutel, den Beutel in den Karton. Voll wird der Karton nicht, sagte er.

Dieser grauenhafte Tod, dachte Joséphine. Dass ausgerechnet de Vriend bei diesem Anschlag – Andererseits: Was heißt ausgerechnet er? Für jeden. Für alle, die zur falschen Zeit … für alle … zwanzig Tote, einhundertdreißig Schwerverletzte.

Sie faltete die Namensliste zusammen, steckte sie in die Tasche ihres weißen Arbeitsmantels, klopfte mit der Hand auf die Tasche und dachte: Solange sein Name nicht durchgestrichen ist, so lange –

Das war alles, sagte Monsieur Hugo.

Epilog

Den Protest der Tierschützer hatte die Redaktion der Metro-Zeitung erwartet. Kurt van der Koot hatte, bevor er seine Serie begann, die Redaktion davor gewarnt. Der Chefredakteur hatte nur gelacht: Der Protest von Radikalen stärke nur die Leser-Blatt-Bindung.

Erstaunlich war nur, wie spät der Protest kam. Erst nach Wochen, nach einem Artikel in Le Soir, der ein Angriff auf Metro und den aufsehenerregenden Kampagnen-Journalismus der Gratis-Zeitung war.

Es war ein zynischer Artikel, in dem Le Soir die Vermutung in den Raum stellte, dass das Schwein, das durch Brüssel lief, wahrscheinlich gar nicht existierte und die unscharfen Bilder von Überwachungskameras Fälschungen waren. Diese Metro-Serie sei wohl nur ein neues Beispiel dafür, wie die Gratiszeitungen arbeiteten: mit erfundenen Geschichten Aufregung erzeugen. Dieser Artikel war illustriert mit einem Foto, aufgenommen in der Slagerij Van Kampen, das zwei Schweinehälften zeigte, die auf Fleischerhaken hingen. Untertitelt: »Das Ende des Brüsseler Schweins?«

Angefügt an diesen Artikel war ein Interview mit Michel Moreau, Präsident der »Tierhilfe Belgien«, der die Aktion von Metro als »größten Skandal seit Marc Dutroux« bezeichnete. Es sei schändlich, ein durch die Stadt laufendes Schwein für eine Zeitungs-Werbekampagne zu missbrauchen, statt dieses Schwein, so es überhaupt existiert, zu retten. Die Straßen der Stadt seien kein natürlicher Lebensraum für ein Schwein, das sich gegenüber den Herausforderungen von Asphalt, Menschenmassen und Autoverkehr in einem Dauerstress befinden dürfte, der wohl noch quälender für das Tier sei als die

Kastenhaltung in den Tierfabriken. Und er rief »die verantwortlichen Stellen« dazu auf, sich endlich Klarheit darüber zu verschaffen, ob es sich um »ein real existierendes« Schwein handle, und sollte dies tatsächlich der Fall sein, das Tier von Amts wegen einzufangen, von einem Veterinär untersuchen zu lassen und auf einen Hof zu bringen, wo es artgerecht gehalten werden könne. »Als Tierschützer bin ich auch sehr vorsichtig mit Tiermetaphern, aber was hier abgeht, kann man nur als Schweinerei bezeichnen«, so Moreau.

Nun hatte auch Le Soir ihren Shitstorm. Dutzende Leser protestierten in Leserbriefen und Postings dagegen, dass Tierquälerei mit dem Kindesmissbrauch und den Morden von Marc Dutroux verglichen wurde. Auf Facebook bekam das Interview mit Michel Moreau innerhalb weniger Stunden Hunderte Wut-Emojis.

Der Angriff auf Metro ging nach hinten los und wurde kurzfristig zum Problem von Le Soir. Dennoch hatte die Metro-Redaktion ein noch größeres Problem, das unbedingt gelöst werden musste, bevor die Öffentlichkeit auch noch darauf aufmerksam wurde: Die Kampagne »Brüssel sucht einen Namen für sein Schwein« lief völlig aus dem Ruder. Die Leser konnten online ihre Vorschläge machen oder Vorschläge von anderen liken, gleichzeitig aktualisierte sich mit jeder Nennung und jedem Klick regelmäßig das Ranking der Vorschläge, entsprechend der Anzahl der Nennungen eines Namens und der Anzahl der Likes. Dieses Ranking war als Grundlage gedacht, auf der die Jury nun die Longlist erstellen sollte. Anfangs waren naheliegende Vorschläge gekommen: Miss Piggy, Madame Cochon, Schweinchen Schlau.

Brüssel-Bezug hatte nur Varkentje Pis (17 Likes), eventuell noch Catherine, weil das Schwein in Sainte-Catherine zum ersten Mal gesehen worden war (21 Likes). Aber dann geschah etwas Unfassbares. Hundertfach wurde ein Name genannt, der sich mit Tausenden Likes überlegen an die Spitze des Rankings setzte: Mohamed. Das konnte nur eine organisierte Aktion sein. Als die Redaktion das merkte, nahm sie die Seite aus dem Netz. Mehrere Juroren traten aus der Jury aus. Bei einer Aktion, die in einen Akt der Aggression gegen muslimische Mitbürger mündete, wollten sie nicht mehr dabei sein.

Wir stoppen das, sagte der Chefredakteur. Wir halten still. In kurzer Zeit ist das vergessen. Übrigens Kurt, sagte er zu van der Koot, ist Ihnen aufgefallen, dass seit zwei Wochen keine neuen Bilder mehr von dem Schwein kommen? Und keine Meldung, dass es irgendwo gesehen wurde. Es ist verschwunden. Spurlos verschwunden.

À suivre.